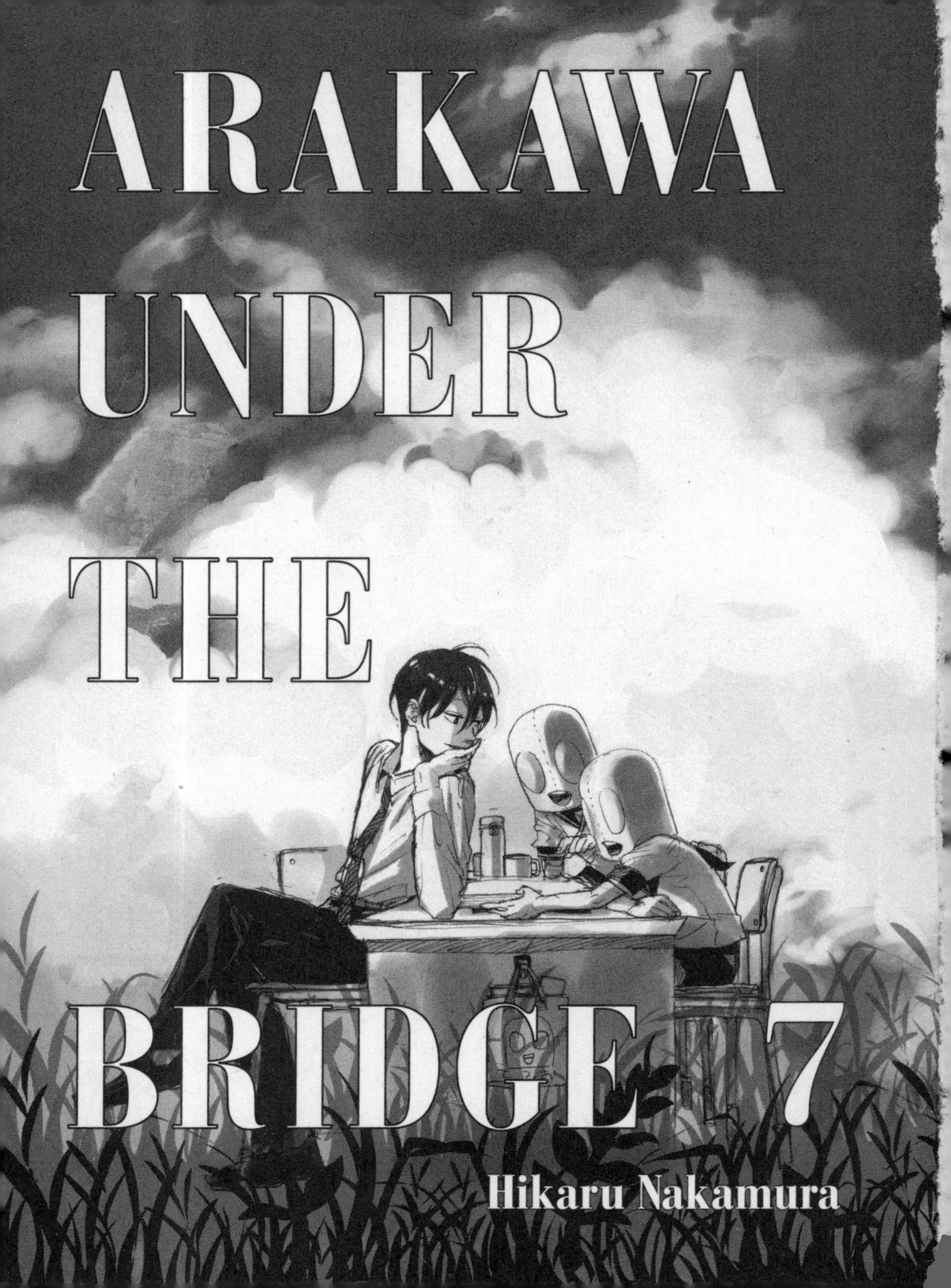
ARAKAWA
UNDER
THE
BRIDGE 7
Hikaru Nakamura

C O N T E N T S

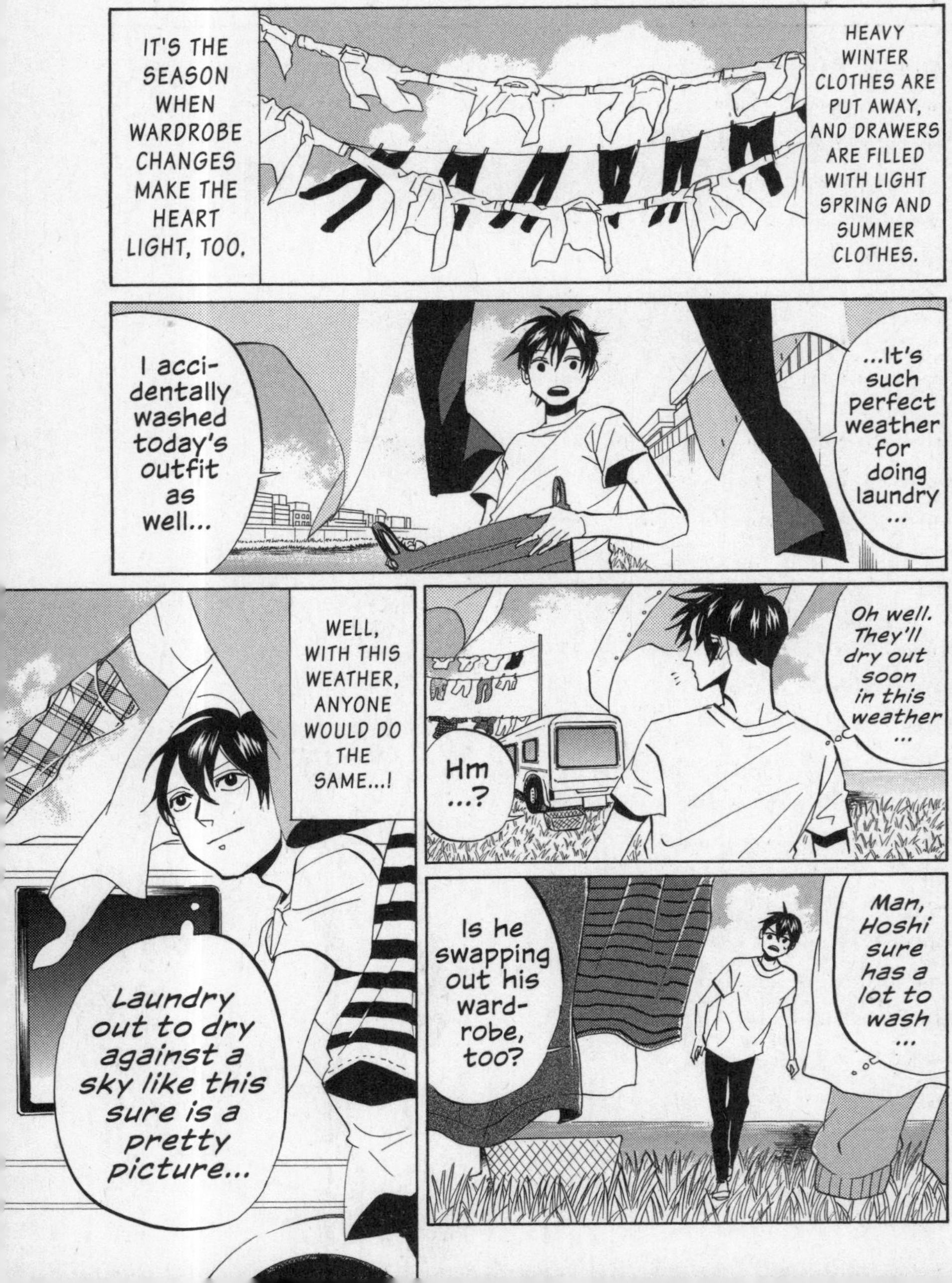
HEAVY WINTER CLOTHES ARE PUT AWAY, AND DRAWERS ARE FILLED WITH LIGHT SPRING AND SUMMER CLOTHES.
IT'S THE SEASON WHEN WARDROBE CHANGES MAKE THE HEART LIGHT, TOO.
...It's such perfect weather for doing laundry ...
I acci-dentally washed today's outfit as well...
Oh well. They'll dry out soon in this weather ...
Hm ...?
Man, Hoshi sure has a lot to wash ...
Is he swapping out his ward-robe, too?
WELL, WITH THIS WEATHER, ANYONE WOULD DO THE SAME...!
Laundry out to dry against a sky like this sure is a pretty picture...

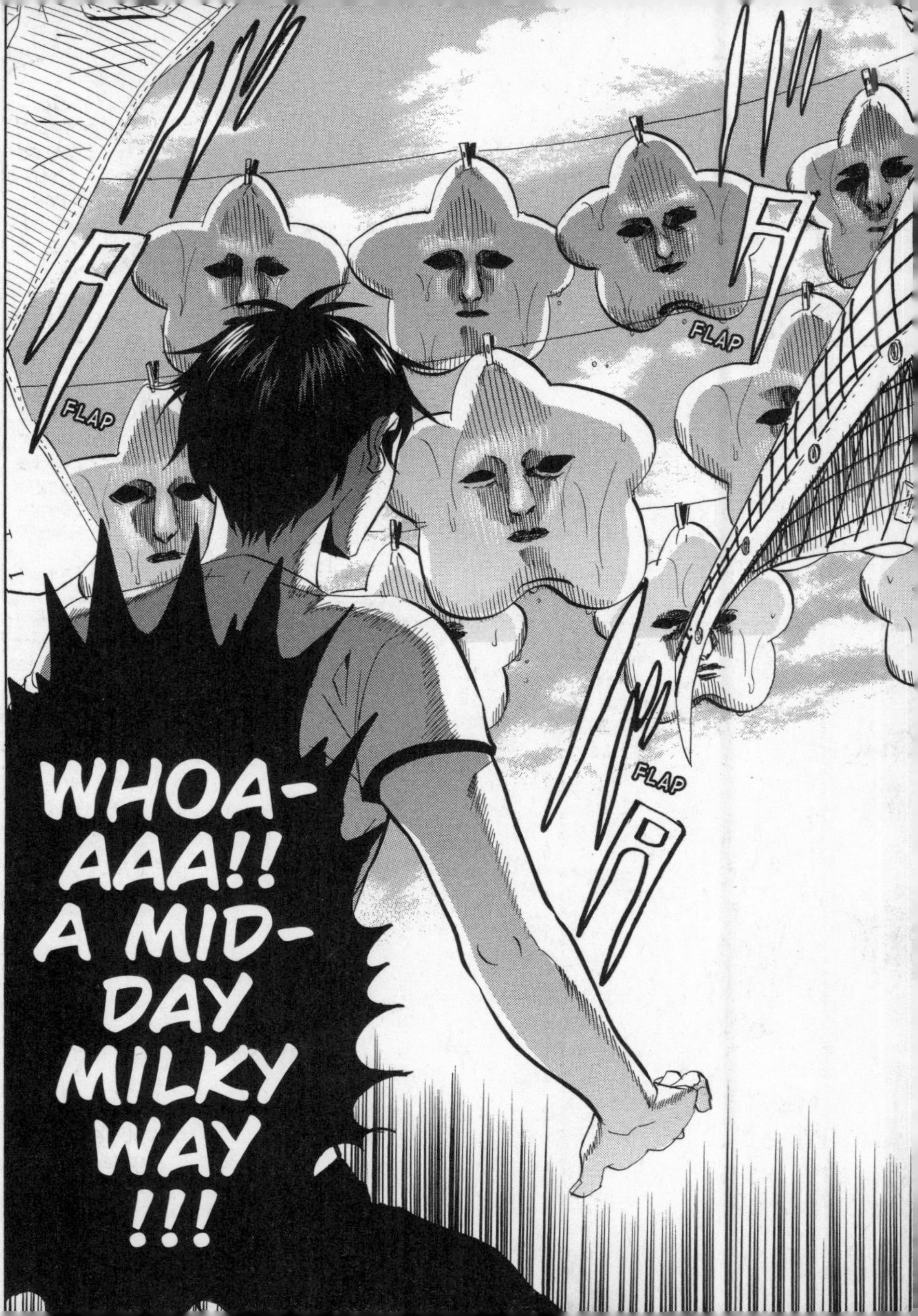
FLAP
FLAP
FLAP
WHOA-AAA!! A MID-DAY MILKY WAY!!!

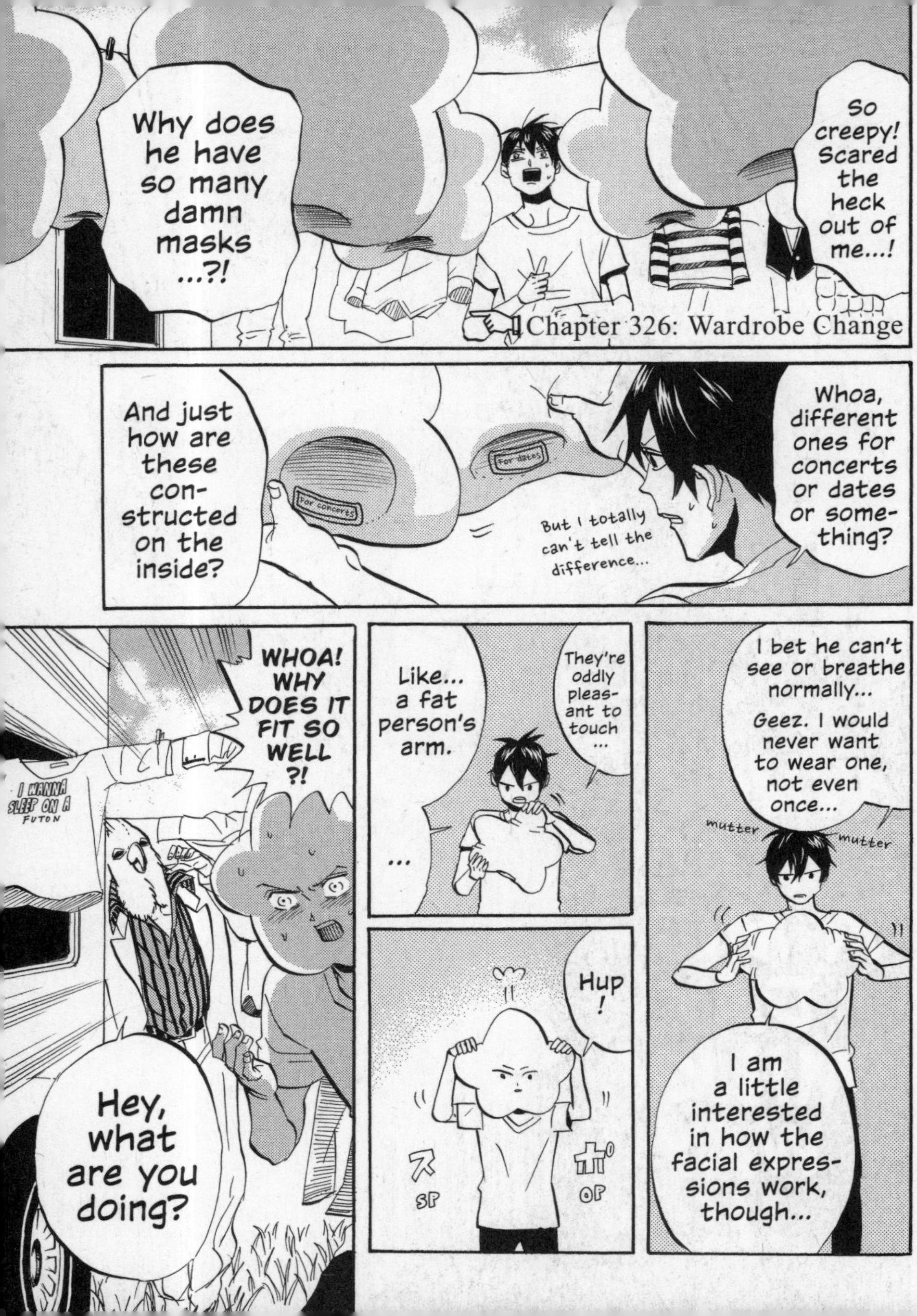
So creepy! Scared the heck out of me...!
Why does he have so many damn masks ...?!
Chapter 326: Wardrobe Change
Whoa, different ones for concerts or dates or something?
But I totally can't tell the difference...
For dates
For concerts
And just how are these constructed on the inside?
I bet he can't see or breathe normally...
Geez. I would never want to wear one, not even once...
mutter mutter
I am a little interested in how the facial expressions work, though...
They're oddly pleasant to touch ...
Like... a fat person's arm.
...
Hup!
SP
OP
WHOA! WHY DOES IT FIT SO WELL ?!
I WANNA SLEEP ON A FUTON
Hey, what are you doing?

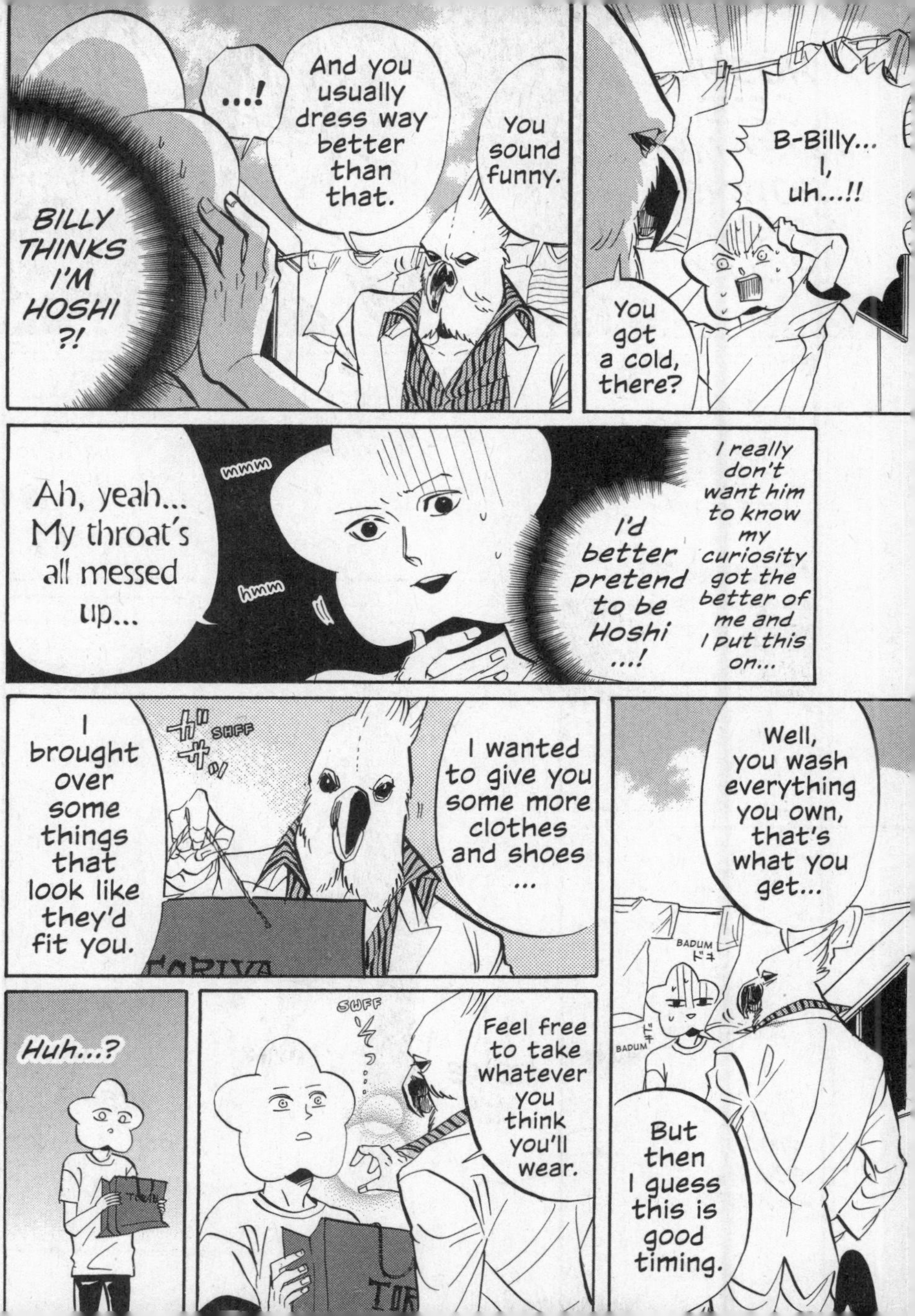
B-Billy... I, uh...!!
You got a cold, there?
You sound funny.
And you usually dress way better than that.
...!
BILLY THINKS I'M HOSHI ?!
I really don't want him to know my curiosity got the better of me and I put this on...
I'd better pretend to be Hoshi ...!
mmm
hmm
Ah, yeah... My throat's all messed up...
Well, you wash everything you own, that's what you get...
BADUM
BADUM
But then I guess this is good timing.
I wanted to give you some more clothes and shoes ...
SHFF
I brought over some things that look like they'd fit you.
SHFF
Feel free to take whatever you think you'll wear.
Huh...?

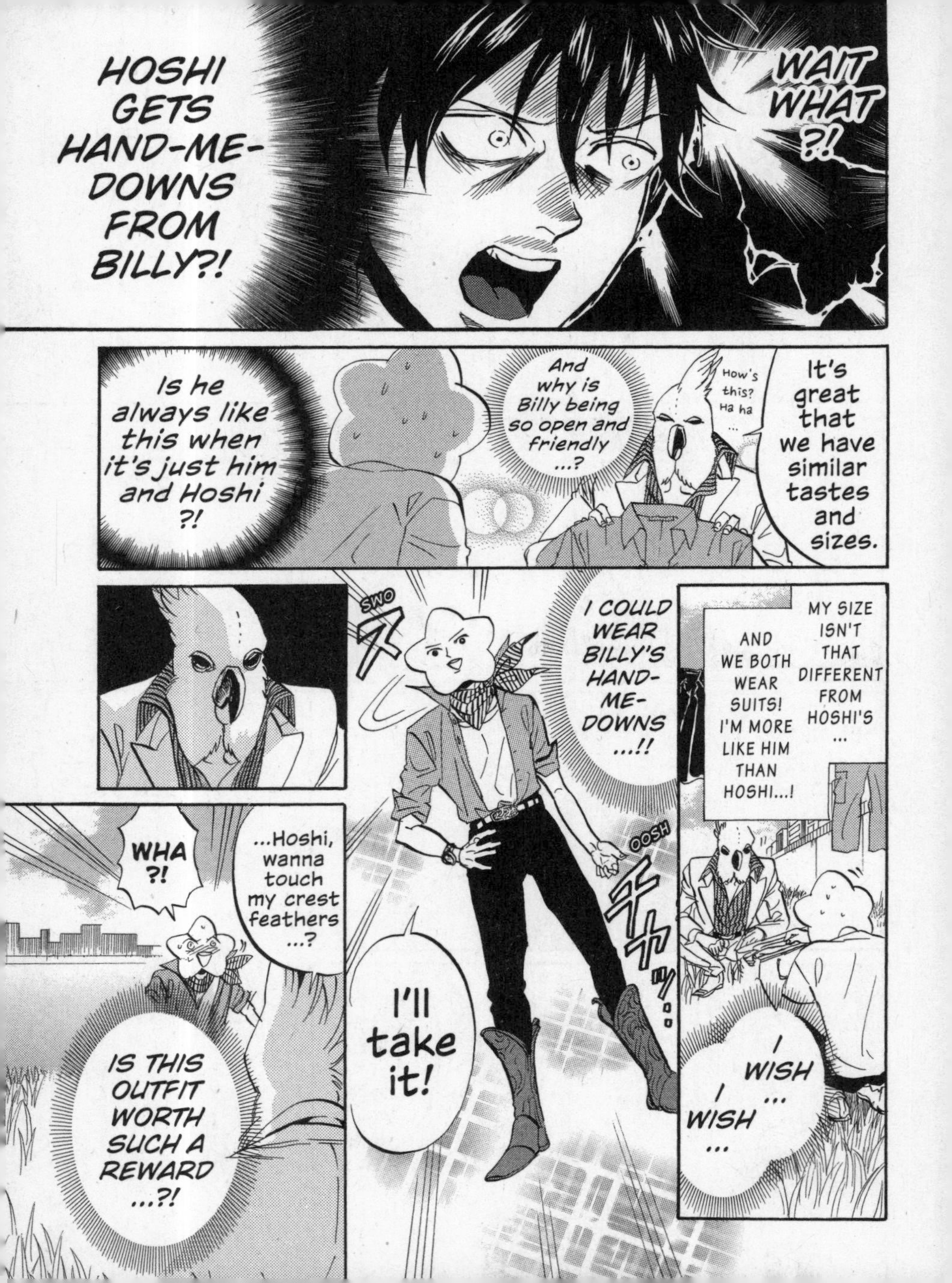
WAIT WHAT ?!
HOSHI GETS HAND-ME-DOWNS FROM BILLY?!
It's great that we have similar tastes and sizes.
How's this? Ha ha ...
And why is Billy being so open and friendly ...?
Is he always like this when it's just him and Hoshi ?!
MY SIZE ISN'T THAT DIFFERENT FROM HOSHI'S ...
AND WE BOTH WEAR SUITS! I'M MORE LIKE HIM THAN HOSHI...!
I COULD WEAR BILLY'S HAND-ME-DOWNS ...!!
SWOOSH
I'll take it!
I WISH ...
I WISH ...
WHA ?!
...Hoshi, wanna touch my crest feathers ...?
IS THIS OUTFIT WORTH SUCH A REWARD ...?!

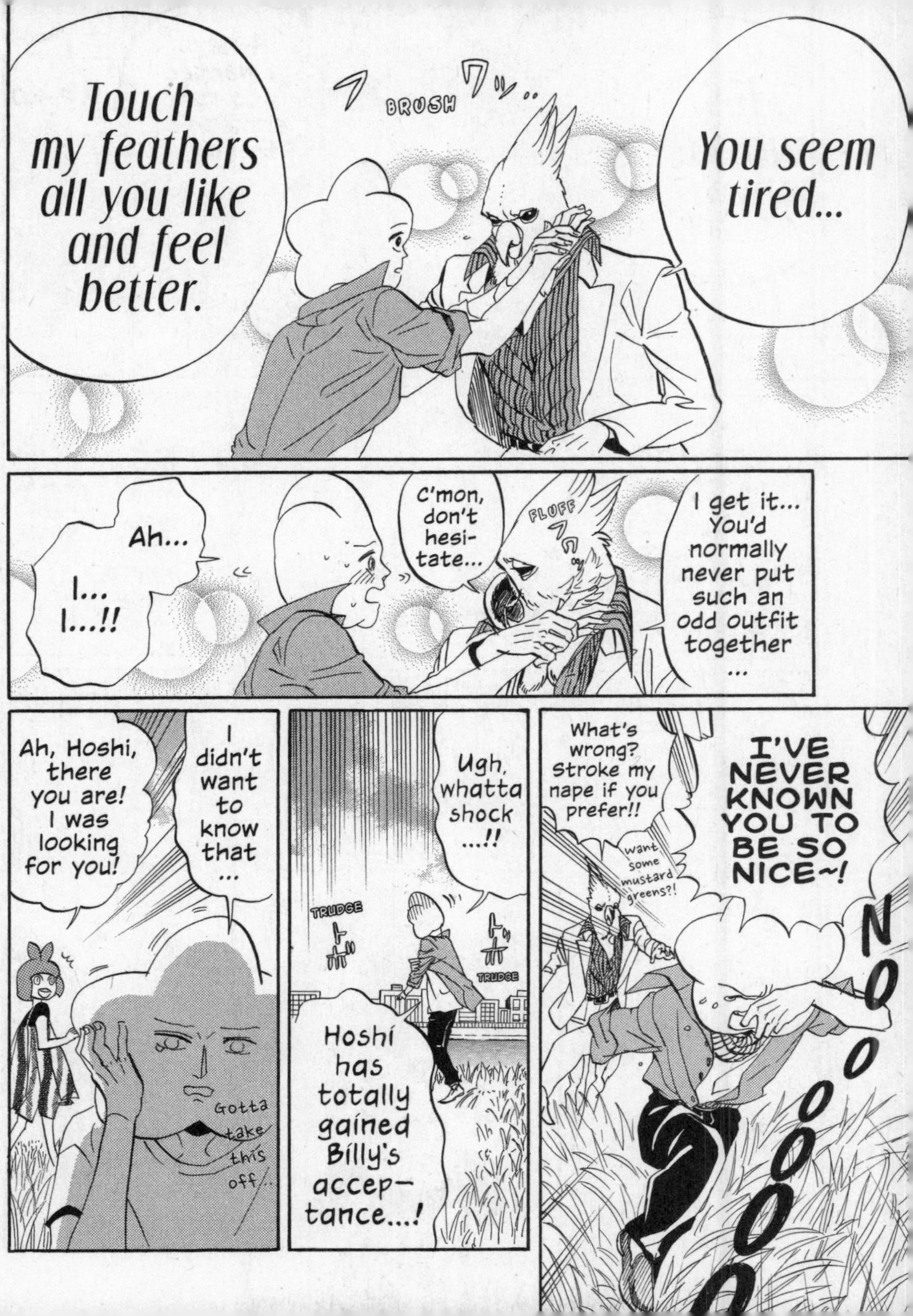
You seem tired...
BRUSH
Touch my feathers all you like and feel better.
I get it... You'd normally never put such an odd outfit together ...
FLUFF
C'mon, don't hesi-tate...
Ah... I... I...!!
What's wrong? Stroke my nape if you prefer!!
I'VE NEVER KNOWN YOU TO BE SO NICE~!
Want some mustard greens?!
NOOOOOOO
Ugh, whatta shock ...!!
TRUDGE
TRUDGE
Hoshi has totally gained Billy's accep-tance...!
I didn't want to know that ...
Ah, Hoshi, there you are! I was looking for you!
Gotta take this off...

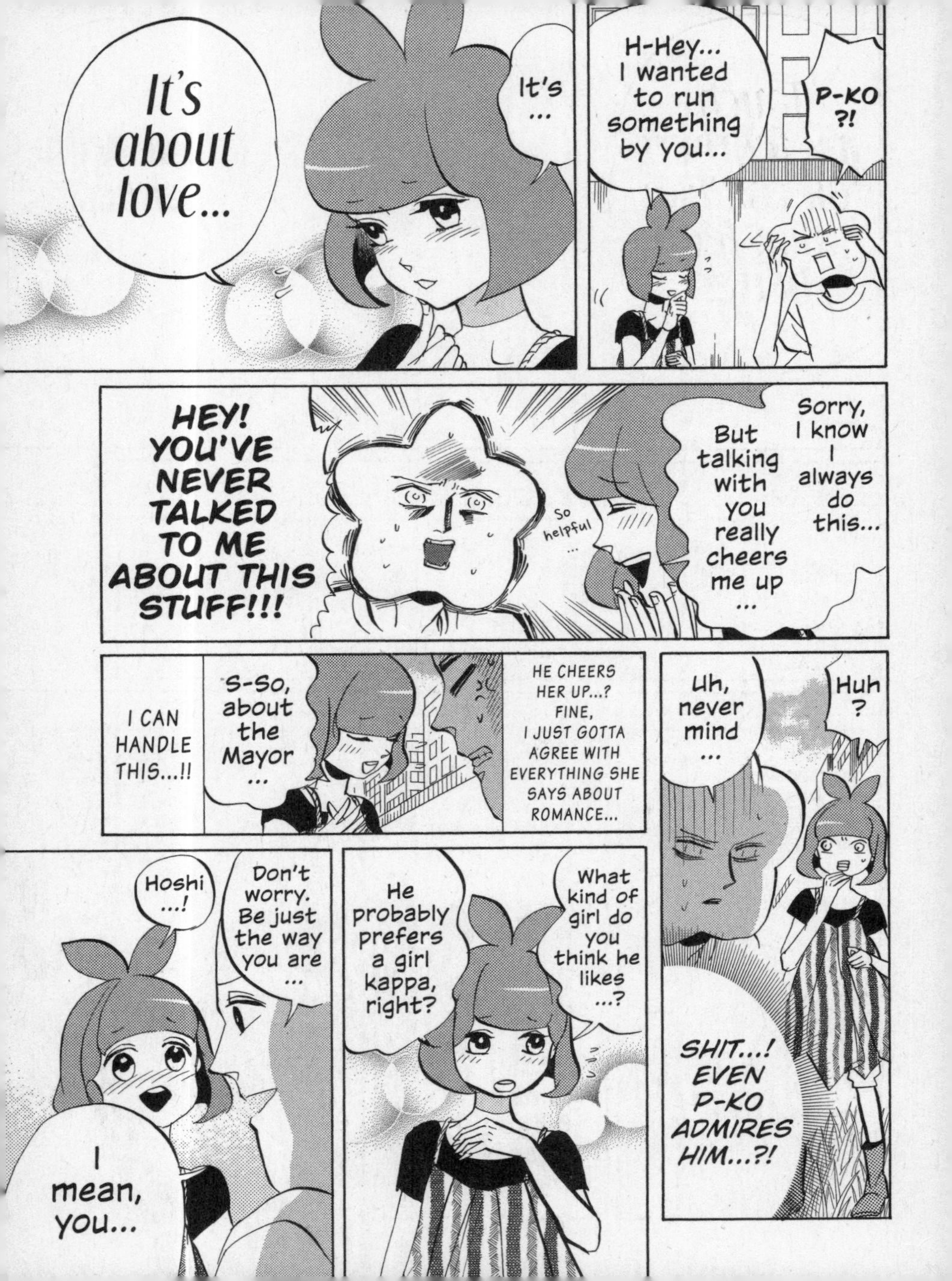
P-KO ?!
H-Hey... I wanted to run something by you...
It's ...
It's about love...
Sorry, I know I always do this...
But talking with you really cheers me up ...
So helpful ...
HEY! YOU'VE NEVER TALKED TO ME ABOUT THIS STUFF!!!
Huh ?
Uh, never mind ...
SHIT...! EVEN P-KO ADMIRES HIM...?!
HE CHEERS HER UP...? FINE, I JUST GOTTA AGREE WITH EVERYTHING SHE SAYS ABOUT ROMANCE...
S-So, about the Mayor ...
I CAN HANDLE THIS...!!
What kind of girl do you think he likes ...?
He probably prefers a girl kappa, right?
Don't worry. Be just the way you are ...
Hoshi ...!
I mean, you...

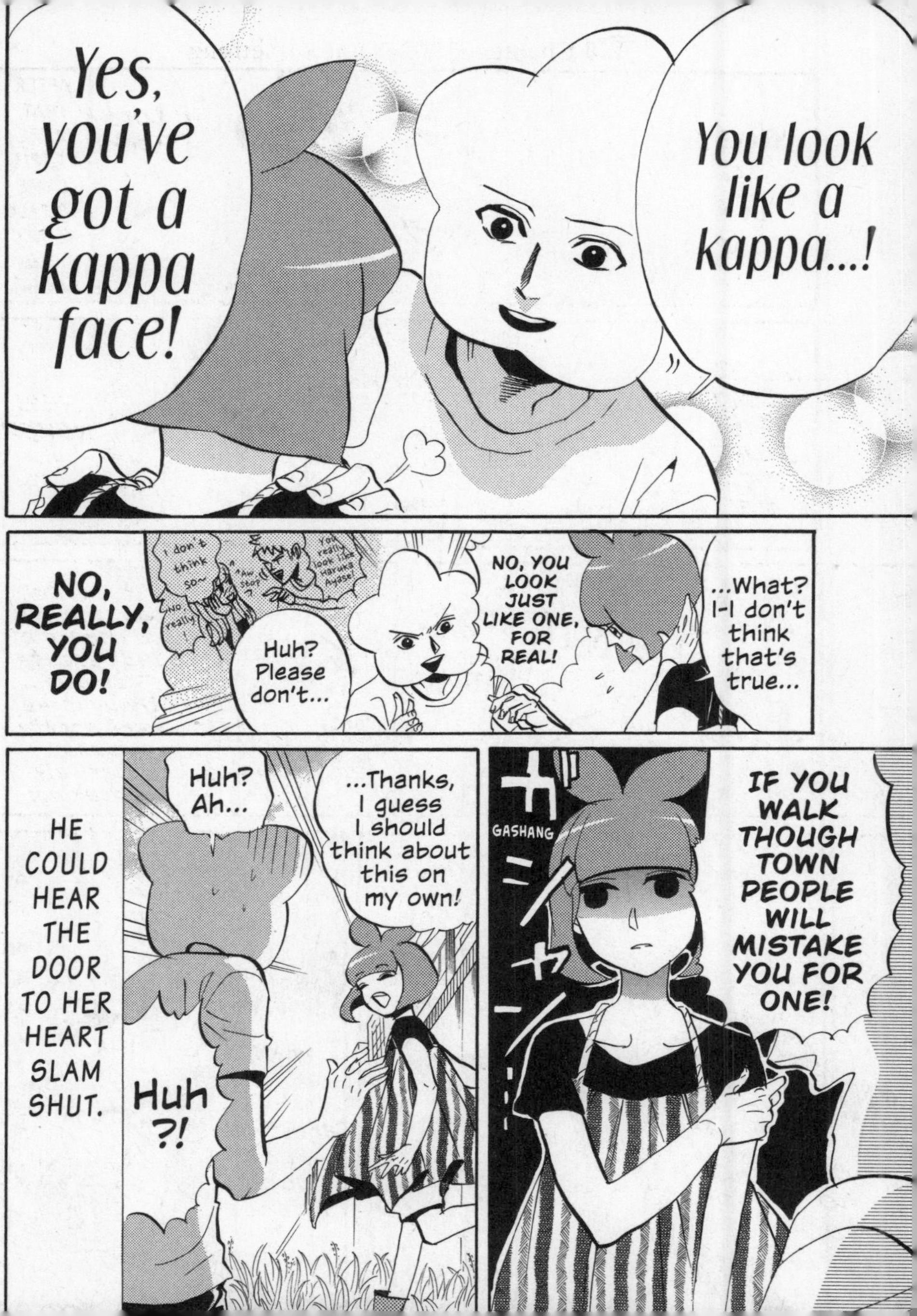
You look like a kappa...!
Yes, you've got a kappa face!
...What? I-I don't think that's true...
NO, YOU LOOK JUST LIKE ONE, FOR REAL!
Huh? Please don't...
NO, REALLY, YOU DO!
IF YOU WALK THOUGH TOWN PEOPLE WILL MISTAKE YOU FOR ONE!
GASHANG
...Thanks, I guess I should think about this on my own!
Huh? Ah...
HE COULD HEAR THE DOOR TO HER HEART SLAM SHUT.
Huh ?!

Chapter 327: Special Something

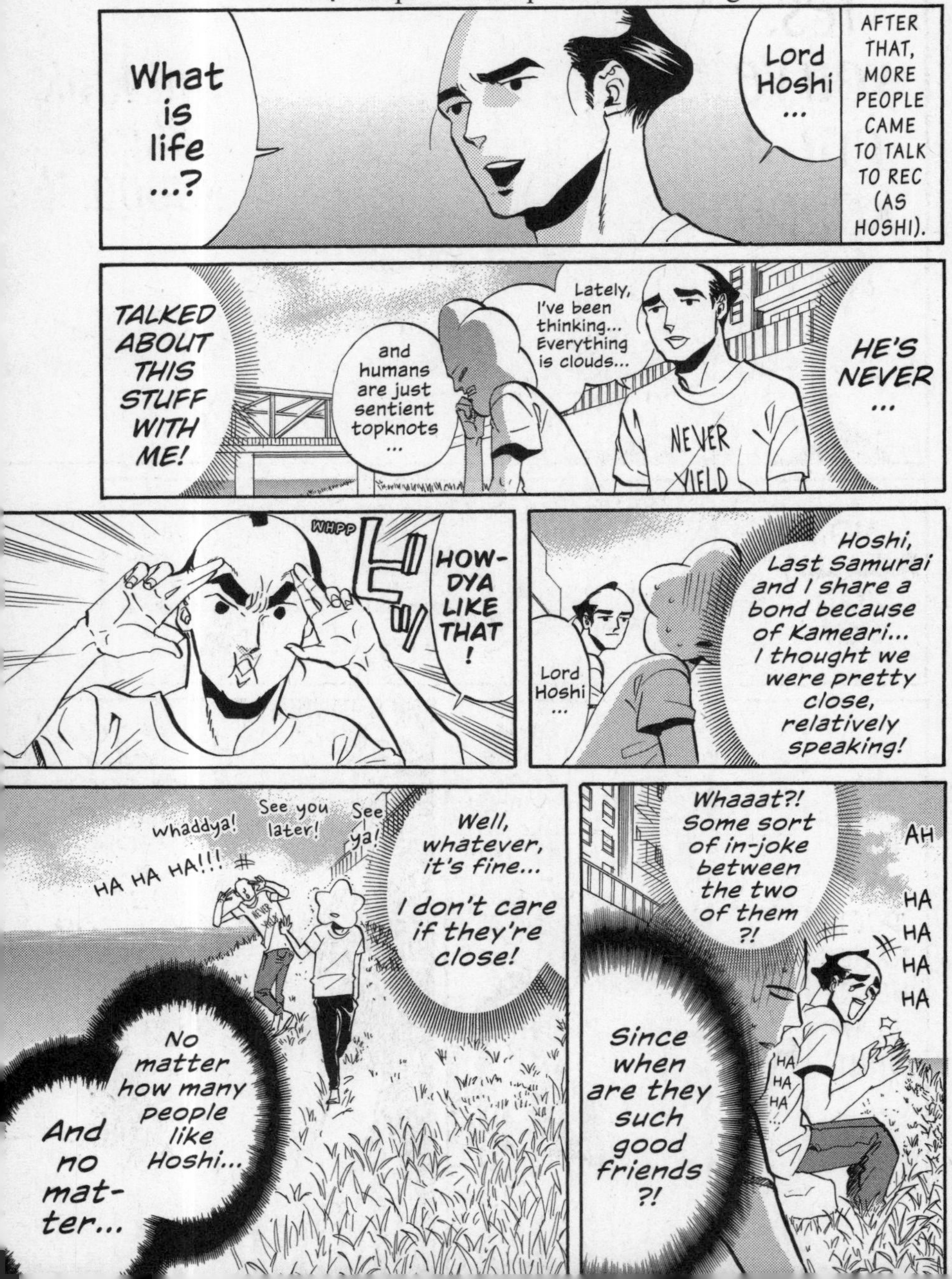

AFTER THAT, MORE PEOPLE CAME TO TALK TO REC (AS HOSHI).
Lord Hoshi ...
What is life ...?
HE'S NEVER ...
Lately, I've been thinking... Everything is clouds...
and humans are just sentient topknots ...
NEVER YIELD
TALKED ABOUT THIS STUFF WITH ME!
Hoshi, Last Samurai and I share a bond because of Kameari... I thought we were pretty close, relatively speaking!
Lord Hoshi ...
HOW-DYA LIKE THAT !
WHPP
Whaaat?! Some sort of in-joke between the two of them ?!
AH HA HA HA HA
HA HA HA
Since when are they such good friends ?!
Well, whatever, it's fine...
I don't care if they're close!
See ya!
See you later!
whaddya!
HA HA HA!!!
No matter how many people like Hoshi...
And no mat-ter...

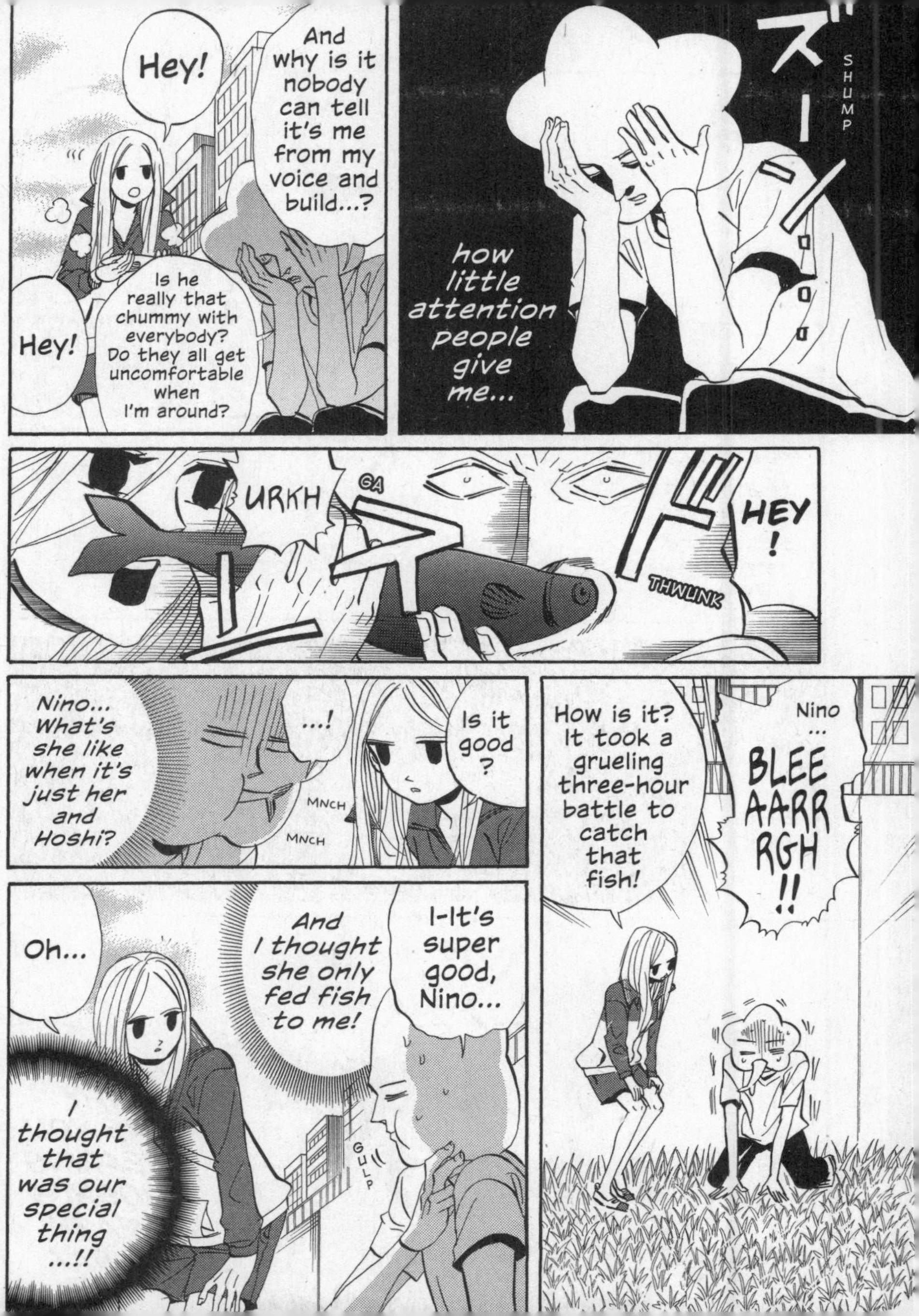
SHUMP
how little attention people give me...
And why is it nobody can tell it's me from my voice and build...?
Hey!
Is he really that chummy with everybody? Do they all get uncomfortable when I'm around?
Hey!
HEY!
THWUNK
GA
URKH
Nino...
BLEEAARRRGH!!
How is it? It took a grueling three-hour battle to catch that fish!
Is it good?
...!
MNCH
MNCH
Nino... What's she like when it's just her and Hoshi?
I-It's super good, Nino...
GULP
And I thought she only fed fish to me!
Oh...
I thought that was our special thing...!!

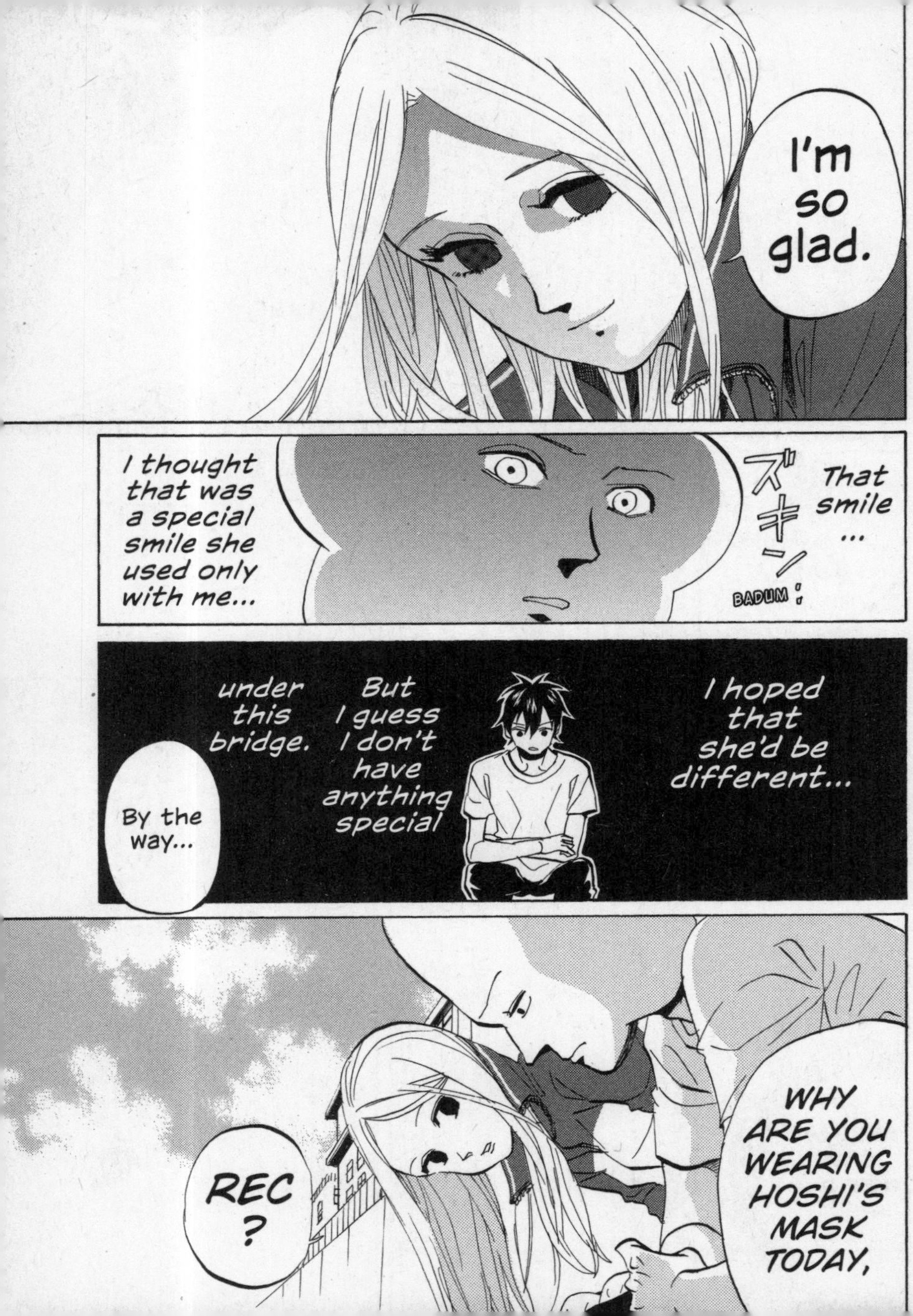
I'm so glad.
That smile...
ズキン
BADUM
I thought that was a special smile she used only with me...
I hoped that she'd be different...
But I guess I don't have anything special
under this bridge.
By the way...
WHY ARE YOU WEARING HOSHI'S MASK TODAY,
REC?

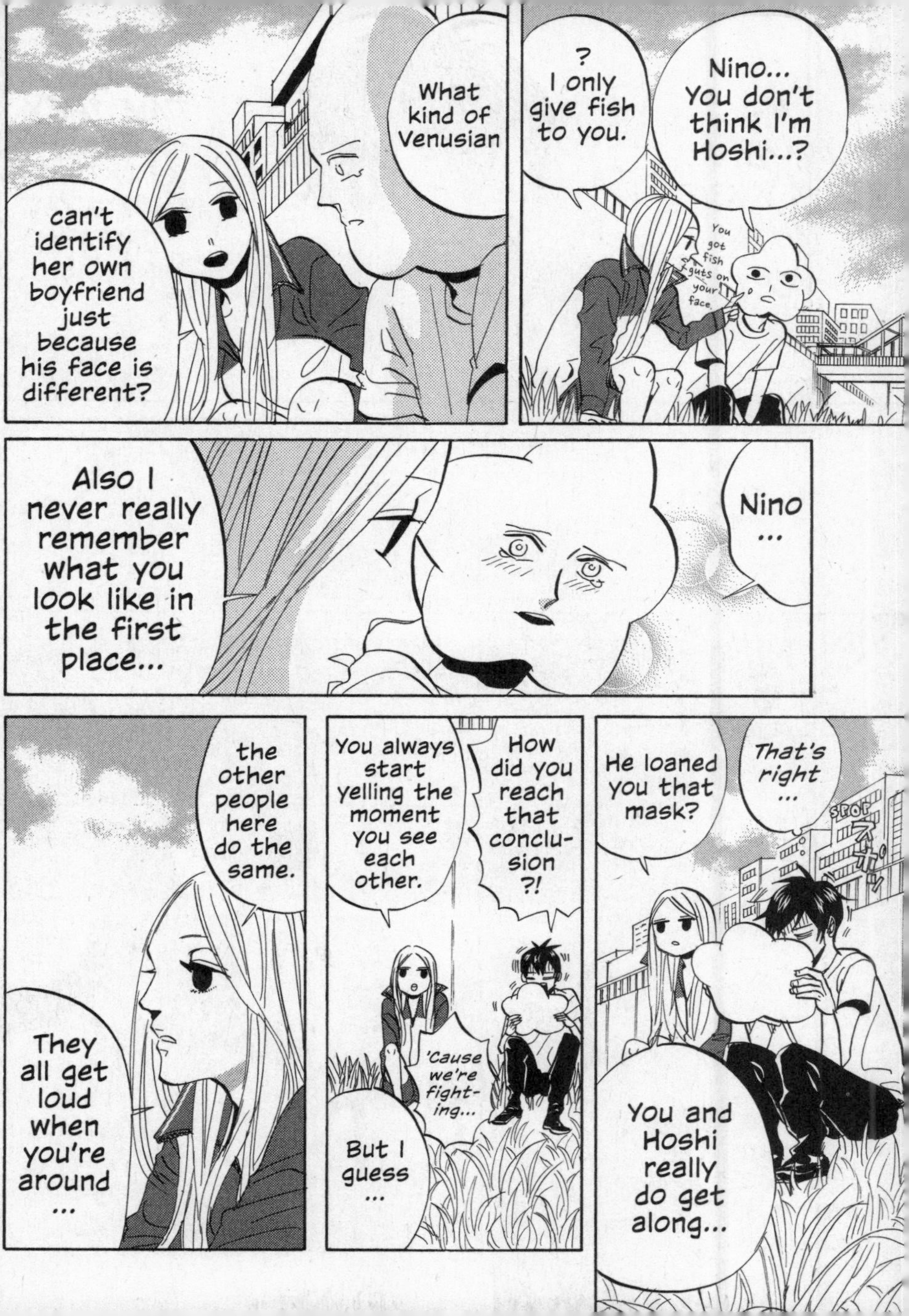
Nino... You don't think I'm Hoshi...?
You got fish guts on your face.
? I only give fish to you.
What kind of Venusian
can't identify her own boyfriend just because his face is different?
Nino ...
Also I never really remember what you look like in the first place...
That's right ...
SPOP
He loaned you that mask?
You and Hoshi really do get along...
How did you reach that conclusion ?!
You always start yelling the moment you see each other.
'Cause we're fighting...
But I guess ...
the other people here do the same.
They all get loud when you're around ...

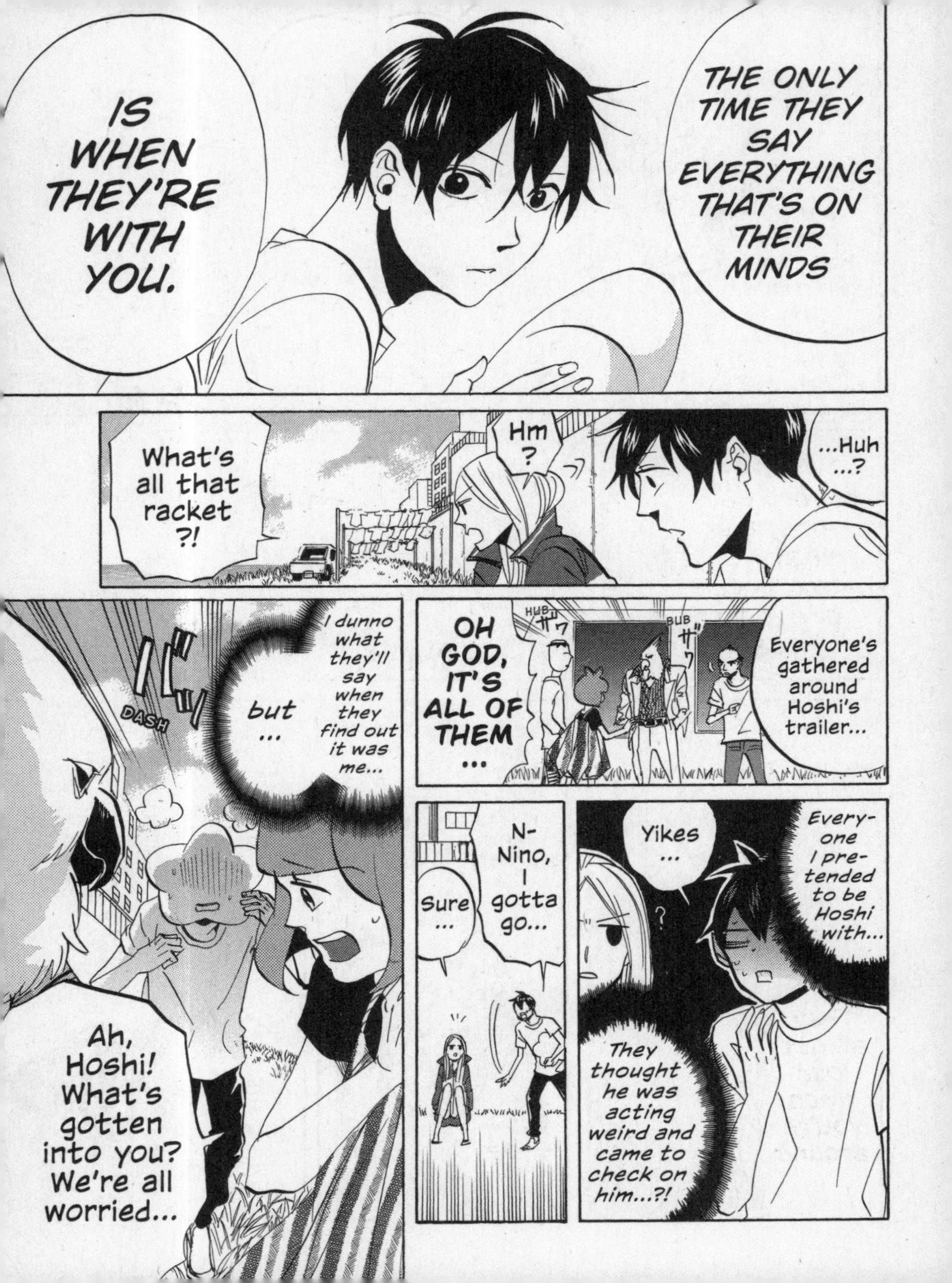
THE ONLY TIME THEY SAY EVERYTHING THAT'S ON THEIR MINDS
IS WHEN THEY'RE WITH YOU.
...Huh ...?
Hm ?
What's all that racket ?!
Everyone's gathered around Hoshi's trailer...
HUB
BUB
OH GOD, IT'S ALL OF THEM ...
Everyone I pretended to be Hoshi with...
Yikes ...
They thought he was acting weird and came to check on him...?!
N-Nino, I gotta go...
Sure ...
I dunno what they'll say when they find out it was me...
but ...
DASH
Ah, Hoshi! What's gotten into you? We're all worried...

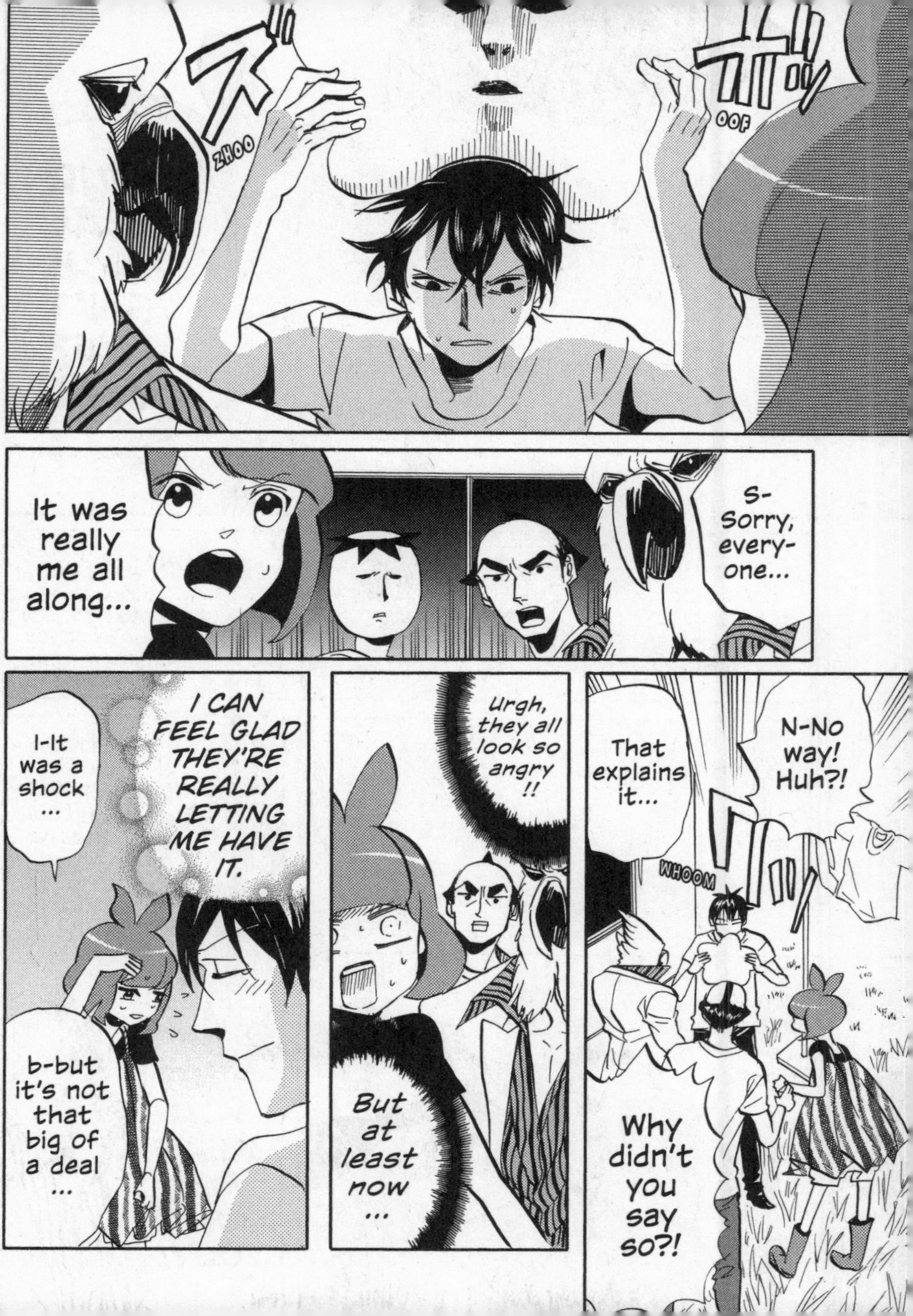
OOF
ZHOO
S-Sorry, every-one...
It was really me all along...
N-No way! Huh?!
That explains it...
WHOOM
Why didn't you say so?!
Urgh, they all look so angry !!
But at least now ...
I CAN FEEL GLAD THEY'RE REALLY LETTING ME HAVE IT.
I-It was a shock ...
b-but it's not that big of a deal ...

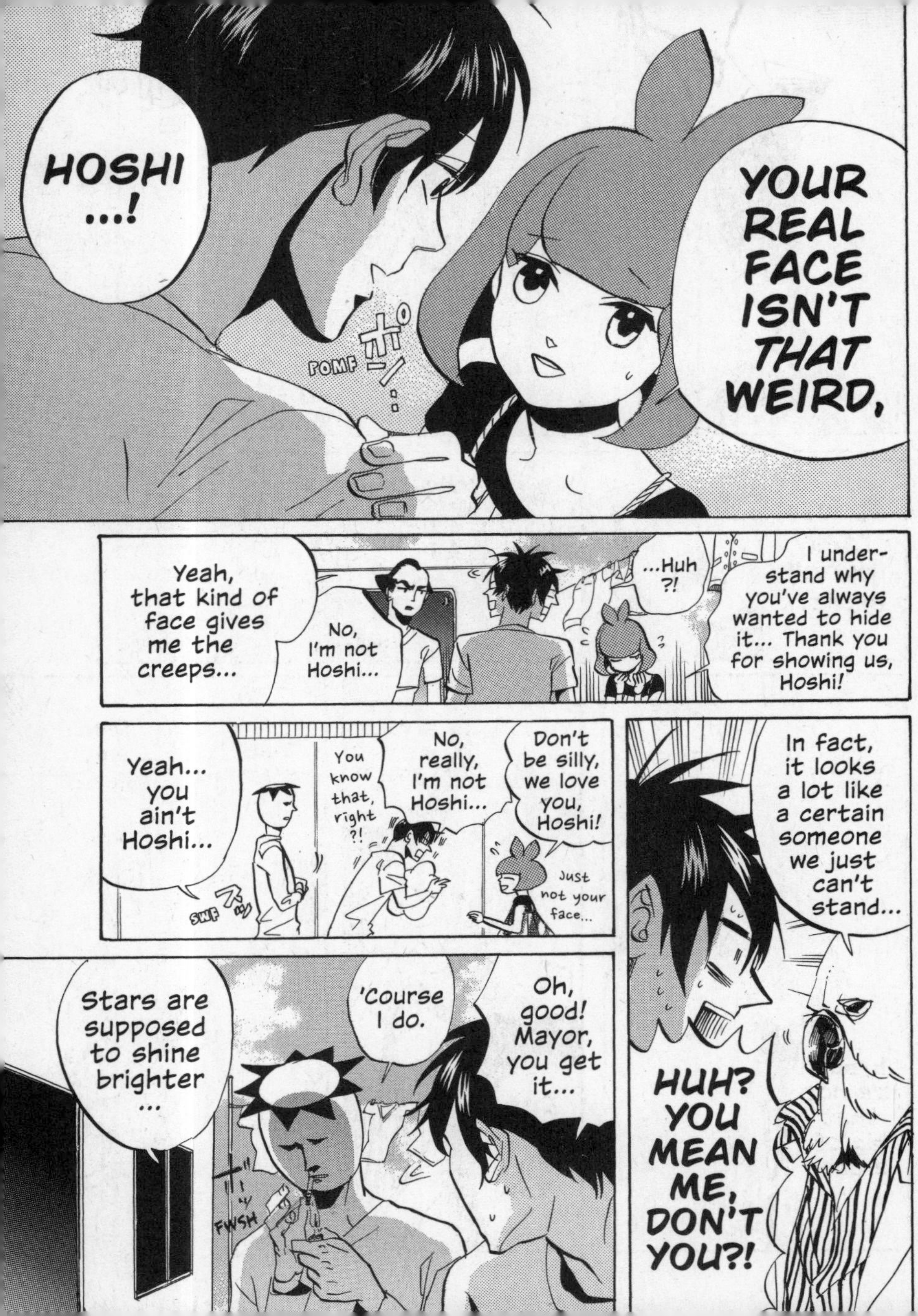
YOUR REAL FACE ISN'T THAT WEIRD,
POMF
HOSHI ...!
I under-stand why you've always wanted to hide it... Thank you for showing us, Hoshi!
...Huh ?!
No, I'm not Hoshi...
Yeah, that kind of face gives me the creeps...
In fact, it looks a lot like a certain someone we just can't stand...
HUH? YOU MEAN ME, DON'T YOU?!
Don't be silly, we love you, Hoshi!
Just not your face...
No, really, I'm not Hoshi...
You know that, right ?!
Yeah... you ain't Hoshi...
SWF
Oh, good! Mayor, you get it...
'Course I do.
Stars are supposed to shine brighter ...
FWSH

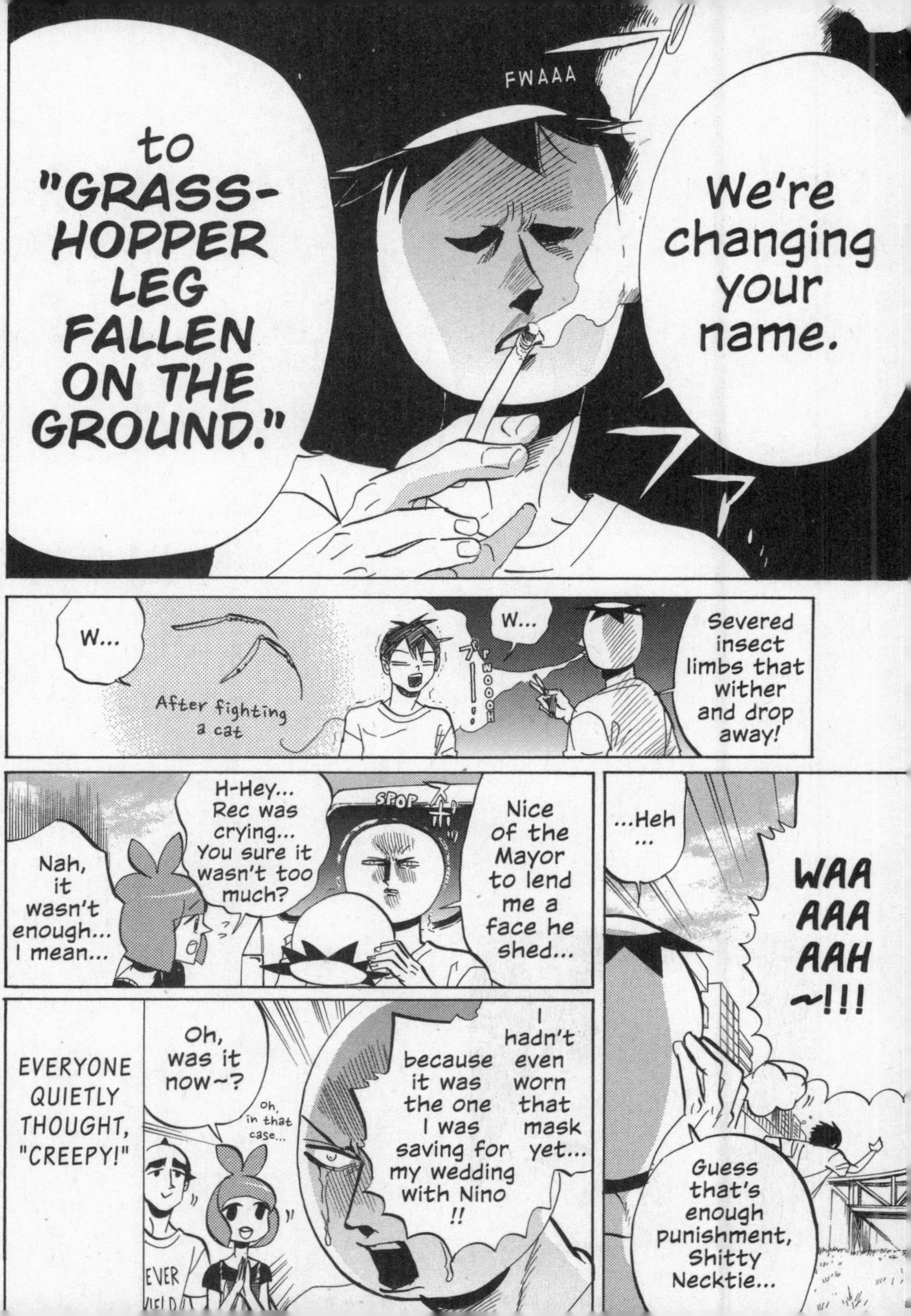
FWAAA
We're changing your name.
to "GRASS-HOPPER LEG FALLEN ON THE GROUND."
Severed insect limbs that wither and drop away!
W...
W...
After fighting a cat
...Heh ...
WAA AAA AAH ~!!!
Nice of the Mayor to lend me a face he shed...
H-Hey... Rec was crying... You sure it wasn't too much?
Nah, it wasn't enough... I mean...
I hadn't even worn that mask yet...
because it was the one I was saving for my wedding with Nino !!
Oh, was it now~?
Oh, in that case...
EVERYONE QUIETLY THOUGHT, "CREEPY!"
Guess that's enough punishment, Shitty Necktie...

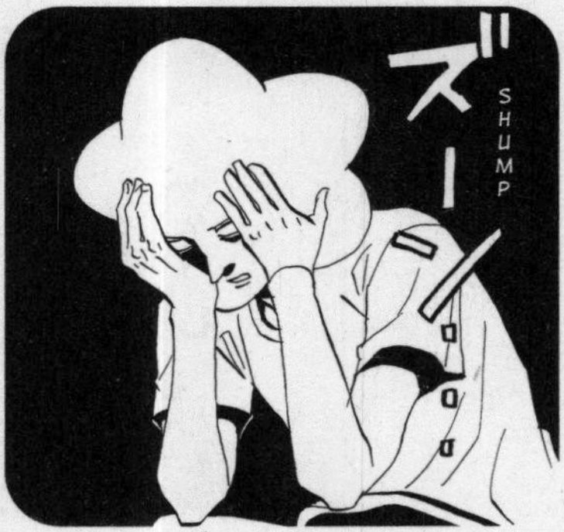
ズーン
SHUMP

ARAKAWA
UNDER
THE BRIDGE

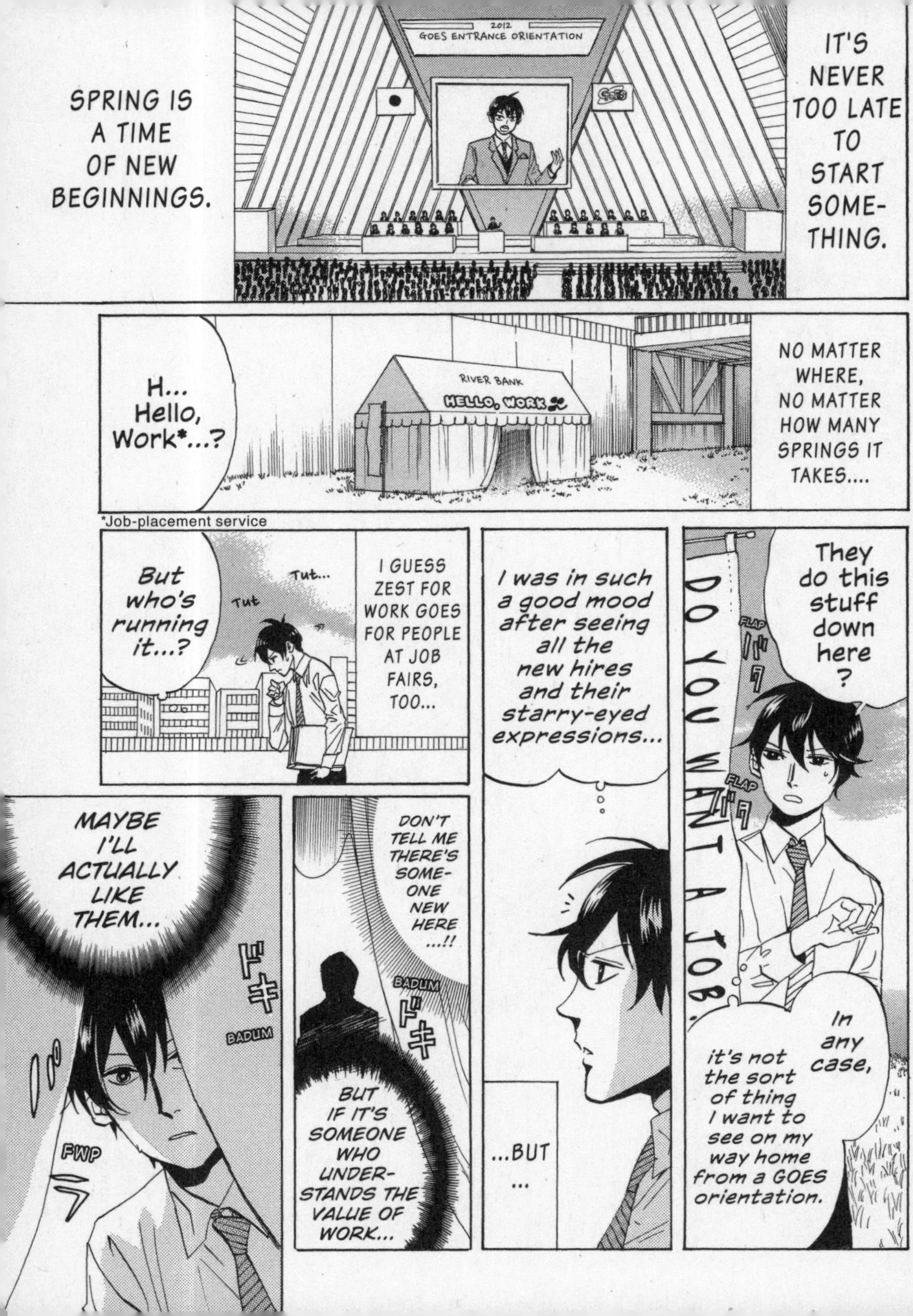
IT'S NEVER TOO LATE TO START SOME-THING.
2012 GOES ENTRANCE ORIENTATION
SPRING IS A TIME OF NEW BEGINNINGS.
NO MATTER WHERE, NO MATTER HOW MANY SPRINGS IT TAKES....
RIVER BANK
HELLO, WORK
H... Hello, Work*...?
They do this stuff down here?
FLAP
DO YOU WANT A JOB.
FLAP
In any case,
it's not the sort of thing I want to see on my way home from a GOES orientation.
I was in such a good mood after seeing all the new hires and their starry-eyed expressions...
...BUT ...
I GUESS ZEST FOR WORK GOES FOR PEOPLE AT JOB FAIRS, TOO...
Tut...
Tut
But who's running it...?
DON'T TELL ME THERE'S SOME-ONE NEW HERE ...!!
BADUM
BUT IF IT'S SOMEONE WHO UNDER-STANDS THE VALUE OF WORK...
MAYBE I'LL ACTUALLY LIKE THEM...
BADUM
FWP

*Job-placement service

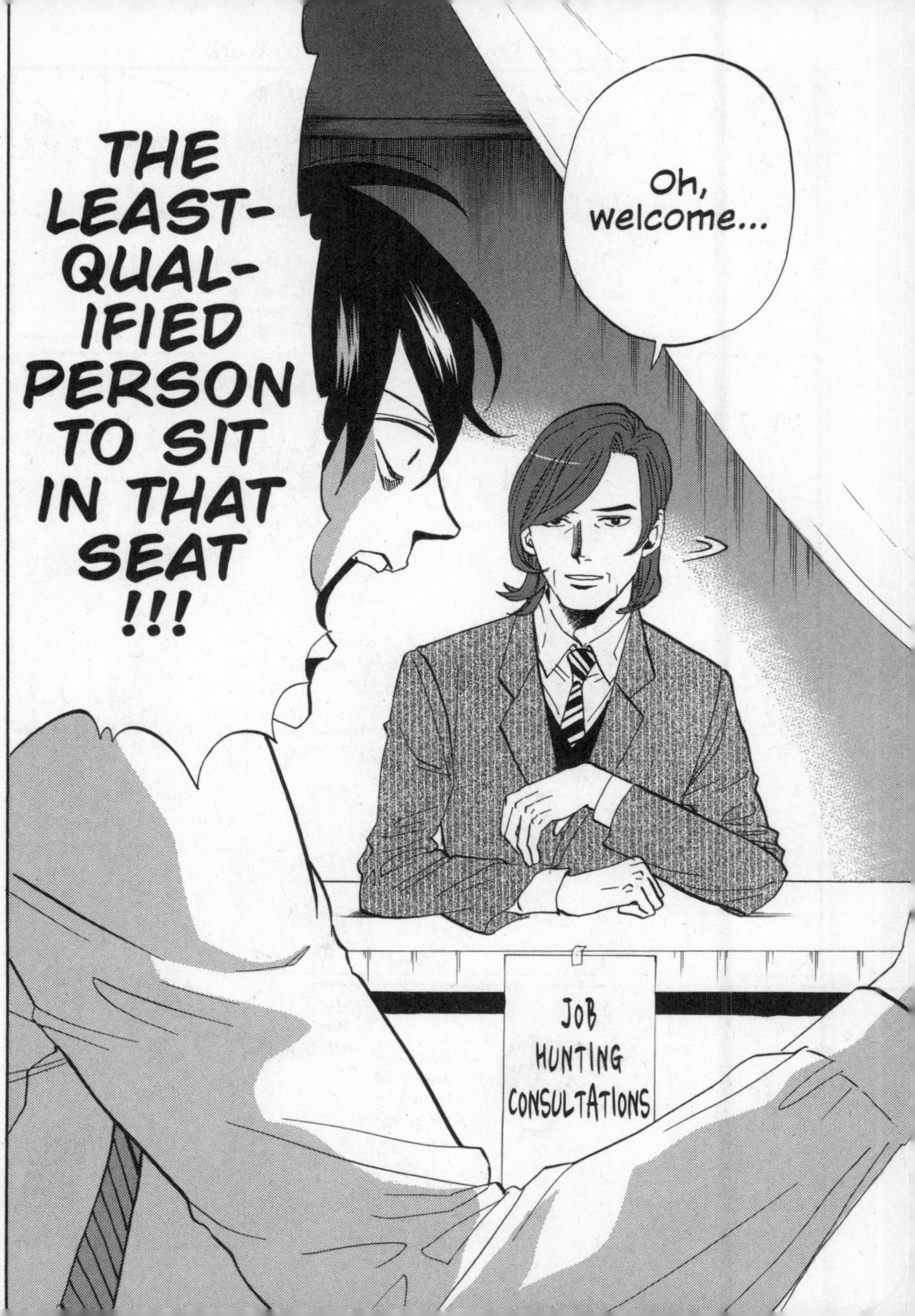
Oh, welcome...
THE LEAST-QUALIFIED PERSON TO SIT IN THAT SEAT!!!
JOB HUNTING CONSULTATIONS

Chapter 328: Arakawa Hello, Work

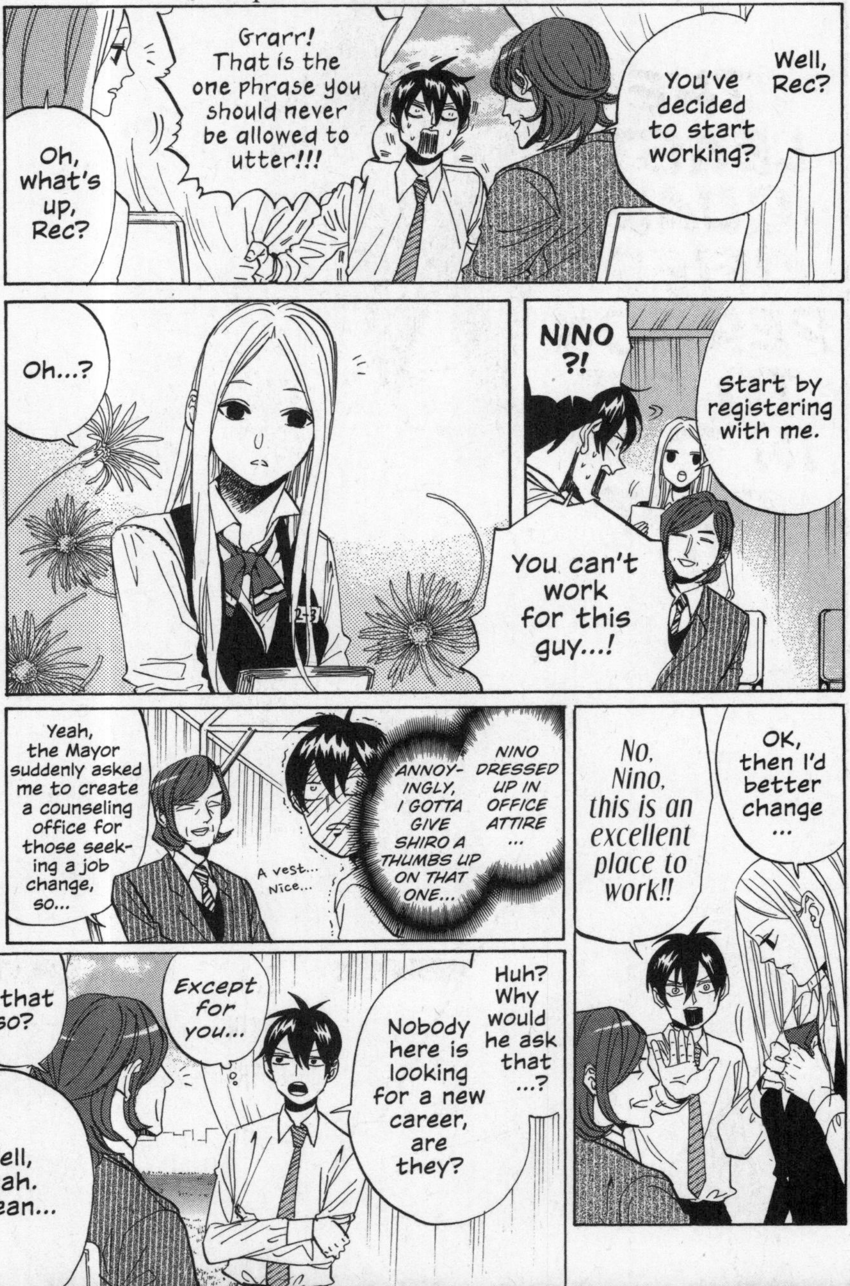
Well, Rec?
You've decided to start working?
Grarr! That is the one phrase you should never be allowed to utter!!!
Oh, what's up, Rec?
NINO ?!
Start by registering with me.
You can't work for this guy...!
Oh...?
OK, then I'd better change ...
No, Nino, this is an excellent place to work!!
NINO DRESSED UP IN OFFICE ATTIRE ...
ANNOY-INGLY, I GOTTA GIVE SHIRO A THUMBS UP ON THAT ONE...
A vest... Nice...
Yeah, the Mayor suddenly asked me to create a counseling office for those seek-ing a job change, so...
Huh? Why would he ask that ...?
Nobody here is looking for a new career, are they?
Except for you...
Is that so?
Well, yeah. I mean...

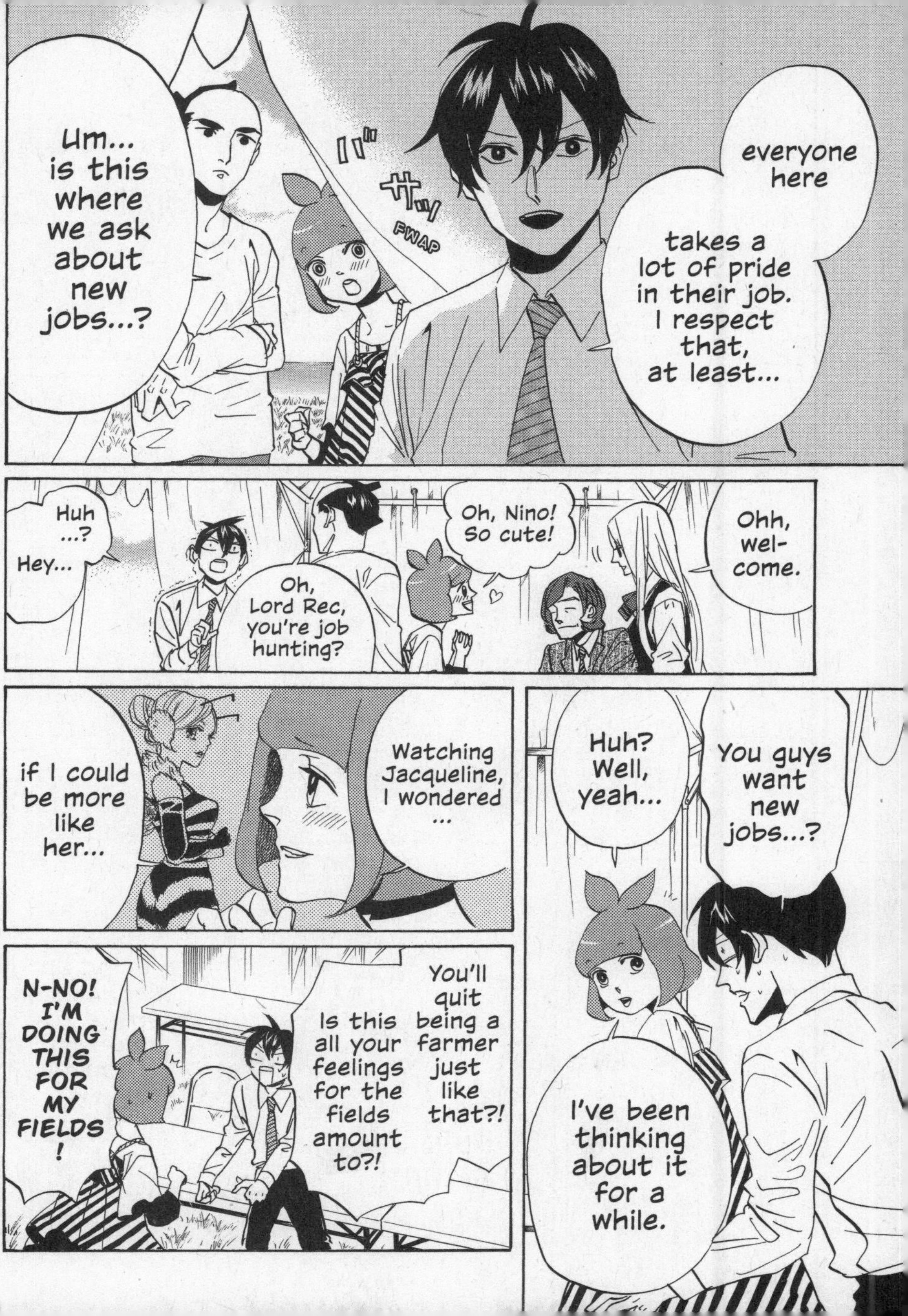
everyone here
takes a lot of pride in their job. I respect that, at least...
FWAP
Um... is this where we ask about new jobs...?
Ohh, wel-come.
Oh, Nino! So cute!
Oh, Lord Rec, you're job hunting?
Huh ...?
Hey...
You guys want new jobs...?
Huh? Well, yeah...
I've been thinking about it for a while.
Watching Jacqueline, I wondered ...
if I could be more like her...
You'll quit being a farmer just like that?!
Is this all your feelings for the fields amount to?!
N-NO! I'M DOING THIS FOR MY FIELDS!

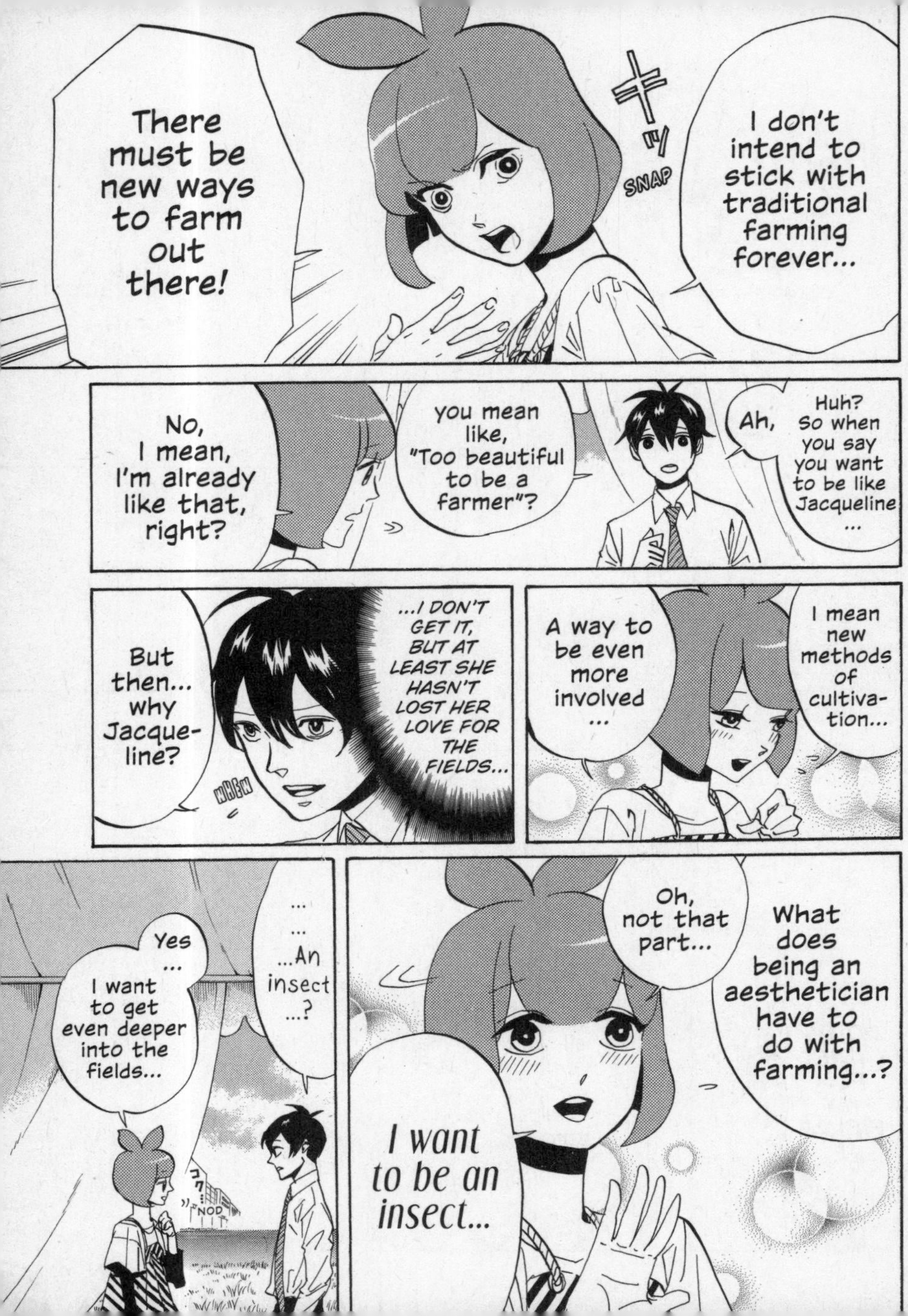
I don't intend to stick with traditional farming forever...
SNAP
There must be new ways to farm out there!
Huh? So when you say you want to be like Jacqueline ...
Ah,
you mean like, "Too beautiful to be a farmer"?
No, I mean, I'm already like that, right?
I mean new methods of cultiva-tion...
A way to be even more involved ...
...I DON'T GET IT, BUT AT LEAST SHE HASN'T LOST HER LOVE FOR THE FIELDS...
WHEW
But then... why Jacque-line?
What does being an aesthetician have to do with farming...?
Oh, not that part...
I want to be an insect...
... ...An insect ...?
Yes ... I want to get even deeper into the fields...
NOD

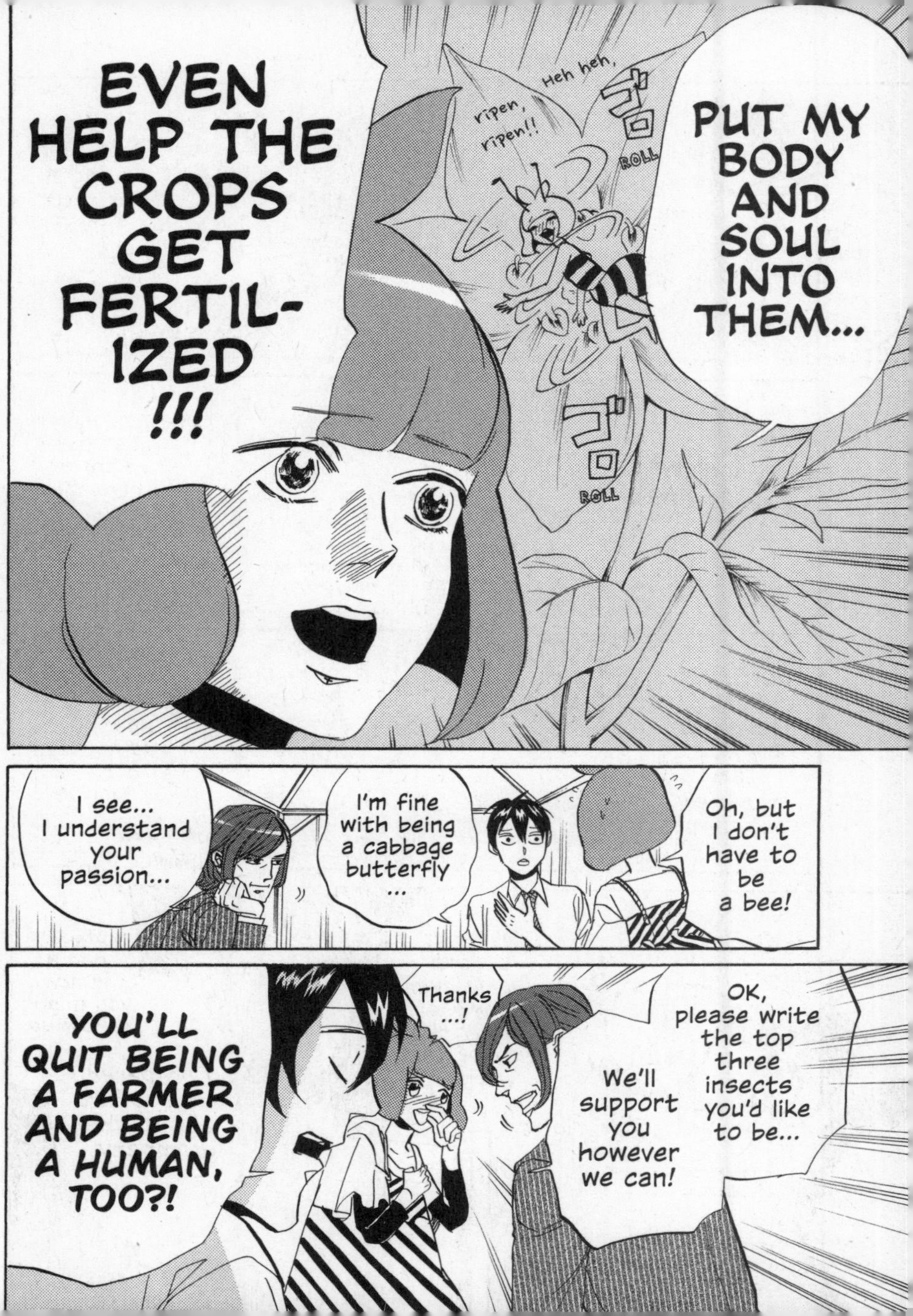
PUT MY BODY AND SOUL INTO THEM...
Heh heh,
ripen, ripen!!
ゴロ ROLL
ゴロ ROLL
EVEN HELP THE CROPS GET FERTIL-IZED!!!
Oh, but I don't have to be a bee!
I'm fine with being a cabbage butterfly ...
I see... I understand your passion...
OK, please write the top three insects you'd like to be...
We'll support you however we can!
Thanks ...!
YOU'LL QUIT BEING A FARMER AND BEING A HUMAN, TOO?!

Chapter 329: Career Upgrade

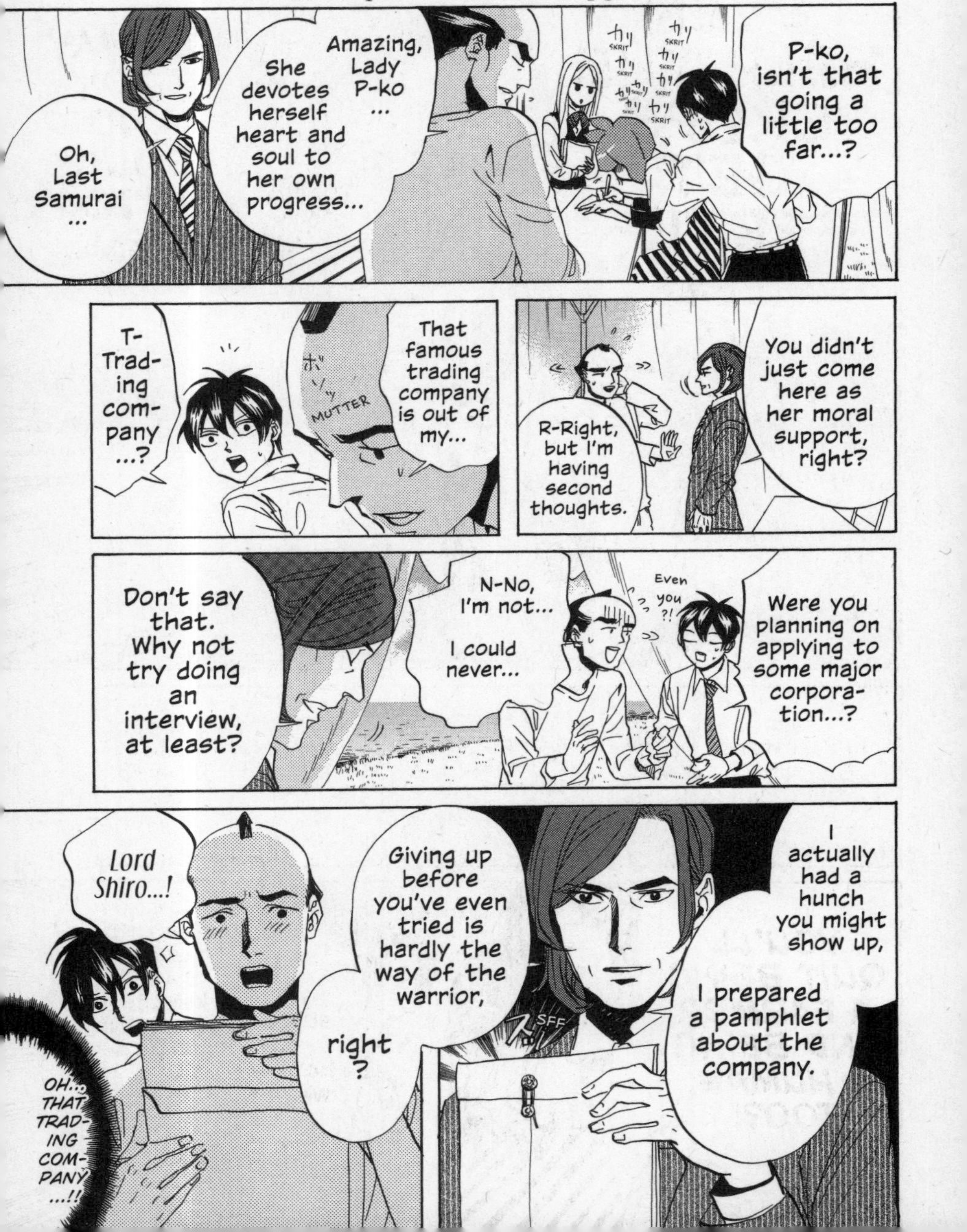
P-ko, isn't that going a little too far...?
SKRIT SKRIT SKRIT SKRIT SKRIT SKRIT SKRIT SKRIT
Amazing, Lady P-ko ...
She devotes herself heart and soul to her own progress...
Oh, Last Samurai ...
You didn't just come here as her moral support, right?
R-Right, but I'm having second thoughts.
That famous trading company is out of my...
MUTTER
T-Trading company ...?
Were you planning on applying to some major corporation...?
Even you ?!
N-No, I'm not...
I could never...
Don't say that. Why not try doing an interview, at least?
I actually had a hunch you might show up,
I prepared a pamphlet about the company.
SFF
Giving up before you've even tried is hardly the way of the warrior,
right ?
Lord Shiro...!
OH... THAT TRADING COMPANY ...!!

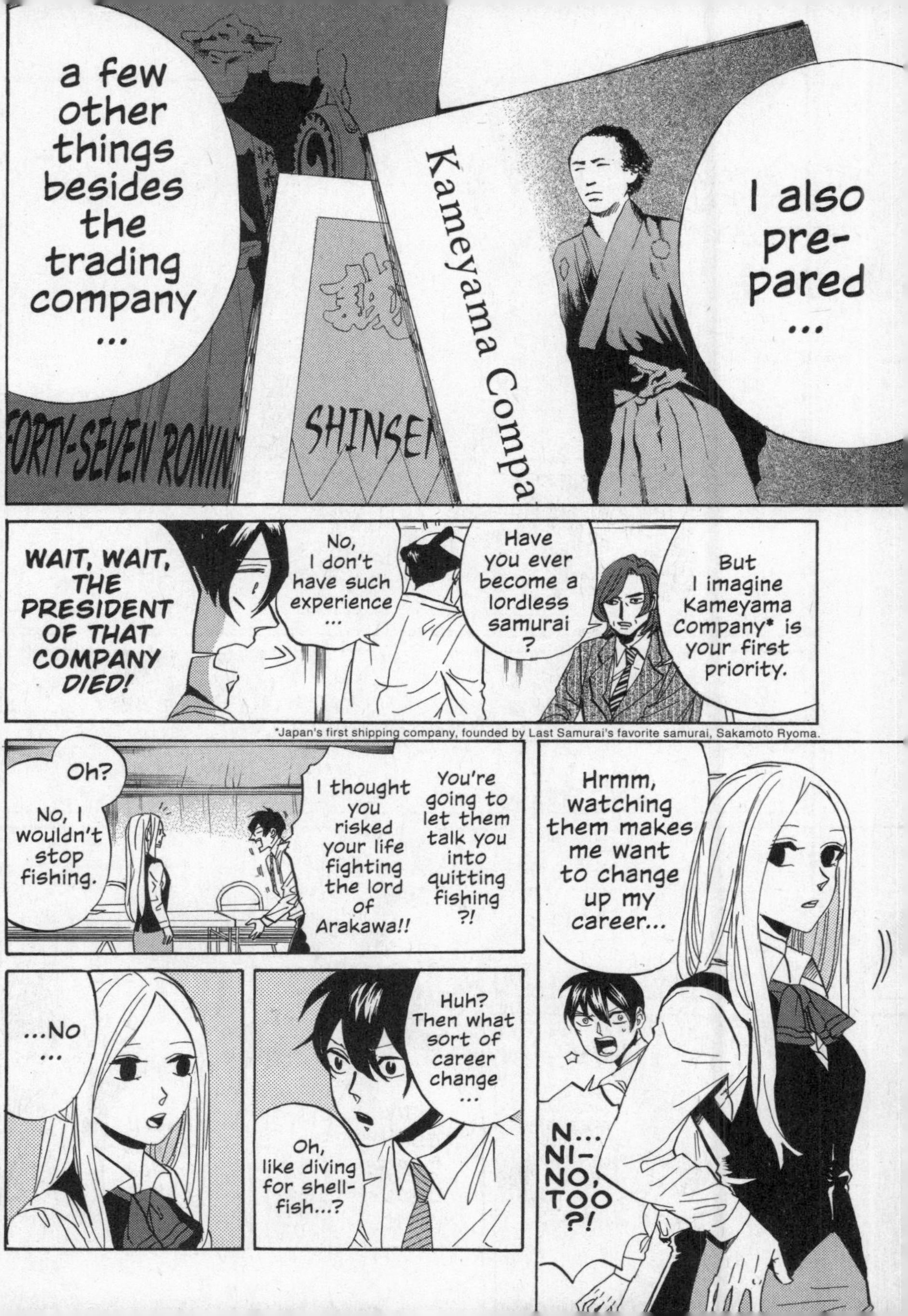
I also pre-pared ...
a few other things besides the trading company ...
Kameyama Compa
SHINSEI
FORTY-SEVEN RONIN
But I imagine Kameyama Company* is your first priority.
Have you ever become a lordless samurai ?
No, I don't have such experience ...
WAIT, WAIT, THE PRESIDENT OF THAT COMPANY DIED!
Hrmm, watching them makes me want to change up my career...
N... NI-NO, TOO ?!
You're going to let them talk you into quitting fishing ?!
I thought you risked your life fighting the lord of Arakawa!!
Oh?
No, I wouldn't stop fishing.
Huh? Then what sort of career change ...
Oh, like diving for shell-fish...?
...No ...

*Japan's first shipping company, founded by Last Samurai's favorite samurai, Sakamoto Ryoma.

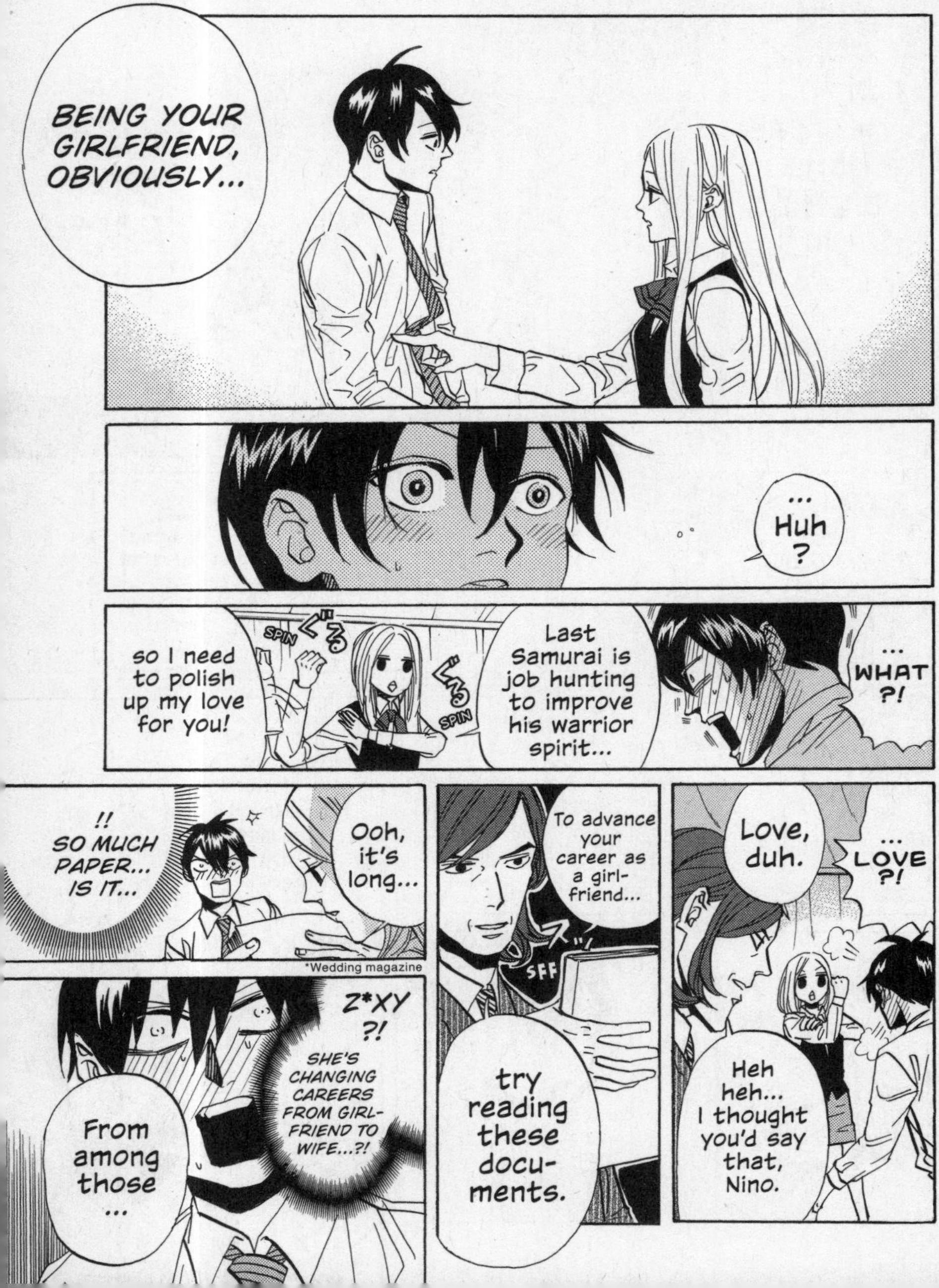
BEING YOUR GIRLFRIEND, OBVIOUSLY...
... Huh ?
... WHAT ?!
Last Samurai is job hunting to improve his warrior spirit...
SPIN
SPIN
so I need to polish up my love for you!
Love, duh.
... LOVE ?!
Heh heh... I thought you'd say that, Nino.
To advance your career as a girl-friend...
SFF
try reading these docu-ments.
Ooh, it's long...
!! SO MUCH PAPER... IS IT...
*Wedding magazine
Z*XY ?!
SHE'S CHANGING CAREERS FROM GIRL-FRIEND TO WIFE...?!
From among those ...

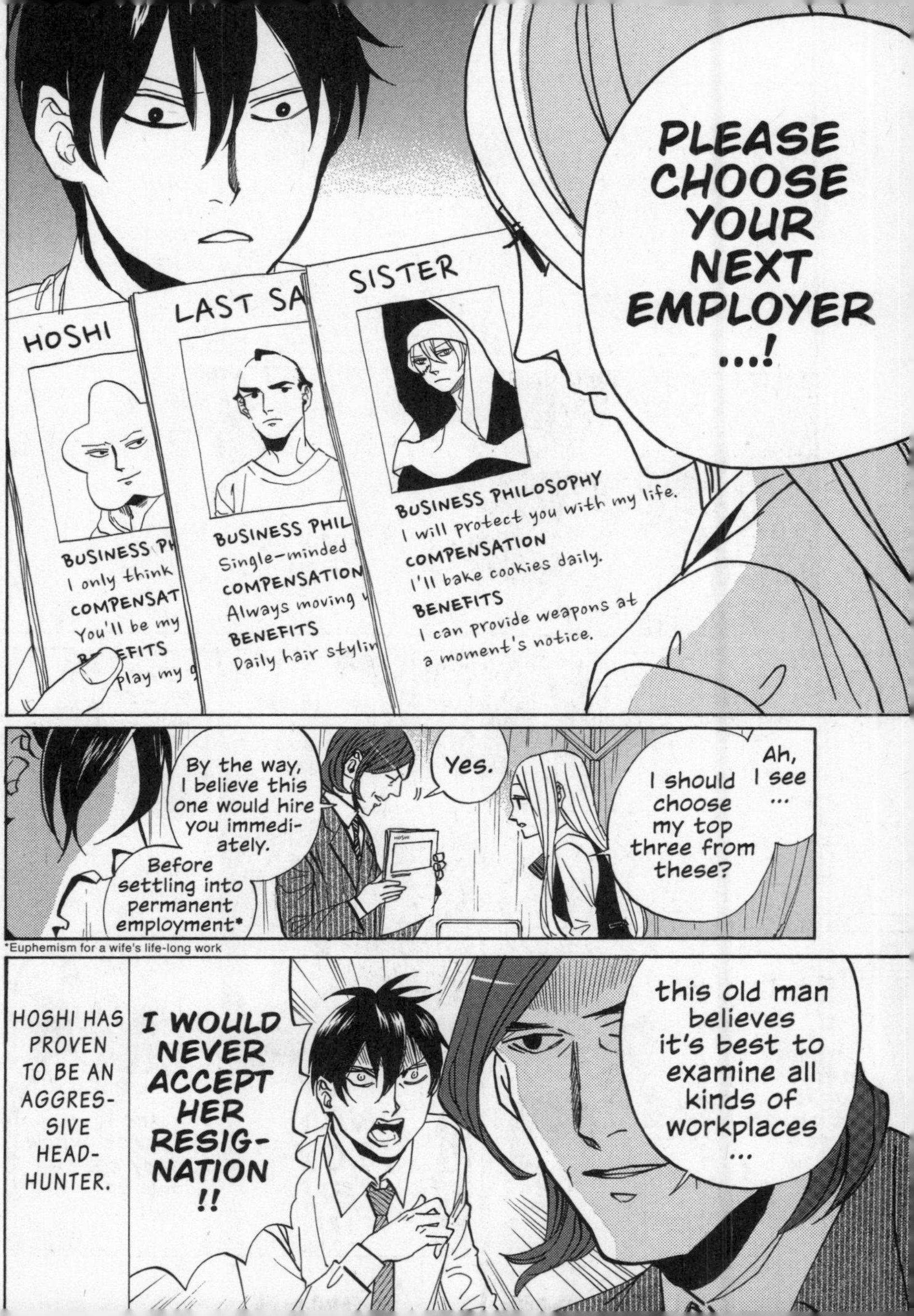
PLEASE CHOOSE YOUR NEXT EMPLOYER ...!
SISTER
BUSINESS PHILOSOPHY
I will protect you with my life.
COMPENSATION
I'll bake cookies daily.
BENEFITS
I can provide weapons at a moment's notice.
LAST SA
BUSINESS PHIL
Single-minded
COMPENSATION
Always moving
BENEFITS
Daily hair stylin
HOSHI
BUSINESS P
I only think
COMPENSAT
You'll be my
EFITS
play my
Ah, I see ...
I should choose my top three from these?
Yes.
By the way, I believe this one would hire you immediately.
Before settling into permanent employment*
this old man believes it's best to examine all kinds of workplaces ...
I WOULD NEVER ACCEPT HER RESIGNATION !!
HOSHI HAS PROVEN TO BE AN AGGRESSIVE HEAD-HUNTER.

*Euphemism for a wife's life-long work

Chapter 330: True Unemployment

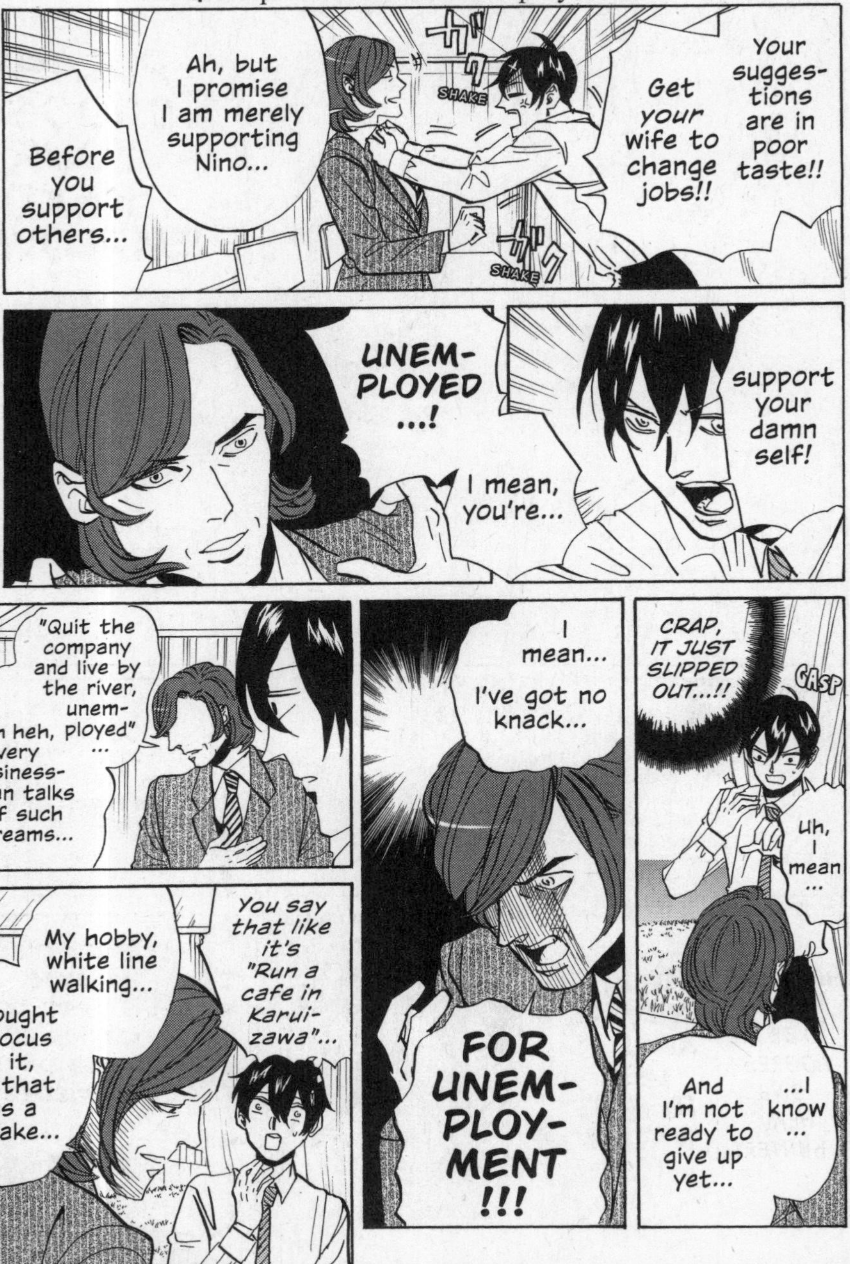
Your sugges-tions are in poor taste!!
Get your wife to change jobs!!
SHAKE
SHAKE
Ah, but I promise I am merely supporting Nino...
Before you support others...
support your damn self!
I mean, you're...
UNEM-PLOYED ...!
CRAP, IT JUST SLIPPED OUT...!!
GASP
Uh, I mean ...
...I know ...
And I'm not ready to give up yet...
I mean...
I've got no knack...
FOR UNEM-PLOY-MENT !!!
"Quit the company and live by the river, unem-ployed" ...
Heh heh, every business-man talks of such dreams...
You say that like it's "Run a cafe in Karui-zawa"...
My hobby, white line walking...
I thought I'd focus on it, but that was a mistake...

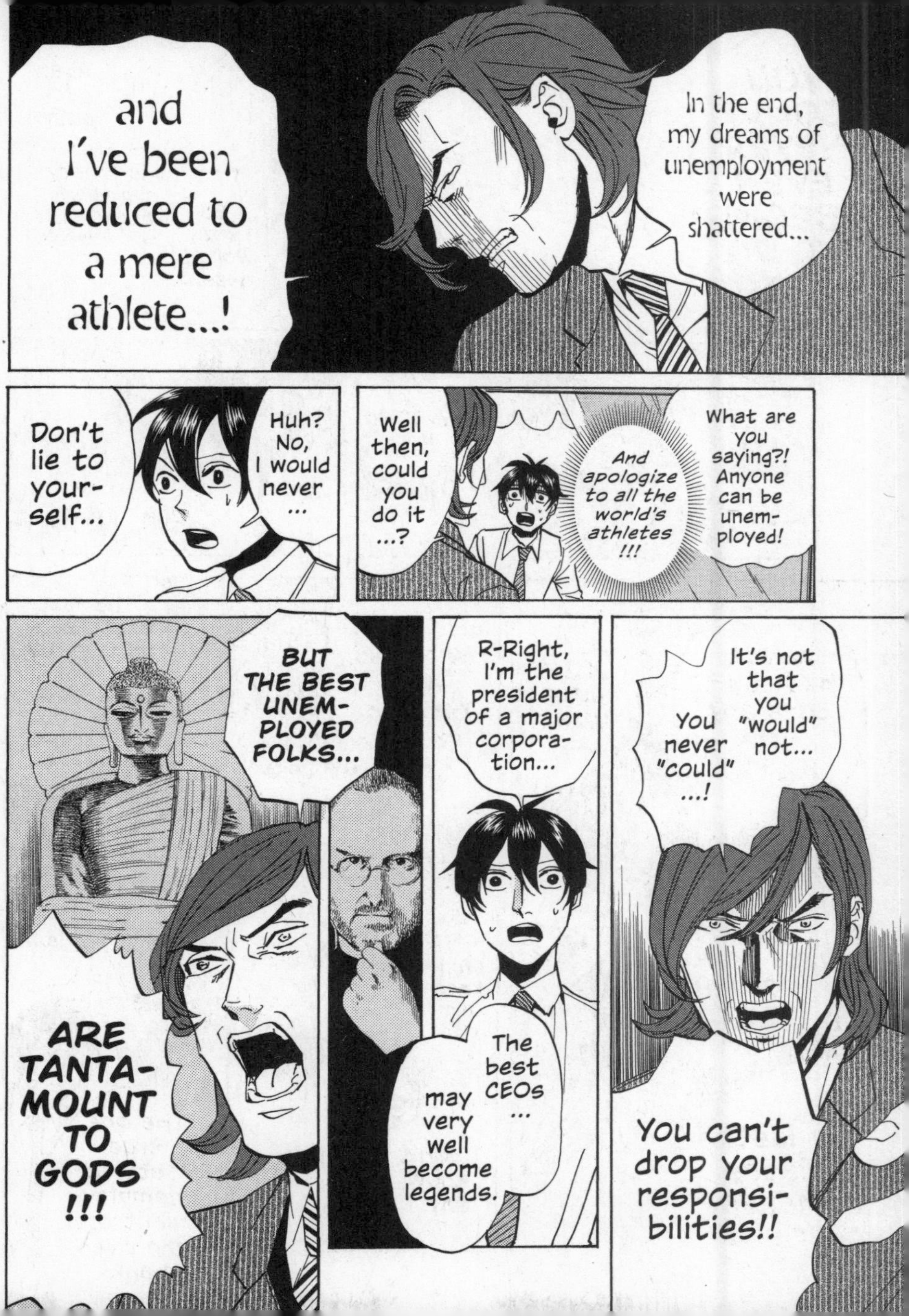
In the end, my dreams of unemployment were shattered...
and I've been reduced to a mere athlete...!
What are you saying?! Anyone can be unemployed!
And apologize to all the world's athletes !!!
Well then, could you do it ...?
Huh? No, I would never ...
Don't lie to yourself...
It's not that you "would" not...
You never "could" ...!
You can't drop your responsibilities!!
R-Right, I'm the president of a major corporation...
The best CEOs ...
may very well become legends.
BUT THE BEST UNEMPLOYED FOLKS...
ARE TANTAMOUNT TO GODS !!!

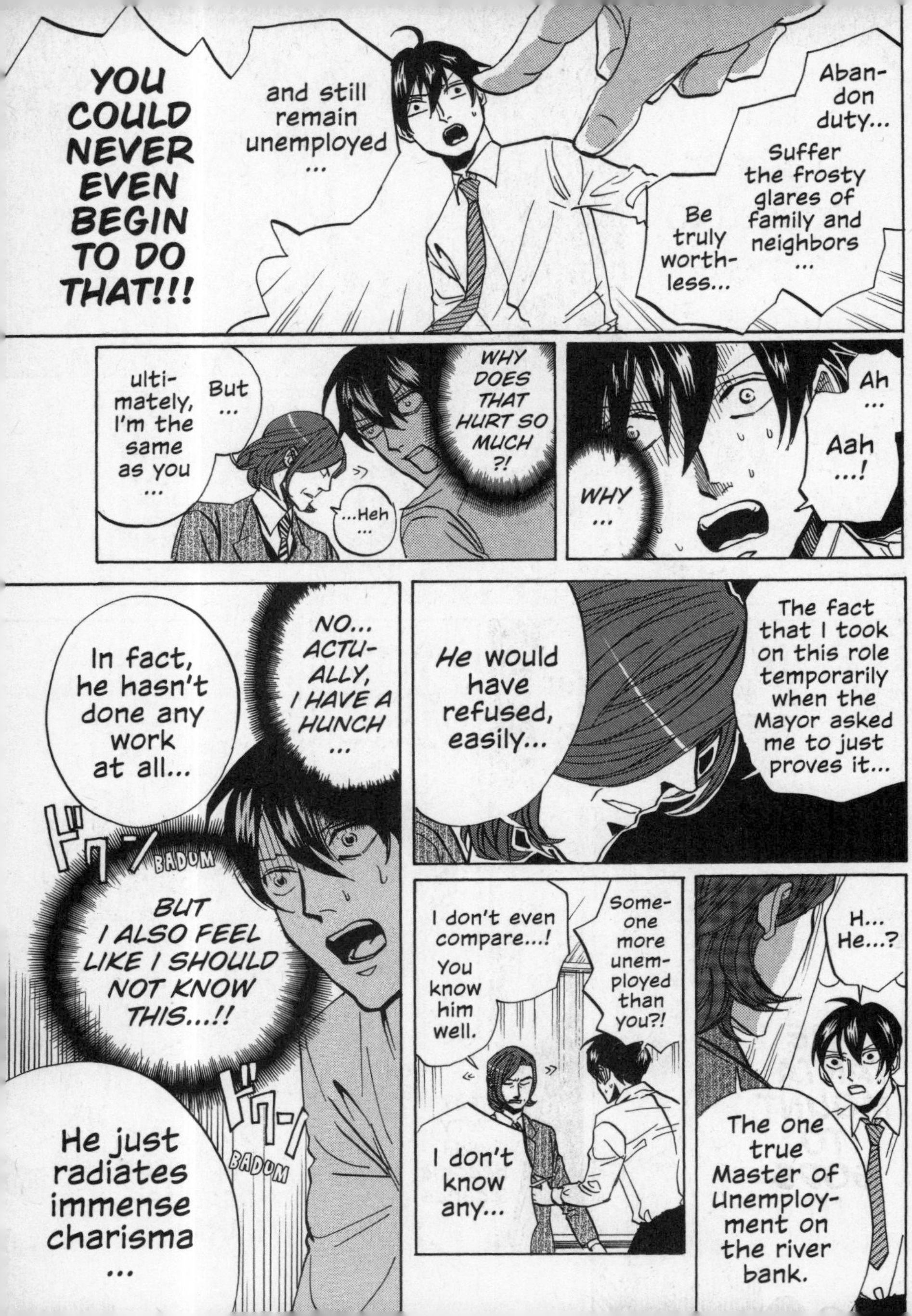
Abandon duty...
Suffer the frosty glares of family and neighbors ...
Be truly worthless...
and still remain unemployed ...
YOU COULD NEVER EVEN BEGIN TO DO THAT!!!
Ah ...
Aah ...!
WHY ...
WHY DOES THAT HURT SO MUCH ?!
But ...
ultimately, I'm the same as you ...
...Heh ...
The fact that I took on this role temporarily when the Mayor asked me to just proves it...
He would have refused, easily...
NO... ACTUALLY, I HAVE A HUNCH ...
In fact, he hasn't done any work at all...
BADUM
BUT I ALSO FEEL LIKE I SHOULD NOT KNOW THIS...!!
BADUM
He just radiates immense charisma ...
H... He...?
The one true Master of Unemployment on the river bank.
Someone more unemployed than you?!
I don't even compare...!
You know him well.
I don't know any...

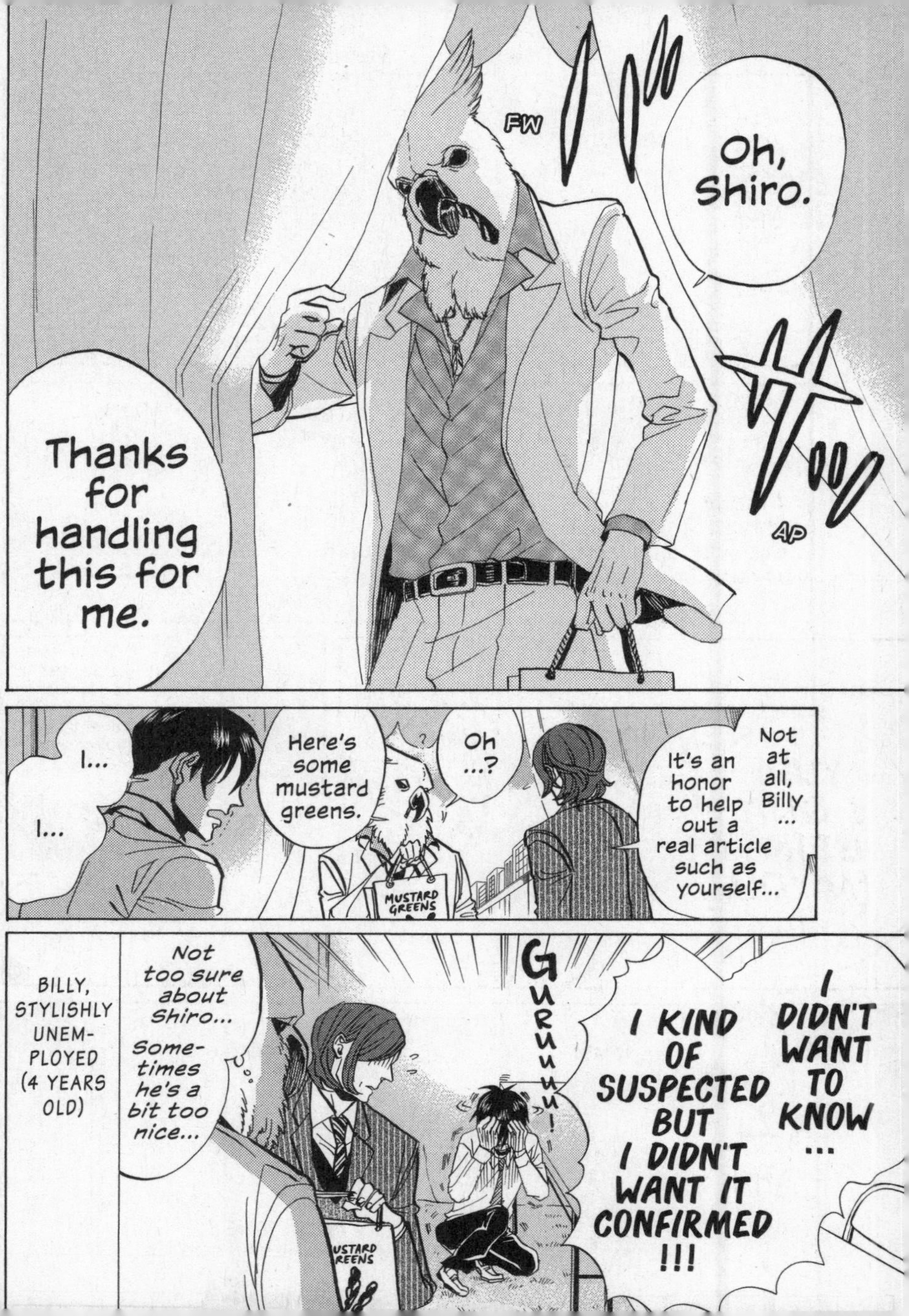
FWOOSH
FW
Oh, Shiro.
AP
Thanks for handling this for me.
Not at all, Billy...
It's an honor to help out a real article such as yourself...
Oh ...?
Here's some mustard greens.
MUSTARD GREENS
I... I...
I DIDN'T WANT TO KNOW...
I KIND OF SUSPECTED BUT I DIDN'T WANT IT CONFIRMED!!!
Guruuuuu!
Not too sure about Shiro...
Some-times he's a bit too nice...
BILLY, STYLISHLY UNEMPLOYED (4 YEARS OLD)

Chapter 331: Spring HR

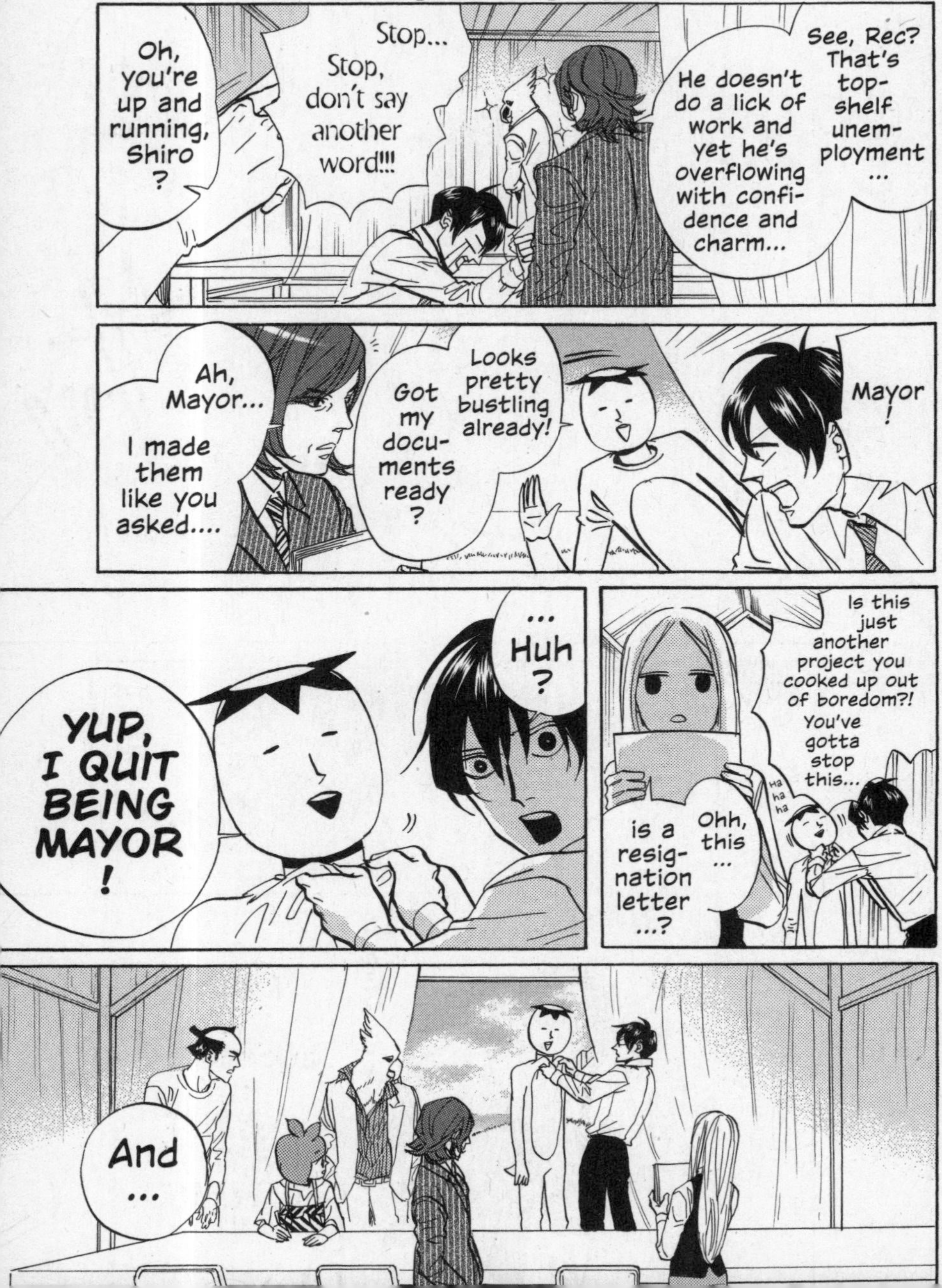
See, Rec? That's top-shelf unemployment...
He doesn't do a lick of work and yet he's overflowing with confidence and charm...
Stop...
Stop, don't say another word!!!
Oh, you're up and running, Shiro?
Mayor!
Looks pretty bustling already!
Got my documents ready?
Ah, Mayor...
I made them like you asked....
Is this just another project you cooked up out of boredom?! You've gotta stop this...
Ha ha ha
Ohh, this...
is a resignation letter...?
... Huh?
YUP, I QUIT BEING MAYOR!
And...

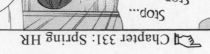

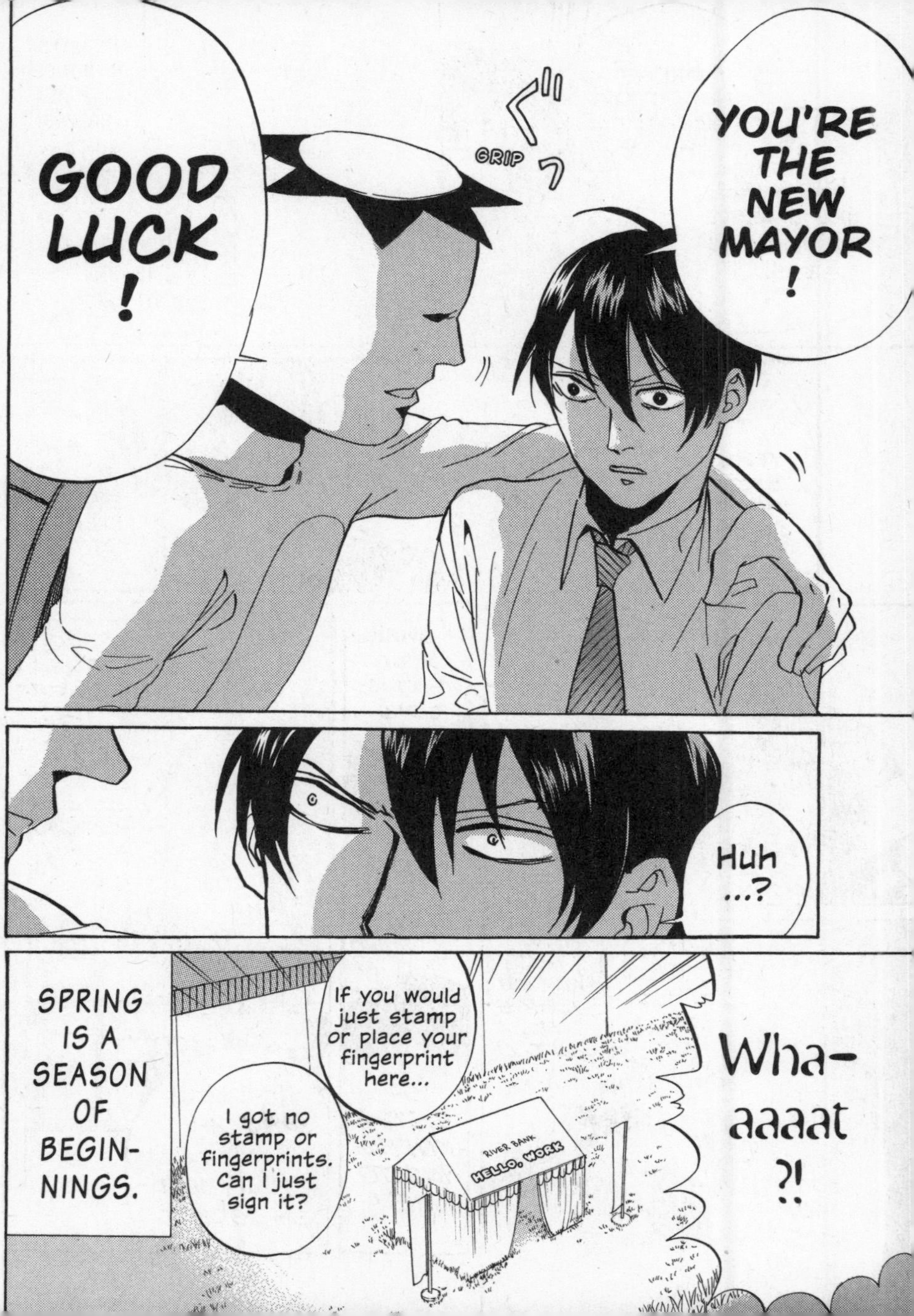
YOU'RE THE NEW MAYOR!
GRIP
GOOD LUCK!
Huh...?
Wha-aaaat?!
If you would just stamp or place your fingerprint here...
I got no stamp or fingerprints. Can I just sign it?
RIVER BANK
HELLO, WORK
SPRING IS A SEASON OF BEGIN-NINGS.

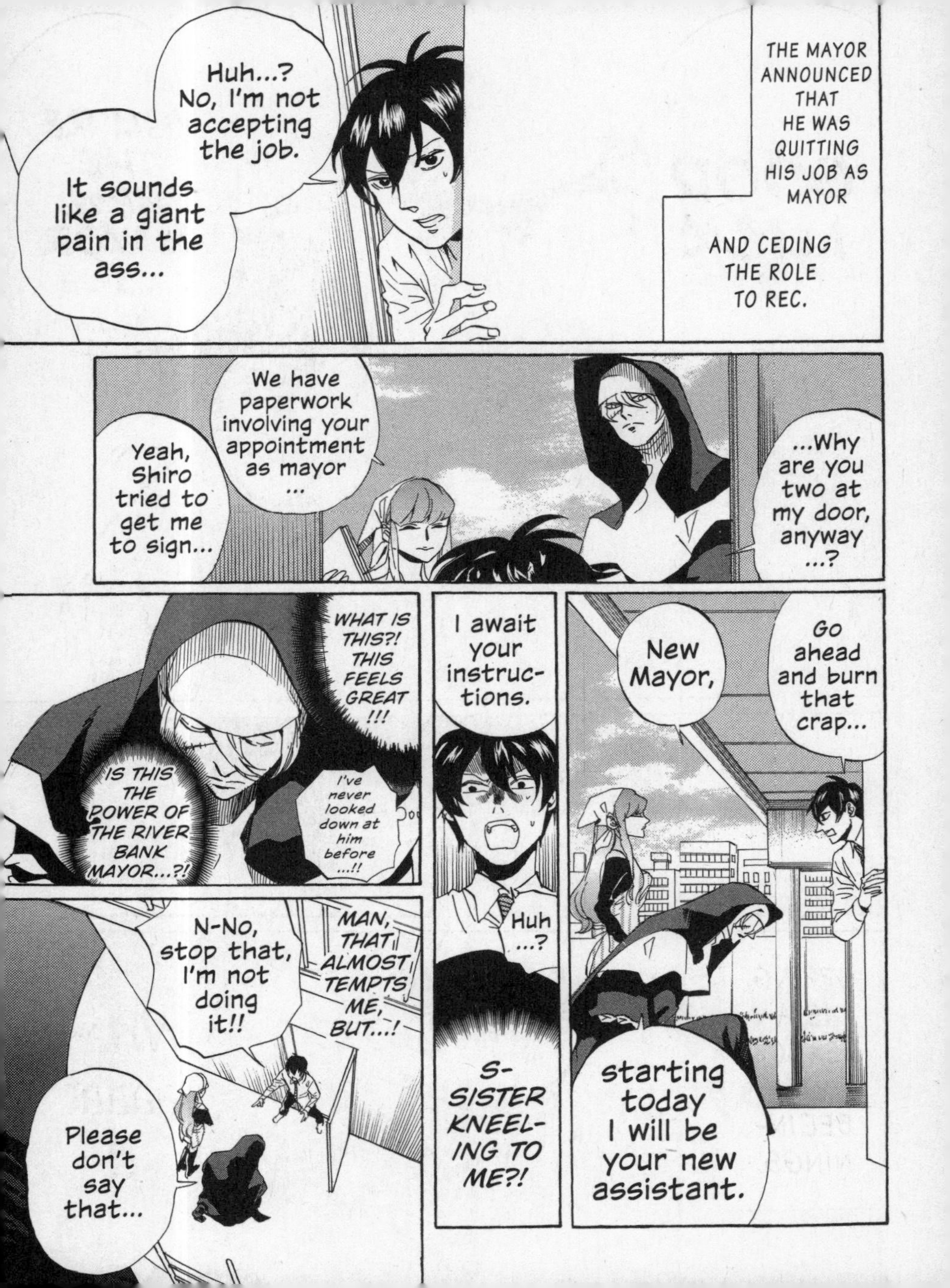
THE MAYOR ANNOUNCED THAT HE WAS QUITTING HIS JOB AS MAYOR
AND CEDING THE ROLE TO REC.
Huh...? No, I'm not accepting the job.
It sounds like a giant pain in the ass...
...Why are you two at my door, anyway ...?
We have paperwork involving your appointment as mayor ...
Yeah, Shiro tried to get me to sign...
Go ahead and burn that crap...
New Mayor,
starting today I will be your new assistant.
I await your instructions.
Huh ...?
S-SISTER KNEELING TO ME?!
WHAT IS THIS?! THIS FEELS GREAT !!!
IS THIS THE POWER OF THE RIVER BANK MAYOR...?!
I've never looked down at him before ...!!
MAN, THAT ALMOST TEMPTS ME, BUT...!
N-No, stop that, I'm not doing it!!
Please don't say that...

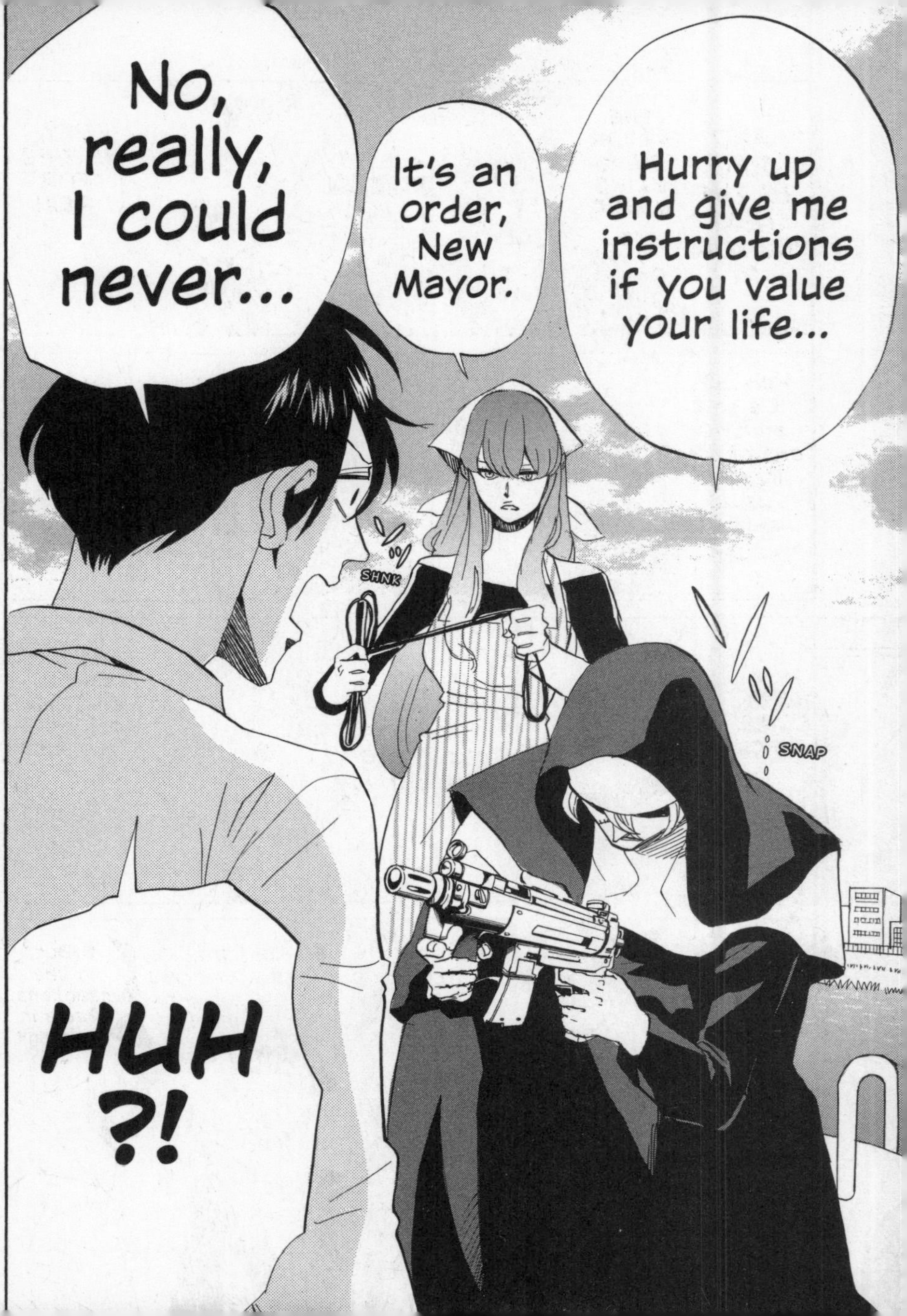
Hurry up and give me instructions if you value your life...
It's an order, New Mayor.
No, really, I could never...
SHNK
SNAP
HUH ?!

Chapter 332: Birth of a New Mayor

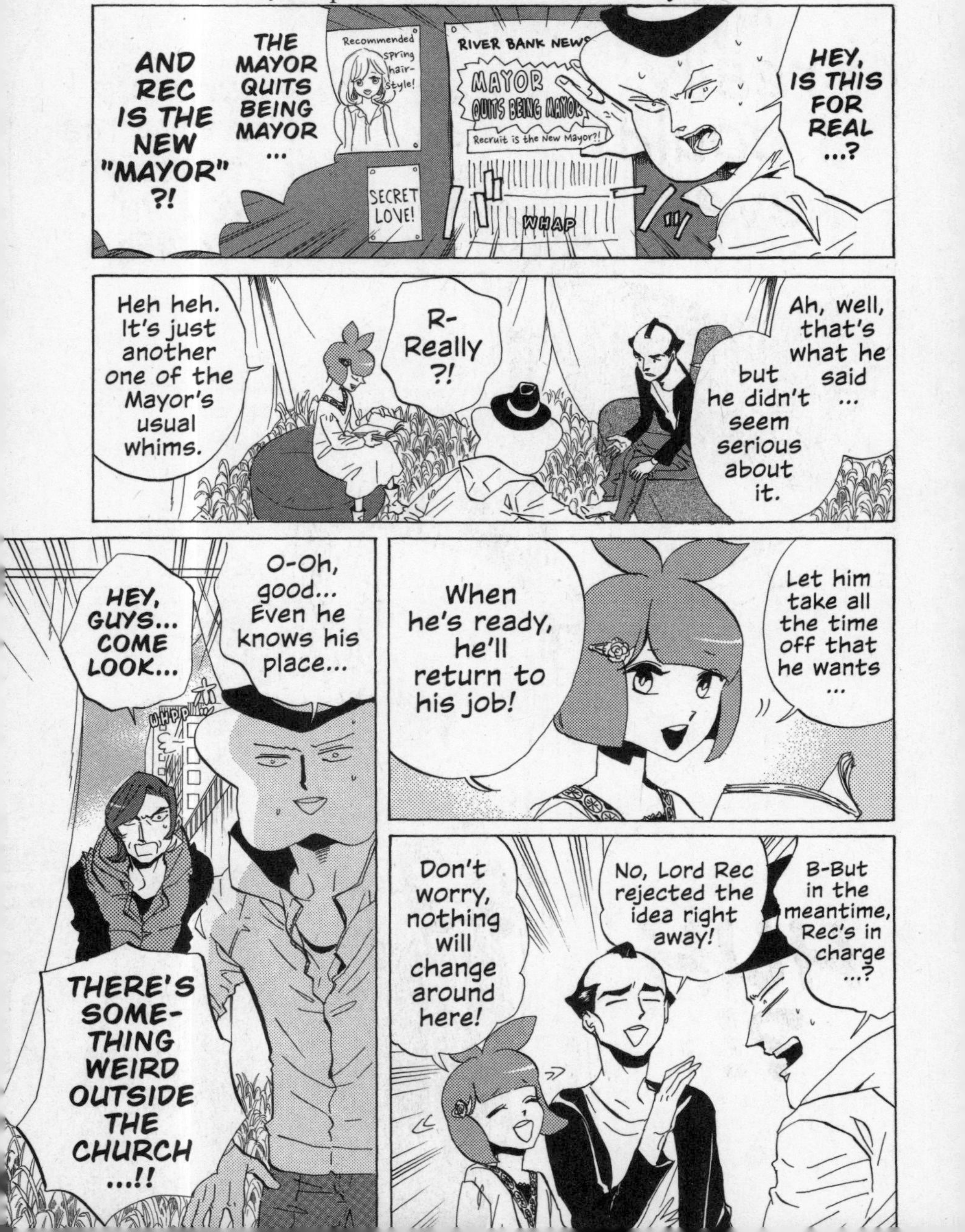
HEY, IS THIS FOR REAL ...?
RIVER BANK NEWS
MAYOR QUITS BEING MAYOR
Recruit is the New Mayor?!
WHAP
Recommended spring hair-style!
SECRET LOVE!
THE MAYOR QUITS BEING MAYOR ...
AND REC IS THE NEW "MAYOR" ?!
Ah, well, that's what he said ... but he didn't seem serious about it.
R-Really ?!
Heh heh. It's just another one of the Mayor's usual whims.
Let him take all the time off that he wants ...
When he's ready, he'll return to his job!
B-But in the meantime, Rec's in charge ...?
No, Lord Rec rejected the idea right away!
Don't worry, nothing will change around here!
O-Oh, good... Even he knows his place...
HEY, GUYS... COME LOOK...
THERE'S SOME-THING WEIRD OUTSIDE THE CHURCH ...!!

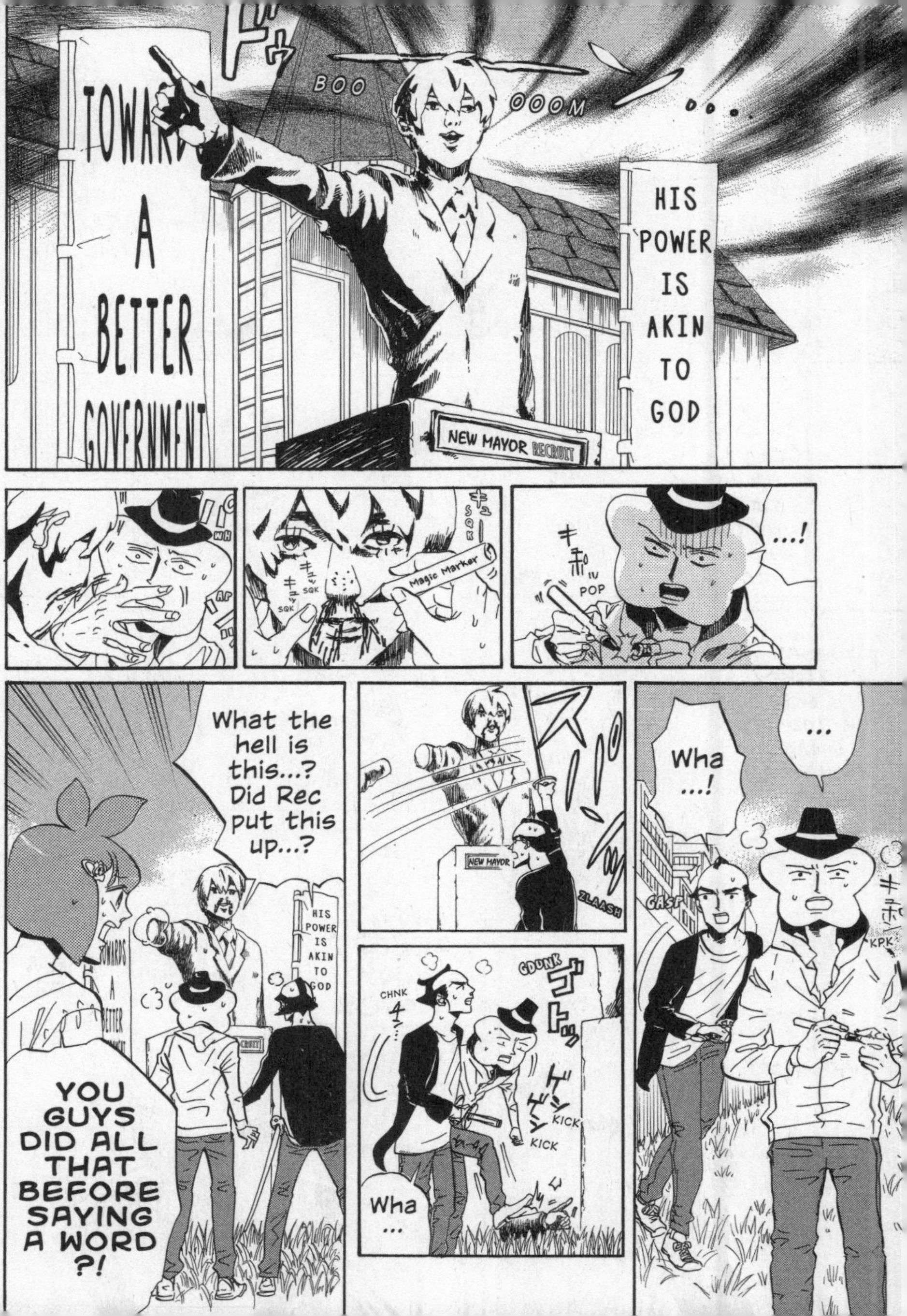
BOO
OOOM
...
TOWARD A BETTER GOVERNMENT
HIS POWER IS AKIN TO GOD
NEW MAYOR RECRUIT
...!
POP
SQK
SQK
SQK
Magic Marker
WH
AP
...
Wha ...!
GASP
KPK
NEW MAYOR
ZLAASH
GDUNK
CHNK
KICK
KICK
Wha ...
What the hell is this...? Did Rec put this up...?
TOWARDS A BETTER
HIS POWER IS AKIN TO GOD
YOU GUYS DID ALL THAT BEFORE SAYING A WORD ?!

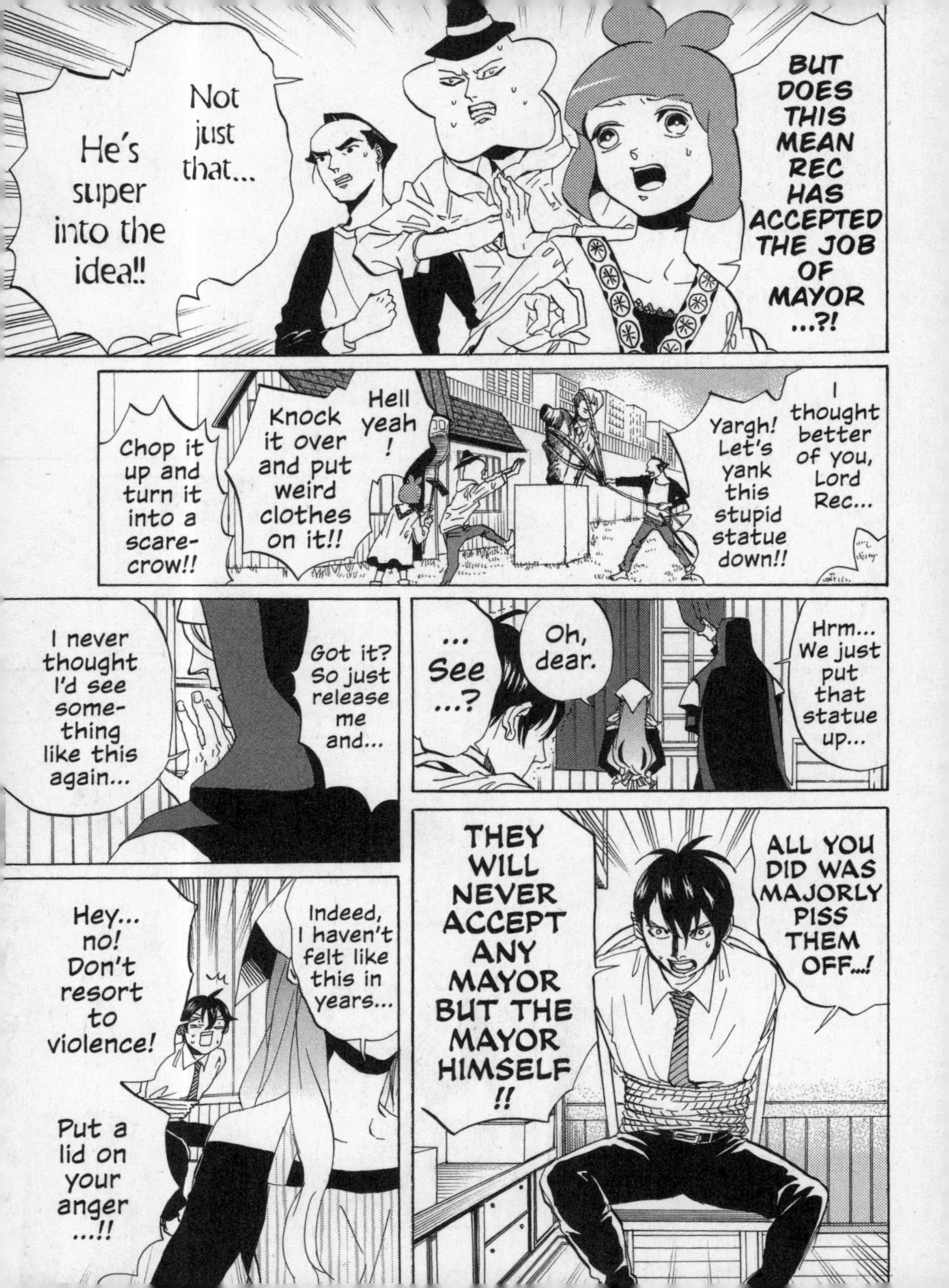
BUT DOES THIS MEAN REC HAS ACCEPTED THE JOB OF MAYOR ...?!
Not just that...
He's super into the idea!!
I thought better of you, Lord Rec...
Yargh! Let's yank this stupid statue down!!
Hell yeah!
Knock it over and put weird clothes on it!!
Chop it up and turn it into a scare-crow!!
Hrm... We just put that statue up...
Oh, dear.
... See ...?
Got it? So just release me and...
I never thought I'd see some-thing like this again...
ALL YOU DID WAS MAJORLY PISS THEM OFF...!
THEY WILL NEVER ACCEPT ANY MAYOR BUT THE MAYOR HIMSELF !!
Indeed, I haven't felt like this in years...
Hey... no! Don't resort to violence!
Put a lid on your anger ...!!

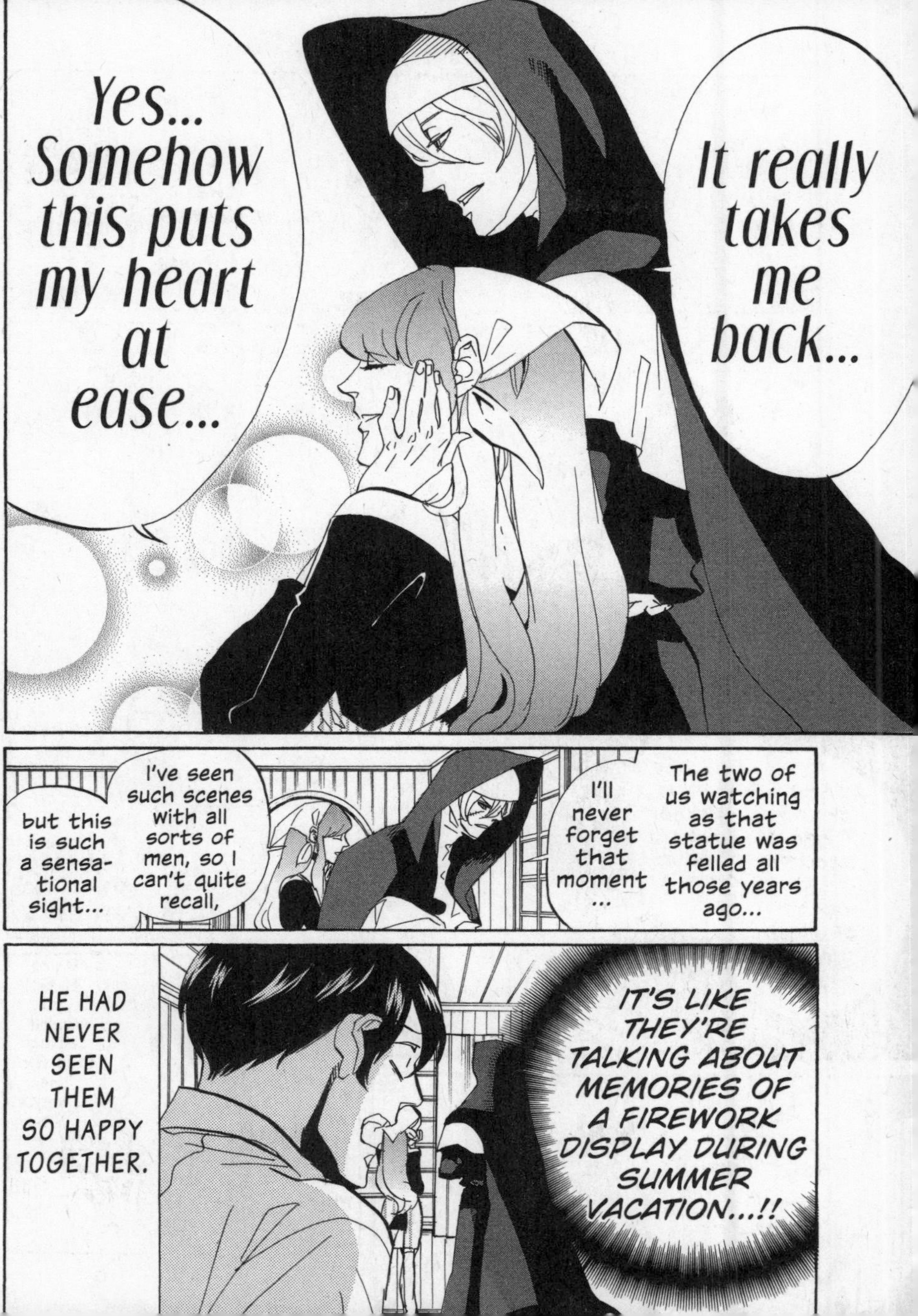
It really takes me back...
Yes... Somehow this puts my heart at ease...
The two of us watching as that statue was felled all those years ago...
I'll never forget that moment ...
I've seen such scenes with all sorts of men, so I can't quite recall,
but this is such a sensational sight...
IT'S LIKE THEY'RE TALKING ABOUT MEMORIES OF A FIREWORK DISPLAY DURING SUMMER VACATION...!!
HE HAD NEVER SEEN THEM SO HAPPY TOGETHER.

Chapter 333: Public Opinion Poll

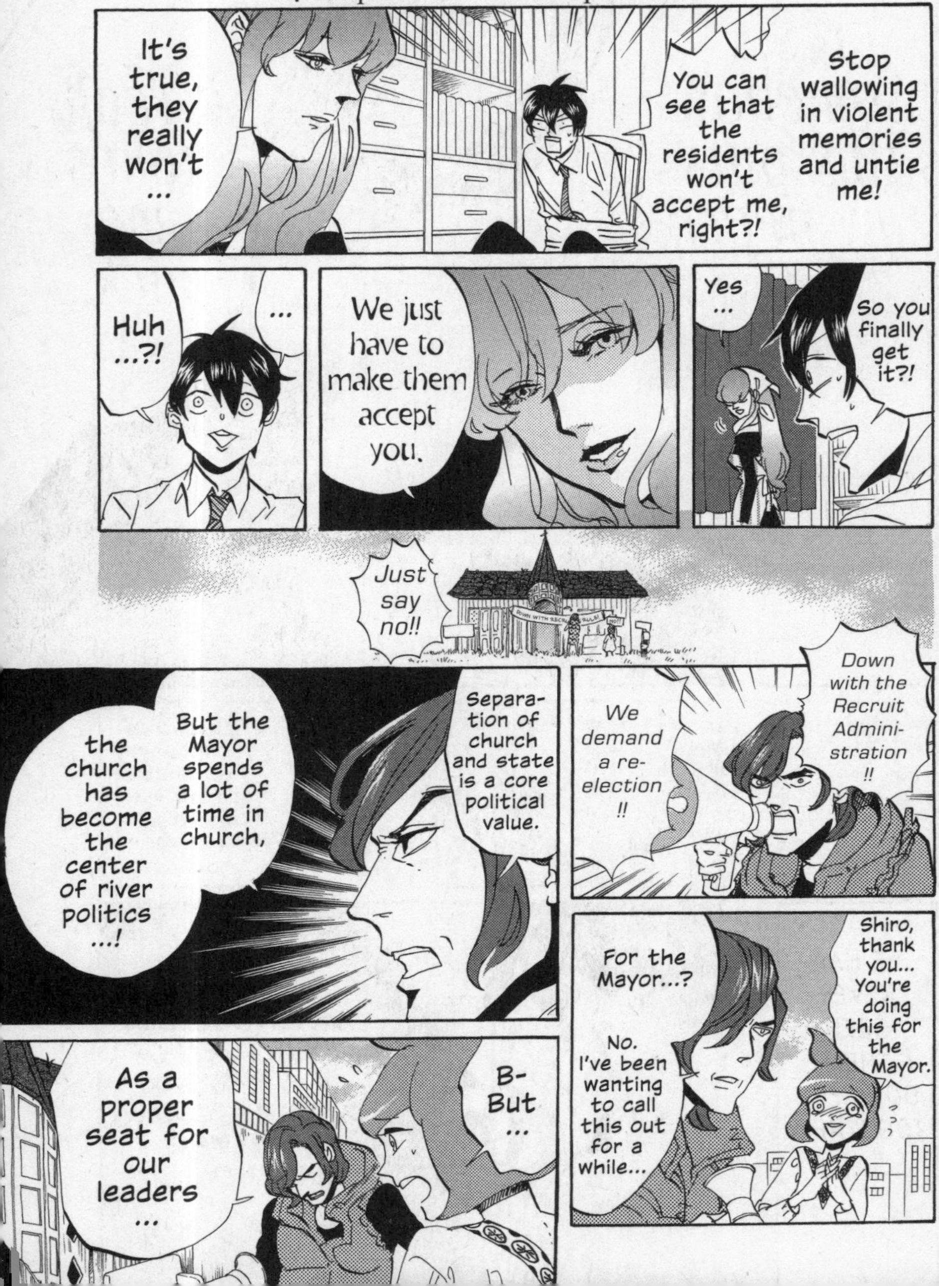
Stop wallowing in violent memories and untie me!
You can see that the residents won't accept me, right?!
It's true, they really won't ...
So you finally get it?!
Yes ...
We just have to make them accept you.
...
Huh ...?!
Just say no!!
Down with the Recruit Administration !!
We demand a re-election !!
Shiro, thank you... You're doing this for the Mayor.
For the Mayor...?
No. I've been wanting to call this out for a while...
Separation of church and state is a core political value.
But the Mayor spends a lot of time in church,
the church has become the center of river politics ...!
B-But ...
As a proper seat for our leaders ...

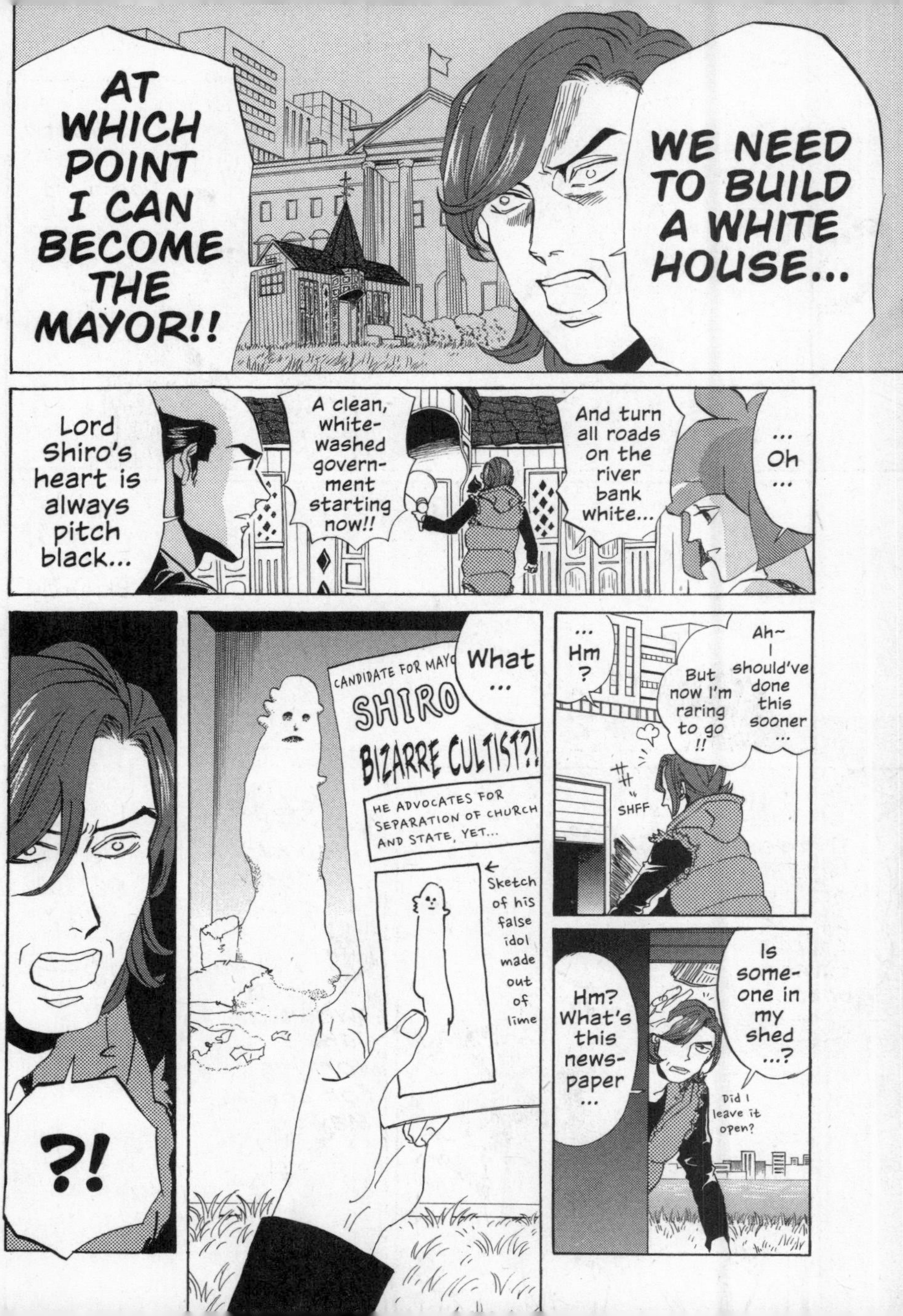
WE NEED TO BUILD A WHITE HOUSE...
AT WHICH POINT I CAN BECOME THE MAYOR!!
...Oh...
And turn all roads on the river bank white...
A clean, white-washed govern-ment starting now!!
Lord Shiro's heart is always pitch black...
Ah~ I should've done this sooner...
But now I'm raring to go!!
SHFF
...Hm?
Is some-one in my shed...?
Did I leave it open?
Hm? What's this news-paper...
What...
CANDIDATE FOR MAYO
SHIRO
BIZARRE CULTIST?!
HE ADVOCATES FOR SEPARATION OF CHURCH AND STATE, YET...
Sketch of his false idol made out of lime
?!

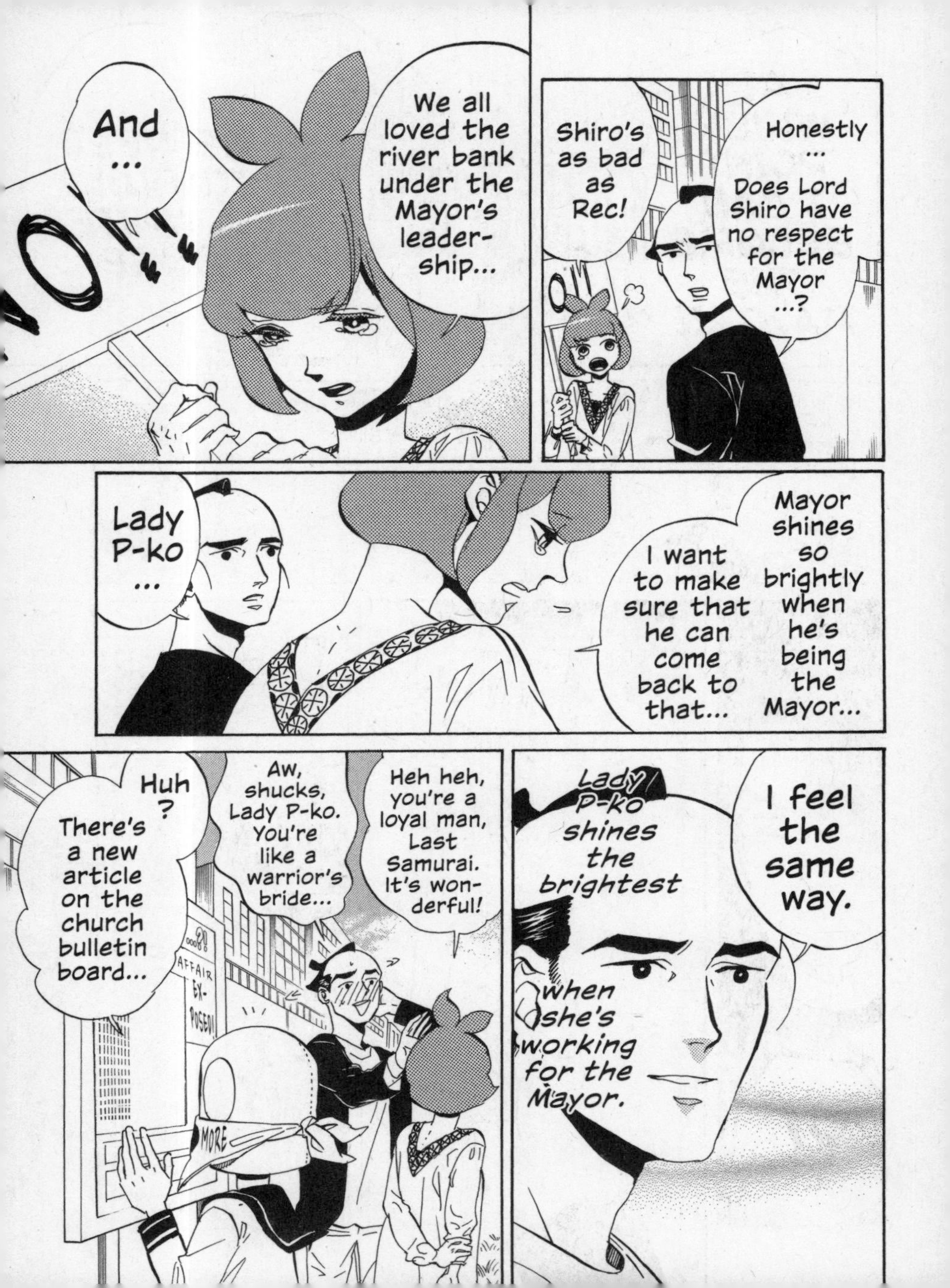
Honestly ... Does Lord Shiro have no respect for the Mayor ...?
Shiro's as bad as Rec!
We all loved the river bank under the Mayor's leadership...
And ...
Mayor shines so brightly when he's being the Mayor...
I want to make sure that he can come back to that...
Lady P-ko ...
I feel the same way.
Lady P-ko shines the brightest
when she's working for the Mayor.
Heh heh, you're a loyal man, Last Samurai. It's wonderful!
Aw, shucks, Lady P-ko. You're like a warrior's bride...
Huh ? There's a new article on the church bulletin board...
AFFAIR EX-POSED!!
MORE

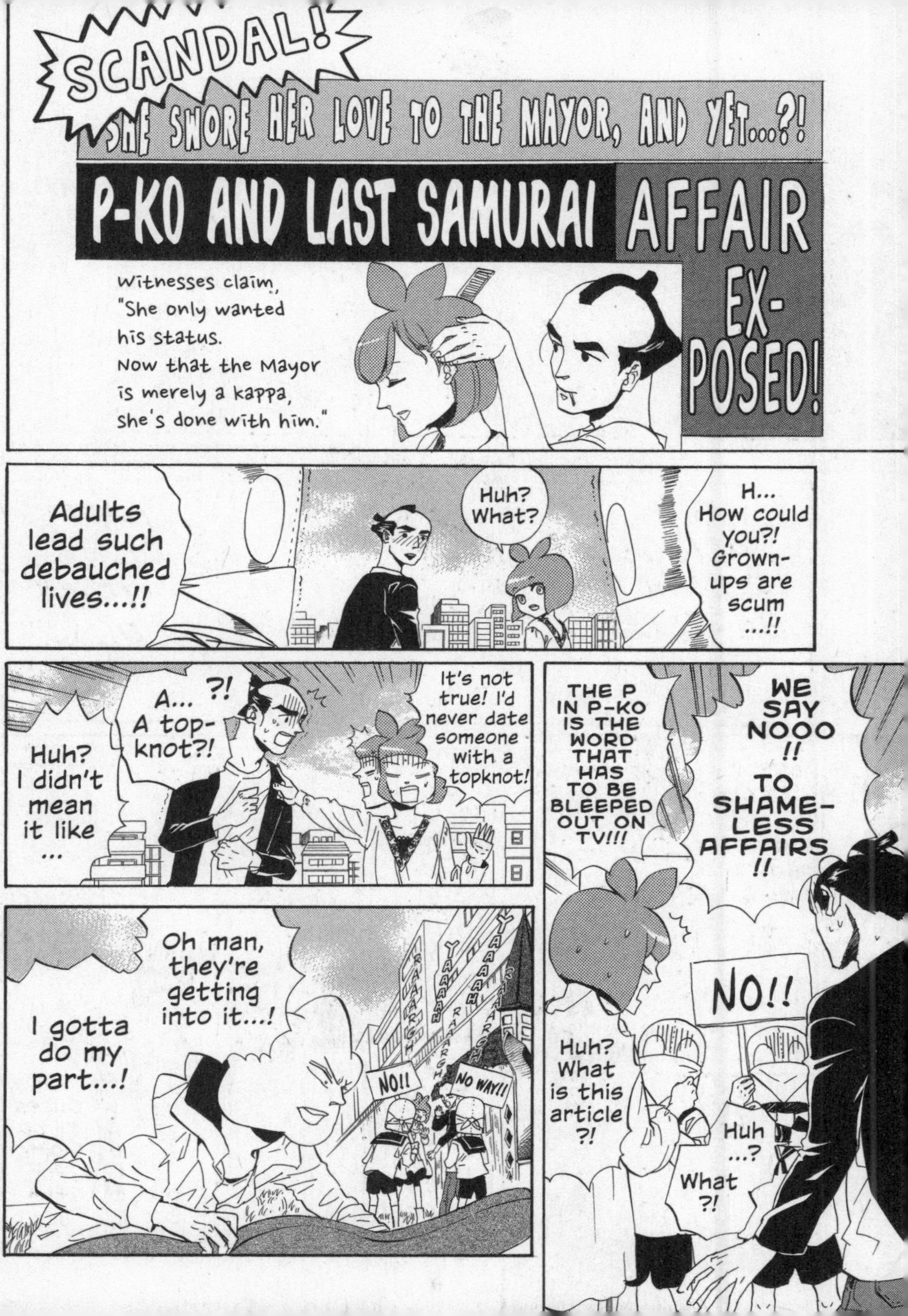
SCANDAL!
SHE SWORE HER LOVE TO THE MAYOR, AND YET...?!
P-KO AND LAST SAMURAI AFFAIR EX-POSED!
Witnesses claim, "She only wanted his status. Now that the Mayor is merely a kappa, she's done with him."
H... How could you?! Grown-ups are scum ...!!
Huh? What?
Adults lead such debauched lives...!!
WE SAY NOOO!! TO SHAME-LESS AFFAIRS!!
THE P IN P-KO IS THE WORD THAT HAS TO BE BLEEPED OUT ON TV!!!
NO!!
Huh? What is this article ?!
Huh ...?
What ?!
It's not true! I'd never date someone with a topknot!
A... ?! A top-knot?!
Huh? I didn't mean it like ...
Oh man, they're getting into it...!
I gotta do my part...!
YAAAAH
RAAARGH
NO!!
NO WAY!!

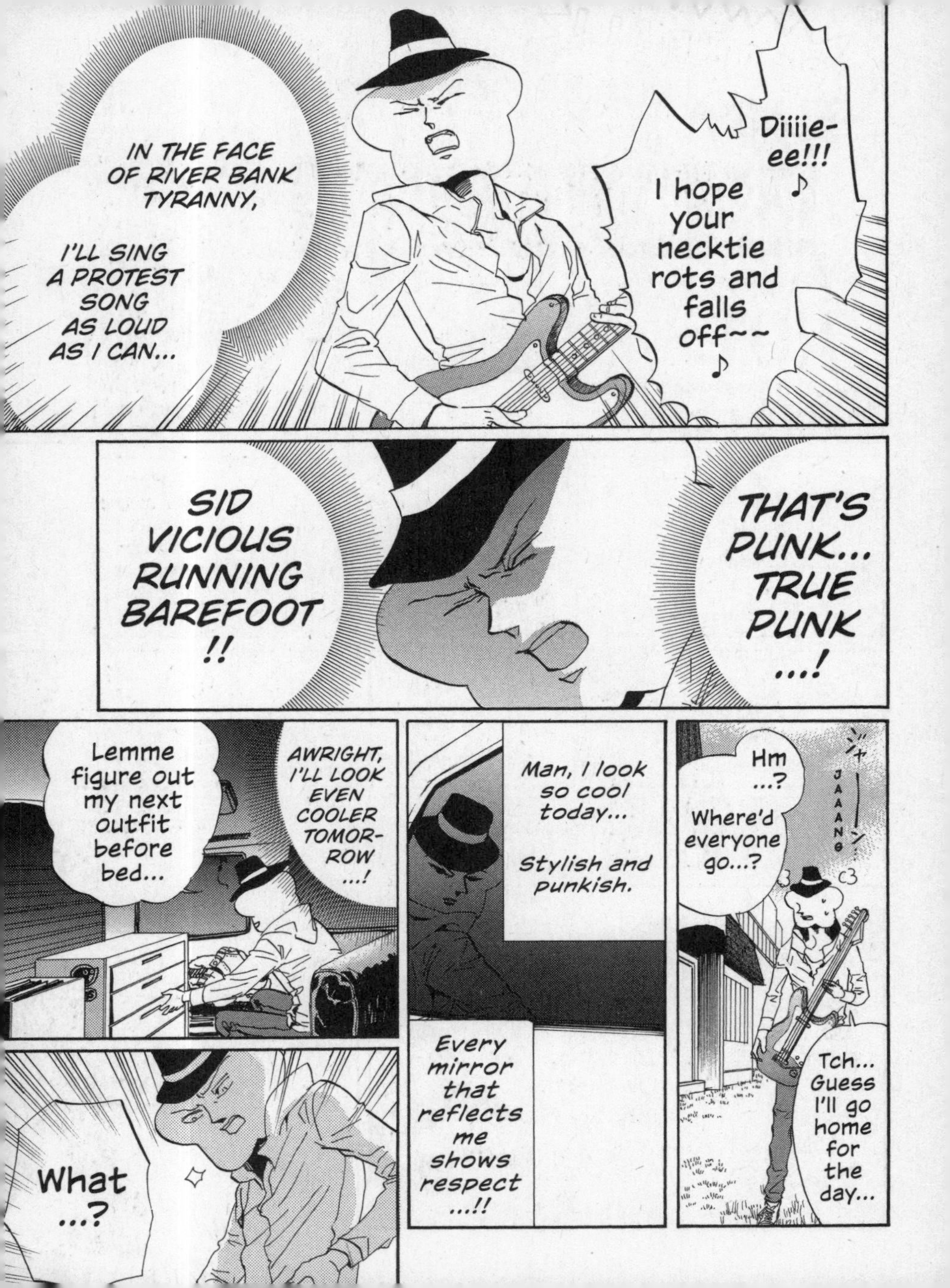
Diiiie-ee!!! ♪
I hope your necktie rots and falls off~~ ♪
IN THE FACE OF RIVER BANK TYRANNY,
I'LL SING A PROTEST SONG AS LOUD AS I CAN...
THAT'S PUNK... TRUE PUNK ...!
SID VICIOUS RUNNING BAREFOOT !!
JAAANG
Hm ...?
Where'd everyone go...?
Tch... Guess I'll go home for the day...
Man, I look so cool today...
Stylish and punkish.
Every mirror that reflects me shows respect ...!!
AWRIGHT, I'LL LOOK EVEN COOLER TOMORROW ...!
Lemme figure out my next outfit before bed...
What ...?

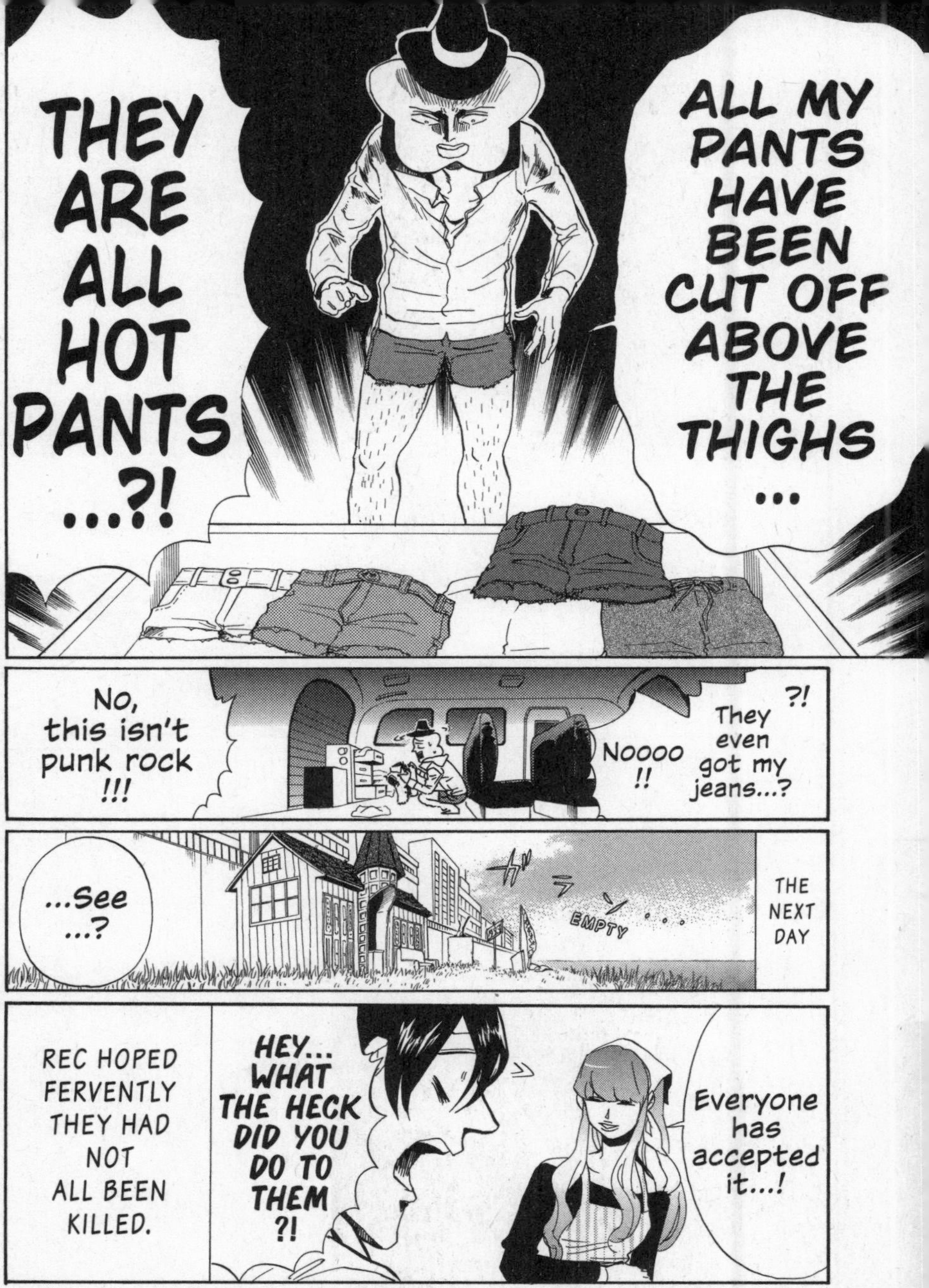
ALL MY PANTS HAVE BEEN CUT OFF ABOVE THE THIGHS ...
THEY ARE ALL HOT PANTS ...?!
?! They even got my jeans...?
Noooo !!
No, this isn't punk rock !!!
THE NEXT DAY
EMPTY
...See ...?
Everyone has accepted it...!
HEY... WHAT THE HECK DID YOU DO TO THEM ?!
REC HOPED FERVENTLY THEY HAD NOT ALL BEEN KILLED.

Chapter 334: River Bank Imperial Education

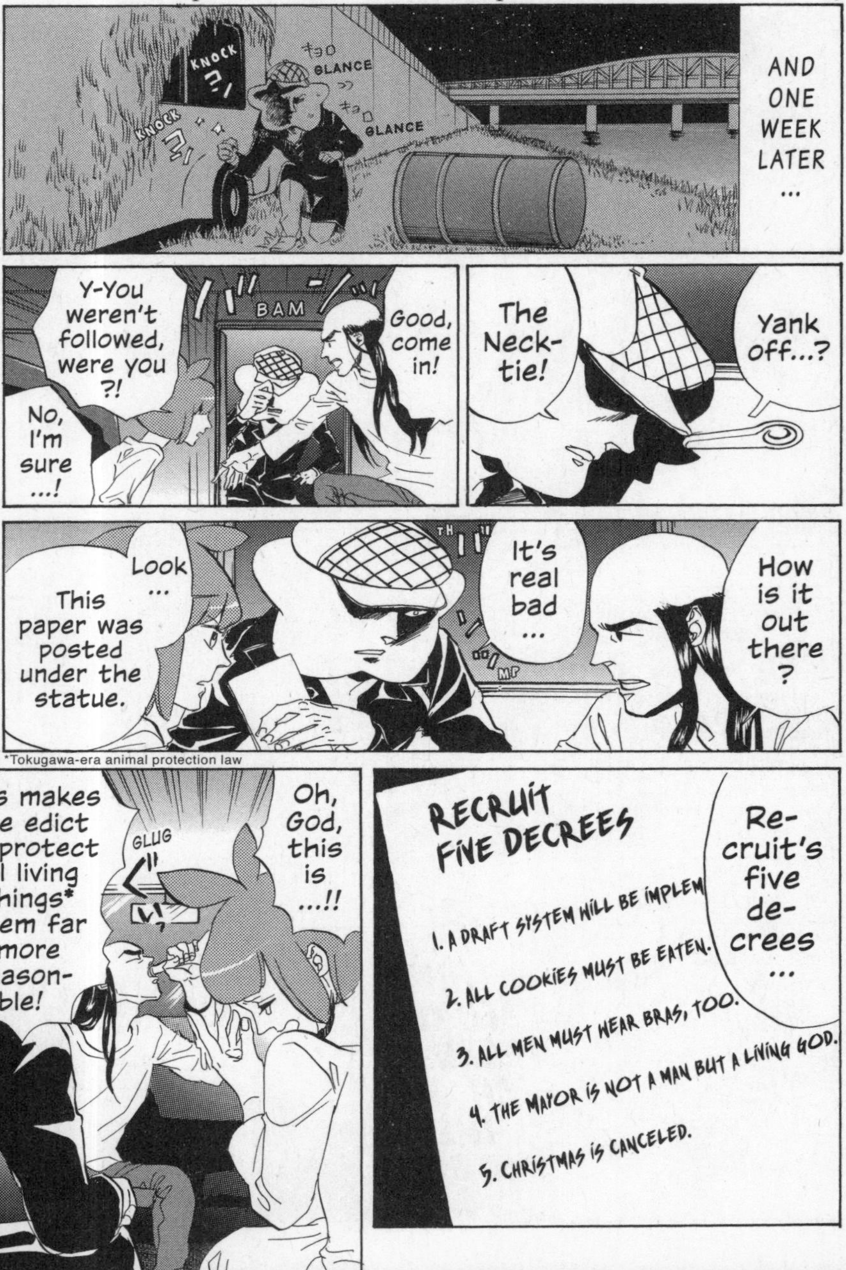
AND ONE WEEK LATER ...
KNOCK
KNOCK
GLANCE
GLANCE
Yank off...?
The Neck-tie!
Good, come in!
BAM
Y-You weren't followed, were you ?!
No, I'm sure ...!
How is it out there ?
It's real bad ...
TH
MP
Look ...
This paper was posted under the statue.
Re-cruit's five de-crees ...
RECRUIT FIVE DECREES
1. A DRAFT SYSTEM WILL BE IMPLEM
2. ALL COOKIES MUST BE EATEN.
3. ALL MEN MUST WEAR BRAS, TOO.
4. THE MAYOR IS NOT A MAN BUT A LIVING GOD.
5. CHRISTMAS IS CANCELED.
Oh, God, this is ...!!
GLUG
This makes the edict to protect all living things* seem far more reason-able!

*Tokugawa-era animal protection law

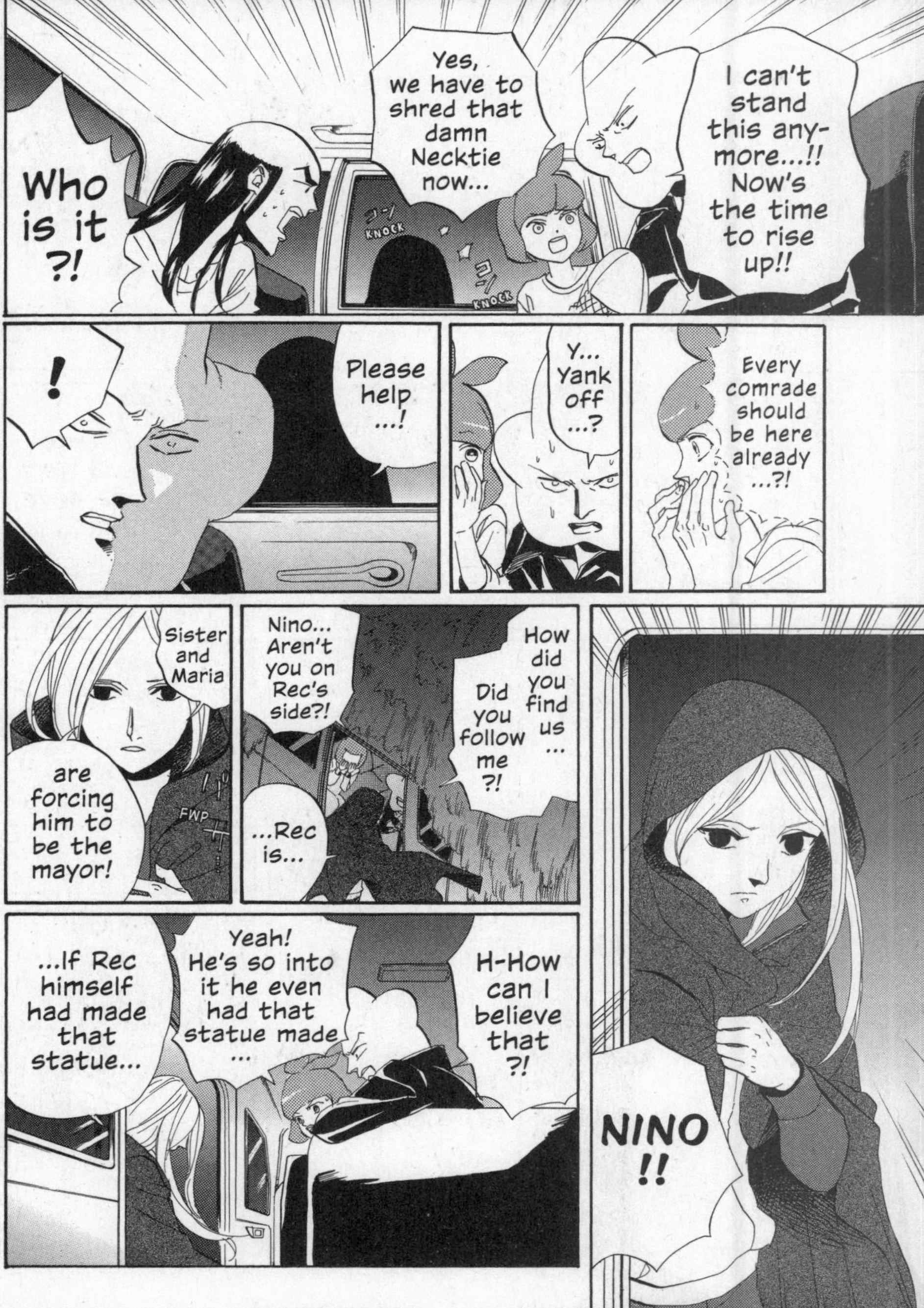
I can't stand this any-more...!! Now's the time to rise up!!
Yes, we have to shred that damn Necktie now...
KNOCK
KNOCK
Who is it ?!
Every comrade should be here already ...?!
Y... Yank off ...?
Please help ...!
!
NINO !!
How did you find us ...
Did you follow me ?!
Nino... Aren't you on Rec's side?!
...Rec is...
Sister and Maria
are forcing him to be the mayor!
FWP
H-How can I believe that ?!
Yeah! He's so into it he even had that statue made ...
...If Rec himself had made that statue...

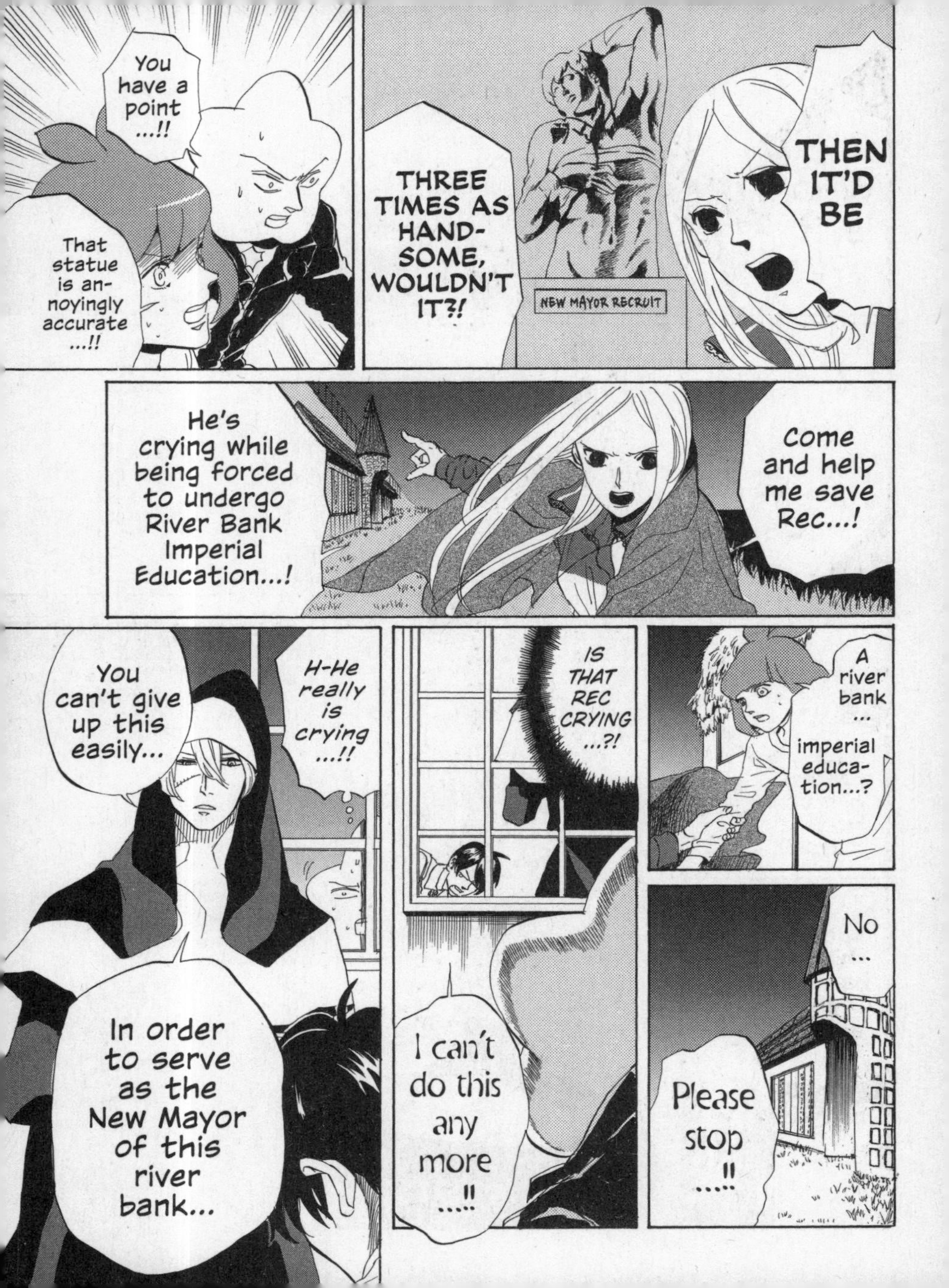
THEN IT'D BE
NEW MAYOR RECRUIT
THREE TIMES AS HAND-SOME, WOULDN'T IT?!
You have a point ...!!
That statue is an-noyingly accurate ...!!
Come and help me save Rec...!
He's crying while being forced to undergo River Bank Imperial Education...!
A river bank ... imperial educa-tion...?
IS THAT REC CRYING ...?!
H-He really is crying ...!!
You can't give up this easily...
In order to serve as the New Mayor of this river bank...
No ...
Please stop !! .....
I can't do this any more !! .....

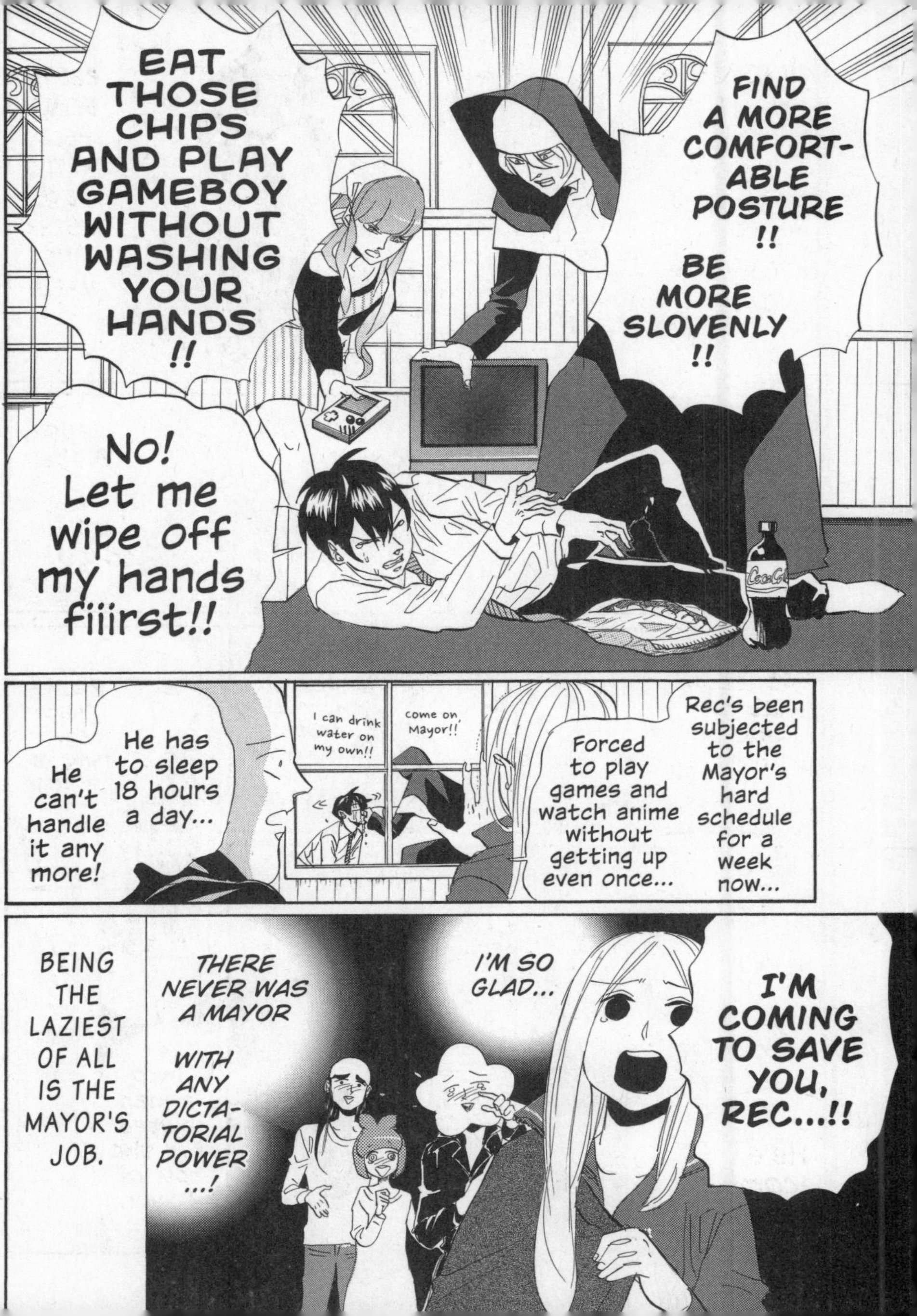
FIND A MORE COMFORTABLE POSTURE !!
BE MORE SLOVENLY !!
EAT THOSE CHIPS AND PLAY GAMEBOY WITHOUT WASHING YOUR HANDS !!
No! Let me wipe off my hands fiiirst!!
Rec's been subjected to the Mayor's hard schedule for a week now...
Forced to play games and watch anime without getting up even once...
come on, Mayor!!
I can drink water on my own!!
He has to sleep 18 hours a day...
He can't handle it any more!
I'M COMING TO SAVE YOU, REC...!!
I'M SO GLAD...
THERE NEVER WAS A MAYOR
WITH ANY DICTATORIAL POWER ...!
BEING THE LAZIEST OF ALL IS THE MAYOR'S JOB.

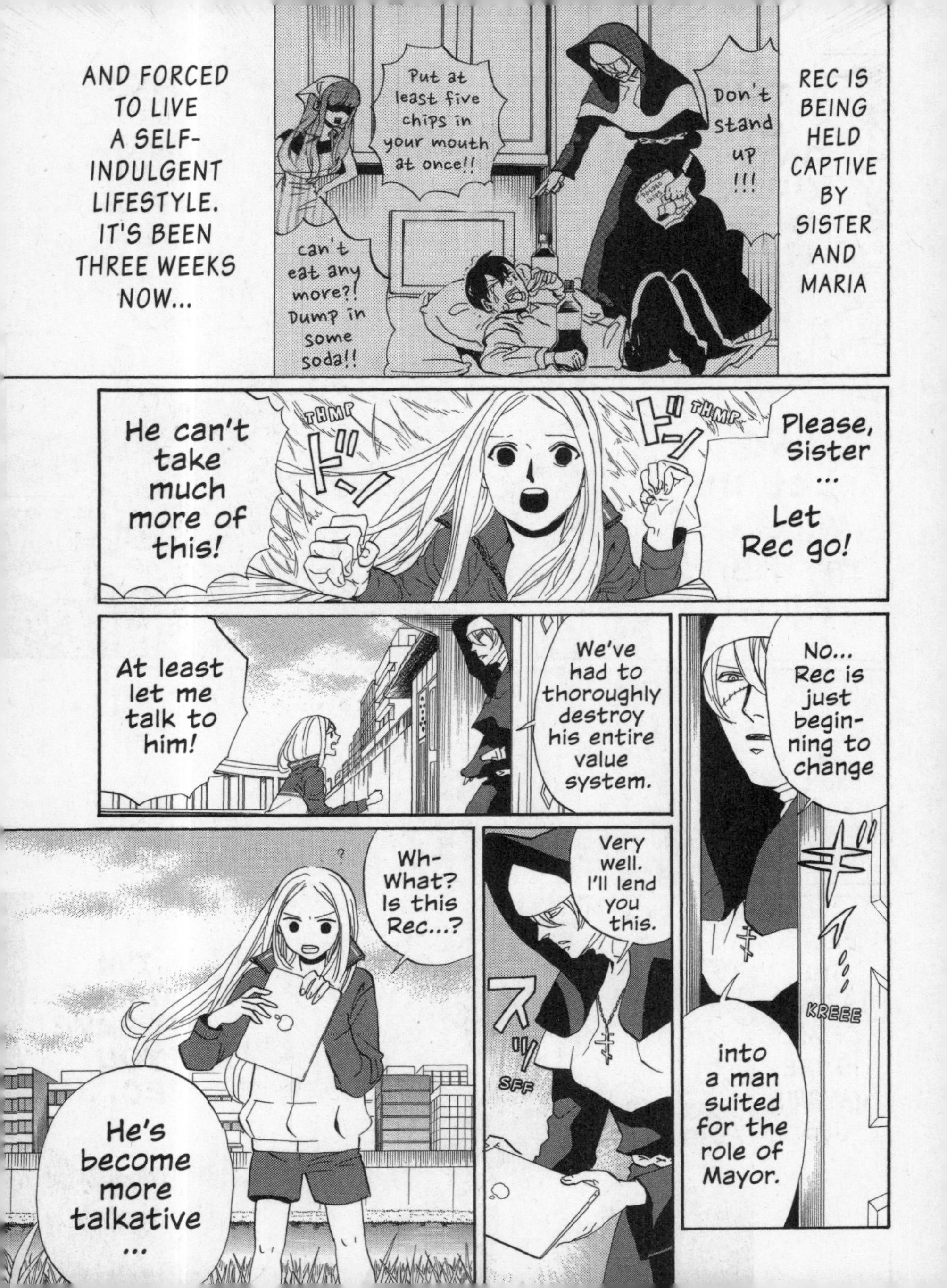
REC IS BEING HELD CAPTIVE BY SISTER AND MARIA
Don't stand up !!!
Put at least five chips in your mouth at once!!
can't eat any more?! Dump in some soda!!
AND FORCED TO LIVE A SELF-INDULGENT LIFESTYLE. IT'S BEEN THREE WEEKS NOW...
Please, Sister ... Let Rec go!
THMP
THMP
He can't take much more of this!
No... Rec is just begin-ning to change
KREEE
into a man suited for the role of Mayor.
We've had to thoroughly destroy his entire value system.
At least let me talk to him!
Very well. I'll lend you this.
SFF
Wh-What? Is this Rec...?
He's become more talkative ...

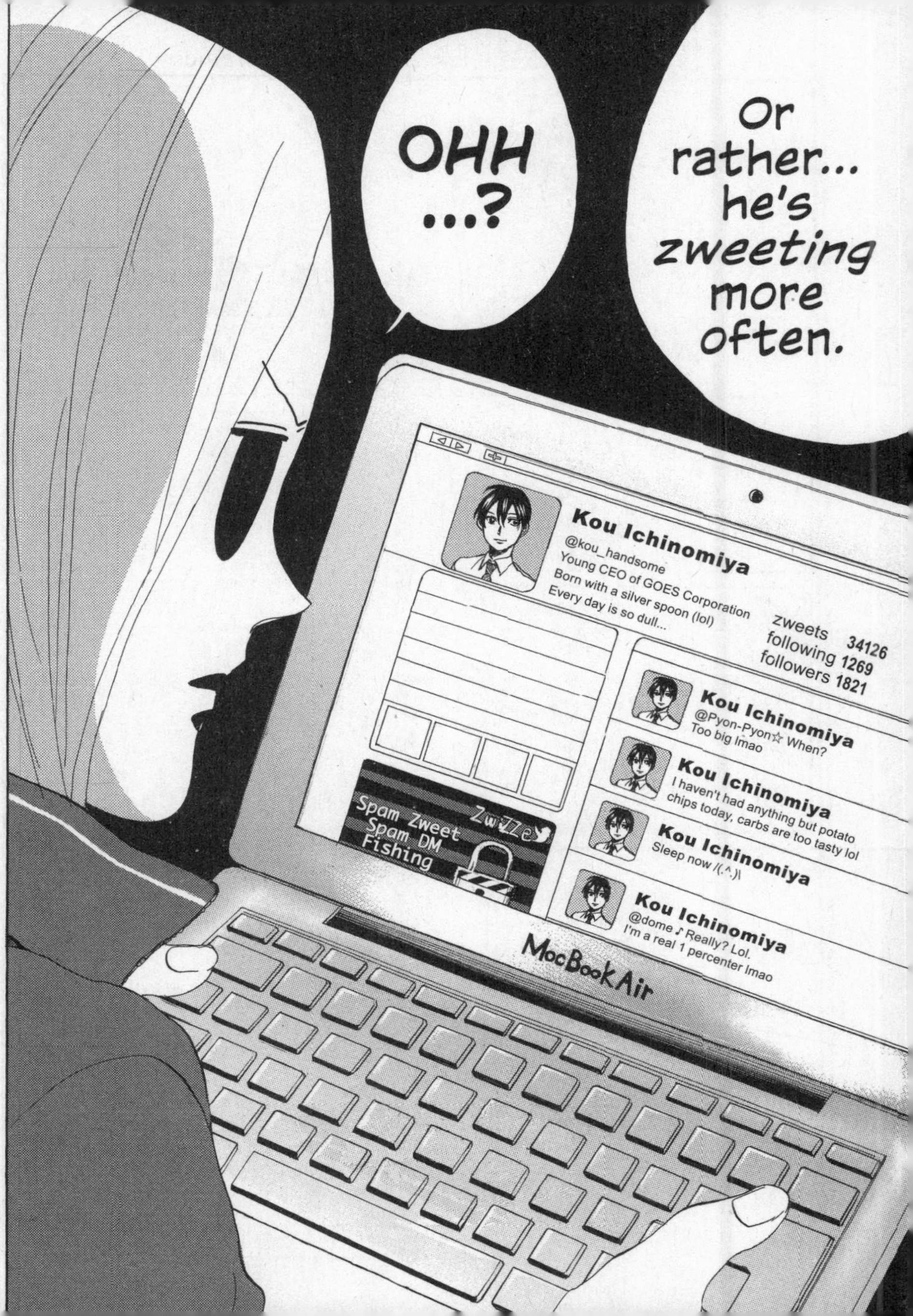
Or rather... he's zweeting more often.
OHH ...?
Kou Ichinomiya
@kou_handsome
Young CEO of GOES Corporation
Born with a silver spoon (lol)
Every day is so dull...
zweets 34126
following 1269
followers 1821
Kou Ichinomiya
@Pyon-Pyon☆ When?
Too big lmao
Kou Ichinomiya
I haven't had anything but potato chips today, carbs are too tasty lol
Kou Ichinomiya
Sleep now /(.^.)\
Kou Ichinomiya
@dome♪ Really? Lol.
I'm a real 1 percenter lmao
Spam Zweet
Spam DM
Fishing
MocBookAir

Chapter 335: New Mayor's New Values

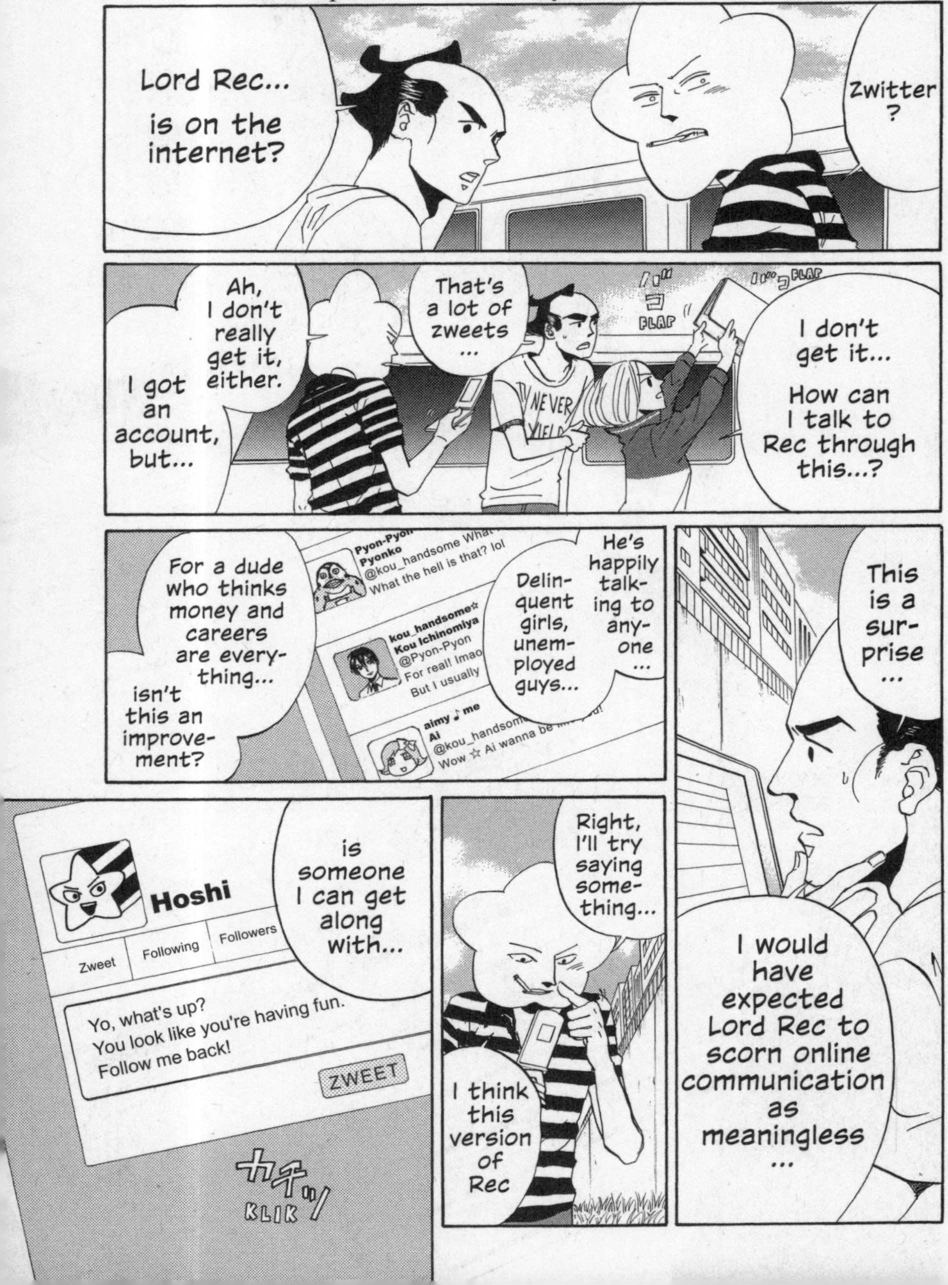

Zwitter?
Lord Rec... is on the internet?
I don't get it... How can I talk to Rec through this...?
FLAP
FLAP
That's a lot of zweets...
Ah, I don't really get it, either.
I got an account, but...
This is a surprise...
He's happily talking to anyone...
Delinquent girls, unemployed guys...
For a dude who thinks money and careers are everything... isn't this an improvement?
Pyon-Pyon Pyonko
@kou_handsome What the hell is that? lol
kou_handsome☆ Kou Ichinomiya
@Pyon-Pyon For real! lmao But I usually
aimy♪me Ai
Wow ☆ Ai wanna be
I would have expected Lord Rec to scorn online communication as meaningless...
Right, I'll try saying something...
I think this version of Rec
is someone I can get along with...
Hoshi
Zweet
Following
Followers
Yo, what's up?
You look like you're having fun.
Follow me back!
ZWEET
KLIK

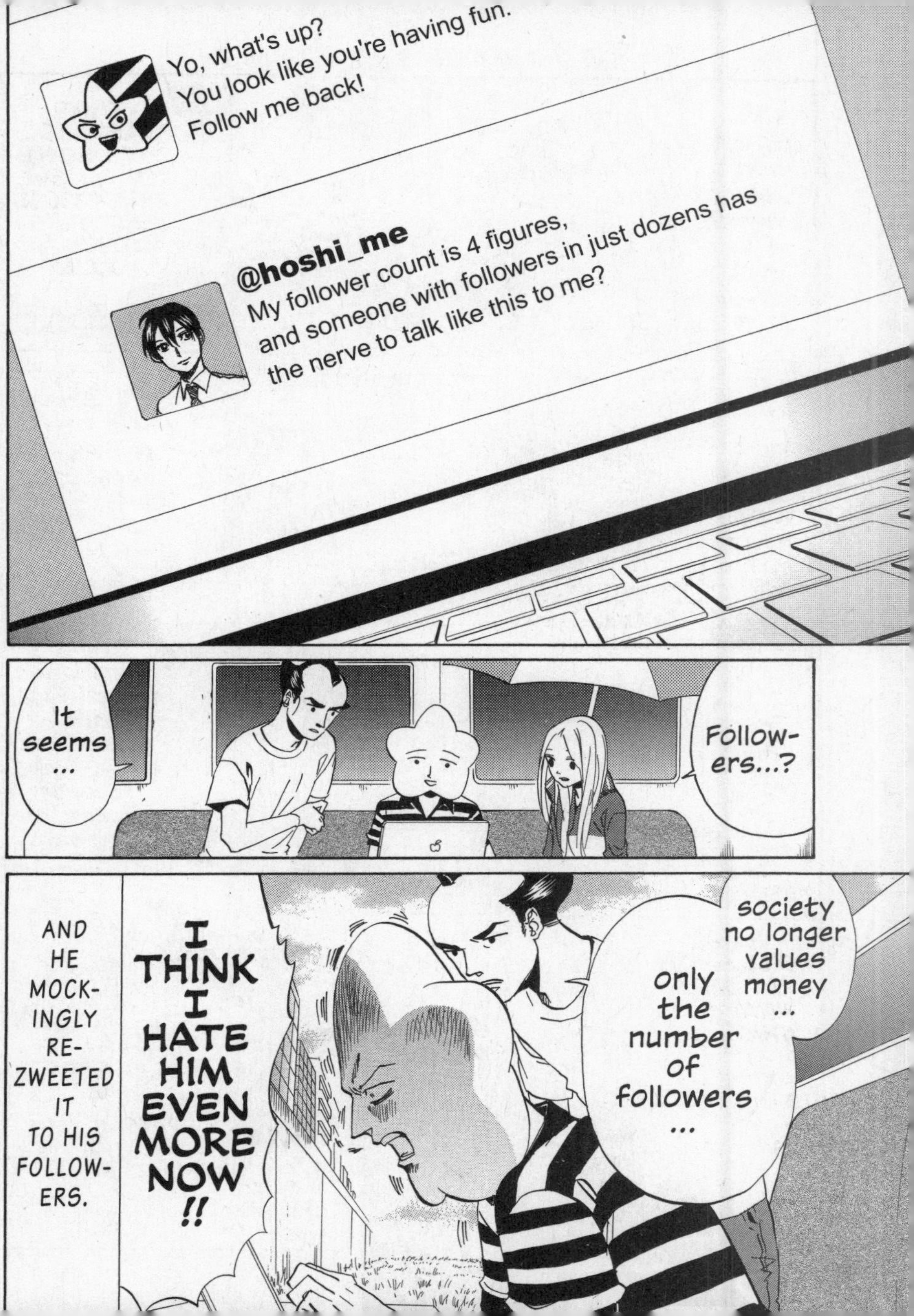
Yo, what's up?
You look like you're having fun.
Follow me back!
@hoshi_me
My follower count is 4 figures, and someone with followers in just dozens has the nerve to talk like this to me?
Follow-ers...?
It seems ...
society no longer values money ...
only the number of followers ...
I THINK I HATE HIM EVEN MORE NOW !!
AND HE MOCKINGLY RE-ZWEETED IT TO HIS FOLLOWERS.

Chapter 336: Light of Hope

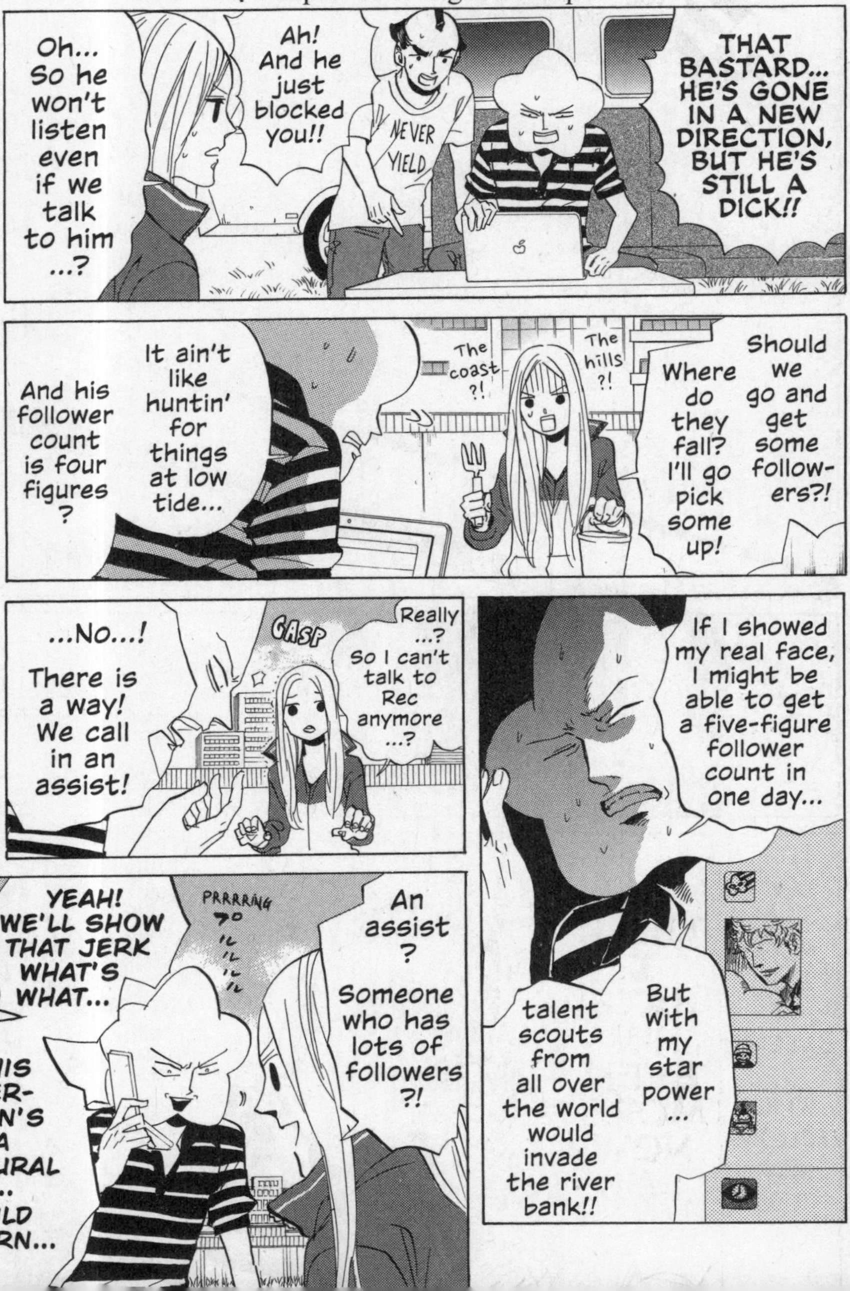

THAT BASTARD... HE'S GONE IN A NEW DIRECTION, BUT HE'S STILL A DICK!!
Ah! And he just blocked you!!
NEVER YIELD
Oh... So he won't listen even if we talk to him ...?
Should we go and get some followers?!
Where do they fall? I'll go pick some up!
The hills?!
The coast?!
It ain't like huntin' for things at low tide...
And his follower count is four figures?
If I showed my real face, I might be able to get a five-figure follower count in one day...
But with my star power...
talent scouts from all over the world would invade the river bank!!
Really...? So I can't talk to Rec anymore...?
GASP
...No...!
There is a way! We call in an assist!
An assist?
Someone who has lots of followers?!
PRRRRING
YEAH! WE'LL SHOW THAT JERK WHAT'S WHAT...
THIS PERSON'S A NATURAL... WILD BORN...

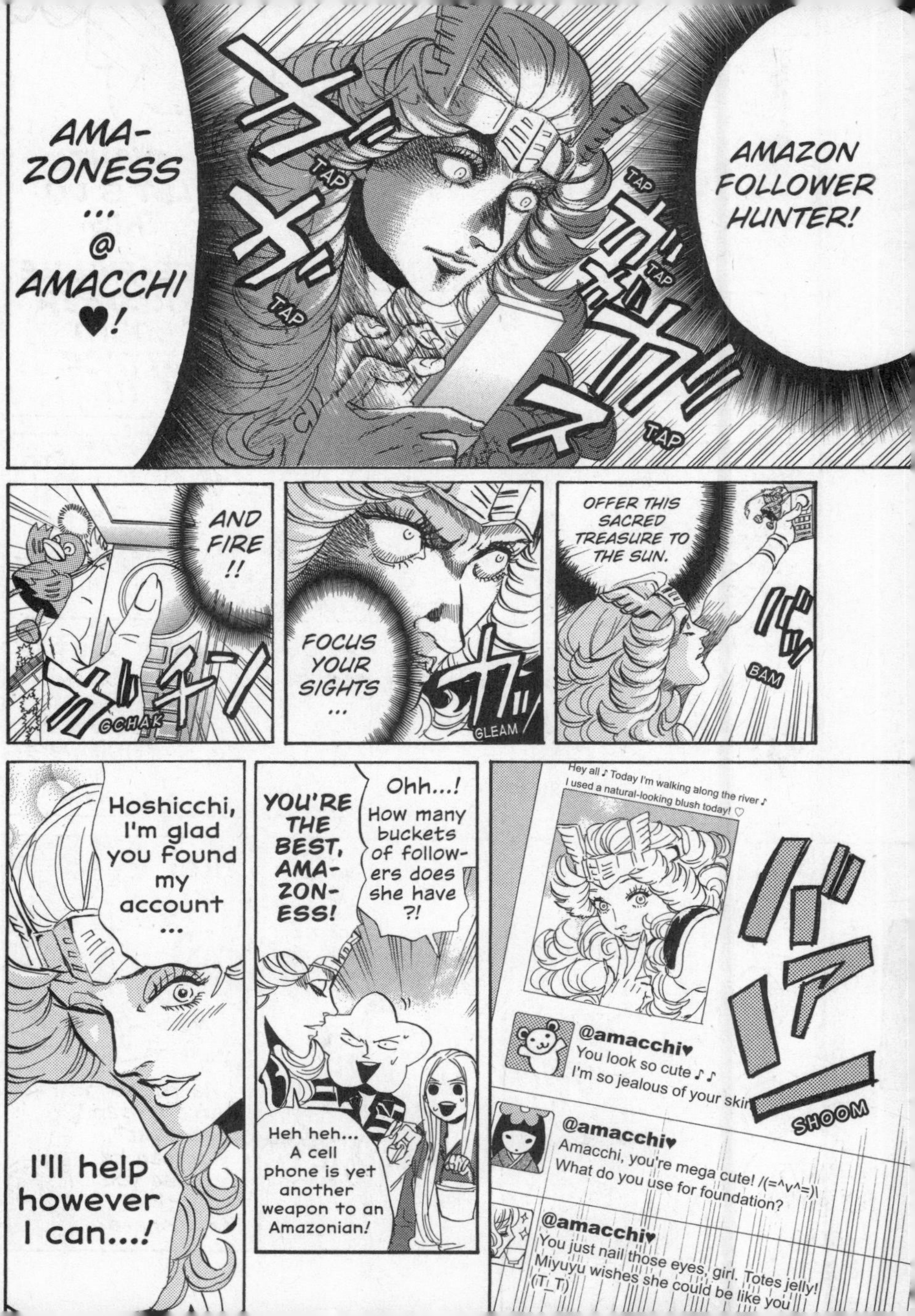
AMAZON FOLLOWER HUNTER!
TAP
TAP
TAP
TAP
AMA-ZONESS ... @ AMACCHI ♥!
OFFER THIS SACRED TREASURE TO THE SUN.
BAM
FOCUS YOUR SIGHTS ...
GLEAM
AND FIRE !!
GCHAK
Hey all ♪ Today I'm walking along the river ♪
I used a natural-looking blush today! ♡
@amacchi♥
You look so cute ♪ ♪
I'm so jealous of your skin
@amacchi♥
Amacchi, you're mega cute! /(=^v^=)\
What do you use for foundation?
@amacchi♥
You just nail those eyes, girl. Totes jelly!
Miyuyu wishes she could be like you
(T_T)
SHOOM
Ohh...! How many buckets of followers does she have ?!
YOU'RE THE BEST, AMA-ZON-ESS!
Heh heh... A cell phone is yet another weapon to an Amazonian!
Hoshicchi, I'm glad you found my account ...
I'll help however I can...!

Amacchi
@amacchi♡

Zweet	Following	Followers
2169	216	12812

Recchi, hey-oh ♪ It's Amazoness! (o^-^o)
Followers, he's a real-life friend of mine...!!

TAP
TAP

RIGHT, LET'S DO THIS!

FIVE-FIGURE FOLLOWER COUNT ATTACK !!!

In his current state of mind...

Now he'll have to talk to you!

Ohh...!

That's a powerful endorsement !!

?!

kou_handsome☆
spammer

he'll be bowled over by how many followers you have...

HUH ?!

I've pretended to buy things I've created myself...!

I always felt guilty about it...

That idiot!

Just because you're talking about what kind of make-up you use...

No... he's actually right...

HUH ?!

He thinks you're a spam account? How can he accuse you of that, Amazoness?

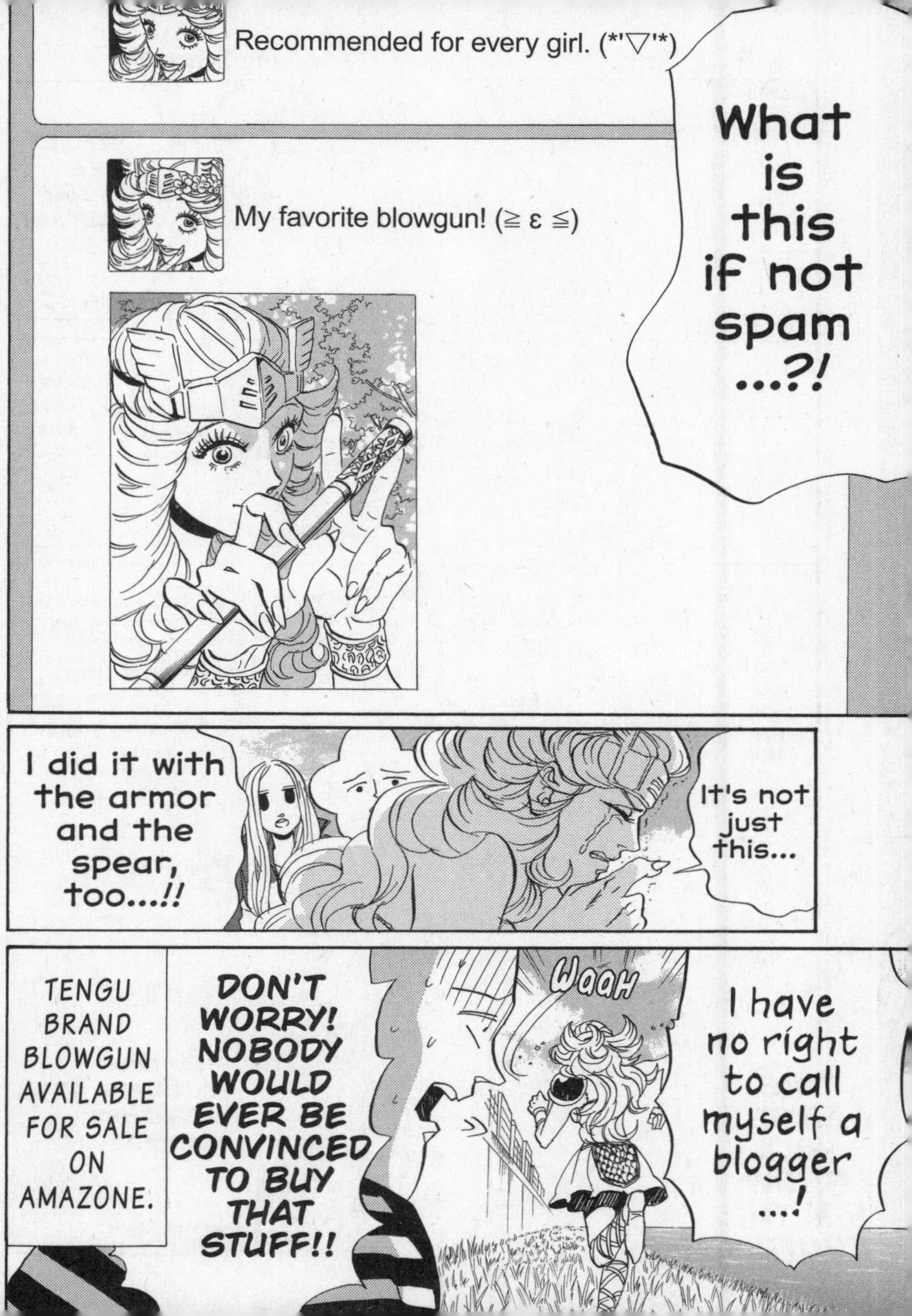
What is this if not spam ...?!
Recommended for every girl. (*'▽'*)
My favorite blowgun! (≧ ε ≦)
It's not just this...
I did it with the armor and the spear, too...!!
I have no right to call myself a blogger ...!
Waah
DON'T WORRY! NOBODY WOULD EVER BE CONVINCED TO BUY THAT STUFF!!
TENGU BRAND BLOWGUN AVAILABLE FOR SALE ON AMAZONE.

Chapter 337: Last Samurai's Cunning Scheme

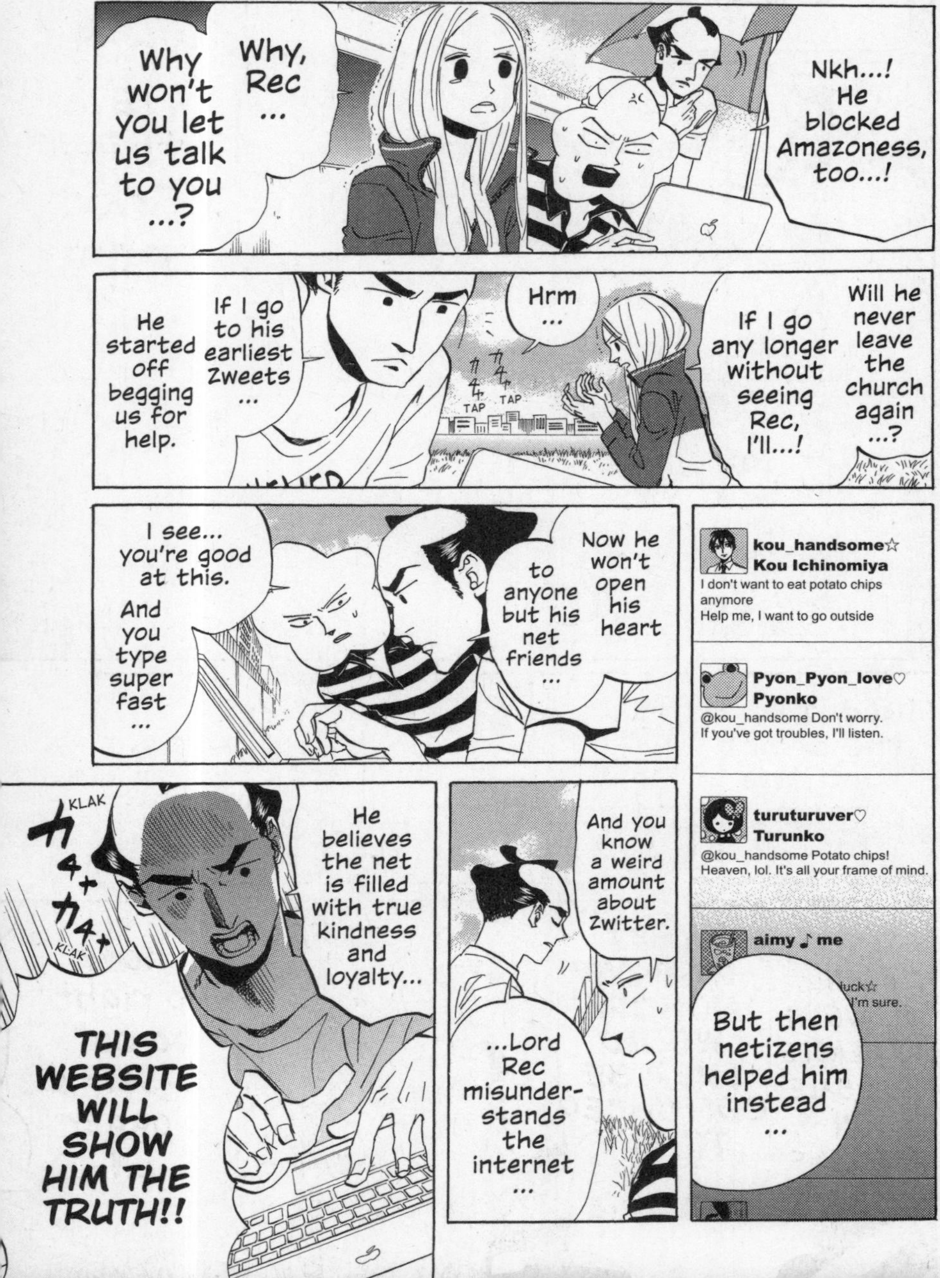

Nkh...! He blocked Amazoness, too...!
Why, Rec ...
Why won't you let us talk to you ...?
Will he never leave the church again ...?
If I go any longer without seeing Rec, I'll...!
Hrm ...
TAP TAP
If I go to his earliest Zweets ...
He started off begging us for help.
kou_handsome☆
Kou Ichinomiya
I don't want to eat potato chips anymore
Help me, I want to go outside
Pyon_Pyon_love♡
Pyonko
@kou_handsome Don't worry.
If you've got troubles, I'll listen.
turuturuver♡
Turunko
@kou_handsome Potato chips!
Heaven, lol. It's all your frame of mind.
aimy♪me
But then netizens helped him instead ...
Now he won't open his heart
to anyone but his net friends ...
I see... you're good at this.
And you type super fast ...
And you know a weird amount about Zwitter.
...Lord Rec misunder-stands the internet ...
He believes the net is filled with true kindness and loyalty...
KLAK KLAK
THIS WEBSITE WILL SHOW HIM THE TRUTH!!

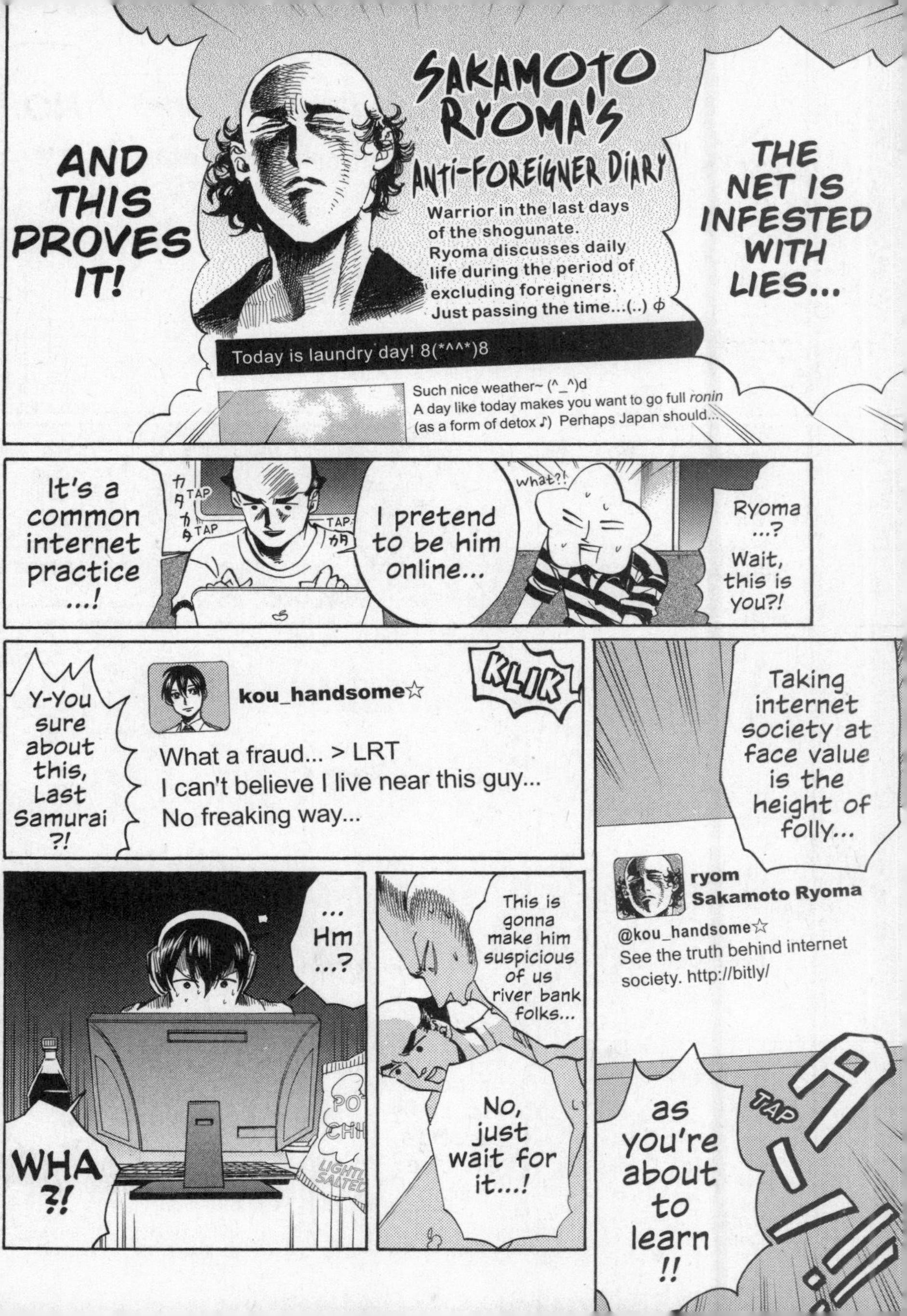
THE NET IS INFESTED WITH LIES...
SAKAMOTO RYOMA'S
ANTI-FOREIGNER DIARY
Warrior in the last days of the shogunate. Ryoma discusses daily life during the period of excluding foreigners. Just passing the time...(..) ϕ
Today is laundry day! 8(*^^*)8
Such nice weather~ (^_^)d
A day like today makes you want to go full ronin (as a form of detox ♪) Perhaps Japan should...
AND THIS PROVES IT!
Ryoma ...? Wait, this is you?!
what?!
I pretend to be him online...
TAP TAP TAP
It's a common internet practice ...!
Taking internet society at face value is the height of folly...
ryom
Sakamoto Ryoma
@kou_handsome☆
See the truth behind internet society. http://bitly/
TAP
as you're about to learn !!
KLIK
kou_handsome☆
What a fraud... > LRT
I can't believe I live near this guy...
No freaking way...
Y-You sure about this, Last Samurai ?!
This is gonna make him suspicious of us river bank folks...
No, just wait for it...!
... Hm ...?
WHA ?!

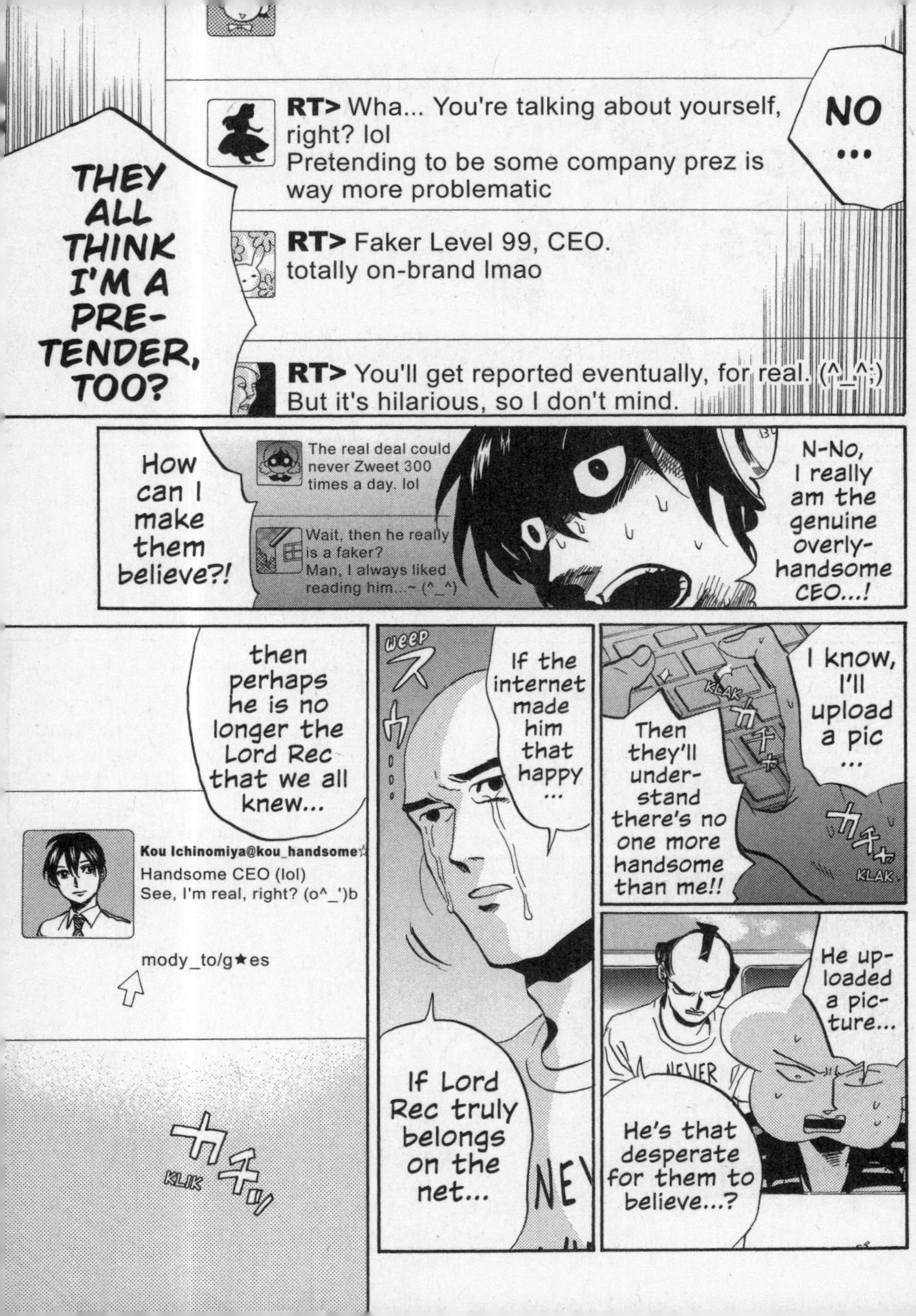
NO ...
THEY ALL THINK I'M A PRE-TENDER, TOO?
RT> Wha... You're talking about yourself, right? lol
Pretending to be some company prez is way more problematic
RT> Faker Level 99, CEO.
totally on-brand lmao
RT> You'll get reported eventually, for real. (^_^;)
But it's hilarious, so I don't mind.
N-No, I really am the genuine overly-handsome CEO...!
The real deal could never Zweet 300 times a day. lol
Wait, then he really is a faker?
Man, I always liked reading him...~ (^_^)
How can I make them believe?!
I know, I'll upload a pic ...
KLAK
Then they'll under-stand there's no one more handsome than me!!
KLAK
He up-loaded a pic-ture...
He's that desperate for them to believe...?
WEEP
If the internet made him that happy ...
If Lord Rec truly belongs on the net...
then perhaps he is no longer the Lord Rec that we all knew...
Kou Ichinomiya@kou_handsome☆
Handsome CEO (lol)
See, I'm real, right? (o^_')b
mody_to/g★es
KLIK

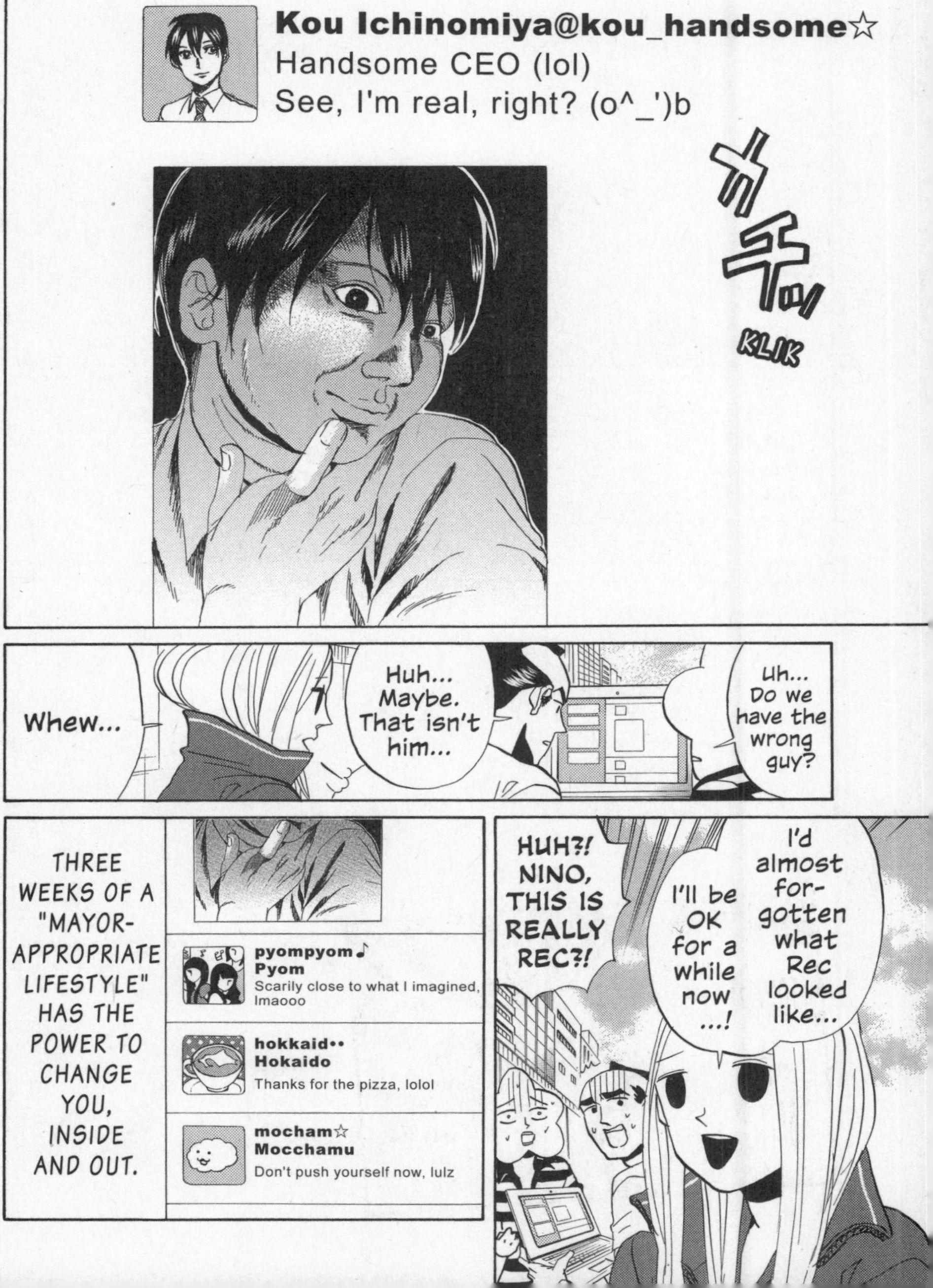
Kou Ichinomiya@kou_handsome☆
Handsome CEO (lol)
See, I'm real, right? (o^_')b
KLIK
Uh... Do we have the wrong guy?
Huh... Maybe. That isn't him...
Whew...
I'd almost for-gotten what Rec looked like...
I'll be OK for a while now ...!
HUH?! NINO, THIS IS REALLY REC?!
pyompyom♪
Pyom
Scarily close to what I imagined, lmaooo
hokkaid••
Hokaido
Thanks for the pizza, lolol
mocham☆
Mocchamu
Don't push yourself now, lulz
THREE WEEKS OF A "MAYOR-APPROPRIATE LIFESTYLE" HAS THE POWER TO CHANGE YOU, INSIDE AND OUT.

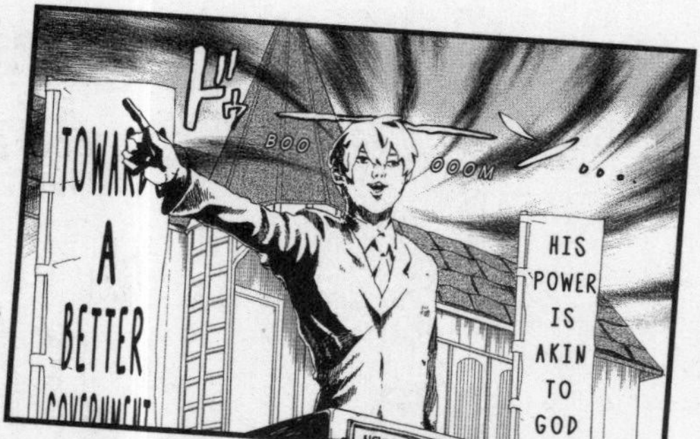
BOO
OOOM
. .
TOWARD A BETTER GOVERNMENT
HIS POWER IS AKIN TO GOD

ARAKAWA
UNDER
THE BRIDGE

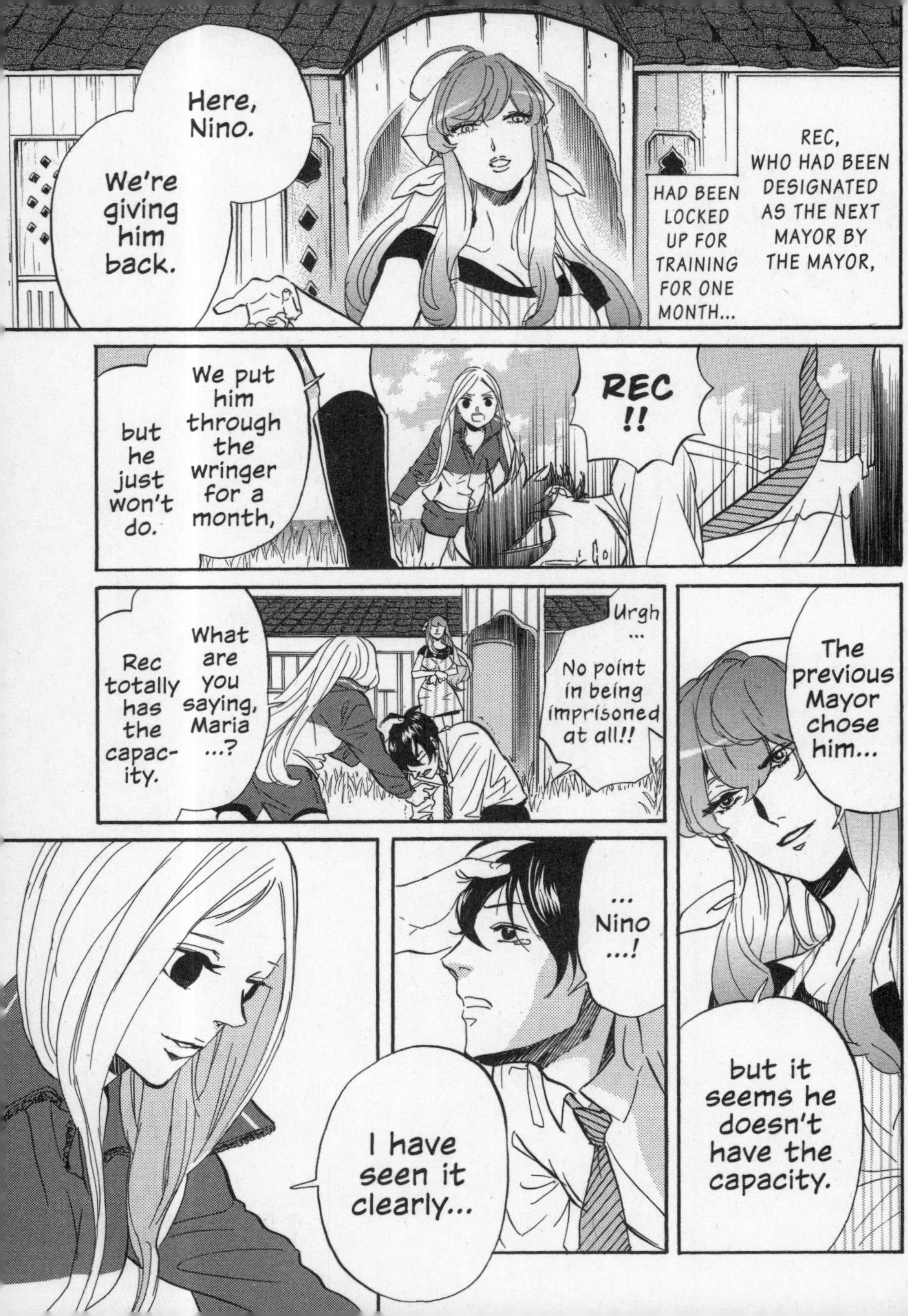
REC, WHO HAD BEEN DESIGNATED AS THE NEXT MAYOR BY THE MAYOR,
HAD BEEN LOCKED UP FOR TRAINING FOR ONE MONTH...
Here, Nino.
We're giving him back.
REC !!
We put him through the wringer for a month,
but he just won't do.
The previous Mayor chose him...
but it seems he doesn't have the capacity.
Urgh ...
No point in being imprisoned at all!!
What are you saying, Maria ...?
Rec totally has the capac- ity.
... Nino ...!
I have seen it clearly...

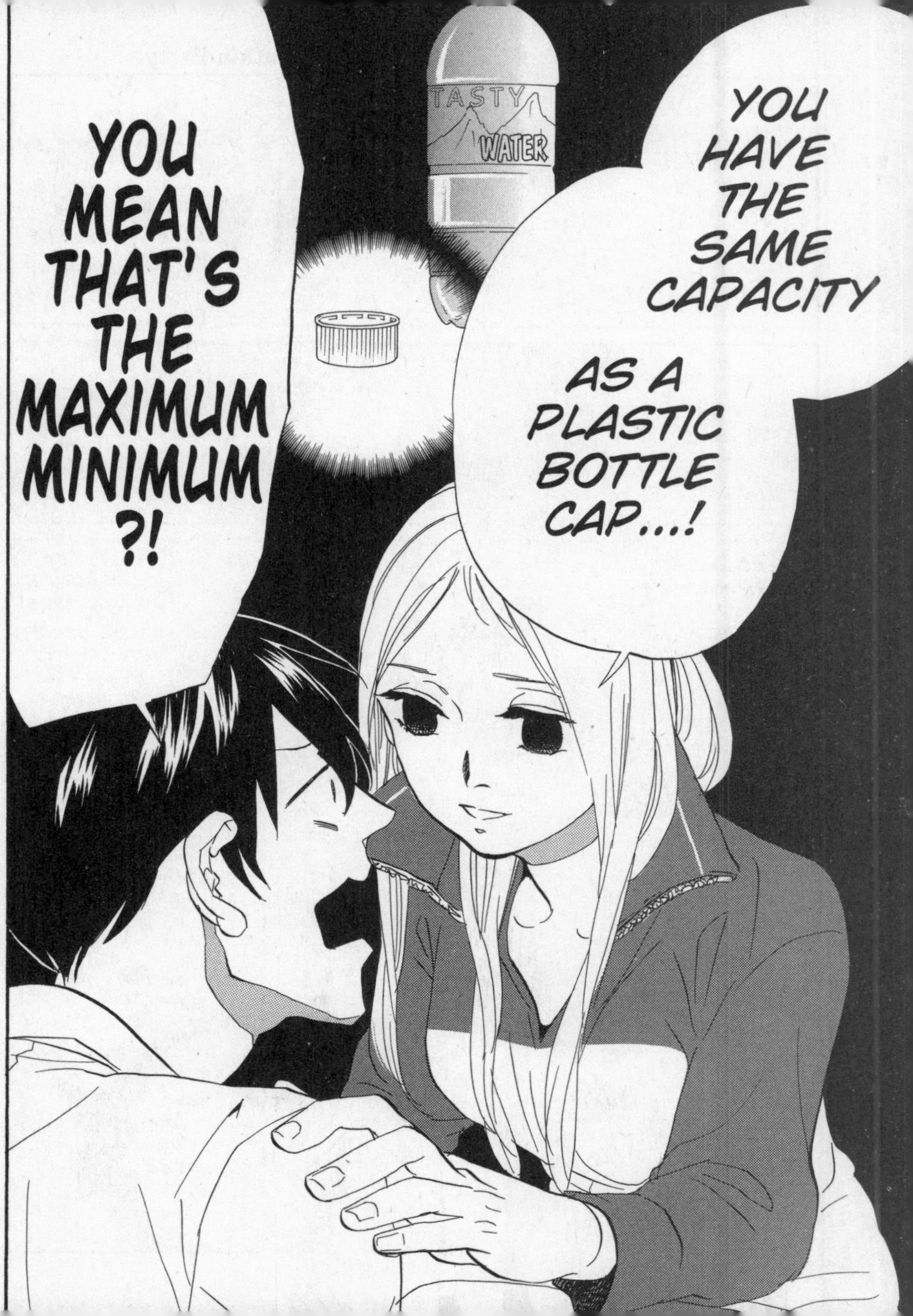
TASTY WATER
YOU HAVE THE SAME CAPACITY
AS A PLASTIC BOTTLE CAP...!
YOU MEAN THAT'S THE MAXIMUM MINIMUM ?!

Chapter 338: New Mayor Inauguration Party

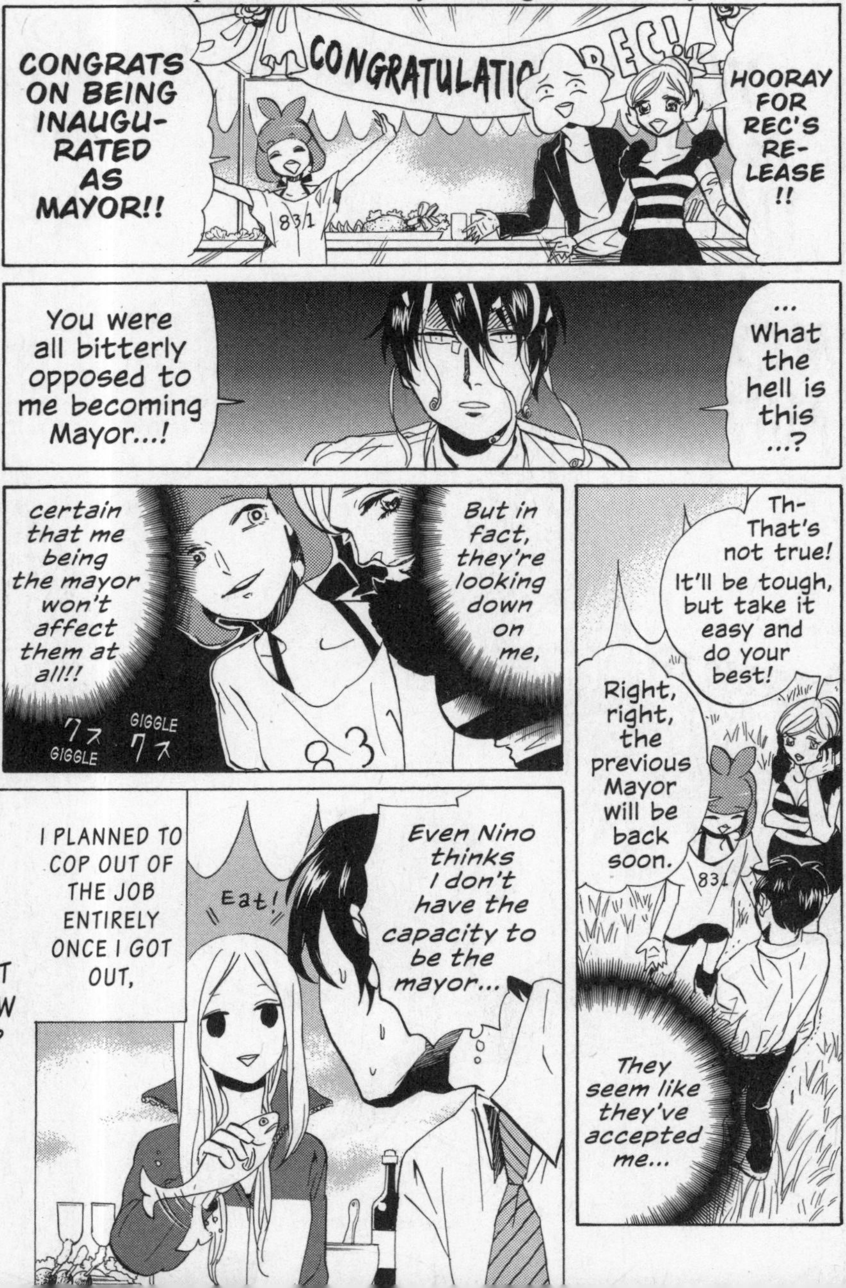
HOORAY FOR REC'S RE-LEASE!!
CONGRATULATIO
REC!
CONGRATS ON BEING INAUGU-RATED AS MAYOR!!
831
...What the hell is this...?
You were all bitterly opposed to me becoming Mayor...!
Th-That's not true! It'll be tough, but take it easy and do your best!
Right, right, the previous Mayor will be back soon.
831
They seem like they've accepted me...
But in fact, they're looking down on me,
certain that me being the mayor won't affect them at all!!
GIGGLE
GIGGLE
83
Even Nino thinks I don't have the capacity to be the mayor...
Eat!
I PLANNED TO COP OUT OF THE JOB ENTIRELY ONCE I GOT OUT,
BUT NOW...?

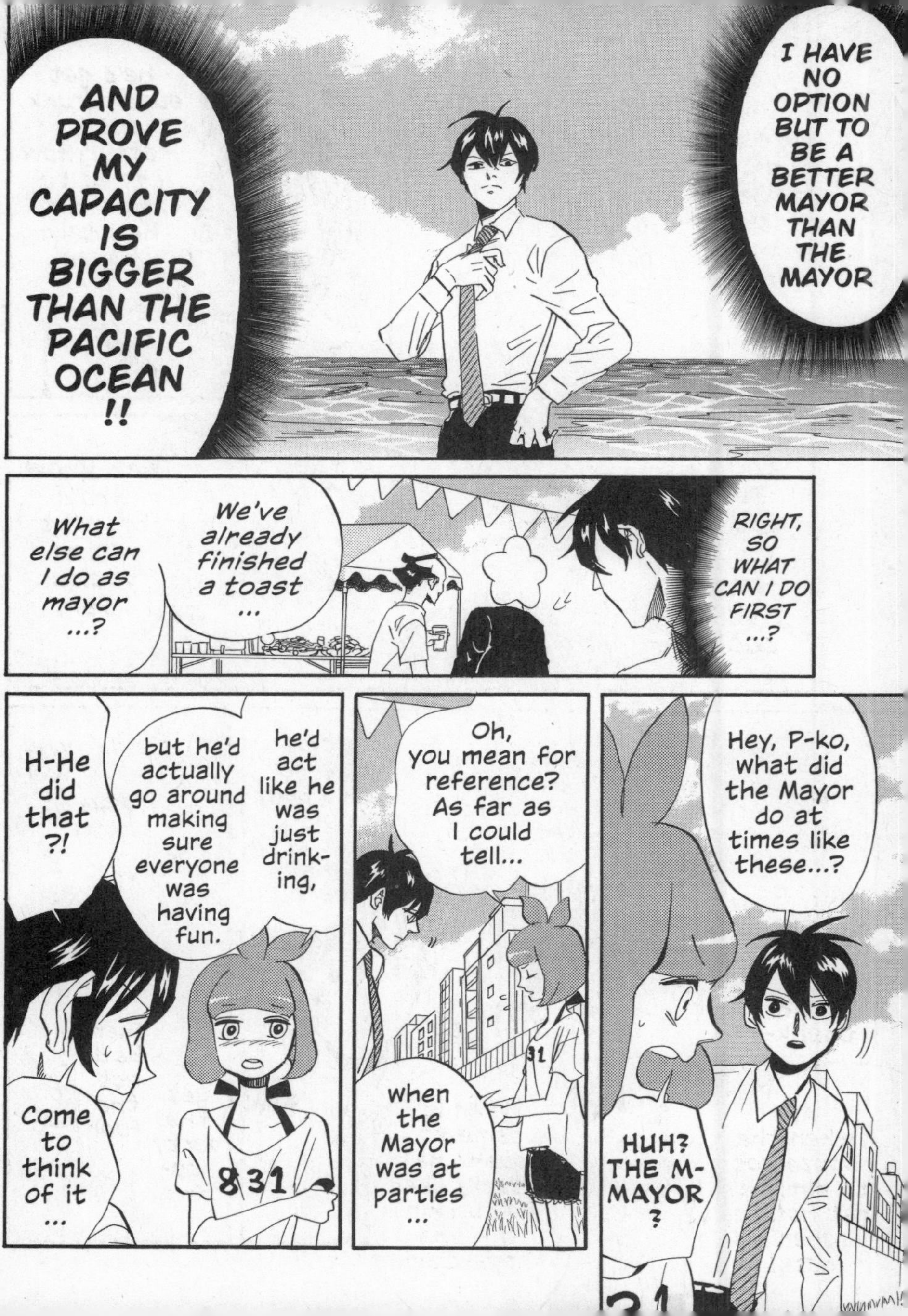
I HAVE NO OPTION BUT TO BE A BETTER MAYOR THAN THE MAYOR
AND PROVE MY CAPACITY IS BIGGER THAN THE PACIFIC OCEAN !!
RIGHT, SO WHAT CAN I DO FIRST ...?
We've already finished a toast ...
What else can I do as mayor ...?
Hey, P-ko, what did the Mayor do at times like these...?
HUH? THE M-MAYOR ?
Oh, you mean for reference? As far as I could tell...
when the Mayor was at parties ...
he'd act like he was just drinking,
but he'd actually go around making sure everyone was having fun.
H-He did that ?!
Come to think of it ...

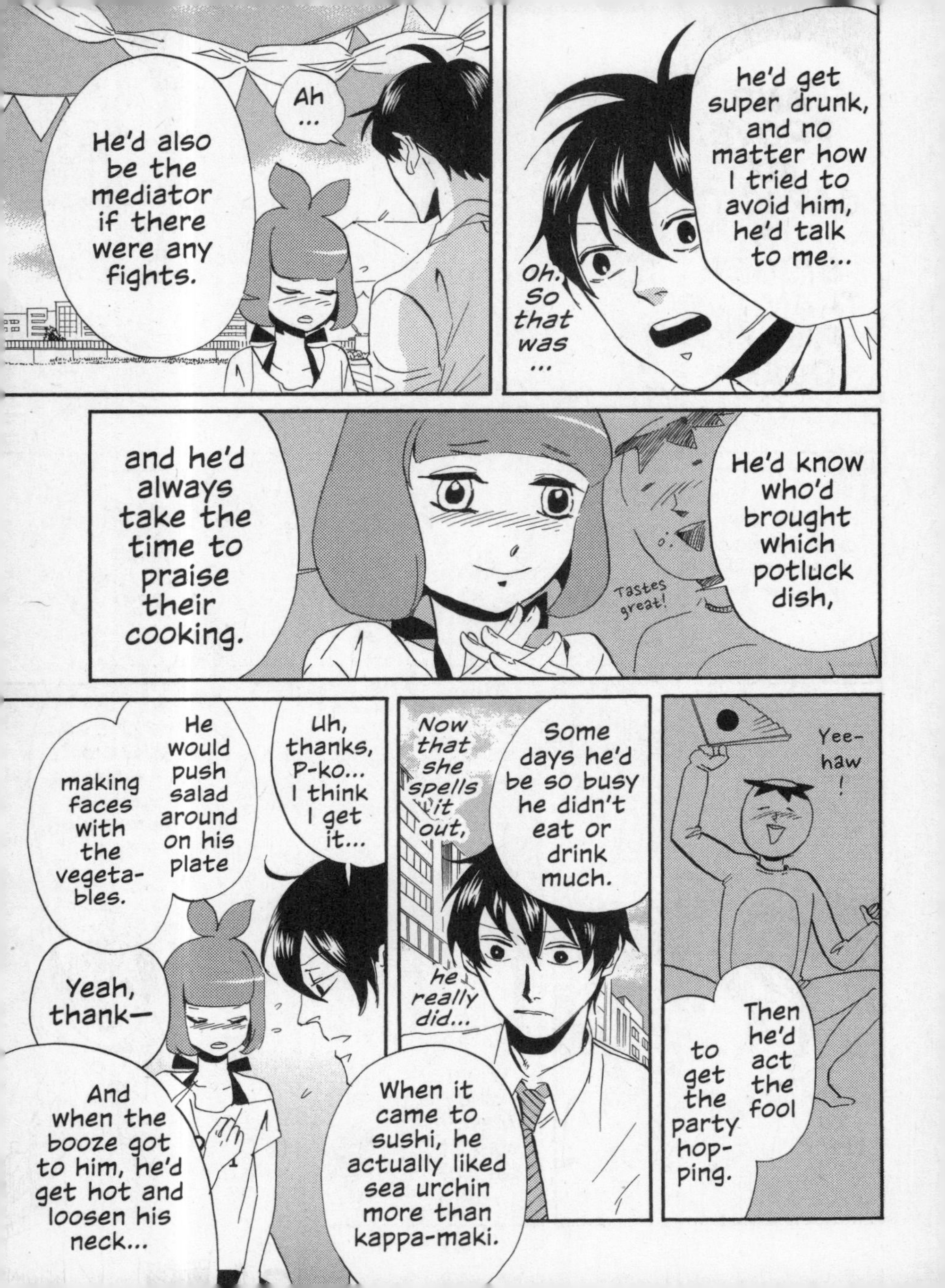
he'd get super drunk, and no matter how I tried to avoid him, he'd talk to me...
Oh. So that was...
Ah...
He'd also be the mediator if there were any fights.
He'd know who'd brought which potluck dish,
Tastes great!
and he'd always take the time to praise their cooking.
Yee-haw!
Then he'd act the fool to get the party hop-ping.
Some days he'd be so busy he didn't eat or drink much.
Now that she spells it out,
he really did...
When it came to sushi, he actually liked sea urchin more than kappa-maki.
He would push salad around on his plate
making faces with the vegeta-bles.
Uh, thanks, P-ko... I think I get it...
Yeah, thank—
And when the booze got to him, he'd get hot and loosen his neck...

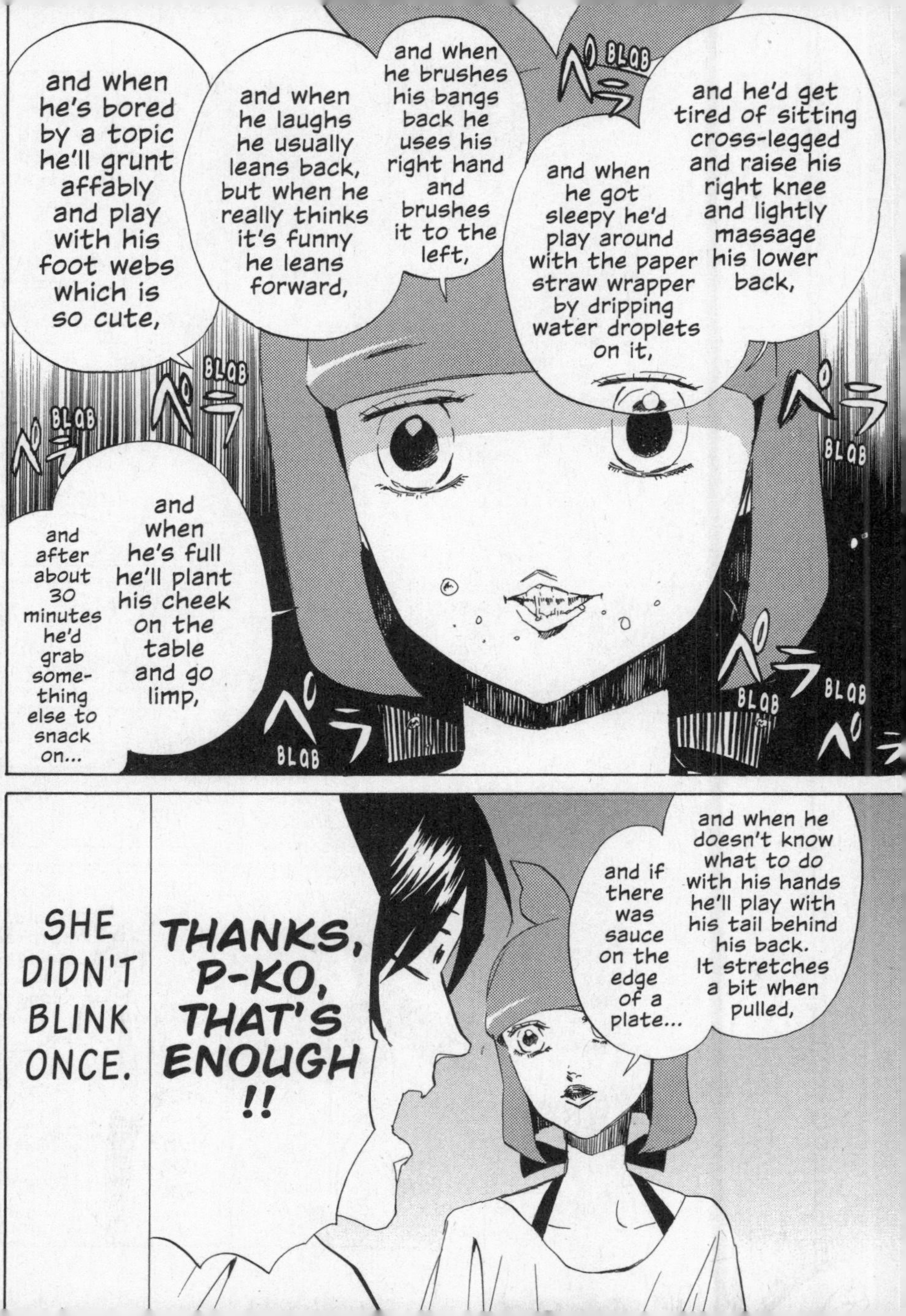
and he'd get tired of sitting cross-legged and raise his right knee and lightly massage his lower back,
BLAB
and when he brushes his bangs back he uses his right hand and brushes it to the left,
and when he got sleepy he'd play around with the paper straw wrapper by dripping water droplets on it,
and when he laughs he usually leans back, but when he really thinks it's funny he leans forward,
and when he's bored by a topic he'll grunt affably and play with his foot webs which is so cute,
BLAB
BLAB
BLAB
BLAB
BLAB
BLAB
and when he's full he'll plant his cheek on the table and go limp,
and after about 30 minutes he'd grab some-thing else to snack on...
BLAB
and when he doesn't know what to do with his hands he'll play with his tail behind his back. It stretches a bit when pulled,
and if there was sauce on the edge of a plate...
THANKS, P-KO, THAT'S ENOUGH !!
SHE DIDN'T BLINK ONCE.

Chapter 339: New Mayor's First Job

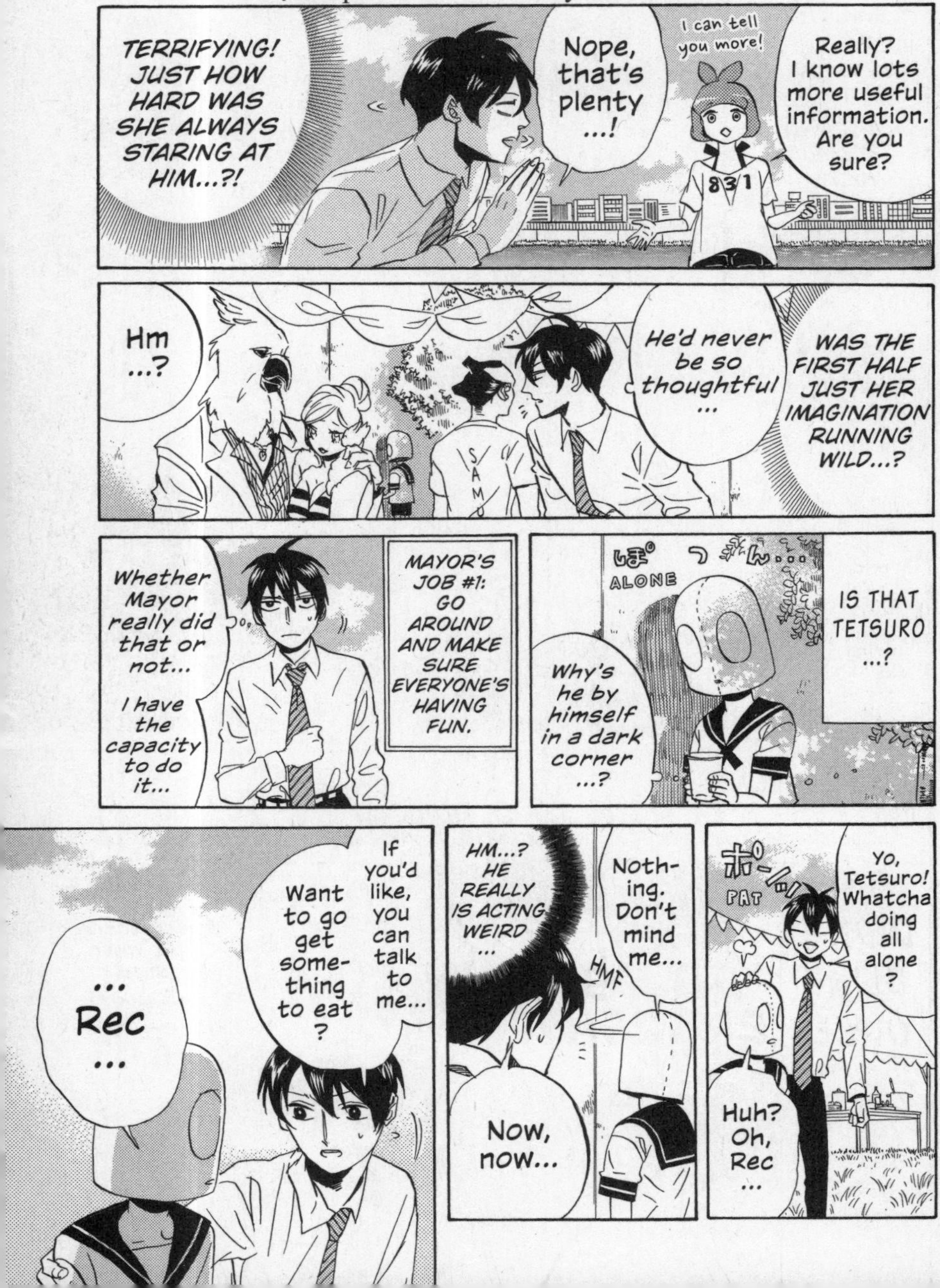
Really? I know lots more useful information. Are you sure?
I can tell you more!
Nope, that's plenty ...!
TERRIFYING! JUST HOW HARD WAS SHE ALWAYS STARING AT HIM...?!
WAS THE FIRST HALF JUST HER IMAGINATION RUNNING WILD...?
He'd never be so thoughtful ...
Hm ...?
IS THAT TETSURO ...?
ALONE
Why's he by himself in a dark corner ...?
MAYOR'S JOB #1: GO AROUND AND MAKE SURE EVERYONE'S HAVING FUN.
Whether Mayor really did that or not...
I have the capacity to do it...
Yo, Tetsuro! Whatcha doing all alone ?
PAT
Huh? Oh, Rec ...
Noth-ing. Don't mind me...
HM...? HE REALLY IS ACTING WEIRD ...
HMF
Now, now...
If you'd like, you can talk to me...
Want to go get some-thing to eat ?
... Rec ...

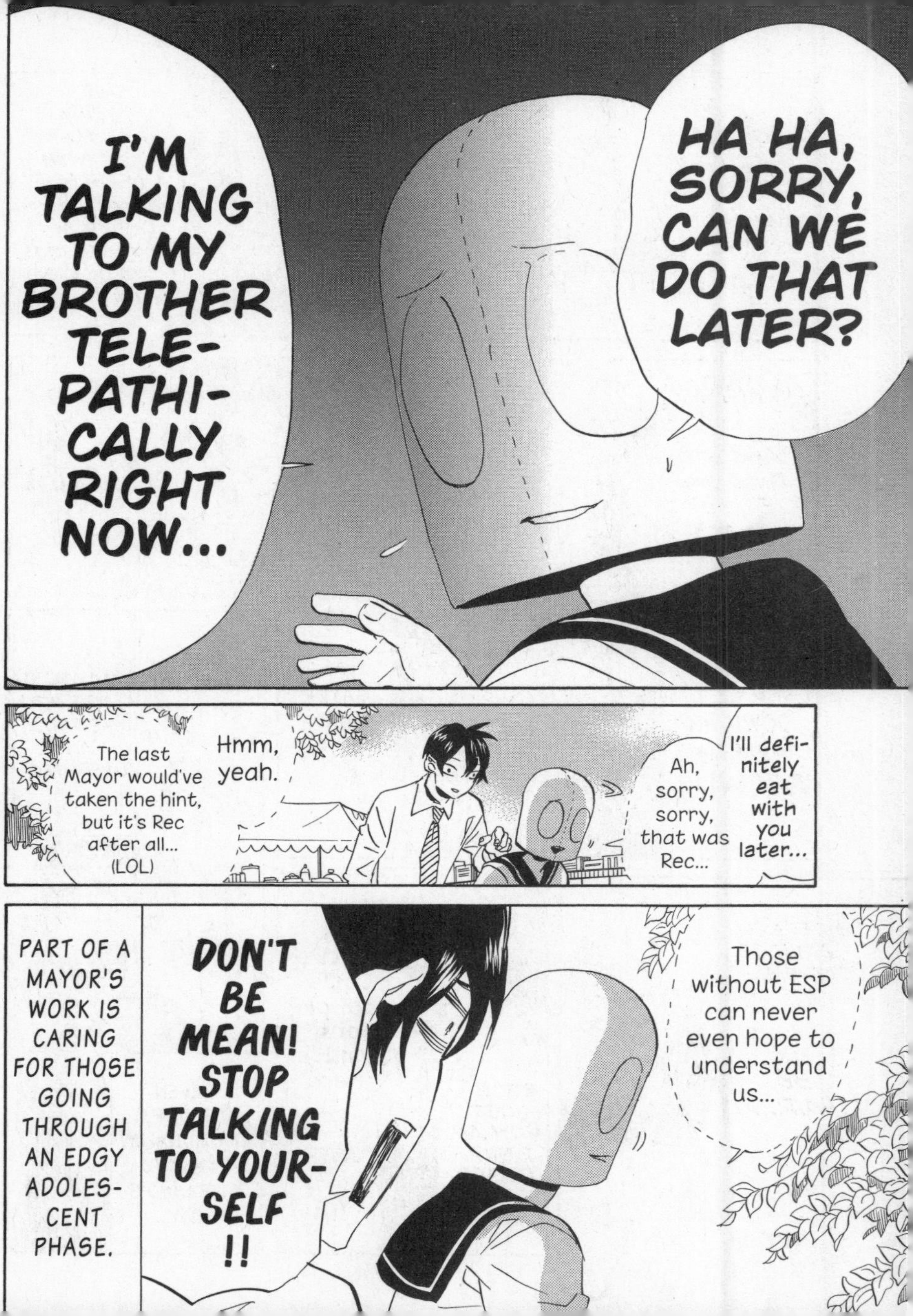
HA HA, SORRY, CAN WE DO THAT LATER?
I'M TALKING TO MY BROTHER TELEPATHICALLY RIGHT NOW...
I'll definitely eat with you later...
Ah, sorry, sorry, that was Rec...
Hmm, yeah.
The last Mayor would've taken the hint, but it's Rec after all... (LOL)
Those without ESP can never even hope to understand us...
DON'T BE MEAN! STOP TALKING TO YOURSELF !!
PART OF A MAYOR'S WORK IS CARING FOR THOSE GOING THROUGH AN EDGY ADOLESCENT PHASE.

Chapter 340: Sense of Humor

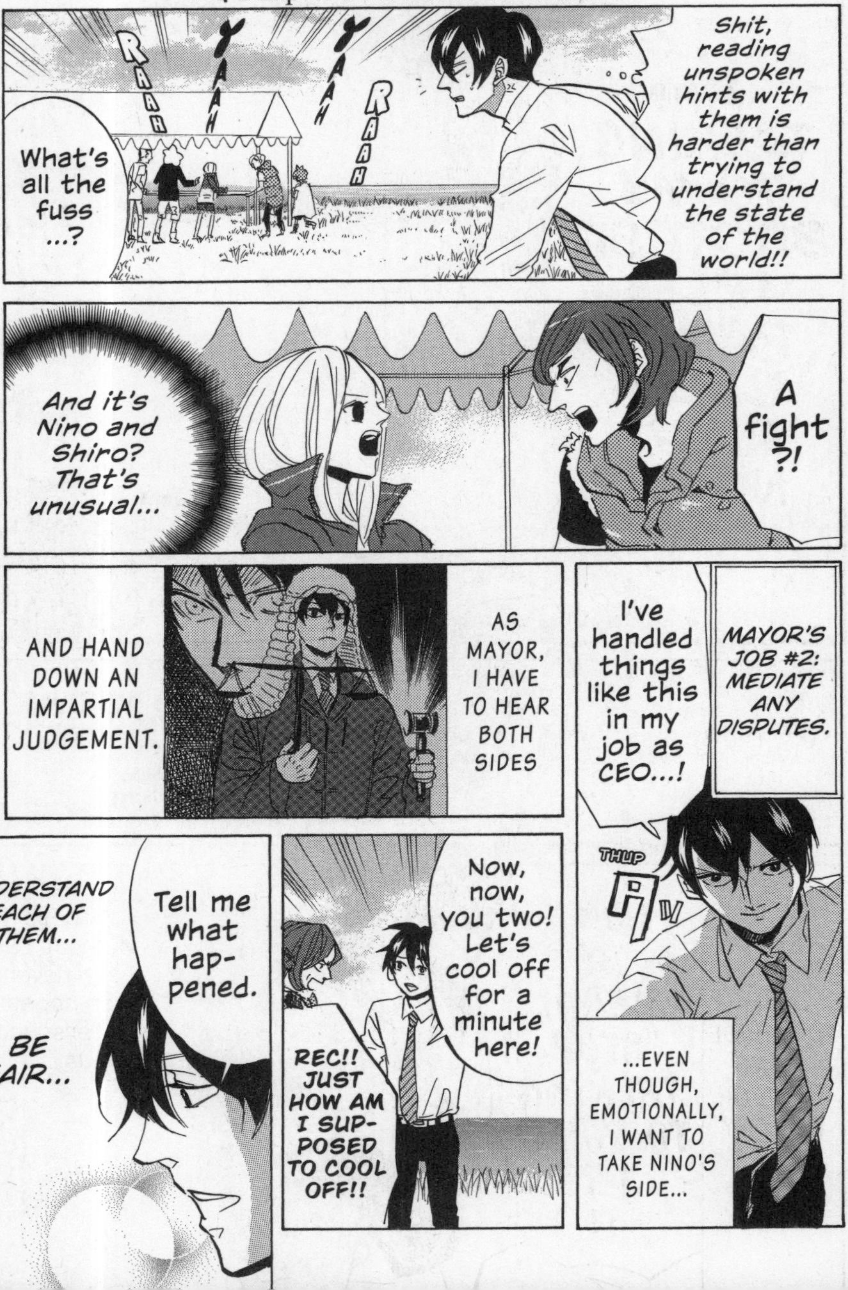

Shit, reading unspoken hints with them is harder than trying to understand the state of the world!!
RAAAH
YAAAH
YAAAH
RAAAH
What's all the fuss ...?
A fight ?!
And it's Nino and Shiro? That's unusual...
MAYOR'S JOB #2: MEDIATE ANY DISPUTES.
I've handled things like this in my job as CEO...!
THUP
...EVEN THOUGH, EMOTIONALLY, I WANT TO TAKE NINO'S SIDE...
AS MAYOR, I HAVE TO HEAR BOTH SIDES
AND HAND DOWN AN IMPARTIAL JUDGEMENT.
Now, now, you two! Let's cool off for a minute here!
REC!! JUST HOW AM I SUP-POSED TO COOL OFF!!
UNDERSTAND EACH OF THEM...
Tell me what hap-pened.
BE FAIR...

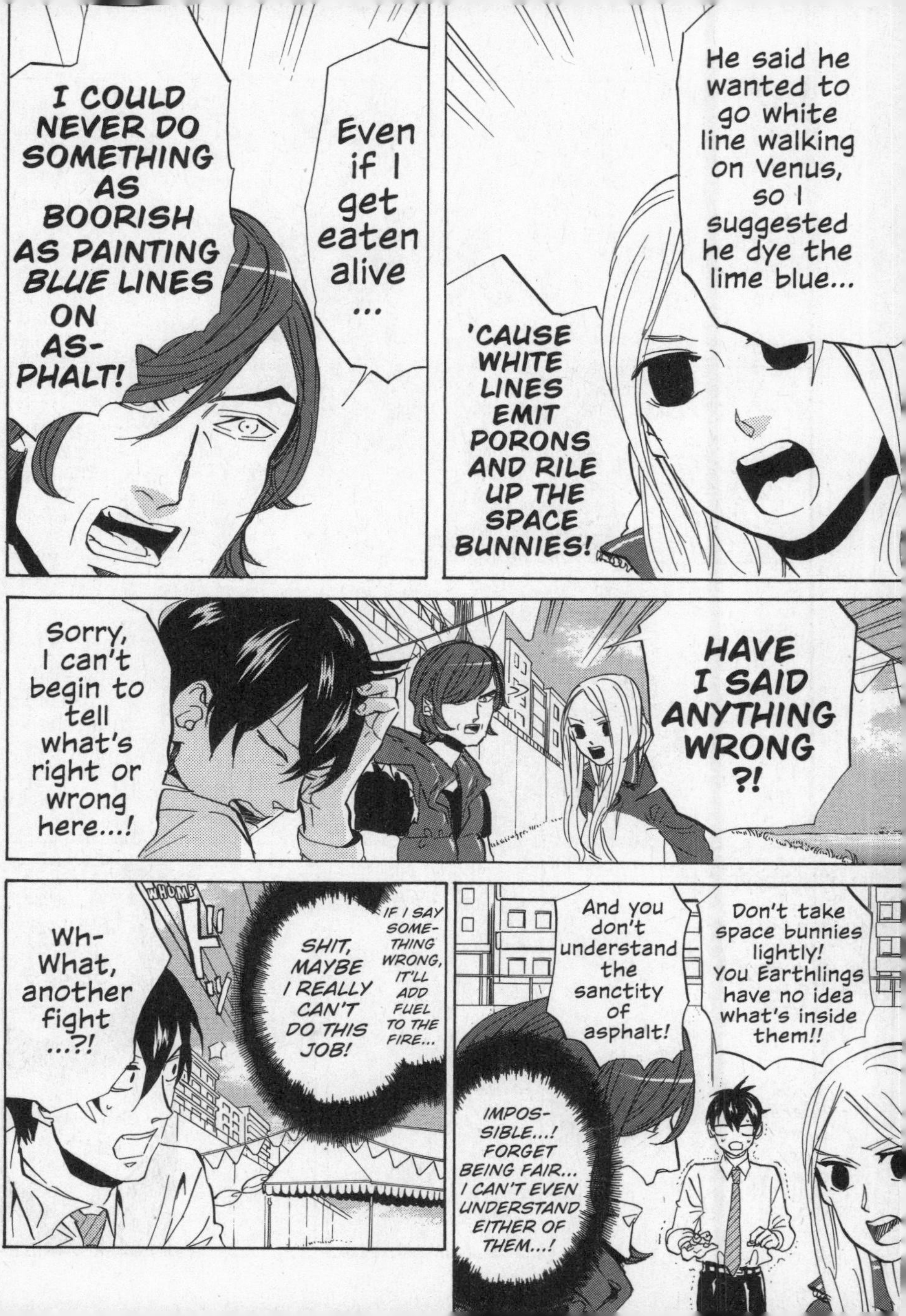
He said he wanted to go white line walking on Venus, so I suggested he dye the lime blue...
'CAUSE WHITE LINES EMIT PORONS AND RILE UP THE SPACE BUNNIES!
Even if I get eaten alive ...
I COULD NEVER DO SOMETHING AS BOORISH AS PAINTING BLUE LINES ON AS-PHALT!
HAVE I SAID ANYTHING WRONG ?!
Sorry, I can't begin to tell what's right or wrong here...!
Don't take space bunnies lightly! You Earthlings have no idea what's inside them!!
And you don't understand the sanctity of asphalt!
IMPOS-SIBLE...! FORGET BEING FAIR... I CAN'T EVEN UNDERSTAND EITHER OF THEM...!
IF I SAY SOME-THING WRONG, IT'LL ADD FUEL TO THE FIRE...
SHIT, MAYBE I REALLY CAN'T DO THIS JOB!
WHOMP
Wh-What, another fight ...?!

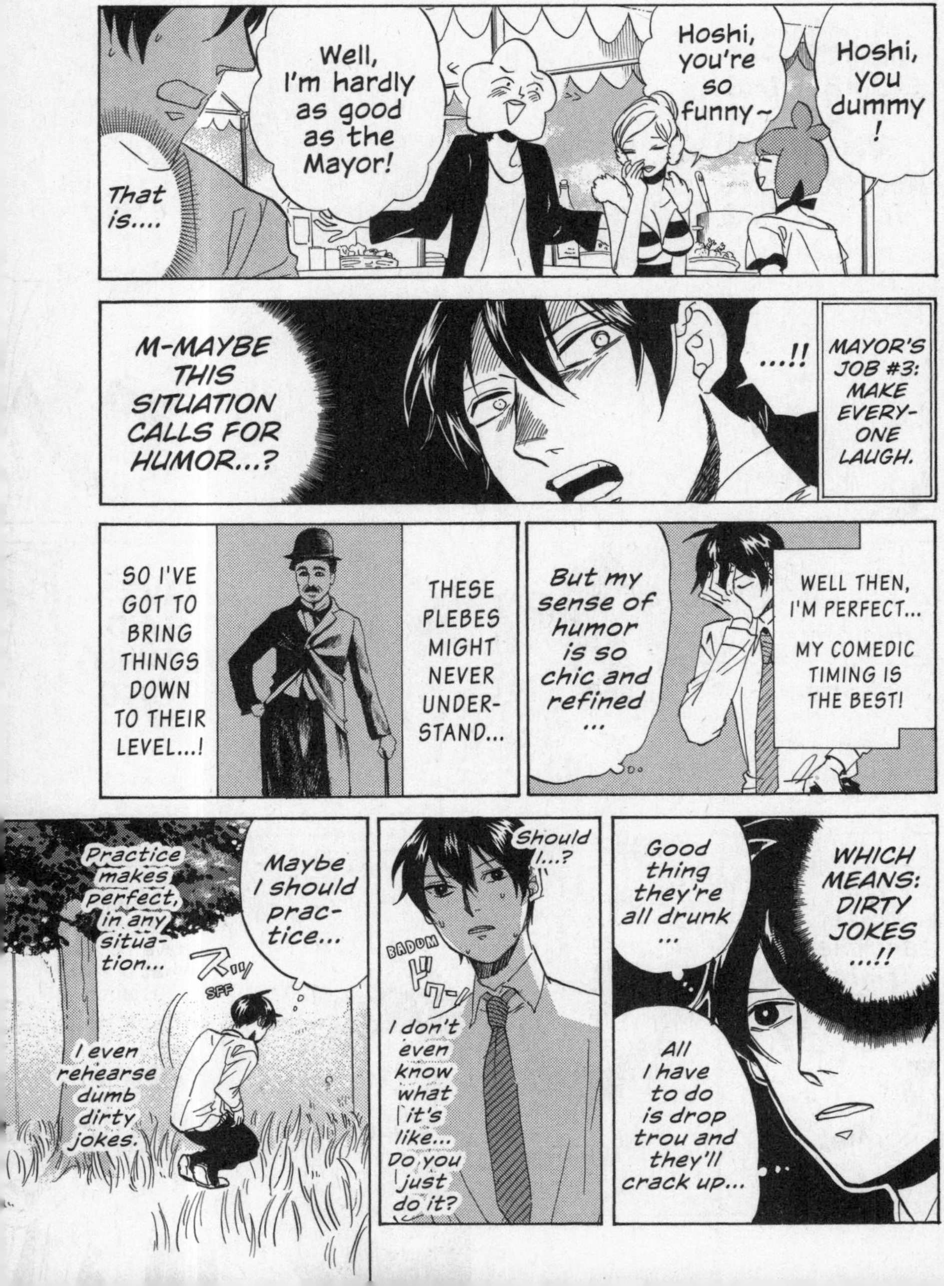
Hoshi, you dummy!
Hoshi, you're so funny~
Well, I'm hardly as good as the Mayor!
That is....
MAYOR'S JOB #3: MAKE EVERY-ONE LAUGH.
...!!
M-MAYBE THIS SITUATION CALLS FOR HUMOR...?
WELL THEN, I'M PERFECT...
MY COMEDIC TIMING IS THE BEST!
But my sense of humor is so chic and refined ...
THESE PLEBES MIGHT NEVER UNDER-STAND...
SO I'VE GOT TO BRING THINGS DOWN TO THEIR LEVEL...!
WHICH MEANS: DIRTY JOKES ...!!
Good thing they're all drunk ...
All I have to do is drop trou and they'll crack up...
Should I...?
BADUM
I don't even know what it's like... Do you just do it?
Maybe I should prac-tice...
Practice makes perfect, in any situa-tion...
SFF
I even rehearse dumb dirty jokes.

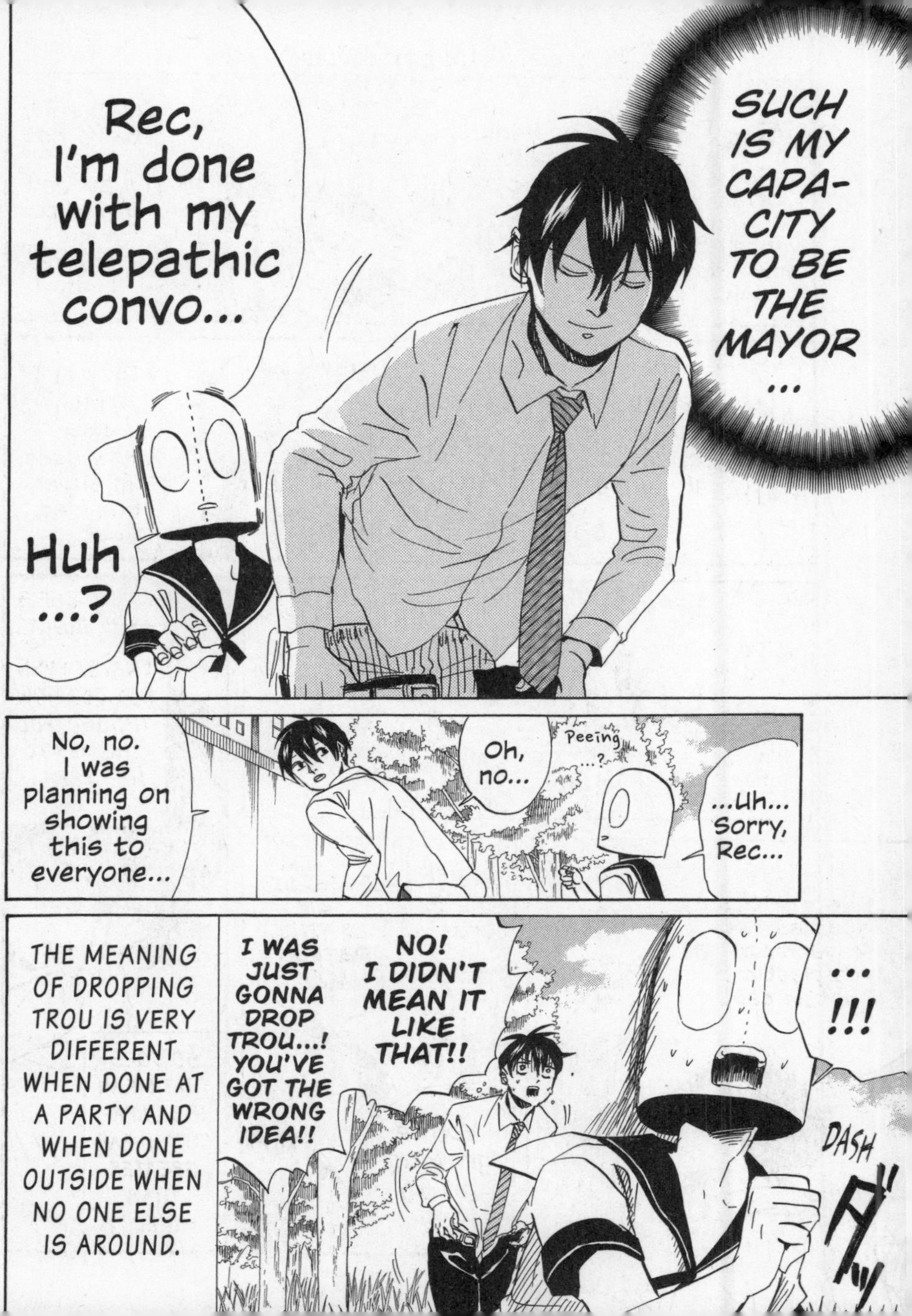
SUCH IS MY CAPA-CITY TO BE THE MAYOR ...
Rec, I'm done with my telepathic convo...
Huh ...?
...Uh... Sorry, Rec...
Peeing ...?
Oh, no...
No, no. I was planning on showing this to everyone...
... !!!
DASH
NO! I DIDN'T MEAN IT LIKE THAT!!
I WAS JUST GONNA DROP TROU...! YOU'VE GOT THE WRONG IDEA!!
THE MEANING OF DROPPING TROU IS VERY DIFFERENT WHEN DONE AT A PARTY AND WHEN DONE OUTSIDE WHEN NO ONE ELSE IS AROUND.

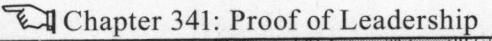

Chapter 341: Proof of Leadership

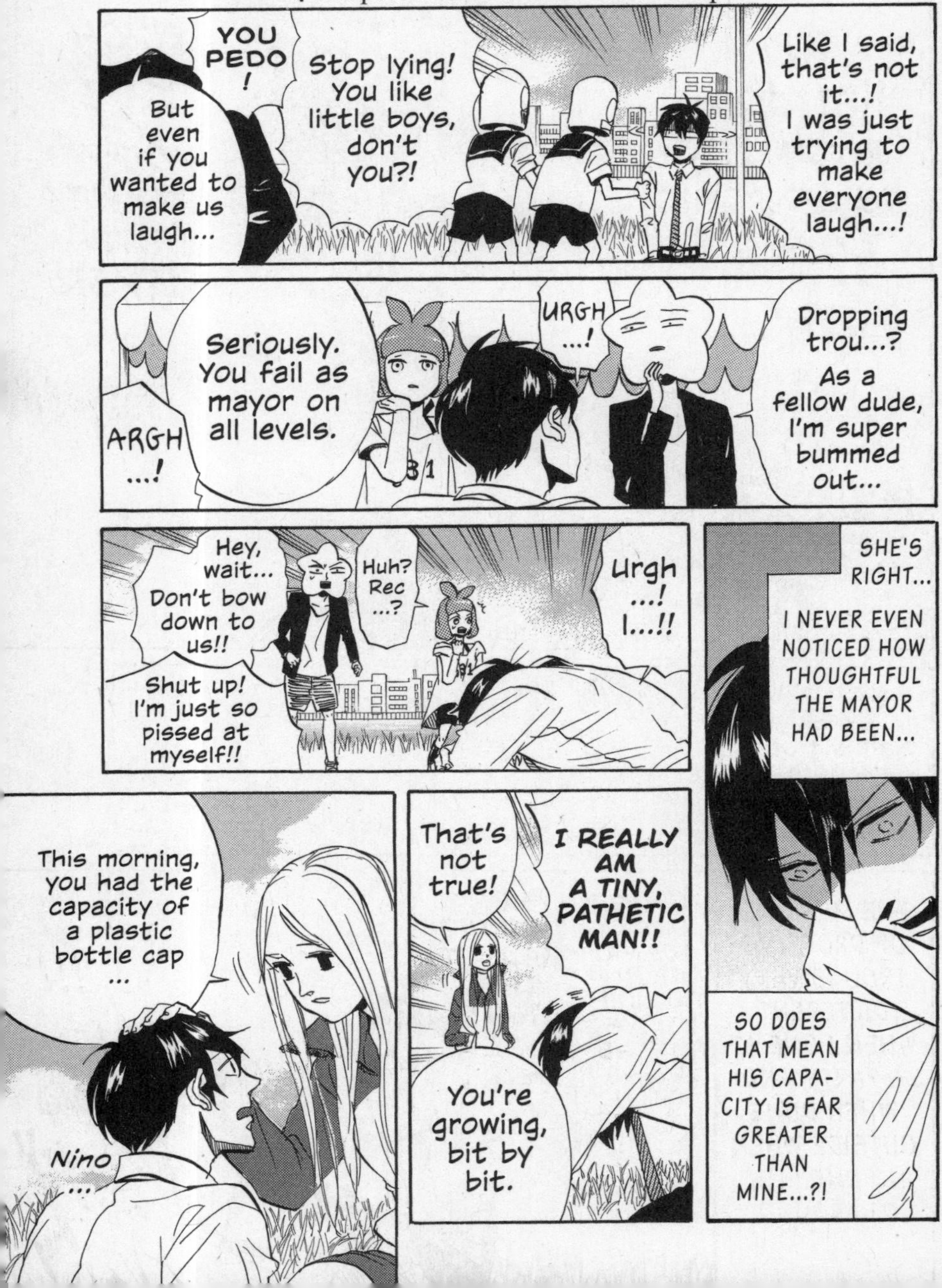
Like I said, that's not it...! I was just trying to make everyone laugh...!
Stop lying! You like little boys, don't you?!
YOU PEDO!
But even if you wanted to make us laugh...
Dropping trou...?
As a fellow dude, I'm super bummed out...
URGH ...!
Seriously. You fail as mayor on all levels.
ARGH ...!
SHE'S RIGHT...
I NEVER EVEN NOTICED HOW THOUGHTFUL THE MAYOR HAD BEEN...
SO DOES THAT MEAN HIS CAPA-CITY IS FAR GREATER THAN MINE...?!
Urgh ...! I...!!
Huh? Rec ...?
Hey, wait...
Don't bow down to us!!
Shut up! I'm just so pissed at myself!!
That's not true!
I REALLY AM A TINY, PATHETIC MAN!!
You're growing, bit by bit.
This morning, you had the capacity of a plastic bottle cap ...
Nino ...

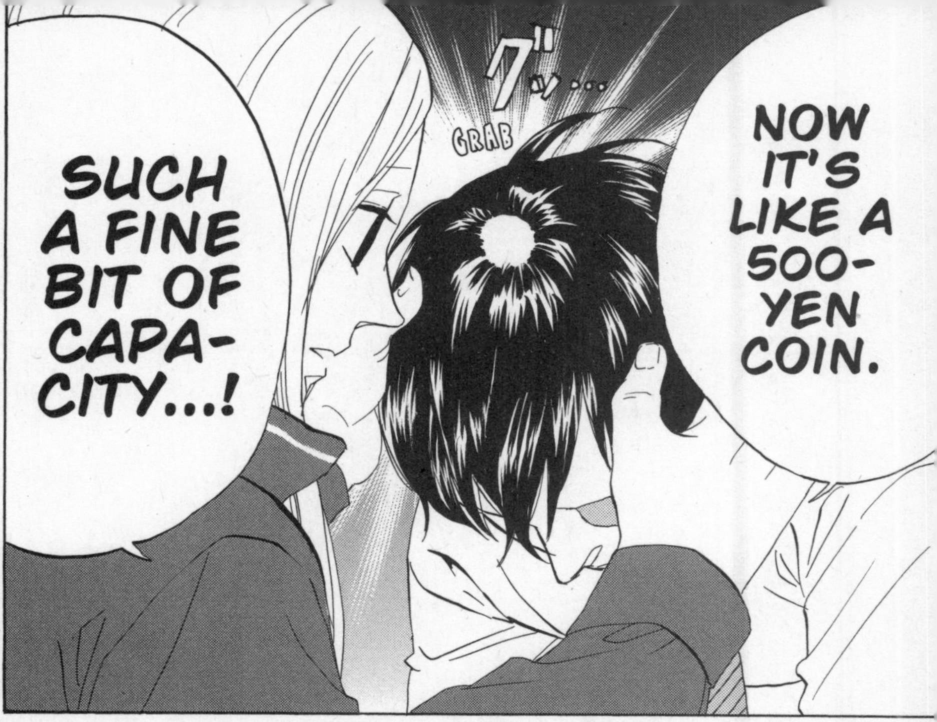
NOW IT'S LIKE A 500-YEN COIN.
GRAB
SUCH A FINE BIT OF CAPA-CITY...!

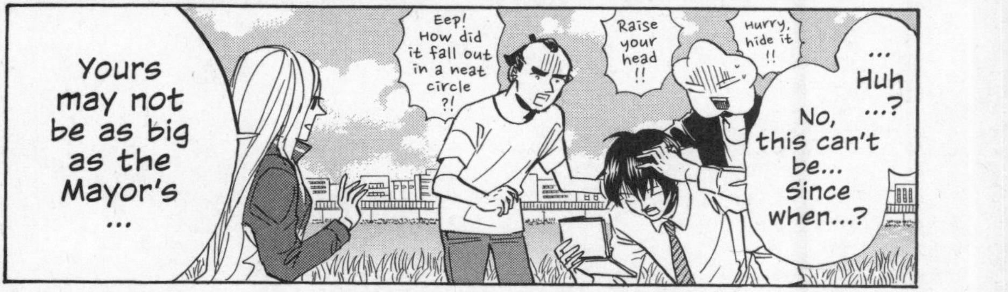
... Huh ...?
No, this can't be... Since when...?
Hurry, hide it !!
Raise your head !!
Eep! How did it fall out in a neat circle ?!
Yours may not be as big as the Mayor's ...

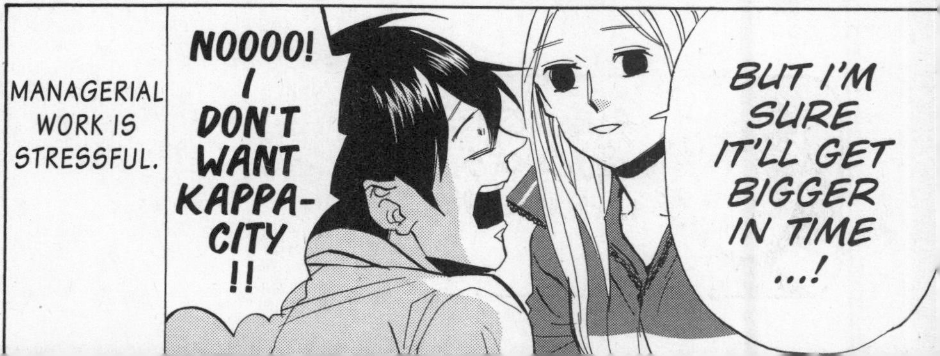
BUT I'M SURE IT'LL GET BIGGER IN TIME ...!
NOOOO! I DON'T WANT KAPPA-CITY !!
MANAGERIAL WORK IS STRESSFUL.

SAKAMOTO RYOMA'S ANTI-FOREIGNER DIARY

ARAKAWA
UNDER
THE BRIDGE

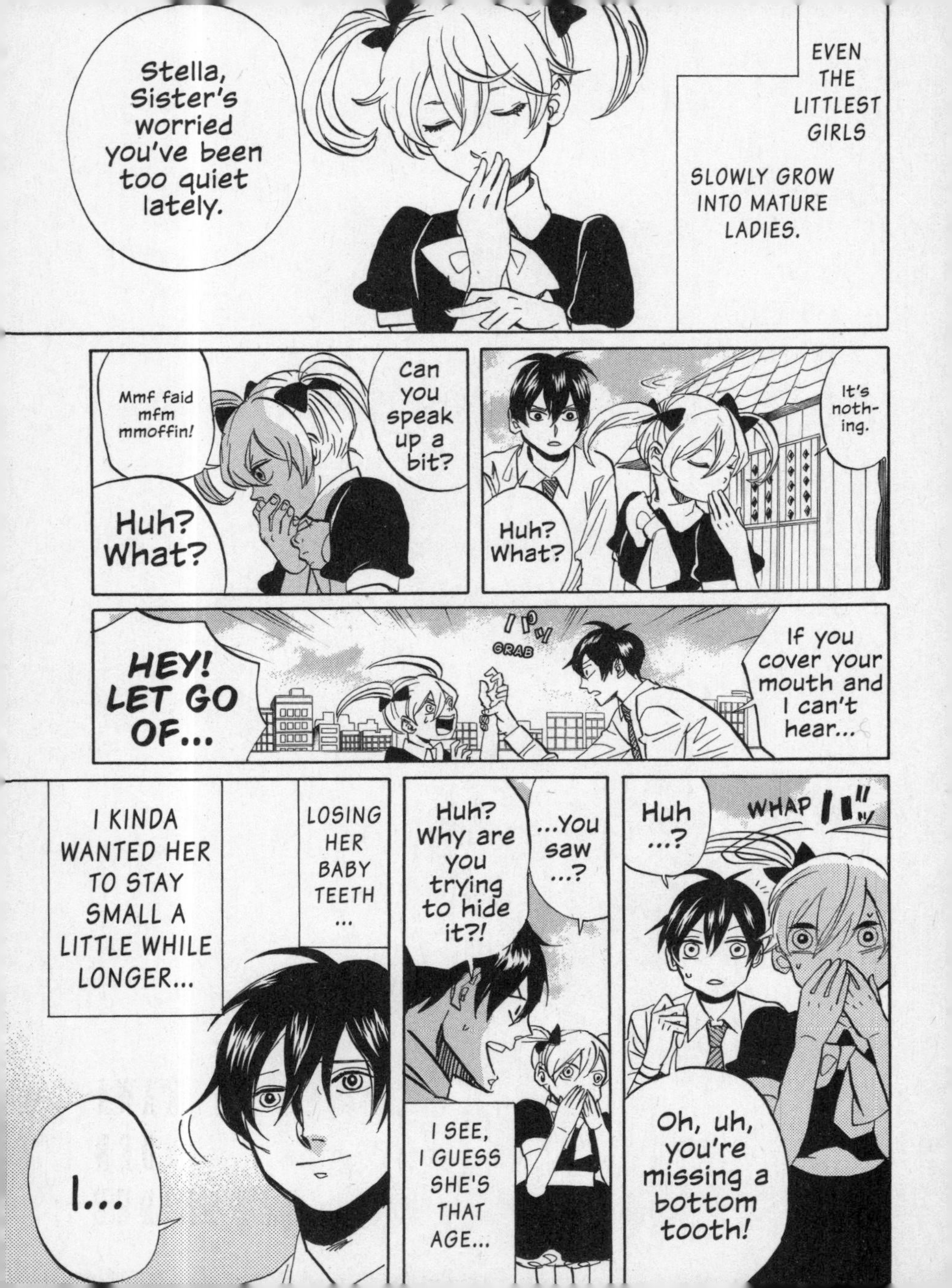
EVEN THE LITTLEST GIRLS
SLOWLY GROW INTO MATURE LADIES.
Stella, Sister's worried you've been too quiet lately.
It's noth-ing.
Huh? What?
Can you speak up a bit?
Mmf faid mfm mmoffin!
Huh? What?
If you cover your mouth and I can't hear...
GRAB
HEY! LET GO OF...
WHAP
Huh ...?
Oh, uh, you're missing a bottom tooth!
...You saw ...?
Huh? Why are you trying to hide it?!
I SEE, I GUESS SHE'S THAT AGE...
LOSING HER BABY TEETH ...
I KINDA WANTED HER TO STAY SMALL A LITTLE WHILE LONGER...
I...

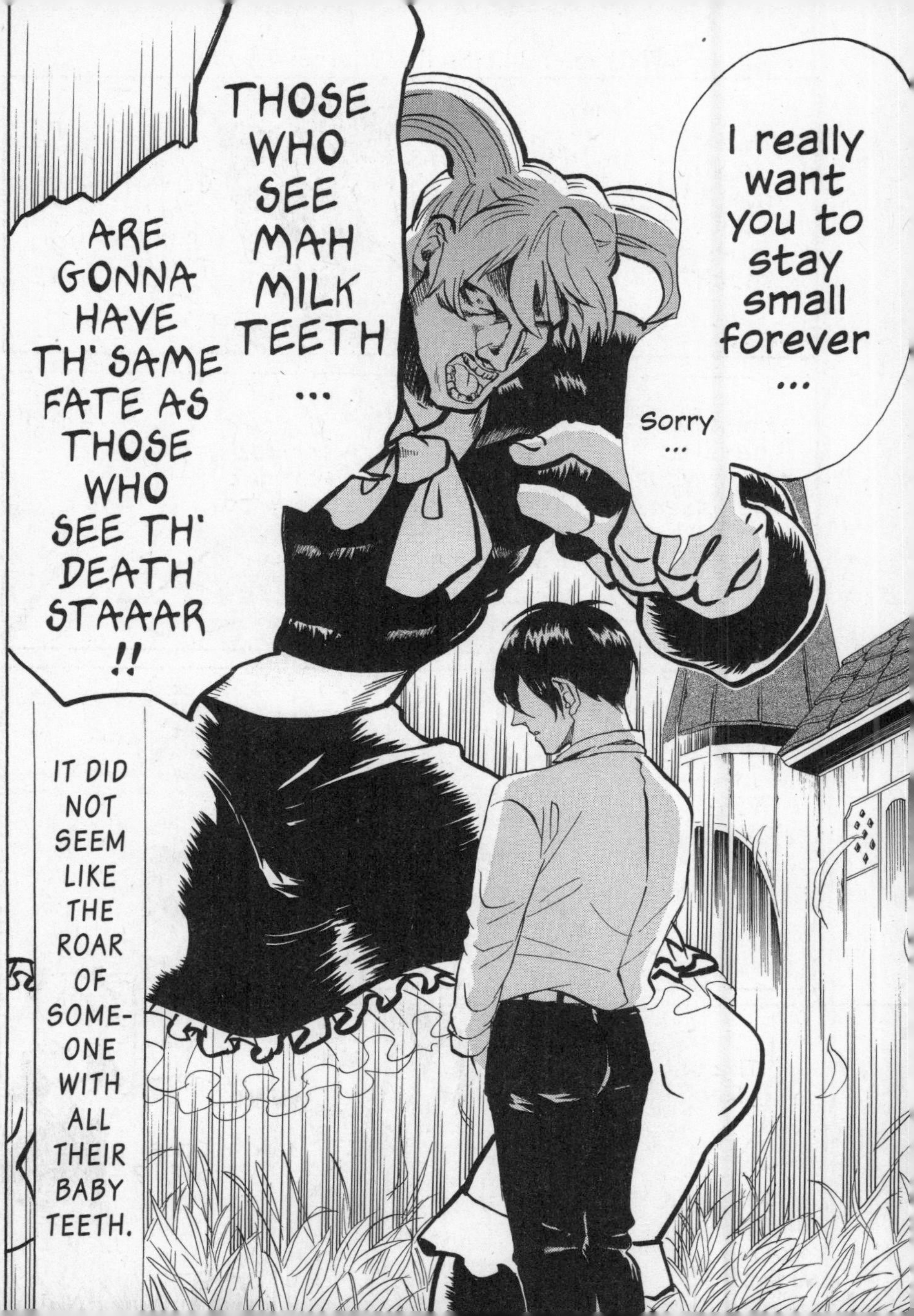
I really want you to stay small forever ...
Sorry ...
THOSE WHO SEE MAH MILK TEETH ...
ARE GONNA HAVE TH' SAME FATE AS THOSE WHO SEE TH' DEATH STAAAR !!
IT DID NOT SEEM LIKE THE ROAR OF SOME-ONE WITH ALL THEIR BABY TEETH.

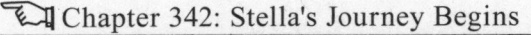

Chapter 342: Stella's Journey Begins

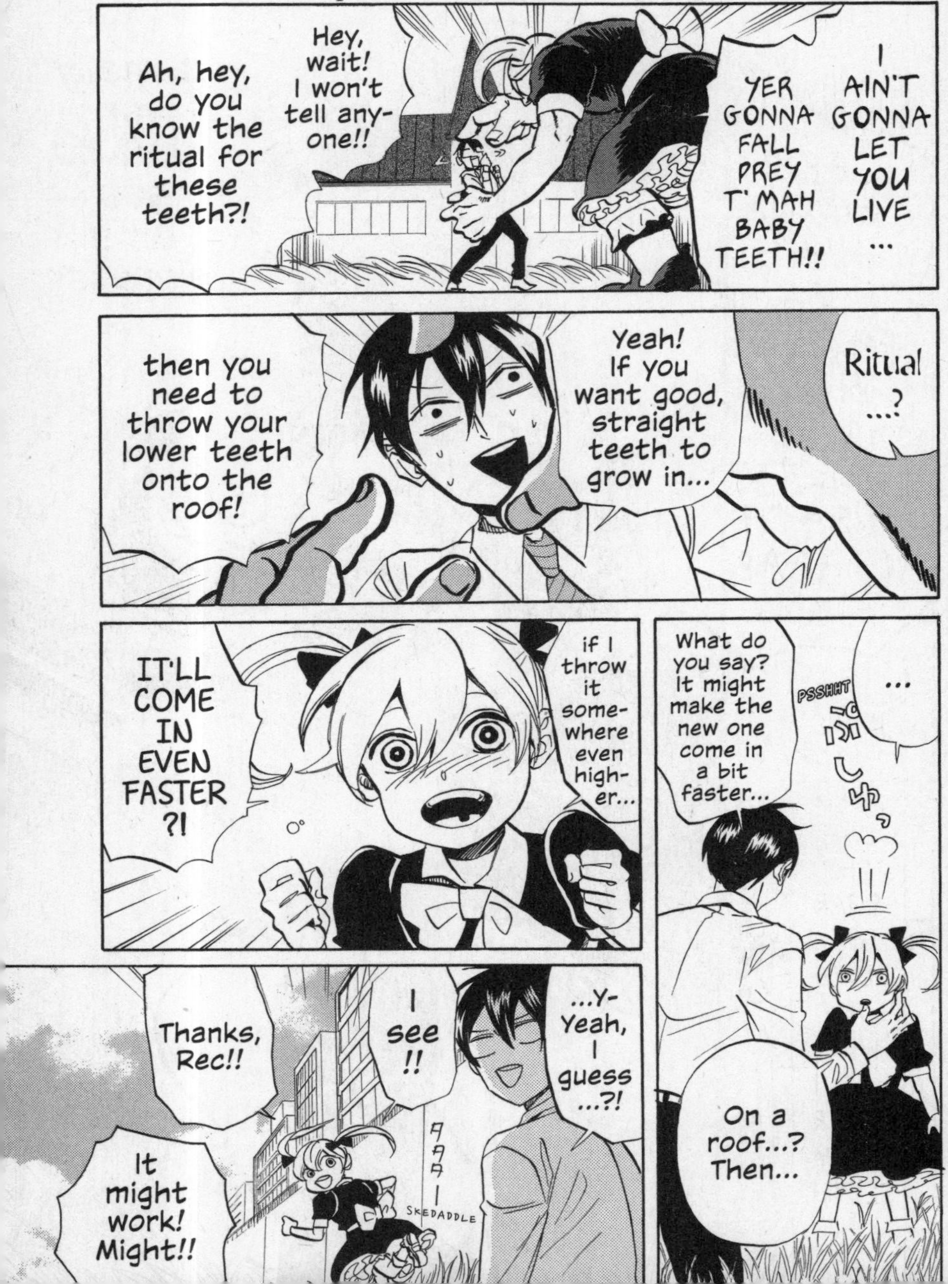

I AIN'T GONNA LET YOU LIVE ...
YER GONNA FALL PREY T' MAH BABY TEETH!!
Hey, wait! I won't tell any-one!!
Ah, hey, do you know the ritual for these teeth?!
Ritual ...?
Yeah! If you want good, straight teeth to grow in...
then you need to throw your lower teeth onto the roof!
...
What do you say? It might make the new one come in a bit faster...
PSSHHT
if I throw it some-where even high-er...
IT'LL COME IN EVEN FASTER ?!
On a roof...? Then...
...Y-Yeah, I guess ...?!
I see !!
Thanks, Rec!!
It might work! Might!!
SKEDADDLE

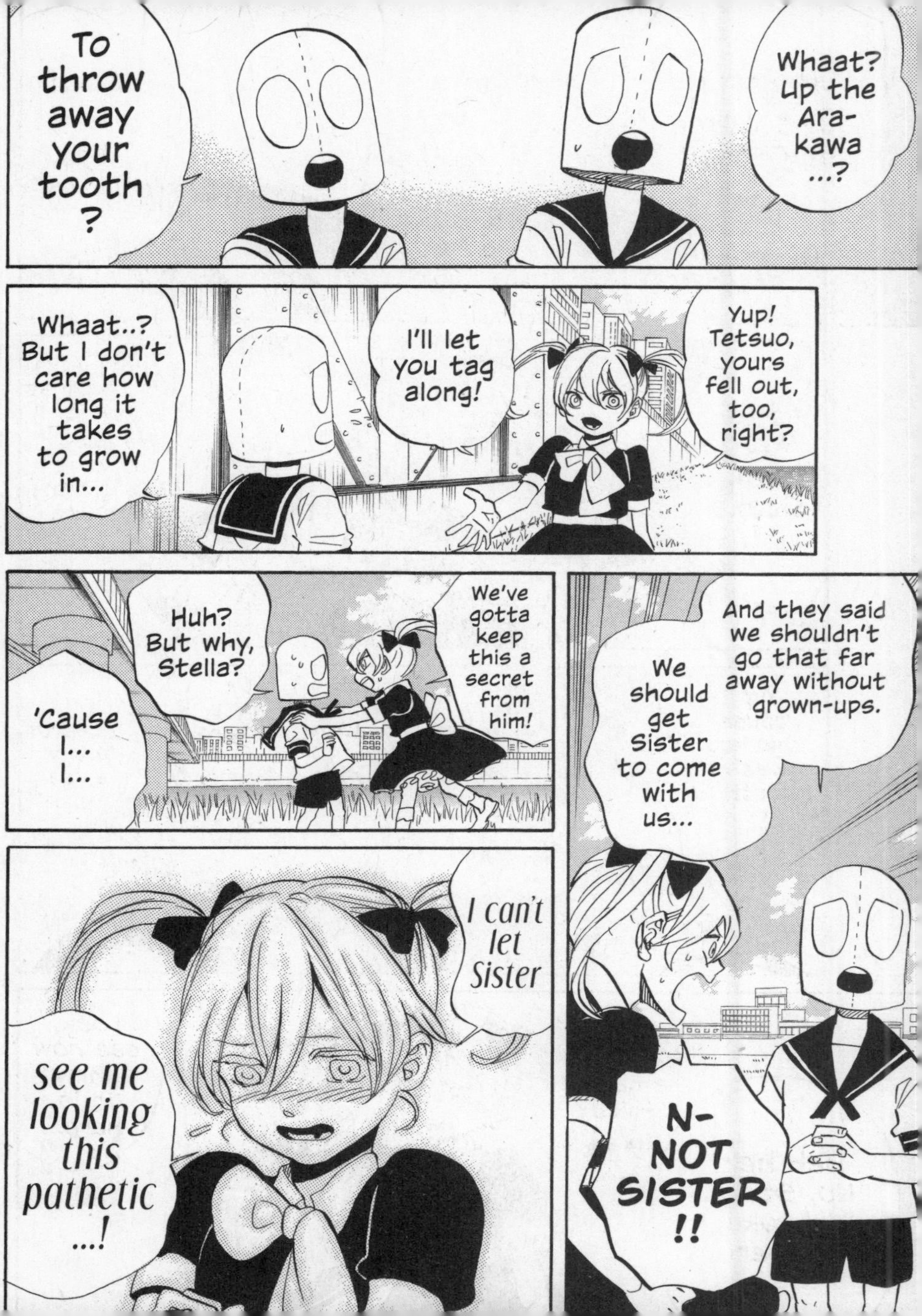
Whaat? Up the Ara-kawa ...?
To throw away your tooth ?
Yup! Tetsuo, yours fell out, too, right?
I'll let you tag along!
Whaat..? But I don't care how long it takes to grow in...
And they said we shouldn't go that far away without grown-ups.
We should get Sister to come with us...
N- NOT SISTER !!
We've gotta keep this a secret from him!
Huh? But why, Stella?
'Cause I... I...
I can't let Sister
see me looking this pathetic ...!

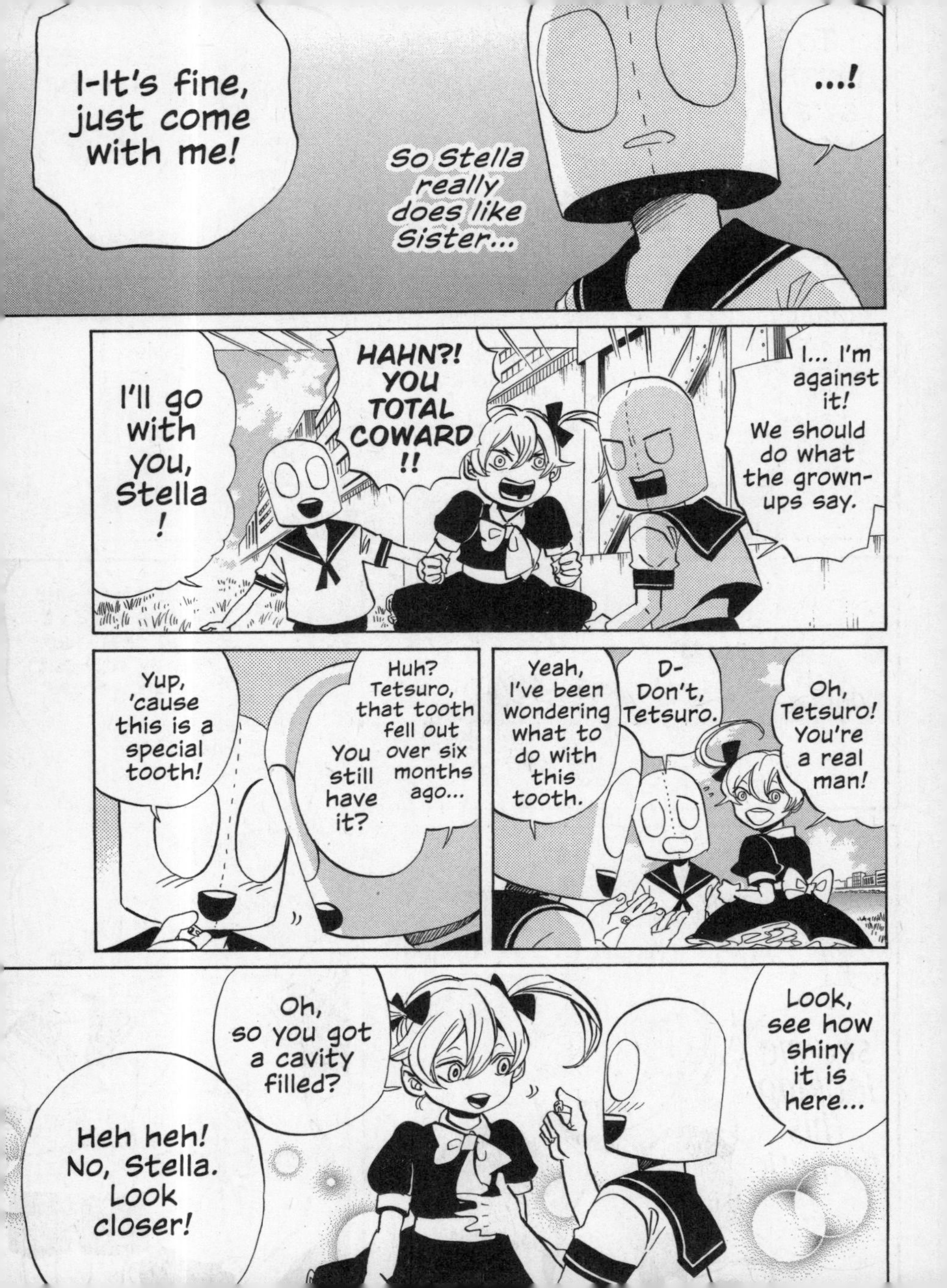
...!
So Stella really does like Sister...
I-It's fine, just come with me!
I... I'm against it! We should do what the grown-ups say.
HAHN?! YOU TOTAL COWARD !!
I'll go with you, Stella !
Oh, Tetsuro! You're a real man!
D- Don't, Tetsuro.
Yeah, I've been wondering what to do with this tooth.
Huh? Tetsuro, that tooth fell out over six months ago... You still have it?
Yup, 'cause this is a special tooth!
Look, see how shiny it is here...
Oh, so you got a cavity filled?
Heh heh! No, Stella. Look closer!

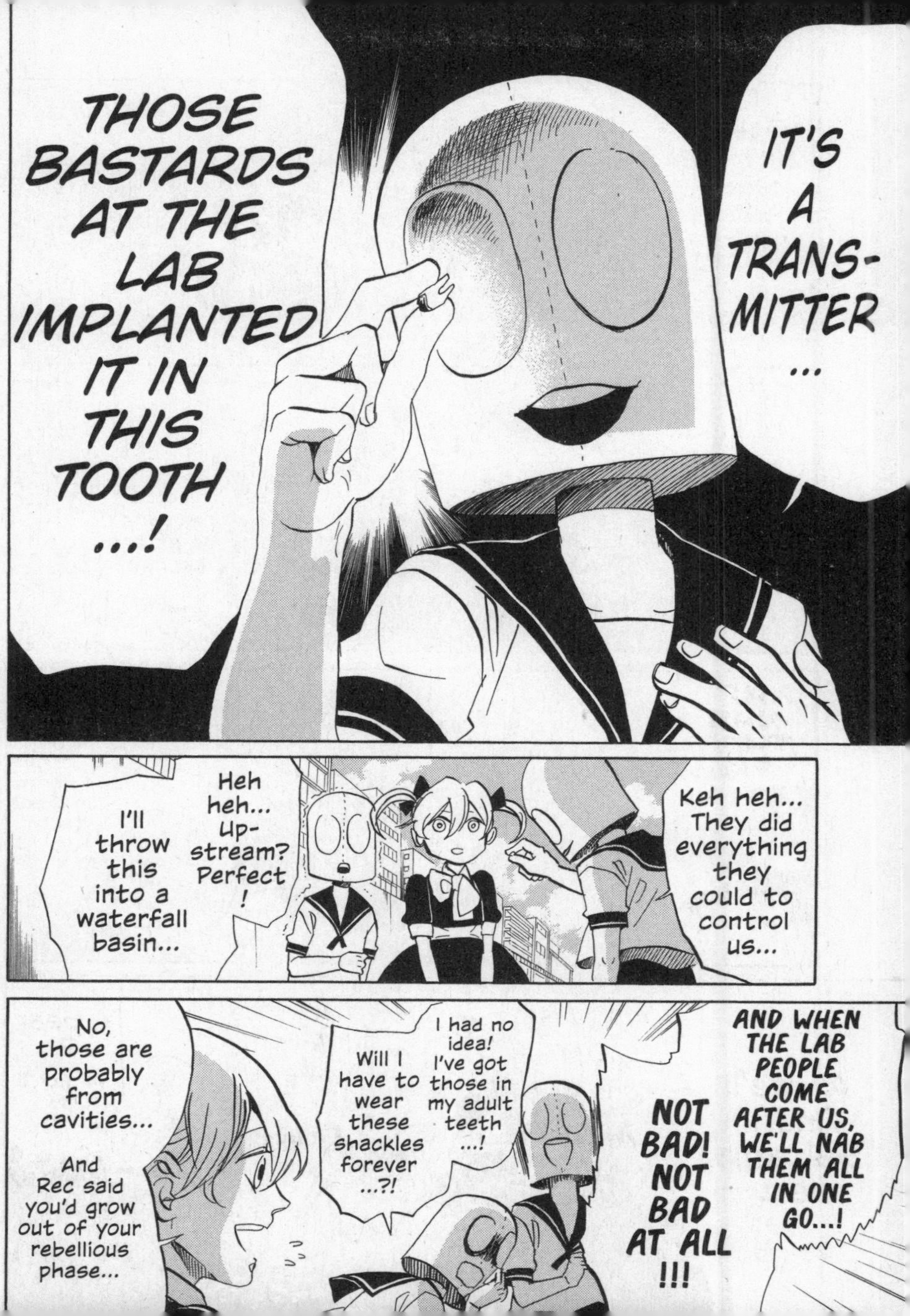
IT'S A TRANS-MITTER ...
THOSE BASTARDS AT THE LAB IMPLANTED IT IN THIS TOOTH ...!
Keh heh... They did everything they could to control us...
Heh heh... Up-stream? Perfect !
I'll throw this into a waterfall basin...
AND WHEN THE LAB PEOPLE COME AFTER US, WE'LL NAB THEM ALL IN ONE GO...!
NOT BAD! NOT BAD AT ALL !!!
I had no idea! I've got those in my adult teeth ...!
Will I have to wear these shackles forever ...?!
No, those are probably from cavities...
And Rec said you'd grow out of your rebellious phase...

Chapter 343: Whither the Baby Teeth

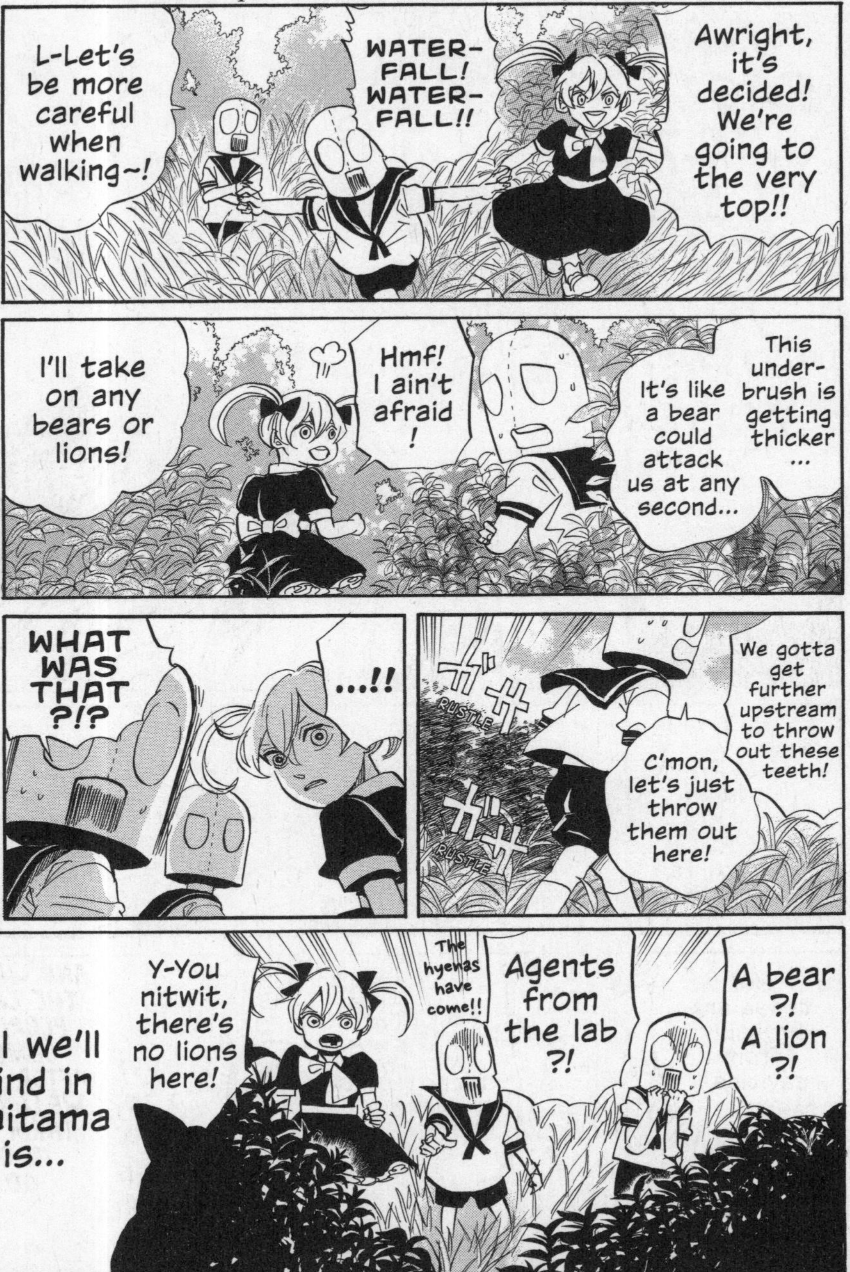

Awright, it's decided! We're going to the very top!!
WATER-FALL! WATER-FALL!!
L-Let's be more careful when walking~!
This under-brush is getting thicker ...
It's like a bear could attack us at any second...
Hmf! I ain't afraid !
I'll take on any bears or lions!
We gotta get further upstream to throw out these teeth!
RUSTLE
C'mon, let's just throw them out here!
RUSTLE
...!!
WHAT WAS THAT ?!?
A bear ?! A lion ?!
Agents from the lab ?!
The hyenas have come!!
Y-You nitwit, there's no lions here!
All we'll find in Saitama is...

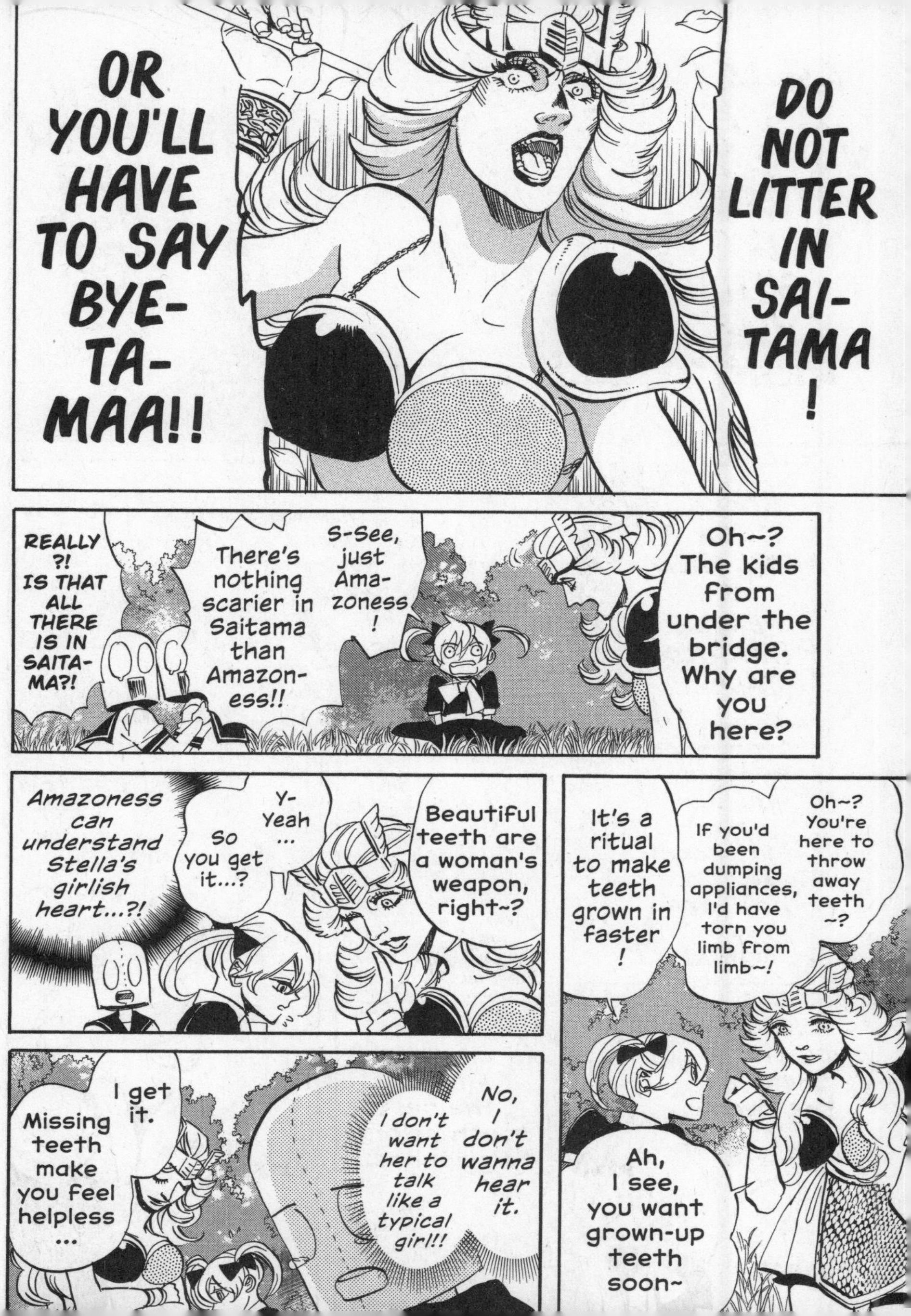
DO NOT LITTER IN SAITAMA!
OR YOU'LL HAVE TO SAY BYE-TA-MAA!!
Oh~? The kids from under the bridge. Why are you here?
S-See, just Amazoness!
There's nothing scarier in Saitama than Amazoness!!
REALLY?! IS THAT ALL THERE IS IN SAITAMA?!
Oh~? You're here to throw away teeth~?
If you'd been dumping appliances, I'd have torn you limb from limb~!
It's a ritual to make teeth grown in faster!
Ah, I see, you want grown-up teeth soon~
Beautiful teeth are a woman's weapon, right~?
Y-Yeah...
So you get it...?
Amazoness can understand Stella's girlish heart...?!
No, I don't wanna hear it.
I don't want her to talk like a typical girl!!
I get it.
Missing teeth make you feel helpless...

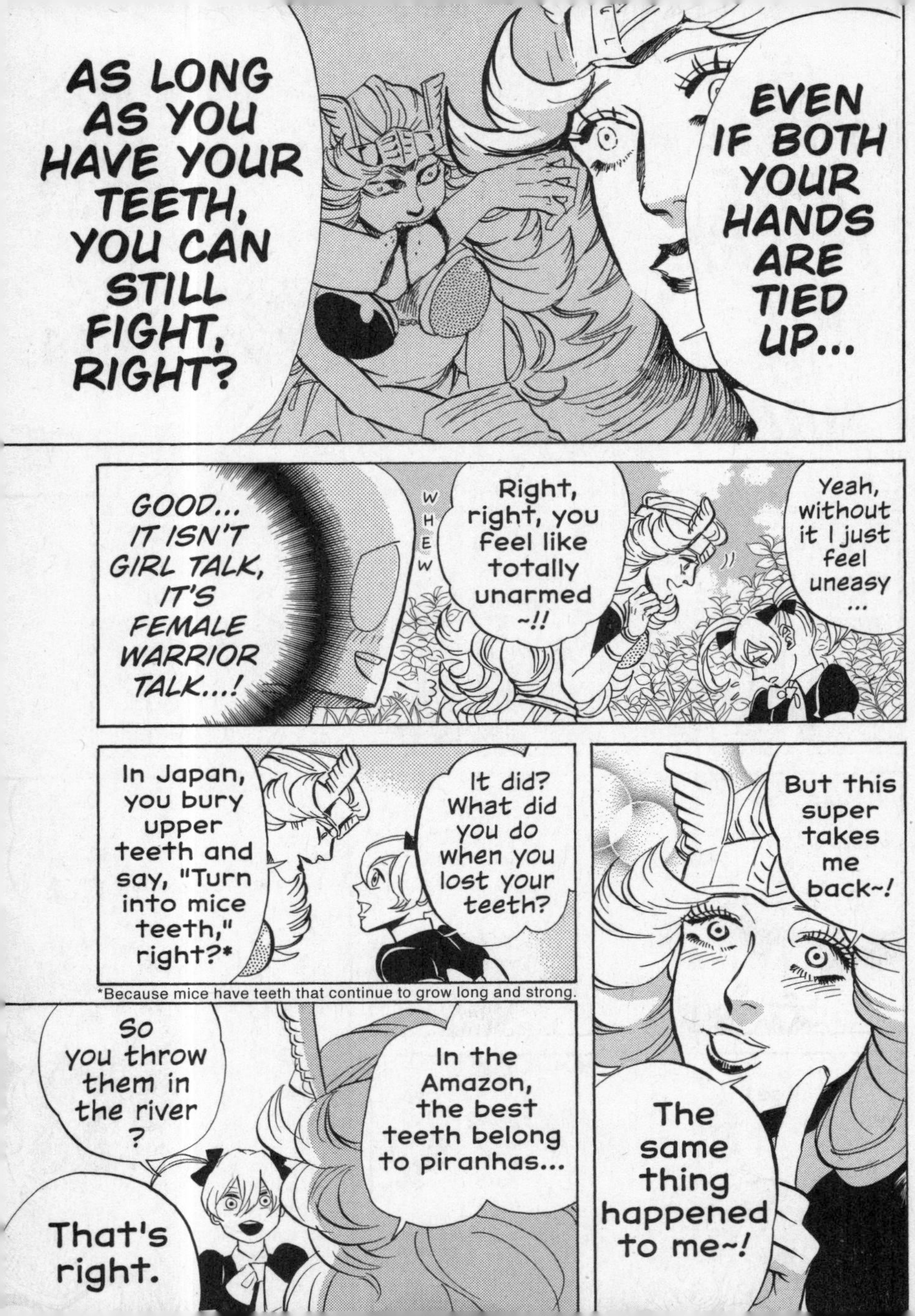
EVEN IF BOTH YOUR HANDS ARE TIED UP...
AS LONG AS YOU HAVE YOUR TEETH, YOU CAN STILL FIGHT, RIGHT?
Yeah, without it I just feel uneasy...
Right, right, you feel like totally unarmed ~!!
WHEW
GOOD... IT ISN'T GIRL TALK, IT'S FEMALE WARRIOR TALK...!
But this super takes me back~!
The same thing happened to me~!
It did? What did you do when you lost your teeth?
In Japan, you bury upper teeth and say, "Turn into mice teeth," right?*
*Because mice have teeth that continue to grow long and strong.
In the Amazon, the best teeth belong to piranhas...
So you throw them in the river?
That's right.

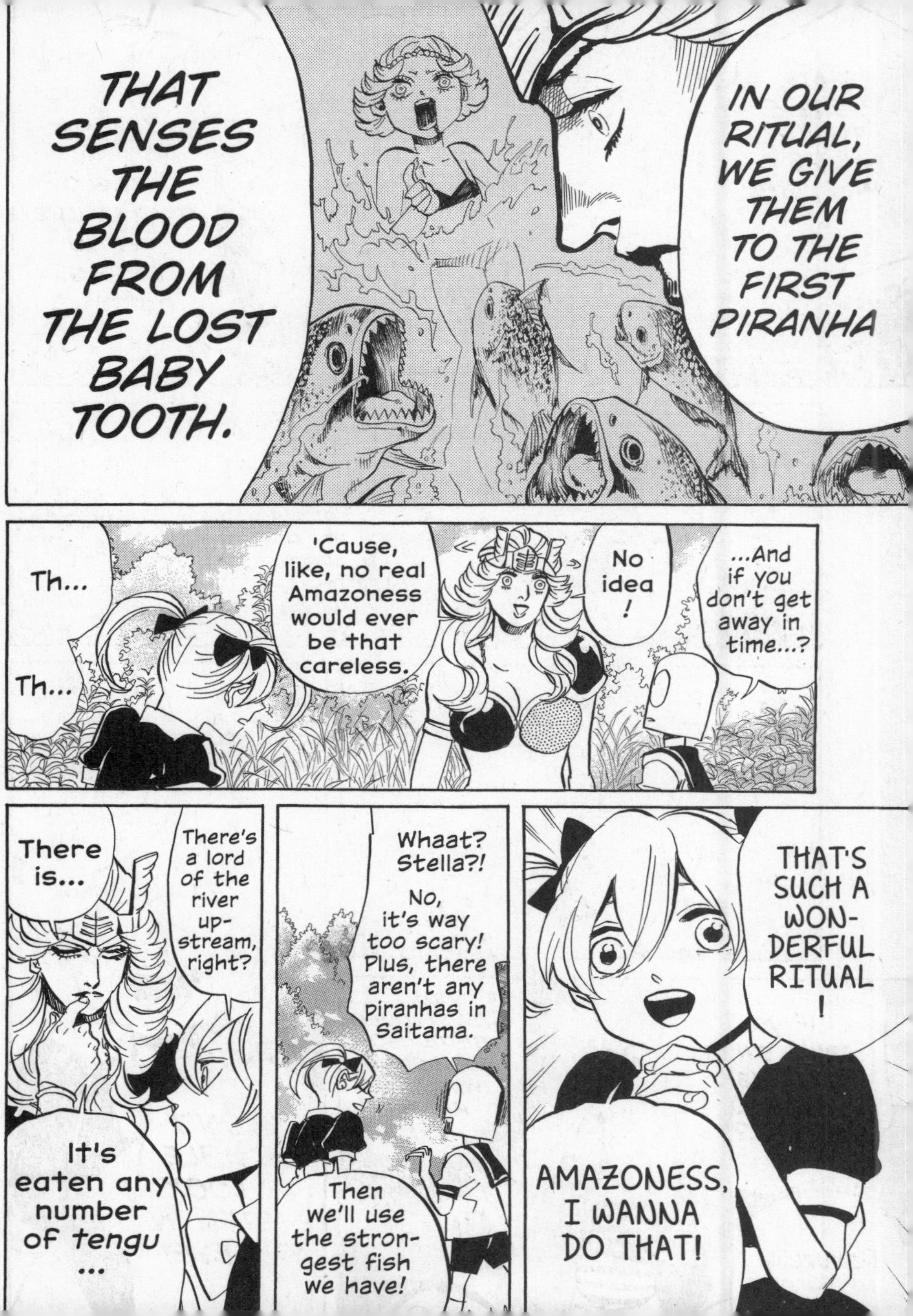
IN OUR RITUAL, WE GIVE THEM TO THE FIRST PIRANHA
THAT SENSES THE BLOOD FROM THE LOST BABY TOOTH.
...And if you don't get away in time...?
No idea!
'Cause, like, no real Amazoness would ever be that careless.
Th...
Th...
THAT'S SUCH A WON-DERFUL RITUAL!
AMAZONESS, I WANNA DO THAT!
Whaat? Stella?!
No, it's way too scary! Plus, there aren't any piranhas in Saitama.
Then we'll use the strong-est fish we have!
There's a lord of the river up-stream, right?
There is...
It's eaten any number of tengu ...

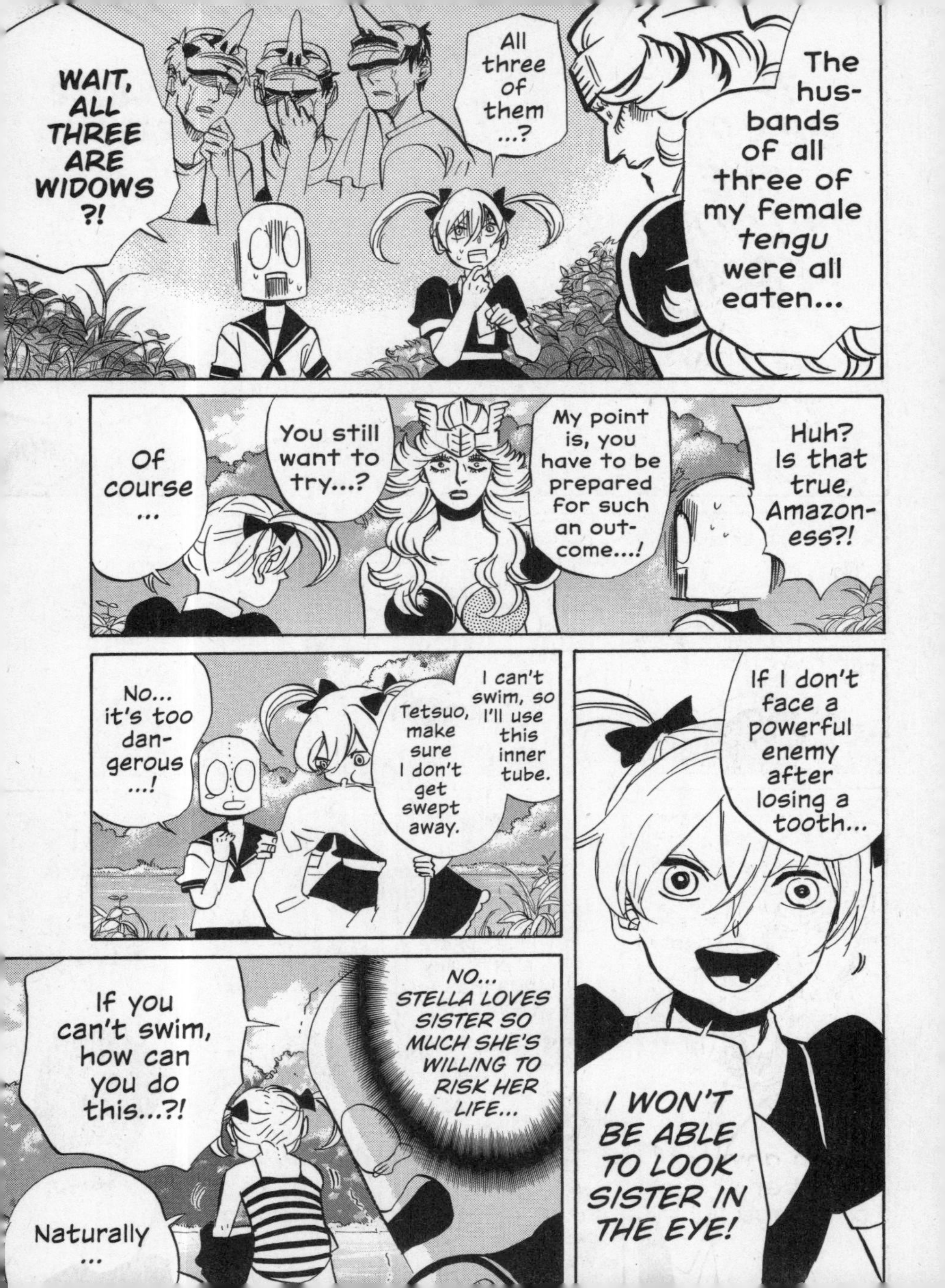
The husbands of all three of my female tengu were all eaten...
All three of them ...?
WAIT, ALL THREE ARE WIDOWS ?!
Huh? Is that true, Amazoness?!
My point is, you have to be prepared for such an outcome...!
You still want to try...?
Of course ...
If I don't face a powerful enemy after losing a tooth...
I WON'T BE ABLE TO LOOK SISTER IN THE EYE!
I can't swim, so I'll use this inner tube.
Tetsuo, make sure I don't get swept away.
No... it's too dangerous ...!
NO... STELLA LOVES SISTER SO MUCH SHE'S WILLING TO RISK HER LIFE...
If you can't swim, how can you do this...?!
Naturally ...

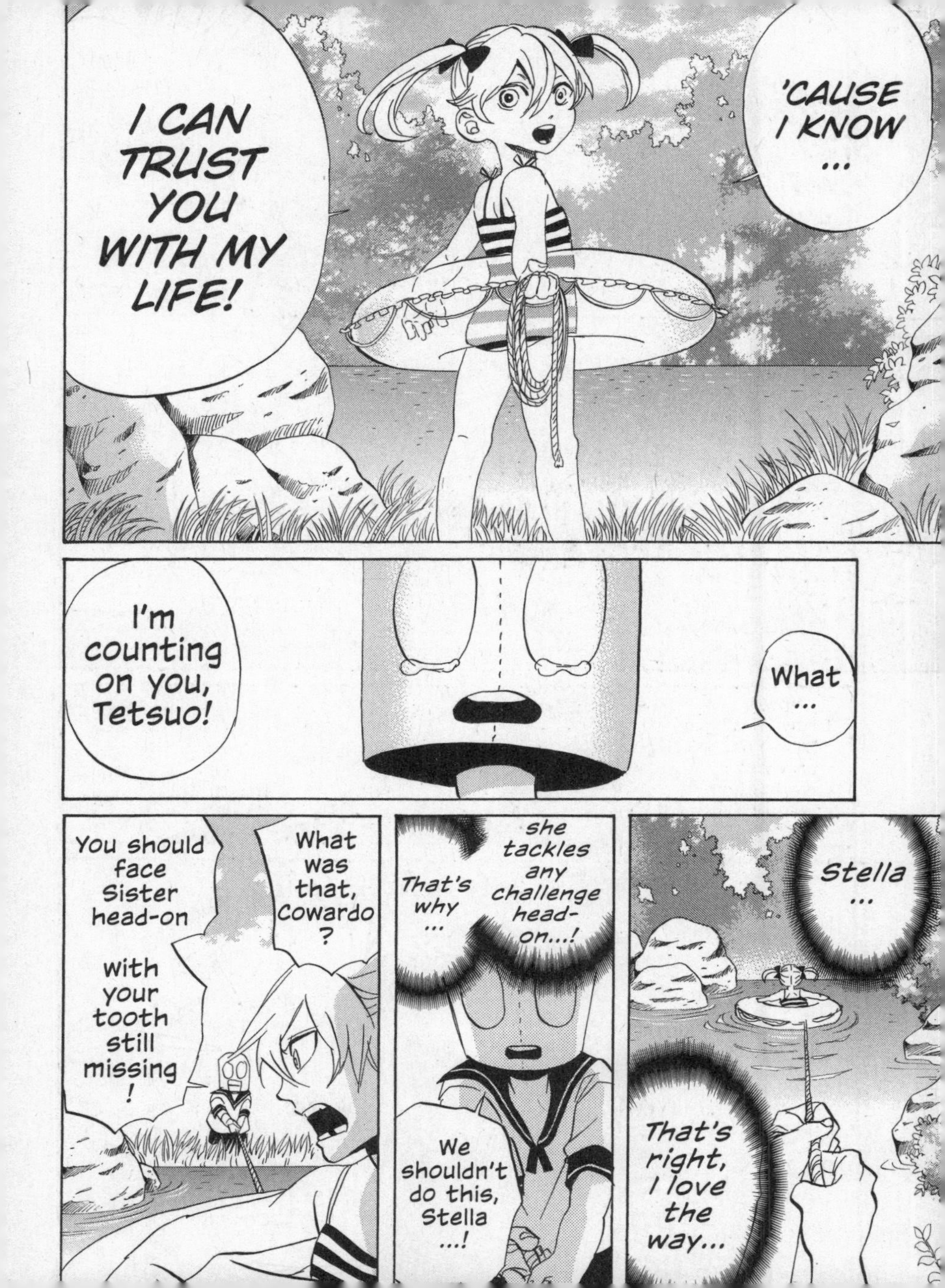
'CAUSE I KNOW ...
I CAN TRUST YOU WITH MY LIFE!
What ...
I'm counting on you, Tetsuo!
Stella ...
That's right, I love the way...
That's why ...
she tackles any challenge head-on...!
We shouldn't do this, Stella ...!
What was that, Cowardo?
You should face Sister head-on
with your tooth still missing!

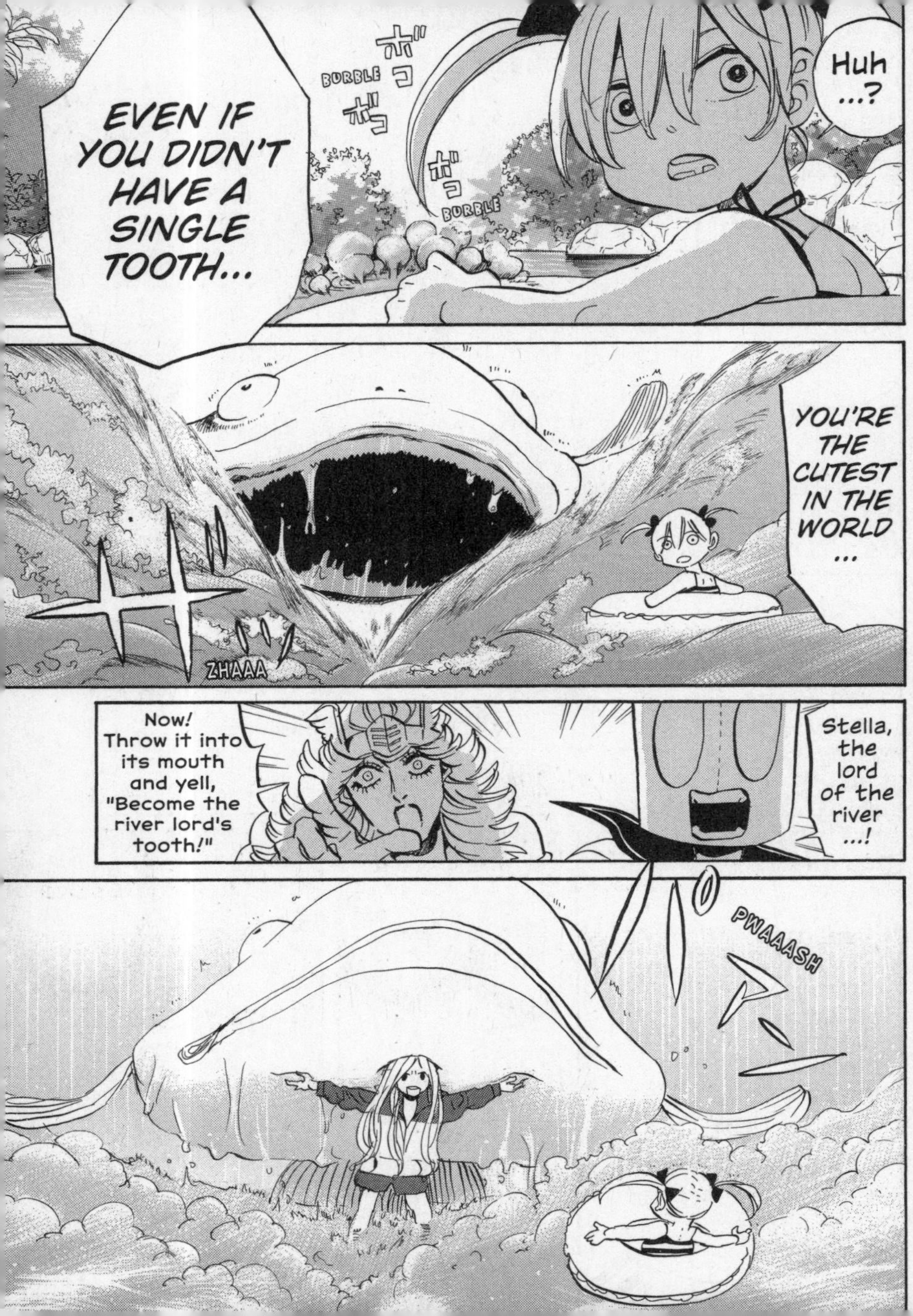
Huh ...?
ボコ BURBLE
ボコ
ボコ BURBLE
EVEN IF YOU DIDN'T HAVE A SINGLE TOOTH...
YOU'RE THE CUTEST IN THE WORLD ...
ZHAAA
Stella, the lord of the river ...!
Now! Throw it into its mouth and yell, "Become the river lord's tooth!"
PWAAASH

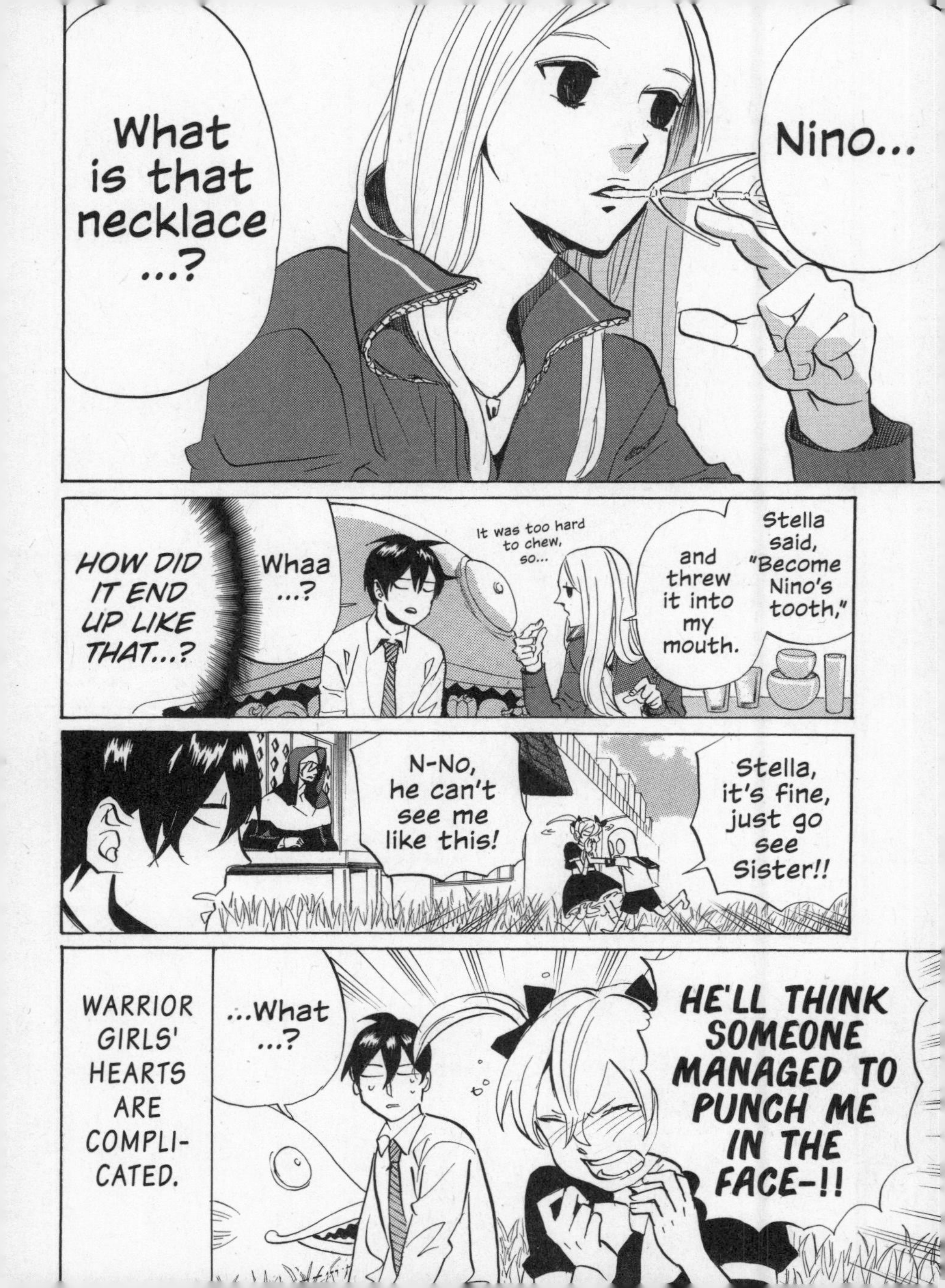
Nino...
What is that necklace ...?
Stella said, "Become Nino's tooth,"
and threw it into my mouth.
It was too hard to chew, so...
Whaa ...?
HOW DID IT END UP LIKE THAT...?
Stella, it's fine, just go see Sister!!
N-No, he can't see me like this!
HE'LL THINK SOMEONE MANAGED TO PUNCH ME IN THE FACE-!!
...What ...?
WARRIOR GIRLS' HEARTS ARE COMPLI-CATED.

ARAKAWA
UNDER
THE BRIDGE

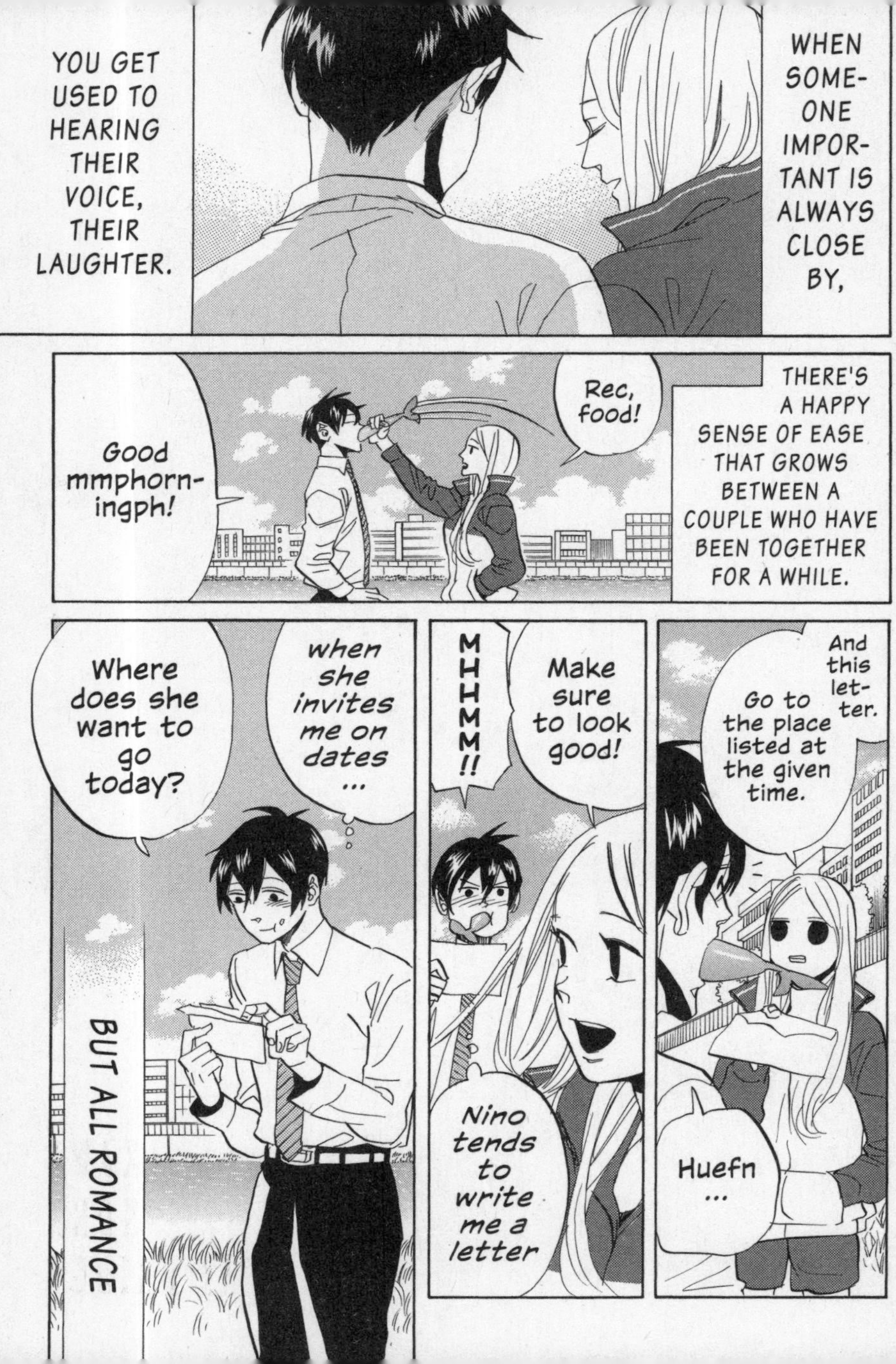
WHEN SOME-ONE IMPOR-TANT IS ALWAYS CLOSE BY,
YOU GET USED TO HEARING THEIR VOICE, THEIR LAUGHTER.
THERE'S A HAPPY SENSE OF EASE THAT GROWS BETWEEN A COUPLE WHO HAVE BEEN TOGETHER FOR A WHILE.
Rec, food!
Good mmphorn-ingph!
And this let-ter.
Go to the place listed at the given time.
Huefn ...
Make sure to look good!
MHHMM!!
Nino tends to write me a letter
when she invites me on dates ...
Where does she want to go today?
BUT ALL ROMANCE

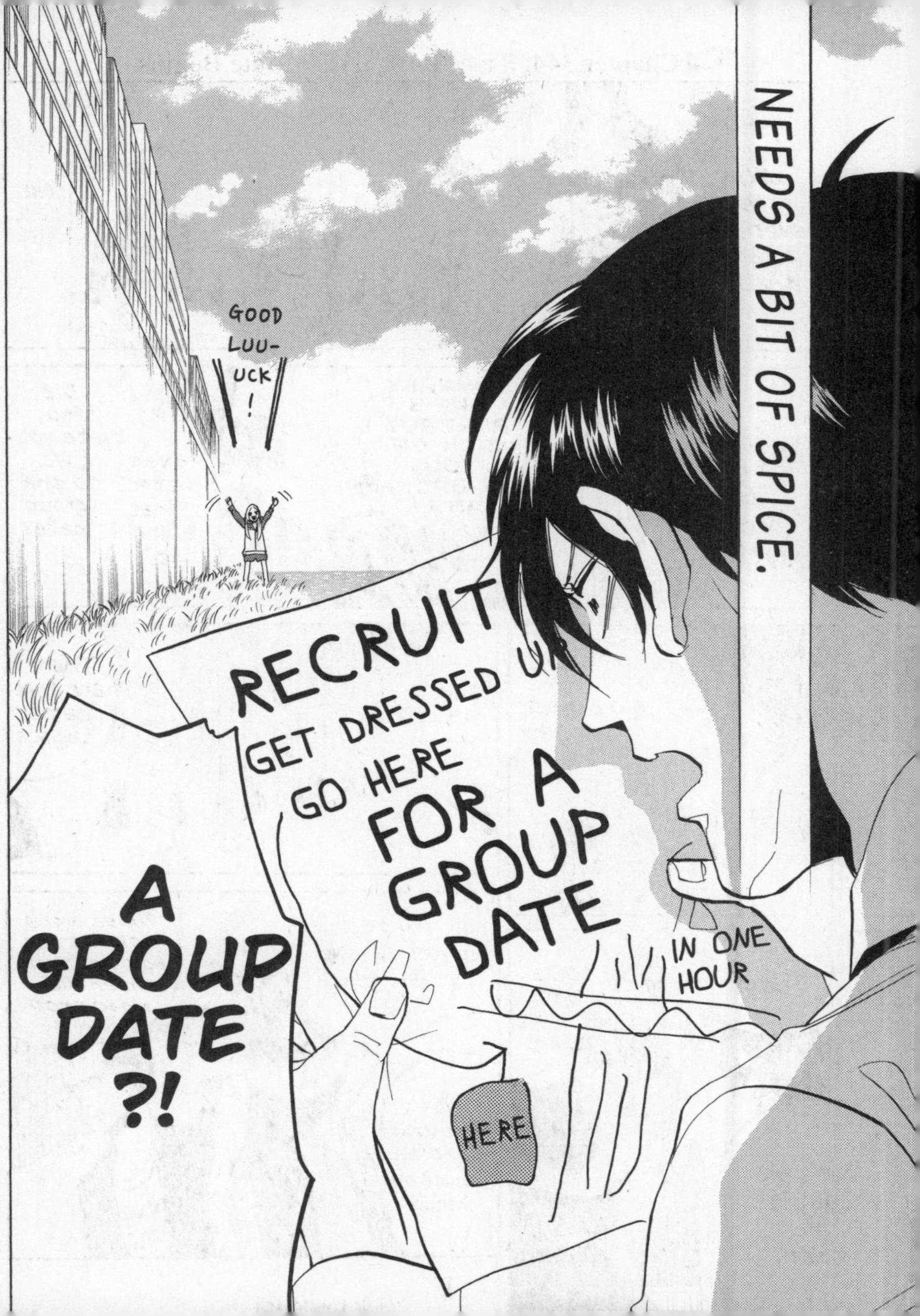
NEEDS A BIT OF SPICE.
GOOD LUU-UCK !
RECRUIT
GET DRESSED U
GO HERE
FOR A GROUP DATE
IN ONE HOUR
HERE
A GROUP DATE ?!

Chapter 344: River Bank Group Date Begins

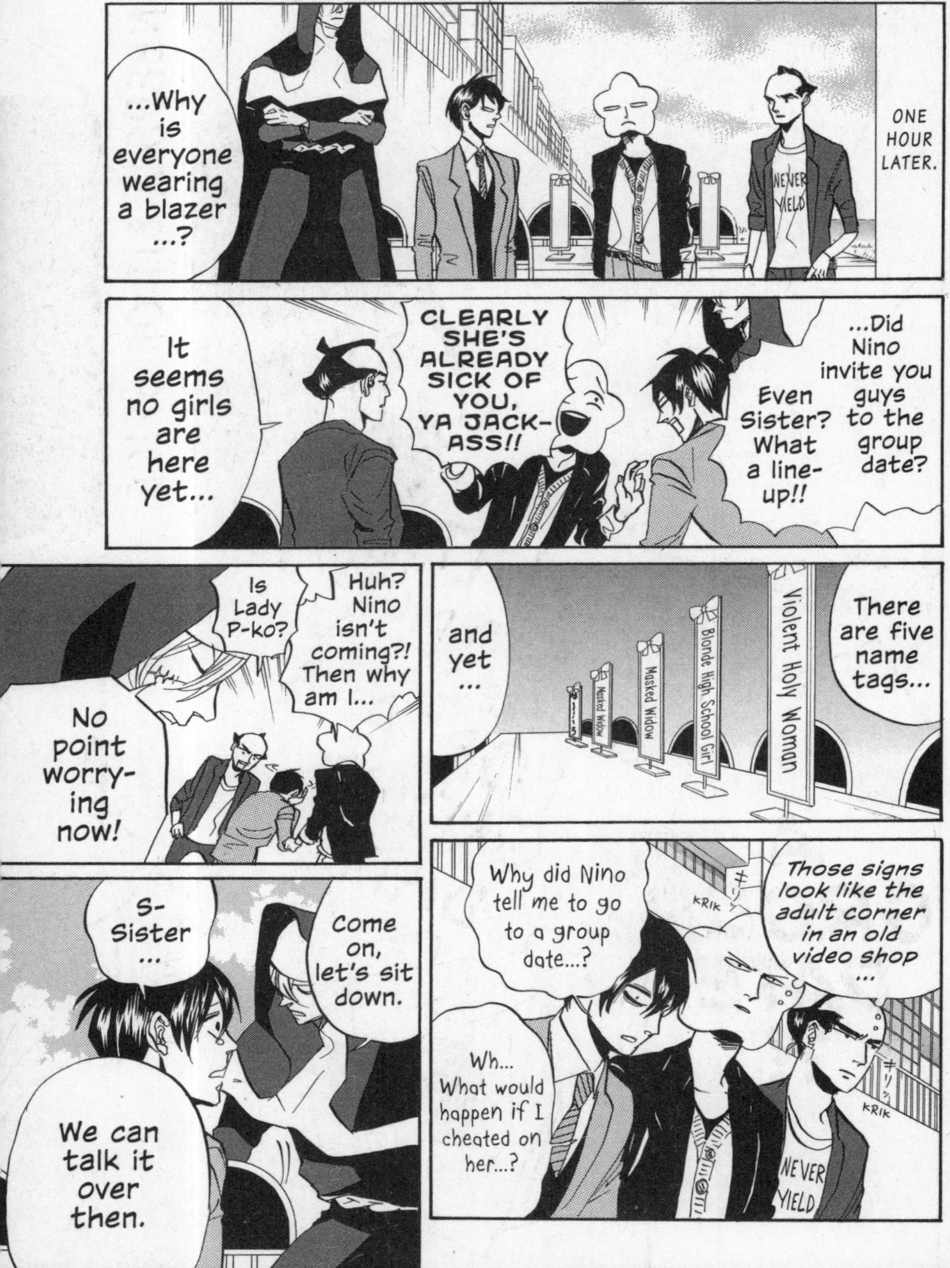
ONE HOUR LATER.
NEVER YIELD
...Why is everyone wearing a blazer ...?
...Did Nino invite you guys to the group date?
Even Sister? What a line-up!!
CLEARLY SHE'S ALREADY SICK OF YOU, YA JACK-ASS!!
It seems no girls are here yet...
There are five name tags...
Violent Holy Woman
Blonde High School Girl
Masked Widow
Masked Widow
and yet ...
Huh? Nino isn't coming?! Then why am I...
Is Lady P-ko?
No point worrying now!
Those signs look like the adult corner in an old video shop ...
KRIK
Why did Nino tell me to go to a group date...?
Wh... What would happen if I cheated on her...?
KRIK
NEVER YIELD
S-Sister ...
Come on, let's sit down.
We can talk it over then.

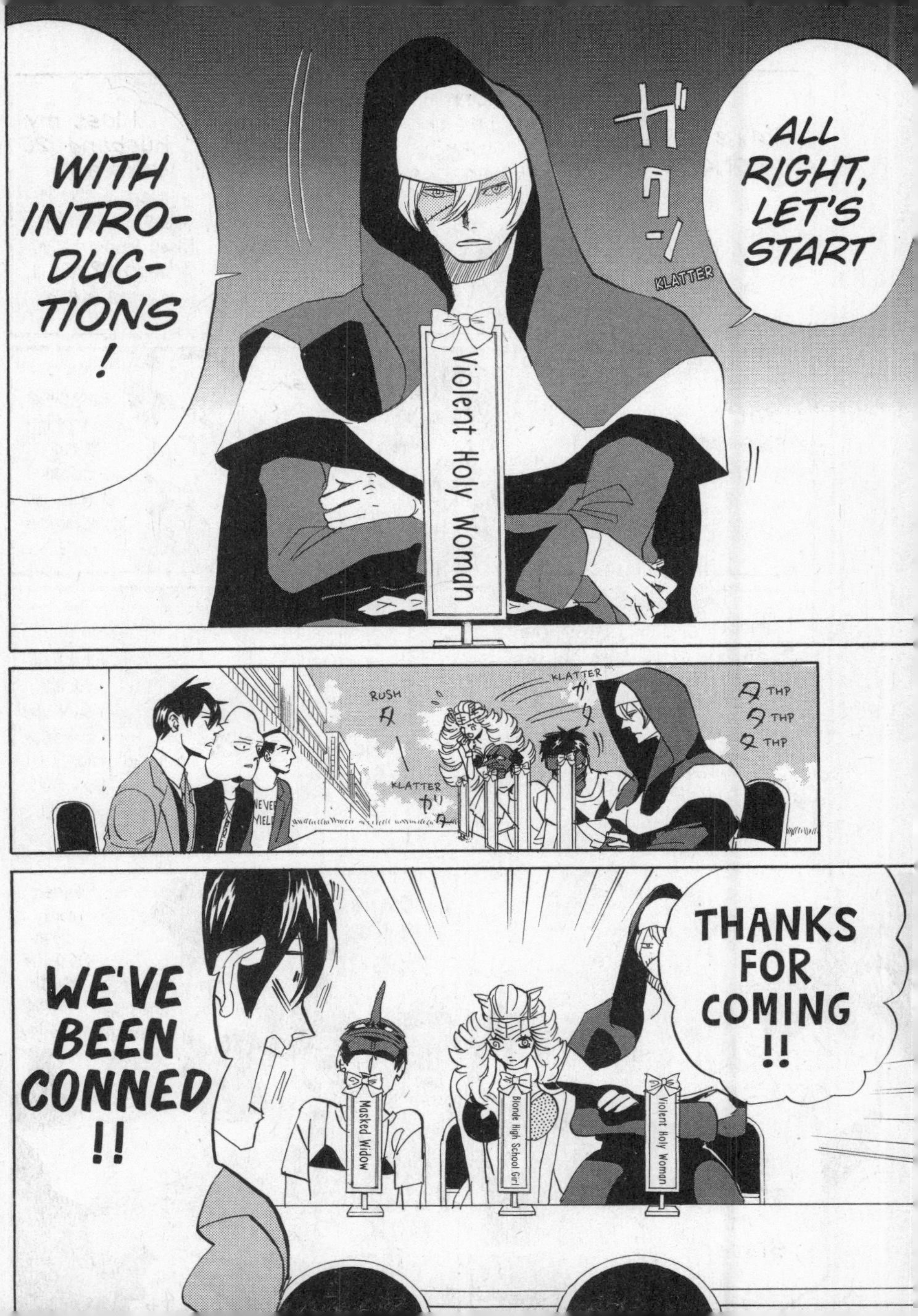
ALL RIGHT, LET'S START
ガタ
KLATTER
WITH INTRO-DUC-TIONS!
Violent Holy Woman
タ THP
タ THP
タ THP
ガタ
KLATTER
RUSH
タ
ガタ
KLATTER
THANKS FOR COMING!!
WE'VE BEEN CONNED!!
Violent Holy Woman
Blonde High School Girl
Masked Widow

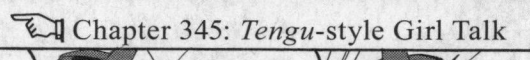

Chapter 345: *Tengu*-style Girl Talk

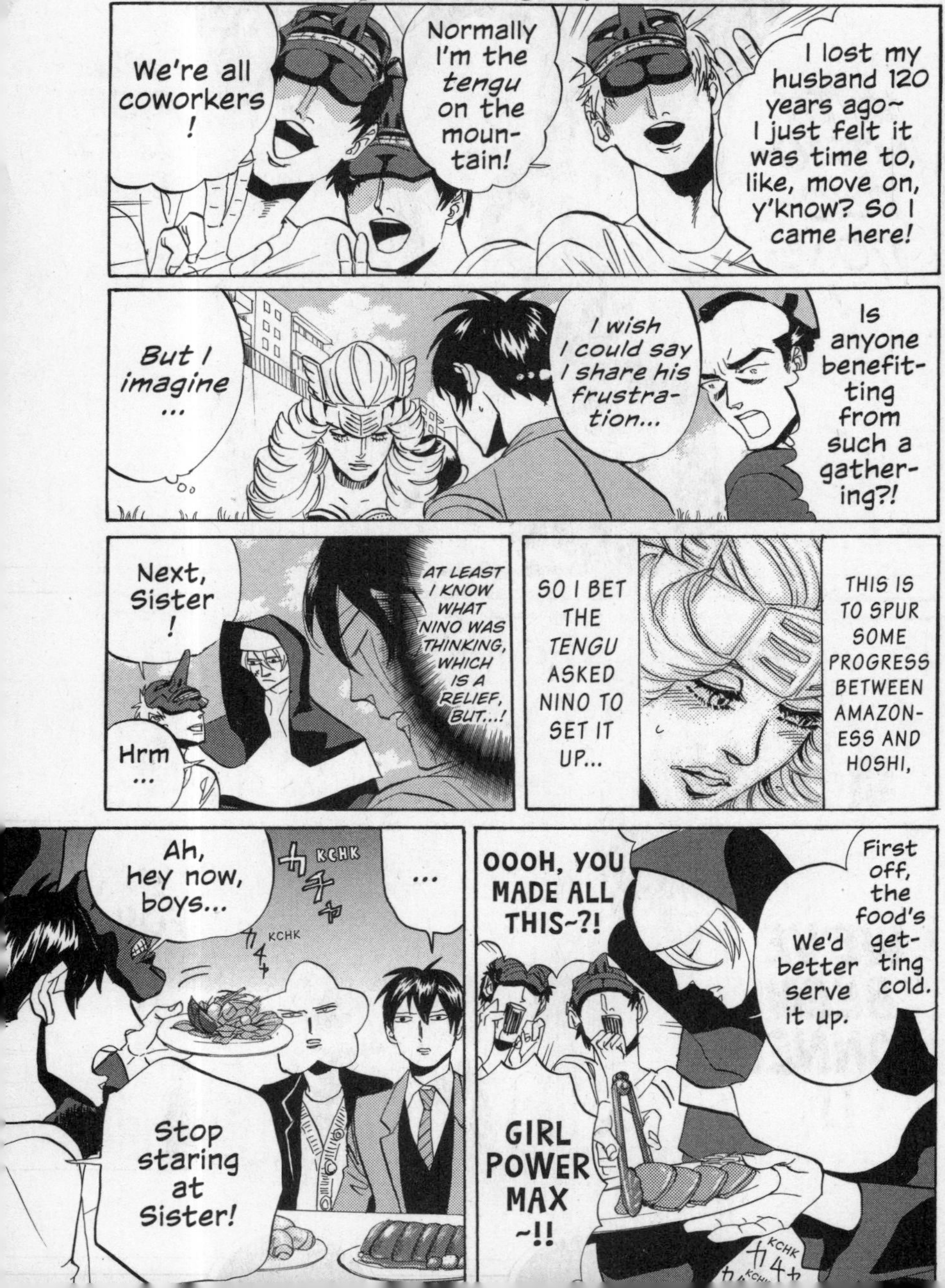
I lost my husband 120 years ago~ I just felt it was time to, like, move on, y'know? So I came here!
Normally I'm the *tengu* on the mountain!
We're all coworkers !
Is anyone benefitting from such a gathering?!
I wish I could say I share his frustration...
But I imagine ...
THIS IS TO SPUR SOME PROGRESS BETWEEN AMAZONESS AND HOSHI,
SO I BET THE TENGU ASKED NINO TO SET IT UP...
AT LEAST I KNOW WHAT NINO WAS THINKING, WHICH IS A RELIEF, BUT...!
Next, Sister !
Hrm ...
First off, the food's getting cold.
We'd better serve it up.
OOOH, YOU MADE ALL THIS~?!
GIRL POWER MAX ~!!
KCHK
KCHK
...
Ah, hey now, boys...
KCHK
Stop staring at Sister!

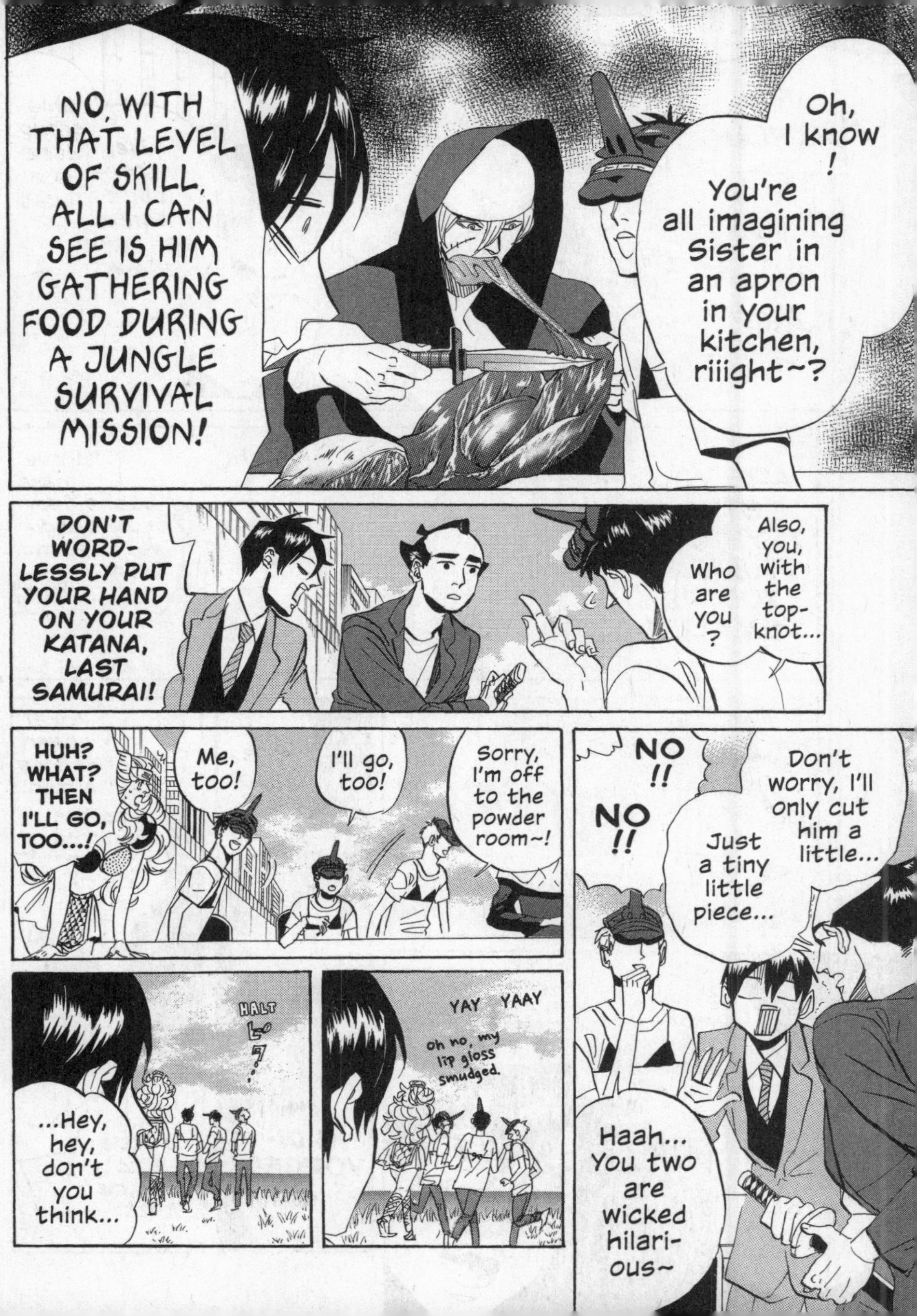
Oh, I know! You're all imagining Sister in an apron in your kitchen, riiight~?
NO, WITH THAT LEVEL OF SKILL, ALL I CAN SEE IS HIM GATHERING FOOD DURING A JUNGLE SURVIVAL MISSION!
Also, you, with the top-knot...
Who are you?
DON'T WORDLESSLY PUT YOUR HAND ON YOUR KATANA, LAST SAMURAI!
Don't worry, I'll only cut him a little...
NO !!
Just a tiny little piece...
NO !!
Haah... You two are wicked hilarious~
Sorry, I'm off to the powder room~!
I'll go, too!
Me, too!
HUH? WHAT? THEN I'LL GO, TOO...!
YAY YAAY
oh no, my lip gloss smudged.
HALT
...Hey, hey, don't you think...

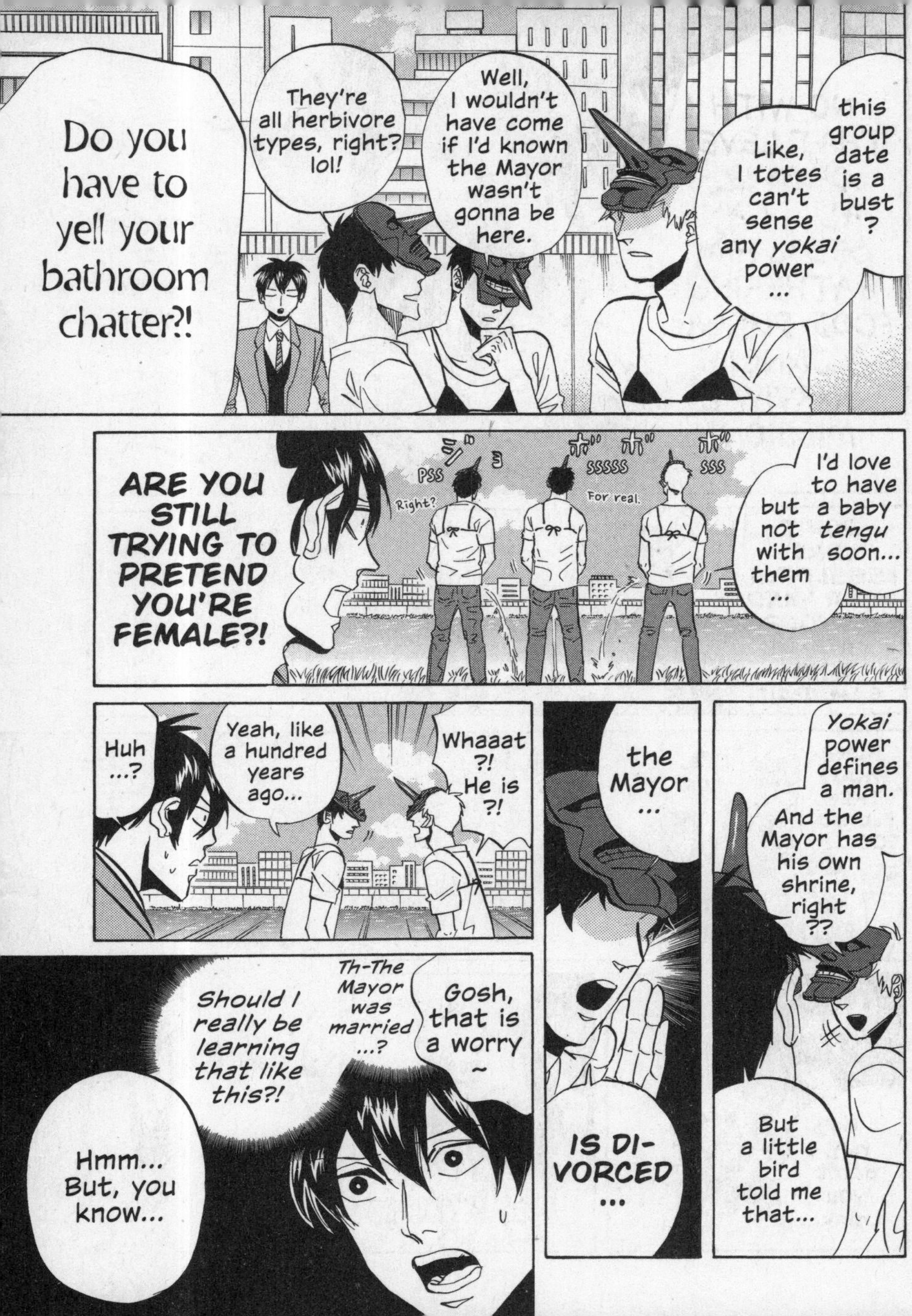
Like, I totes can't sense any yokai power ... this group date is a bust?
Well, I wouldn't have come if I'd known the Mayor wasn't gonna be here.
They're all herbivore types, right? lol!
Do you have to yell your bathroom chatter?!
I'd love to have a baby tengu soon... but not with them ...
SSS
SSSSS
For real.
PSS
Right?
ARE YOU STILL TRYING TO PRETEND YOU'RE FEMALE?!
Yokai power defines a man.
And the Mayor has his own shrine, right ??
But a little bird told me that...
the Mayor ...
IS DI-VORCED ...
Whaaat ?! He is ?!
Yeah, like a hundred years ago...
Huh ...?
Gosh, that is a worry ~
Th-The Mayor was married ...?
Should I really be learning that like this?!
Hmm... But, you know...

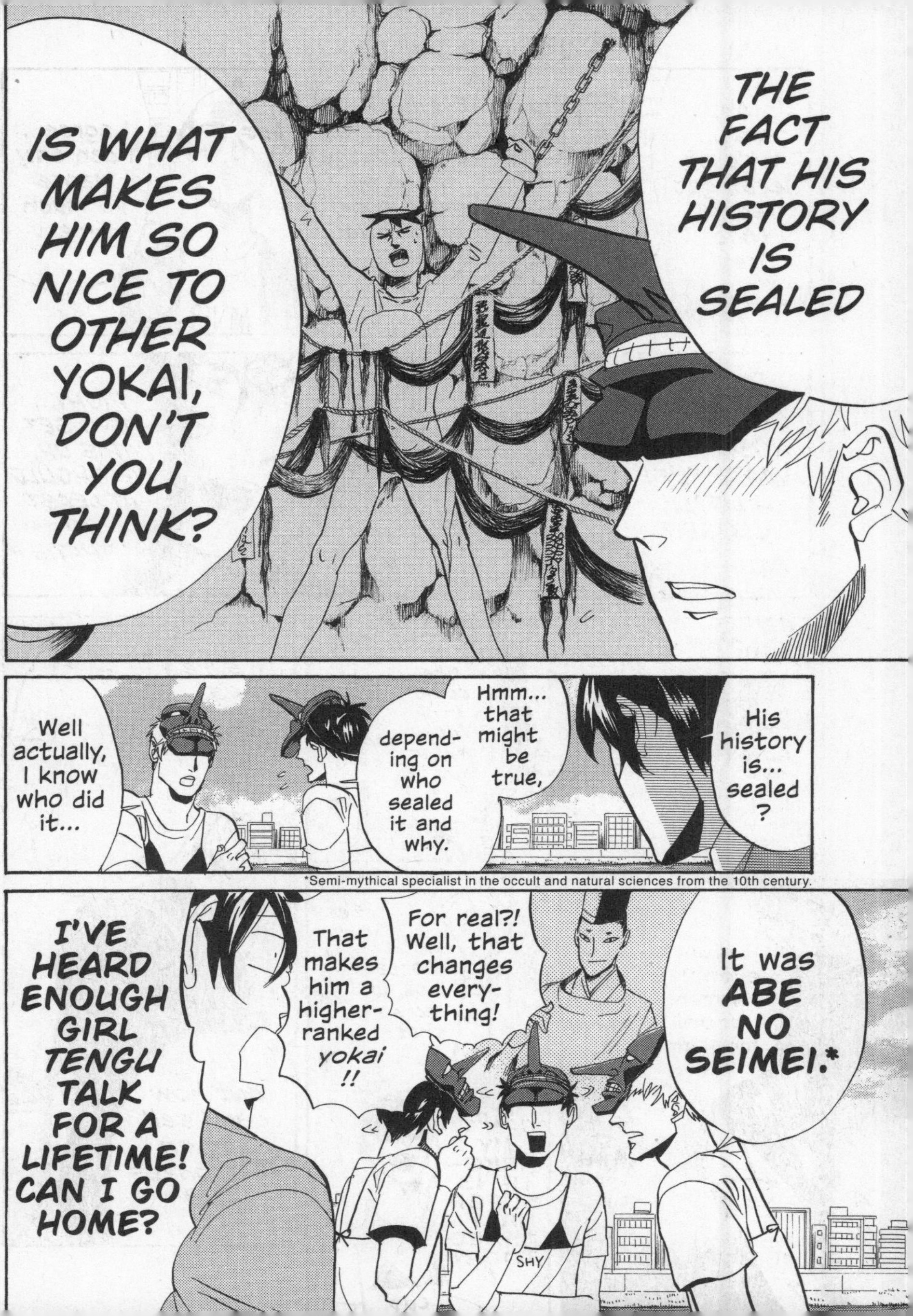
THE FACT THAT HIS HISTORY IS SEALED
IS WHAT MAKES HIM SO NICE TO OTHER YOKAI, DON'T YOU THINK?
His history is... sealed?
Hmm... that might be true,
depending on who sealed it and why.
Well actually, I know who did it...
It was ABE NO SEIMEI.*
For real?! Well, that changes every-thing!
That makes him a higher-ranked yokai!!
SHY
I'VE HEARD ENOUGH GIRL TENGU TALK FOR A LIFETIME! CAN I GO HOME?

*Semi-mythical specialist in the occult and natural sciences from the 10th century.

Chapter 346: Bare-faced

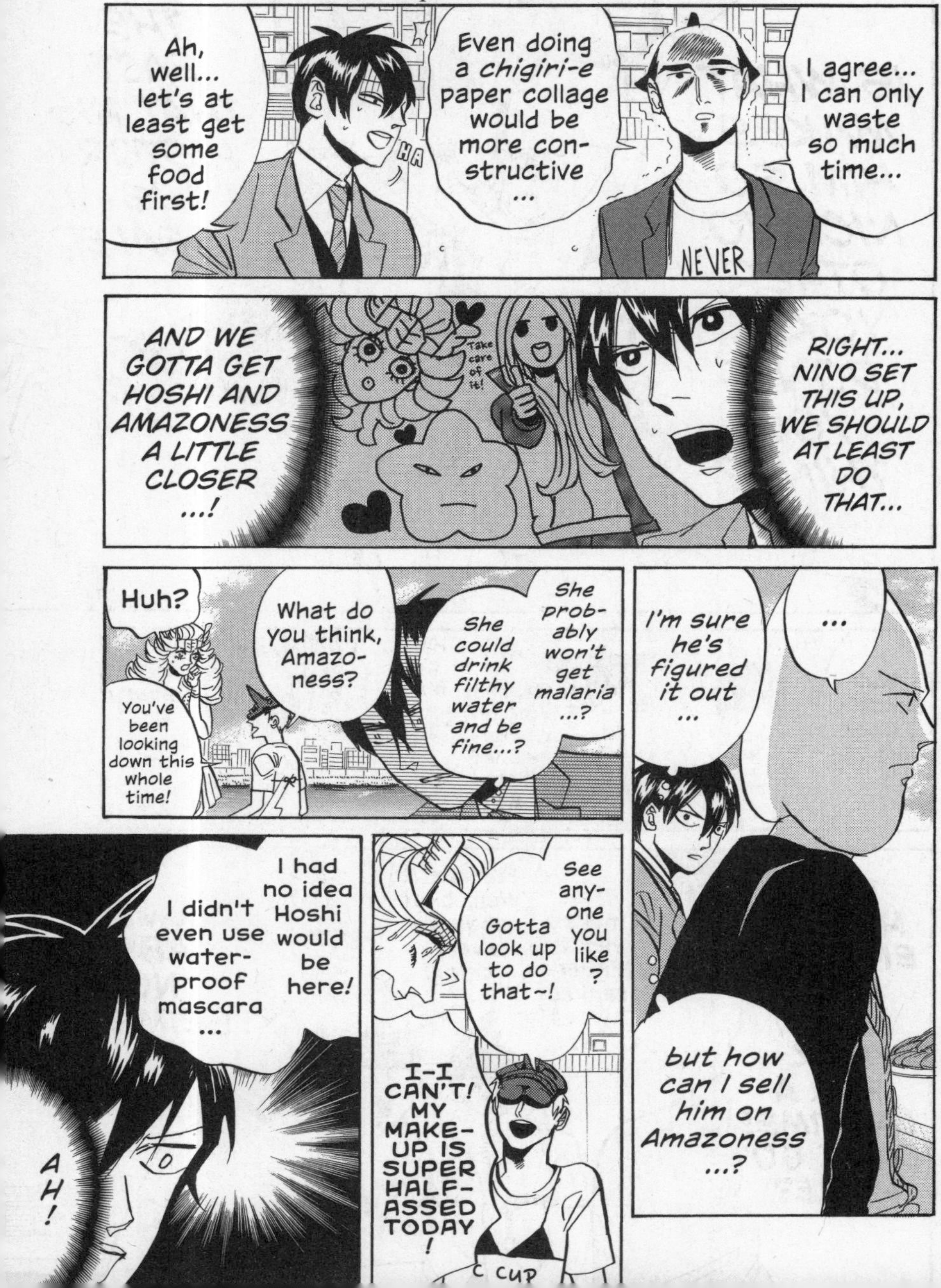

I agree... I can only waste so much time...
NEVER
Even doing a chigiri-e paper collage would be more constructive ...
HA
Ah, well... let's at least get some food first!
RIGHT... NINO SET THIS UP, WE SHOULD AT LEAST DO THAT...
Take care of it!
AND WE GOTTA GET HOSHI AND AMAZONESS A LITTLE CLOSER ...!
...
I'm sure he's figured it out ...
She probably won't get malaria ...?
She could drink filthy water and be fine...?
What do you think, Amazoness?
Huh?
You've been looking down this whole time!
but how can I sell him on Amazoness ...?
See anyone you like ?
Gotta look up to do that~!
I-I CAN'T! MY MAKE-UP IS SUPER HALF-ASSED TODAY !
C CUP
I had no idea Hoshi would be here!
I didn't even use water-proof mascara ...
AH!

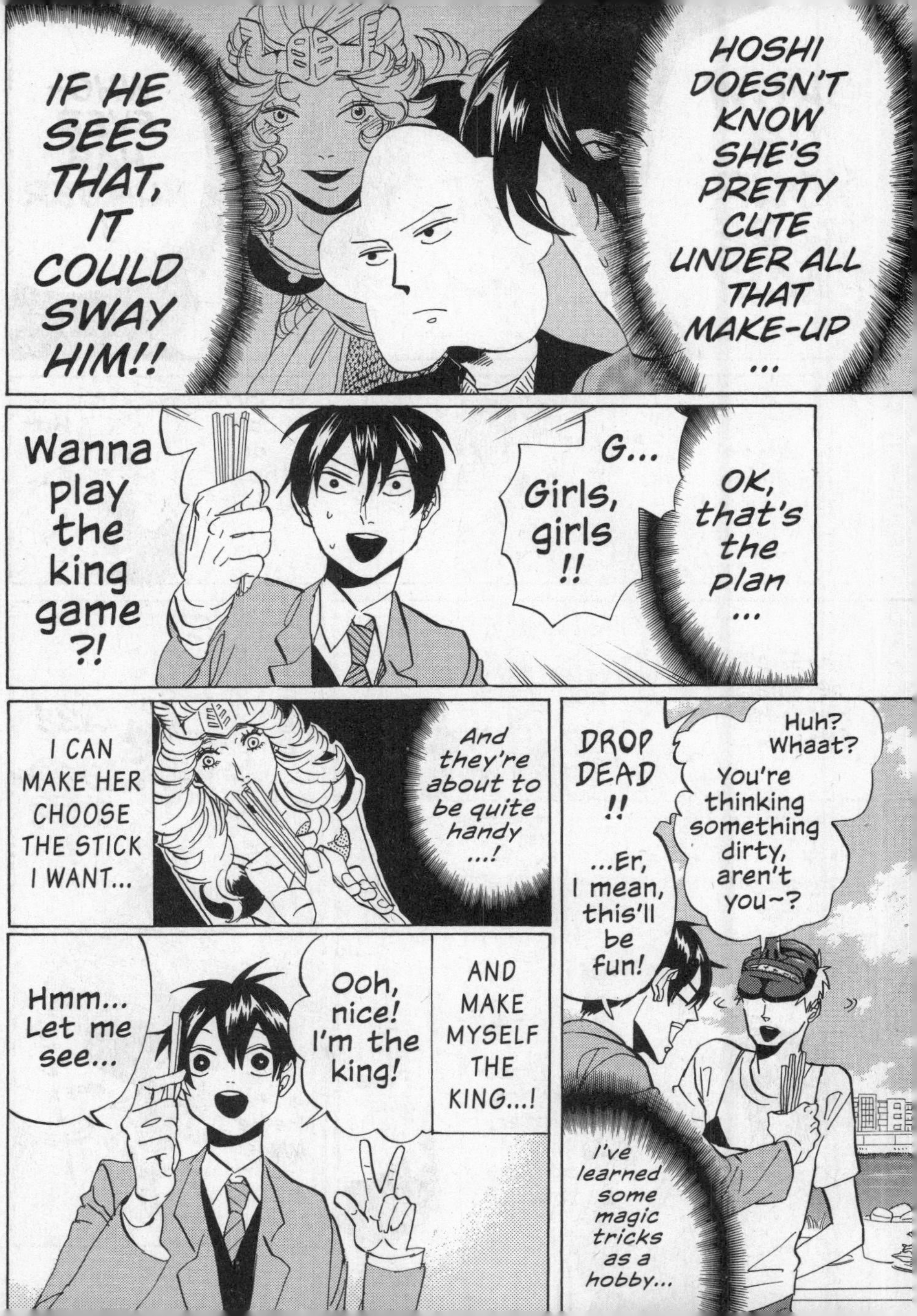
HOSHI DOESN'T KNOW SHE'S PRETTY CUTE UNDER ALL THAT MAKE-UP ...
IF HE SEES THAT, IT COULD SWAY HIM!!
OK, that's the plan ...
G... Girls, girls !!
Wanna play the king game ?!
Huh? Whaat? You're thinking something dirty, aren't you~?
DROP DEAD !!
...Er, I mean, this'll be fun!
I've learned some magic tricks as a hobby...
And they're about to be quite handy ...!
I CAN MAKE HER CHOOSE THE STICK I WANT...
AND MAKE MYSELF THE KING...!
Ooh, nice! I'm the king!
Hmm... Let me see...

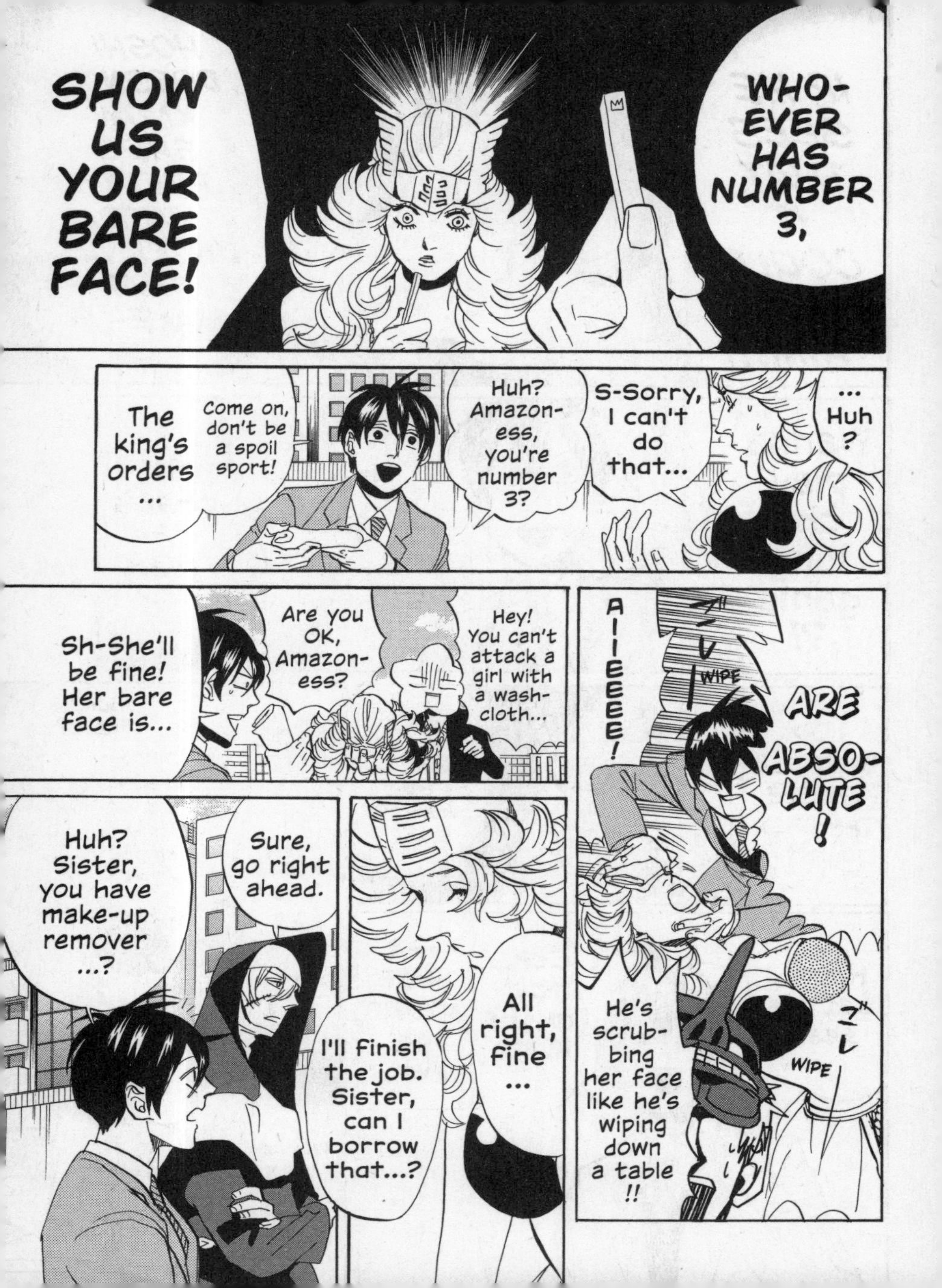
WHO-EVER HAS NUMBER 3,
SHOW US YOUR BARE FACE!
... Huh ?
S-Sorry, I can't do that...
Huh? Amazon-ess, you're number 3?
Come on, don't be a spoil sport!
The king's orders ...
ARE ABSO-LUTE !
A-IEEEE!
WIPE
He's scrub-bing her face like he's wiping down a table !!
WIPE
Hey! You can't attack a girl with a wash-cloth...
Are you OK, Amazon-ess?
Sh-She'll be fine! Her bare face is...
All right, fine ...
I'll finish the job. Sister, can I borrow that...?
Sure, go right ahead.
Huh? Sister, you have make-up remover ...?

PRESS
I'D RATHER SLICE MY FACE OFF...
THAN LET ANYONE SEE ME WITHOUT MAKE-UP...!
Oh, in that case, this knife is easier to use.
Thank you.
No! Sudden displays of deep trauma will drive men away!!
Just show him your face...
C'mon, you can show him your bare face.
No! I'd rather show him my skull...!
P-Put the knife away! I won't look!
No, you'll see!
EEK
EEK
Just stay away!!
Calm down, Amazon-ess!!
YOU'RE THE ONE PERSON I DON'T WANT SEEING ME LIKE THIS, HOSHI!!

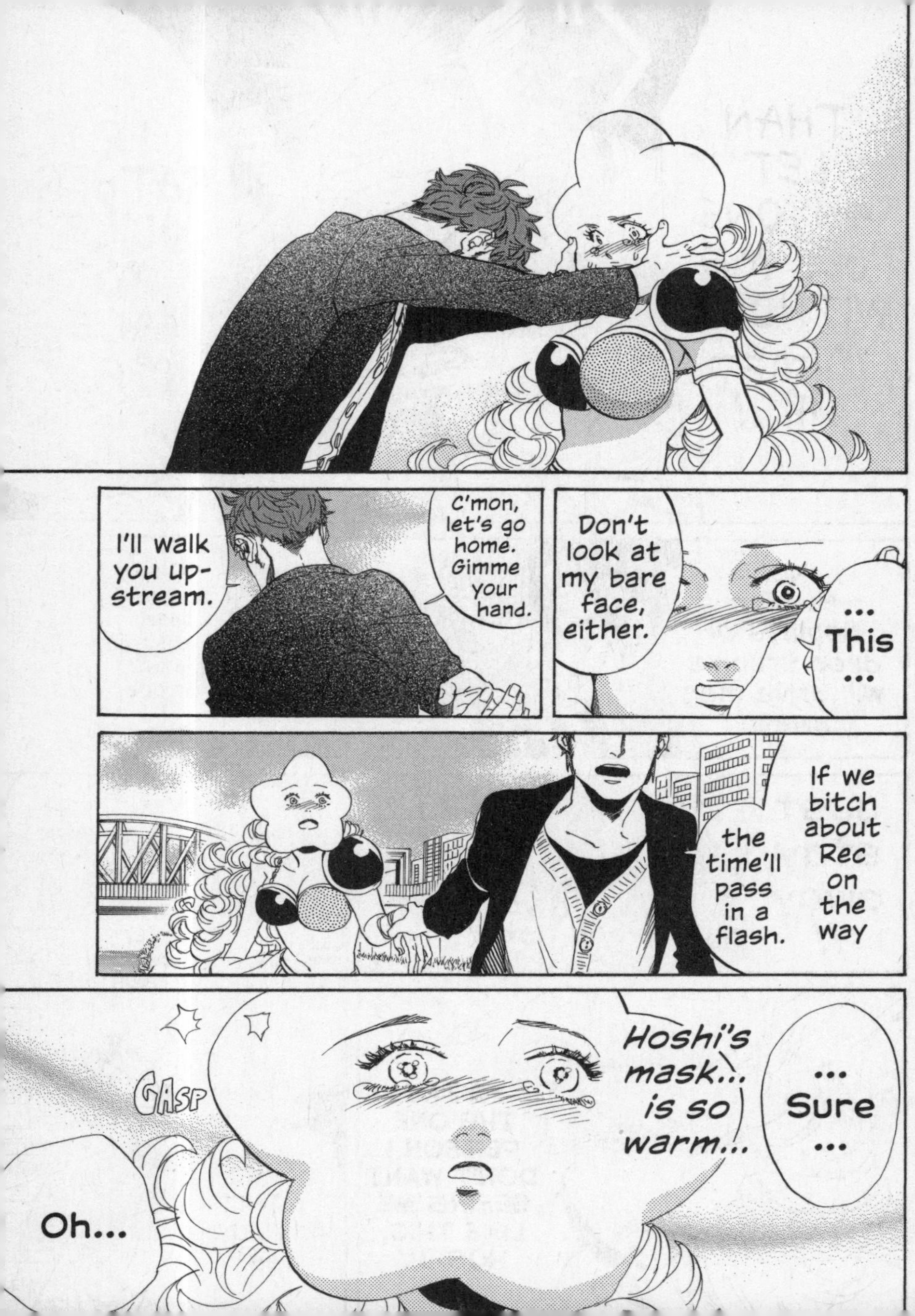
... This ...
Don't look at my bare face, either.
C'mon, let's go home. Gimme your hand.
I'll walk you up-stream.
If we bitch about Rec on the way
the time'll pass in a flash.
... Sure ...
Hoshi's mask... is so warm...
GASP
Oh...

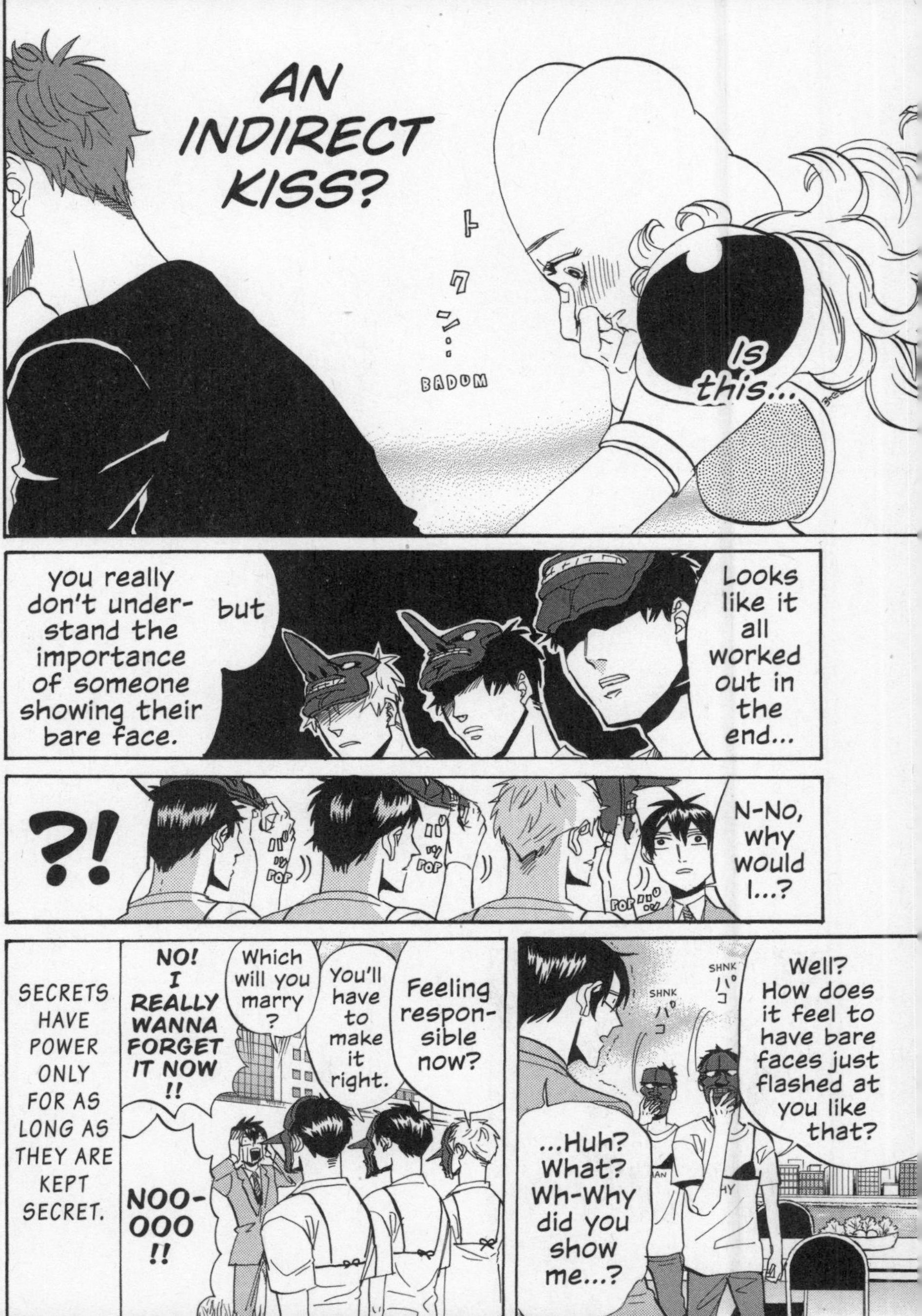
Is this...
BADUM
AN INDIRECT KISS?
Looks like it all worked out in the end...
but
you really don't under-stand the importance of someone showing their bare face.
N-No, why would I...?
POP
POP
POP
?!
Well? How does it feel to have bare faces just flashed at you like that?
SHNK
SHNK
...Huh? What? Wh-Why did you show me...?
Feeling respon-sible now?
You'll have to make it right.
Which will you marry?
NO! I REALLY WANNA FORGET IT NOW !!
NOO-OOO !!
SECRETS HAVE POWER ONLY FOR AS LONG AS THEY ARE KEPT SECRET.

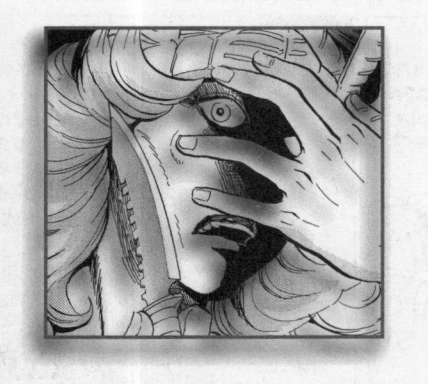

ARAKAWA
UNDER
THE BRIDGE

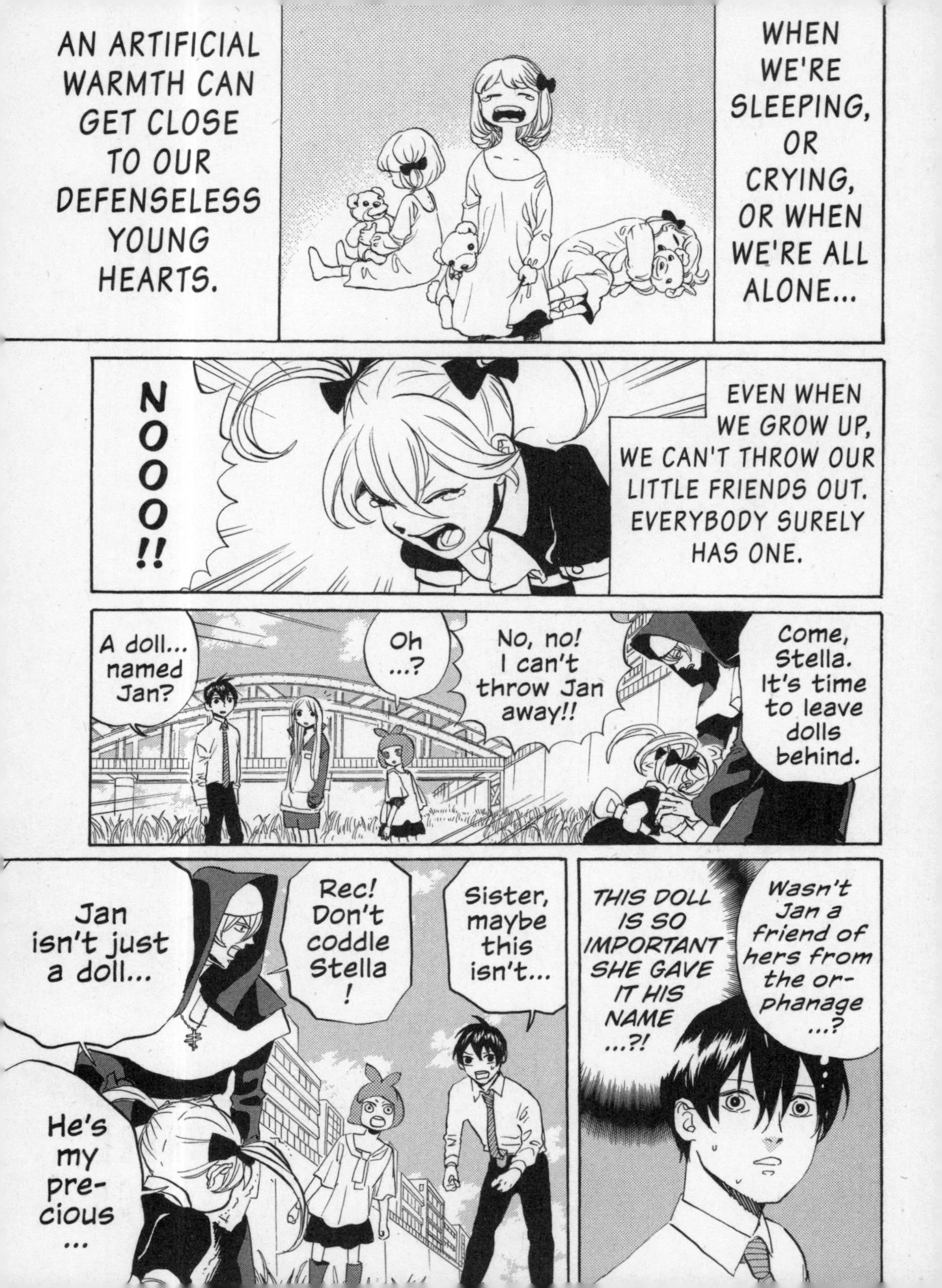
WHEN WE'RE SLEEPING, OR CRYING, OR WHEN WE'RE ALL ALONE...
AN ARTIFICIAL WARMTH CAN GET CLOSE TO OUR DEFENSELESS YOUNG HEARTS.
EVEN WHEN WE GROW UP, WE CAN'T THROW OUR LITTLE FRIENDS OUT. EVERYBODY SURELY HAS ONE.
NOOOO!!
Come, Stella. It's time to leave dolls behind.
No, no! I can't throw Jan away!!
Oh ...?
A doll... named Jan?
Wasn't Jan a friend of hers from the or- phanage ...?
THIS DOLL IS SO IMPORTANT SHE GAVE IT HIS NAME ...?!
Sister, maybe this isn't...
Rec! Don't coddle Stella !
Jan isn't just a doll...
He's my pre- cious ...

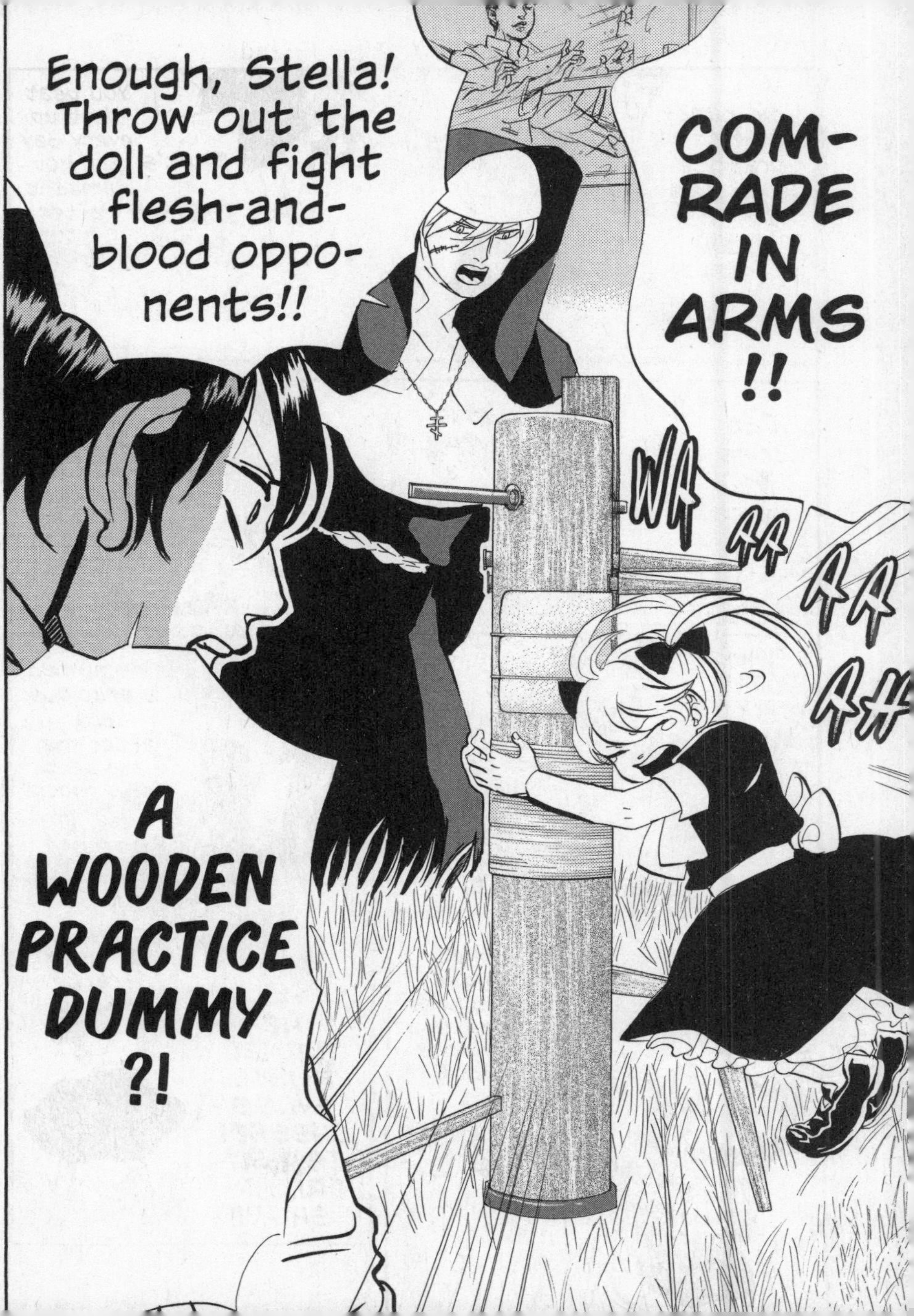
COMRADE IN ARMS!!
WAAAAAAAH
Enough, Stella! Throw out the doll and fight flesh-and-blood opponents!!
A WOODEN PRACTICE DUMMY?!

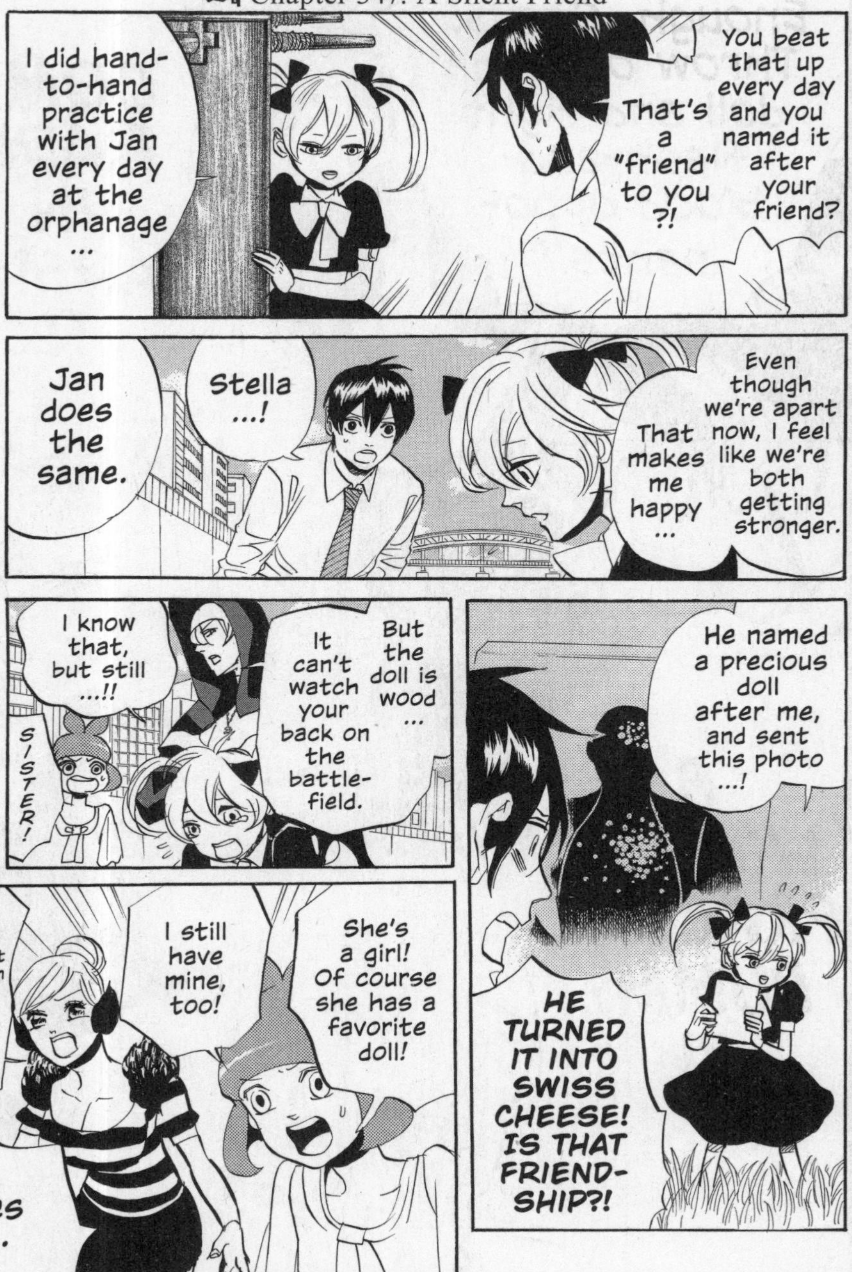
You beat that up every day and you named it after your friend?
That's a "friend" to you ?!
I did hand-to-hand practice with Jan every day at the orphanage ...
Even though we're apart now, I feel like we're both getting stronger.
That makes me happy ...
Stella ...!
Jan does the same.
He named a precious doll after me, and sent this photo ...!
HE TURNED IT INTO SWISS CHEESE! IS THAT FRIENDSHIP?!
But the doll is wood ...
It can't watch your back on the battlefield.
I know that, but still ...!!
SISTER!
She's a girl! Of course she has a favorite doll!
I still have mine, too!
I haven't thrown mine out either ...!
Yes ...

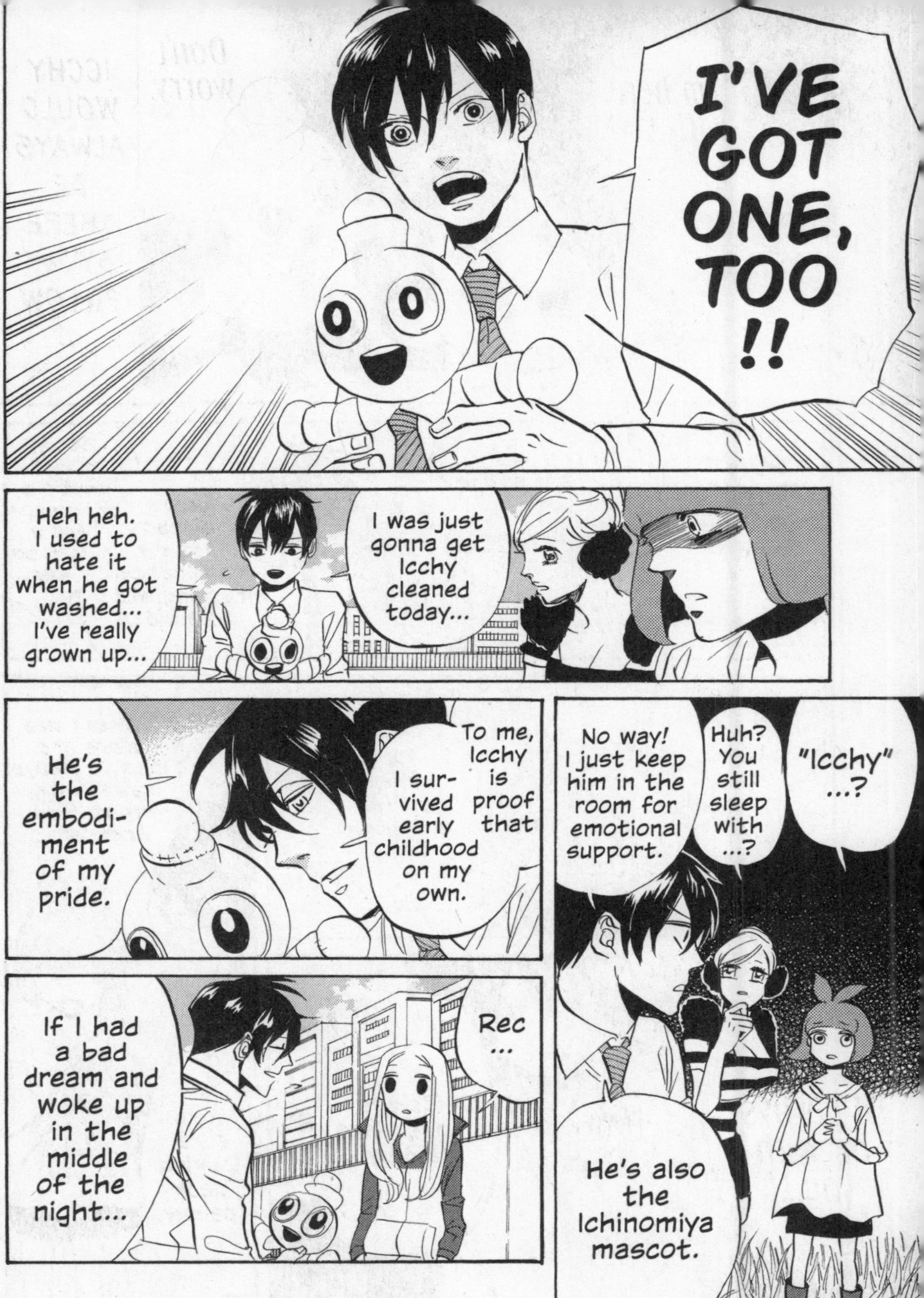
I'VE GOT ONE, TOO!!
I was just gonna get Icchy cleaned today...
Heh heh. I used to hate it when he got washed... I've really grown up...
"Icchy"...?
Huh? You still sleep with...?
No way! I just keep him in the room for emotional support.
He's also the Ichinomiya mascot.
To me, Icchy is proof that I survived early childhood on my own.
He's the embodiment of my pride.
Rec...
If I had a bad dream and woke up in the middle of the night...

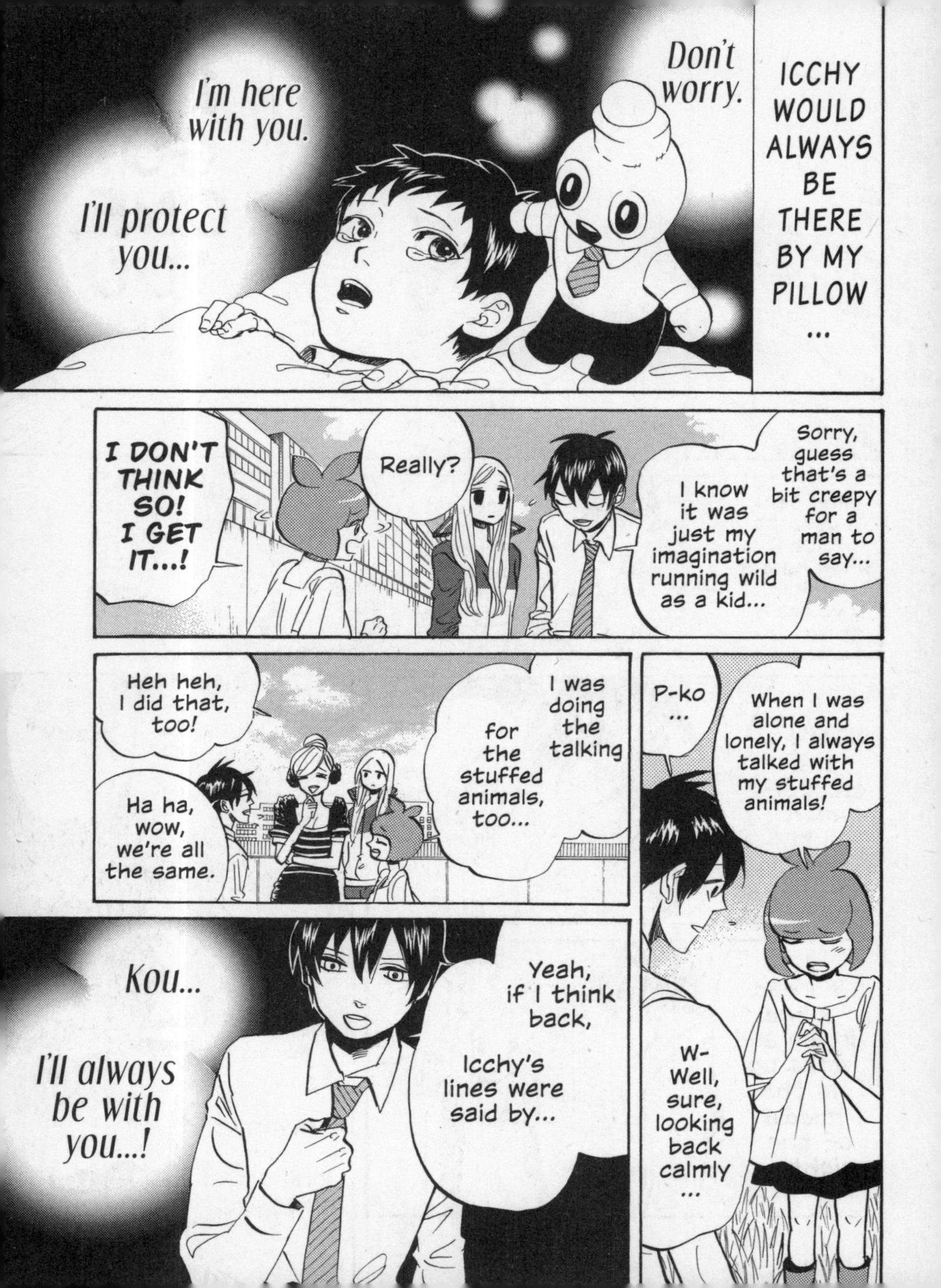
ICCHY WOULD ALWAYS BE THERE BY MY PILLOW ...
Don't worry.
I'm here with you.
I'll protect you...
Sorry, guess that's a bit creepy for a man to say...
I know it was just my imagination running wild as a kid...
Really?
I DON'T THINK SO! I GET IT...!
When I was alone and lonely, I always talked with my stuffed animals!
P-ko ...
I was doing the talking for the stuffed animals, too...
Heh heh, I did that, too!
Ha ha, wow, we're all the same.
W- Well, sure, looking back calmly ...
Yeah, if I think back,
Icchy's lines were said by...
Kou...
I'll always be with you...!

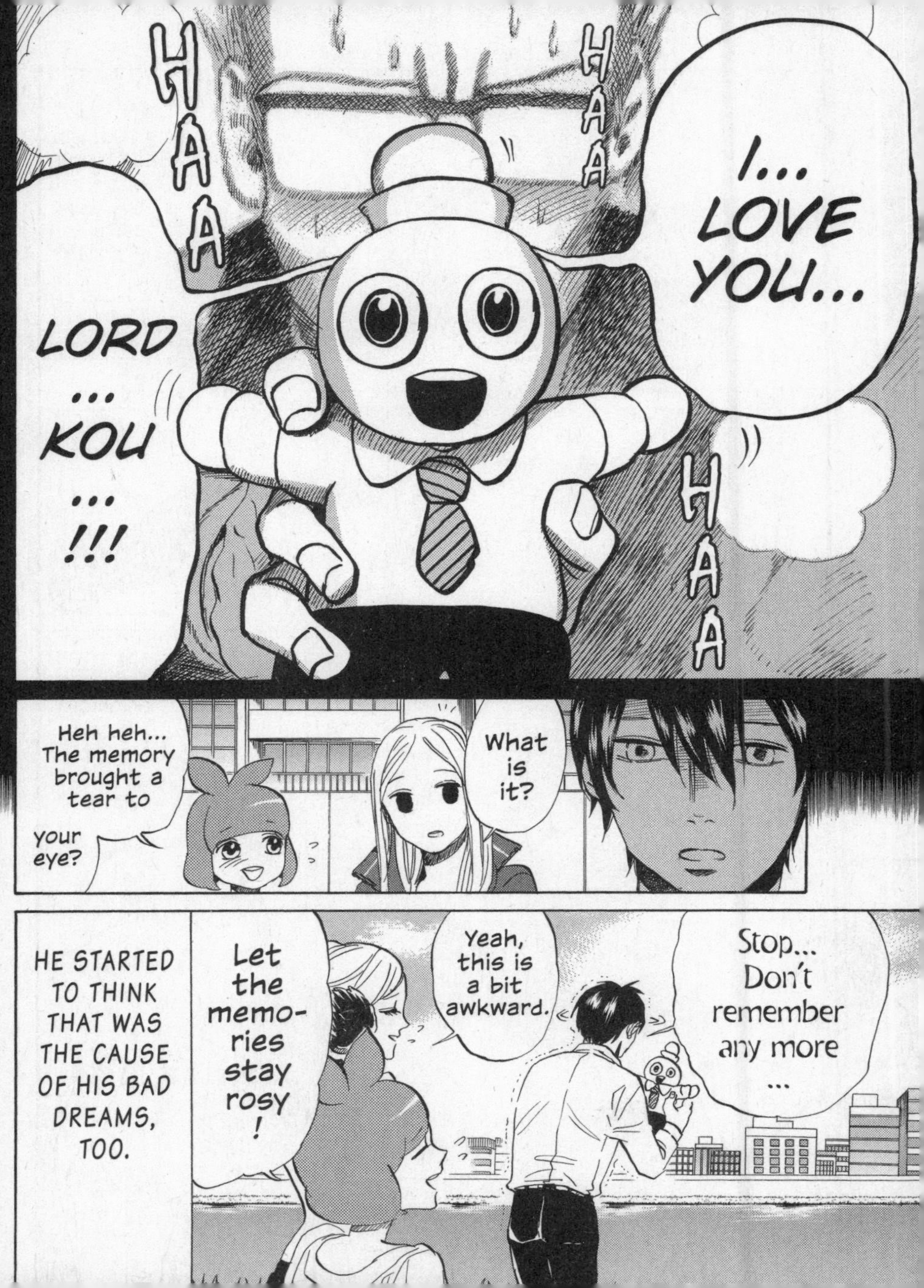
I... LOVE YOU...
HAAA
HAA
LORD ... KOU ... !!!
HAAA
Heh heh... The memory brought a tear to your eye?
What is it?
Stop... Don't remember any more ...
Yeah, this is a bit awkward.
Let the memories stay rosy!
HE STARTED TO THINK THAT WAS THE CAUSE OF HIS BAD DREAMS, TOO.

Chapter 348: Habits

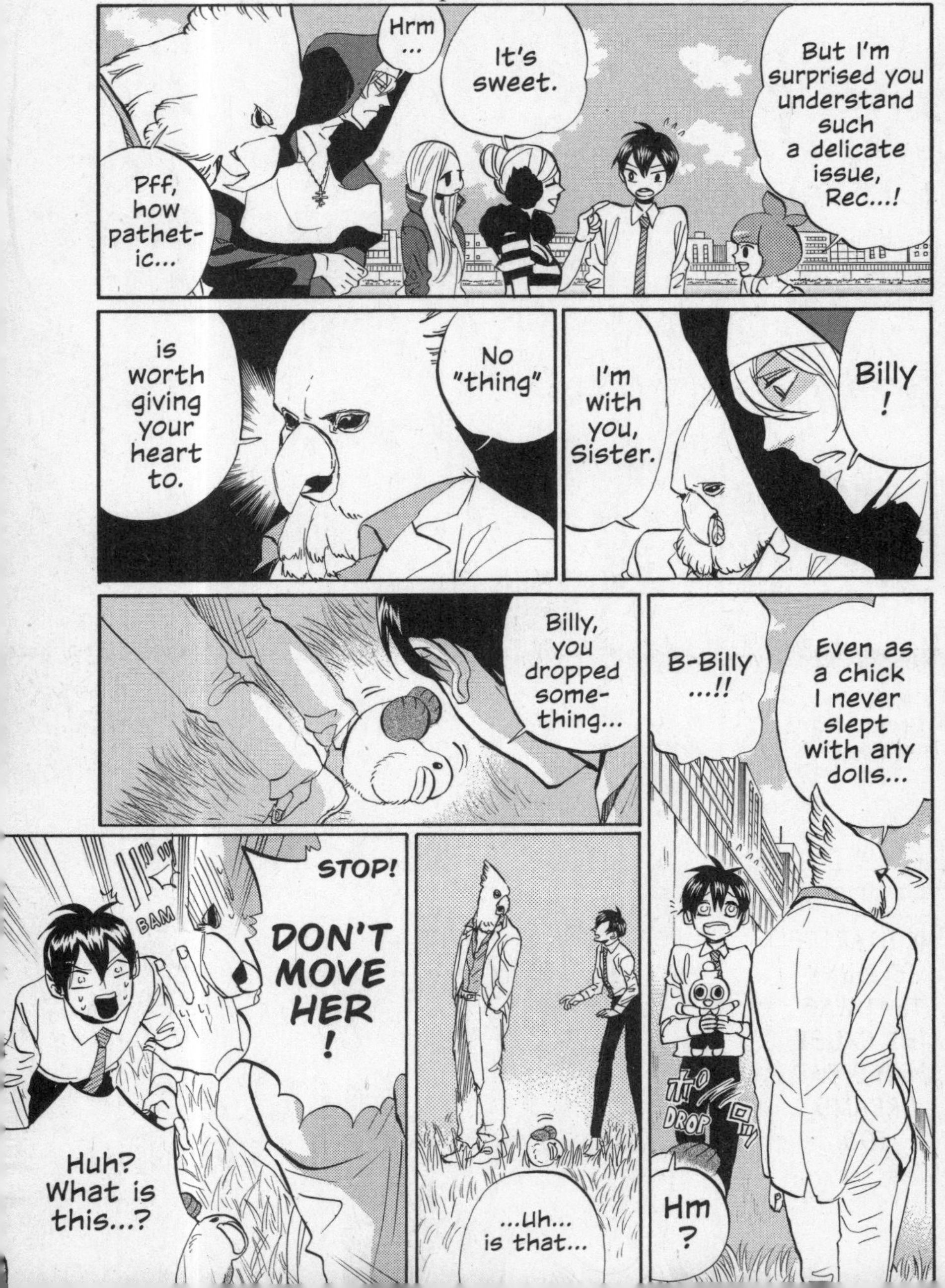
But I'm surprised you understand such a delicate issue, Rec...!
It's sweet.
Hrm ...
Pff, how pathet-ic...
Billy !
I'm with you, Sister.
No "thing"
is worth giving your heart to.
Even as a chick I never slept with any dolls...
B-Billy ...!!
Billy, you dropped some-thing...
DROP
Hm ?
...uh... is that...
STOP!
BAM
DON'T MOVE HER !
Huh? What is this...?

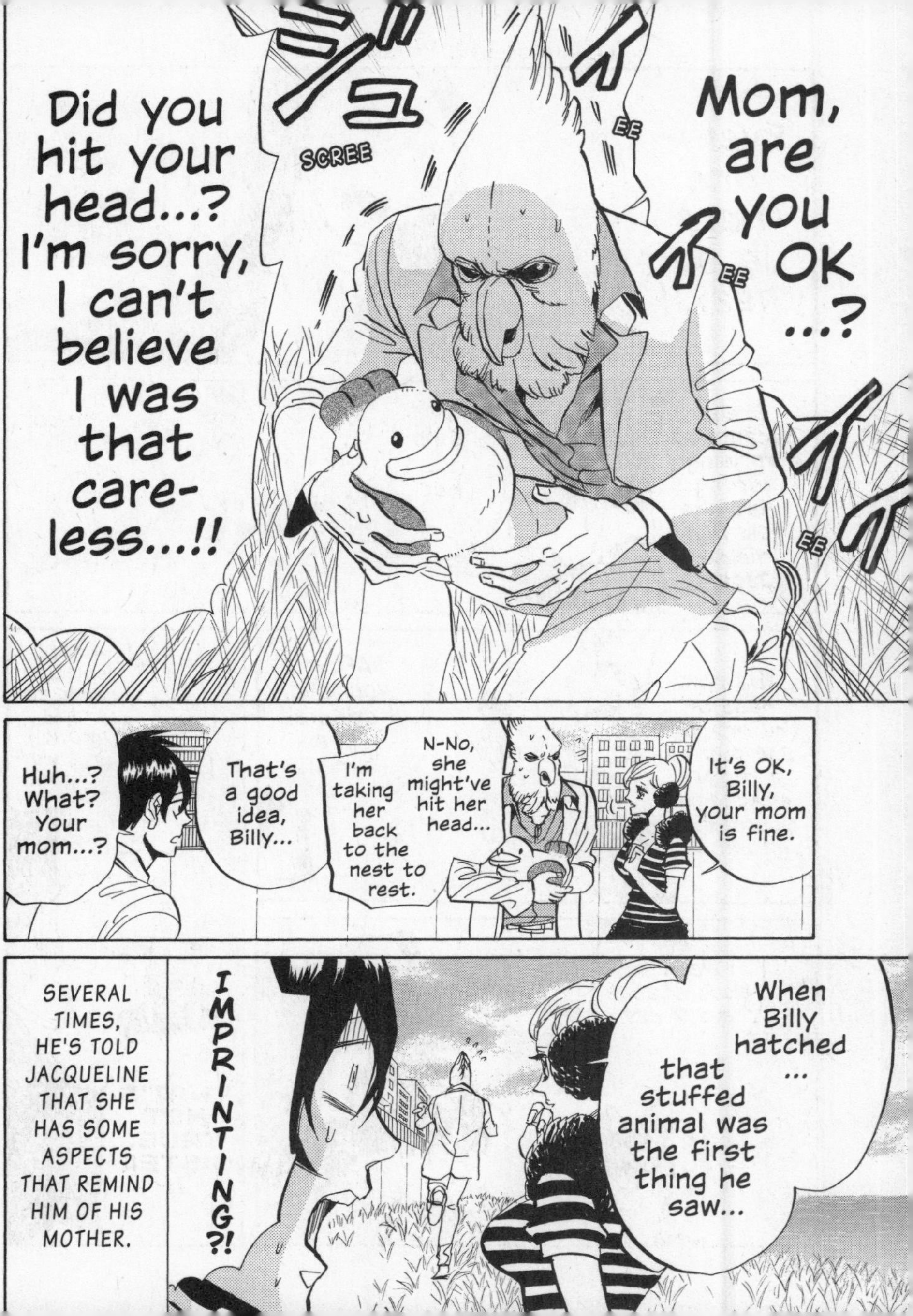
Mom, are you OK ...?
EE
EE
EE
SCREE
Did you hit your head...? I'm sorry, I can't believe I was that care-less...!!
It's OK, Billy, your mom is fine.
N-No, she might've hit her head...
I'm taking her back to the nest to rest.
That's a good idea, Billy...
Huh...? What? Your mom...?
When Billy hatched ... that stuffed animal was the first thing he saw...
IMPRINTING?!
SEVERAL TIMES, HE'S TOLD JACQUELINE THAT SHE HAS SOME ASPECTS THAT REMIND HIM OF HIS MOTHER.

Chapter 349: Pillar of the Heart

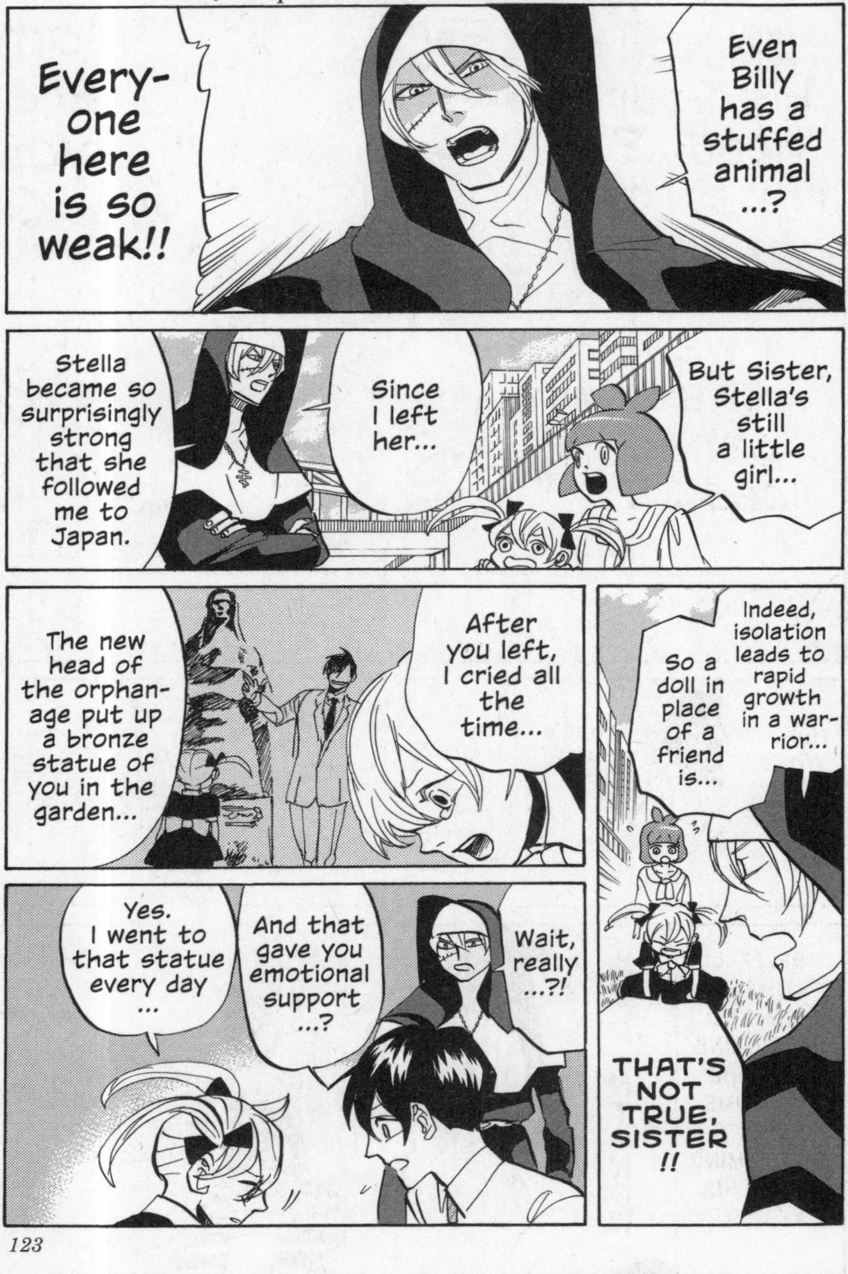

Even Billy has a stuffed animal ...?
Every-one here is so weak!!
But Sister, Stella's still a little girl...
Since I left her...
Stella became so surprisingly strong that she followed me to Japan.
Indeed, isolation leads to rapid growth in a war-rior...
So a doll in place of a friend is...
THAT'S NOT TRUE, SISTER !!
After you left, I cried all the time...
The new head of the orphan-age put up a bronze statue of you in the garden...
Wait, really ...?!
And that gave you emotional support ...?
Yes. I went to that statue every day ...

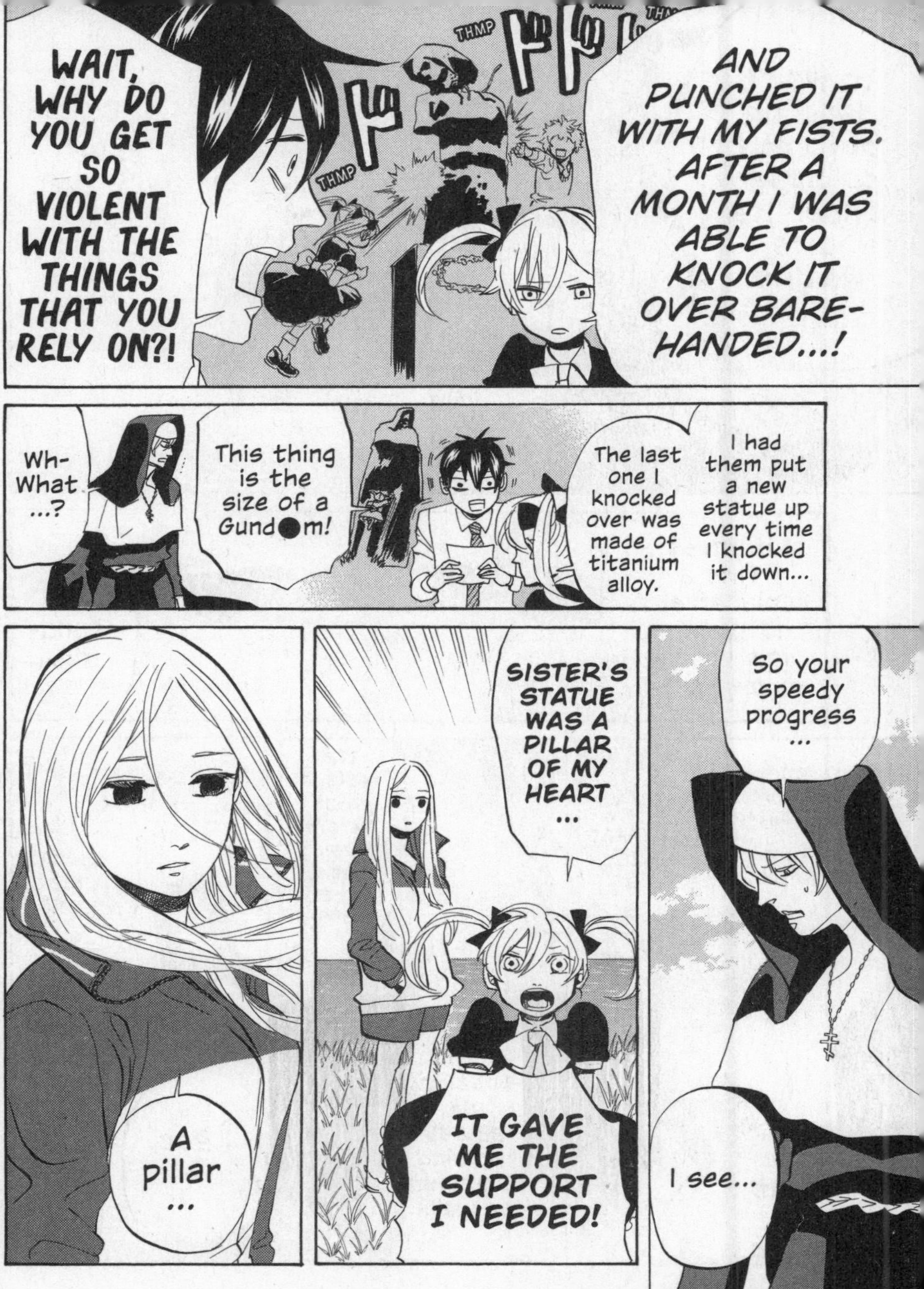
AND PUNCHED IT WITH MY FISTS. AFTER A MONTH I WAS ABLE TO KNOCK IT OVER BARE-HANDED...!
THMP
THMP
WAIT, WHY DO YOU GET SO VIOLENT WITH THE THINGS THAT YOU RELY ON?!
I had them put a new statue up every time I knocked it down...
The last one I knocked over was made of titanium alloy.
This thing is the size of a Gund●m!
Wh-What ...?
So your speedy progress ...
I see...
SISTER'S STATUE WAS A PILLAR OF MY HEART ...
IT GAVE ME THE SUPPORT I NEEDED!
A pillar ...

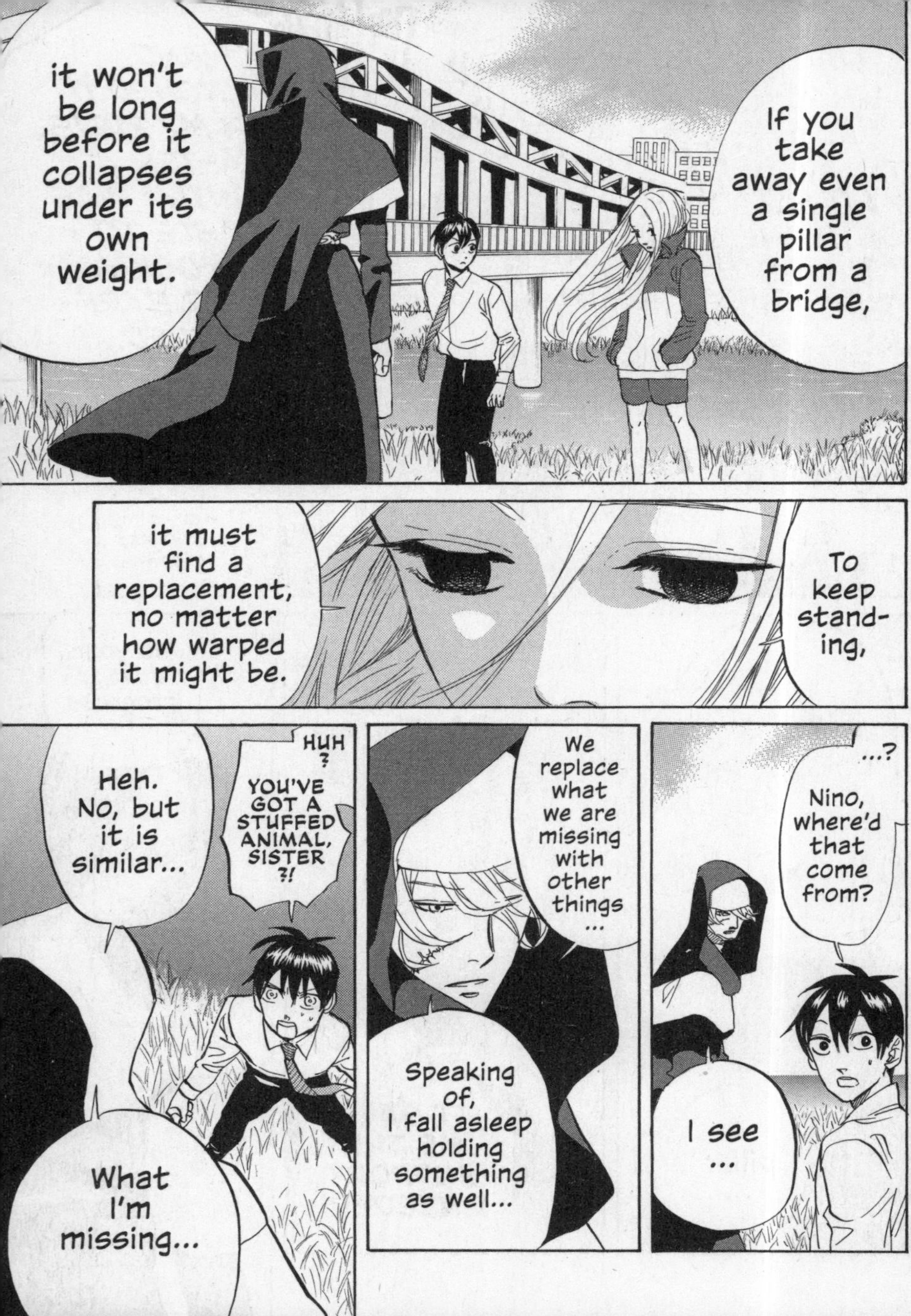
If you take away even a single pillar from a bridge,
it won't be long before it collapses under its own weight.
To keep standing,
it must find a replacement, no matter how warped it might be.
...?
Nino, where'd that come from?
I see ...
We replace what we are missing with other things ...
Speaking of, I fall asleep holding something as well...
HUH?
YOU'VE GOT A STUFFED ANIMAL, SISTER?!
Heh. No, but it is similar...
What I'm missing...

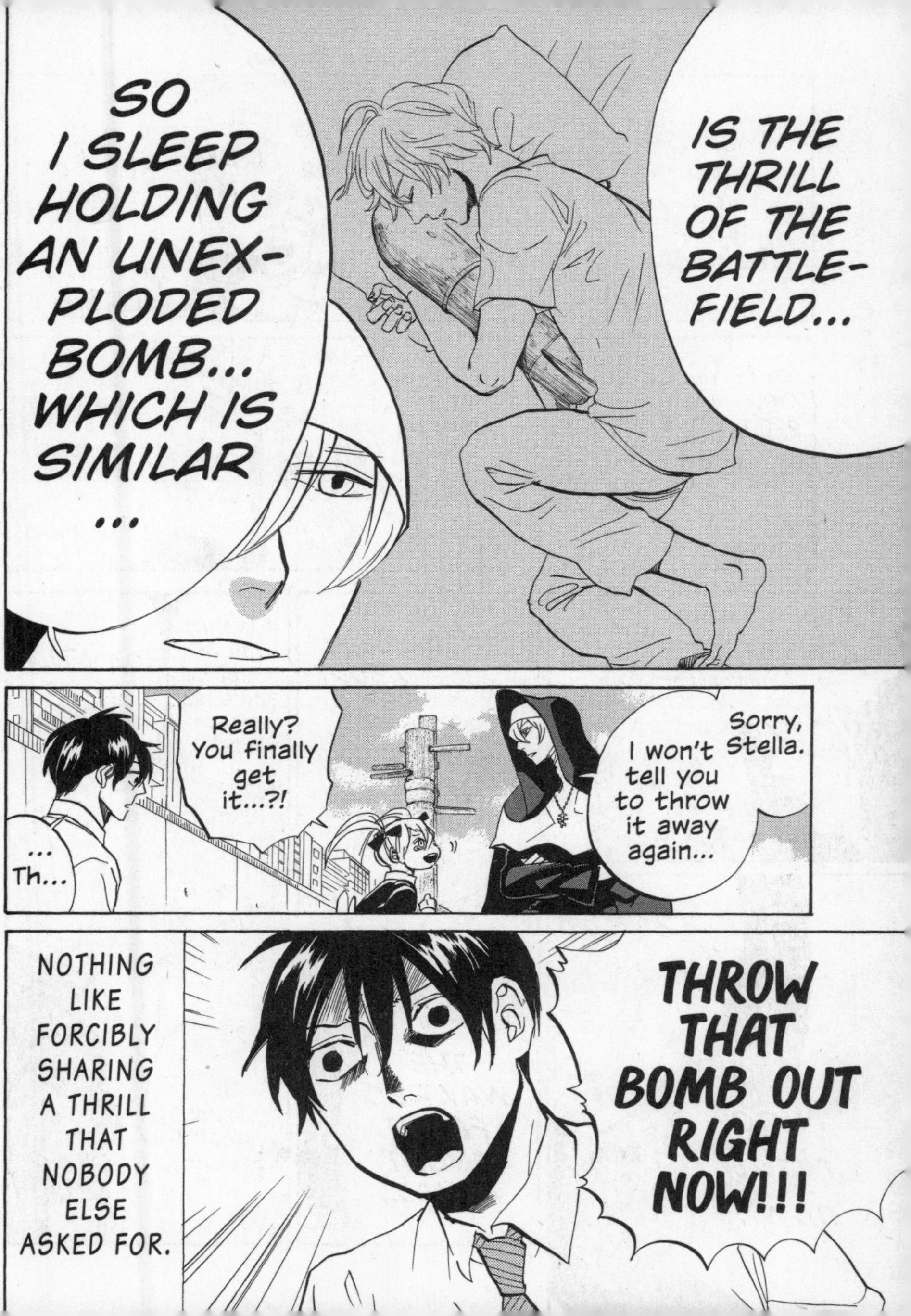
SO I SLEEP HOLDING AN UNEX-PLODED BOMB... WHICH IS SIMILAR ...
IS THE THRILL OF THE BATTLE-FIELD...
Sorry, Stella. I won't tell you to throw it away again...
Really? You finally get it...?!
... Th...
THROW THAT BOMB OUT RIGHT NOW!!!
NOTHING LIKE FORCIBLY SHARING A THRILL THAT NOBODY ELSE ASKED FOR.

Chapter 350: Nino's Answer

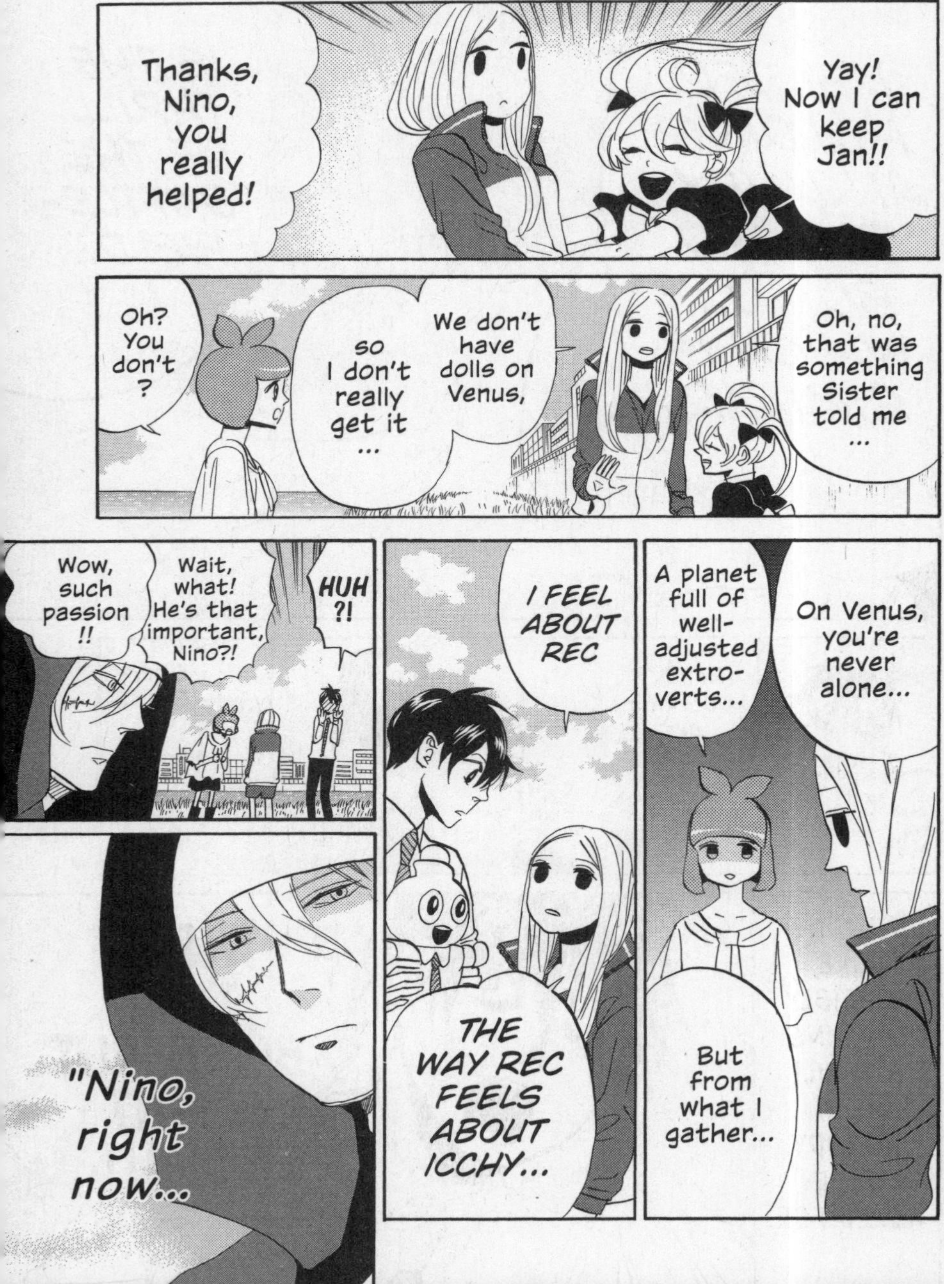

Yay! Now I can keep Jan!!
Thanks, Nino, you really helped!
Oh, no, that was something Sister told me ...
We don't have dolls on Venus,
so I don't really get it ...
Oh? You don't ?
On Venus, you're never alone...
A planet full of well-adjusted extro-verts...
But from what I gather...
I FEEL ABOUT REC
THE WAY REC FEELS ABOUT ICCHY...
HUH ?!
Wait, what! He's that important, Nino?!
Wow, such passion !!
"Nino, right now...

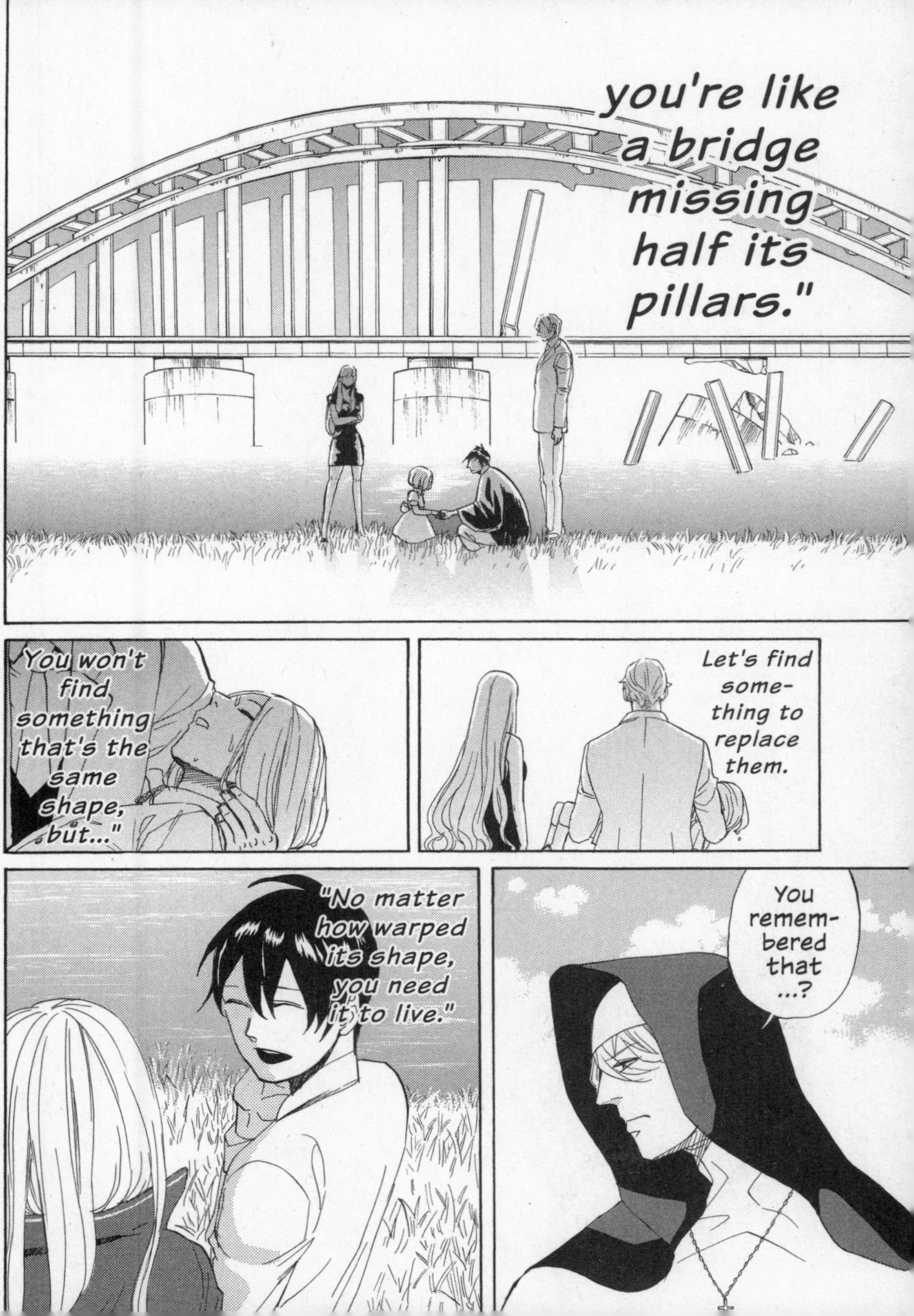
you're like a bridge missing half its pillars."
"You won't find something that's the same shape, but..."
Let's find some-thing to replace them.
"No matter how warped its shape, you need it to live."
You remem-bered that ...?

ARAKAWA
UNDER
THE BRIDGE

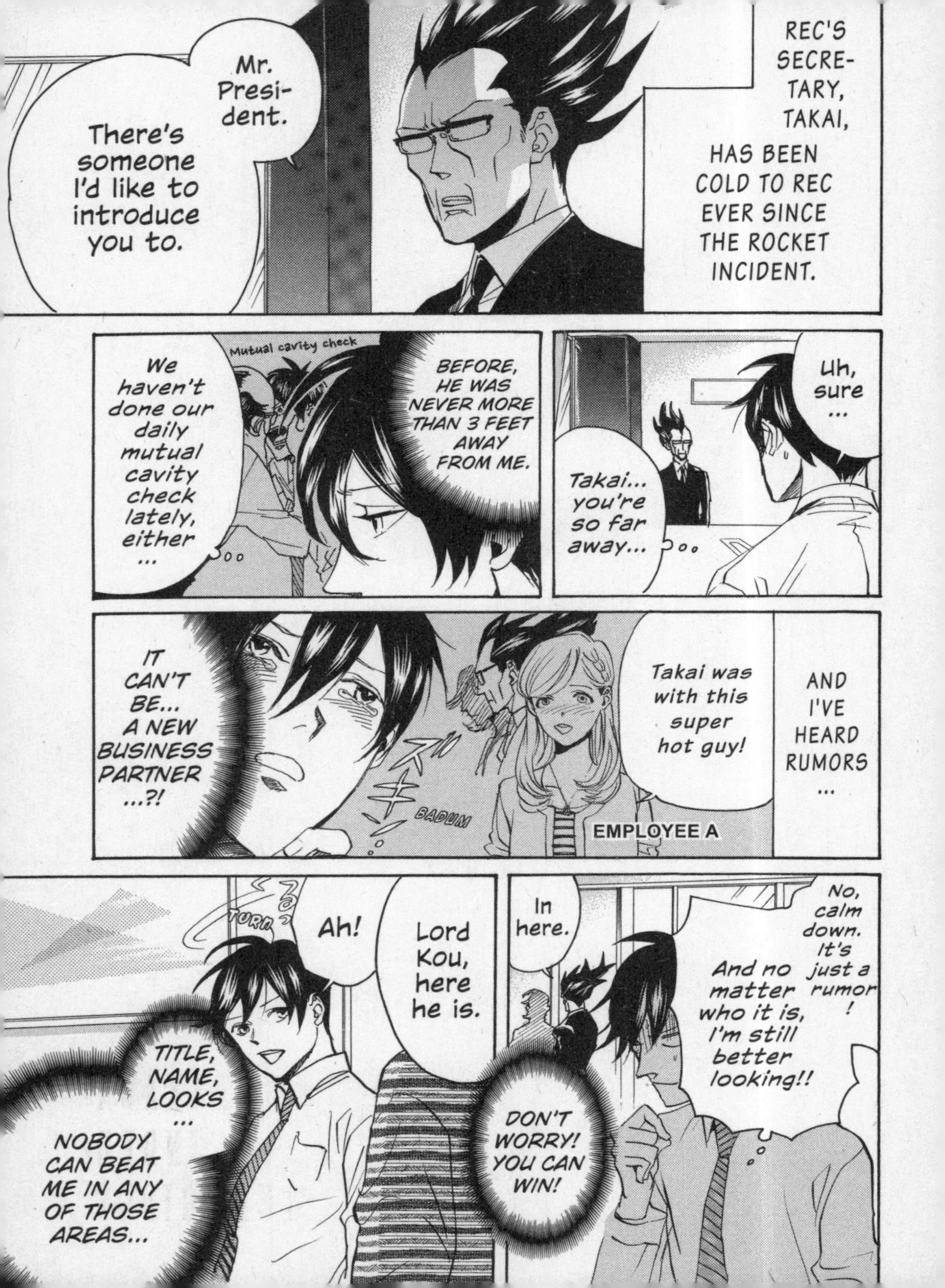

REC'S SECRETARY, TAKAI, HAS BEEN COLD TO REC EVER SINCE THE ROCKET INCIDENT.
Mr. President.
There's someone I'd like to introduce you to.
Uh, sure ...
Takai... you're so far away...
BEFORE, HE WAS NEVER MORE THAN 3 FEET AWAY FROM ME.
Mutual cavity check
We haven't done our daily mutual cavity check lately, either ...
AND I'VE HEARD RUMORS ...
Takai was with this super hot guy!
EMPLOYEE A
BADUM
IT CAN'T BE... A NEW BUSINESS PARTNER ...?!
No, calm down. It's just a rumor!
And no matter who it is, I'm still better looking!!
In here.
DON'T WORRY! YOU CAN WIN!
Lord Kou, here he is.
Ah!
TURN
TITLE, NAME, LOOKS ...
NOBODY CAN BEAT ME IN ANY OF THOSE AREAS...

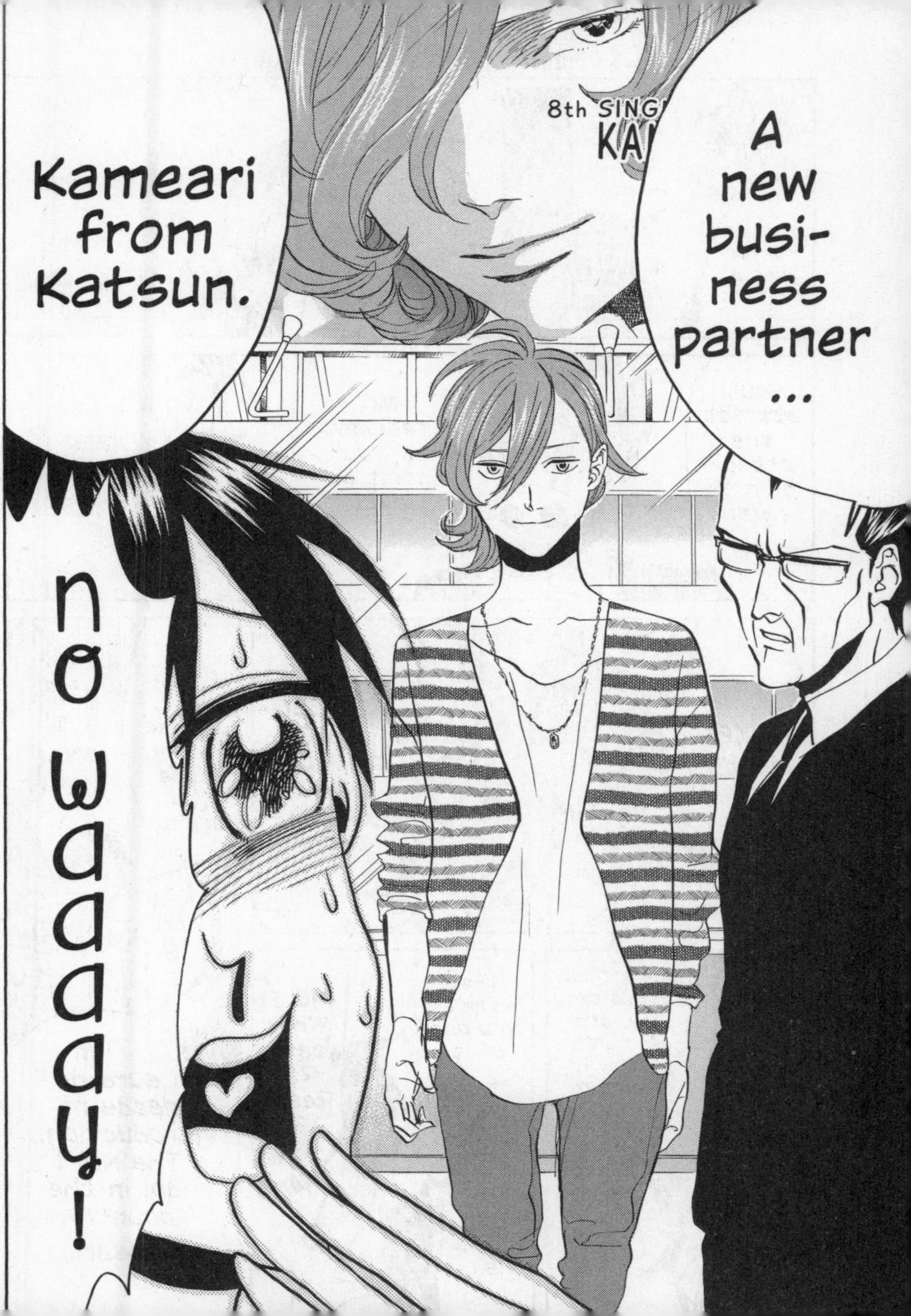
A new business partner ...
Kameari from Katsun.
no waaaay!

Chapter 351: Kameari's Request

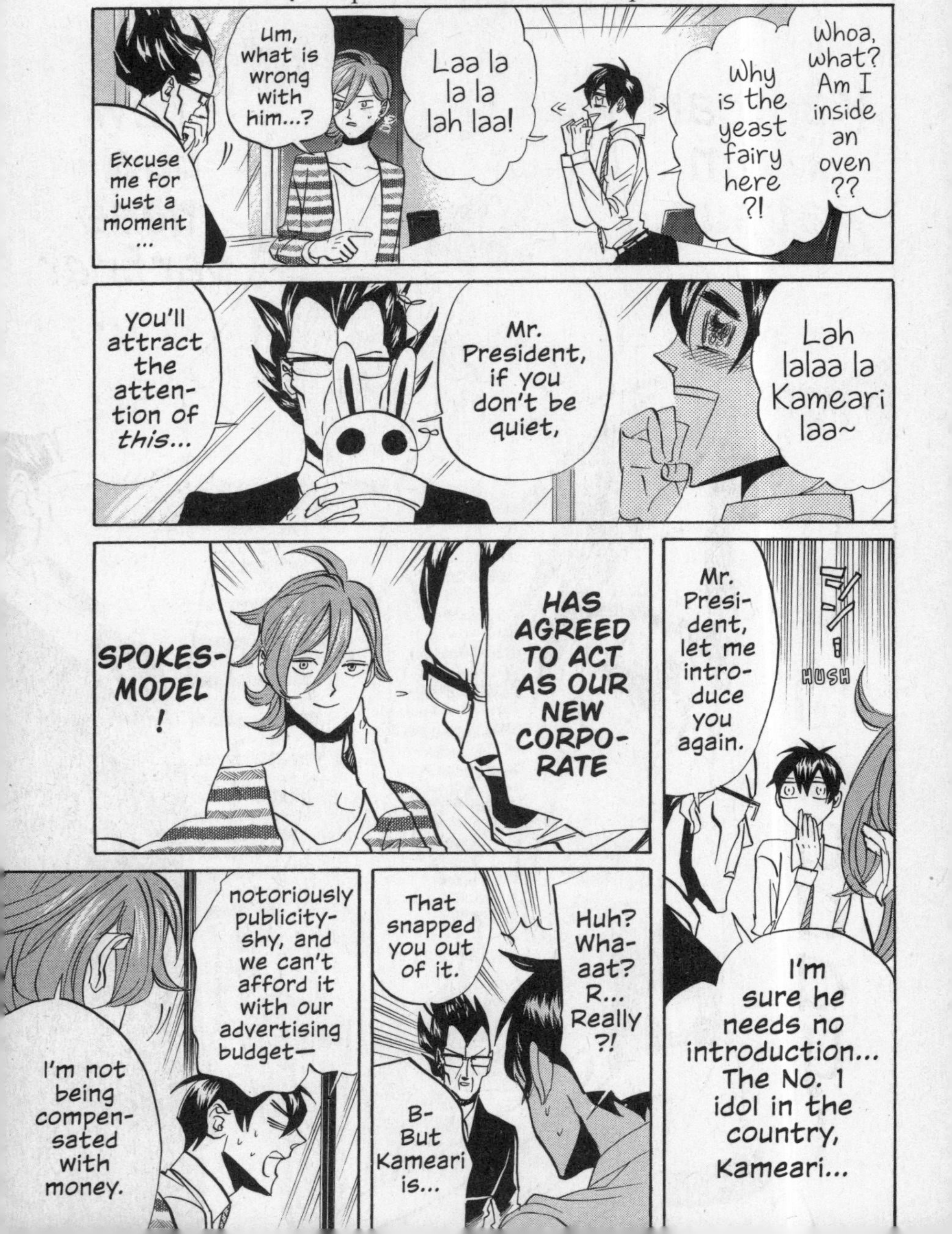

Whoa, what? Am I inside an oven ??
Why is the yeast fairy here ?!
Laa la la la lah laa!
Um, what is wrong with him...?
Excuse me for just a moment ...
Lah lalaa la Kameari laa~
Mr. President, if you don't be quiet,
you'll attract the attention of *this*...
Mr. President, let me introduce you again.
HUSH
I'm sure he needs no introduction... The No. 1 idol in the country, Kameari...
HAS AGREED TO ACT AS OUR NEW CORPORATE
SPOKES-MODEL!
Huh? Wha-aat? R... Really ?!
That snapped you out of it.
B-But Kameari is...
notoriously publicity-shy, and we can't afford it with our advertising budget—
I'm not being compensated with money.

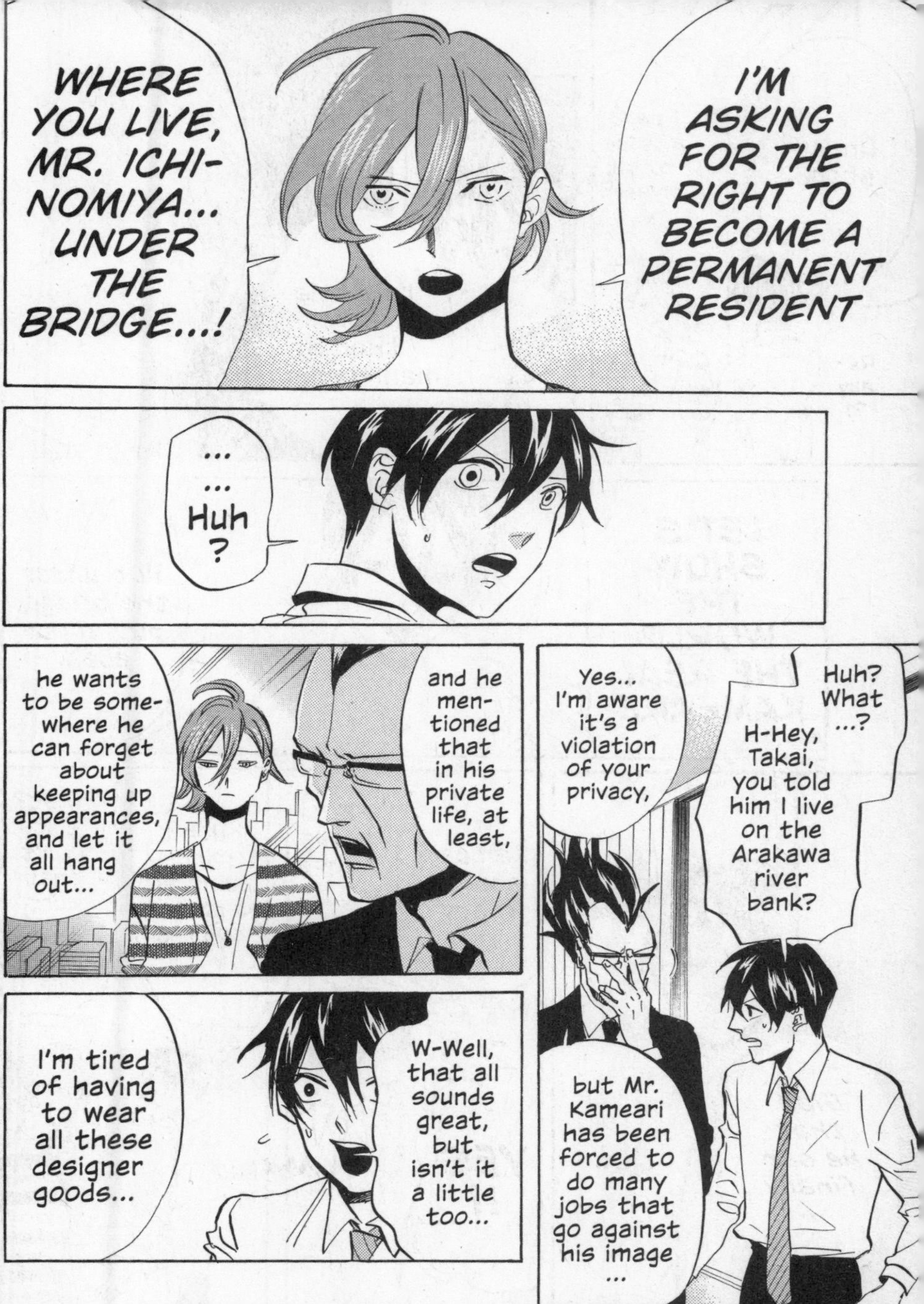
I'M ASKING FOR THE RIGHT TO BECOME A PERMANENT RESIDENT
WHERE YOU LIVE, MR. ICHI-NOMIYA... UNDER THE BRIDGE...!
... ... Huh?
Huh? What ...?
H-Hey, Takai, you told him I live on the Arakawa river bank?
Yes... I'm aware it's a violation of your privacy,
but Mr. Kameari has been forced to do many jobs that go against his image ...
and he mentioned that in his private life, at least,
he wants to be some-where he can forget about keeping up appearances, and let it all hang out...
W-Well, that all sounds great, but isn't it a little too...
I'm tired of having to wear all these designer goods...

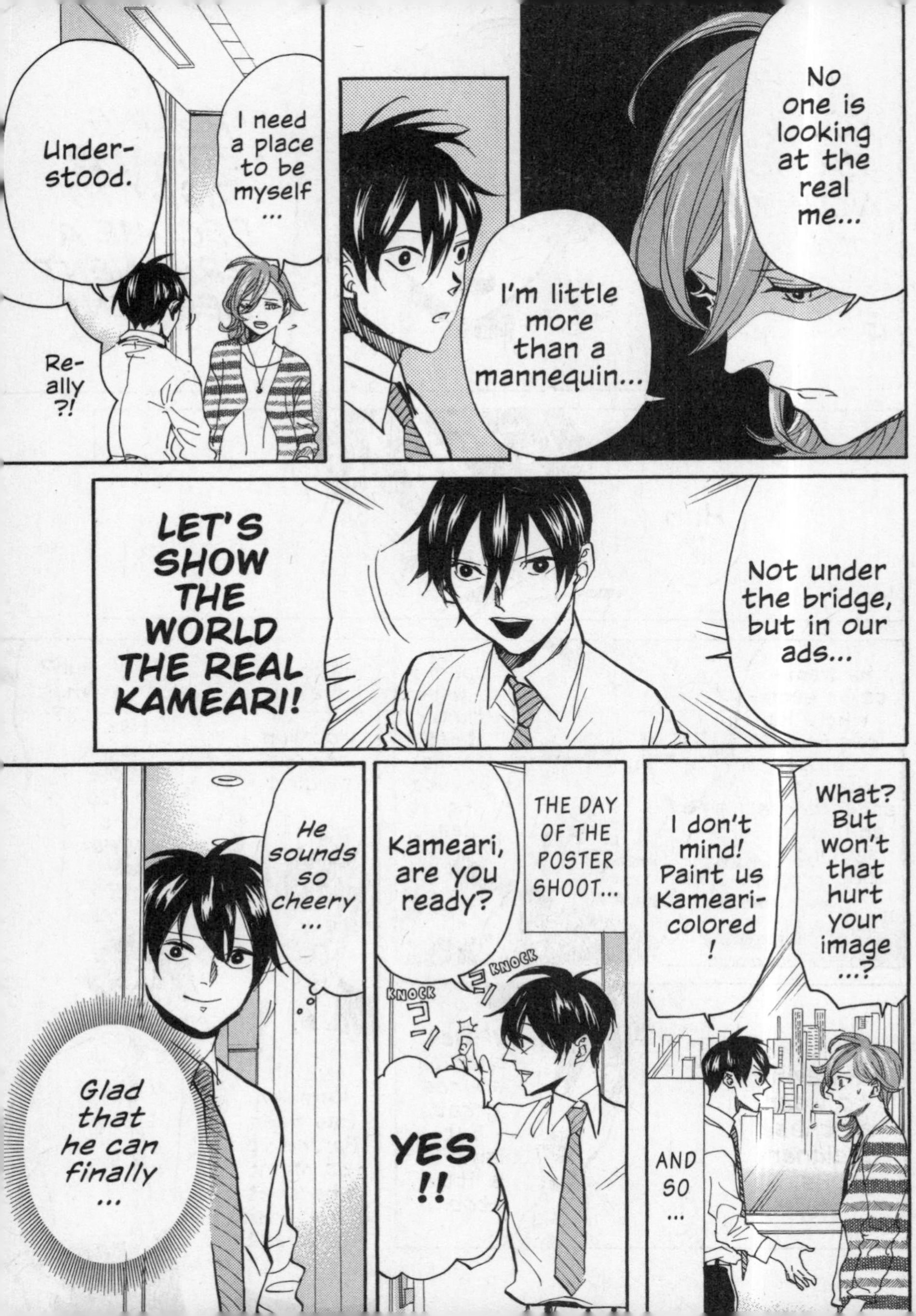
No one is looking at the real me...
I'm little more than a mannequin...
I need a place to be myself ...
Under-stood.
Re-ally?!
Not under the bridge, but in our ads...
LET'S SHOW THE WORLD THE REAL KAMEARI!
What? But won't that hurt your image ...?
I don't mind! Paint us Kameari-colored!
AND SO ...
THE DAY OF THE POSTER SHOOT...
Kameari, are you ready?
KNOCK
KNOCK
YES!!
He sounds so cheery ...
Glad that he can finally ...

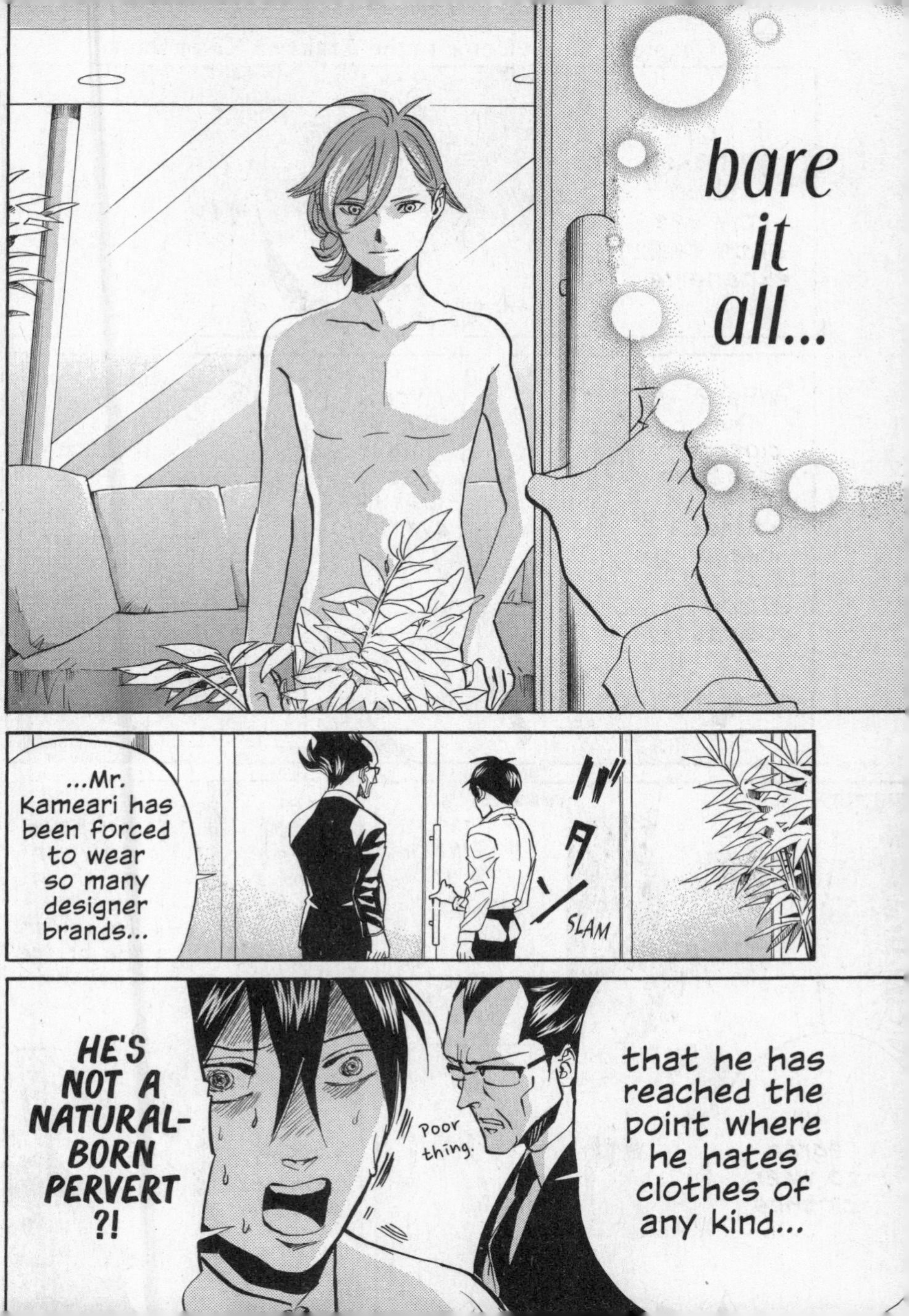
bare it all...
バタン
SLAM
...Mr. Kameari has been forced to wear so many designer brands...
that he has reached the point where he hates clothes of any kind...
Poor thing.
HE'S NOT A NATURAL-BORN PERVERT?!

Chapter 352: Welcome to the Arakawa River Bank

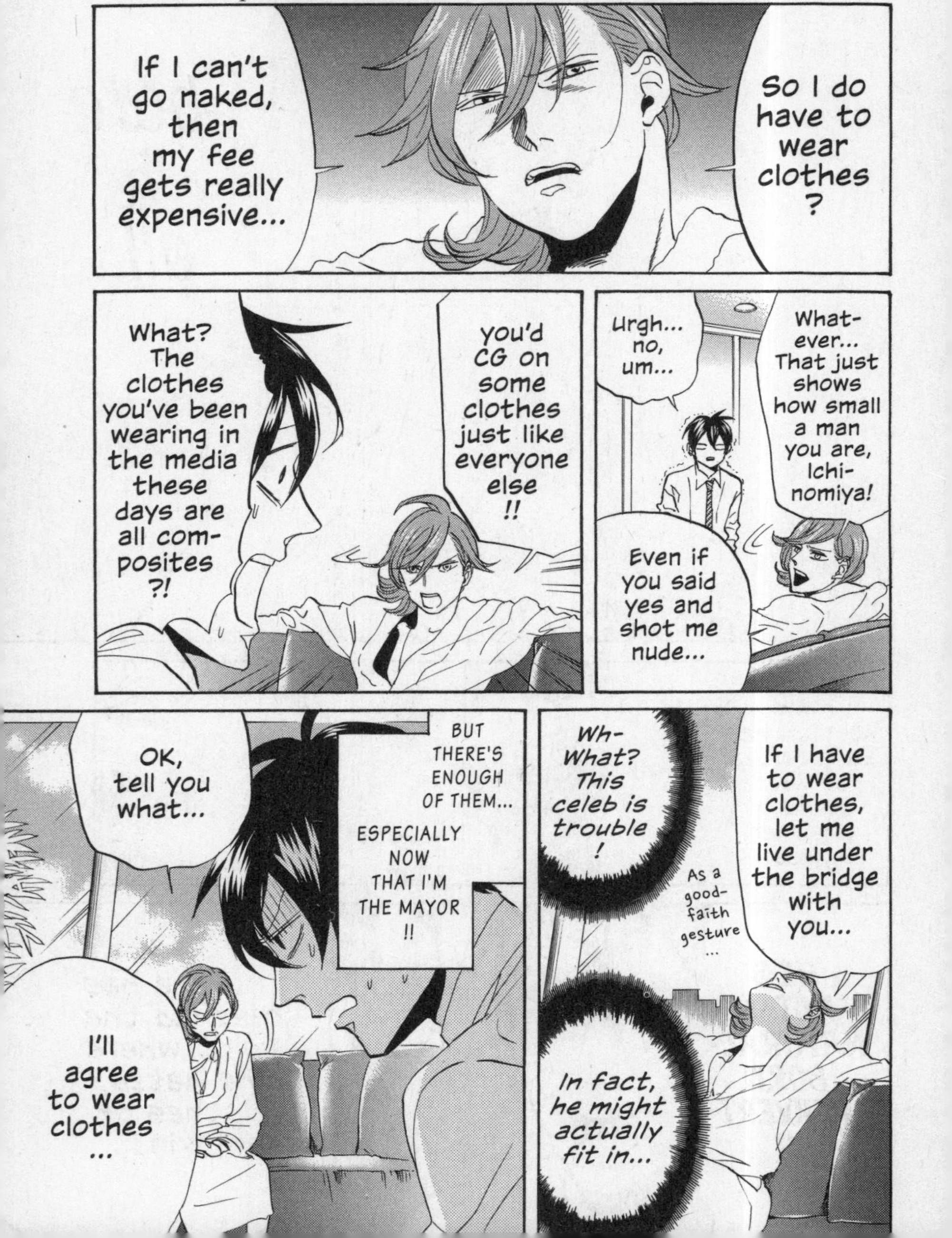
So I do have to wear clothes?
If I can't go naked, then my fee gets really expensive...
What-ever... That just shows how small a man you are, Ichi-nomiya!
Urgh... no, um...
Even if you said yes and shot me nude...
you'd CG on some clothes just like everyone else!!
What? The clothes you've been wearing in the media these days are all com-posites?!
If I have to wear clothes, let me live under the bridge with you...
As a good-faith gesture...
Wh-What? This celeb is trouble!
In fact, he might actually fit in...
BUT THERE'S ENOUGH OF THEM...
ESPECIALLY NOW THAT I'M THE MAYOR!!
OK, tell you what...
I'll agree to wear clothes...

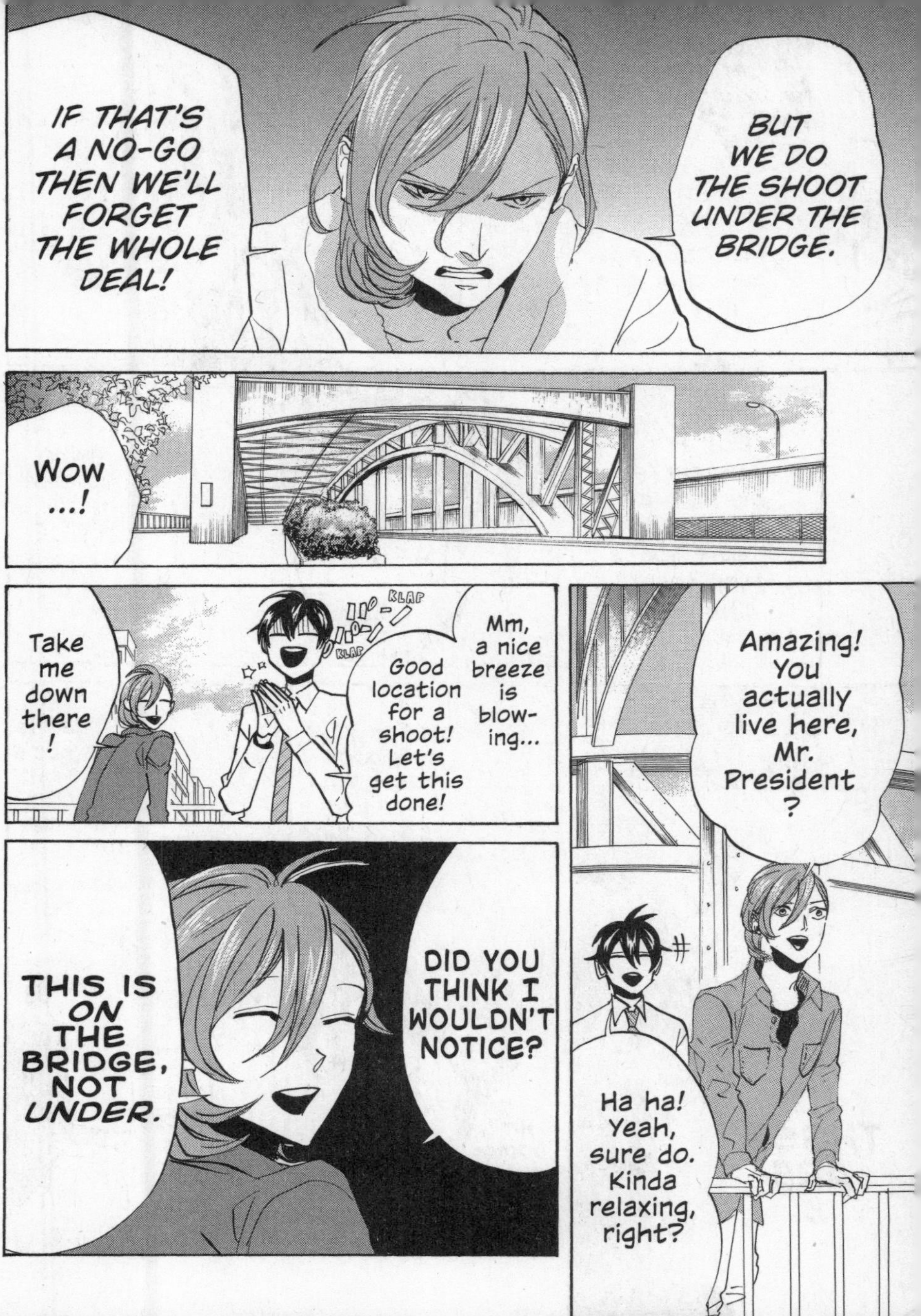
BUT WE DO THE SHOOT UNDER THE BRIDGE.
IF THAT'S A NO-GO THEN WE'LL FORGET THE WHOLE DEAL!
Wow ...!
Amazing! You actually live here, Mr. President?
Ha ha! Yeah, sure do. Kinda relaxing, right?
Mm, a nice breeze is blowing...
Good location for a shoot! Let's get this done!
KLAP
KLAP
Take me down there!
DID YOU THINK I WOULDN'T NOTICE?
THIS IS *ON* THE BRIDGE, NOT *UNDER*.

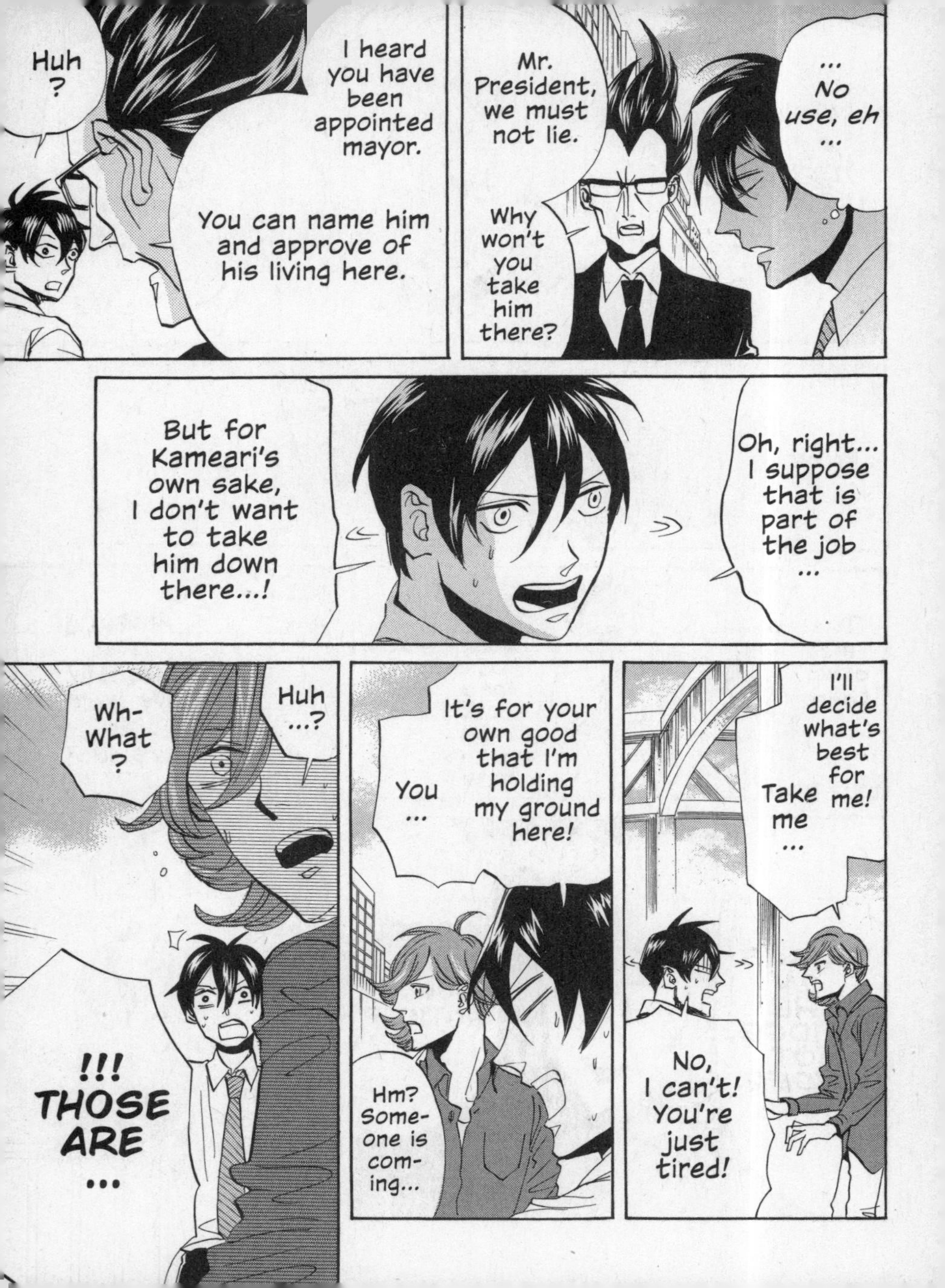
... No use, eh ...
Mr. President, we must not lie.
Why won't you take him there?
I heard you have been appointed mayor.
You can name him and approve of his living here.
Huh?
Oh, right... I suppose that is part of the job ...
But for Kameari's own sake, I don't want to take him down there...!
I'll decide what's best for me!
Take me ...
No, I can't! You're just tired!
It's for your own good that I'm holding my ground here!
You ...
Hm? Some-one is com-ing...
Huh ...?
Wh-What?
!!! THOSE ARE ...

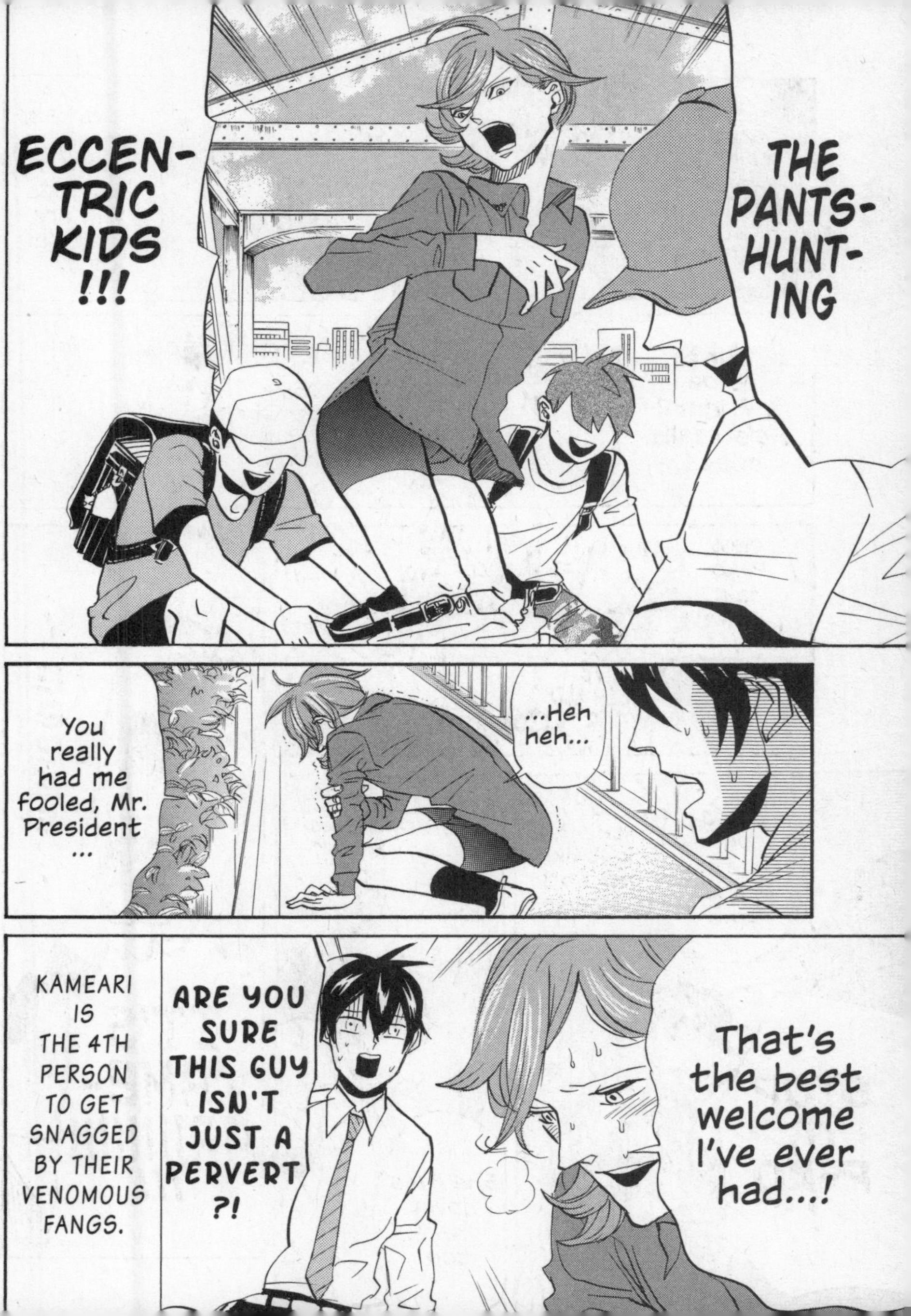

THE PANTS-HUNTING
ECCENTRIC KIDS!!!
...Heh heh...
You really had me fooled, Mr. President...
That's the best welcome I've ever had...!
ARE YOU SURE THIS GUY ISN'T JUST A PERVERT?!
KAMEARI IS THE 4TH PERSON TO GET SNAGGED BY THEIR VENOMOUS FANGS.

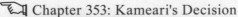

Chapter 353: Kameari's Decision

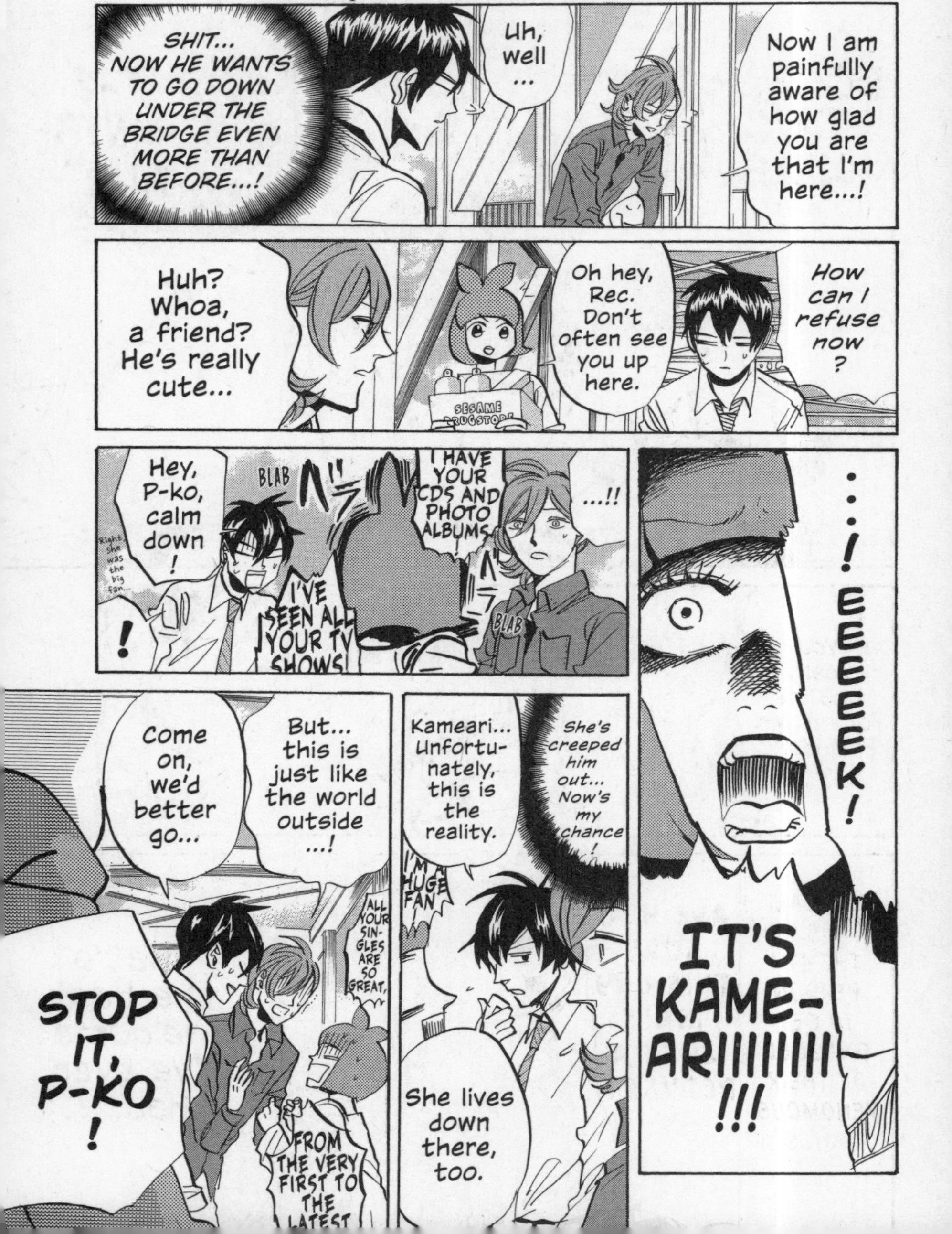
Now I am painfully aware of how glad you are that I'm here...!
Uh, well ...
SHIT... NOW HE WANTS TO GO DOWN UNDER THE BRIDGE EVEN MORE THAN BEFORE...!
How can I refuse now?
Oh hey, Rec. Don't often see you up here.
SESAME DRUGSTORE
Huh? Whoa, a friend? He's really cute...
...!
EEEEEK!
IT'S KAME-ARIIIIIIII!!!
...!!
I HAVE YOUR CDS AND PHOTO ALBUMS!
BLAB
I'VE SEEN ALL YOUR TV SHOWS!
Hey, P-ko, calm down!
Right, she was the big fan...
BLAB
!
She's creeped him out... Now's my chance!
Kameari... Unfortunately, this is the reality.
I'M A HUGE FAN!
She lives down there, too.
But... this is just like the world outside ...!
Come on, we'd better go...
ALL YOUR SINGLES ARE SO GREAT,
FROM THE VERY FIRST TO THE LATEST
STOP IT, P-KO!

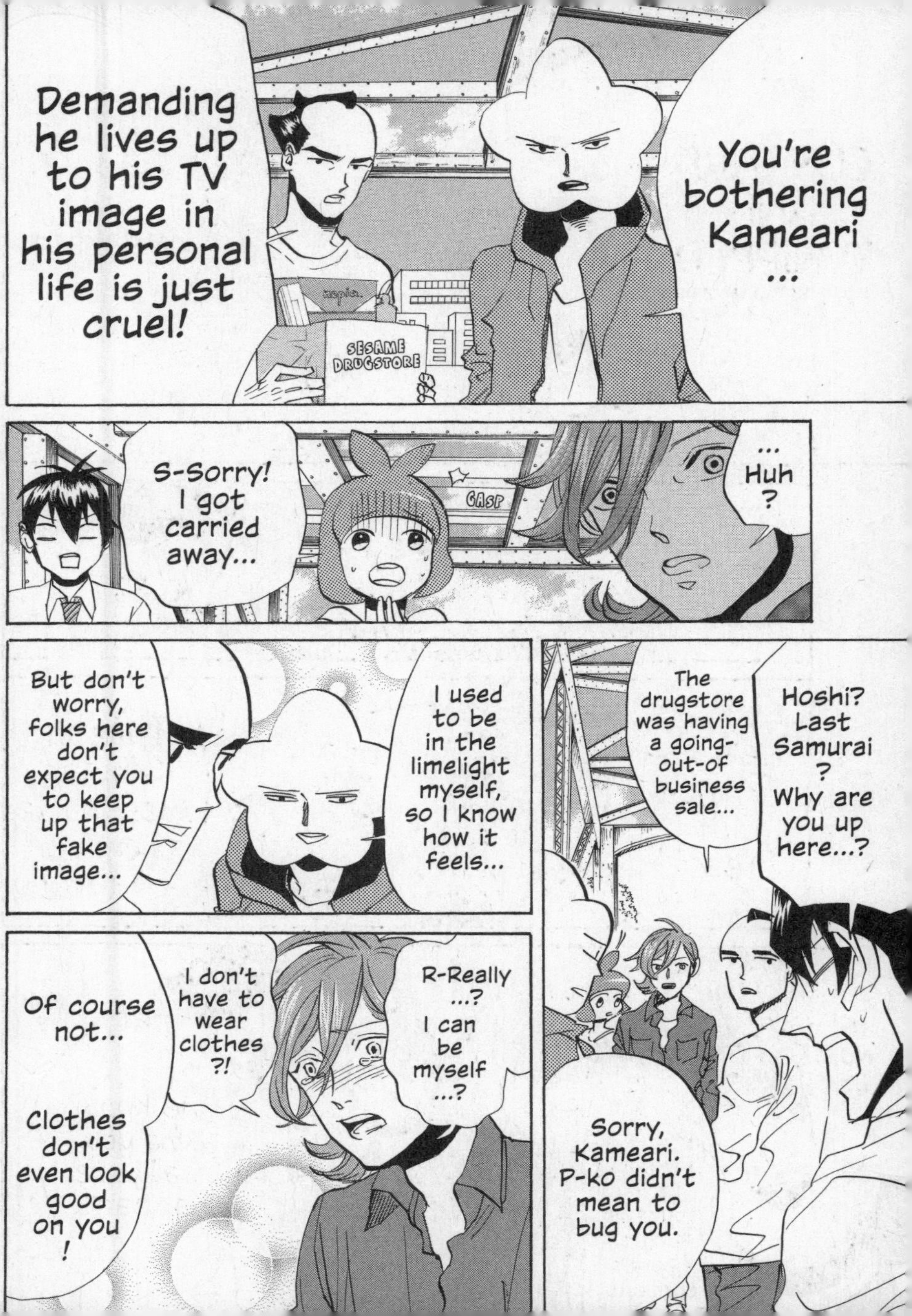

You're bothering Kameari ...
Demanding he lives up to his TV image in his personal life is just cruel!
SESAME DRUGSTORE
... Huh ?
GASP
S-Sorry! I got carried away...
Hoshi? Last Samurai ? Why are you up here...?
The drugstore was having a going-out-of business sale...
Sorry, Kameari. P-ko didn't mean to bug you.
I used to be in the limelight myself, so I know how it feels...
But don't worry, folks here don't expect you to keep up that fake image...
R-Really ...? I can be myself ...?
I don't have to wear clothes ?!
Of course not...
Clothes don't even look good on you !

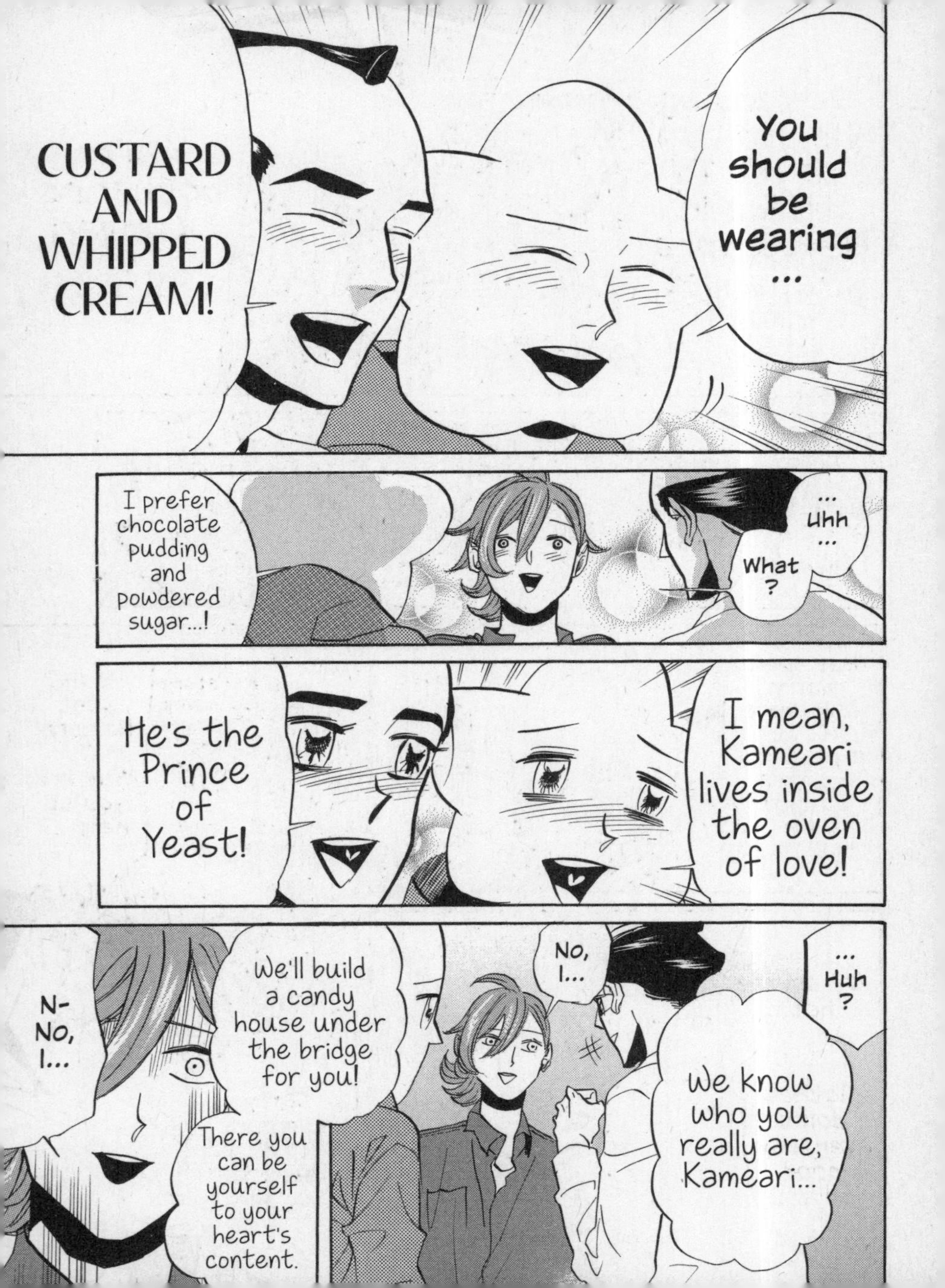
You should be wearing ...
CUSTARD AND WHIPPED CREAM!
... Uhh ... What ?
I prefer chocolate pudding and powdered sugar...!
I mean, Kameari lives inside the oven of love!
He's the Prince of Yeast!
... Huh ?
We know who you really are, Kameari...
No, I...
We'll build a candy house under the bridge for you!
There you can be yourself to your heart's content.
N- No, I...

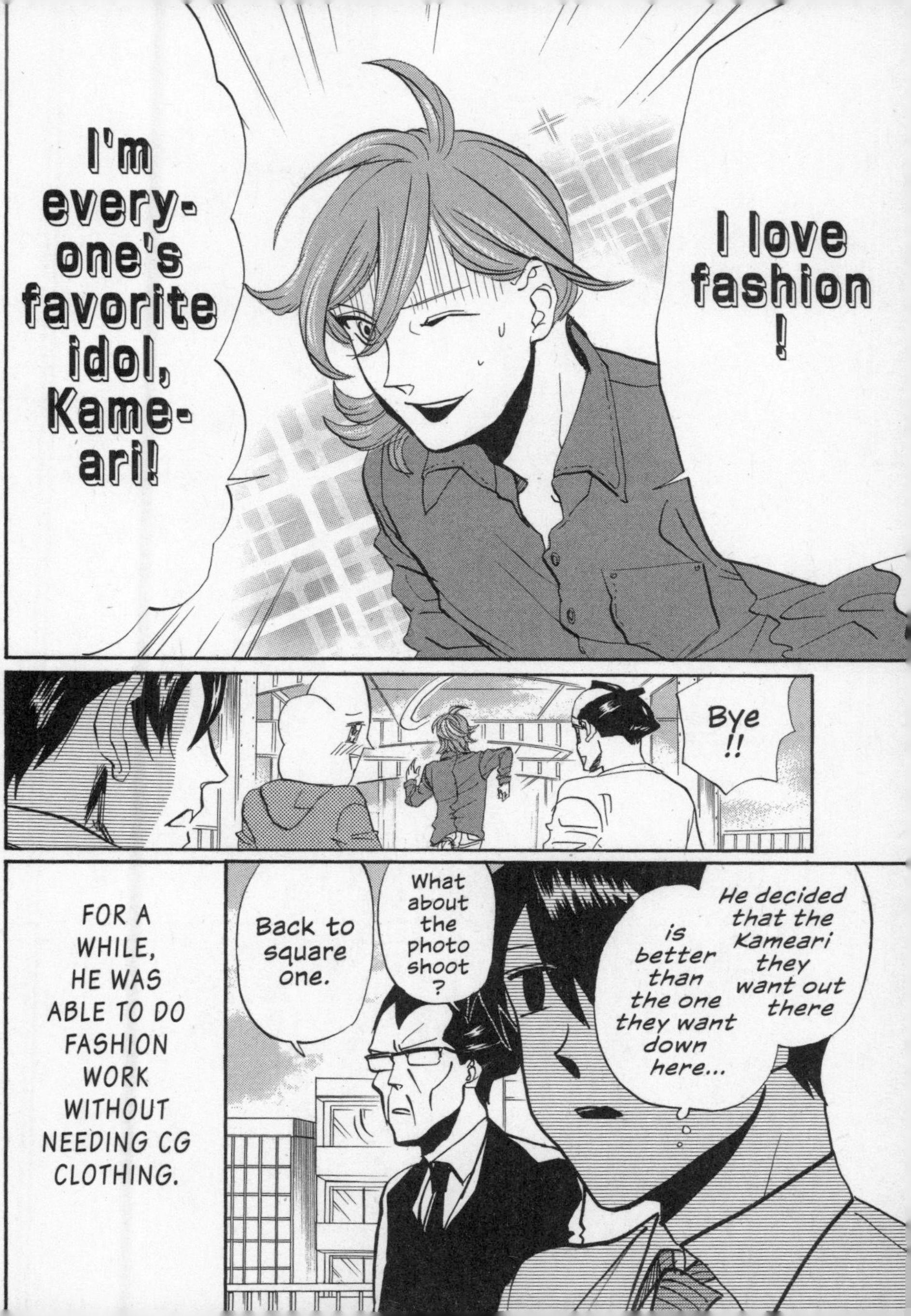
I love fashion!
I'm everyone's favorite idol, Kameari!
Bye!!
He decided that the Kameari they want out there is better than the one they want down here...
What about the photo shoot?
Back to square one.
FOR A WHILE, HE WAS ABLE TO DO FASHION WORK WITHOUT NEEDING CG CLOTHING.

ARAKAWA
UNDER
THE BRIDGE

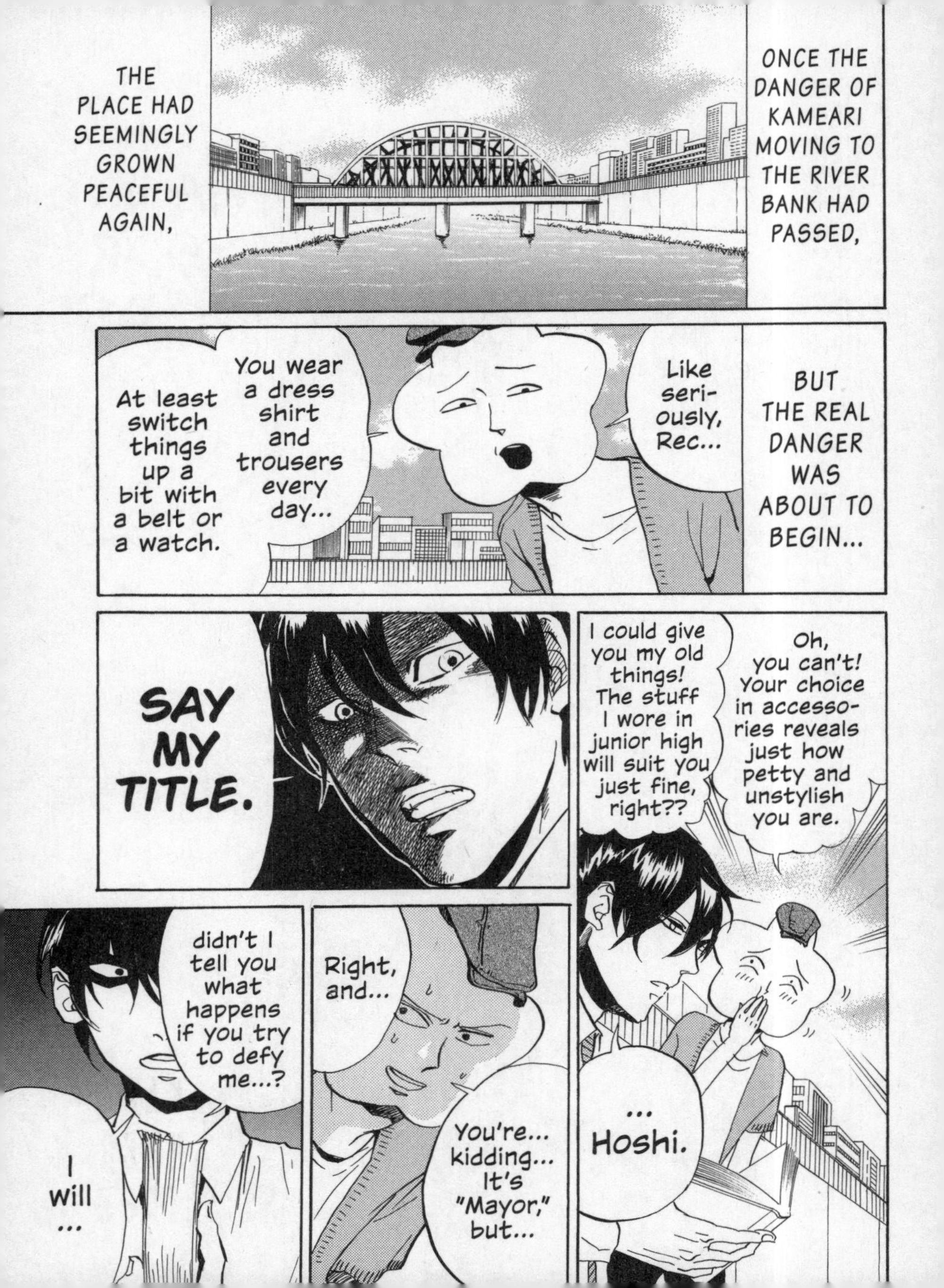
ONCE THE DANGER OF KAMEARI MOVING TO THE RIVER BANK HAD PASSED,
THE PLACE HAD SEEMINGLY GROWN PEACEFUL AGAIN,
BUT THE REAL DANGER WAS ABOUT TO BEGIN...
Like seriously, Rec...
You wear a dress shirt and trousers every day...
At least switch things up a bit with a belt or a watch.
Oh, you can't! Your choice in accessories reveals just how petty and unstylish you are.
I could give you my old things! The stuff I wore in junior high will suit you just fine, right??
... Hoshi.
SAY MY TITLE.
Right, and...
You're... kidding... It's "Mayor," but...
didn't I tell you what happens if you try to defy me...?
I will ...

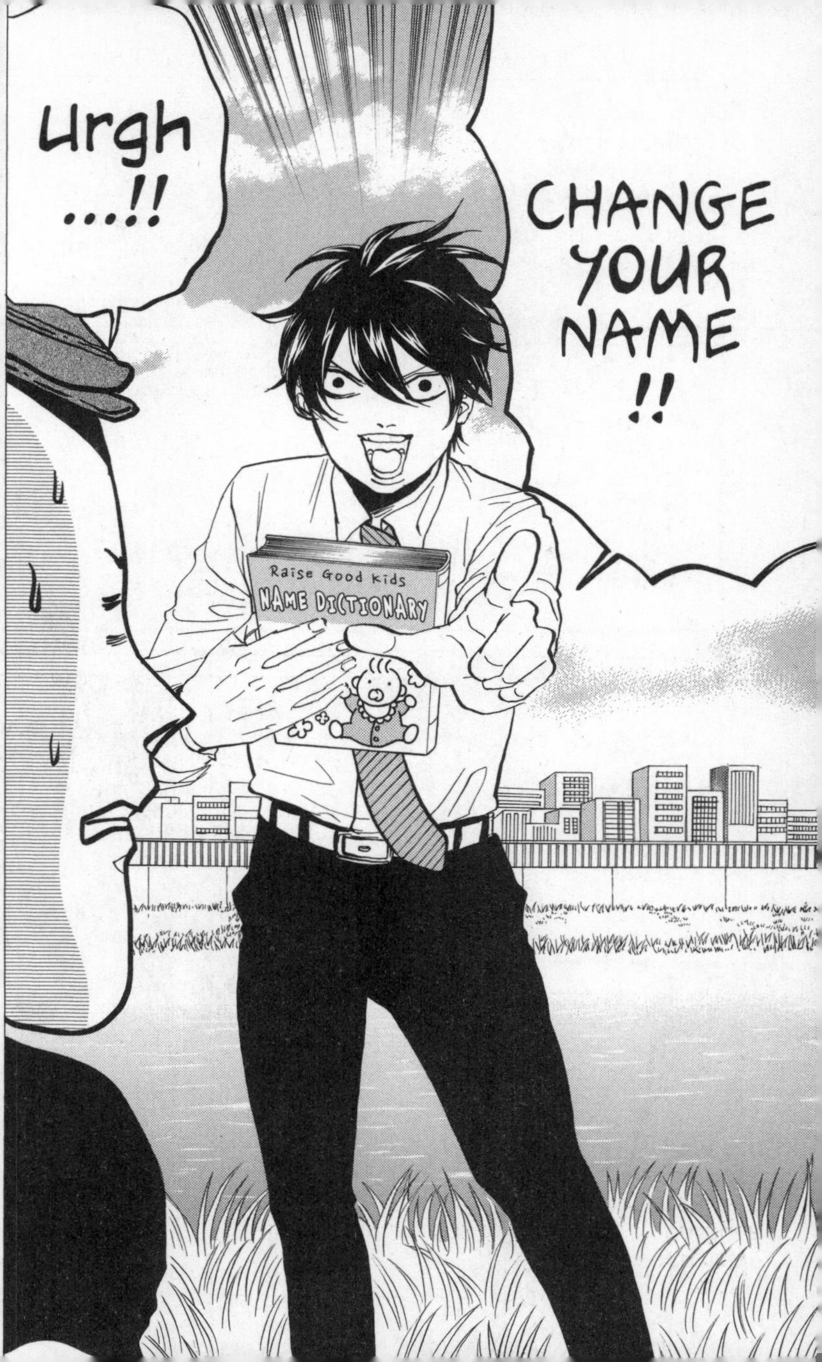

REC HAD REALIZED WHAT HIS GREATEST POWER AS MAYOR WAS...

Chapter 354: Despotic Reign of Terror

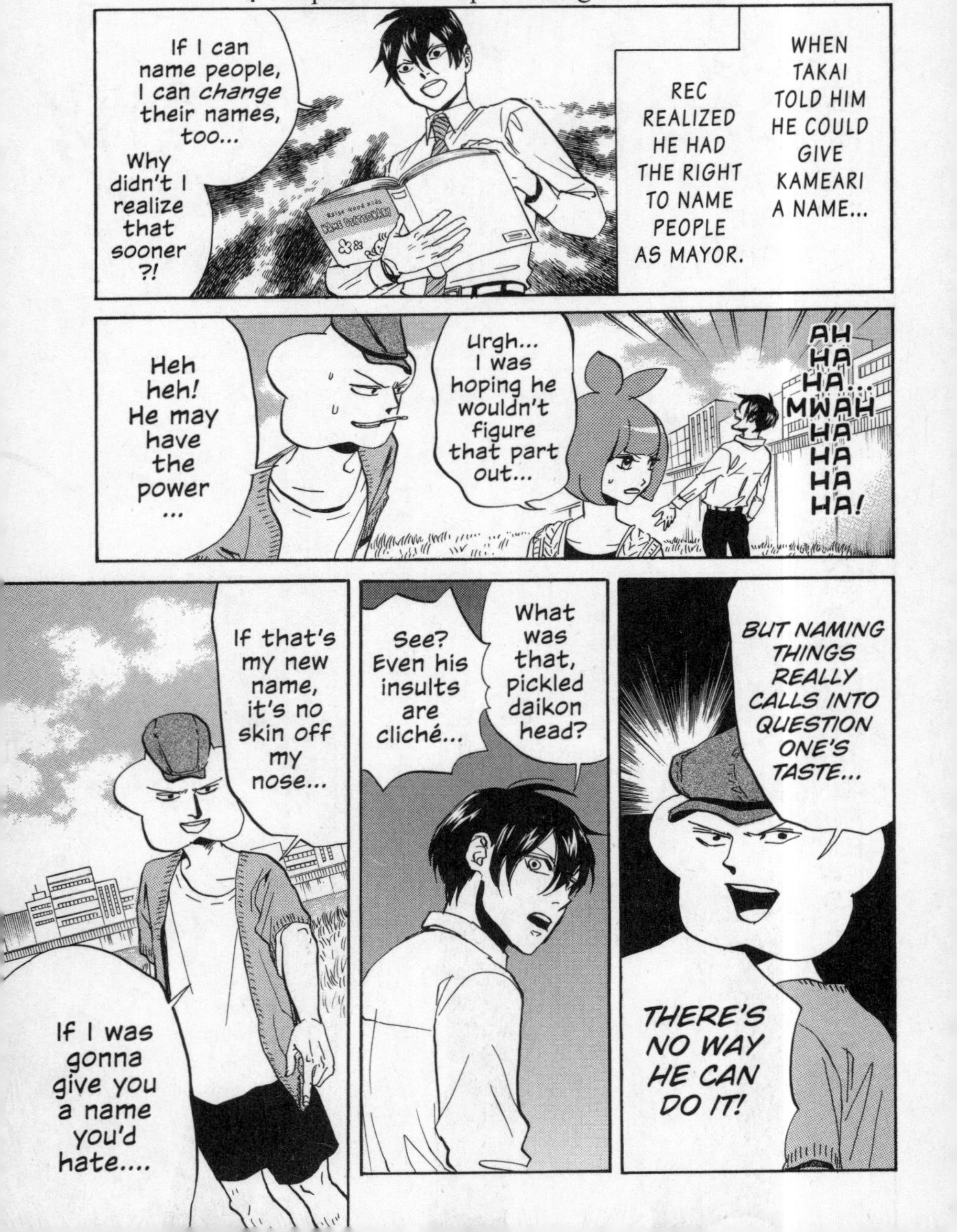
WHEN TAKAI TOLD HIM HE COULD GIVE KAMEARI A NAME...
REC REALIZED HE HAD THE RIGHT TO NAME PEOPLE AS MAYOR.
If I can name people, I can *change* their names, too...
Why didn't I realize that sooner?!
AH HA HA... MWAH HA HA HA HA HA!
Urgh... I was hoping he wouldn't figure that part out...
Heh heh! He may have the power...
BUT NAMING THINGS REALLY CALLS INTO QUESTION ONE'S TASTE...
THERE'S NO WAY HE CAN DO IT!
What was that, pickled daikon head?
See? Even his insults are cliché...
If that's my new name, it's no skin off my nose...
If I was gonna give you a name you'd hate....

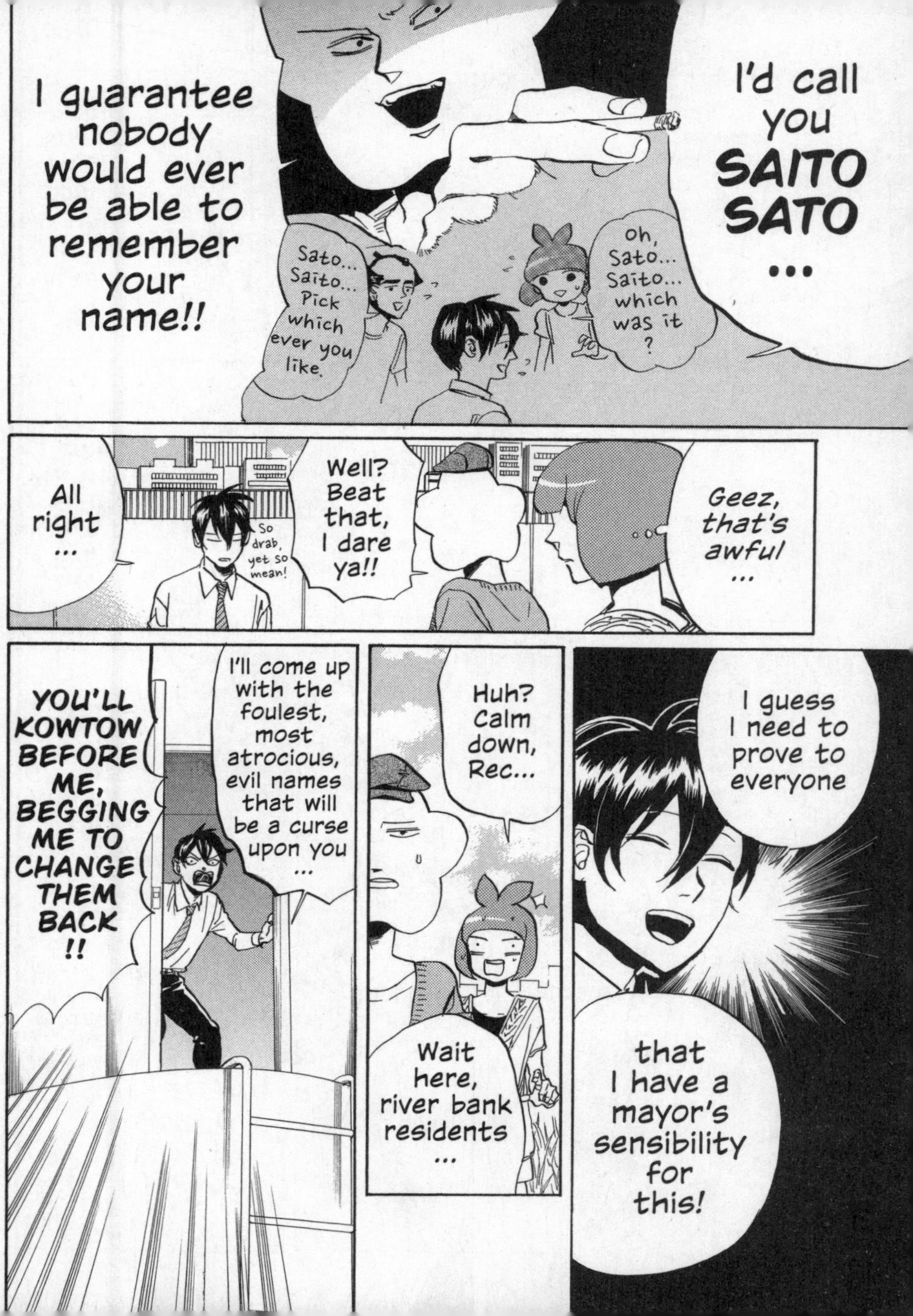
I'd call you SAITO SATO ...
Oh, Sato... Saito... which was it ?
Sato... Saito... Pick which ever you like.
I guarantee nobody would ever be able to remember your name!!
Geez, that's awful ...
Well? Beat that, I dare ya!!
So drab, yet so mean!
All right ...
I guess I need to prove to everyone
that I have a mayor's sensibility for this!
Huh? Calm down, Rec...
Wait here, river bank residents ...
I'll come up with the foulest, most atrocious, evil names that will be a curse upon you ...
YOU'LL KOWTOW BEFORE ME, BEGGING ME TO CHANGE THEM BACK !!

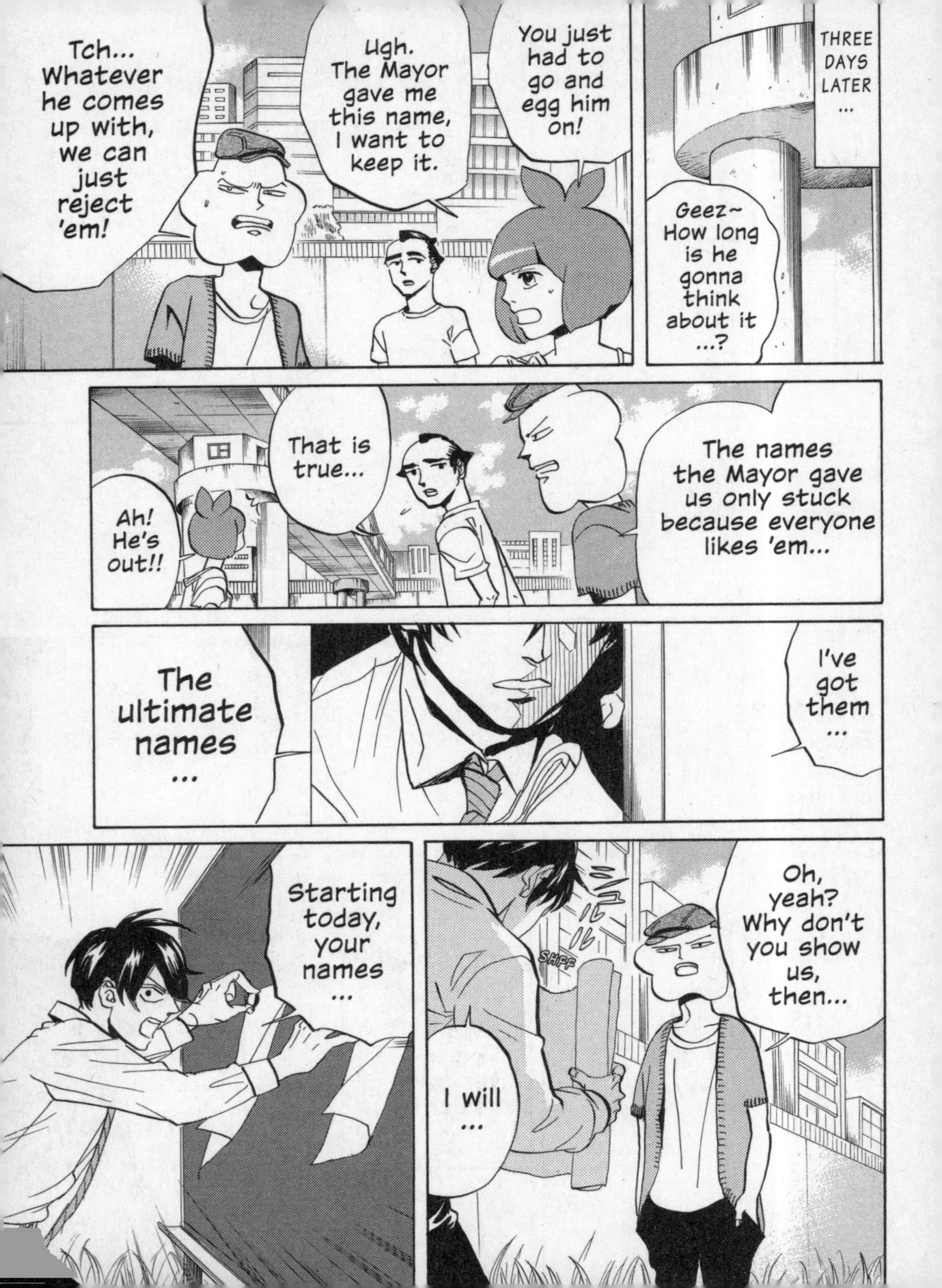
THREE DAYS LATER ...
Geez~ How long is he gonna think about it ...?
You just had to go and egg him on!
Ugh. The Mayor gave me this name, I want to keep it.
Tch... Whatever he comes up with, we can just reject 'em!
The names the Mayor gave us only stuck because everyone likes 'em...
That is true...
Ah! He's out!!
I've got them ...
The ultimate names ...
Oh, yeah? Why don't you show us, then...
SHFF
I will ...
Starting today, your names ...

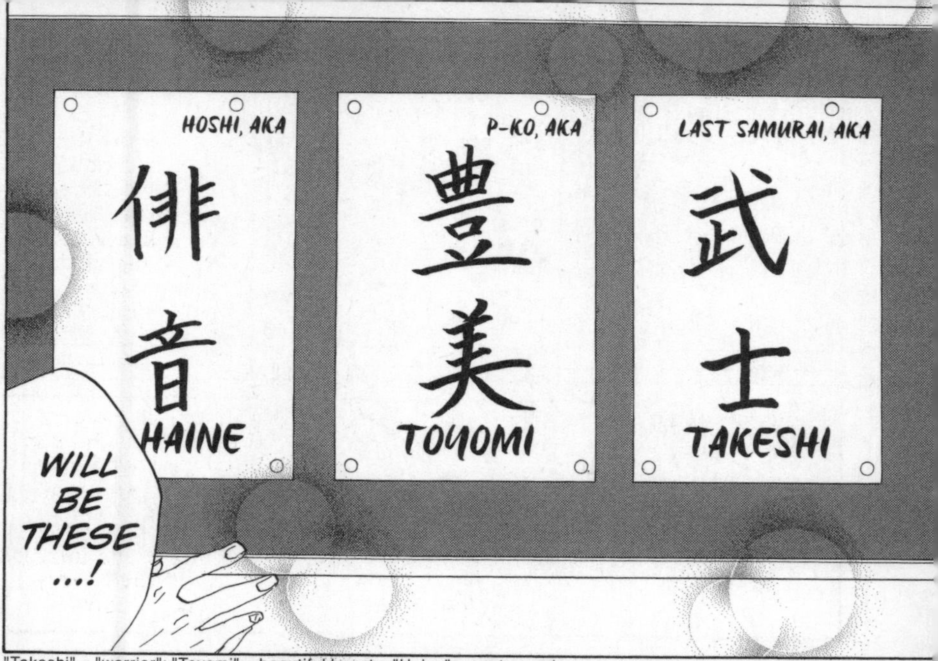
LAST SAMURAI, AKA
武士
TAKESHI
P-KO, AKA
豊美
TOYOMI
HOSHI, AKA
俳音
HAINE
WILL BE THESE ...!

"Takeshi" = "warrior"; "Toyomi" = beautiful bounty; "Haine" = poet sound

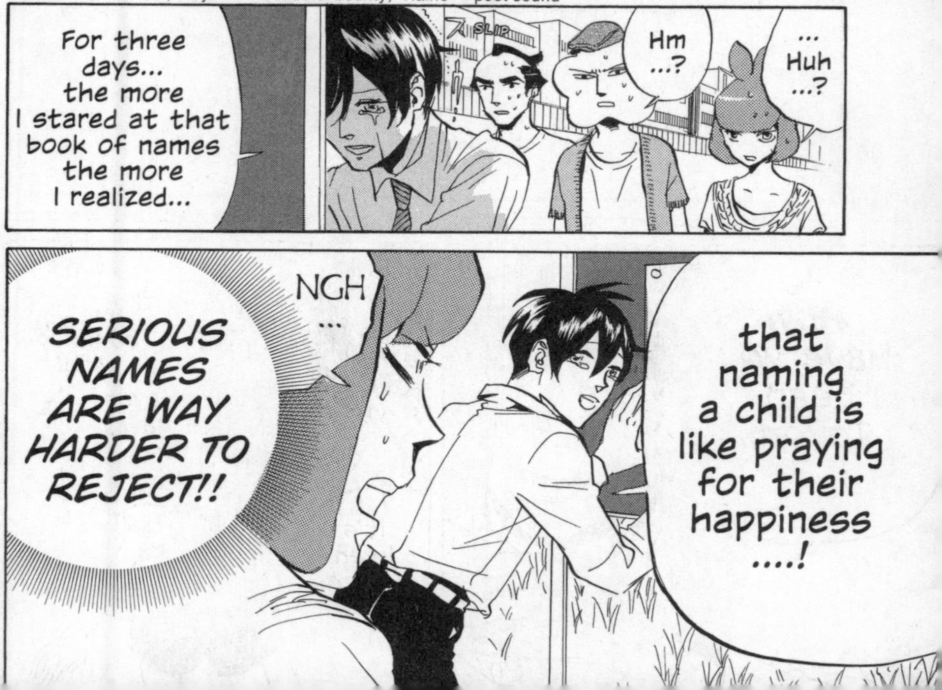
... Huh ...?
Hm ...?
SLIP
For three days... the more I stared at that book of names the more I realized...
that naming a child is like praying for their happiness ....!
NGH ...
SERIOUS NAMES ARE WAY HARDER TO REJECT!!

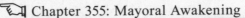

Chapter 355: Mayoral Awakening

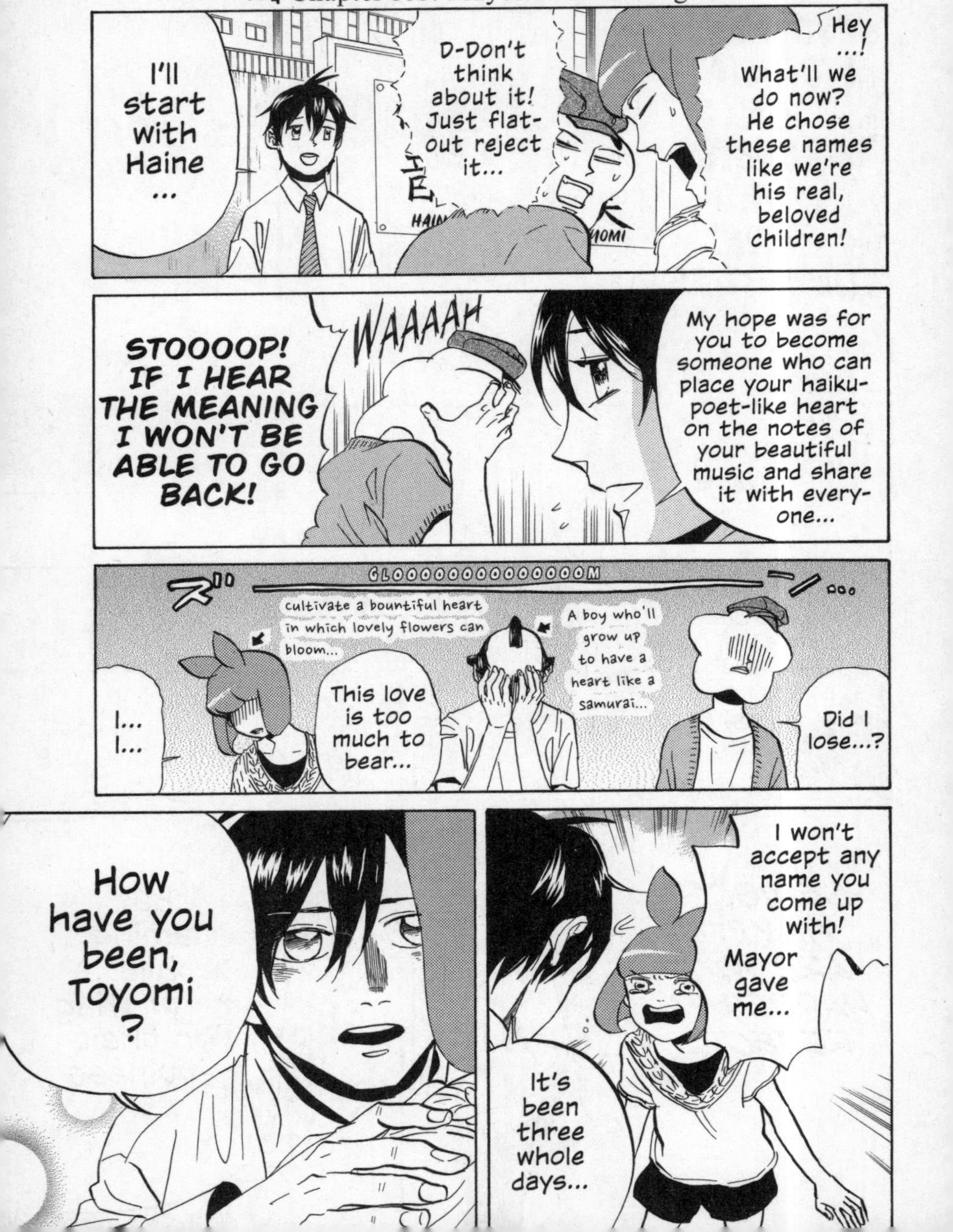
Hey...! What'll we do now? He chose these names like we're his real, beloved children!
D-Don't think about it! Just flat-out reject it...
I'll start with Haine...
My hope was for you to become someone who can place your haiku-poet-like heart on the notes of your beautiful music and share it with every-one...
WAAAAH
STOOOOP! IF I HEAR THE MEANING I WON'T BE ABLE TO GO BACK!
GLOOOOOOOOOOOOOOOM
Did I lose...?
A boy who'll grow up to have a heart like a samurai...
This love is too much to bear...
cultivate a bountiful heart in which lovely flowers can bloom...
I... I...
I won't accept any name you come up with!
Mayor gave me...
It's been three whole days...
How have you been, Toyomi?

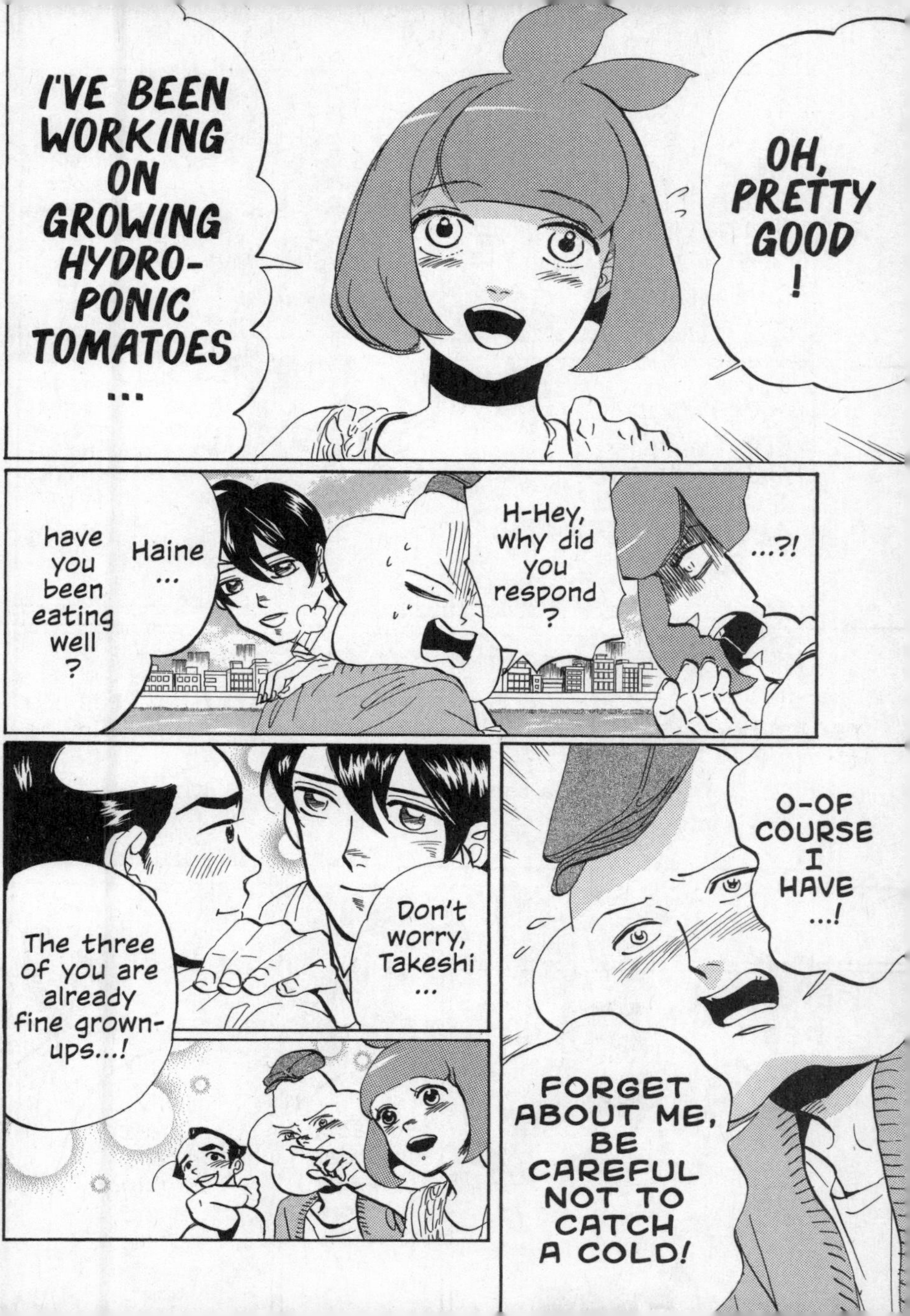
OH, PRETTY GOOD!
I'VE BEEN WORKING ON GROWING HYDRO-PONIC TOMATOES...
...?!
H-Hey, why did you respond?
Haine...
have you been eating well?
O-OF COURSE I HAVE...!
FORGET ABOUT ME, BE CAREFUL NOT TO CATCH A COLD!
Don't worry, Takeshi...
The three of you are already fine grown-ups...!

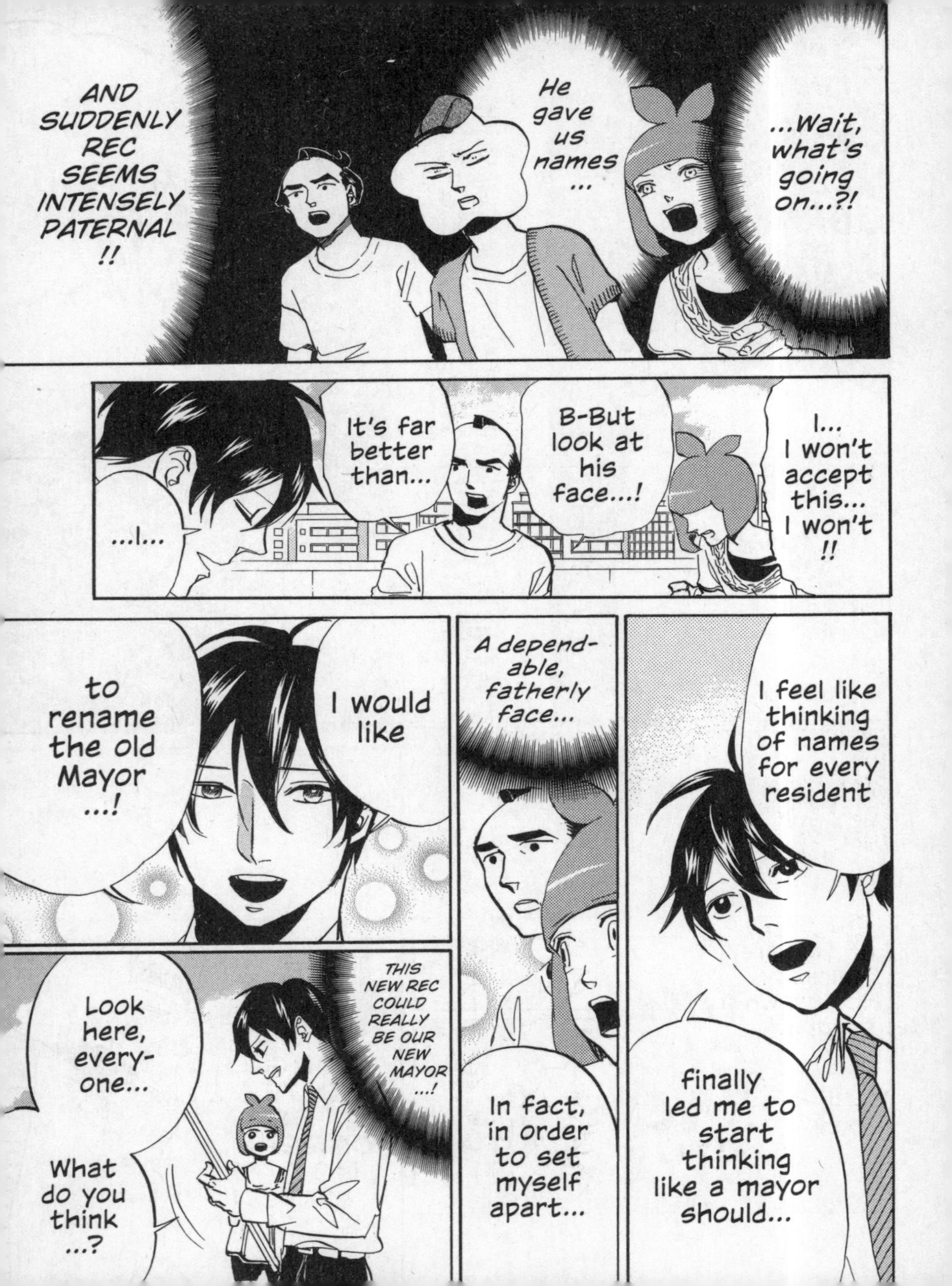
...Wait, what's going on...?!
He gave us names...
AND SUDDENLY REC SEEMS INTENSELY PATERNAL!!
I... I won't accept this... I won't!!
B-But look at his face...!
It's far better than...
...I...
I feel like thinking of names for every resident
finally led me to start thinking like a mayor should...
A dependable, fatherly face...
In fact, in order to set myself apart...
I would like
to rename the old Mayor...!
THIS NEW REC COULD REALLY BE OUR NEW MAYOR...!
Look here, everyone...
What do you think...?

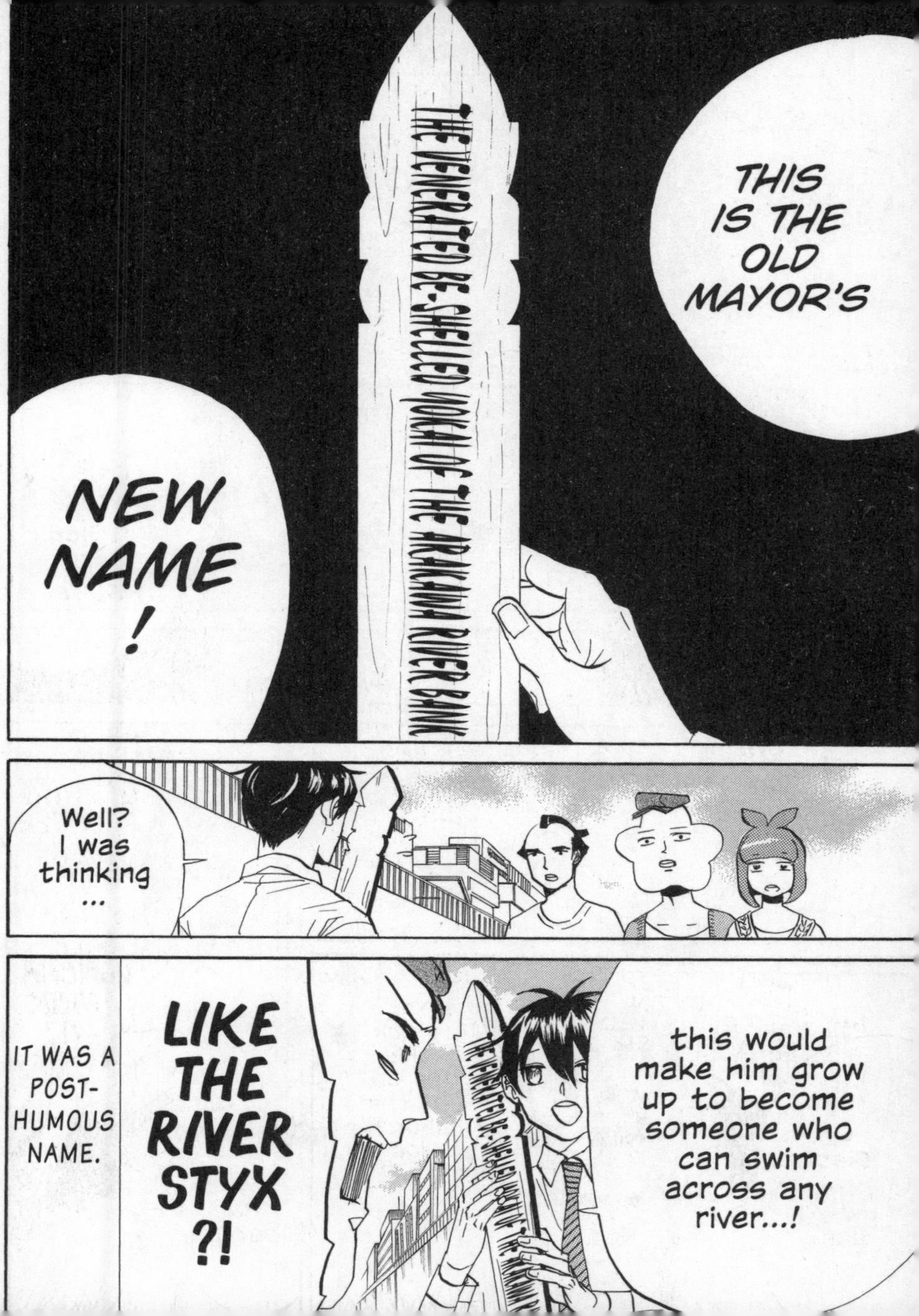
THIS IS THE OLD MAYOR'S
THE VENERATED BE-SHELLED YOKAI OF THE ARAKAWA RIVER BANK
NEW NAME!
Well? I was thinking...
this would make him grow up to become someone who can swim across any river...!
LIKE THE RIVER STYX?!
IT WAS A POST-HUMOUS NAME.

Chapter 356: A Special Name

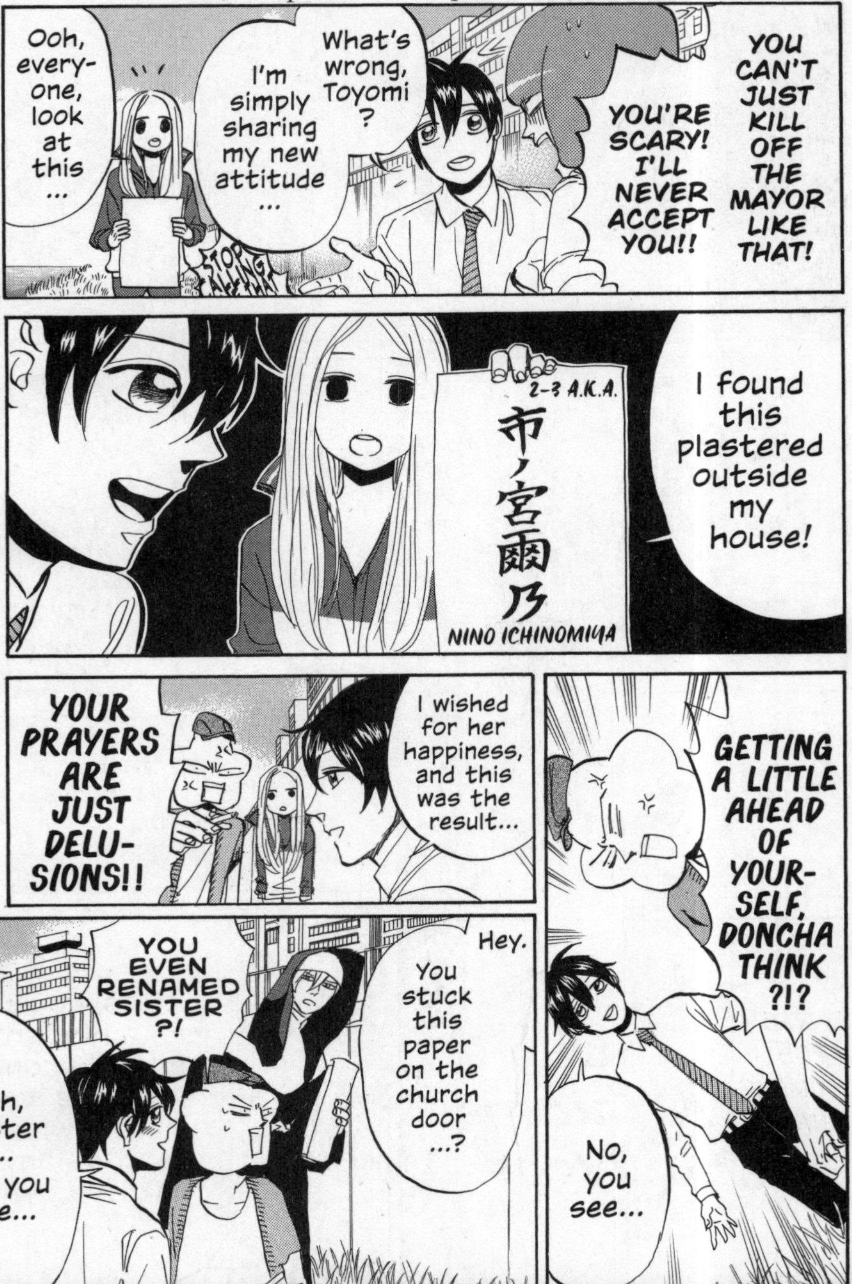

YOU CAN'T JUST KILL OFF THE MAYOR LIKE THAT!
YOU'RE SCARY! I'LL NEVER ACCEPT YOU!!
What's wrong, Toyomi?
I'm simply sharing my new attitude...
Ooh, everyone, look at this...
I found this plastered outside my house!
2-3 A.K.A.
市ノ宮爾乃
NINO ICHINOMIYA
GETTING A LITTLE AHEAD OF YOURSELF, DONCHA THINK?!?
No, you see...
I wished for her happiness, and this was the result...
YOUR PRAYERS ARE JUST DELUSIONS!!
Hey.
You stuck this paper on the church door...?
YOU EVEN RENAMED SISTER?!
Oh, Sister... did you like...

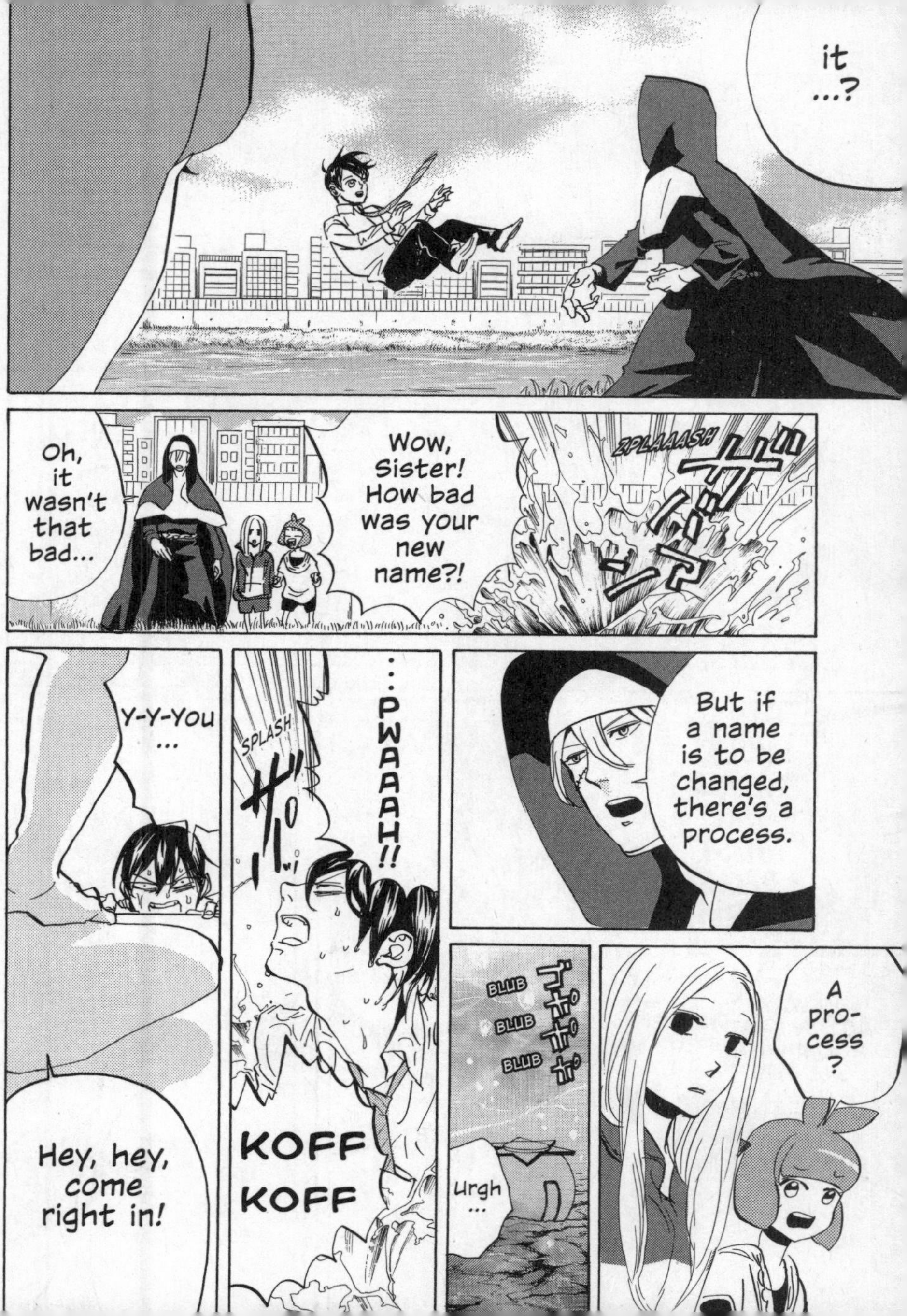
it ...?
ZPLAAASH
Wow, Sister! How bad was your new name?!
Oh, it wasn't that bad...
But if a name is to be changed, there's a process.
A pro-cess?
BLUB
BLUB
BLUB
Urgh ...
SPLASH
...PWAAAAH!!
KOFF
KOFF
Y-Y-You ...
Hey, hey, come right in!

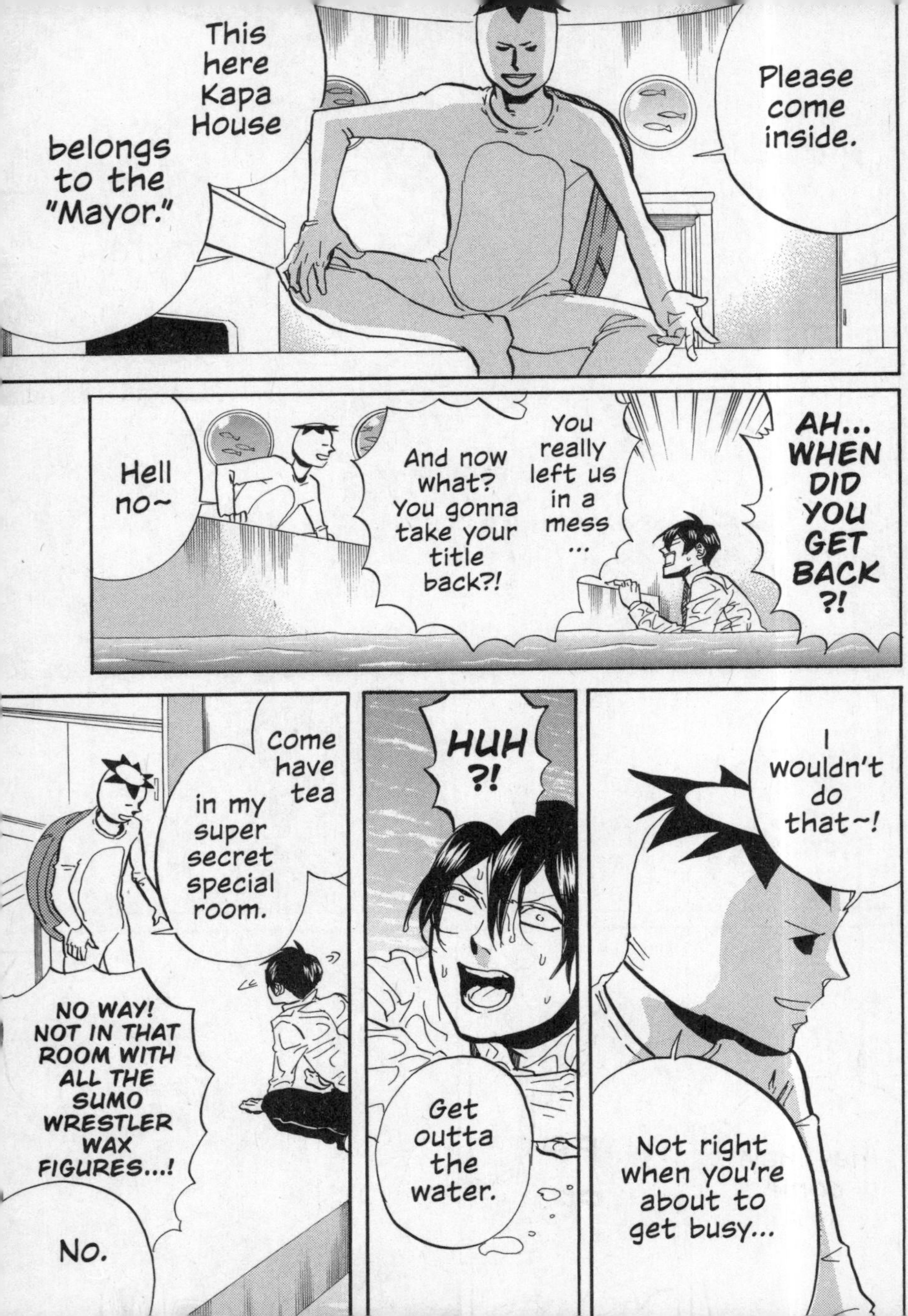
Please come inside.
This here Kapa House
belongs to the "Mayor."
AH... WHEN DID YOU GET BACK?!
You really left us in a mess ...
And now what? You gonna take your title back?!
Hell no~
I wouldn't do that~!
Not right when you're about to get busy...
HUH?!
Get outta the water.
Come have tea in my super secret special room.
NO WAY! NOT IN THAT ROOM WITH ALL THE SUMO WRESTLER WAX FIGURES...!
No.

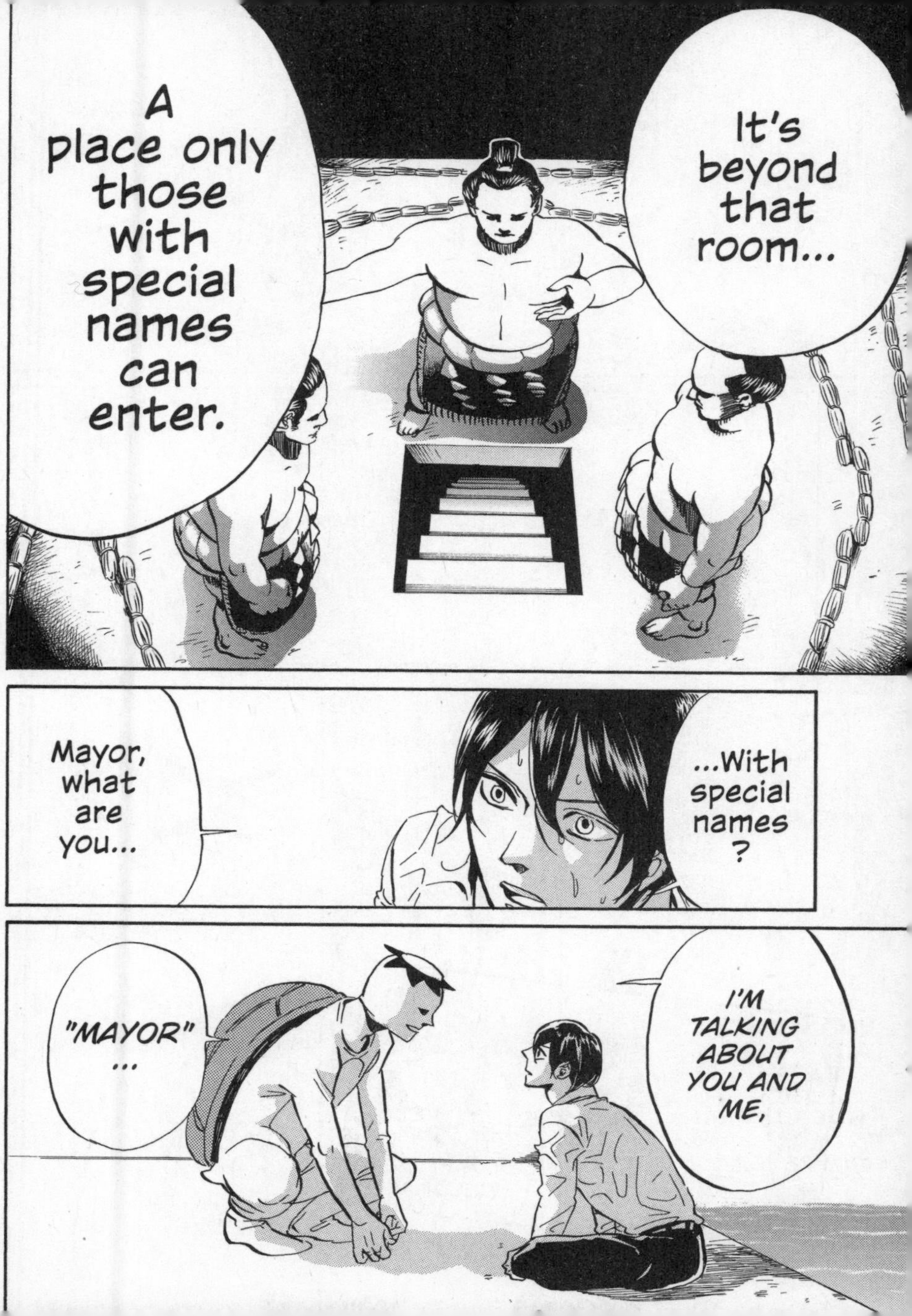
It's beyond that room...
A place only those with special names can enter.
...With special names?
Mayor, what are you...
I'M TALKING ABOUT YOU AND ME,
"MAYOR" ...

ARAKAWA
UNDER
THE BRIDGE

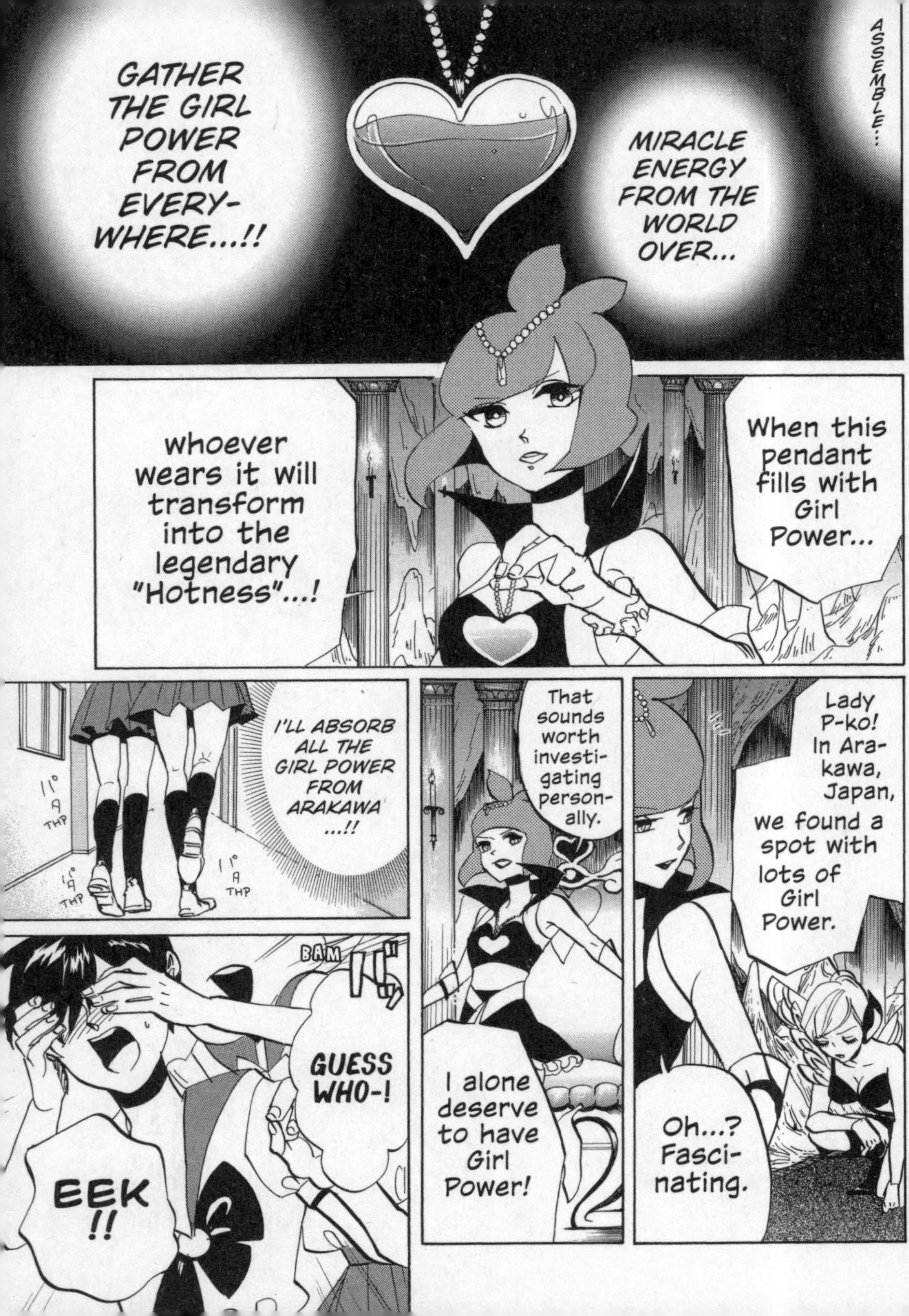
ASSEMBLE...
MIRACLE ENERGY FROM THE WORLD OVER...
GATHER THE GIRL POWER FROM EVERY-WHERE...!!
When this pendant fills with Girl Power...
whoever wears it will transform into the legendary "Hotness"...!
Lady P-ko! In Ara-kawa, Japan, we found a spot with lots of Girl Power.
Oh...? Fasci-nating.
That sounds worth investi-gating person-ally.
I alone deserve to have Girl Power!
I'LL ABSORB ALL THE GIRL POWER FROM ARAKAWA ...!!
THP
THP
THP
BAM
GUESS WHO-!
EEK !!

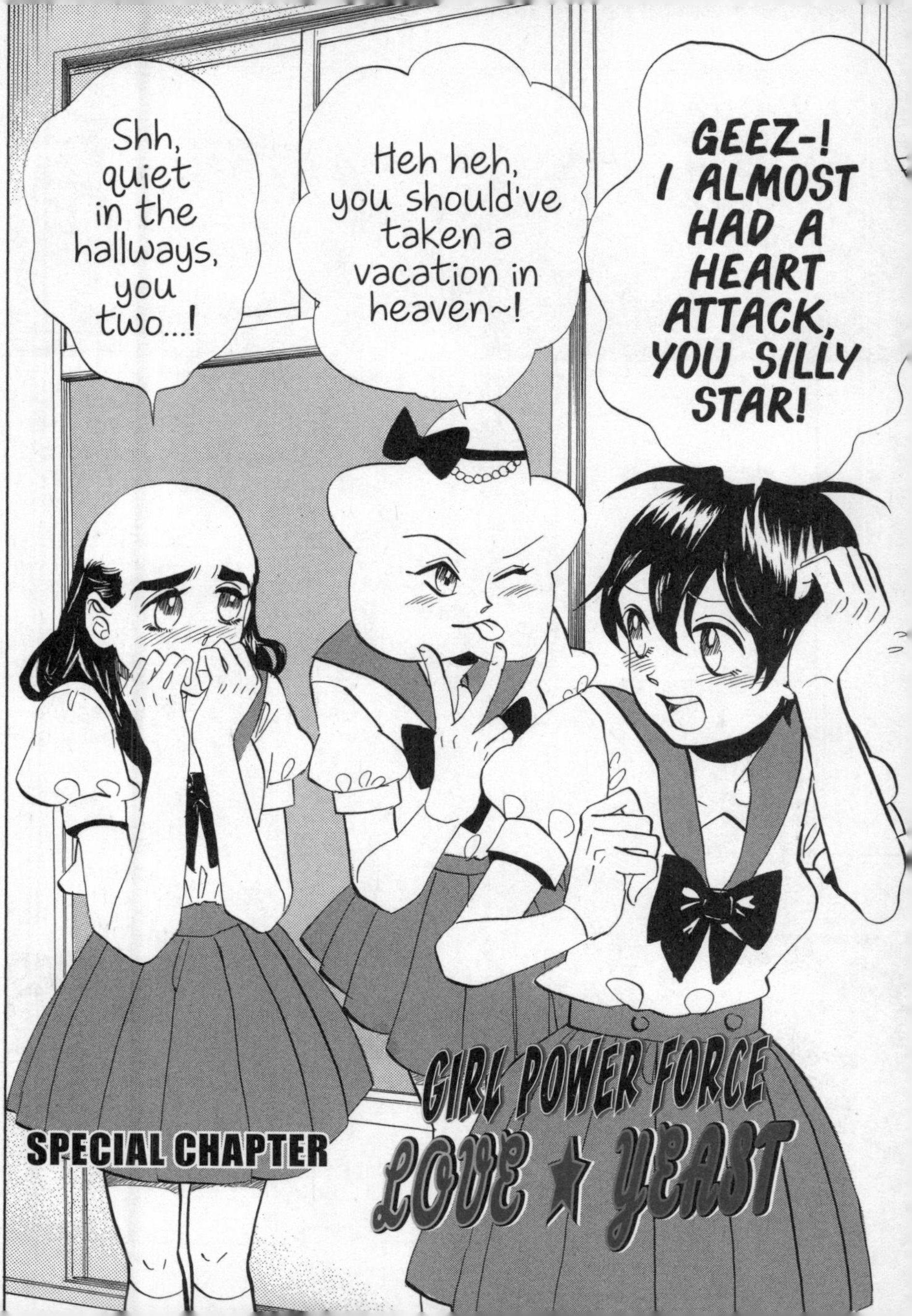
GEEZ-! I ALMOST HAD A HEART ATTACK, YOU SILLY STAR!
Heh heh, you should've taken a vacation in heaven~!
Shh, quiet in the hallways, you two...!
GIRL POWER FORCE LOVE ★ YEAST
SPECIAL CHAPTER

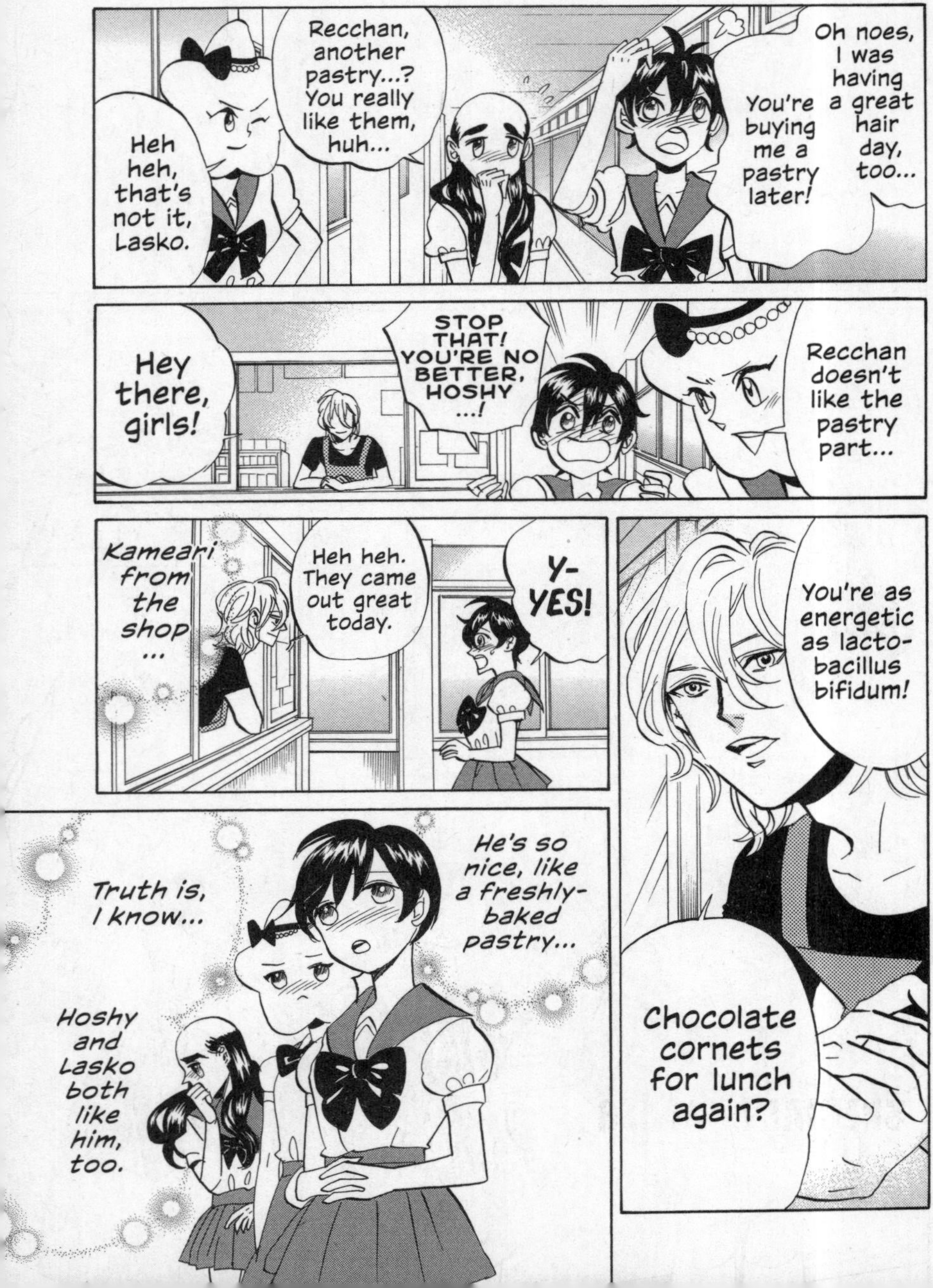
Oh noes, I was having a great hair day, too...
You're buying me a pastry later!
Recchan, another pastry...? You really like them, huh...
Heh heh, that's not it, Lasko.
Recchan doesn't like the pastry part...
STOP THAT! YOU'RE NO BETTER, HOSHY ...!
Hey there, girls!
You're as energetic as lacto-bacillus bifidum!
Chocolate cornets for lunch again?
Y-YES!
Heh heh. They came out great today.
Kameari from the shop ...
He's so nice, like a freshly-baked pastry...
Truth is, I know...
Hoshy and Lasko both like him, too.

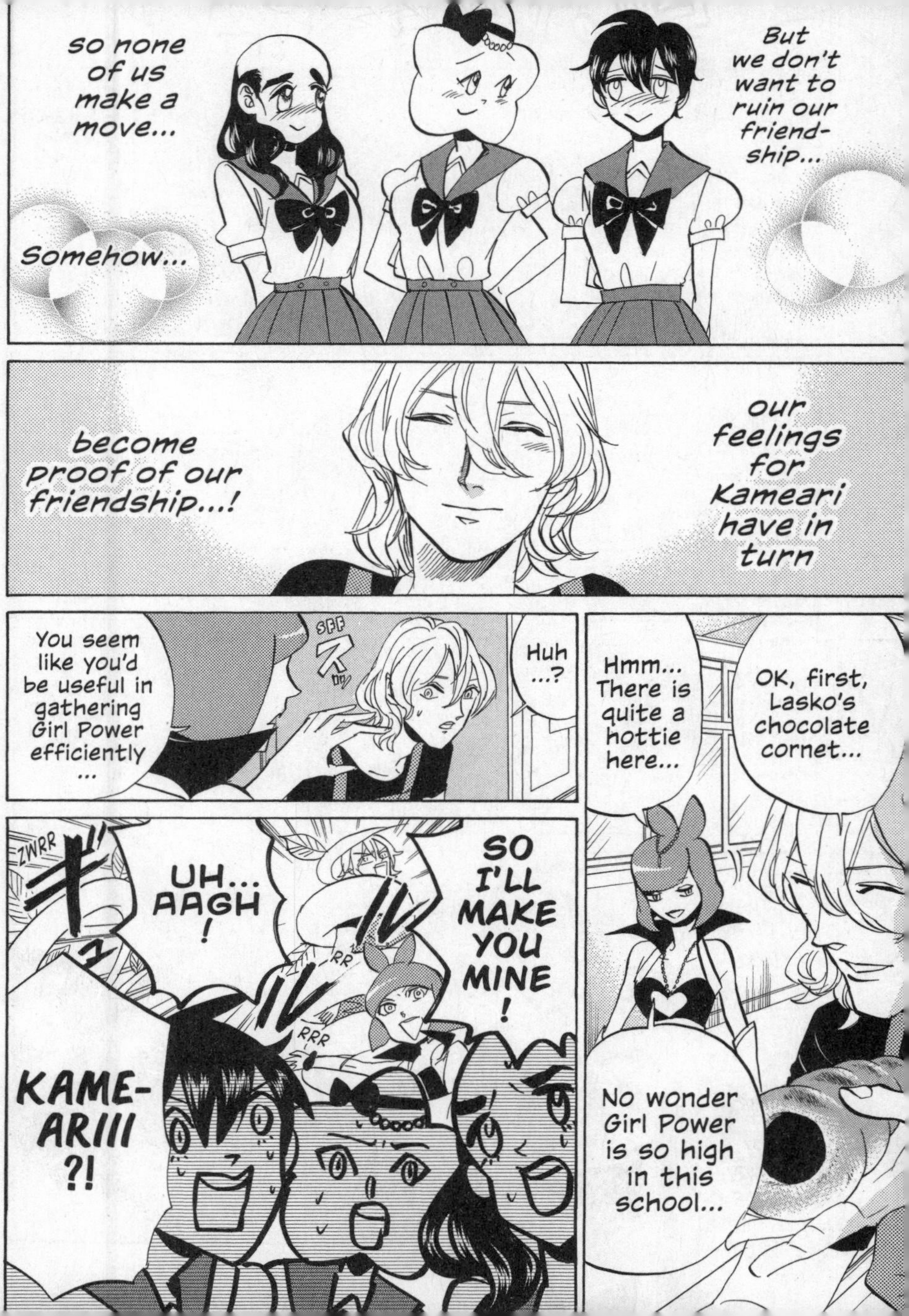
But we don't want to ruin our friendship...
so none of us make a move...
Somehow...
our feelings for Kameari have in turn
become proof of our friendship...!
OK, first, Lasko's chocolate cornet...
Hmm... There is quite a hottie here...
No wonder Girl Power is so high in this school...
Huh ...?
SFF
You seem like you'd be useful in gathering Girl Power efficiently ...
SO I'LL MAKE YOU MINE!
UH... AAGH!
ZWRR
RR
RRR
KAME-ARIII ?!

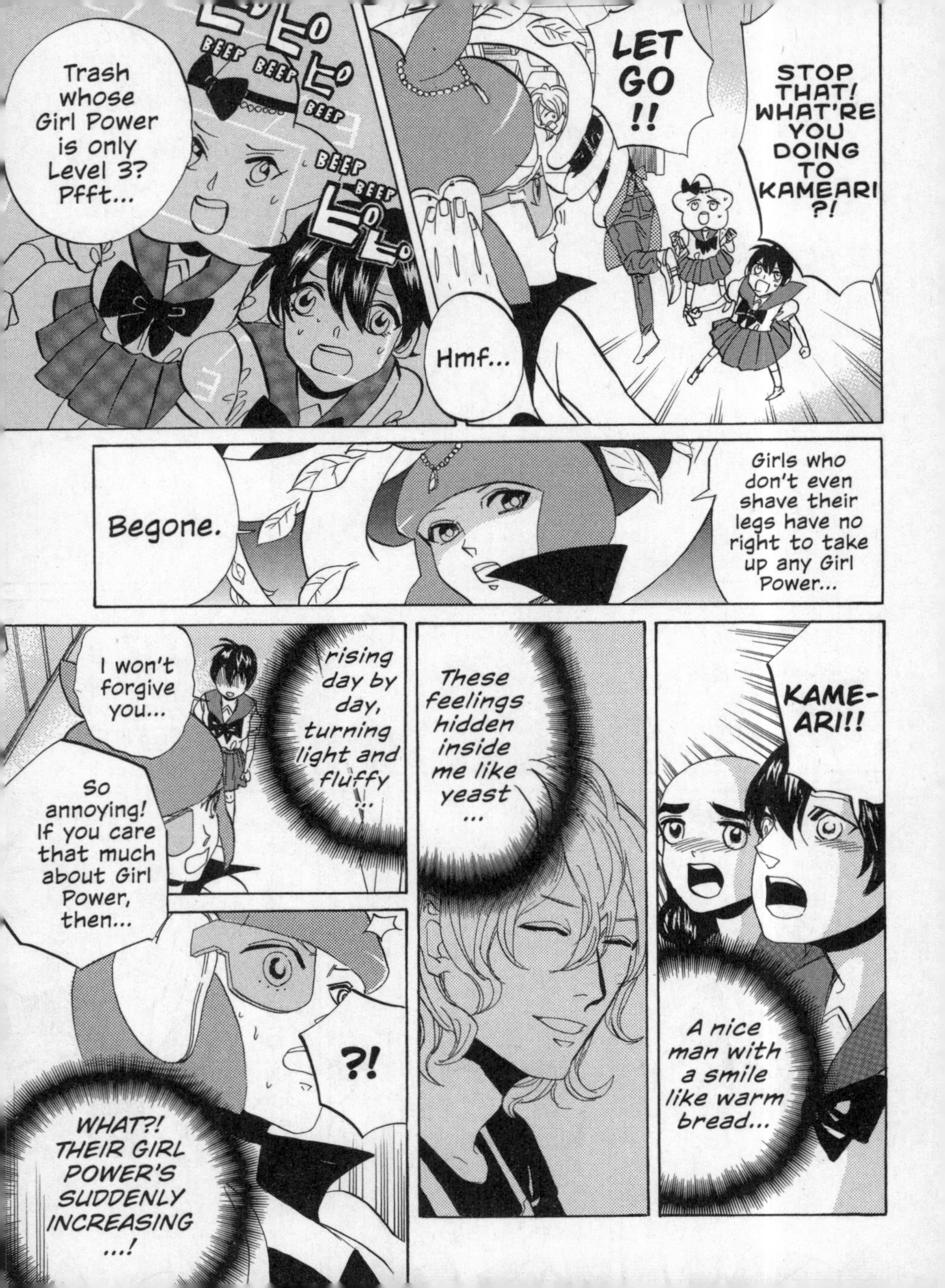
STOP THAT! WHAT'RE YOU DOING TO KAMEARI?!
LET GO!!
Hmf...
BEEP BEEP BEEP
BEEP BEEP
Trash whose Girl Power is only Level 3? Pfft...
Girls who don't even shave their legs have no right to take up any Girl Power...
Begone.
KAME-ARI!!
A nice man with a smile like warm bread...
These feelings hidden inside me like yeast...
rising day by day, turning light and fluffy...
I won't forgive you...
So annoying! If you care that much about Girl Power, then...
?!
WHAT?! THEIR GIRL POWER'S SUDDENLY INCREASING...!

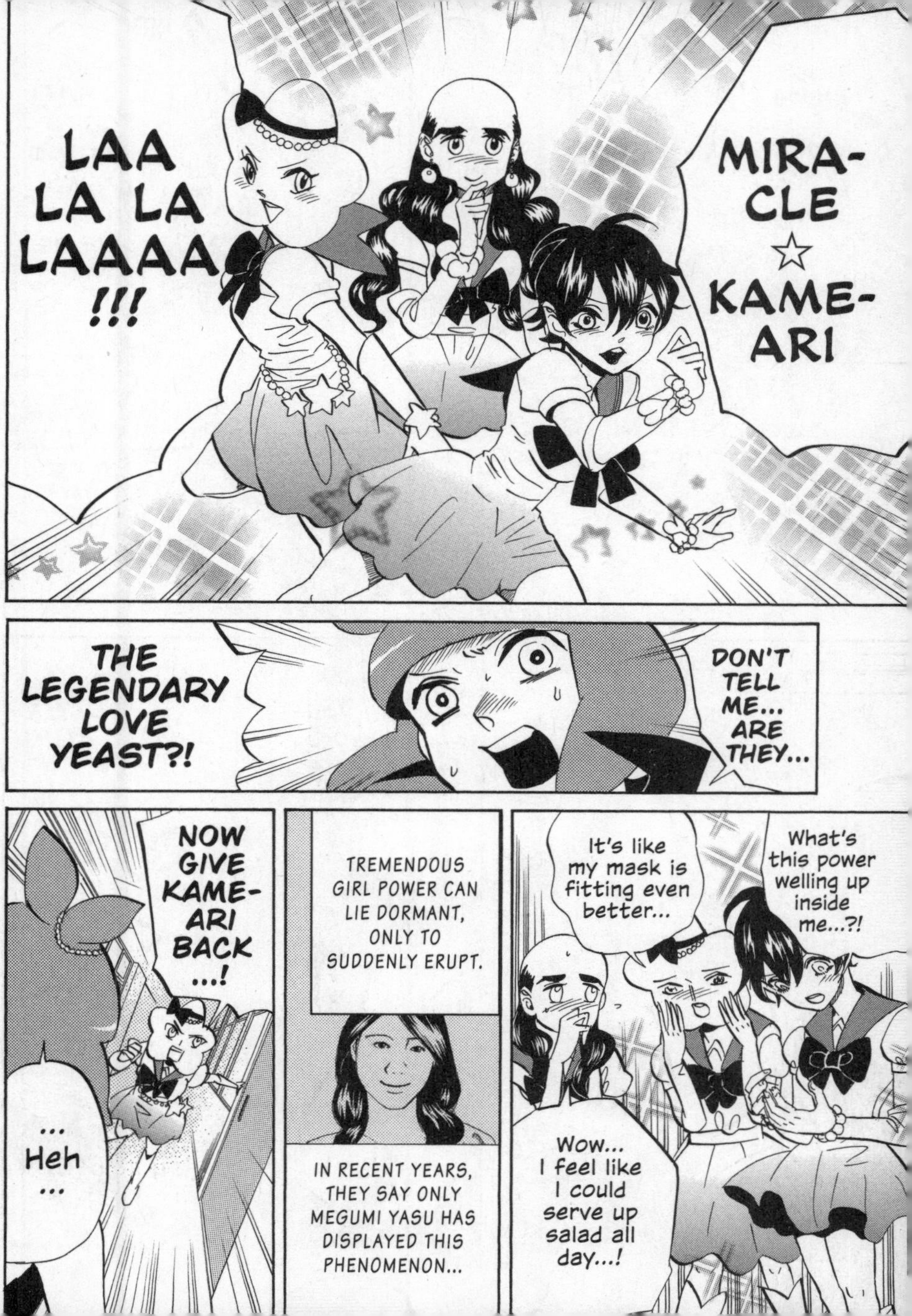
MIRA-CLE ☆ KAME-ARI
LAA LA LA LAAAA!!!
DON'T TELL ME... ARE THEY...
THE LEGENDARY LOVE YEAST?!
What's this power welling up inside me...?!
It's like my mask is fitting even better...
Wow... I feel like I could serve up salad all day...!
TREMENDOUS GIRL POWER CAN LIE DORMANT, ONLY TO SUDDENLY ERUPT.
IN RECENT YEARS, THEY SAY ONLY MEGUMI YASU HAS DISPLAYED THIS PHENOMENON...
NOW GIVE KAME-ARI BACK...!
...Heh...

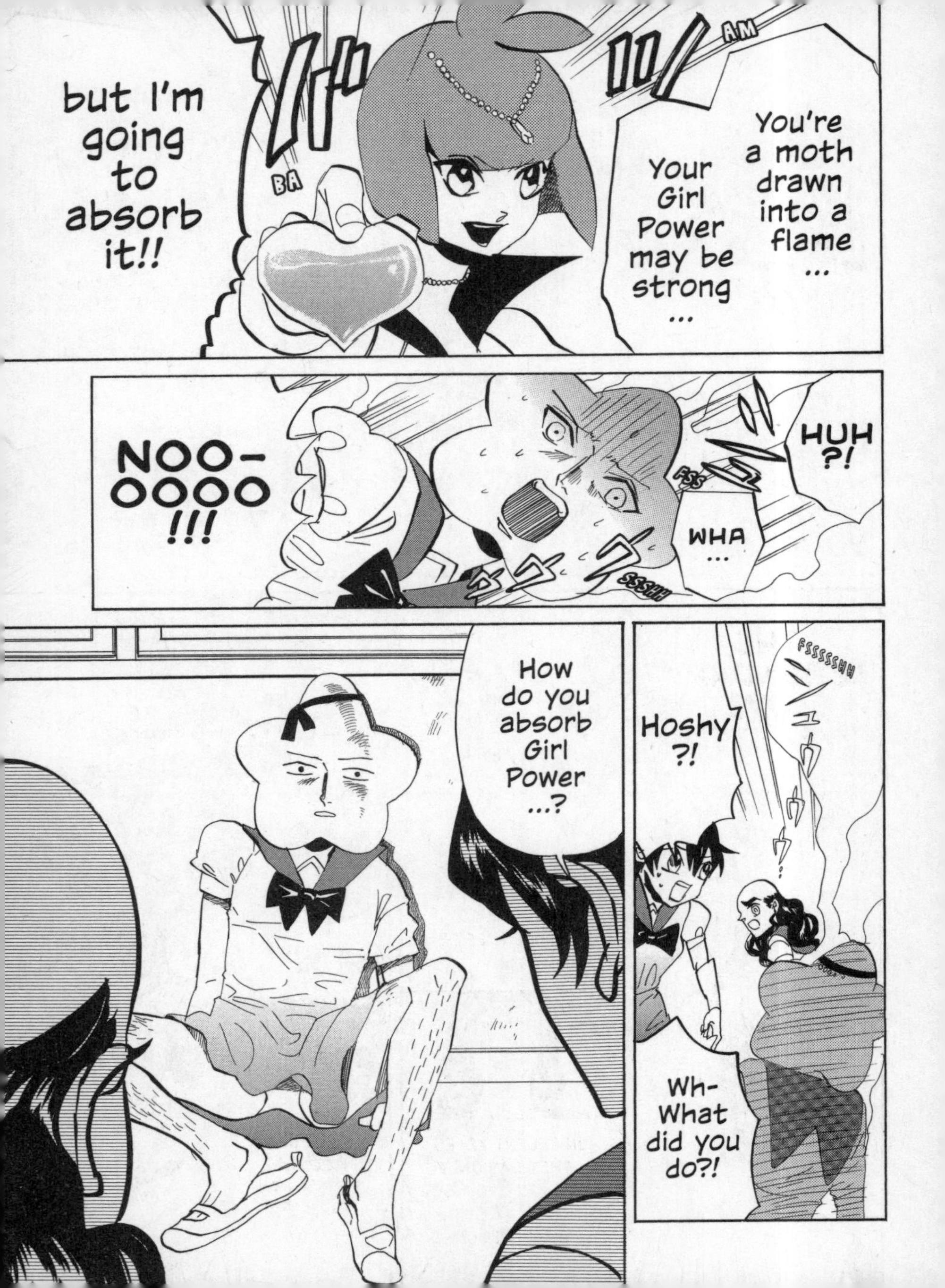
AM
You're a moth drawn into a flame ...
Your Girl Power may be strong ...
BA
but I'm going to absorb it!!
HUH ?!
FSS
WHA ...
NOO-OOOO !!!
FSSSSSHH
Hoshy ?!
Wh- What did you do?!
How do you absorb Girl Power ...?

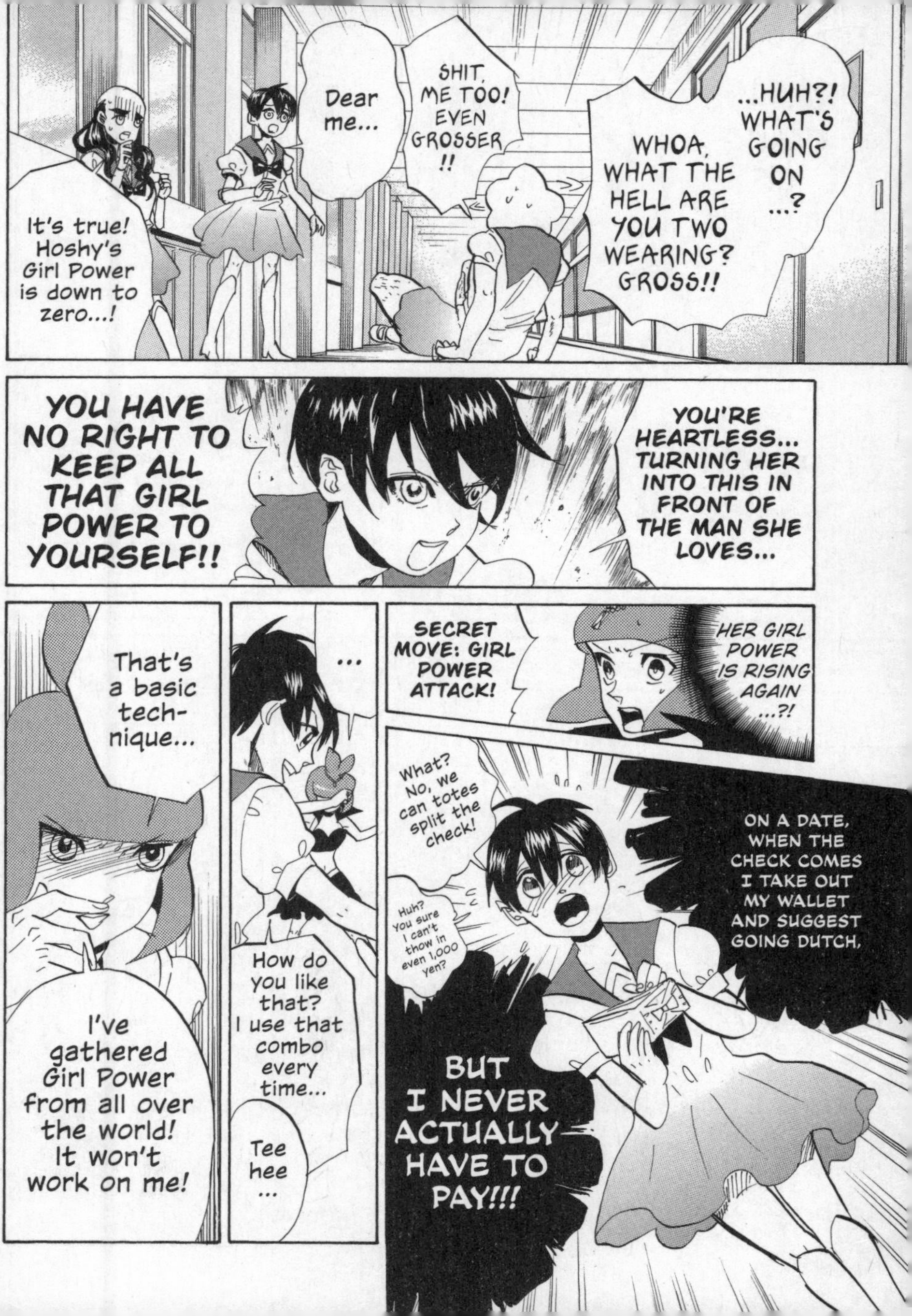
...HUH?! WHAT'S GOING ON ...?
WHOA, WHAT THE HELL ARE YOU TWO WEARING? GROSS!!
SHIT, ME TOO! EVEN GROSSER !!
Dear me...
It's true! Hoshy's Girl Power is down to zero...!
YOU'RE HEARTLESS... TURNING HER INTO THIS IN FRONT OF THE MAN SHE LOVES...
YOU HAVE NO RIGHT TO KEEP ALL THAT GIRL POWER TO YOURSELF!!
HER GIRL POWER IS RISING AGAIN ...?!
SECRET MOVE: GIRL POWER ATTACK!
ON A DATE, WHEN THE CHECK COMES I TAKE OUT MY WALLET AND SUGGEST GOING DUTCH,
What? No, we can totes split the check!
Huh? You sure I can't thow in even 1,000 yen?
BUT I NEVER ACTUALLY HAVE TO PAY!!!
...
How do you like that? I use that combo every time...
Tee hee ...
That's a basic tech-nique...
I've gathered Girl Power from all over the world! It won't work on me!

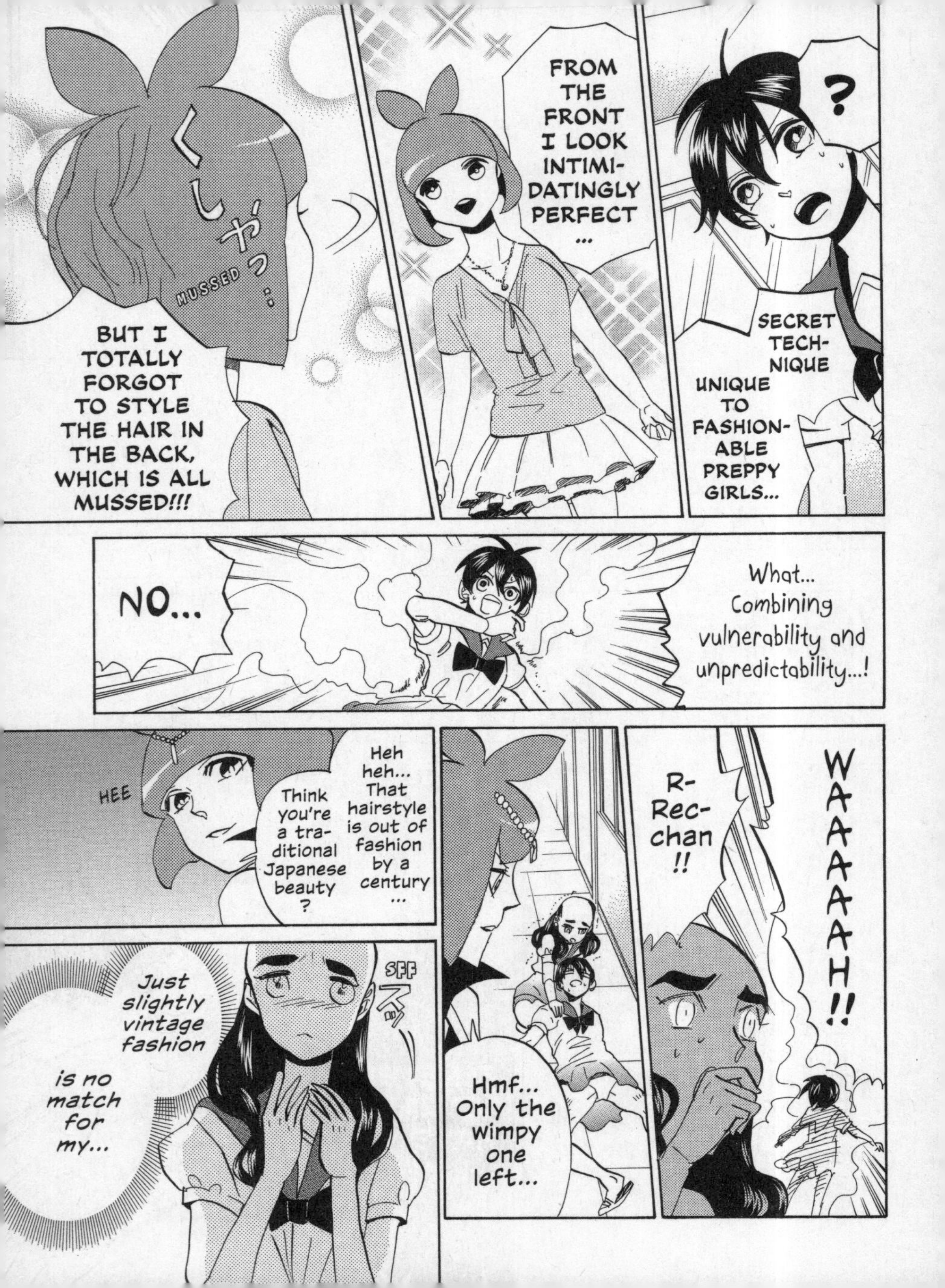
?
SECRET TECHNIQUE
UNIQUE TO FASHIONABLE PREPPY GIRLS...
FROM THE FRONT I LOOK INTIMIDATINGLY PERFECT...
くしゃっ
MUSSED
BUT I TOTALLY FORGOT TO STYLE THE HAIR IN THE BACK, WHICH IS ALL MUSSED!!!
What... Combining vulnerability and unpredictability...!
NO...
WAAAAAAH!!
R-Rec-chan!!
Hmf... Only the wimpy one left...
Heh heh... That hairstyle is out of fashion by a century...
Think you're a traditional Japanese beauty?
HEE
SFF
スッ
Just slightly vintage fashion
is no match for my...

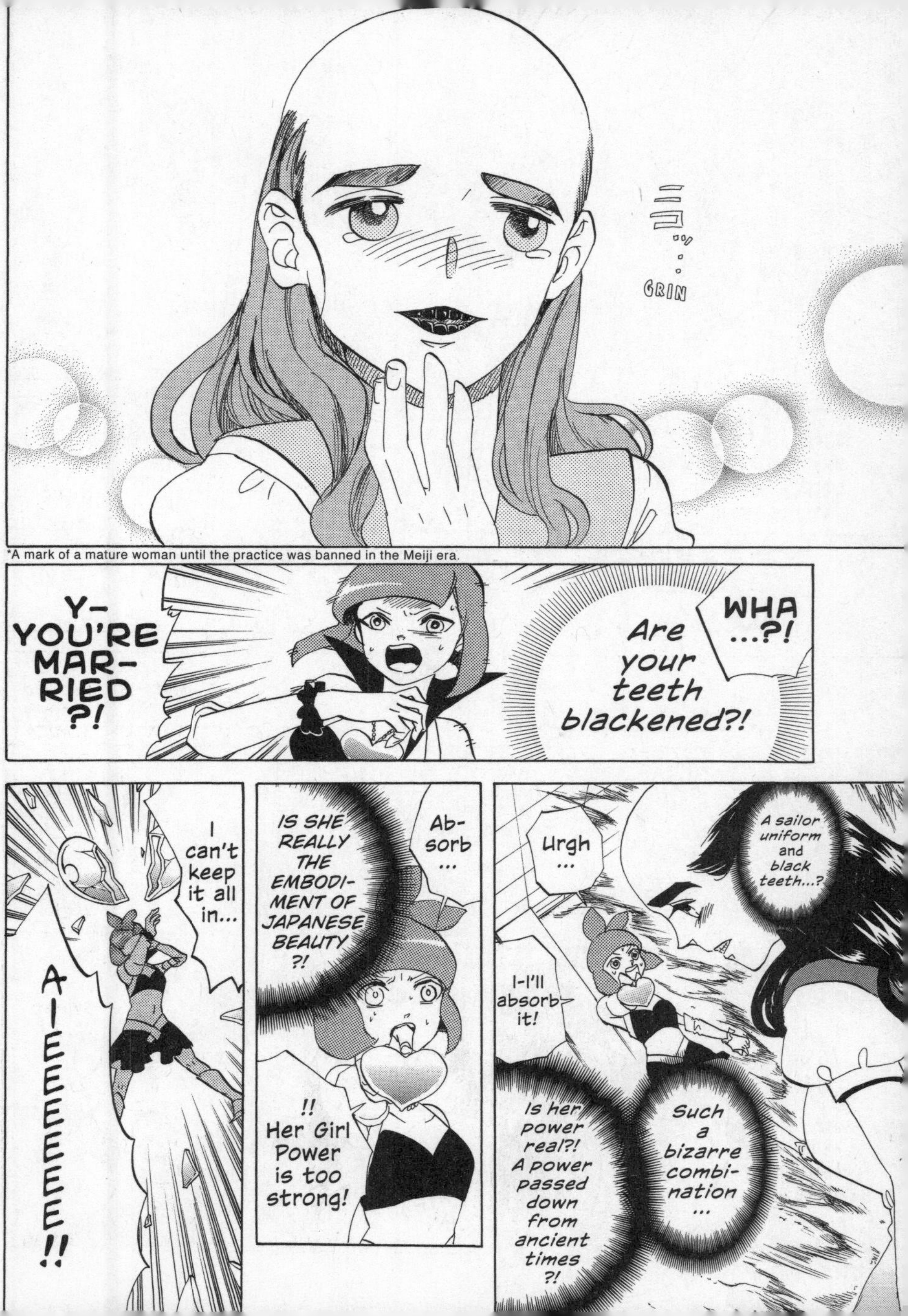
ニコッ
GRIN
WHA...?!
Are your teeth blackened?!
Y-YOU'RE MARRIED?!
A sailor uniform and black teeth...?
Urgh...
I-I'll absorb it!
Such a bizarre combination...
Is her power real?! A power passed down from ancient times?!
Absorb...
IS SHE REALLY THE EMBODIMENT OF JAPANESE BEAUTY?!
!! Her Girl Power is too strong!
I can't keep it all in...
AIEEEEEEE!!

*A mark of a mature woman until the practice was banned in the Meiji era.

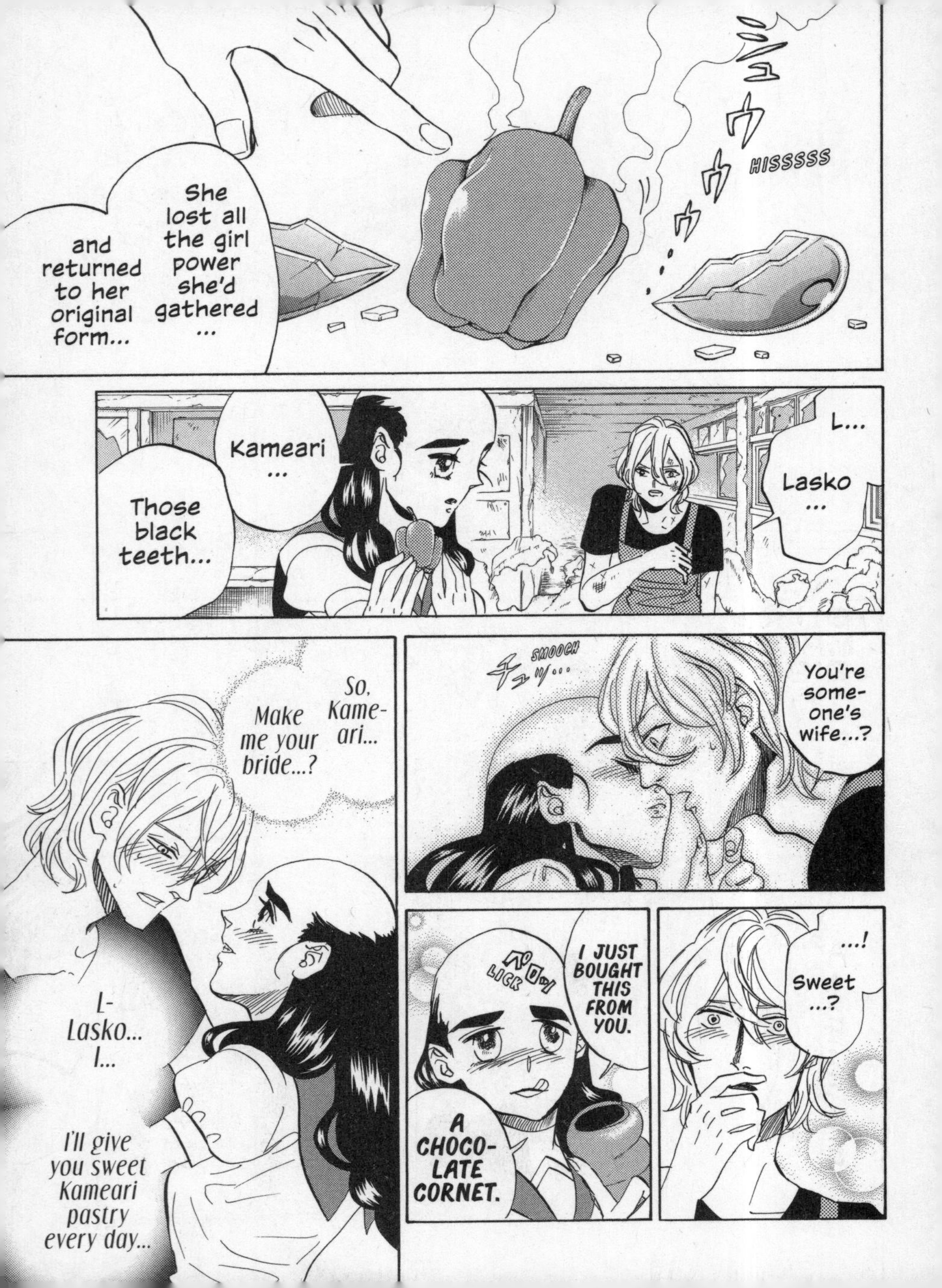

シュウゥゥ
HISSSSS
She lost all the girl power she'd gathered...
and returned to her original form...
L... Lasko...
Kameari...
Those black teeth...
チュッ...
SMOOCH
You're someone's wife...?
...! Sweet...?
I JUST BOUGHT THIS FROM YOU.
ペロッ
LICK
A CHOCOLATE CORNET.
So, Kameari...
Make me your bride...?
L- Lasko... I...
I'll give you sweet Kameari pastry every day...

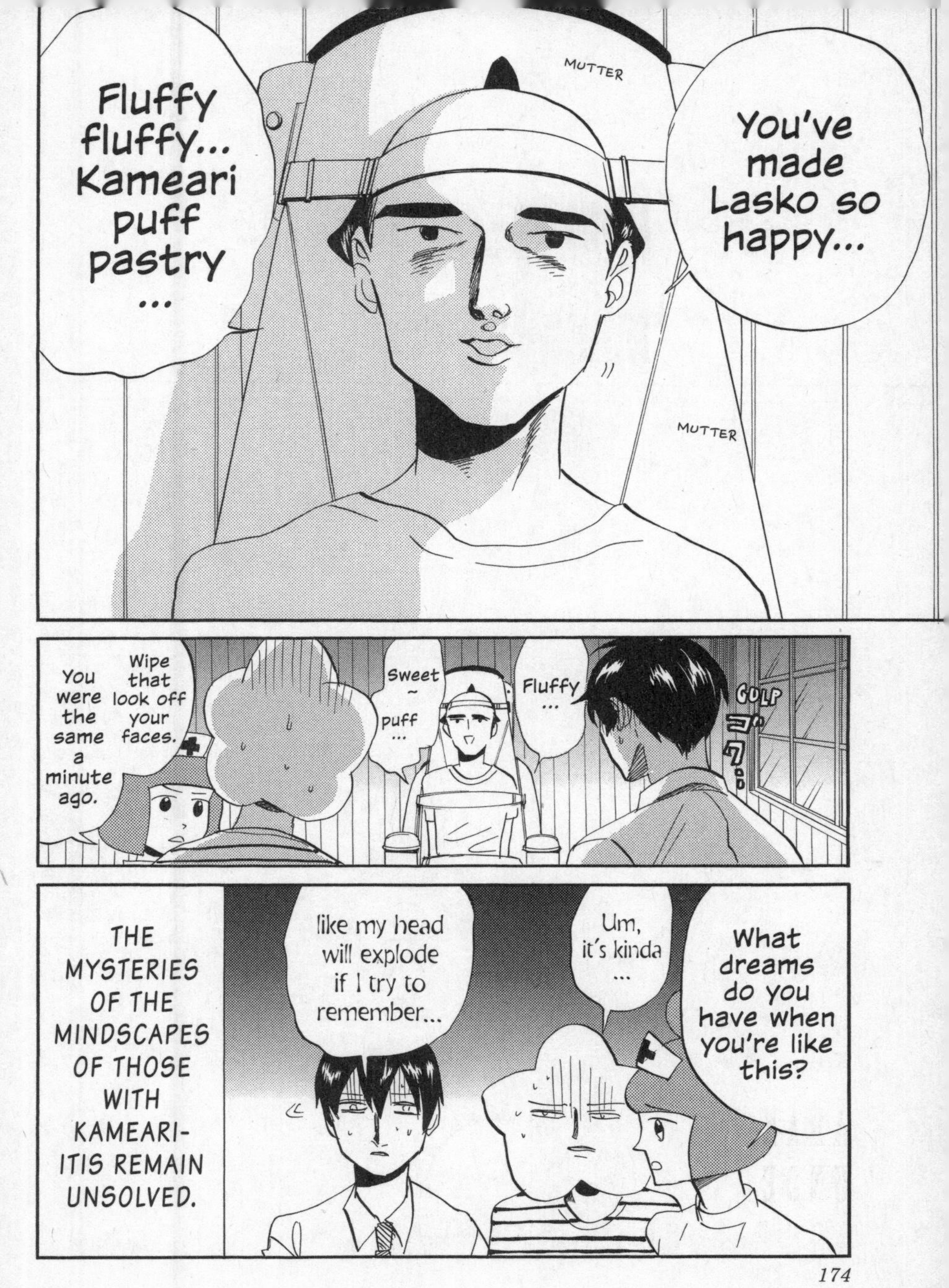
MUTTER
You've made Lasko so happy...
Fluffy fluffy... Kameari puff pastry ...
MUTTER
GULP
Fluffy ...
Sweet ~ puff ...
Wipe that look off your faces.
You were the same a minute ago.
What dreams do you have when you're like this?
Um, it's kinda ...
like my head will explode if I try to remember...
THE MYSTERIES OF THE MINDSCAPES OF THOSE WITH KAMEARI-ITIS REMAIN UNSOLVED.

ARAKAWA
UNDER
THE BRIDGE

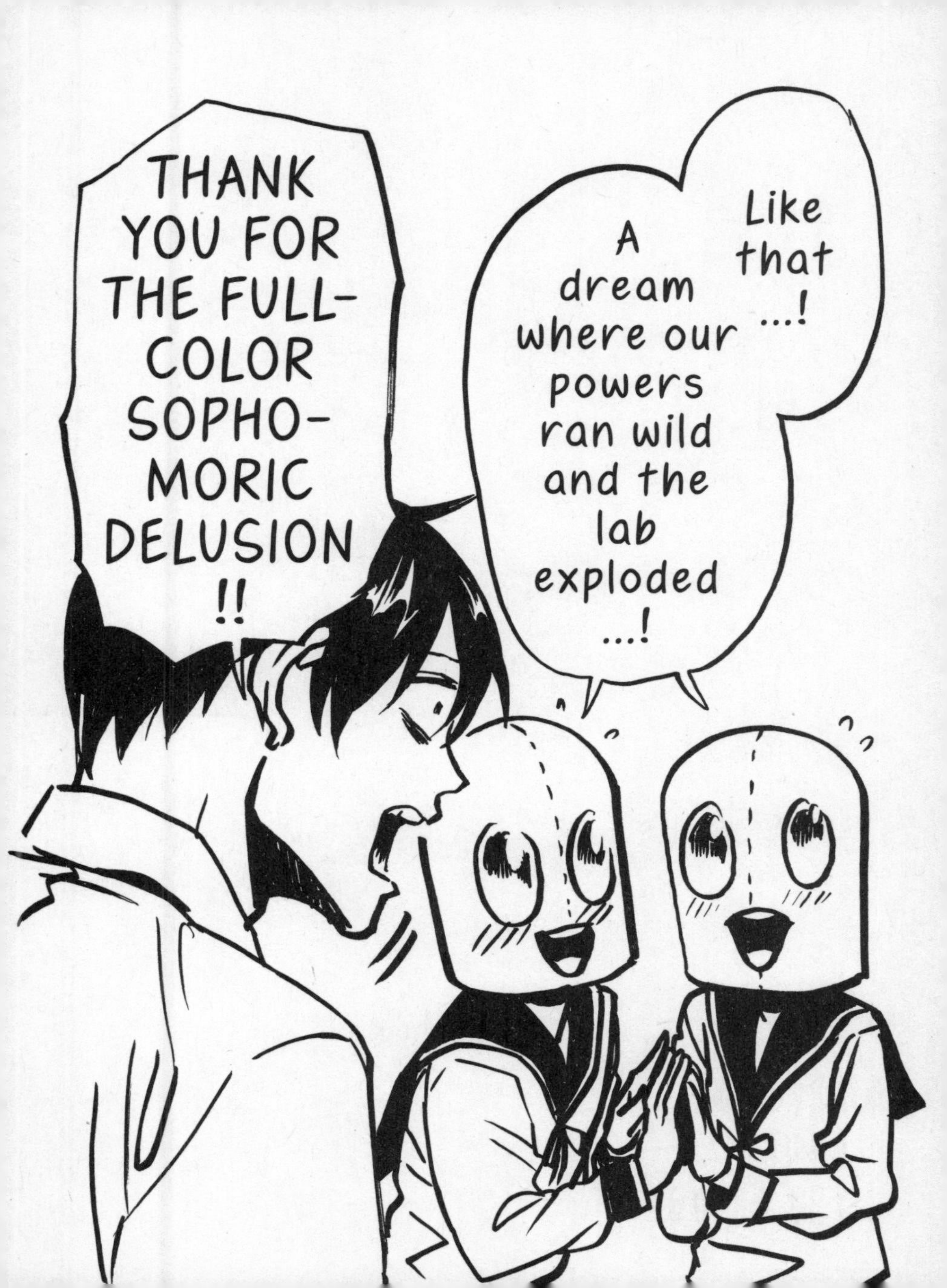

A dream where our powers ran wild and the lab exploded ...!
Like that ...!
THANK YOU FOR THE FULL-COLOR SOPHO-MORIC DELUSION !!

Summer

autumn
spring

winter

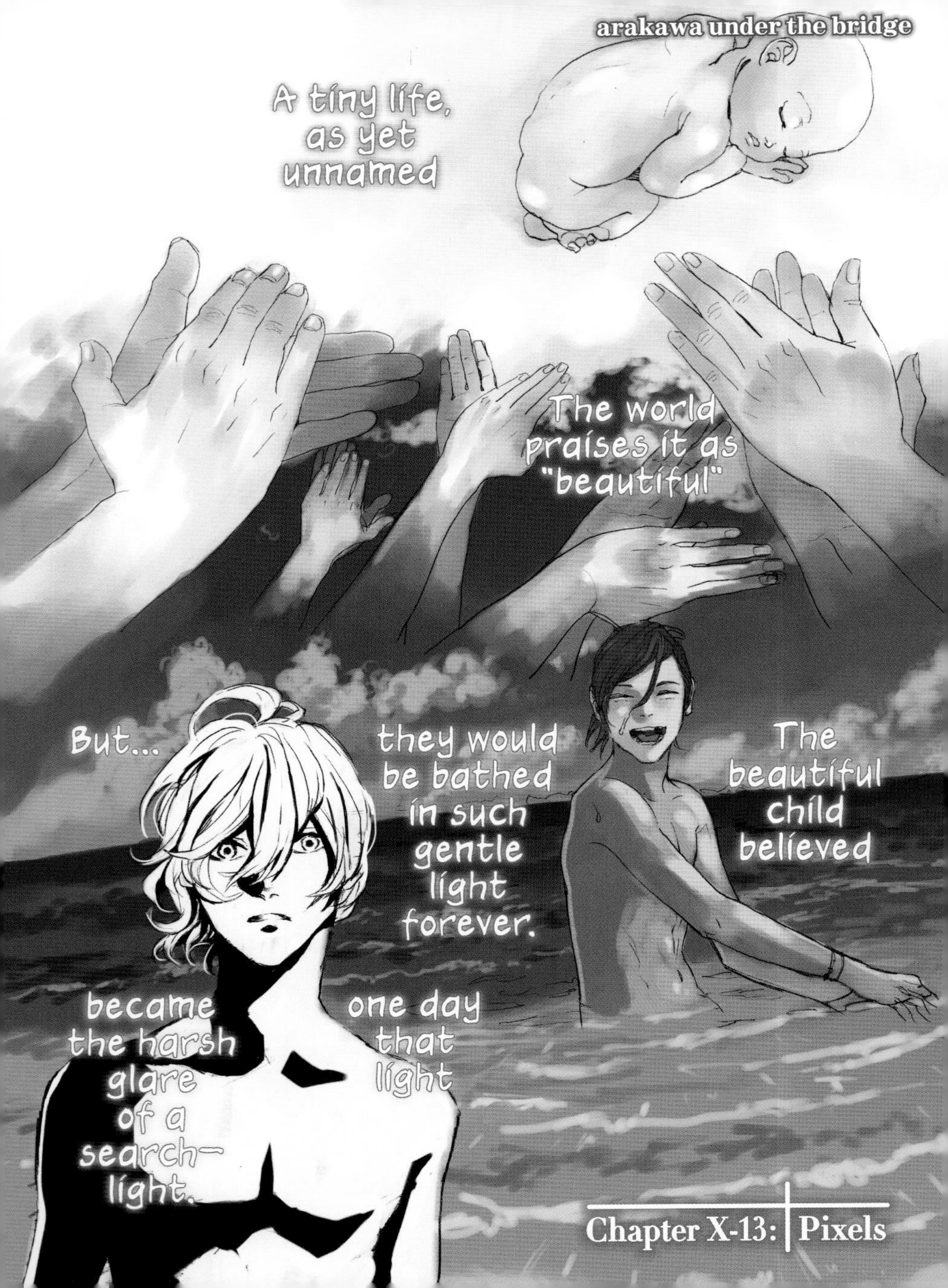
arakawa under the bridge
A tiny life, as yet unnamed
The world praises it as "beautiful"
The beautiful child believed
they would be bathed in such gentle light forever.
But...
one day that light
became the harsh glare of a search-light.
Chapter X-13: Pixels

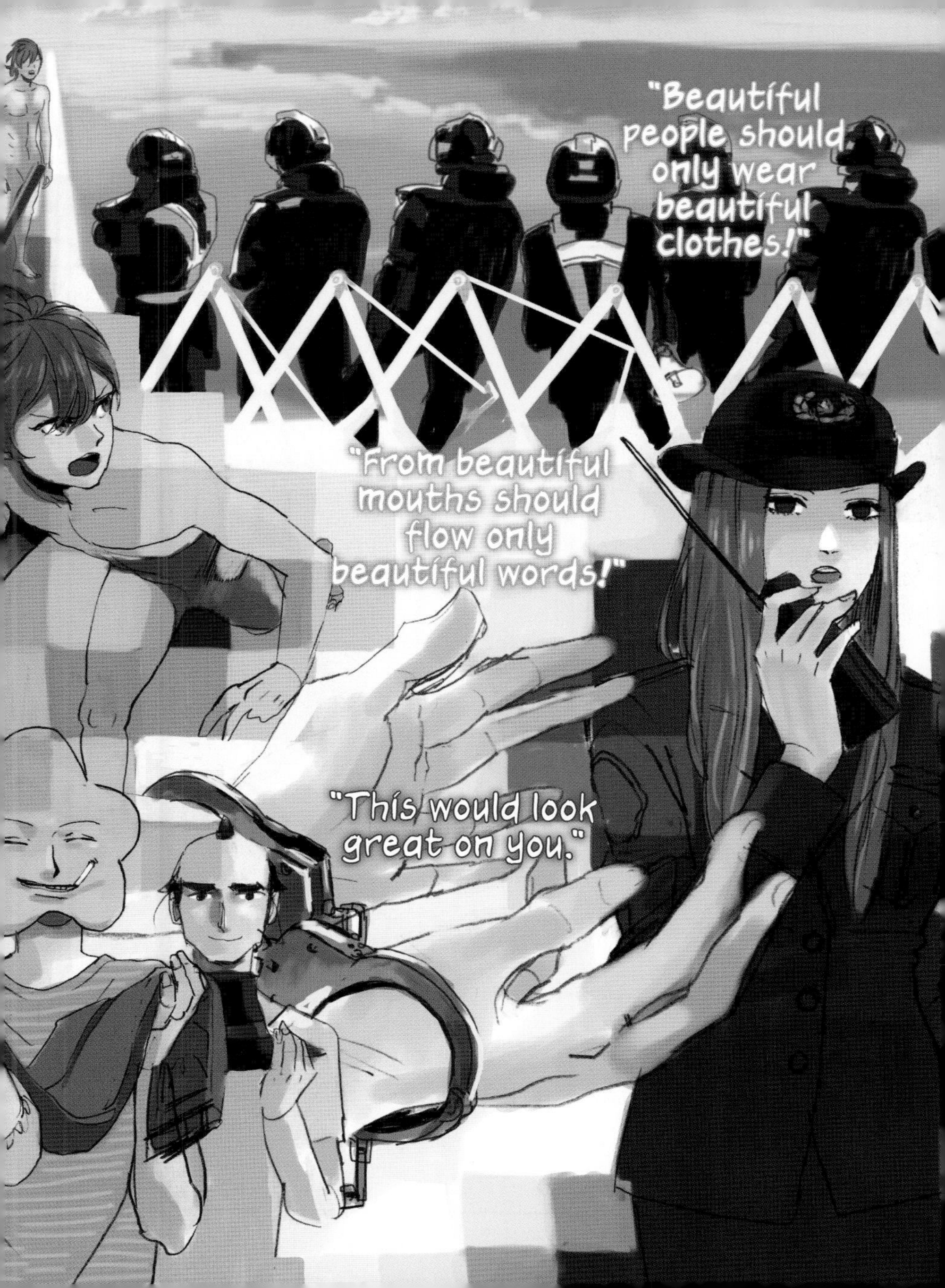
"Beautiful people should only wear beautiful clothes!"
"From beautiful mouths should flow only beautiful words!"
"This would look great on you."

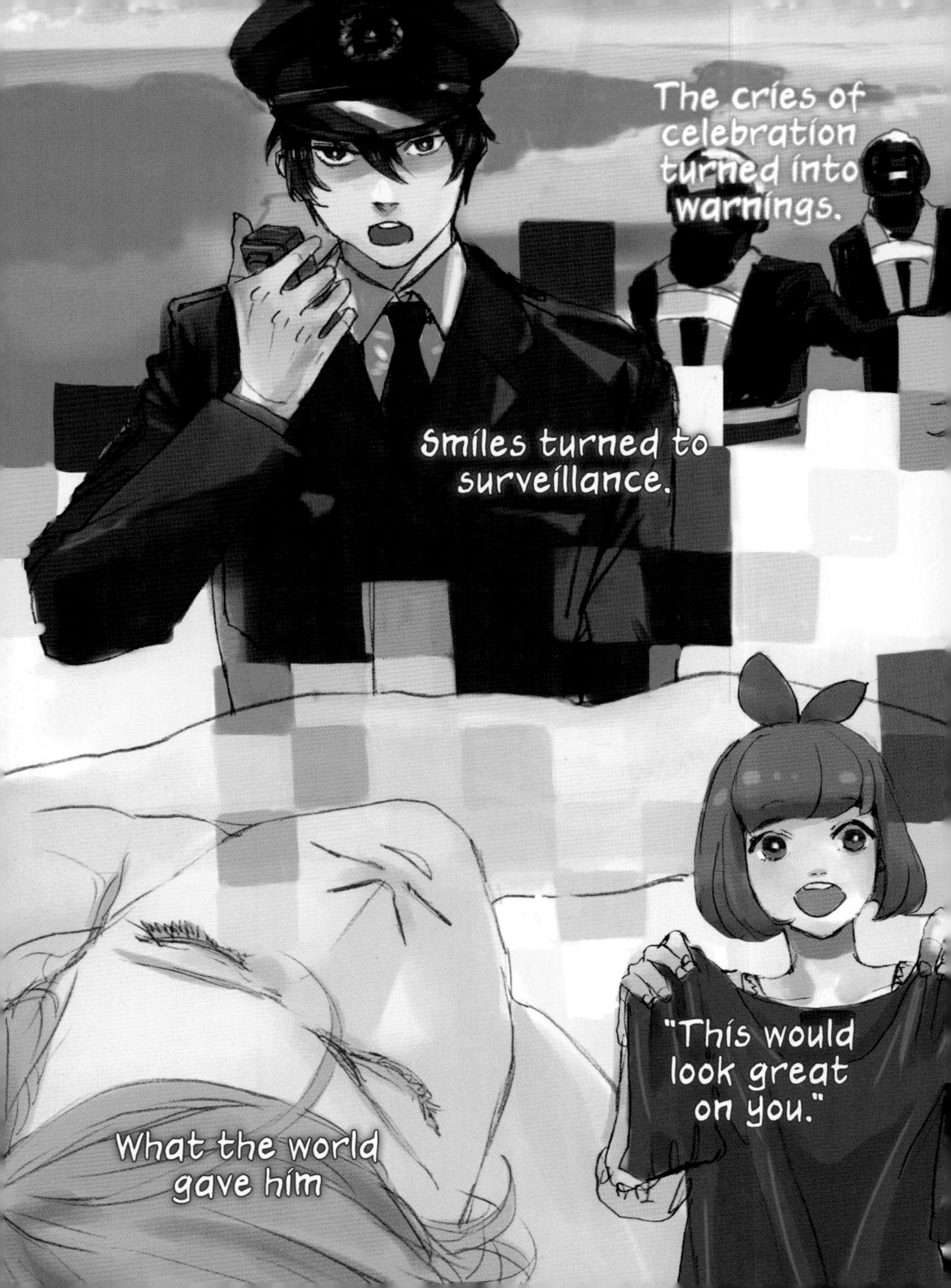
The cries of celebration turned into warnings.
Smiles turned to surveillance.
"This would look great on you."
What the world gave him

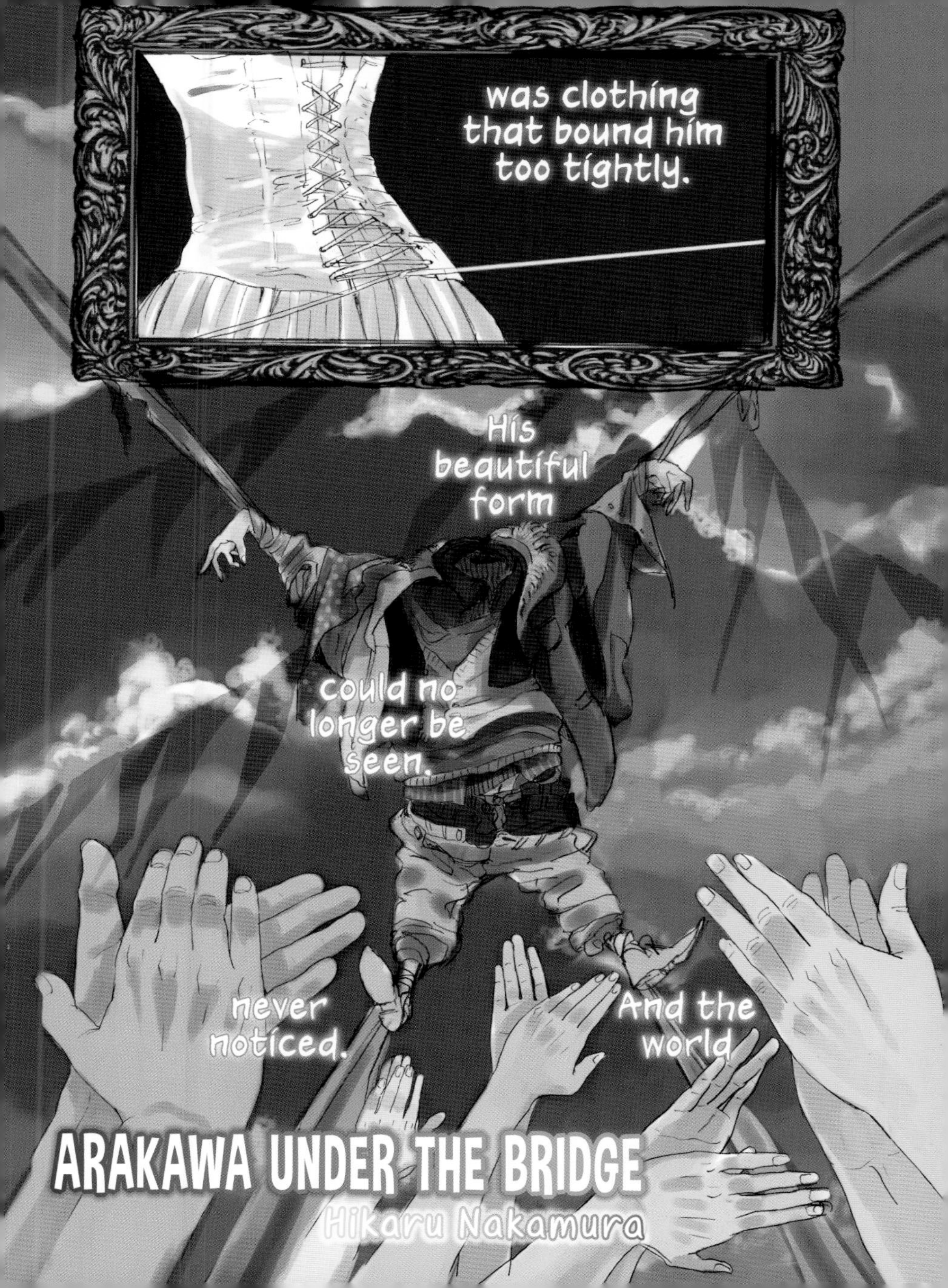
was clothing that bound him too tightly.
His beautiful form
could no longer be seen.
And the world
never noticed.
ARAKAWA UNDER THE BRIDGE
Hikaru Nakamura

Three pointy, humidifying brothers protecting my work place from dryness.

—Hikaru Nakamura

Thank you for picking up this volume! By the time this volume comes out it will be warm, and I feel certain all the pollen will be gone and we can breathe again.

—Hikaru Nakamura

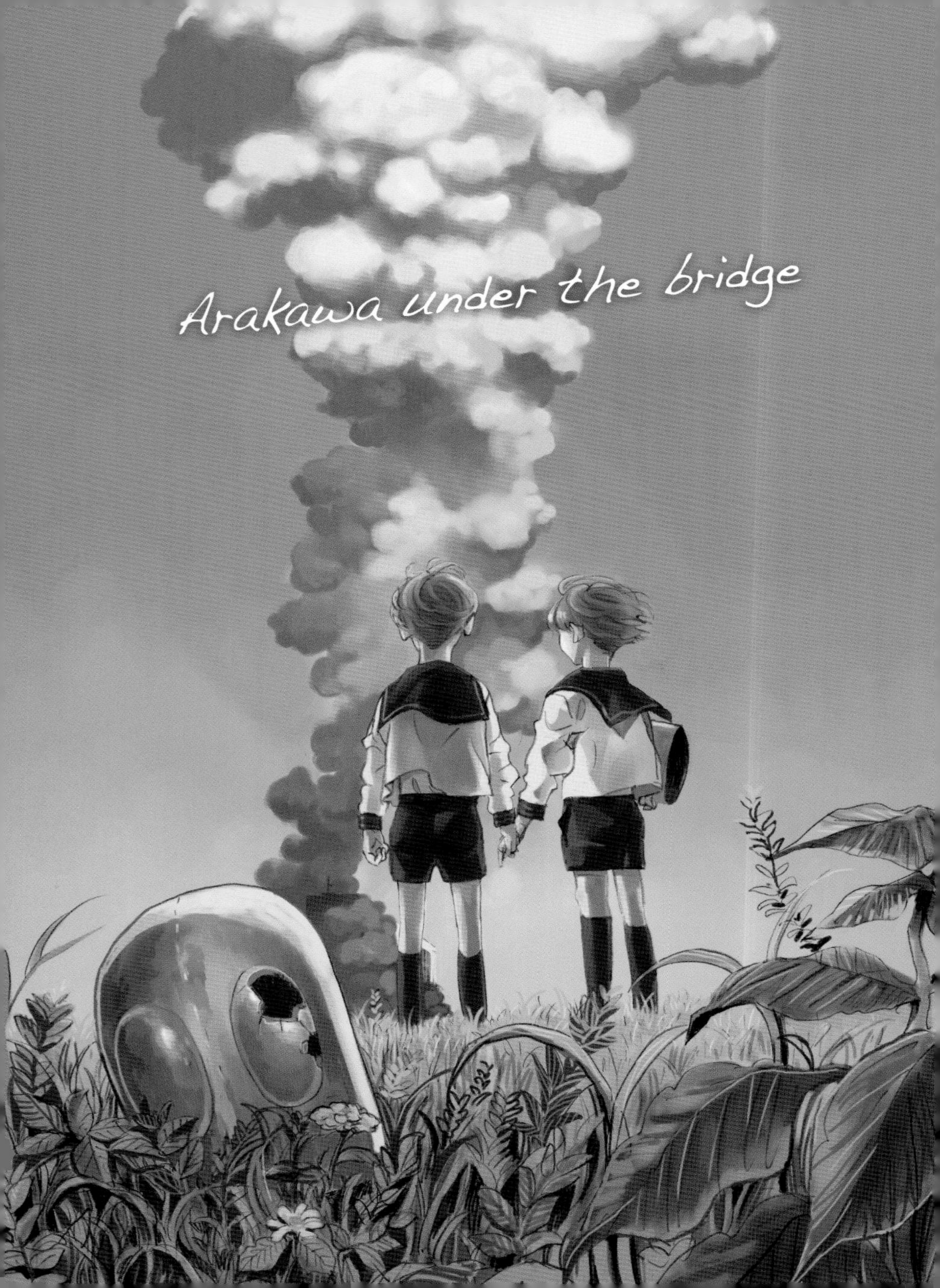
Arakawa under the bridge

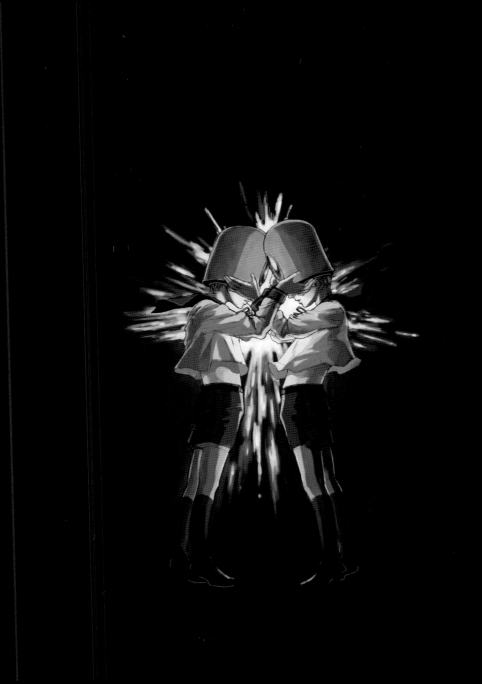

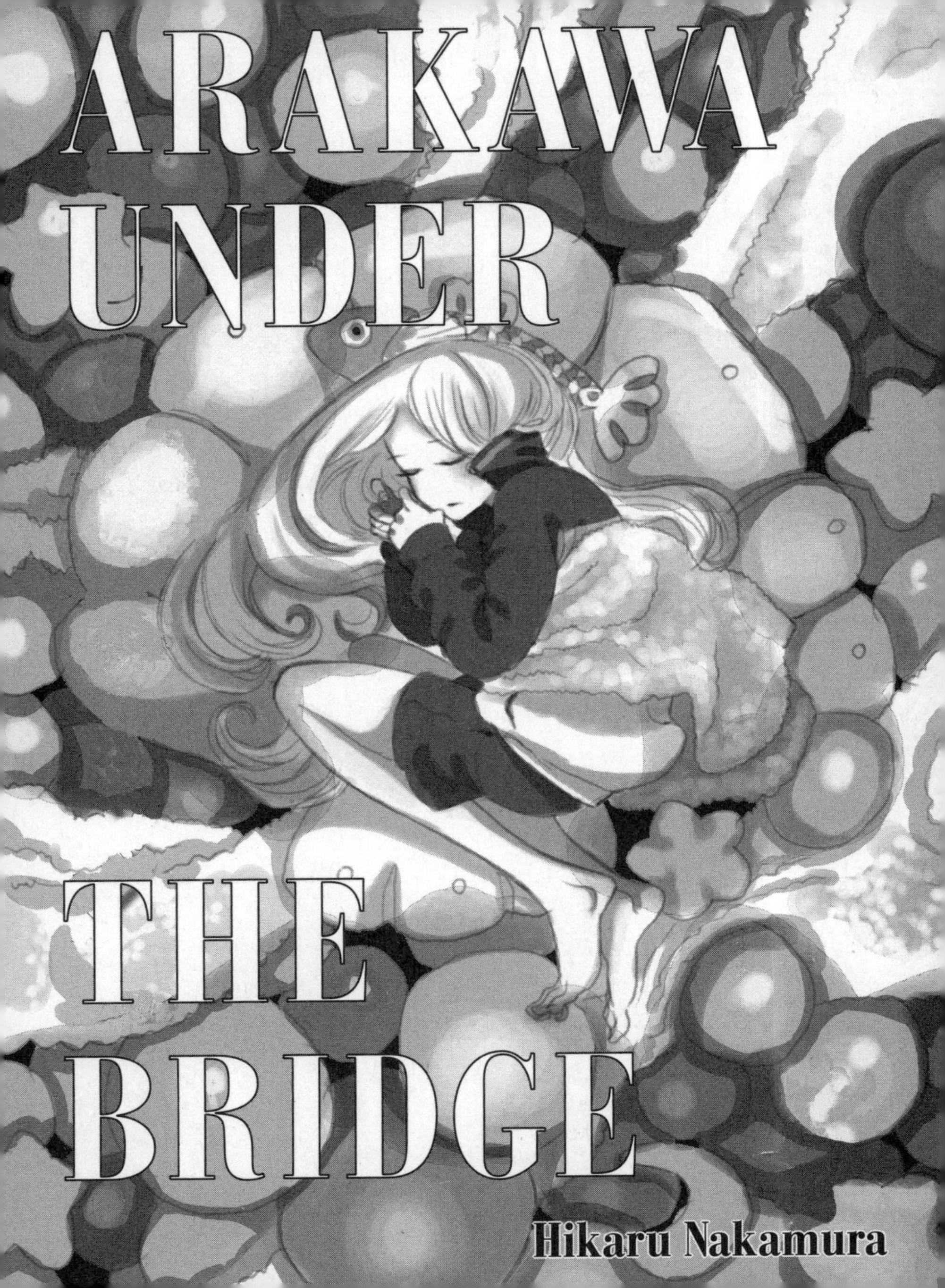
ARAKAWA
UNDER
THE
BRIDGE
Hikaru Nakamura

CONTENTS

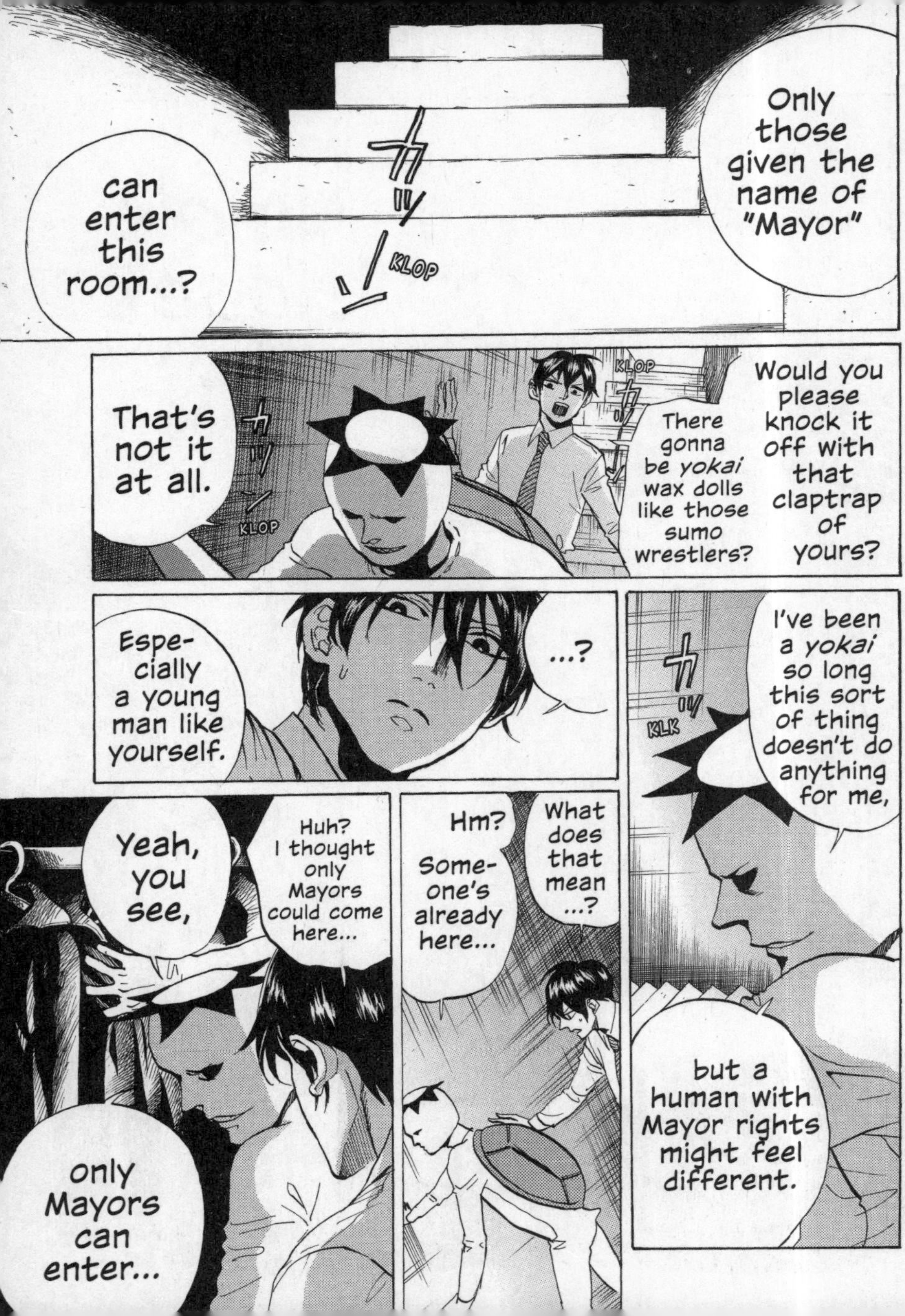
Only those given the name of "Mayor"
KLOP
can enter this room...?
Would you please knock it off with that claptrap of yours?
KLOP
There gonna be *yokai* wax dolls like those sumo wrestlers?
That's not it at all.
KLOP
I've been a *yokai* so long this sort of thing doesn't do anything for me,
KLK
but a human with Mayor rights might feel different.
...?
Espe-cially a young man like yourself.
What does that mean ...?
Hm?
Some-one's already here...
Huh? I thought only Mayors could come here...
Yeah, you see,
only Mayors can enter...

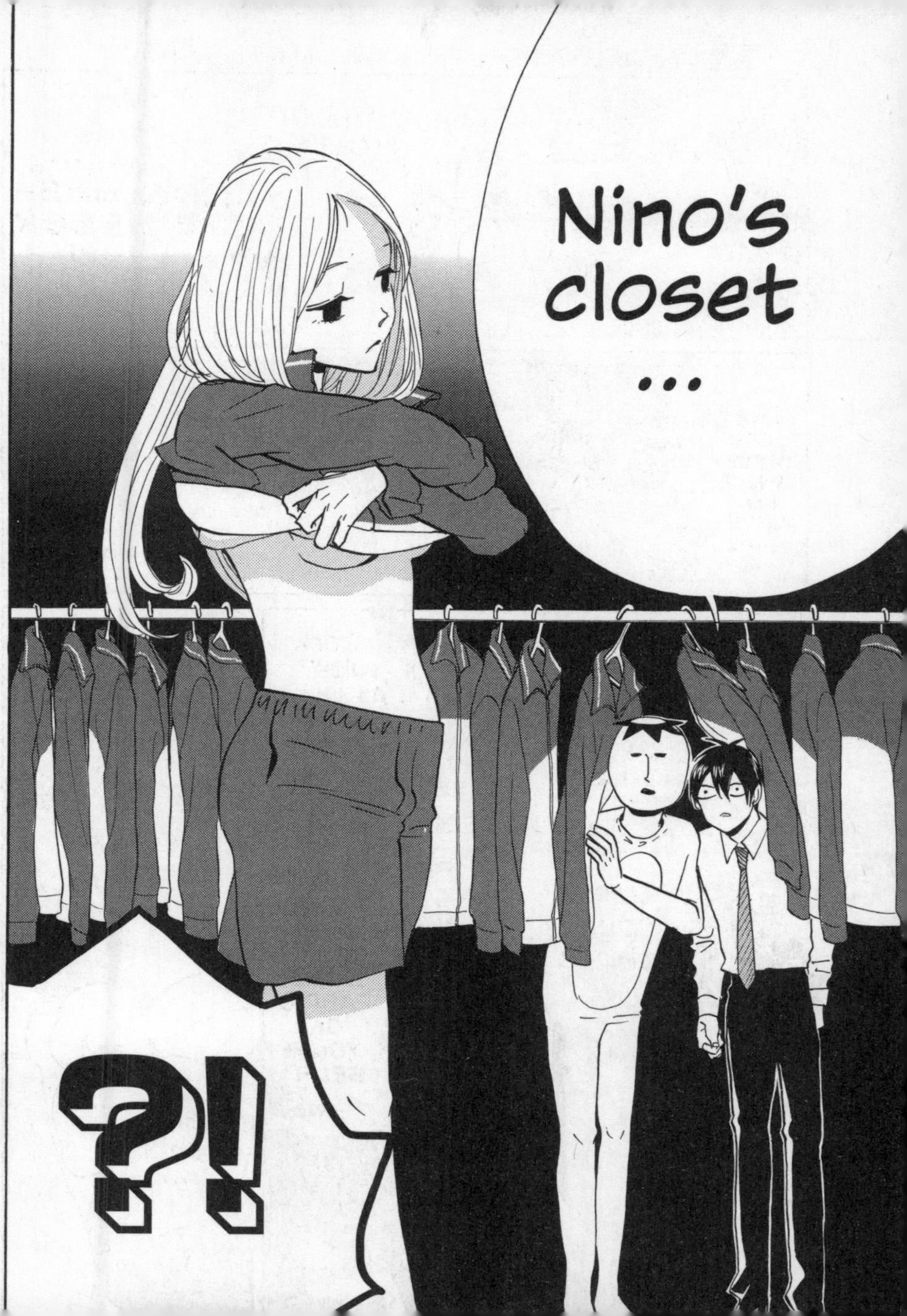
Nino's closet ...
?!

Chapter 357: Nino, Track Suits, and Those Two...

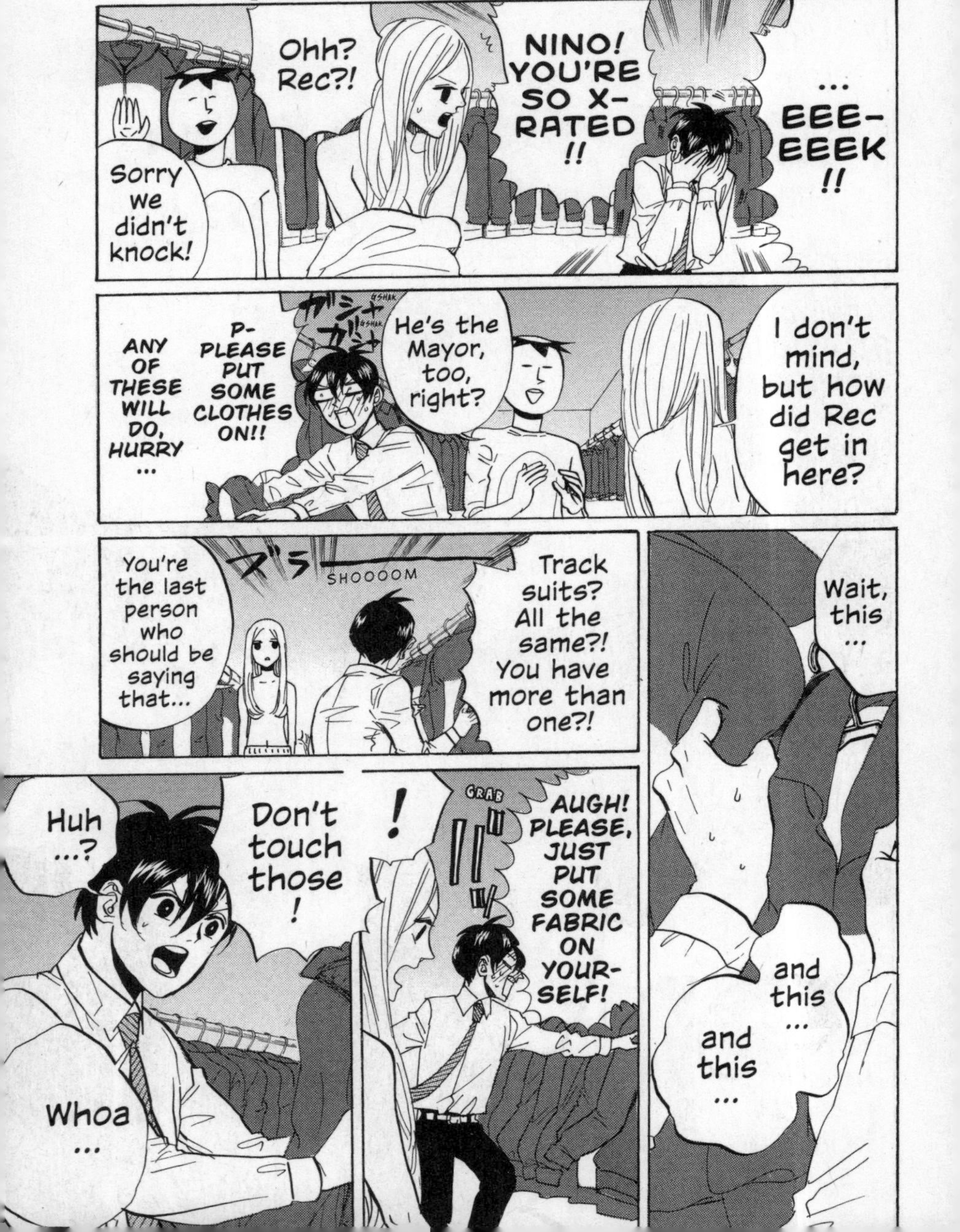
...
EEE-EEEK!!
NINO! YOU'RE SO X-RATED!!
Ohh? Rec?!
Sorry we didn't knock!
I don't mind, but how did Rec get in here?
He's the Mayor, too, right?
GSHAK
GSHAK
P-PLEASE PUT SOME CLOTHES ON!!
ANY OF THESE WILL DO, HURRY...
Wait, this...
and this...
and this...
Track suits? All the same?! You have more than one?!
SHOOOOM
You're the last person who should be saying that...
!
GRAB
AUGH! PLEASE, JUST PUT SOME FABRIC ON YOURSELF!
Don't touch those!
Huh...?
Whoa...

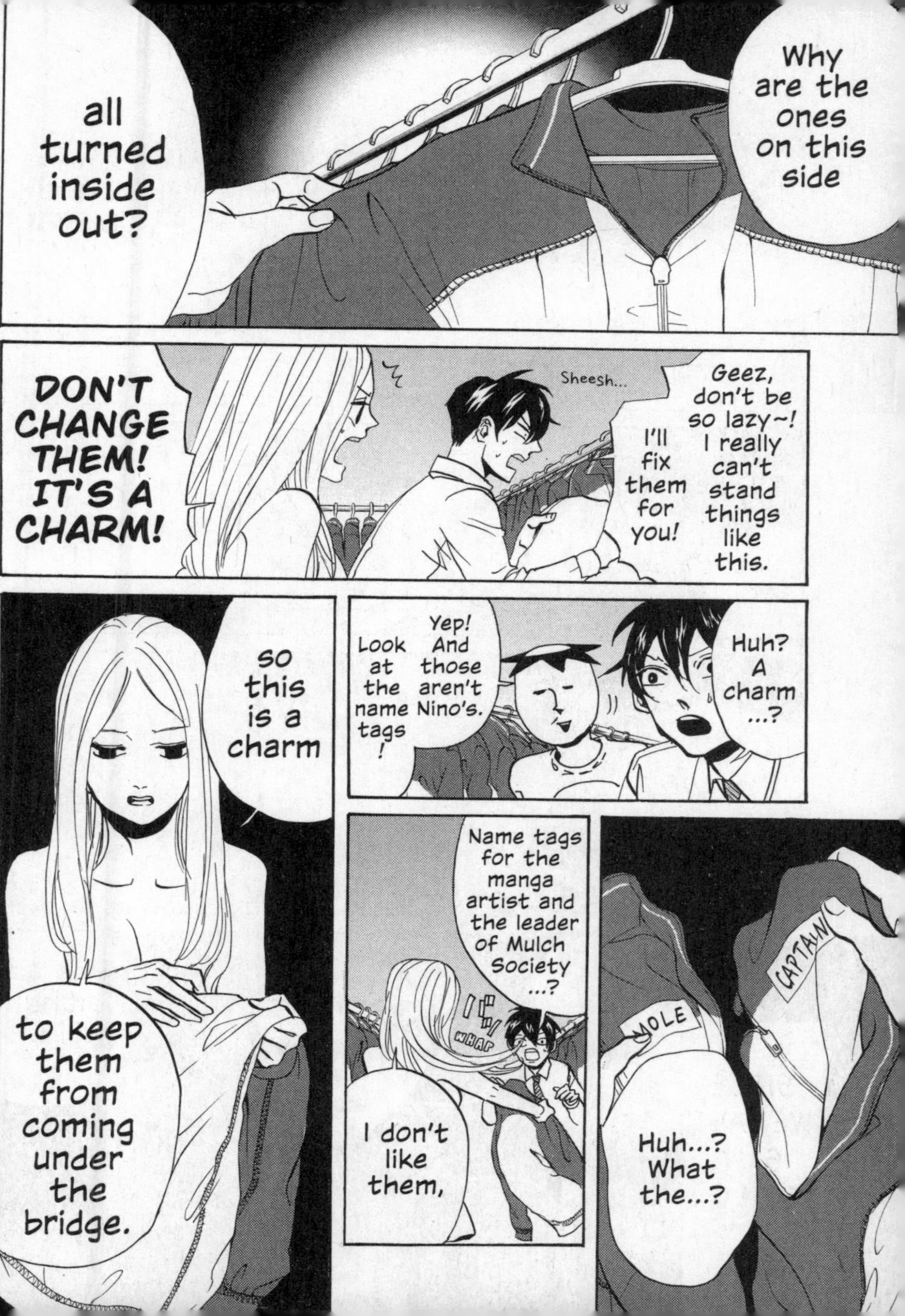
Why are the ones on this side
all turned inside out?
Geez, don't be so lazy~! I really can't stand things like this.
I'll fix them for you!
Sheesh...
DON'T CHANGE THEM! IT'S A CHARM!
Huh? A charm ...?
Yep! And those aren't Nino's.
Look at the name tags!
CAPTAIN
MOLE
Huh...? What the...?
Name tags for the manga artist and the leader of Mulch Society ...?
WHAP
I don't like them,
so this is a charm
to keep them from coming under the bridge.

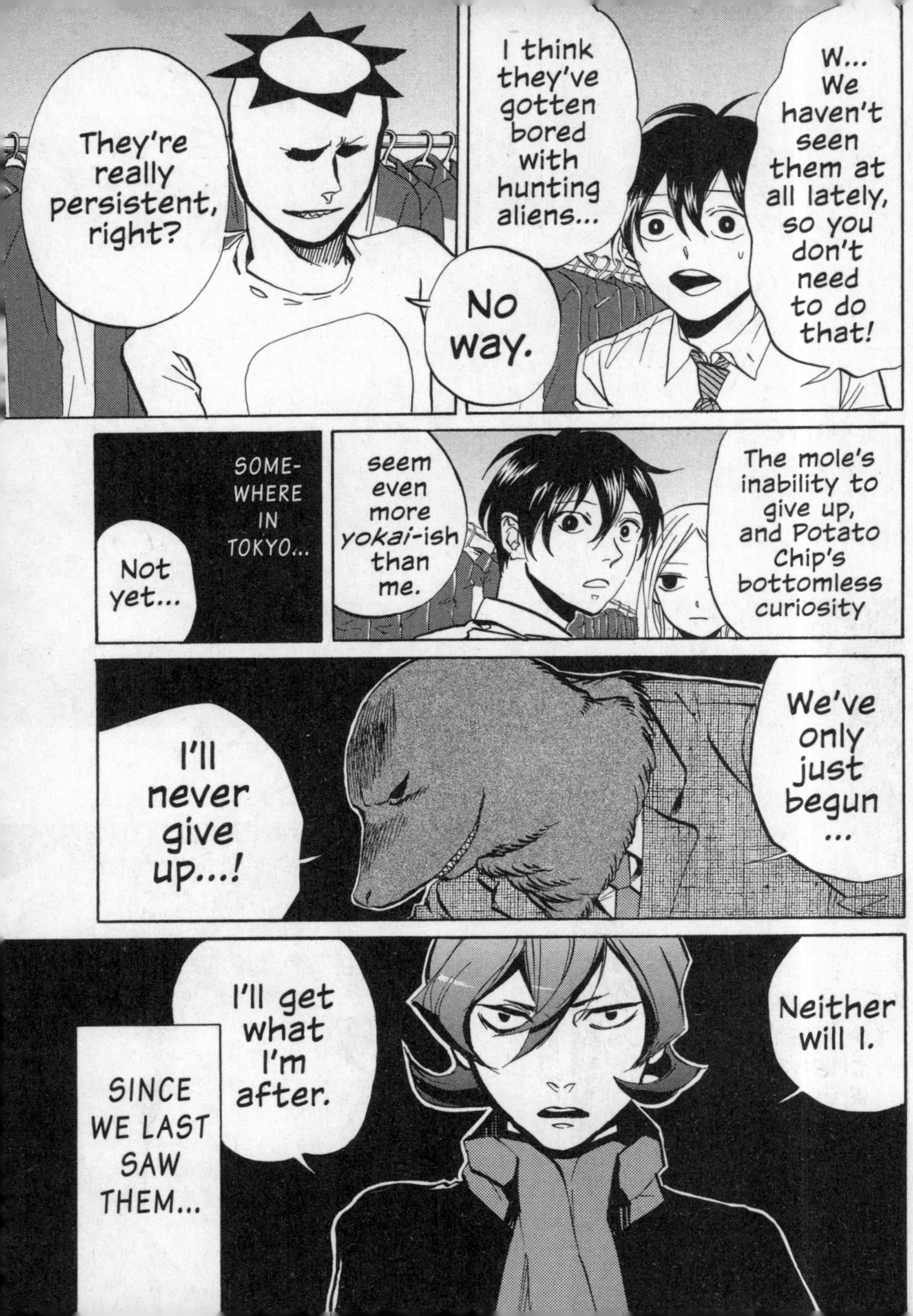
W... We haven't seen them at all lately, so you don't need to do that!
I think they've gotten bored with hunting aliens...
They're really persistent, right?
No way.
The mole's inability to give up, and Potato Chip's bottomless curiosity
seem even more *yokai*-ish than me.
SOME-WHERE IN TOKYO...
Not yet...
We've only just begun ...
I'll never give up...!
Neither will I.
I'll get what I'm after.
SINCE WE LAST SAW THEM...

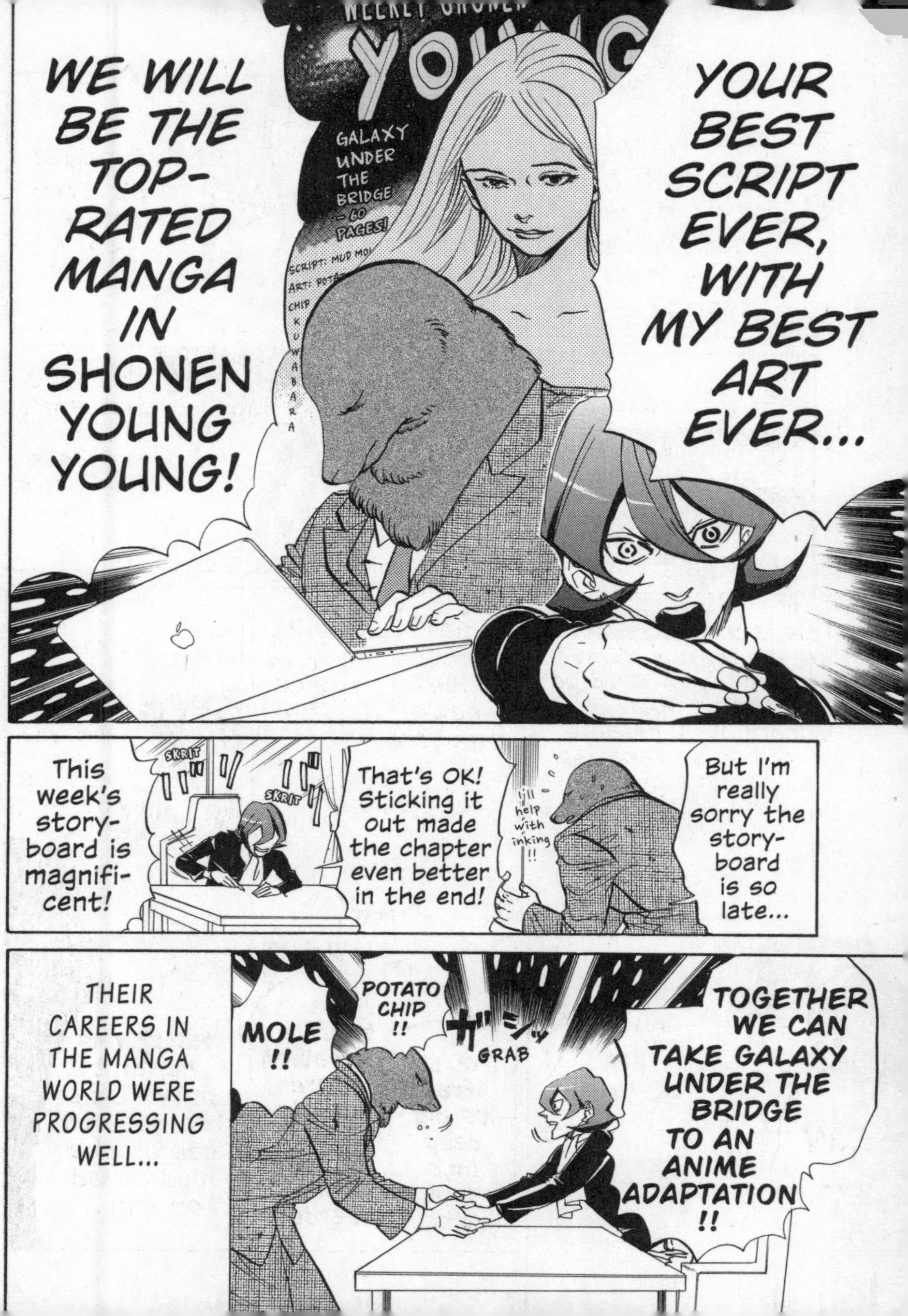
YOUR BEST SCRIPT EVER, WITH MY BEST ART EVER...
YOUNG
GALAXY UNDER THE BRIDGE - 60 PAGES!
KUWABARA
WE WILL BE THE TOP-RATED MANGA IN SHONEN YOUNG YOUNG!
But I'm really sorry the storyboard is so late...
I'll help with inking!!
That's OK! Sticking it out made the chapter even better in the end!
SKRIT
SKRIT
This week's storyboard is magnificent!
TOGETHER WE CAN TAKE GALAXY UNDER THE BRIDGE TO AN ANIME ADAPTATION!!
GRAB
POTATO CHIP!!
MOLE!!
THEIR CAREERS IN THE MANGA WORLD WERE PROGRESSING WELL...

☜ Chapter 358: Their Manga Careers

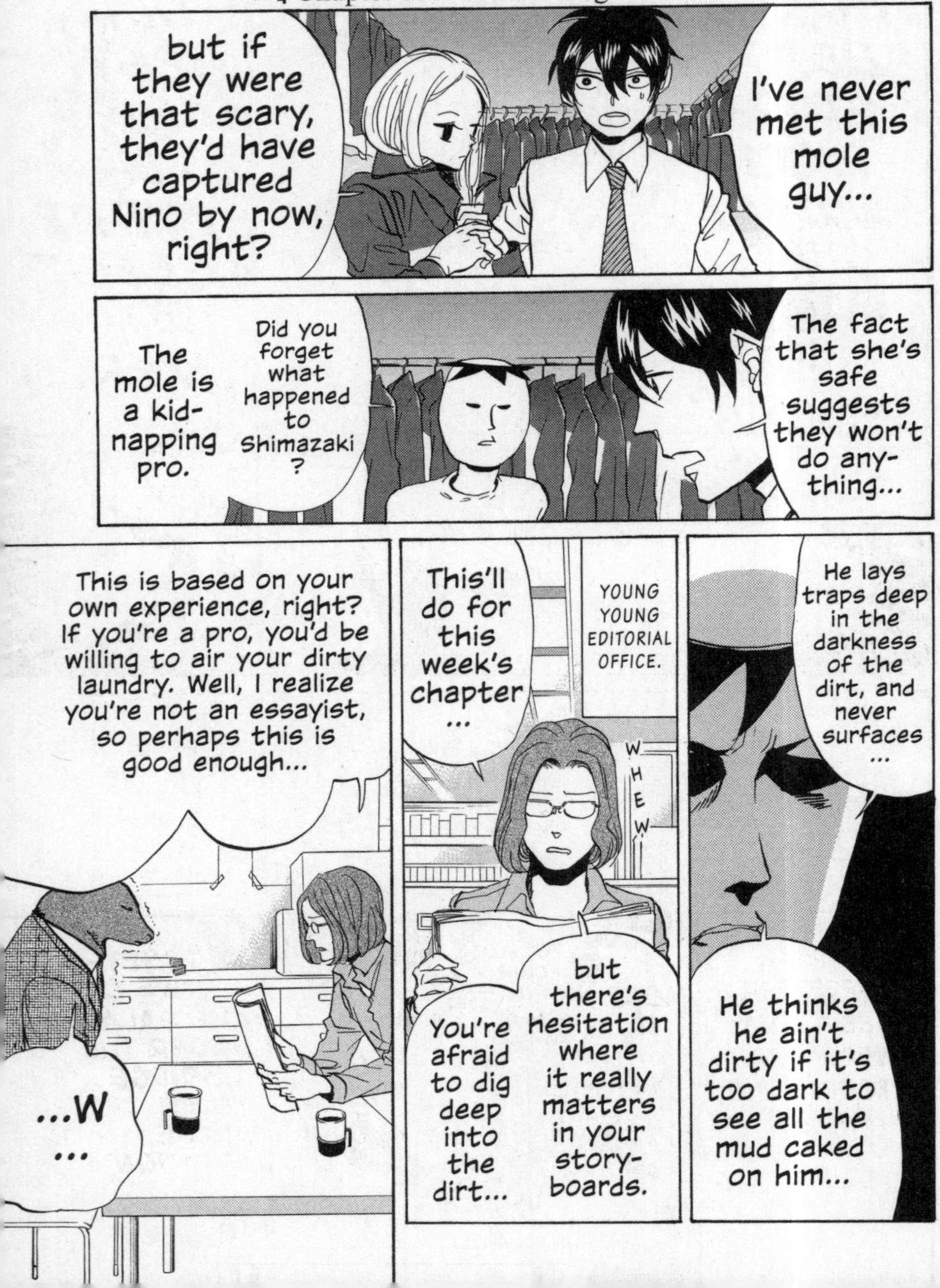

I've never met this mole guy...
but if they were that scary, they'd have captured Nino by now, right?
The fact that she's safe suggests they won't do anything...
Did you forget what happened to Shimazaki?
The mole is a kidnapping pro.
He lays traps deep in the darkness of the dirt, and never surfaces...
He thinks he ain't dirty if it's too dark to see all the mud caked on him...
YOUNG YOUNG EDITORIAL OFFICE.
This'll do for this week's chapter...
WHEW
but there's hesitation where it really matters in your storyboards.
You're afraid to dig deep into the dirt...
This is based on your own experience, right? If you're a pro, you'd be willing to air your dirty laundry. Well, I realize you're not an essayist, so perhaps this is good enough...
...W ...

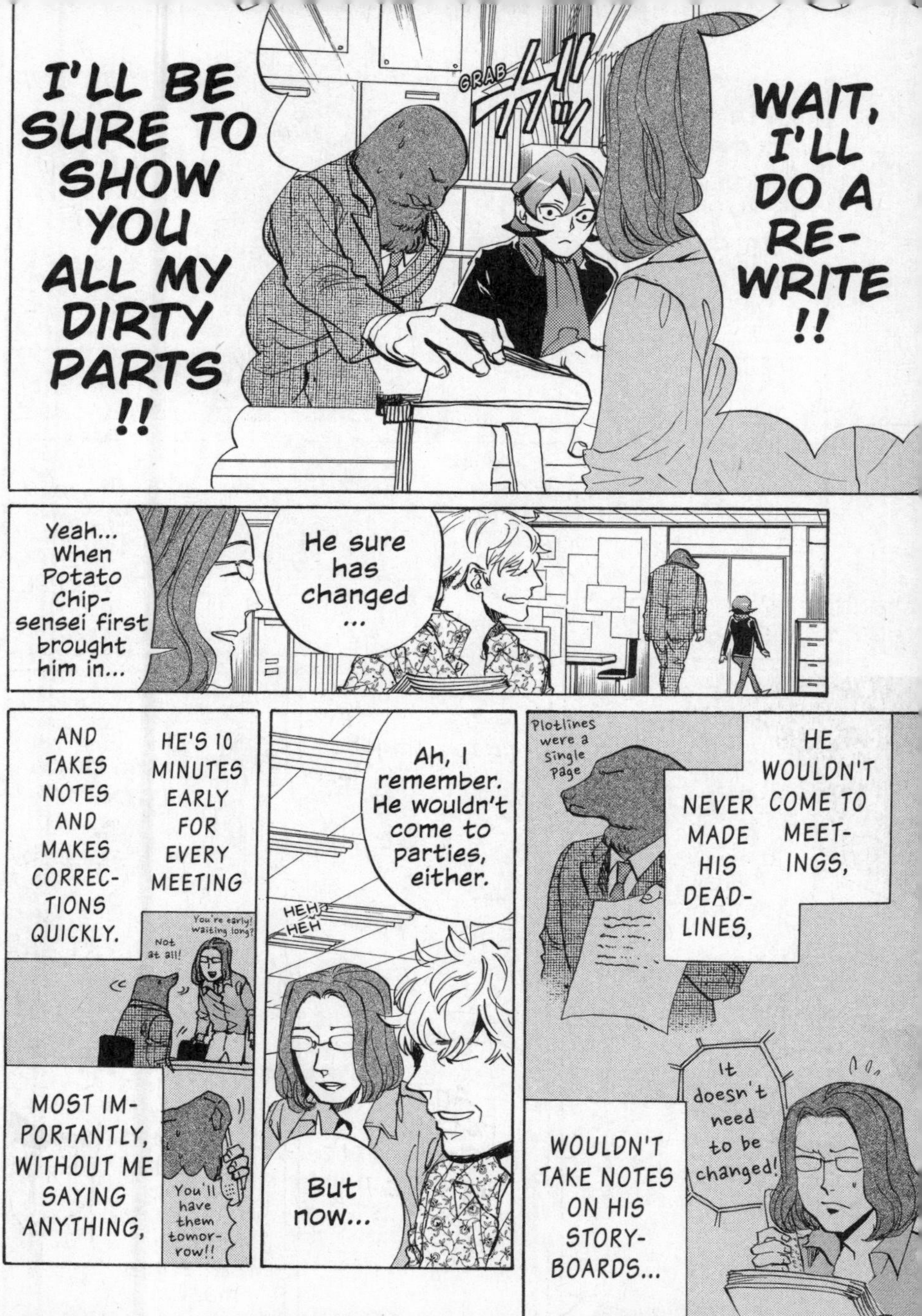
WAIT, I'LL DO A RE-WRITE!!
GRAB
I'LL BE SURE TO SHOW YOU ALL MY DIRTY PARTS!!
He sure has changed...
Yeah... When Potato Chip-sensei first brought him in...
HE WOULDN'T COME TO MEETINGS,
NEVER MADE HIS DEADLINES,
Plotlines were a single page
It doesn't need to be changed!
WOULDN'T TAKE NOTES ON HIS STORYBOARDS...
Ah, I remember. He wouldn't come to parties, either.
HEH HEH
But now...
HE'S 10 MINUTES EARLY FOR EVERY MEETING
AND TAKES NOTES AND MAKES CORRECTIONS QUICKLY.
You're early! Waiting long?
Not at all!
MOST IMPORTANTLY, WITHOUT ME SAYING ANYTHING,
You'll have them tomorrow!!

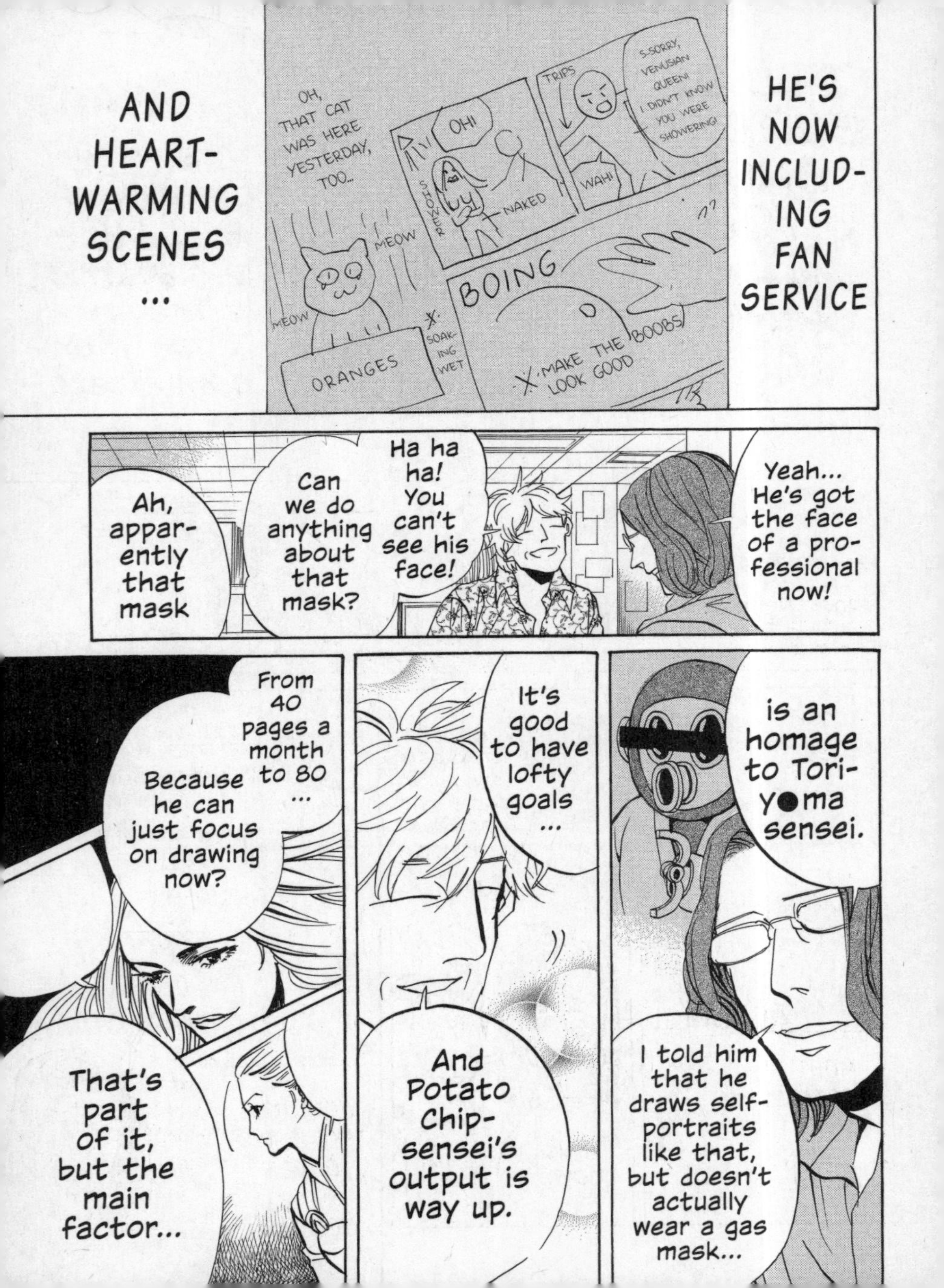
HE'S NOW INCLUDING FAN SERVICE
S-SORRY, VENUSIAN QUEEN! I DIDN'T KNOW YOU WERE SHOWERING!
TRIPS
WAH!
OH!
SHOWER
NAKED
BOING
MAKE THE BOOBS LOOK GOOD
OH, THAT CAT WAS HERE YESTERDAY, TOO...
MEOW
MEOW
SOAKING WET
ORANGES
AND HEART-WARMING SCENES ...
Yeah... He's got the face of a professional now!
Ha ha ha! You can't see his face!
Can we do anything about that mask?
Ah, apparently that mask
is an homage to Tori-y●ma sensei.
I told him that he draws self-portraits like that, but doesn't actually wear a gas mask...
It's good to have lofty goals ...
And Potato Chip-sensei's output is way up.
From 40 pages a month to 80 ...
Because he can just focus on drawing now?
That's part of it, but the main factor...

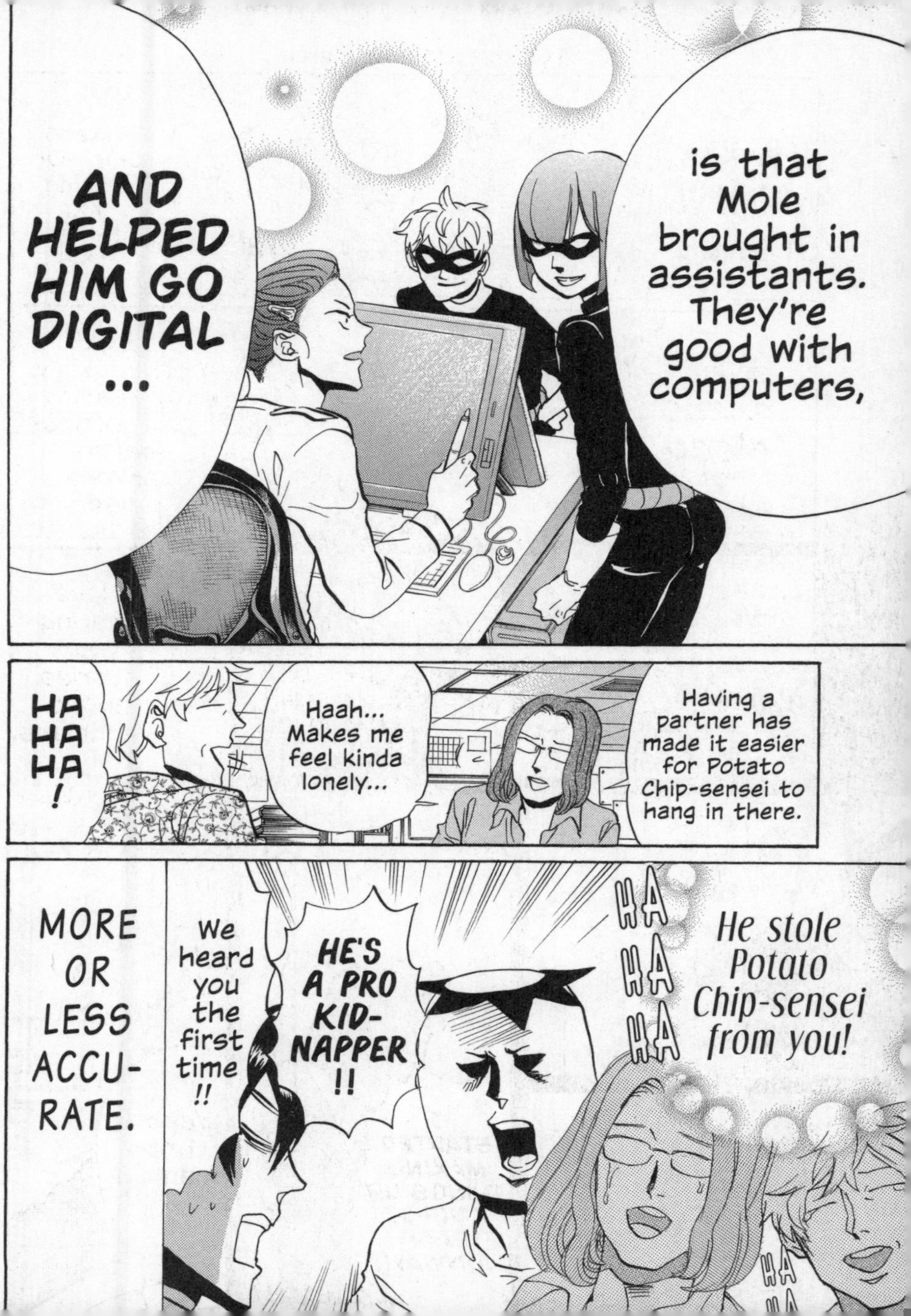
is that Mole brought in assistants. They're good with computers,
AND HELPED HIM GO DIGITAL ...
Having a partner has made it easier for Potato Chip-sensei to hang in there.
Haah... Makes me feel kinda lonely...
HA HA HA !
He stole Potato Chip-sensei from you!
HA HA HA
HE'S A PRO KID-NAPPER !!
We heard you the first time !!
MORE OR LESS ACCU-RATE.
HA HA

Chapter 359: Research

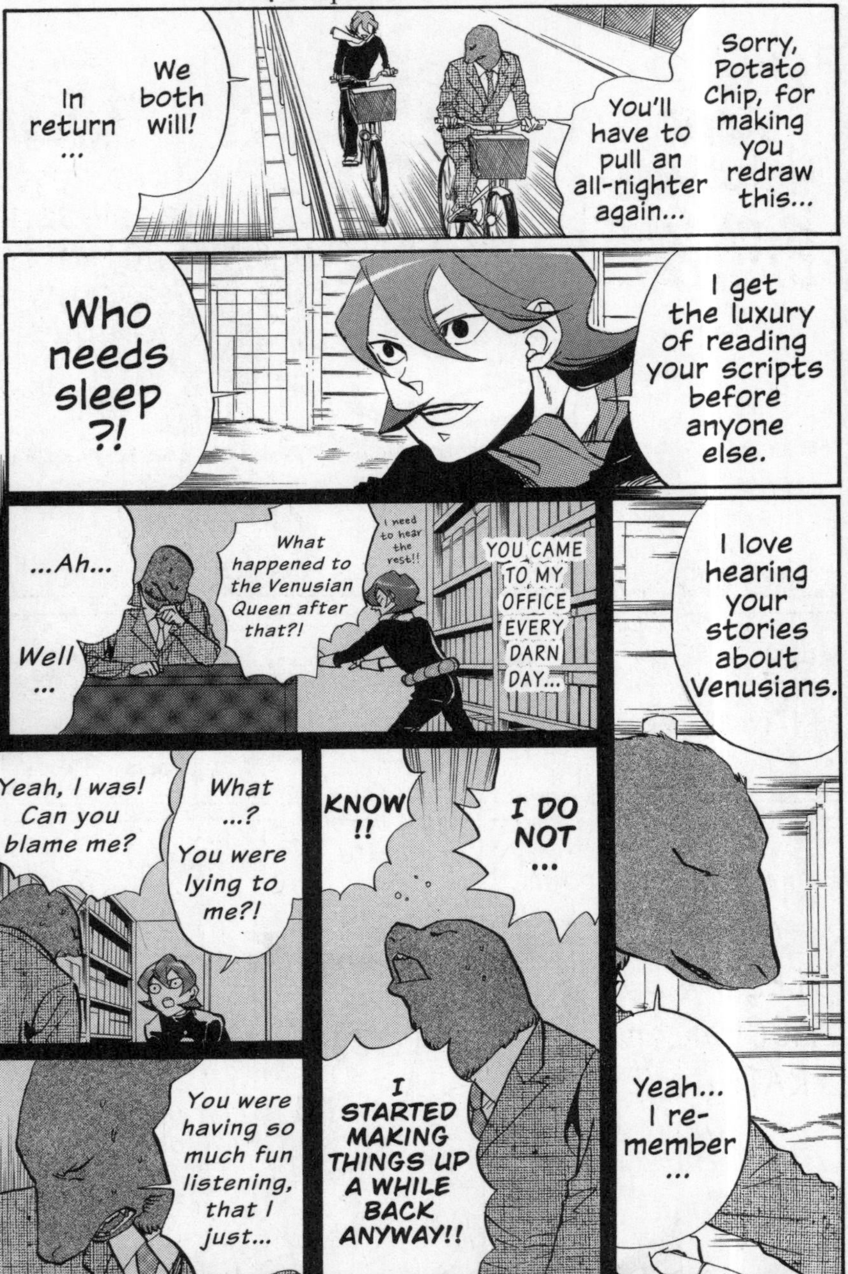

Sorry, Potato Chip, for making you redraw this...
You'll have to pull an all-nighter again...
We both will!
In return...
I get the luxury of reading your scripts before anyone else.
Who needs sleep?!
I love hearing your stories about Venusians.
YOU CAME TO MY OFFICE EVERY DARN DAY...
I need to hear the rest!!
What happened to the Venusian Queen after that?!
...Ah...
Well...
Yeah... I re-member...
I DO NOT...
KNOW!!
I STARTED MAKING THINGS UP A WHILE BACK ANYWAY!!
What...? You were lying to me?!
Yeah, I was! Can you blame me?
You were having so much fun listening, that I just...

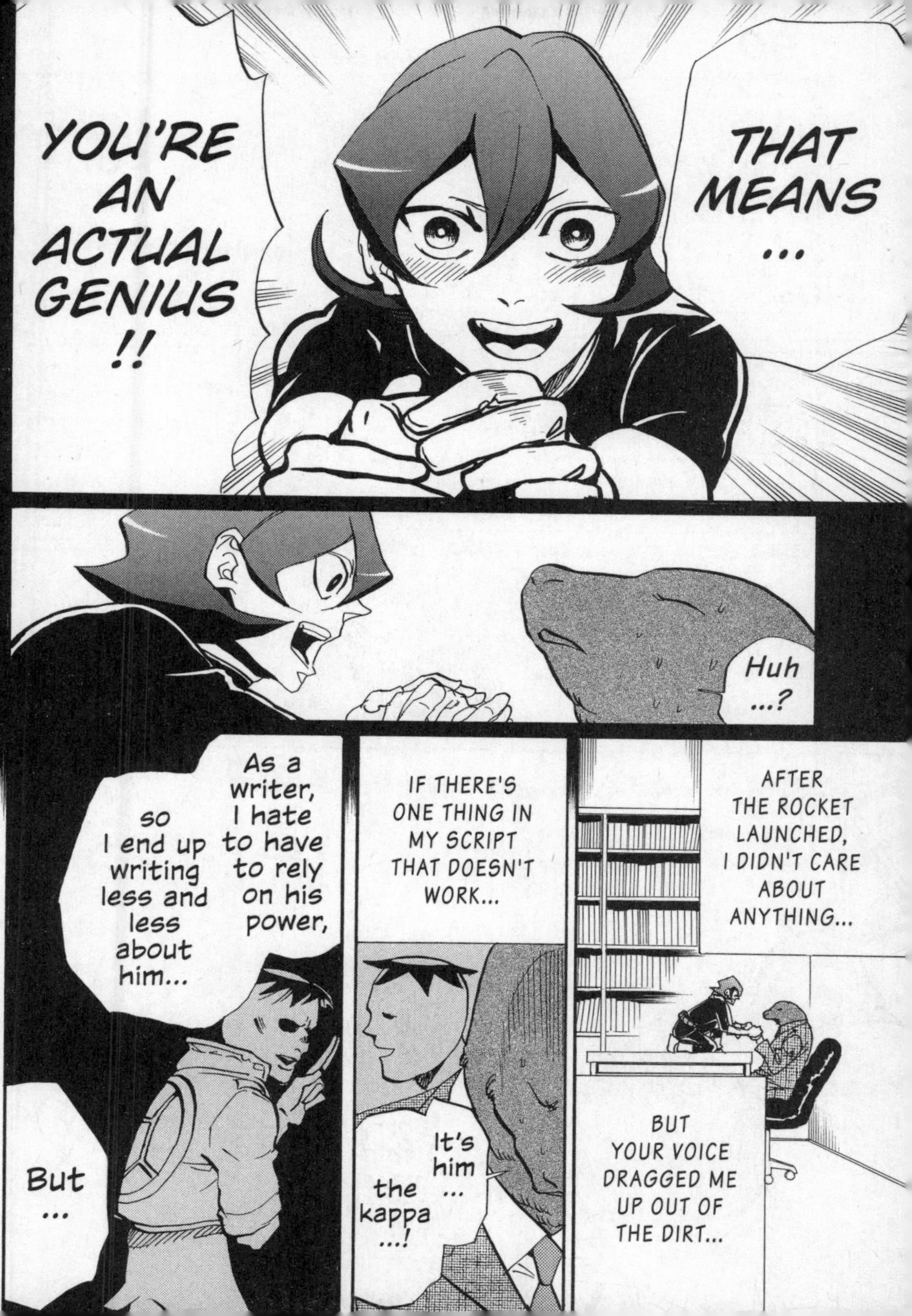
THAT MEANS ...
YOU'RE AN ACTUAL GENIUS !!
Huh ...?
AFTER THE ROCKET LAUNCHED, I DIDN'T CARE ABOUT ANYTHING...
BUT YOUR VOICE DRAGGED ME UP OUT OF THE DIRT...
IF THERE'S ONE THING IN MY SCRIPT THAT DOESN'T WORK...
It's him ... the kappa ...!
As a writer, I hate to have to rely on his power,
so I end up writing less and less about him...
But ...

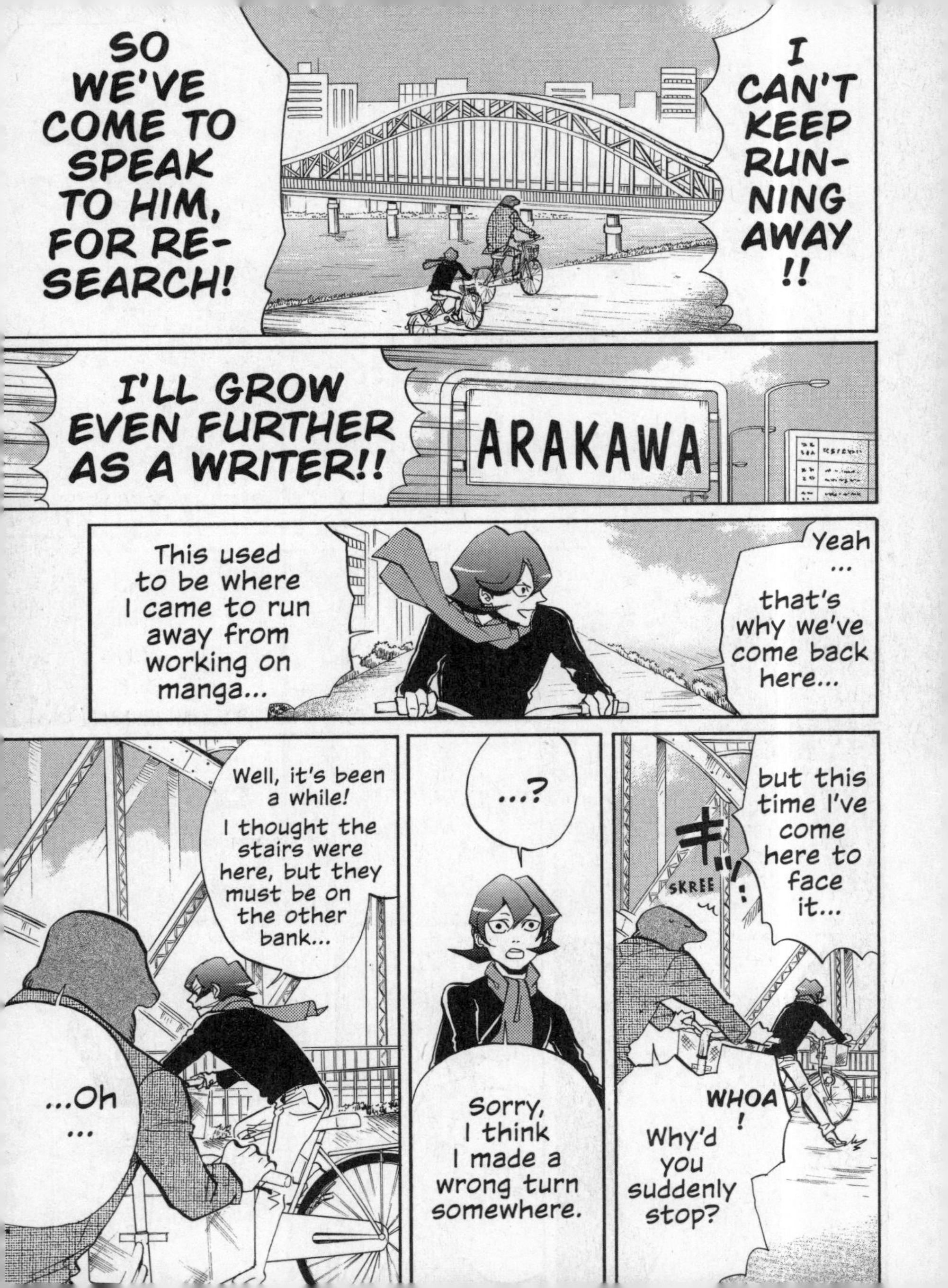
I CAN'T KEEP RUN-NING AWAY !!
SO WE'VE COME TO SPEAK TO HIM, FOR RE-SEARCH!
I'LL GROW EVEN FURTHER AS A WRITER!!
ARAKAWA
Yeah ... that's why we've come back here...
This used to be where I came to run away from working on manga...
but this time I've come here to face it...
SKREE
WHOA !
Why'd you suddenly stop?
...?
Sorry, I think I made a wrong turn somewhere.
Well, it's been a while! I thought the stairs were here, but they must be on the other bank...
...Oh ...

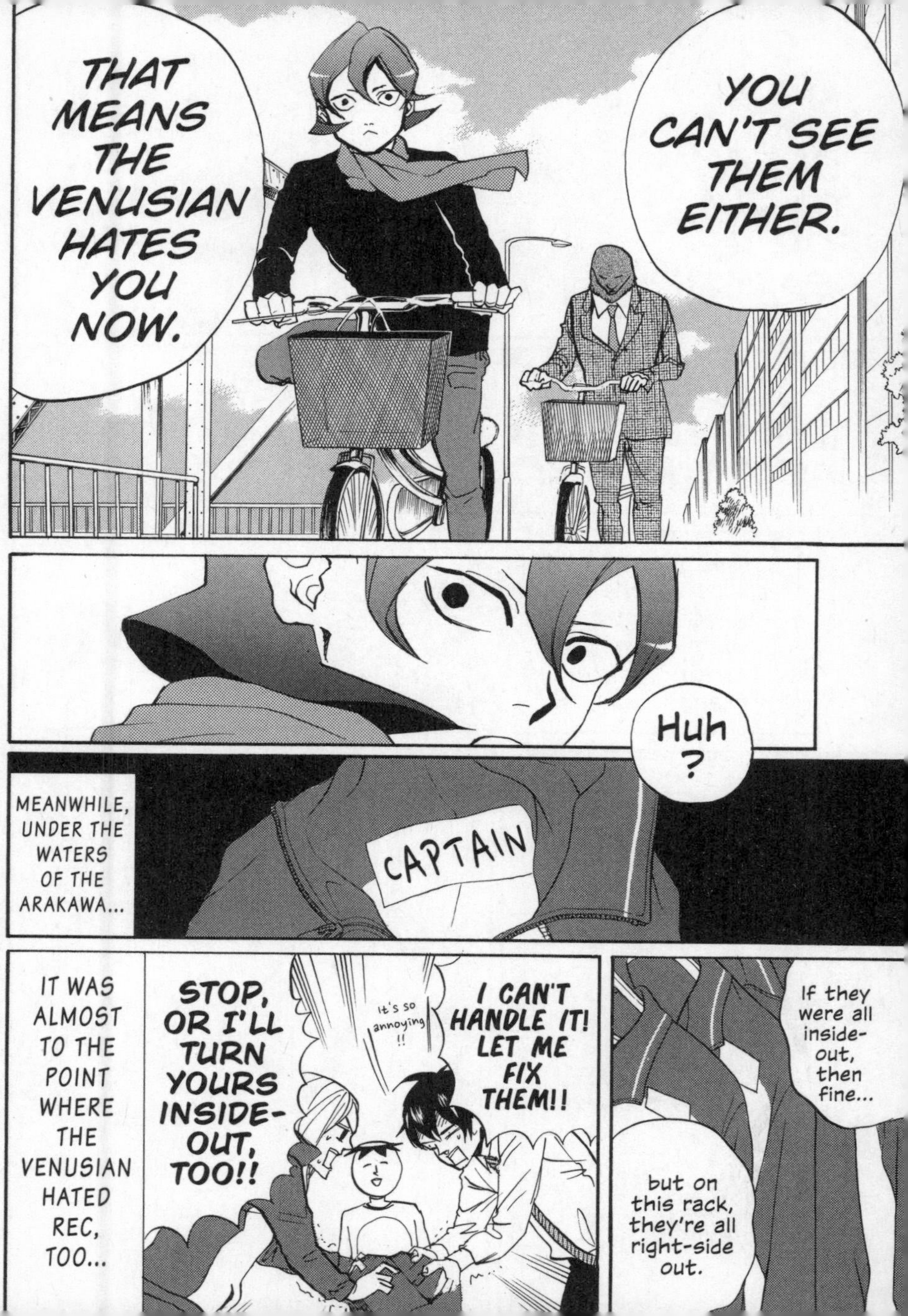
YOU CAN'T SEE THEM EITHER.
THAT MEANS THE VENUSIAN HATES YOU NOW.
Huh?
CAPTAIN
MEANWHILE, UNDER THE WATERS OF THE ARAKAWA...
If they were all inside-out, then fine...
but on this rack, they're all right-side out.
I CAN'T HANDLE IT! LET ME FIX THEM!!
It's so annoying!!
STOP, OR I'LL TURN YOURS INSIDE-OUT, TOO!!
IT WAS ALMOST TO THE POINT WHERE THE VENUSIAN HATED REC, TOO...

ARAKAWA
UNDER
THE BRIDGE

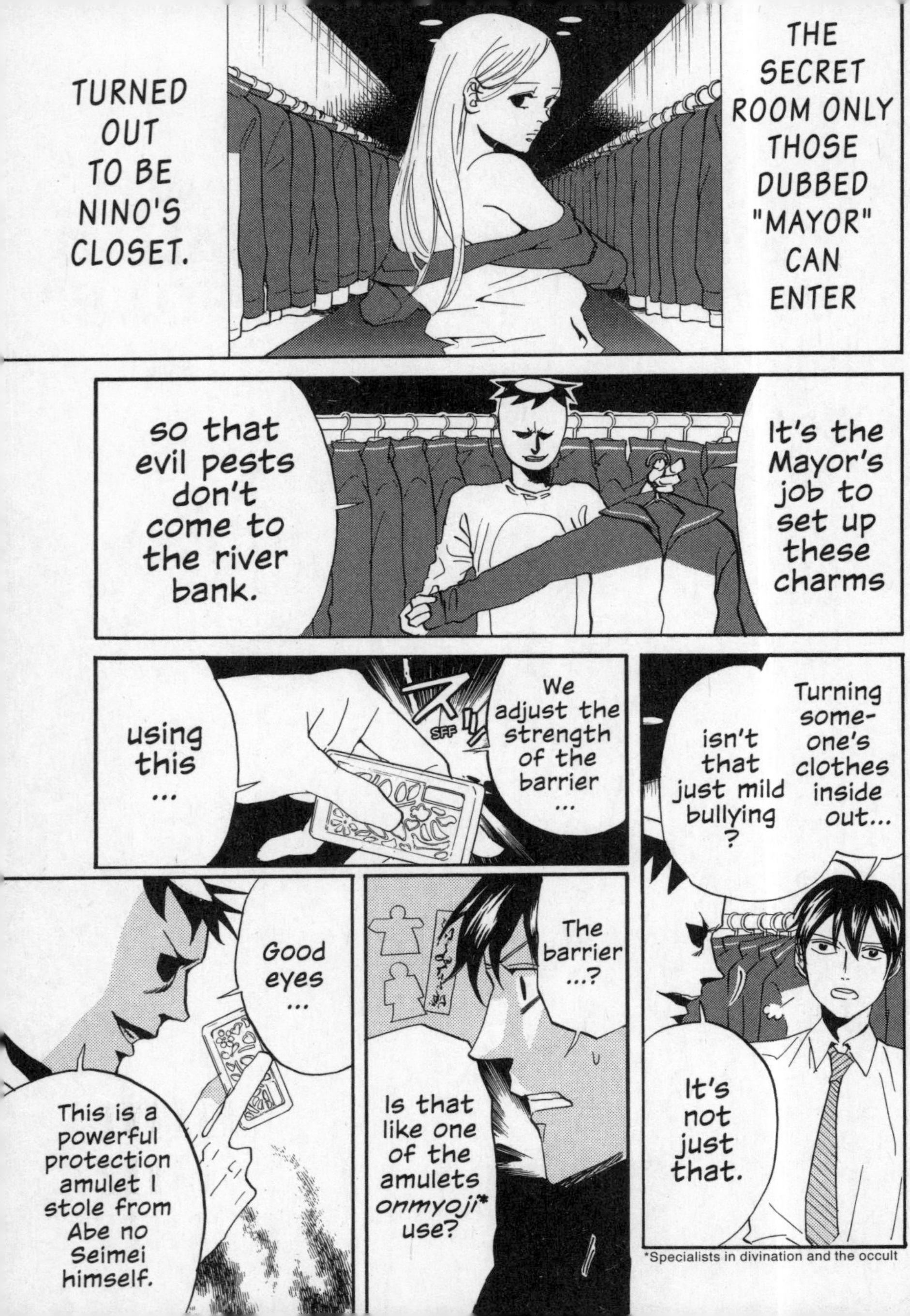
THE SECRET ROOM ONLY THOSE DUBBED "MAYOR" CAN ENTER
TURNED OUT TO BE NINO'S CLOSET.
It's the Mayor's job to set up these charms
so that evil pests don't come to the river bank.
Turning some-one's clothes inside out...
isn't that just mild bullying?
We adjust the strength of the barrier...
SFF
using this...
It's not just that.
The barrier...?
Is that like one of the amulets *onmyoji** use?
Good eyes...
This is a powerful protection amulet I stole from Abe no Seimei himself.

*Specialists in divination and the occult

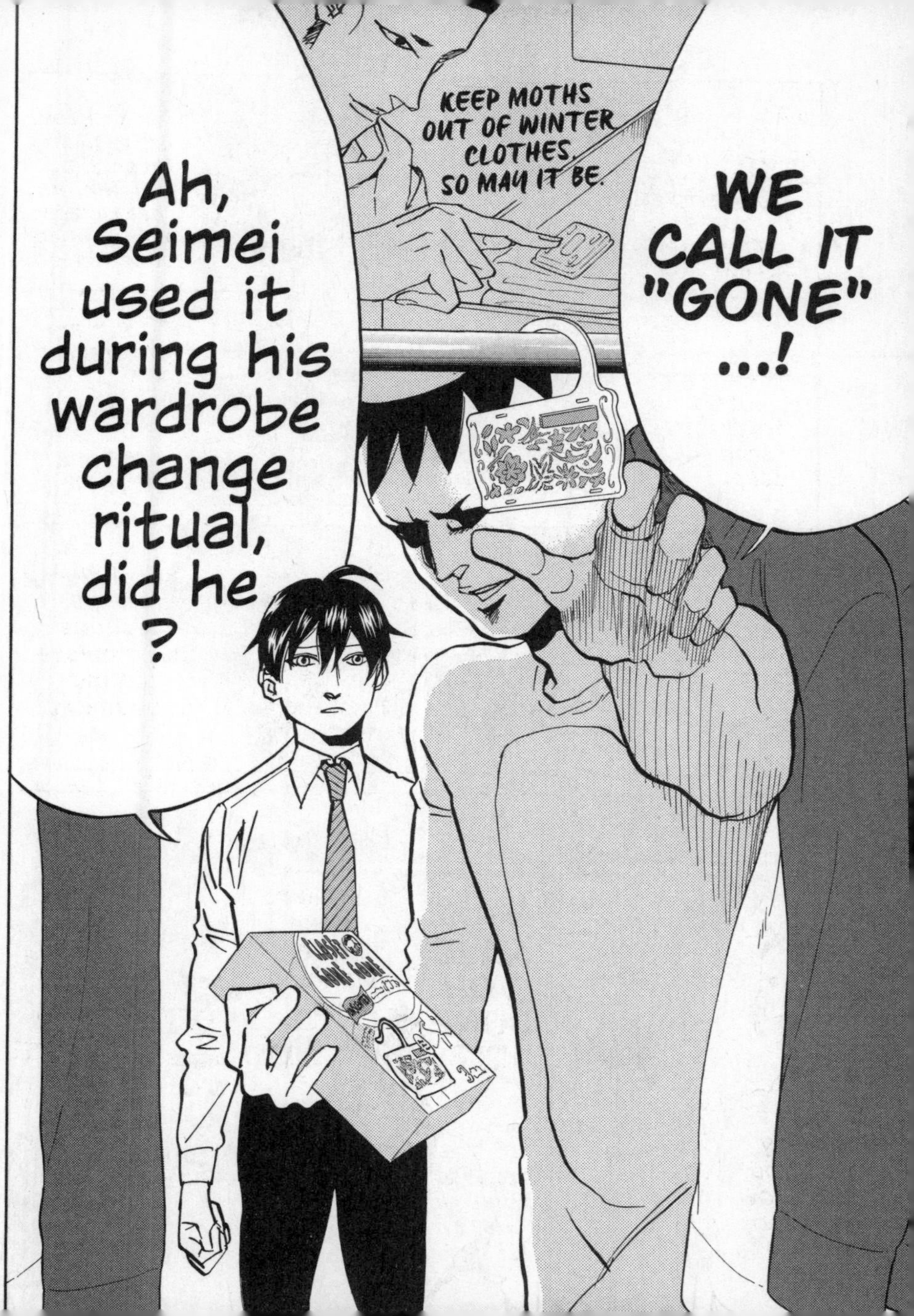
WE CALL IT "GONE" ...!
KEEP MOTHS OUT OF WINTER CLOTHES. SO MAY IT BE.
Ah, Seimei used it during his wardrobe change ritual, did he?

Chapter 360: New Resident Candidate

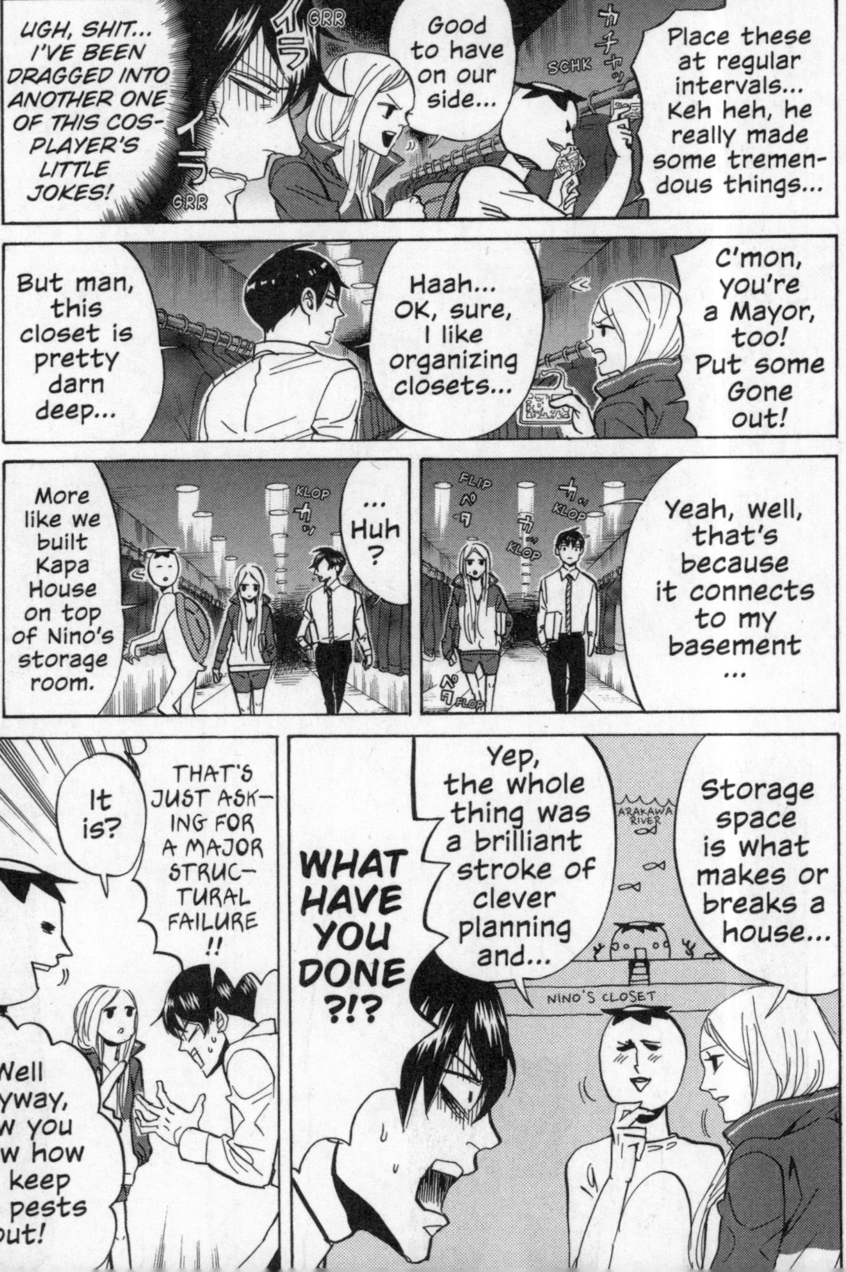
Place these at regular intervals... Keh heh, he really made some tremendous things...
SCHK
Good to have on our side...
GRR
UGH, SHIT... I'VE BEEN DRAGGED INTO ANOTHER ONE OF THIS COS-PLAYER'S LITTLE JOKES!
GRR
C'mon, you're a Mayor, too! Put some Gone out!
Haah... OK, sure, I like organizing closets...
But man, this closet is pretty darn deep...
Yeah, well, that's because it connects to my basement ...
FLIP
KLOP
KLOP
FLOP
... Huh?
KLOP
More like we built Kapa House on top of Nino's storage room.
Storage space is what makes or breaks a house...
Yep, the whole thing was a brilliant stroke of clever planning and...
ARAKAWA RIVER
NINO'S CLOSET
WHAT HAVE YOU DONE ?!?
THAT'S JUST ASKING FOR A MAJOR STRUCTURAL FAILURE !!
It is?
Well anyway, now you know how to keep the pests out!

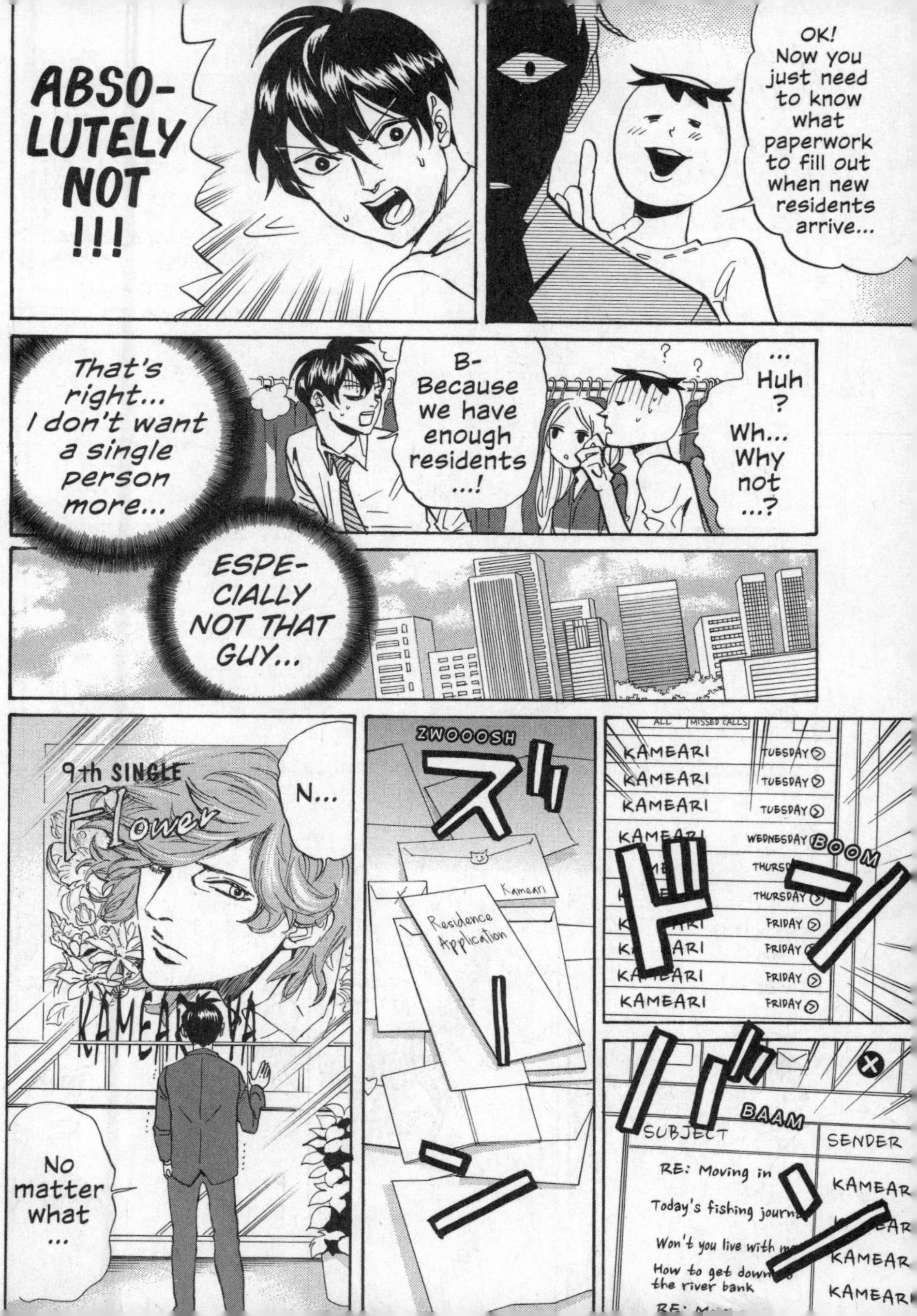
OK! Now you just need to know what paperwork to fill out when new residents arrive...
ABSO-LUTELY NOT !!!
... Huh? Wh... Why not ...?
B- Because we have enough residents ....!
That's right... I don't want a single person more...
ESPE-CIALLY NOT THAT GUY...
ALL
MISSED CALLS
KAMEARI TUESDAY
KAMEARI TUESDAY
KAMEARI TUESDAY
WEDNESDAY
THURSDAY
FRIDAY
FRIDAY
FRIDAY
KAMEARI FRIDAY
BOOM
BAAM
SUBJECT
SENDER
RE: Moving in
KAMEAR
KAMEAR
KAMEARI
ZWOOOSH
Kameari
Residence Application
9th SINGLE
Flower
N...
No matter what ...

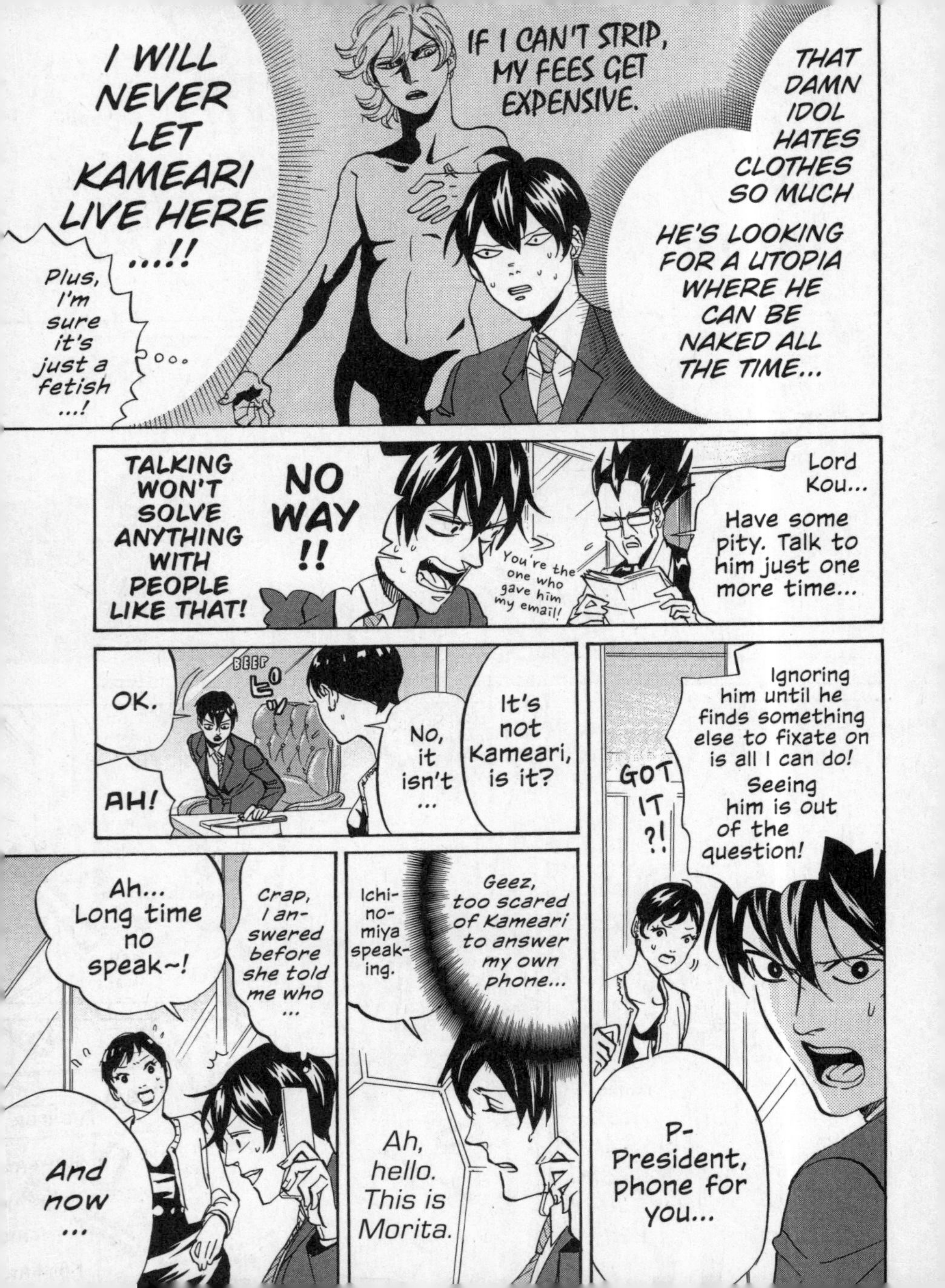
THAT DAMN IDOL HATES CLOTHES SO MUCH
HE'S LOOKING FOR A UTOPIA WHERE HE CAN BE NAKED ALL THE TIME...
IF I CAN'T STRIP, MY FEES GET EXPENSIVE.
I WILL NEVER LET KAMEARI LIVE HERE...!!
Plus, I'm sure it's just a fetish...!
Lord Kou...
Have some pity. Talk to him just one more time...
You're the one who gave him my email!
NO WAY!!
TALKING WON'T SOLVE ANYTHING WITH PEOPLE LIKE THAT!
Ignoring him until he finds something else to fixate on is all I can do!
Seeing him is out of the question!
GOT IT?!
P-President, phone for you...
It's not Kameari, is it?
No, it isn't...
BEEP
OK.
AH!
Geez, too scared of Kameari to answer my own phone...
Ichi-no-miya speak-ing.
Ah, hello. This is Morita.
Ah... Long time no speak~!
Crap, I an-swered before she told me who...
And now...

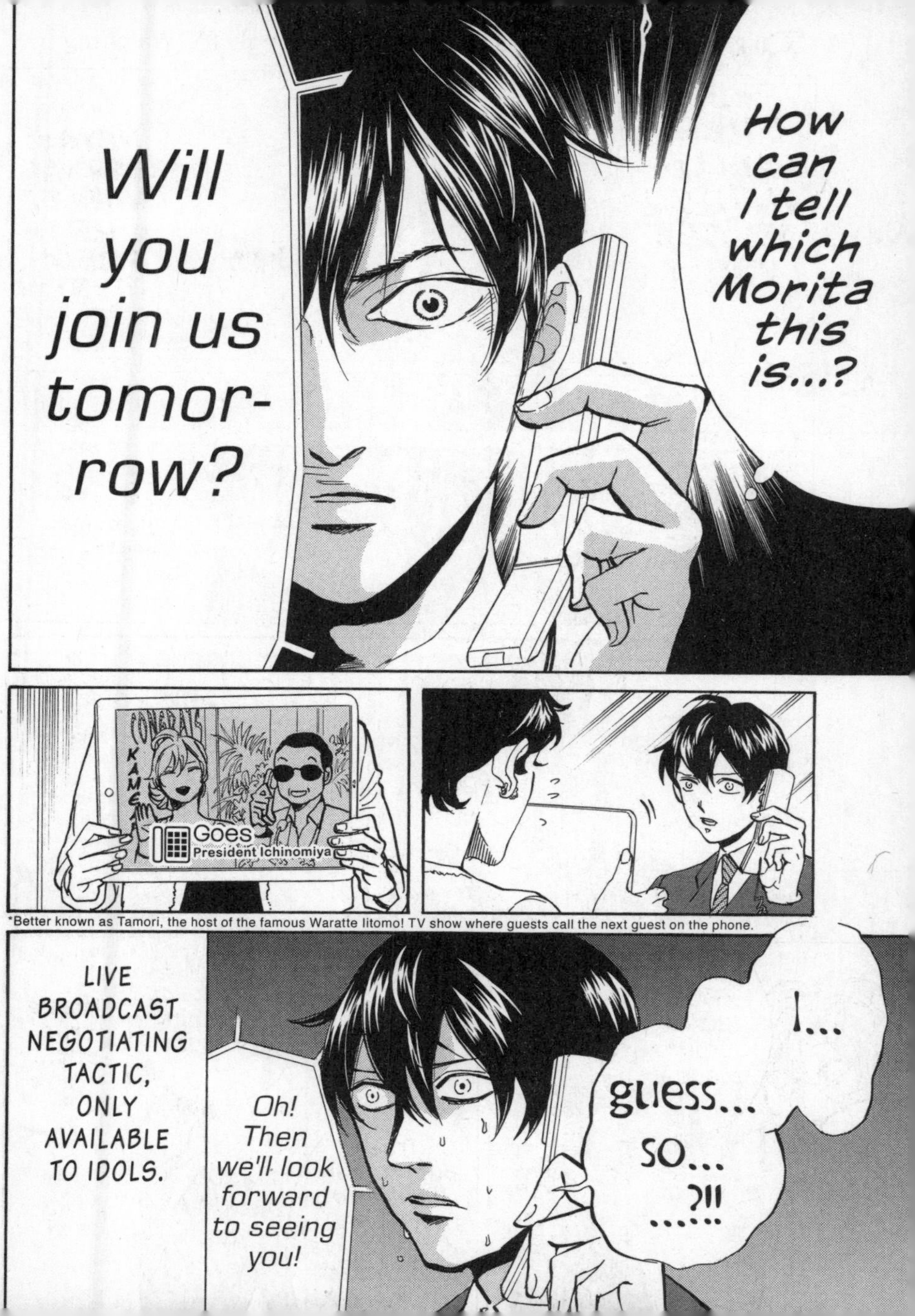
How can I tell which Morita this is...?
Will you join us tomorrow?
Goes
President Ichinomiya
I... guess... so... ...?!!
Oh! Then we'll look forward to seeing you!
LIVE BROADCAST NEGOTIATING TACTIC, ONLY AVAILABLE TO IDOLS.

*Better known as Tamori, the host of the famous Waratte Iitomo! TV show where guests call the next guest on the phone.

Chapter 361: Heart-Pounding Lunch Break TV Watching

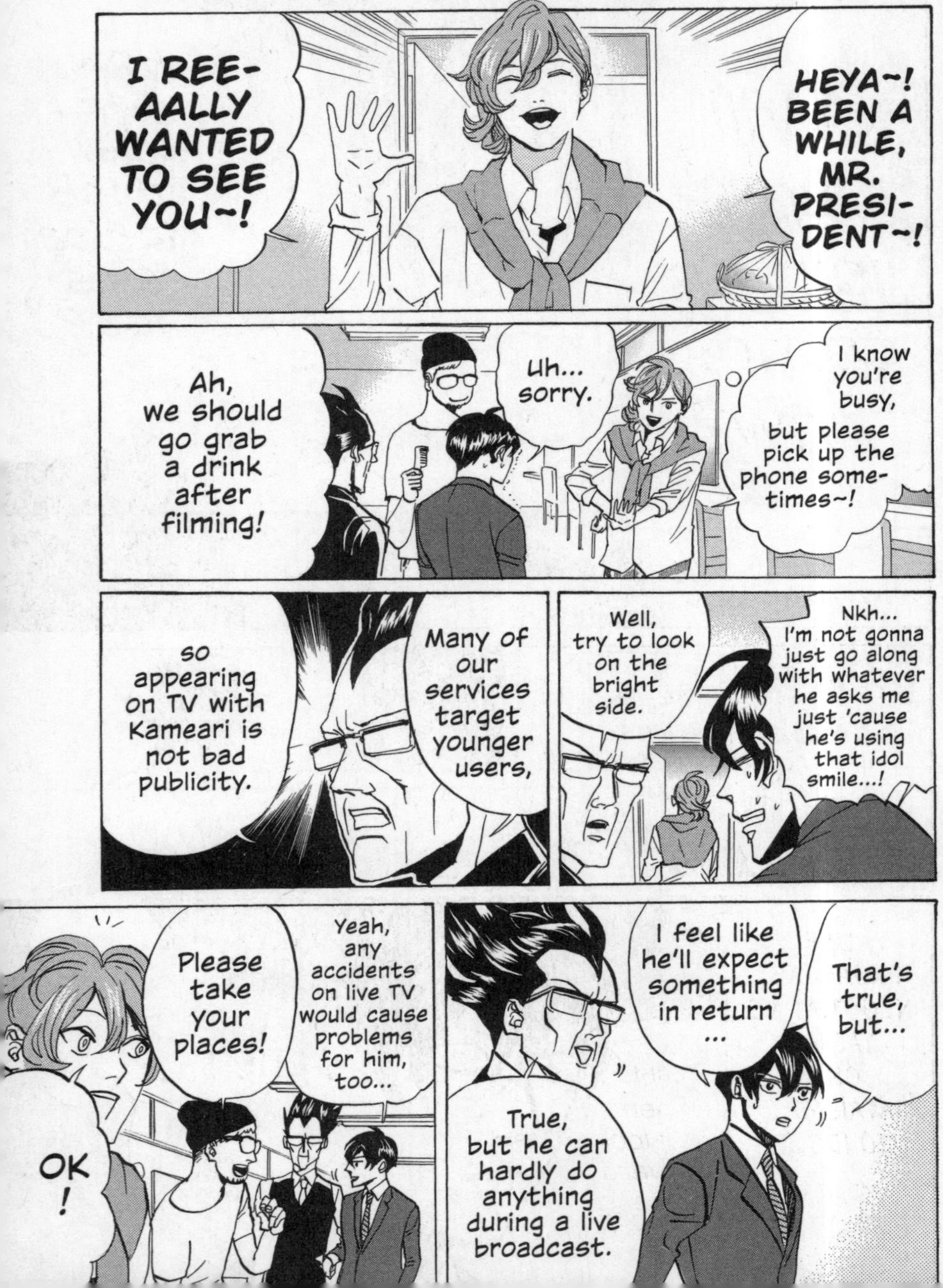
HEYA~! BEEN A WHILE, MR. PRESIDENT~!
I REE-AALLY WANTED TO SEE YOU~!
I know you're busy, but please pick up the phone some-times~!
Uh... sorry.
Ah, we should go grab a drink after filming!
Nkh... I'm not gonna just go along with whatever he asks me just 'cause he's using that idol smile...!
Well, try to look on the bright side.
Many of our services target younger users,
so appearing on TV with Kameari is not bad publicity.
That's true, but...
I feel like he'll expect something in return ...
True, but he can hardly do anything during a live broadcast.
Yeah, any accidents on live TV would cause problems for him, too...
Please take your places!
OK!

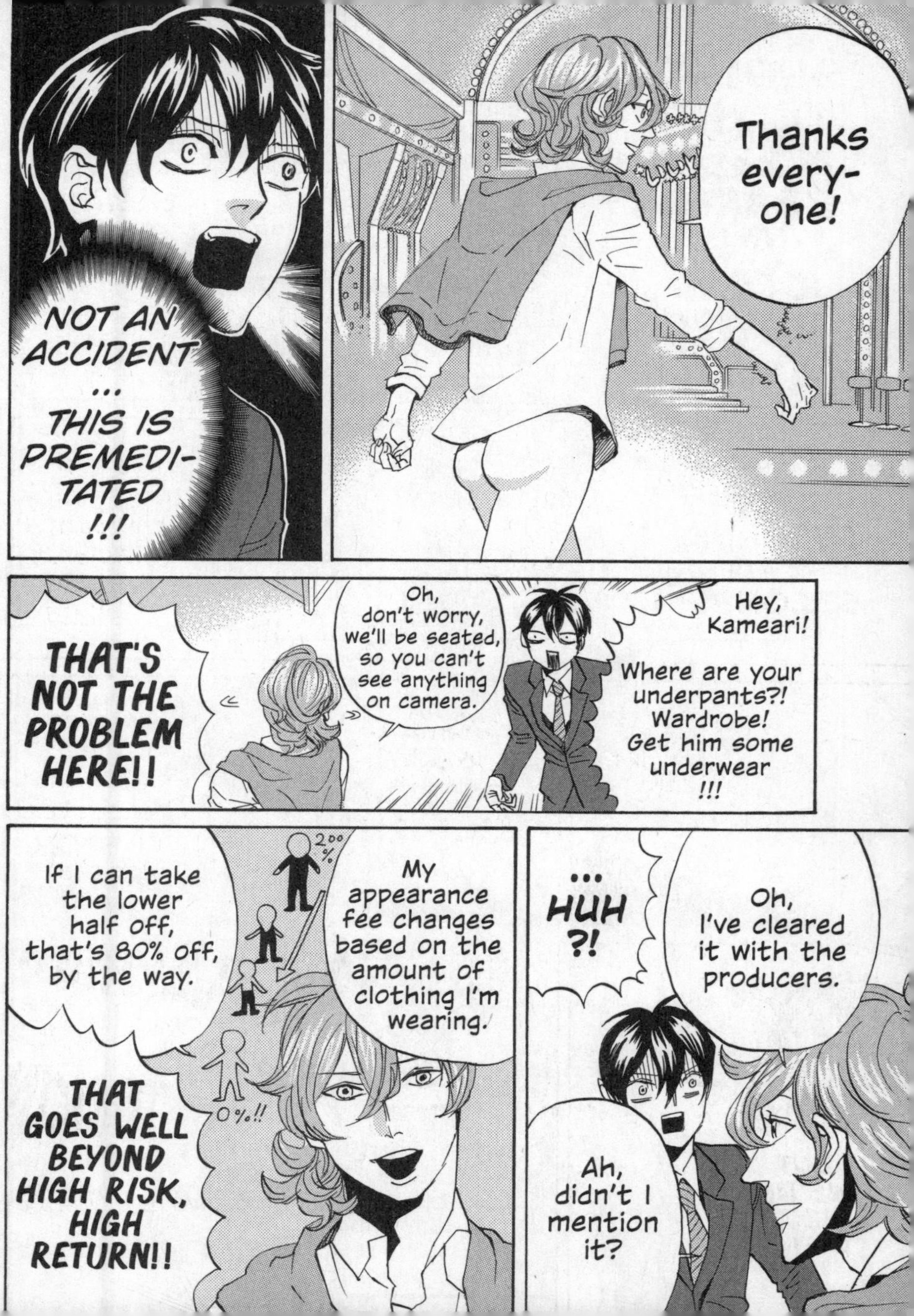
Thanks everyone!
NOT AN ACCIDENT ... THIS IS PREMEDITATED !!!
Hey, Kameari!
Where are your underpants?! Wardrobe! Get him some underwear !!!
Oh, don't worry, we'll be seated, so you can't see anything on camera.
THAT'S NOT THE PROBLEM HERE!!
Oh, I've cleared it with the producers.
... HUH ?!
Ah, didn't I mention it?
My appearance fee changes based on the amount of clothing I'm wearing.
200%
If I can take the lower half off, that's 80% off, by the way.
0%!!
THAT GOES WELL BEYOND HIGH RISK, HIGH RETURN!!

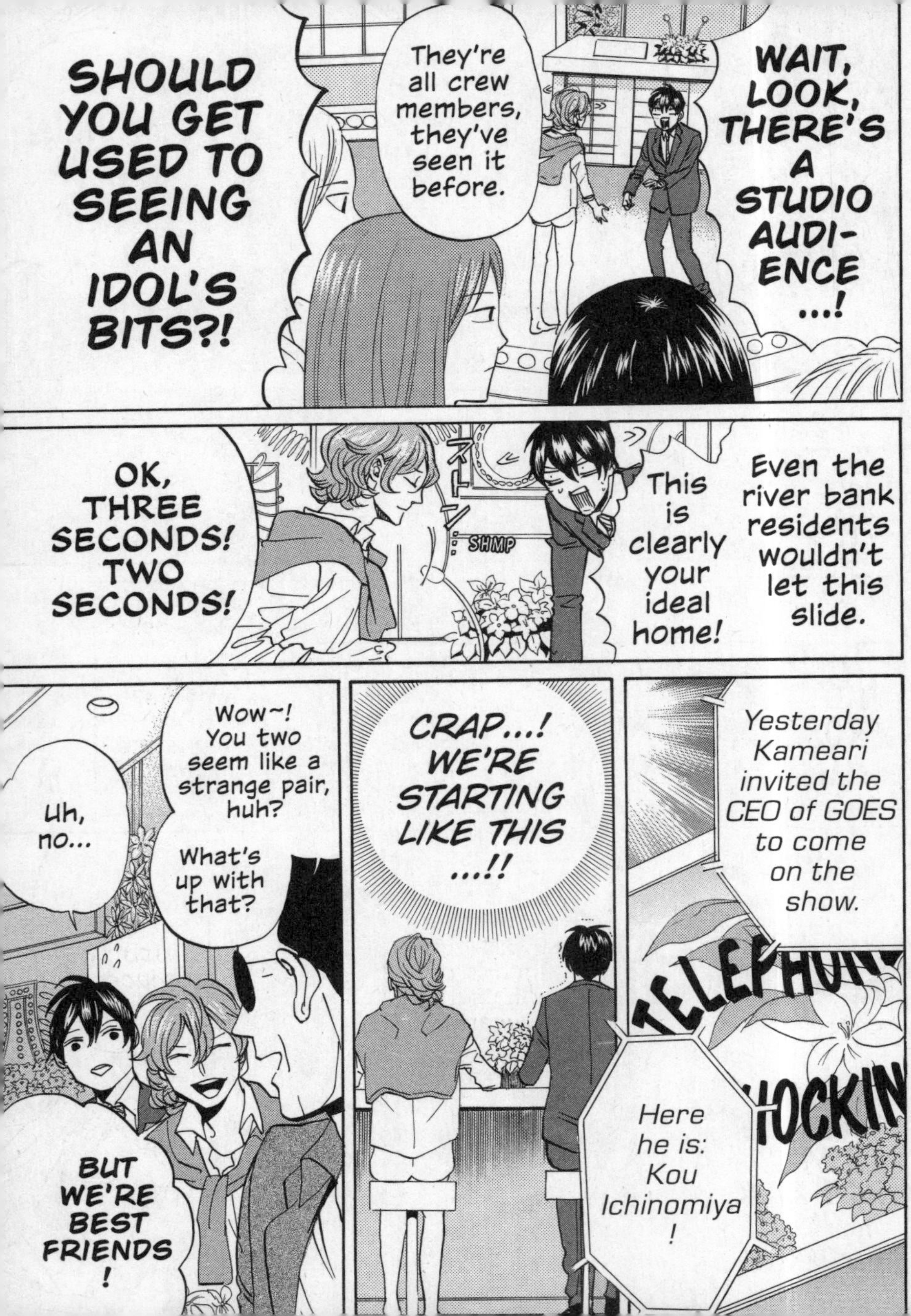
WAIT, LOOK, THERE'S A STUDIO AUDIENCE ...!
They're all crew members, they've seen it before.
SHOULD YOU GET USED TO SEEING AN IDOL'S BITS?!
Even the river bank residents wouldn't let this slide.
This is clearly your ideal home!
SHMP
OK, THREE SECONDS! TWO SECONDS!
Yesterday Kameari invited the CEO of GOES to come on the show.
TELEPHON
HOCKIN
Here he is: Kou Ichinomiya!
CRAP...! WE'RE STARTING LIKE THIS ...!!
Wow~! You two seem like a strange pair, huh?
What's up with that?
Uh, no...
BUT WE'RE BEST FRIENDS!

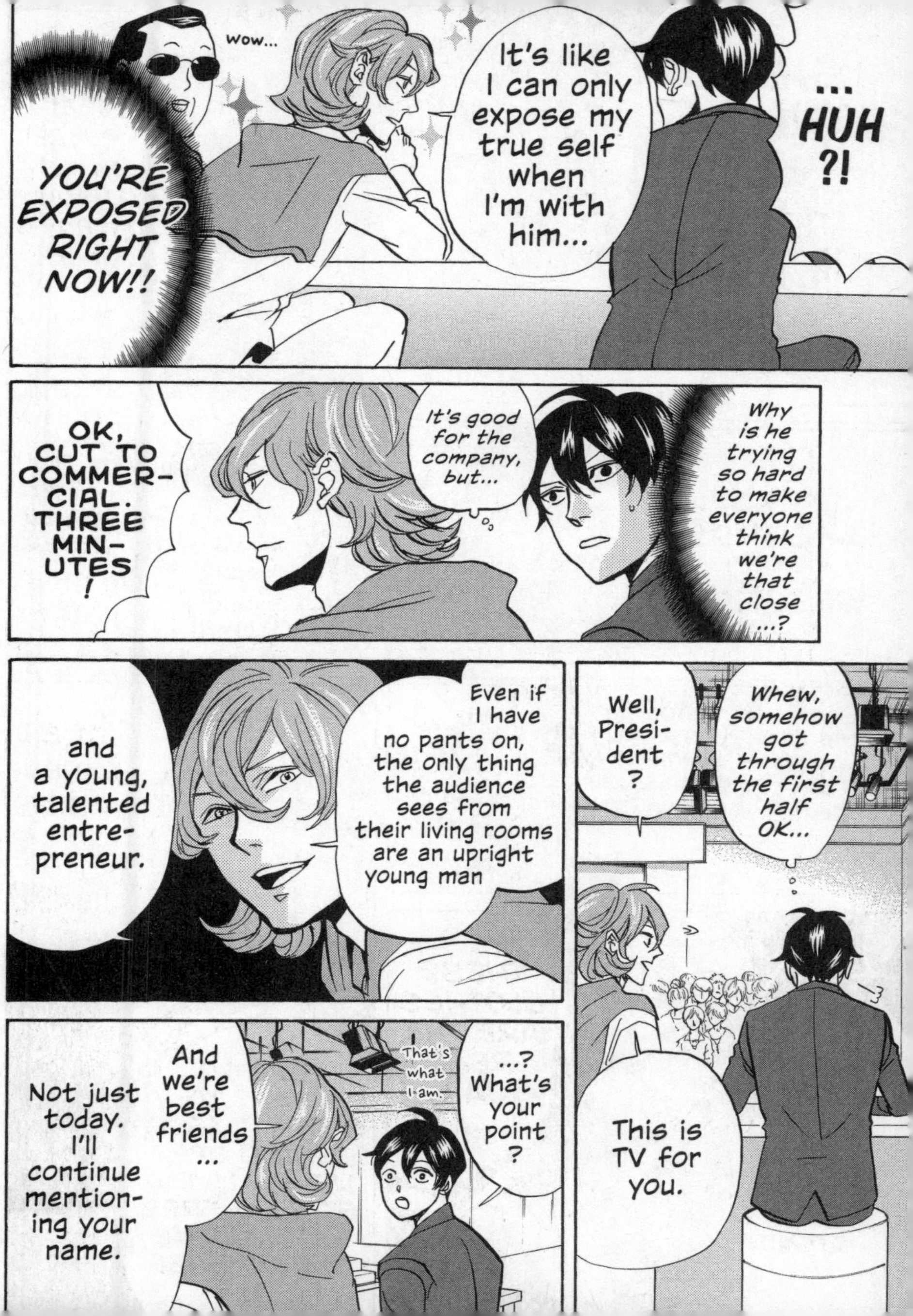
...HUH?!
It's like I can only expose my true self when I'm with him...
wow...
YOU'RE EXPOSED RIGHT NOW!!
Why is he trying so hard to make everyone think we're that close...?
It's good for the company, but...
OK, CUT TO COMMERCIAL. THREE MINUTES!
Whew, somehow got through the first half OK...
Well, President?
This is TV for you.
Even if I have no pants on, the only thing the audience sees from their living rooms are an upright young man
and a young, talented entrepreneur.
...? What's your point?
That's what I am.
And we're best friends...
Not just today. I'll continue mentioning your name.

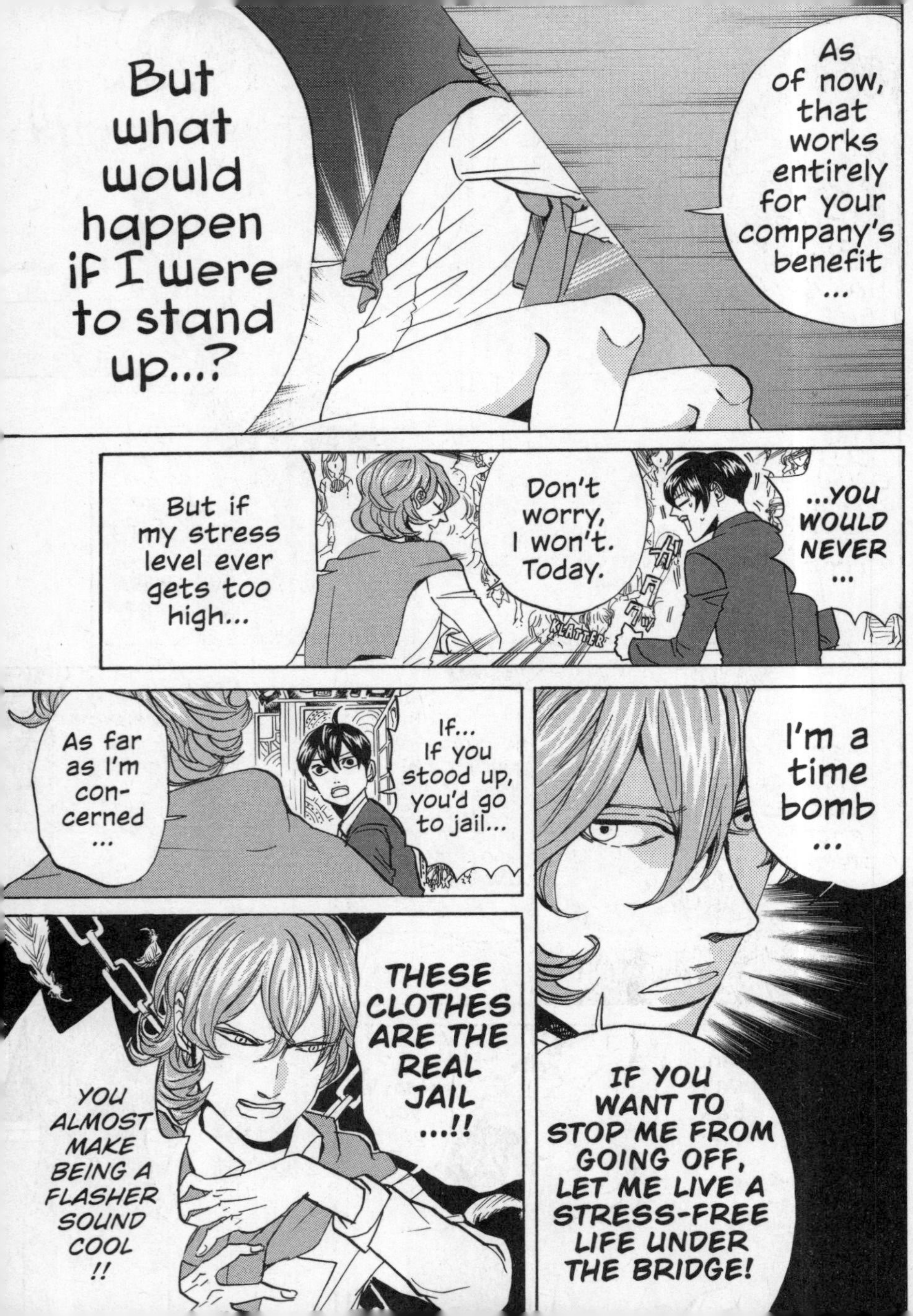
As of now, that works entirely for your company's benefit ...
But what would happen if I were to stand up...?
...YOU WOULD NEVER ...
Don't worry, I won't. Today.
But if my stress level ever gets too high...
KLATTER
I'm a time bomb ...
IF YOU WANT TO STOP ME FROM GOING OFF, LET ME LIVE A STRESS-FREE LIFE UNDER THE BRIDGE!
If... If you stood up, you'd go to jail...
As far as I'm con-cerned ...
THESE CLOTHES ARE THE REAL JAIL ...!!
YOU ALMOST MAKE BEING A FLASHER SOUND COOL !!

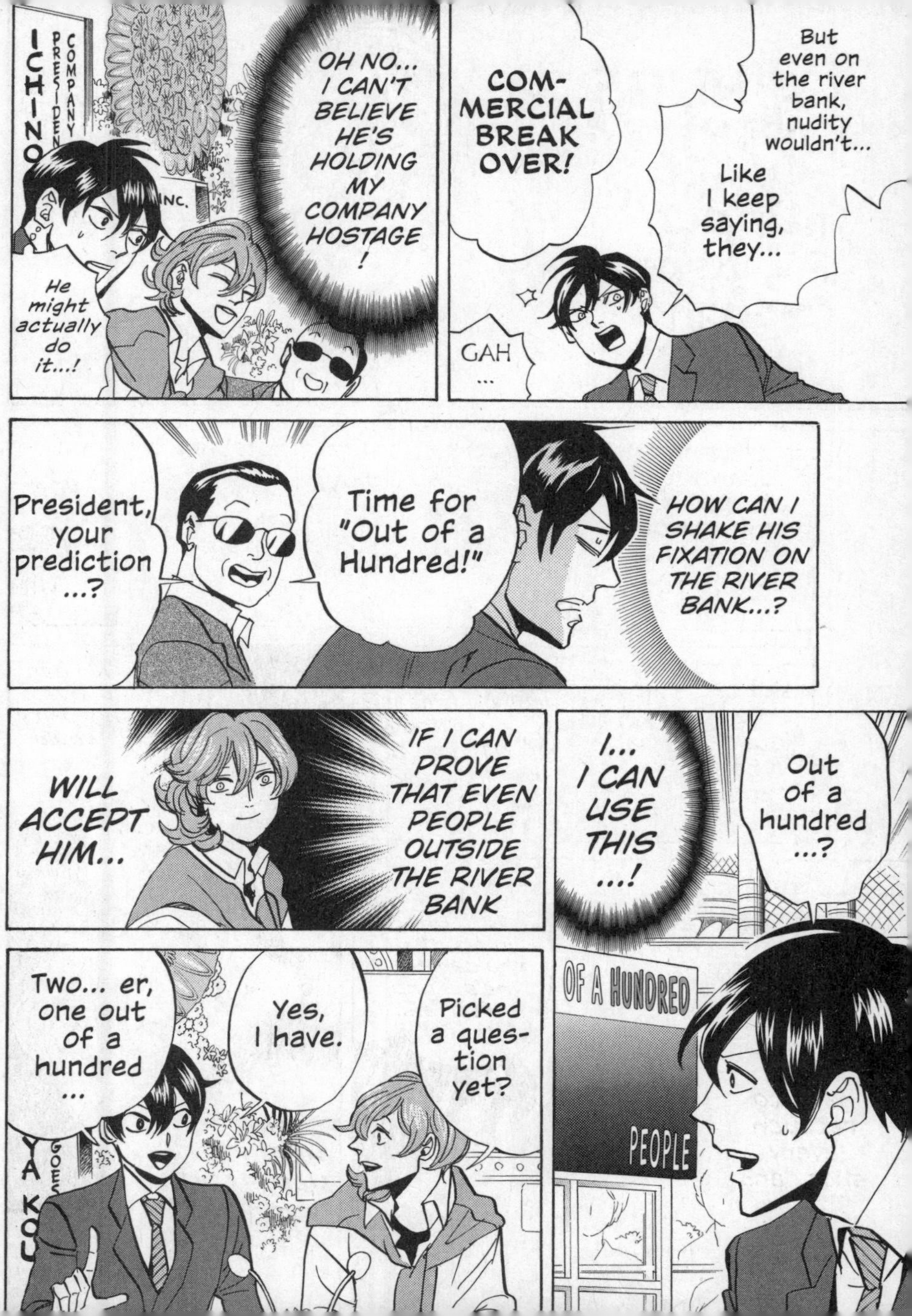

But even on the river bank, nudity wouldn't...
Like I keep saying, they...
COMMERCIAL BREAK OVER!
GAH ...
OH NO... I CAN'T BELIEVE HE'S HOLDING MY COMPANY HOSTAGE!
ICHINO
INC.
He might actually do it...!
HOW CAN I SHAKE HIS FIXATION ON THE RIVER BANK...?
Time for "Out of a Hundred!"
President, your prediction ...?
Out of a hundred ...?
I... I CAN USE THIS ...!
OF A HUNDRED
PEOPLE
IF I CAN PROVE THAT EVEN PEOPLE OUTSIDE THE RIVER BANK
WILL ACCEPT HIM...
Picked a question yet?
Yes, I have.
Two... er, one out of a hundred ...

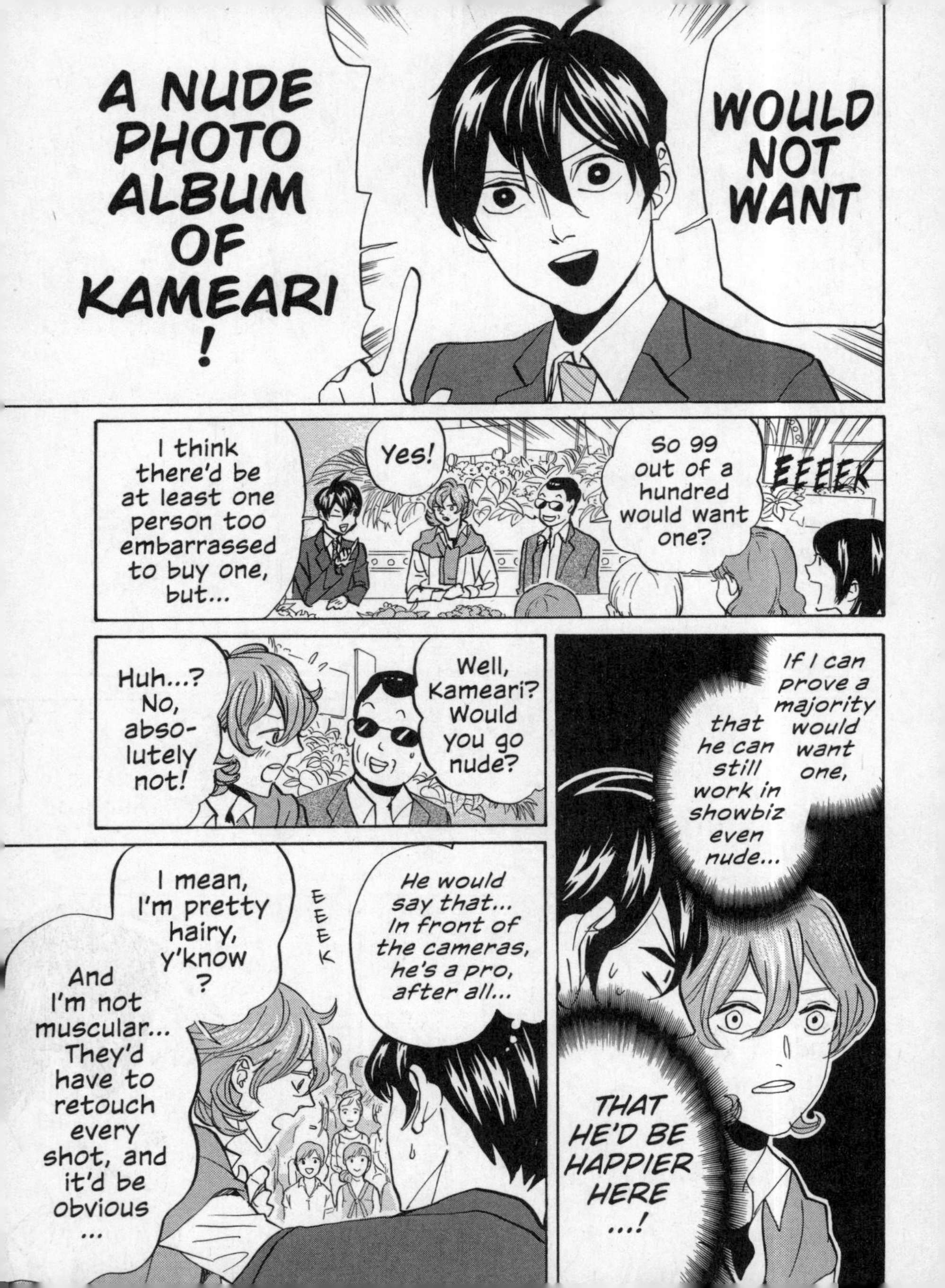
WOULD NOT WANT
A NUDE PHOTO ALBUM OF KAMEARI!
EEEEK
So 99 out of a hundred would want one?
Yes!
I think there'd be at least one person too embarrassed to buy one, but...
If I can prove a majority would want one,
that he can still work in showbiz even nude...
THAT HE'D BE HAPPIER HERE...!
Well, Kameari? Would you go nude?
Huh...? No, absolutely not!
He would say that... In front of the cameras, he's a pro, after all...
EEEK
I mean, I'm pretty hairy, y'know?
And I'm not muscular... They'd have to retouch every shot, and it'd be obvious...

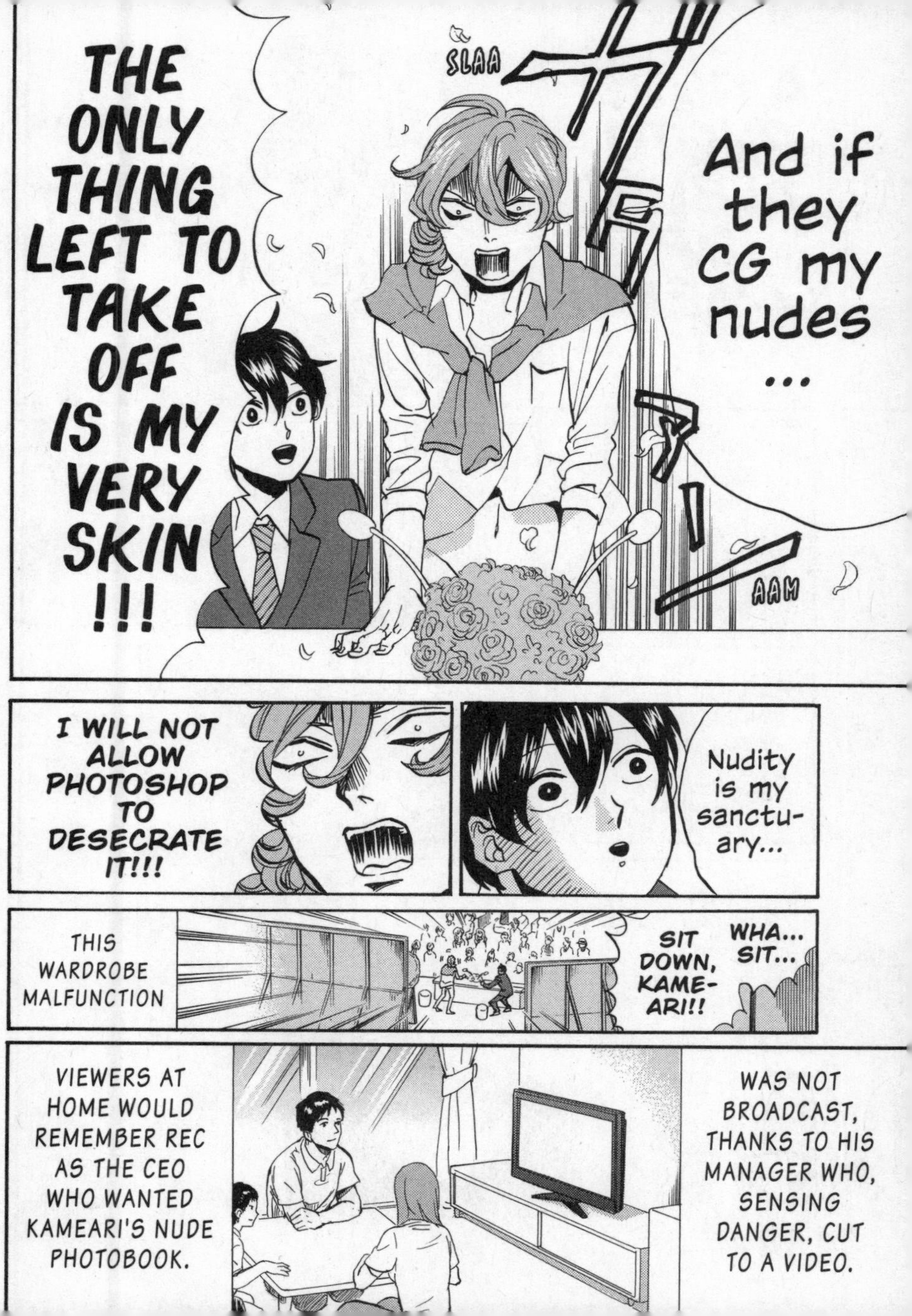
And if they CG my nudes ...
SLAA
AAM
THE ONLY THING LEFT TO TAKE OFF IS MY VERY SKIN !!!
Nudity is my sanctu-ary...
I WILL NOT ALLOW PHOTOSHOP TO DESECRATE IT!!!
WHA... SIT...
SIT DOWN, KAME-ARI!!
THIS WARDROBE MALFUNCTION
WAS NOT BROADCAST, THANKS TO HIS MANAGER WHO, SENSING DANGER, CUT TO A VIDEO.
VIEWERS AT HOME WOULD REMEMBER REC AS THE CEO WHO WANTED KAMEARI'S NUDE PHOTOBOOK.

ARAKAWA
UNDER
THE BRIDGE

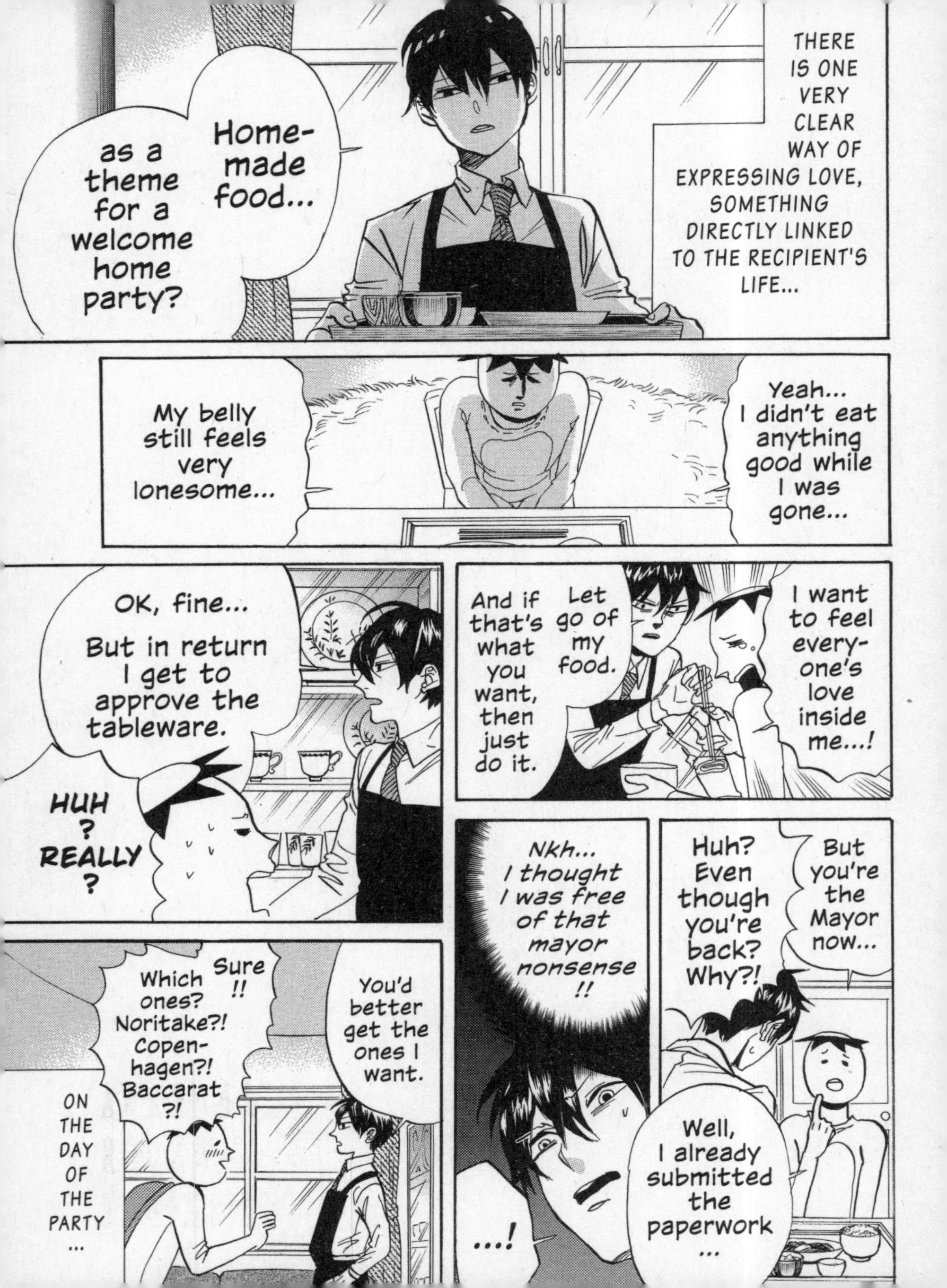
THERE IS ONE VERY CLEAR WAY OF EXPRESSING LOVE, SOMETHING DIRECTLY LINKED TO THE RECIPIENT'S LIFE...
Home-made food...
as a theme for a welcome home party?
Yeah... I didn't eat anything good while I was gone...
My belly still feels very lonesome...
I want to feel every-one's love inside me...!
Let go of my food.
And if that's what you want, then just do it.
OK, fine...
But in return I get to approve the tableware.
HUH? REALLY?
But you're the Mayor now...
Huh? Even though you're back? Why?!
Well, I already submitted the paperwork...
Nkh... I thought I was free of that mayor nonsense!!
...!
You'd better get the ones I want.
Sure!!
Which ones? Noritake?! Copen-hagen?! Baccarat?!
ON THE DAY OF THE PARTY...

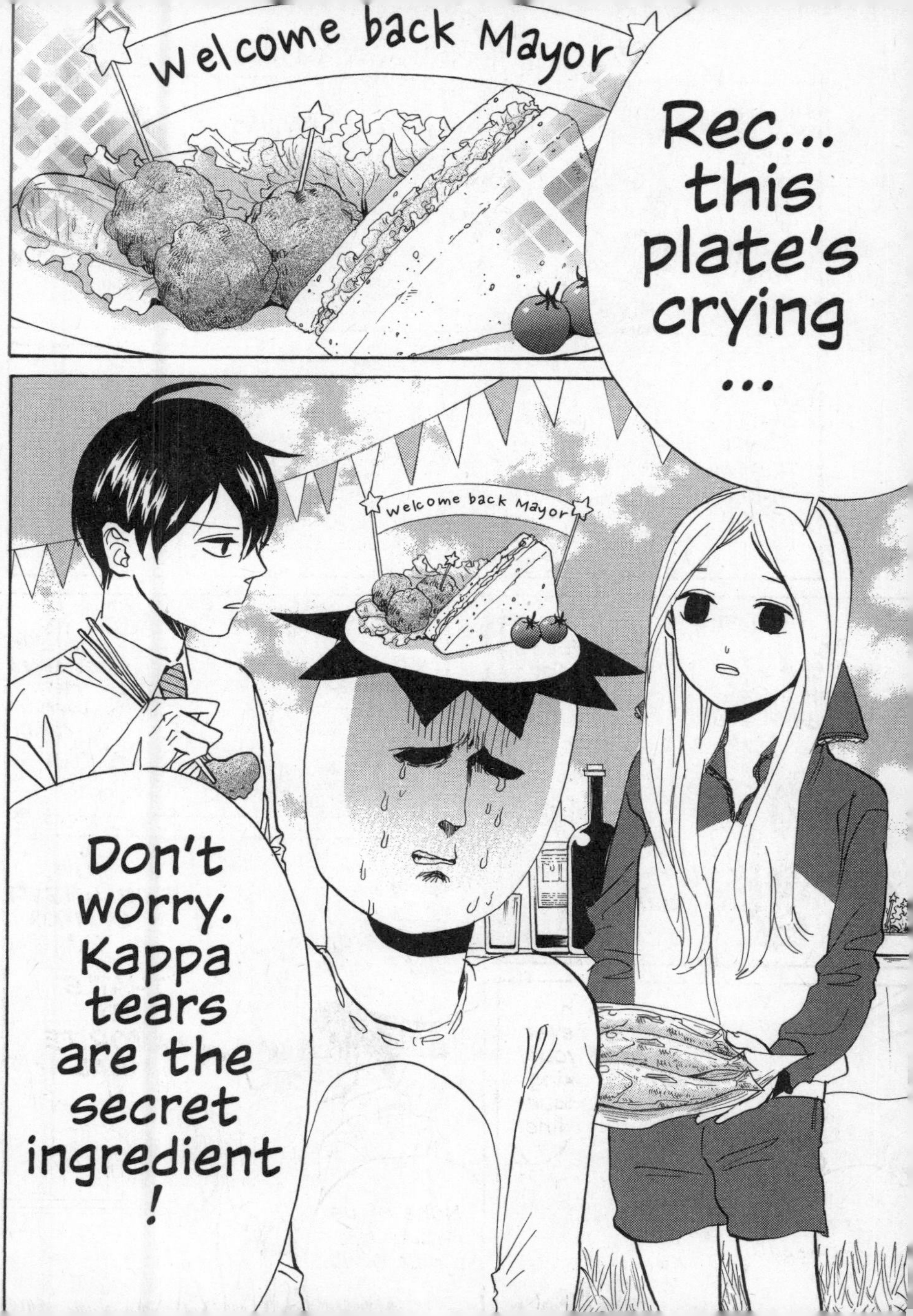
Welcome back Mayor
Rec... this plate's crying ...
welcome back Mayor
Don't worry. Kappa tears are the secret ingredient !

Chapter 362: Love Cooking

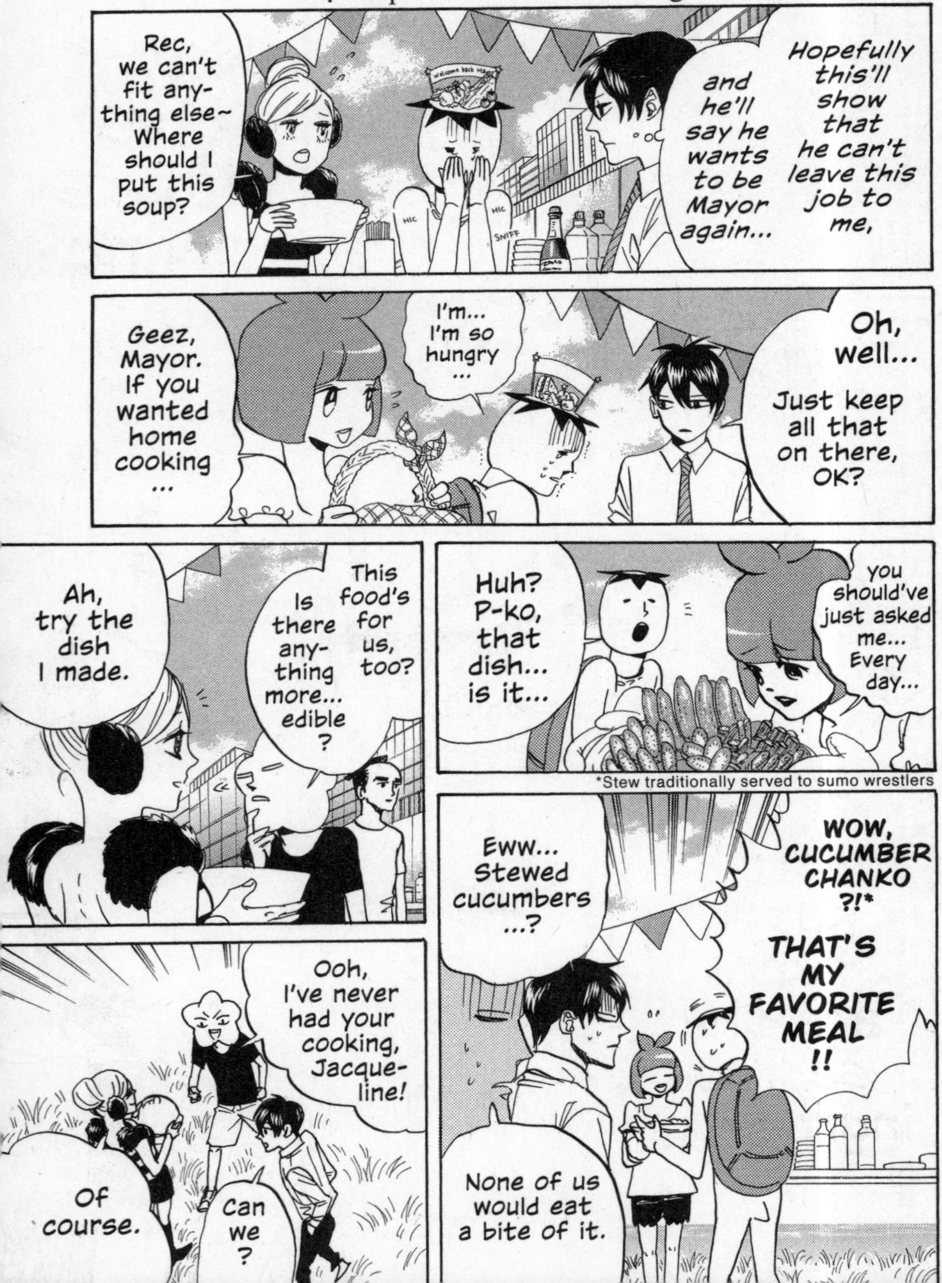
Hopefully this'll show that he can't leave this job to me,
and he'll say he wants to be Mayor again...
Rec, we can't fit any-thing else~ Where should I put this soup?
HIC
HIC
SNIFF
Oh, well...
Just keep all that on there, OK?
I'm... I'm so hungry ...
Geez, Mayor. If you wanted home cooking ...
you should've just asked me... Every day...
Huh? P-ko, that dish... is it...
This food's for us, too?
Is there any-thing more... edible ?
Ah, try the dish I made.
WOW, CUCUMBER CHANKO ?!*
THAT'S MY FAVORITE MEAL !!
Eww... Stewed cucumbers ...?
None of us would eat a bite of it.
Ooh, I've never had your cooking, Jacque-line!
Can we ?
Of course.

*Stew traditionally served to sumo wrestlers

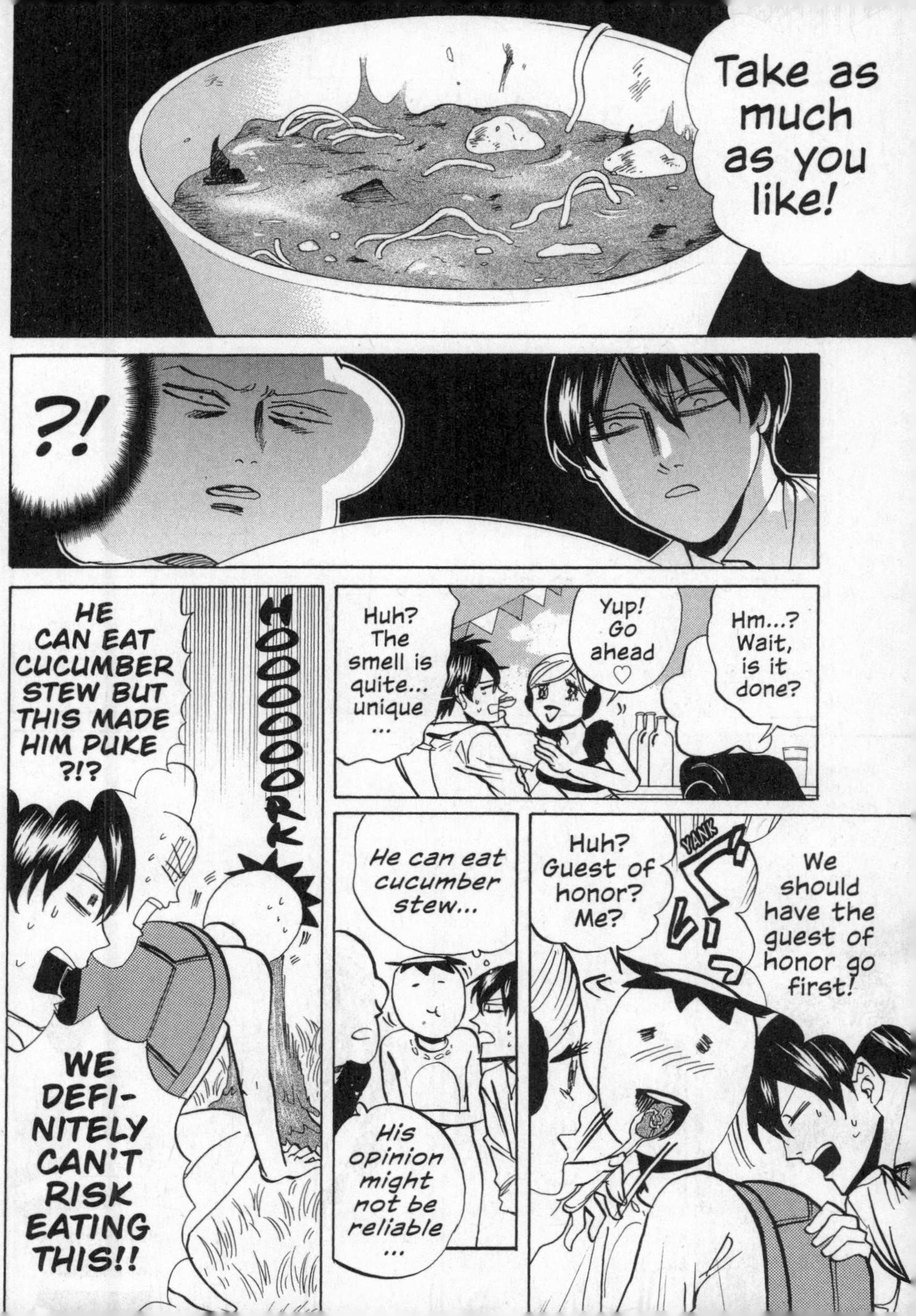
Take as much as you like!
?!
Hm...? Wait, is it done?
Yup! Go ahead ♡
Huh? The smell is quite... unique ...
We should have the guest of honor go first!
YANK
Huh? Guest of honor? Me?
He can eat cucumber stew...
His opinion might not be reliable ...
HOOOOOOORK
HE CAN EAT CUCUMBER STEW BUT THIS MADE HIM PUKE ?!?
WE DEFI-NITELY CAN'T RISK EATING THIS!!

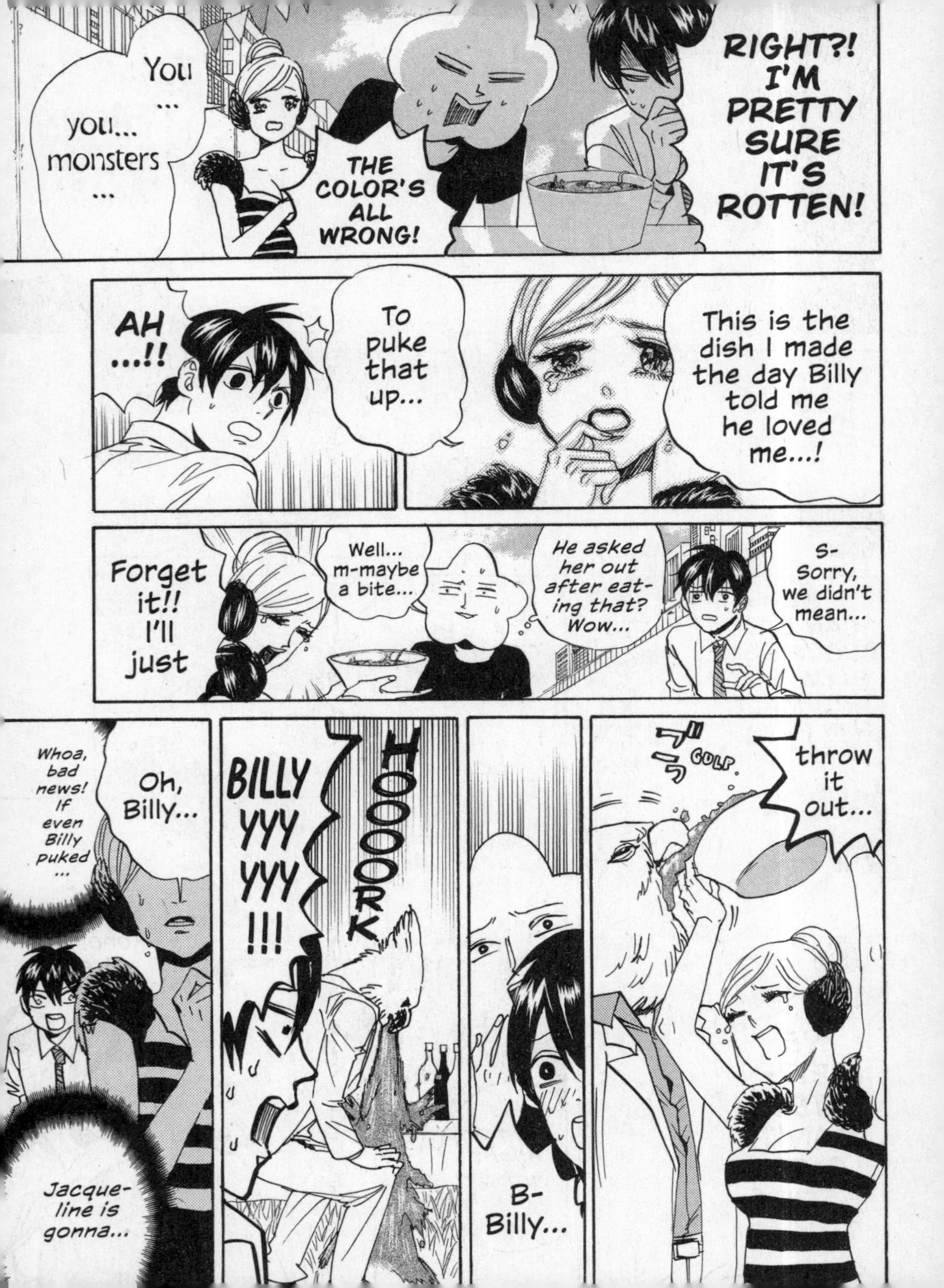
RIGHT?! I'M PRETTY SURE IT'S ROTTEN!
THE COLOR'S ALL WRONG!
You ... you... monsters ...
This is the dish I made the day Billy told me he loved me...!
To puke that up...
AH ...!!
S- Sorry, we didn't mean...
He asked her out after eating that? Wow...
Well... m-maybe a bite...
Forget it!! I'll just
throw it out...
GULP
B- Billy...
BILLY YYY YYY !!!
HOOOOORK
Oh, Billy...
Whoa, bad news! If even Billy puked ...
Jacque- line is gonna...

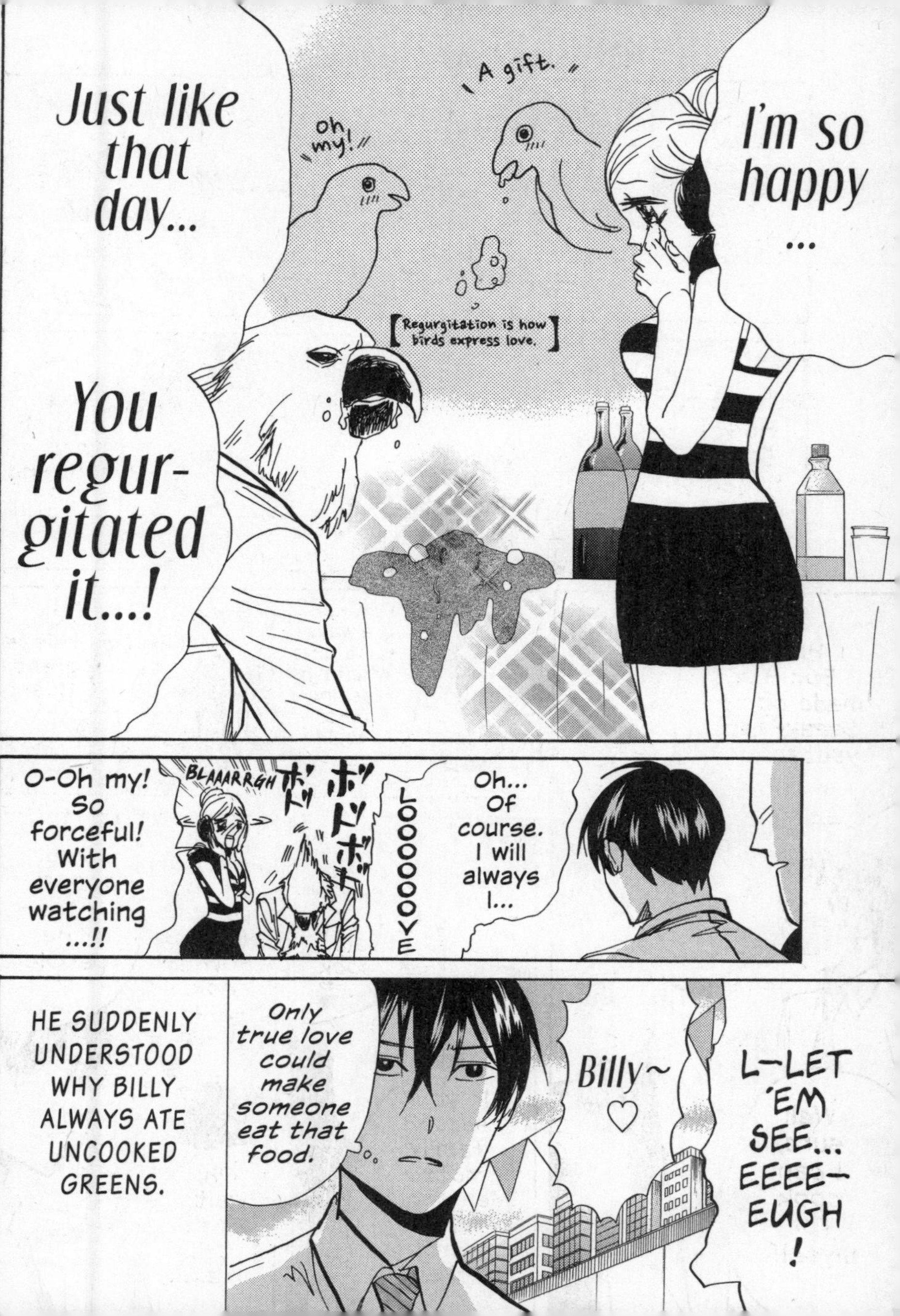
I'm so happy ...
A gift.
oh my!
Just like that day...
Regurgitation is how birds express love.
You regur-gitated it...!
Oh... Of course. I will always l...
LOOOOOOOVE
BLAAARRGH
O-Oh my! So forceful! With everyone watching ...!!
L—LET 'EM SEE... EEEE—EUGH!
Billy~ ♡
Only true love could make someone eat that food.
HE SUDDENLY UNDERSTOOD WHY BILLY ALWAYS ATE UNCOOKED GREENS.

Chapter 363: Cooking History

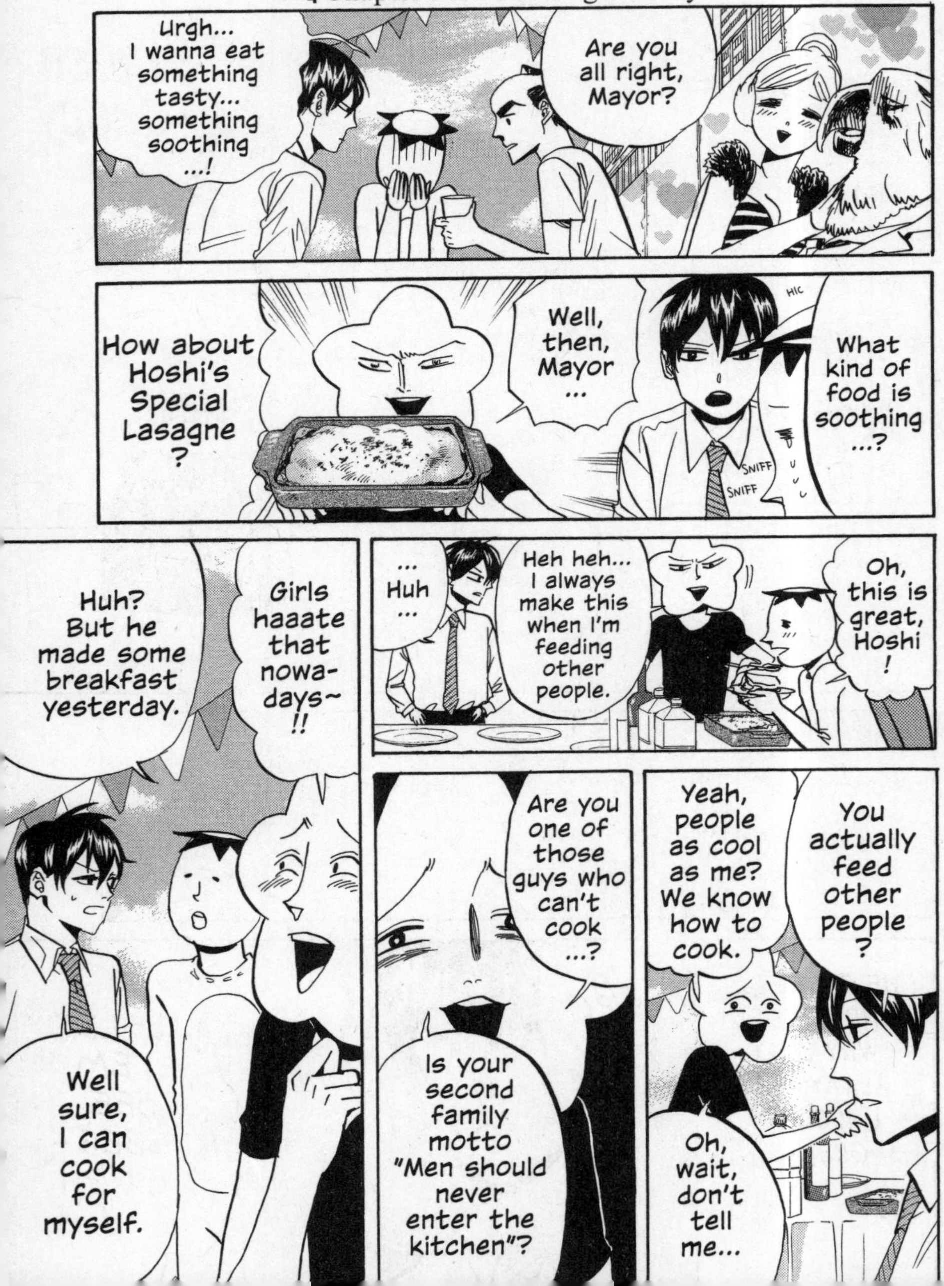

Are you all right, Mayor?
Urgh... I wanna eat something tasty... something soothing ...!
What kind of food is soothing ...?
HIC
SNIFF
SNIFF
Well, then, Mayor ...
How about Hoshi's Special Lasagne ?
Oh, this is great, Hoshi!
Heh heh... I always make this when I'm feeding other people.
... Huh ...
You actually feed other people ?
Yeah, people as cool as me? We know how to cook.
Oh, wait, don't tell me...
Are you one of those guys who can't cook ...?
Is your second family motto "Men should never enter the kitchen"?
Girls haaate that nowa-days~ !!
Huh? But he made some breakfast yesterday.
Well sure, I can cook for myself.

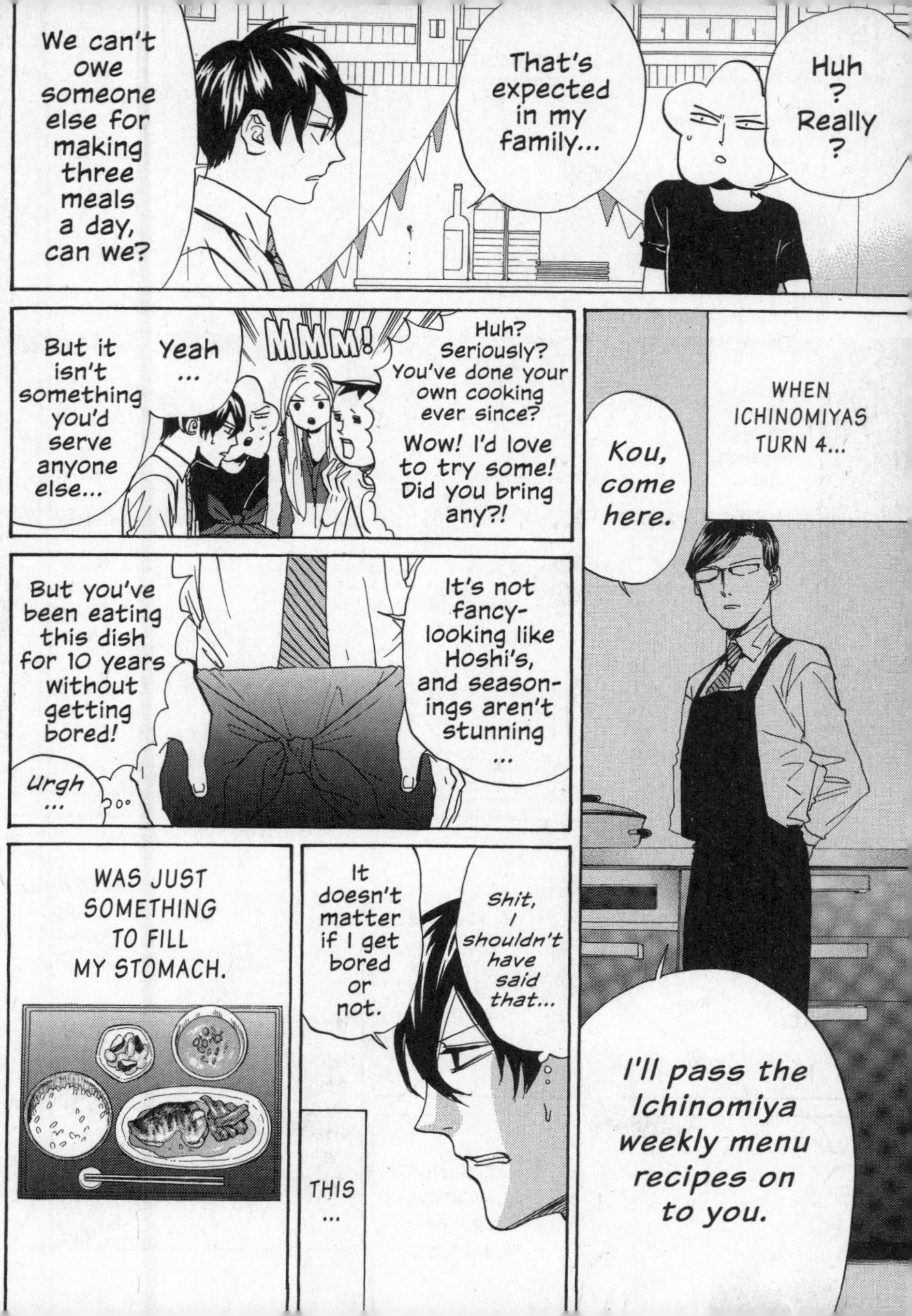

Huh? Really?
That's expected in my family...
We can't owe someone else for making three meals a day, can we?
WHEN ICHINOMIYAS TURN 4...
Kou, come here.
I'll pass the Ichinomiya weekly menu recipes on to you.
MMM!
Huh? Seriously? You've done your own cooking ever since?
Wow! I'd love to try some! Did you bring any?!
Yeah ...
But it isn't something you'd serve anyone else...
It's not fancy-looking like Hoshi's, and seasonings aren't stunning ...
But you've been eating this dish for 10 years without getting bored!
Urgh ...
It doesn't matter if I get bored or not.
Shit, I shouldn't have said that...
THIS ...
WAS JUST SOMETHING TO FILL MY STOMACH.

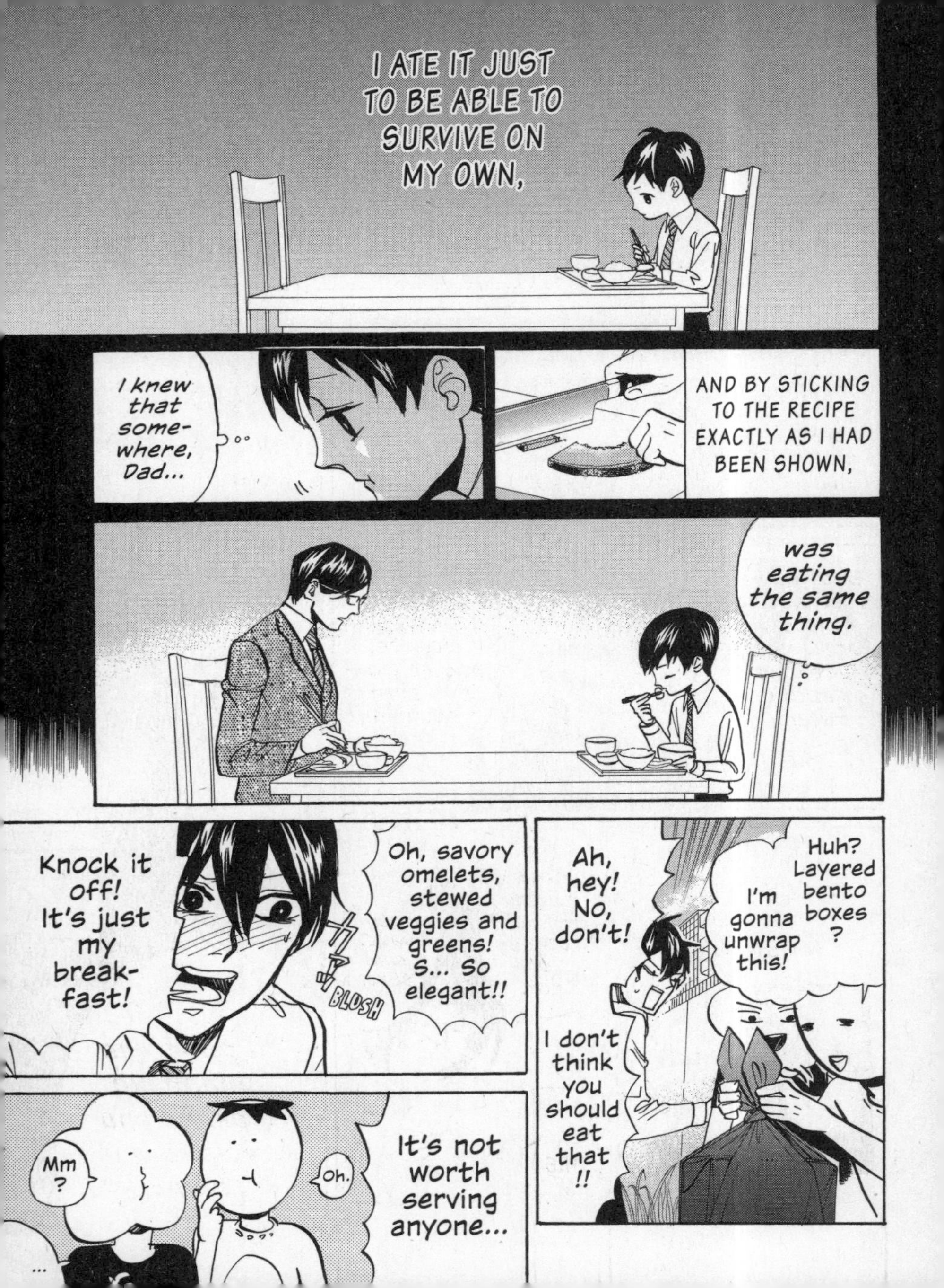
I ATE IT JUST TO BE ABLE TO SURVIVE ON MY OWN,
AND BY STICKING TO THE RECIPE EXACTLY AS I HAD BEEN SHOWN,
I knew that some-where, Dad...
was eating the same thing.
Huh? Layered bento boxes?
I'm gonna unwrap this!
Ah, hey! No, don't!
I don't think you should eat that!!
Oh, savory omelets, stewed veggies and greens! S... So elegant!!
BLUSH
Knock it off! It's just my break-fast!
It's not worth serving anyone...
Oh.
Mm?
...

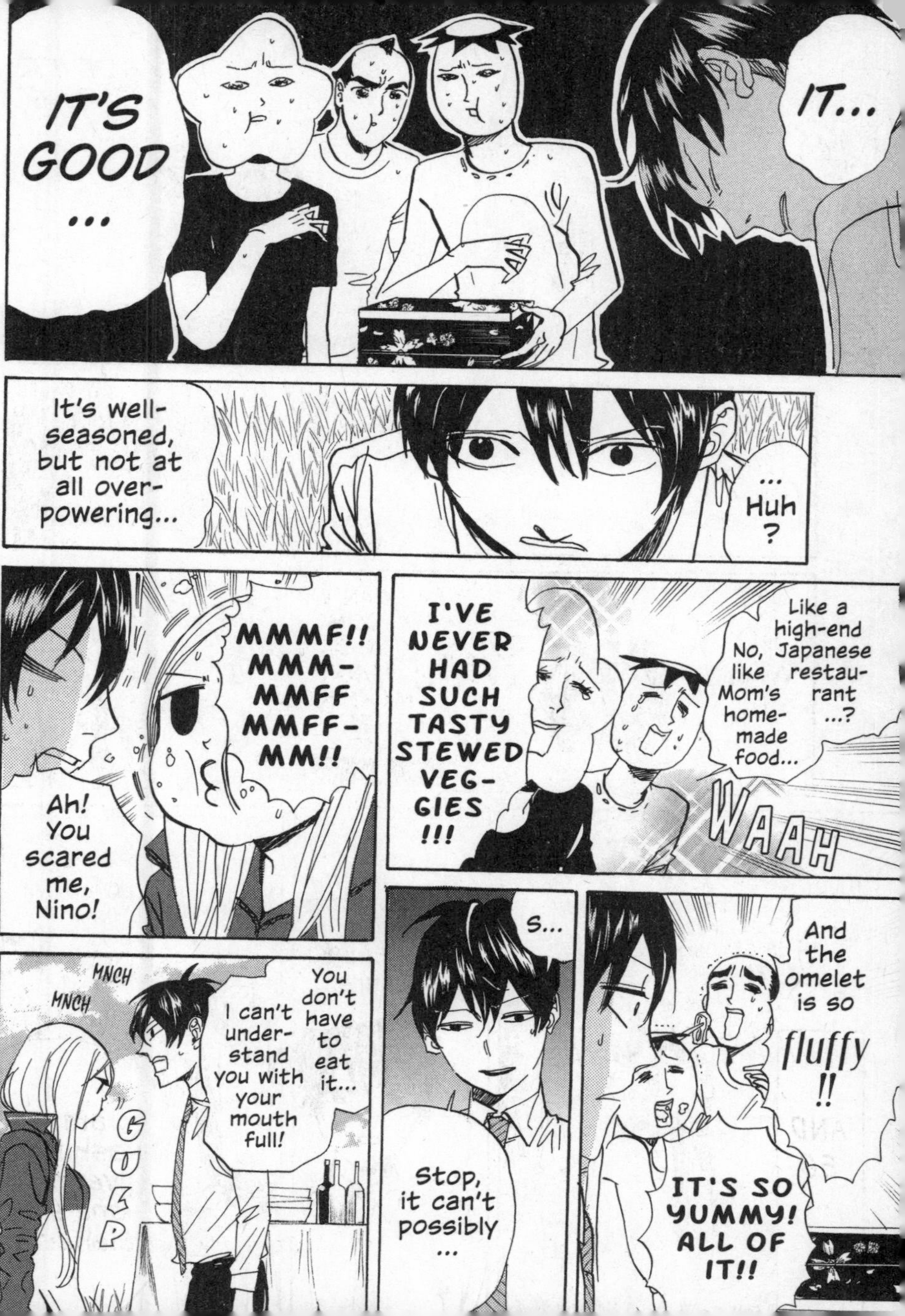
IT...
IT'S GOOD ...
... Huh ?
It's well-seasoned, but not at all over-powering...
Like a high-end Japanese restaurant ...?
No, like Mom's home-made food...
I'VE NEVER HAD SUCH TASTY STEWED VEG-GIES !!!
WAAH
MMMF!! MMM-MMFF MMFF-MM!!
Ah! You scared me, Nino!
And the omelet is so fluffy !!
IT'S SO YUMMY! ALL OF IT!!
S...
Stop, it can't possibly ...
You don't have to eat it...
I can't under-stand you with your mouth full!
MNCH
MNCH
GULP

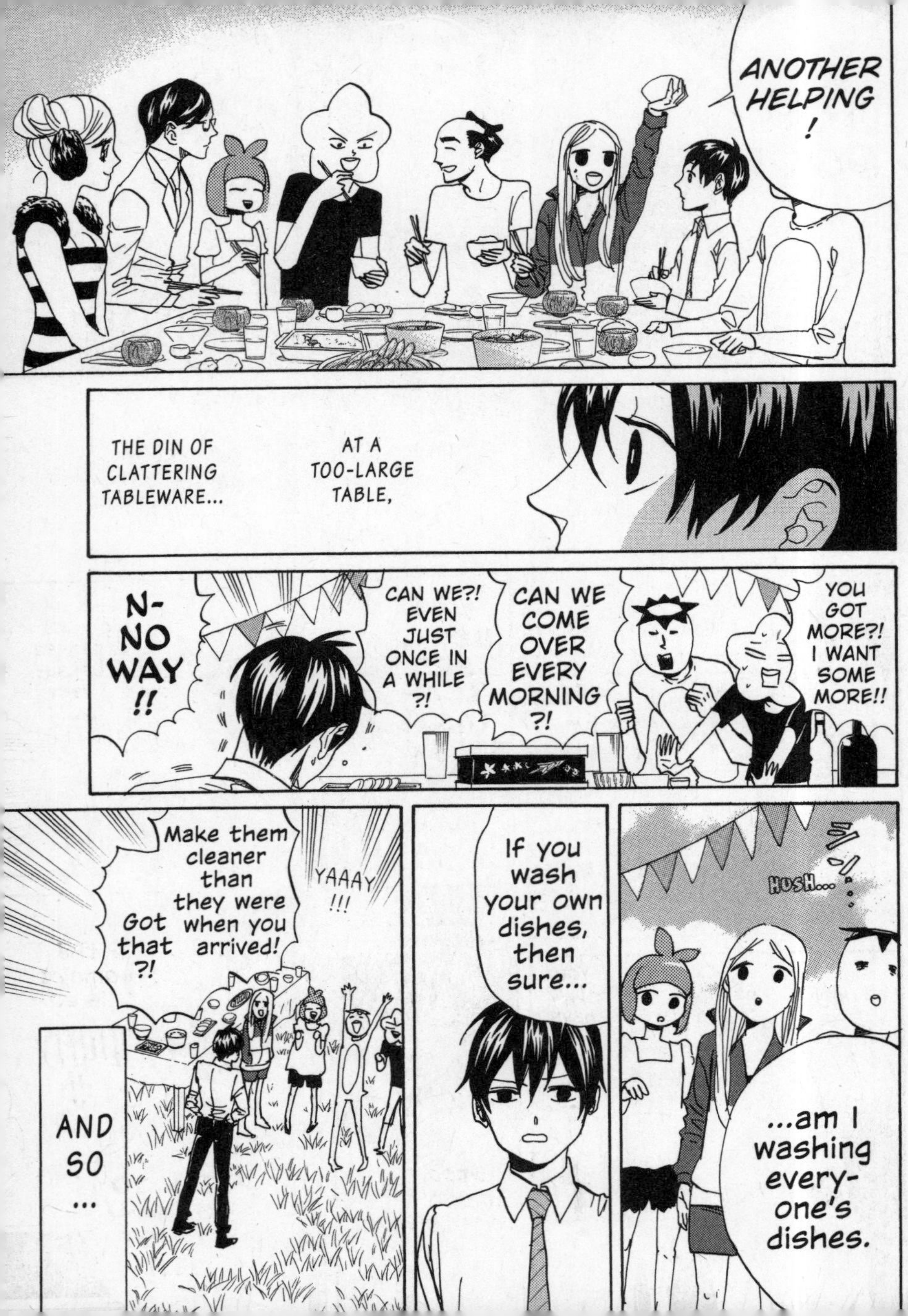
ANOTHER HELPING !
THE DIN OF CLATTERING TABLEWARE...
AT A TOO-LARGE TABLE,
N-NO WAY !!
CAN WE?! EVEN JUST ONCE IN A WHILE ?!
CAN WE COME OVER EVERY MORNING ?!
YOU GOT MORE?! I WANT SOME MORE!!
Make them cleaner than they were when you arrived!
YAAAY !!!
Got that ?!
AND SO ...
If you wash your own dishes, then sure...
HUSH...
...am I washing every-one's dishes.

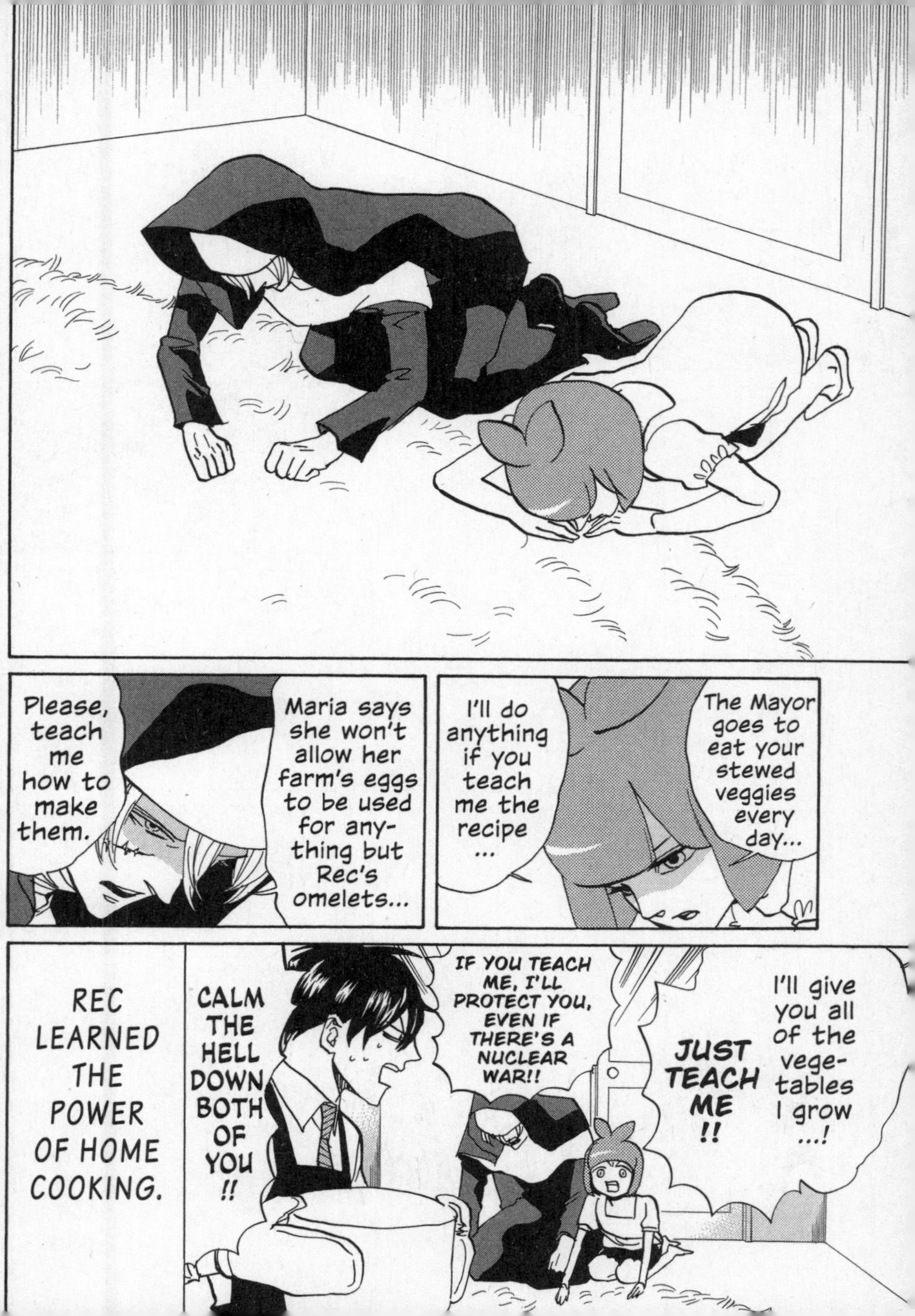
The Mayor goes to eat your stewed veggies every day...
I'll do anything if you teach me the recipe ...
Maria says she won't allow her farm's eggs to be used for anything but Rec's omelets...
Please, teach me how to make them.
I'll give you all of the vegetables I grow ...!
JUST TEACH ME !!
IF YOU TEACH ME, I'LL PROTECT YOU, EVEN IF THERE'S A NUCLEAR WAR!!
CALM THE HELL DOWN BOTH OF YOU !!
REC LEARNED THE POWER OF HOME COOKING.

ARAKAWA
UNDER
THE BRIDGE

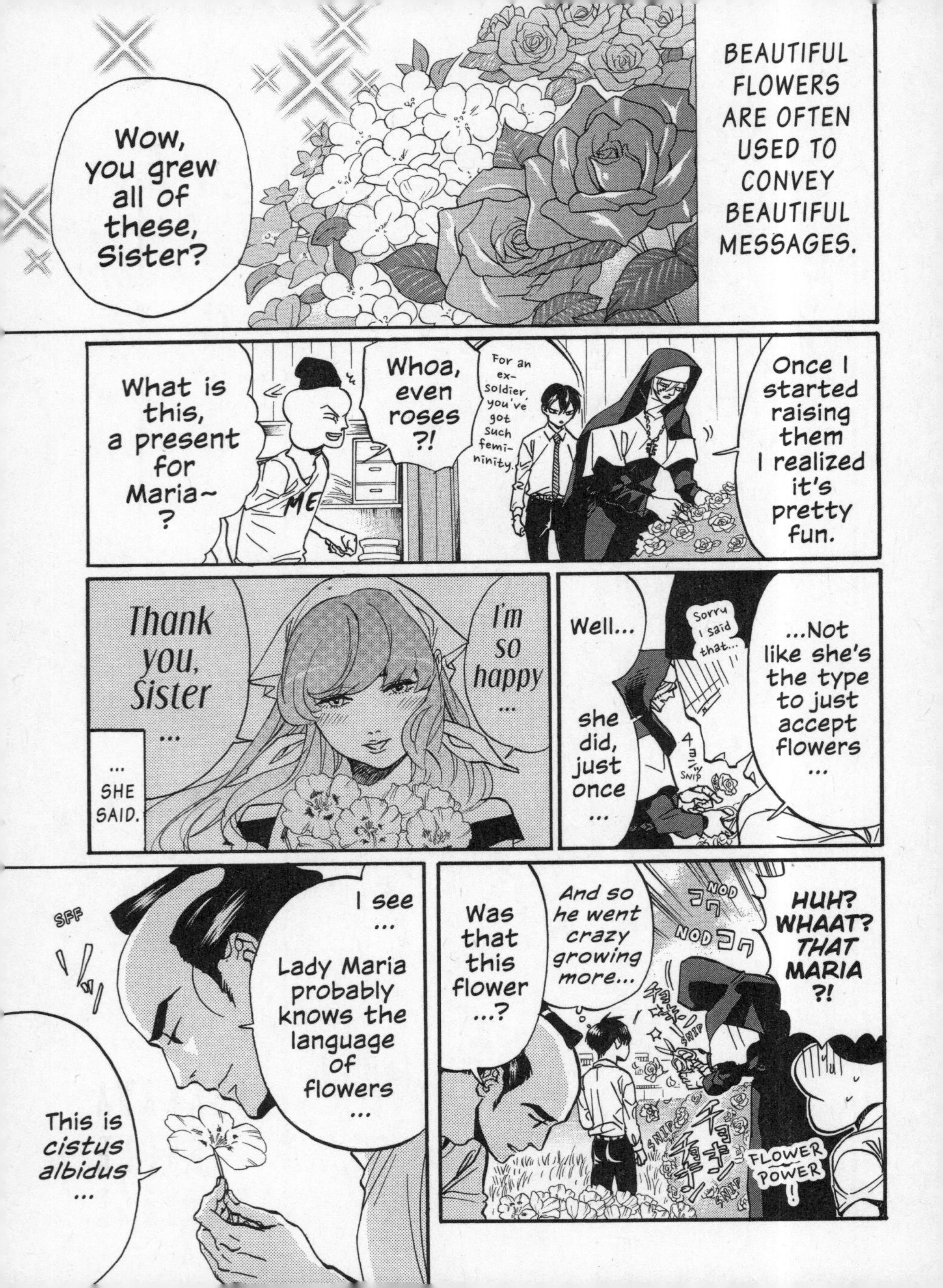

BEAUTIFUL FLOWERS ARE OFTEN USED TO CONVEY BEAUTIFUL MESSAGES.
Wow, you grew all of these, Sister?
Once I started raising them I realized it's pretty fun.
For an ex-soldier, you've got such femininity.
Whoa, even roses?!
What is this, a present for Maria~?
...Not like she's the type to just accept flowers...
Sorry I said that...
Well...
she did, just once...
SNIP
I'm so happy...
Thank you, Sister...
...SHE SAID.
HUH? WHAAT? THAT MARIA?!
NOD
NOD
And so he went crazy growing more...
Was that this flower...?
SNIP
SNIP
FLOWER POWER!
I see... Lady Maria probably knows the language of flowers...
SFF
This is cistus albidus...

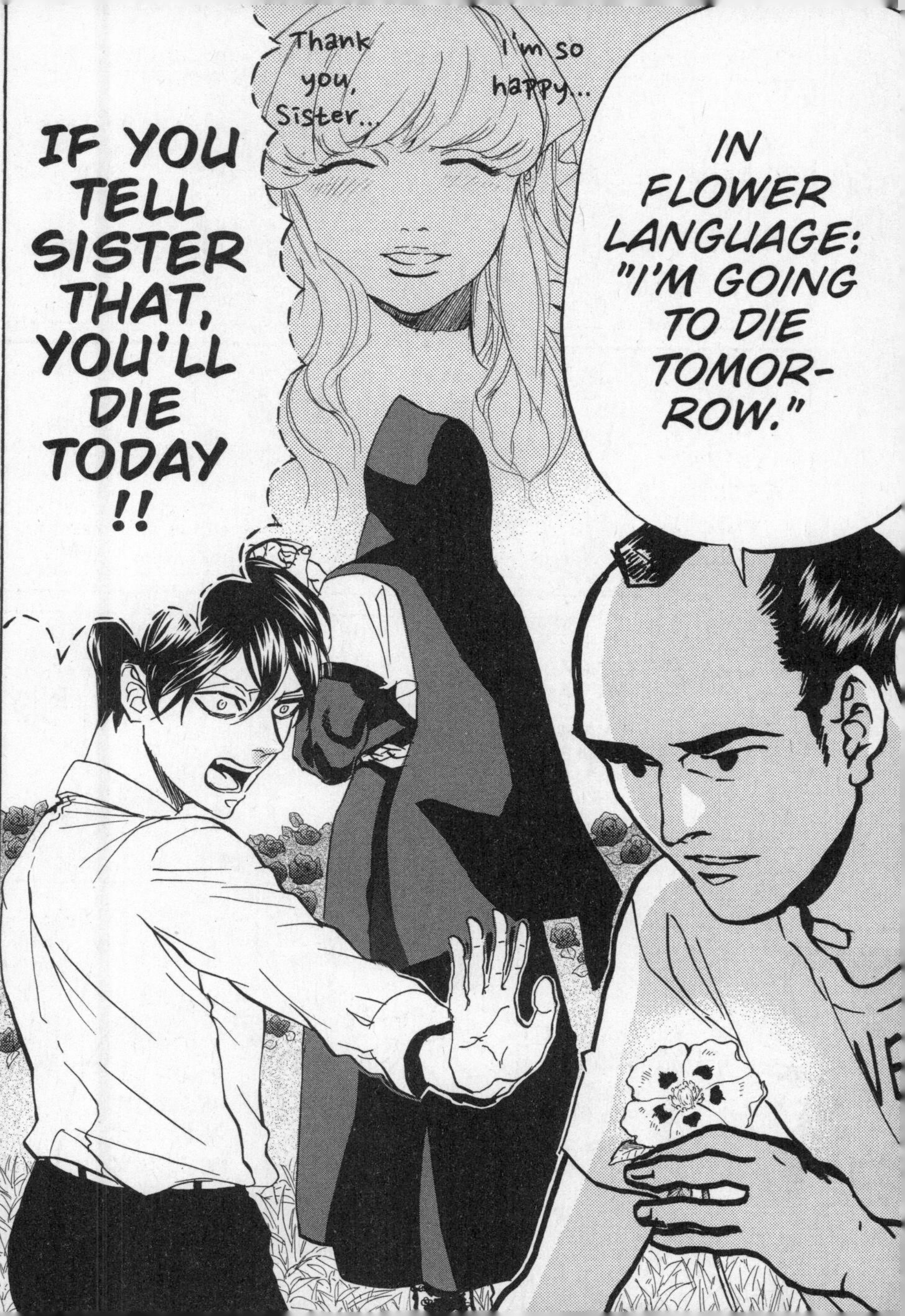
IN FLOWER LANGUAGE: "I'M GOING TO DIE TOMOR-ROW."
Thank you, Sister...
I'm so happy...
IF YOU TELL SISTER THAT, YOU'LL DIE TODAY!!

Chapter 364: Feelings Expressed in Flower Language

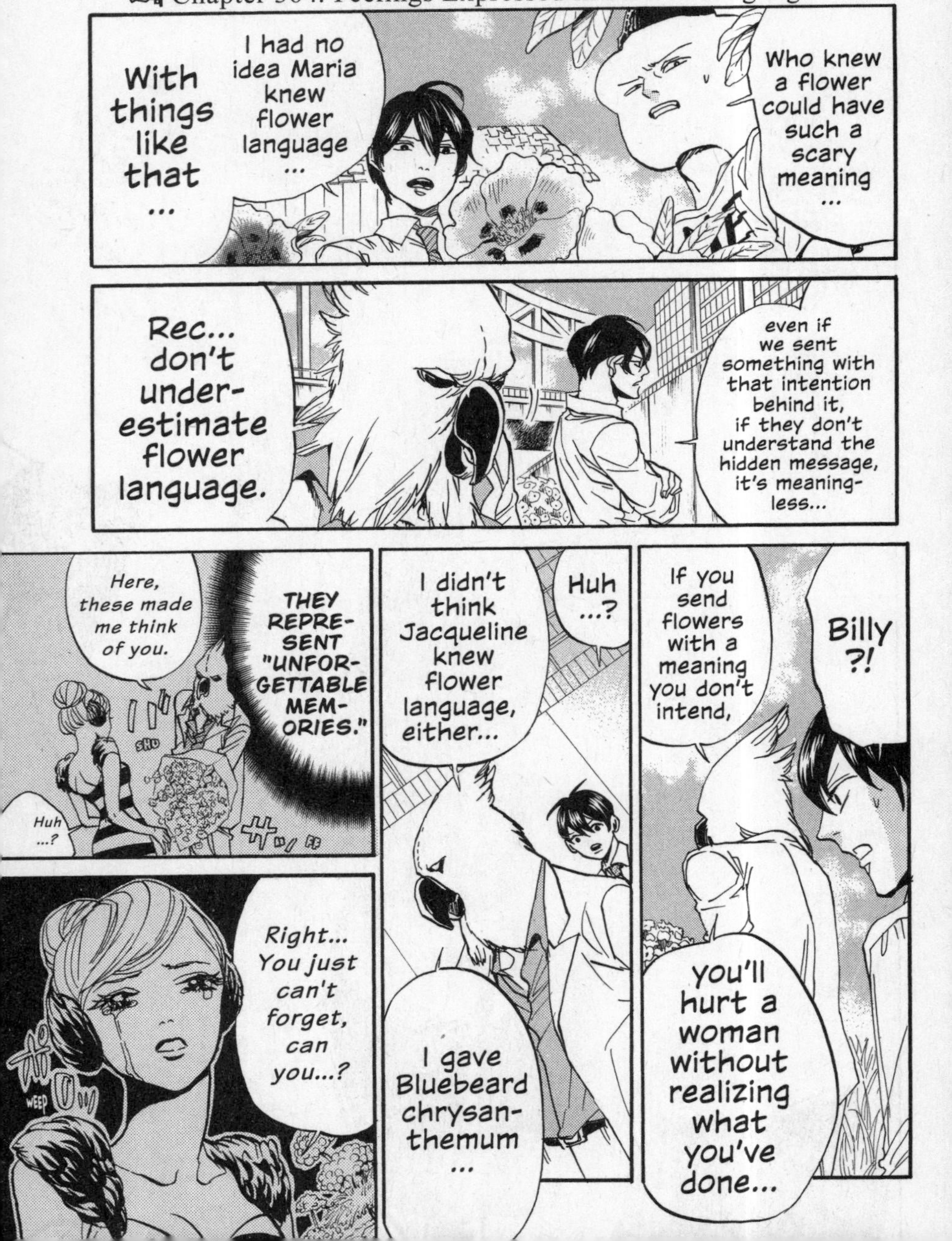

Who knew a flower could have such a scary meaning...
I had no idea Maria knew flower language...
With things like that...
even if we sent something with that intention behind it, if they don't understand the hidden message, it's meaningless...
Rec... don't underestimate flower language.
Billy?!
If you send flowers with a meaning you don't intend,
you'll hurt a woman without realizing what you've done...
Huh...?
I didn't think Jacqueline knew flower language, either...
I gave Bluebeard chrysanthemum...
THEY REPRESENT "UNFORGETTABLE MEMORIES."
Here, these made me think of you.
SHU
Huh...?
Right... You just can't forget, can you...?
WEEP

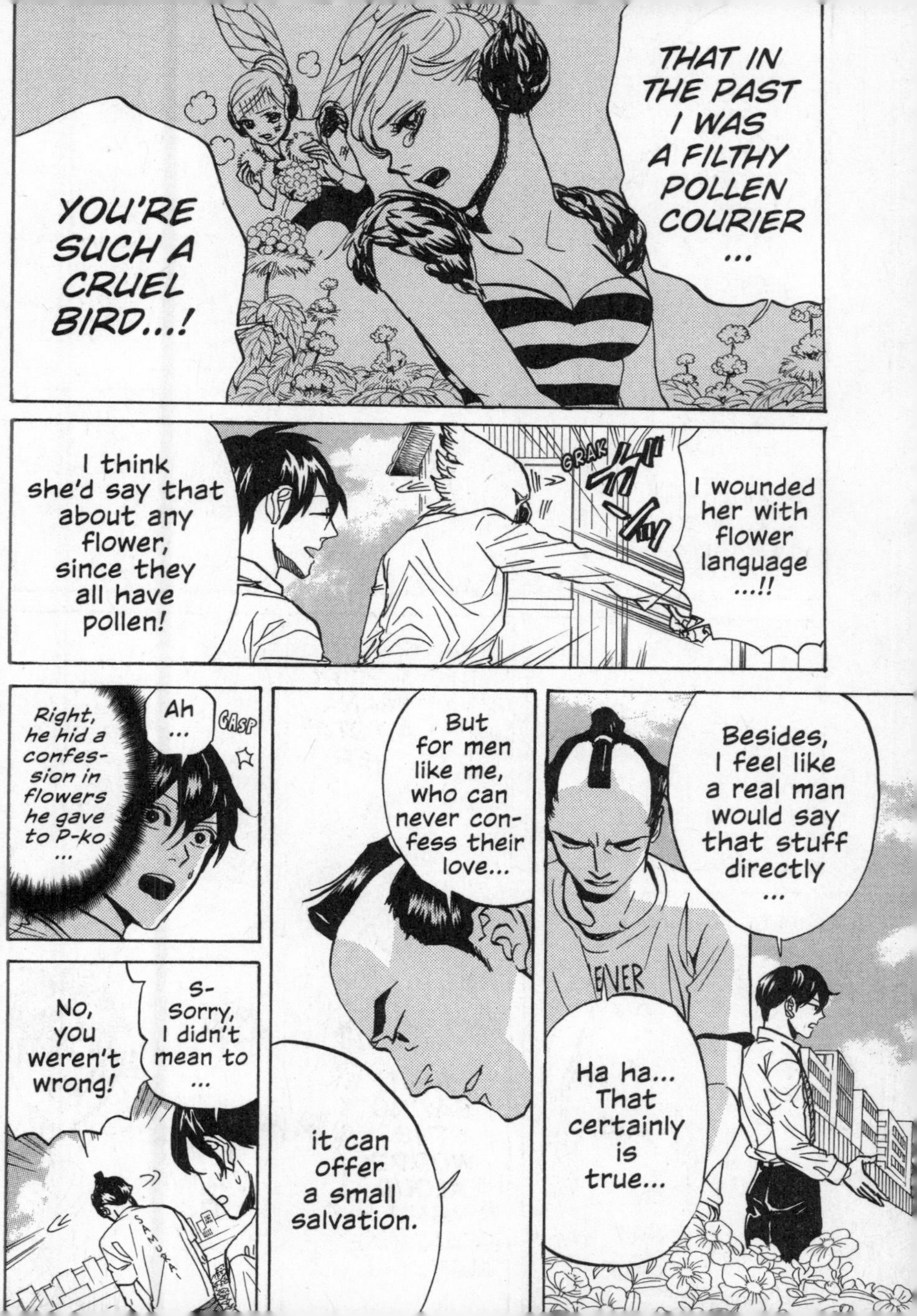
THAT IN THE PAST I WAS A FILTHY POLLEN COURIER ...
YOU'RE SUCH A CRUEL BIRD...!
I wounded her with flower language ...!!
GRAK
I think she'd say that about any flower, since they all have pollen!
Besides, I feel like a real man would say that stuff directly ...
EVER
Ha ha... That certainly is true...
But for men like me, who can never confess their love...
it can offer a small salvation.
GASP
Ah ...
Right, he hid a confession in flowers he gave to P-ko ...
S-Sorry, I didn't mean to ...
No, you weren't wrong!
SAMURAI

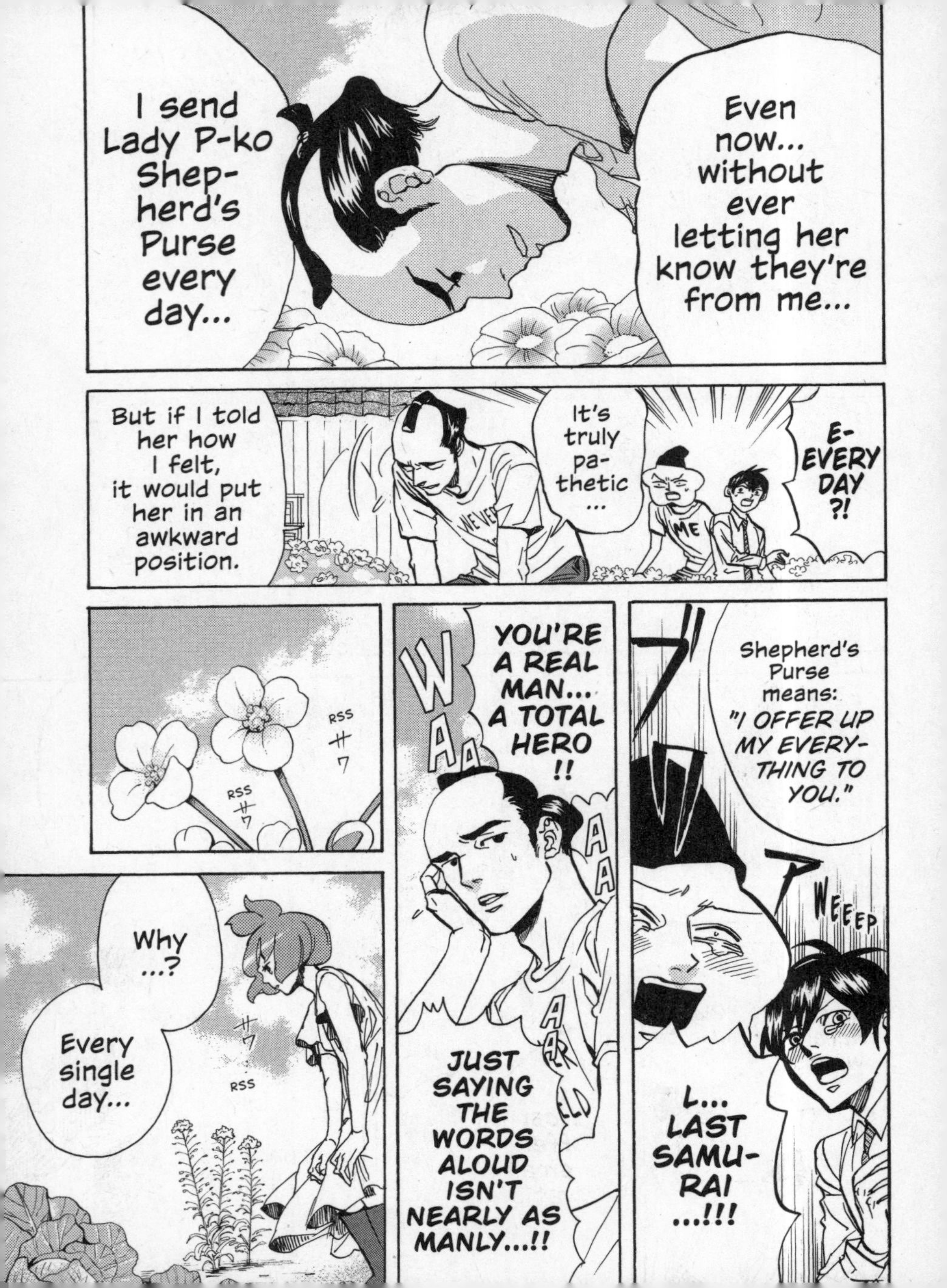
Even now... without ever letting her know they're from me...
I send Lady P-ko Shepherd's Purse every day...
E-EVERY DAY?!
It's truly pathetic...
But if I told her how I felt, it would put her in an awkward position.
Shepherd's Purse means: "I OFFER UP MY EVERYTHING TO YOU."
WEEEP
L... LAST SAMURAI...!!!
YOU'RE A REAL MAN... A TOTAL HERO!!
WAAAAAAA
JUST SAYING THE WORDS ALOUD ISN'T NEARLY AS MANLY...!!
RSS
RSS
Why...?
Every single day...
RSS

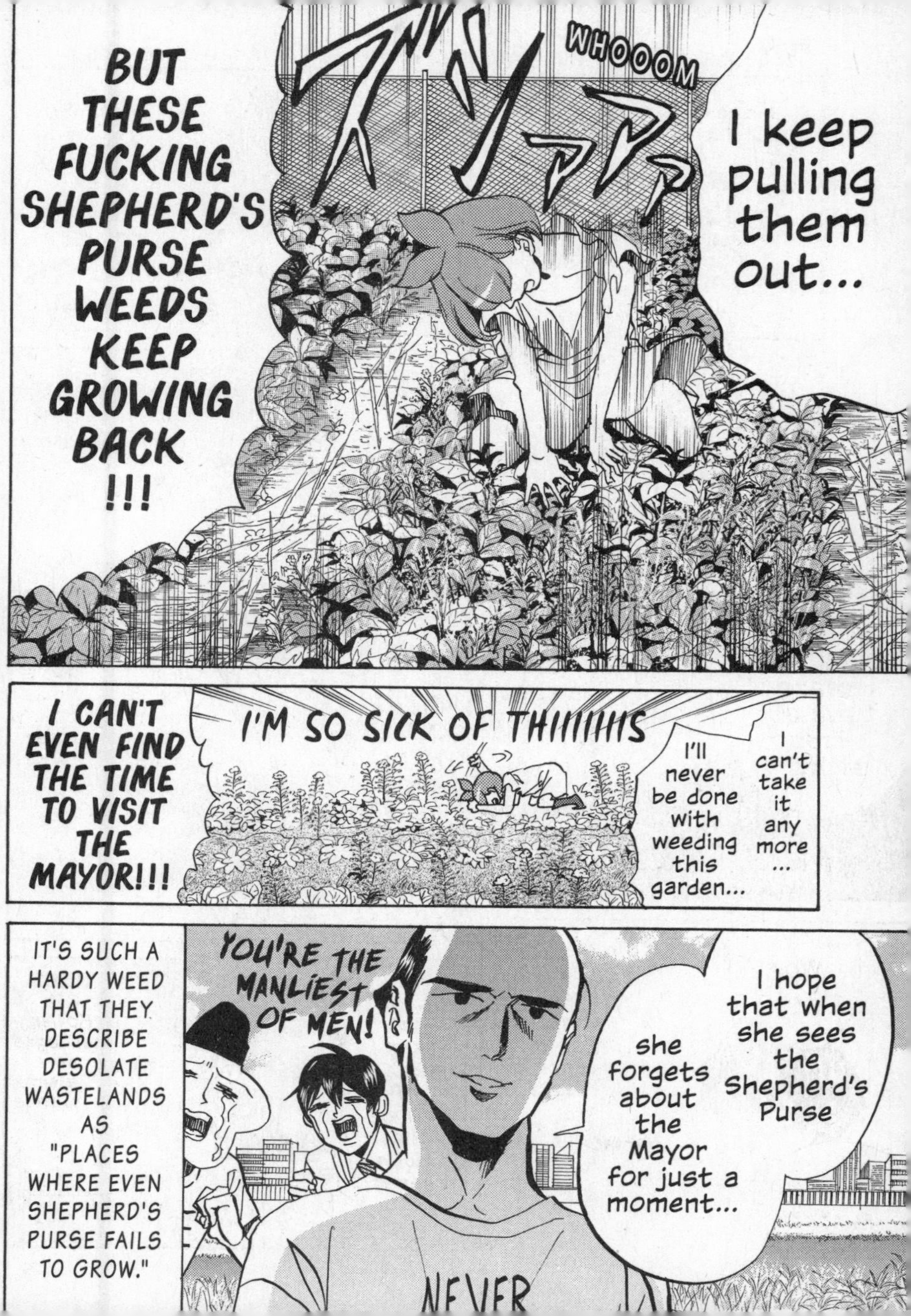

WHOOOM
I keep pulling them out...
BUT THESE FUCKING SHEPHERD'S PURSE WEEDS KEEP GROWING BACK!!!
I can't take it any more...
I'll never be done with weeding this garden...
I'M SO SICK OF THIIIIIIS
I CAN'T EVEN FIND THE TIME TO VISIT THE MAYOR!!!
I hope that when she sees the Shepherd's Purse
she forgets about the Mayor for just a moment...
YOU'RE THE MANLIEST OF MEN!
NEVER
IT'S SUCH A HARDY WEED THAT THEY DESCRIBE DESOLATE WASTELANDS AS "PLACES WHERE EVEN SHEPHERD'S PURSE FAILS TO GROW."

Chapter 365: Last Samurai's Flower Language Lessons

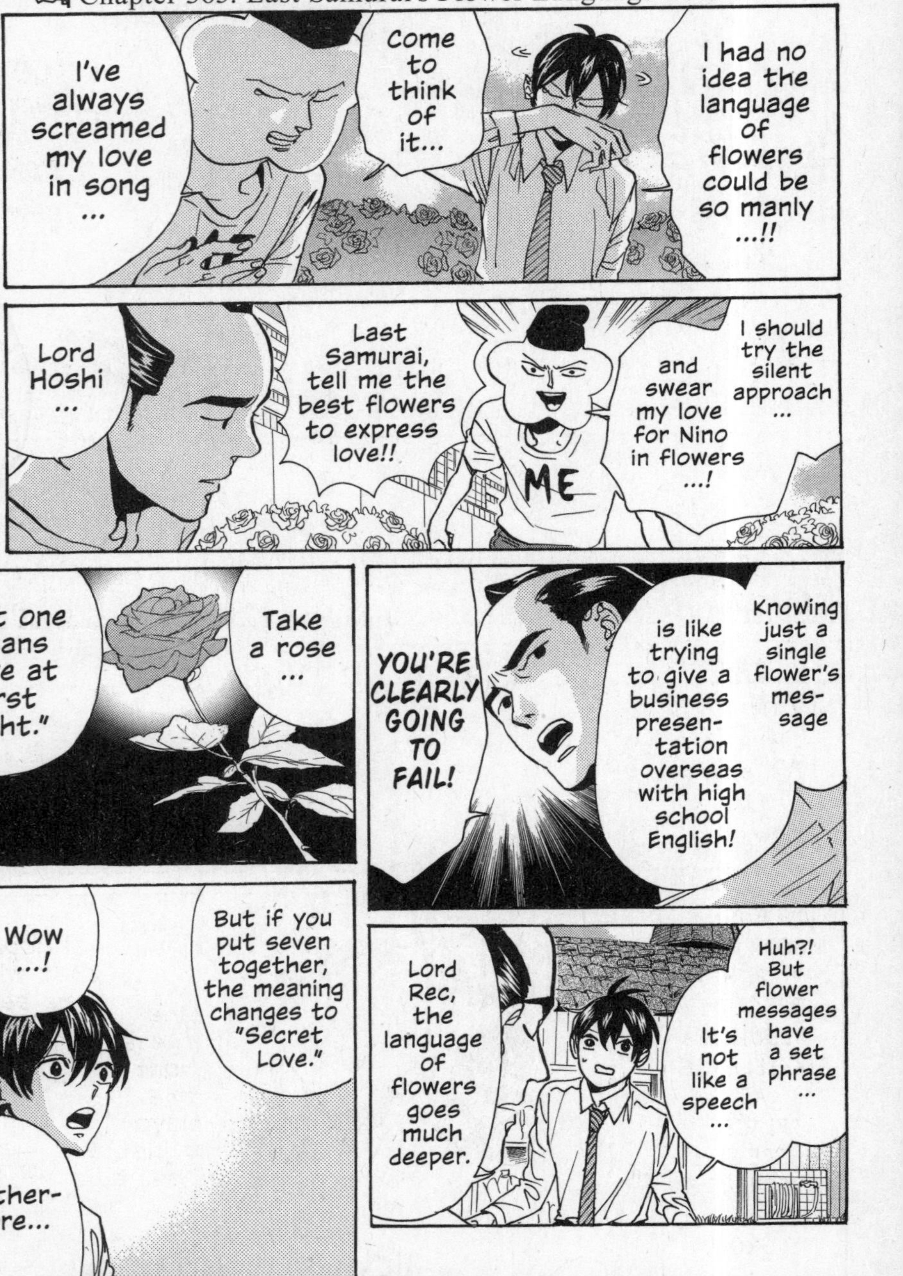

I had no idea the language of flowers could be so manly ...!!
Come to think of it...
I've always screamed my love in song ...
I should try the silent approach ...
and swear my love for Nino in flowers ...!
Last Samurai, tell me the best flowers to express love!!
Lord Hoshi ...
Knowing just a single flower's mes-sage
is like trying to give a business presen-tation overseas with high school English!
YOU'RE CLEARLY GOING TO FAIL!
Take a rose ...
Just one means "love at first sight."
Huh?! But flower messages have a set phrase ...
It's not like a speech ...
Lord Rec, the language of flowers goes much deeper.
But if you put seven together, the meaning changes to "Secret Love."
Wow ...!
Further-more...

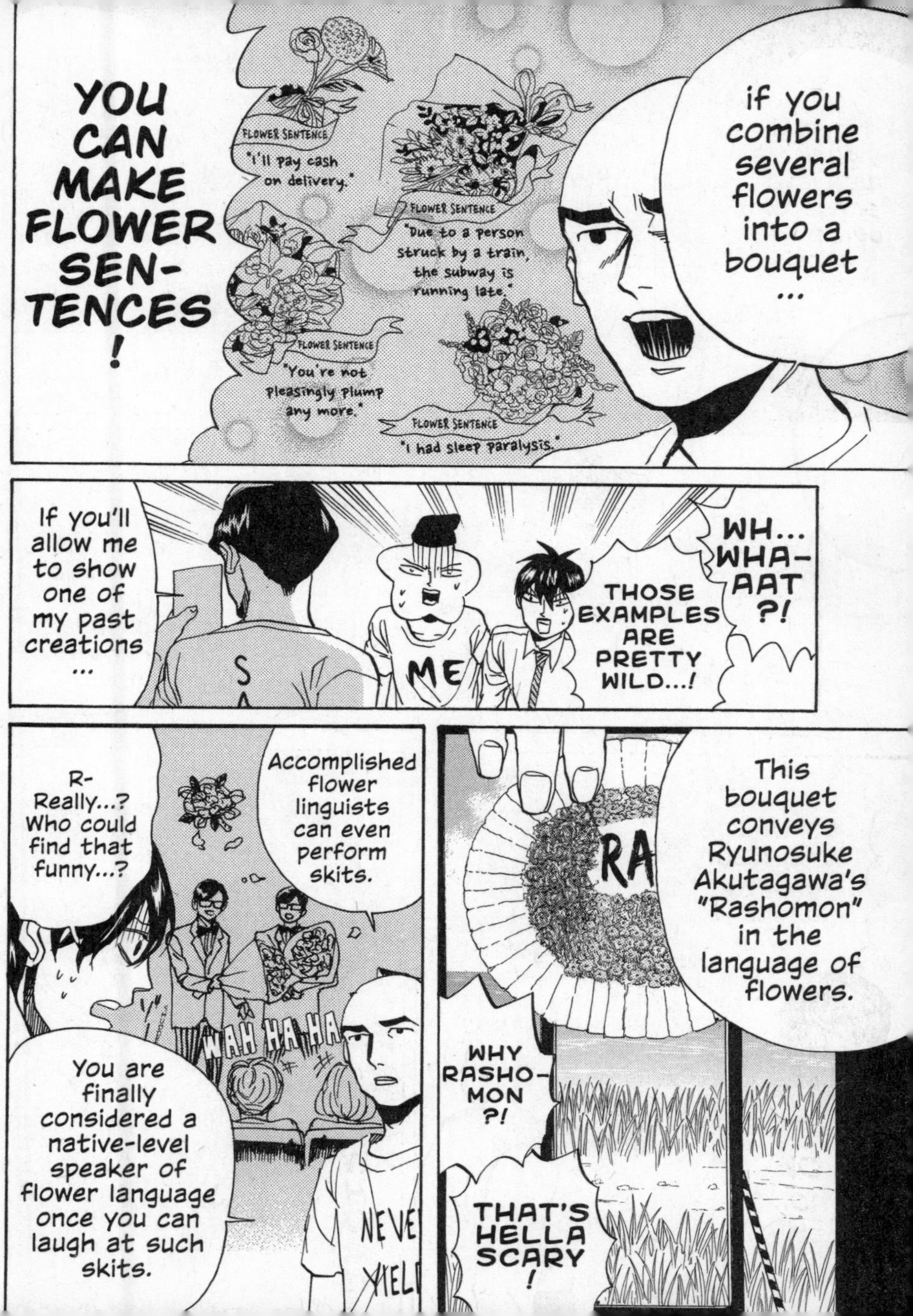
if you combine several flowers into a bouquet ...
FLOWER SENTENCE "I'll pay cash on delivery."
FLOWER SENTENCE "Due to a person struck by a train, the subway is running late."
FLOWER SENTENCE "You're not pleasingly plump any more."
FLOWER SENTENCE "I had sleep paralysis."
YOU CAN MAKE FLOWER SEN-TENCES!
WH... WHA-AAT?!
THOSE EXAMPLES ARE PRETTY WILD...!
ME
If you'll allow me to show one of my past creations ...
This bouquet conveys Ryunosuke Akutagawa's "Rashomon" in the language of flowers.
RA
WHY RASHO-MON?!
THAT'S HELLA SCARY!
Accomplished flower linguists can even perform skits.
R- Really...? Who could find that funny...?
WAH HA HA
You are finally considered a native-level speaker of flower language once you can laugh at such skits.

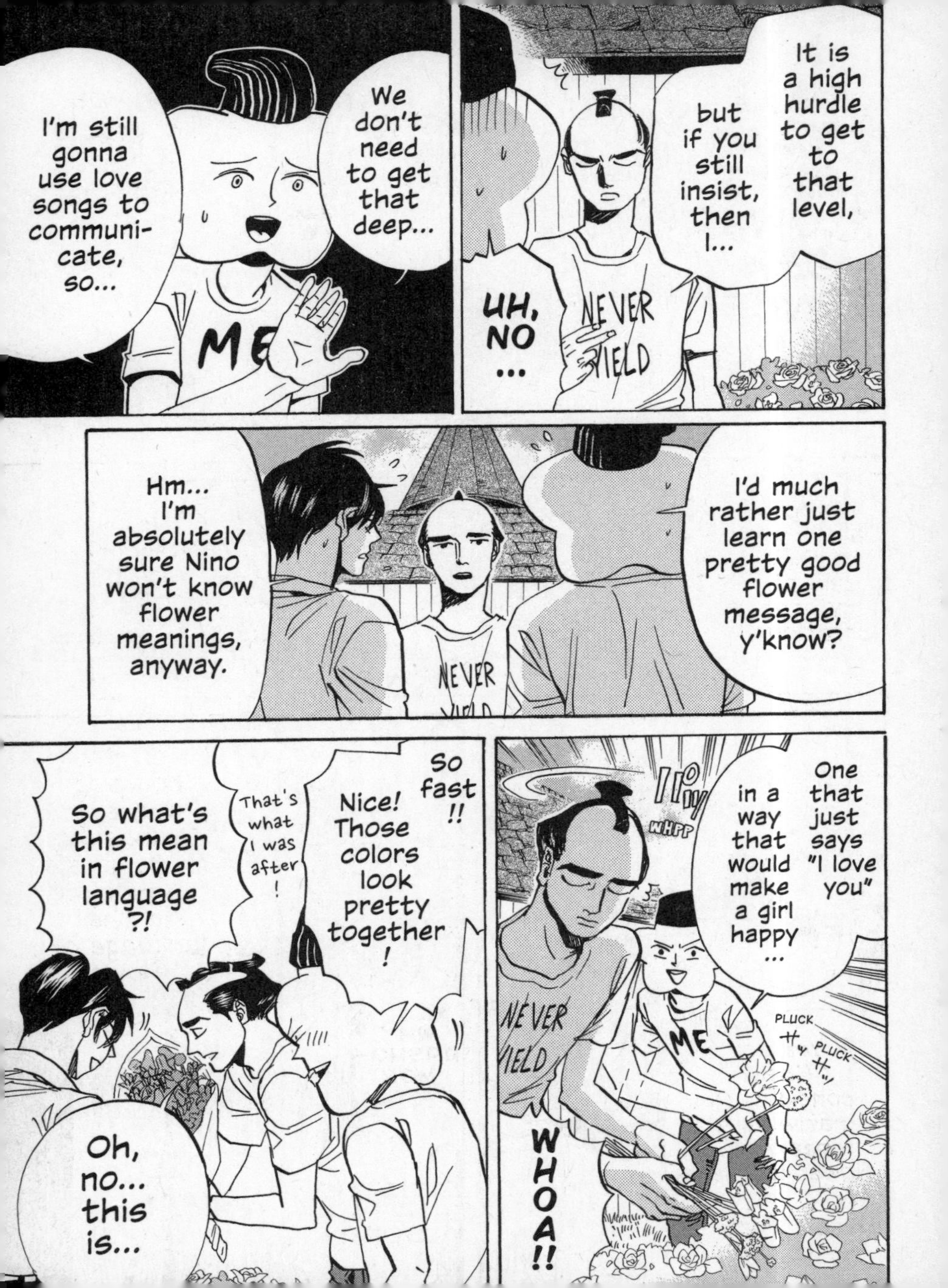
It is a high hurdle to get to that level,
but if you still insist, then I...
UH, NO...
We don't need to get that deep...
I'm still gonna use love songs to communi-cate, so...
I'd much rather just learn one pretty good flower message, y'know?
Hm... I'm absolutely sure Nino won't know flower meanings, anyway.
One that just says "I love you"
in a way that would make a girl happy...
WHPP
PLUCK
PLUCK
WHOA!!
So fast!!
Nice! Those colors look pretty together!
That's what I was after!
So what's this mean in flower language?!
Oh, no... this is...

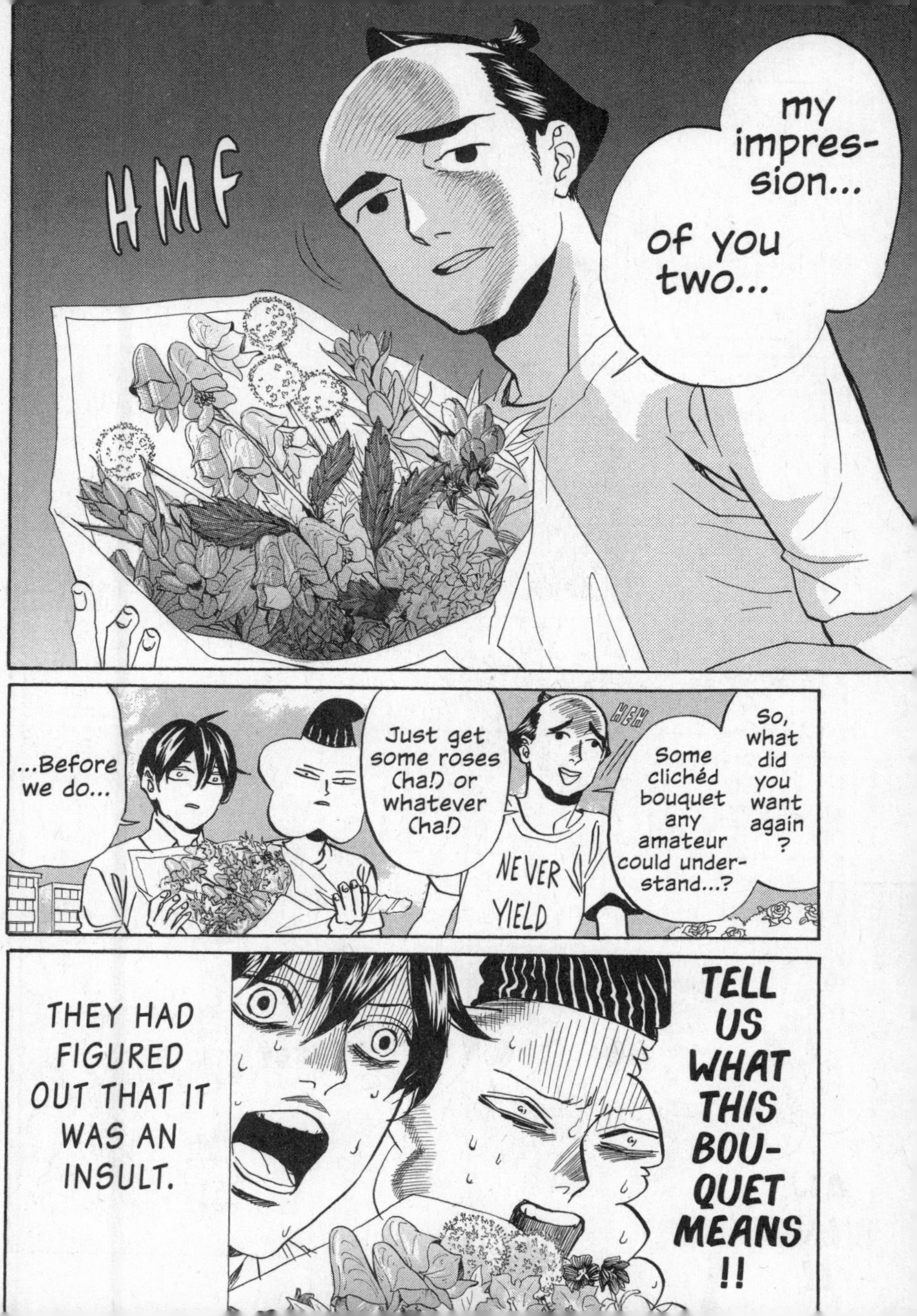
my impres-sion...
of you two...
HMF
So, what did you want again?
Some clichéd bouquet any amateur could under-stand...?
HEH
NEVER YIELD
Just get some roses (ha!) or whatever (ha!)
...Before we do...
TELL US WHAT THIS BOU-QUET MEANS!!
THEY HAD FIGURED OUT THAT IT WAS AN INSULT.

Chapter 366: For You

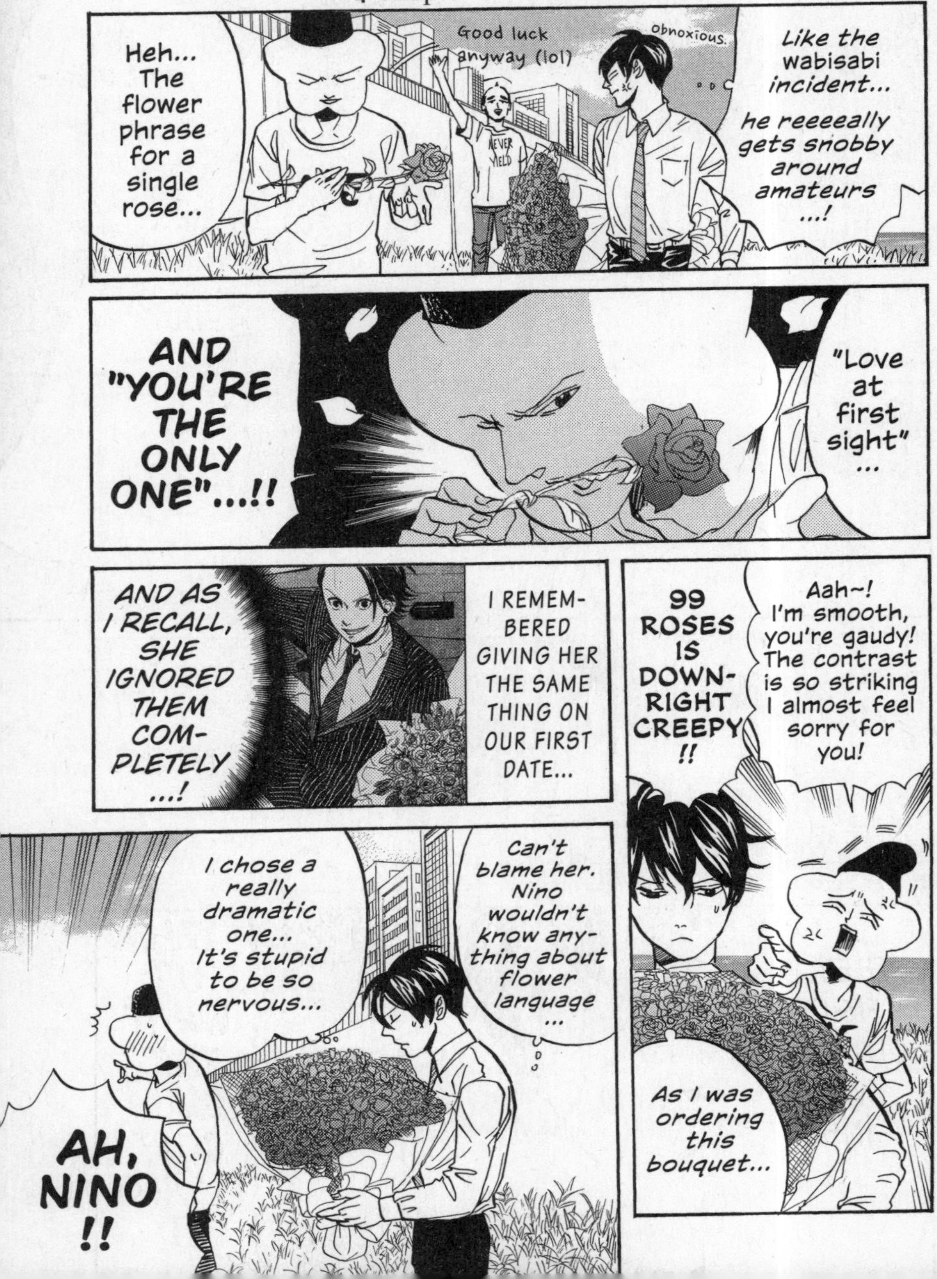
Like the wabisabi incident... he reeeeally gets snobby around amateurs ...!
Obnoxious.
Good luck anyway (lol)
NEVER YIELD
Heh... The flower phrase for a single rose...
"Love at first sight" ...
AND "YOU'RE THE ONLY ONE"...!!
Aah~! I'm smooth, you're gaudy! The contrast is so striking I almost feel sorry for you!
99 ROSES IS DOWN-RIGHT CREEPY !!
As I was ordering this bouquet...
I REMEM-BERED GIVING HER THE SAME THING ON OUR FIRST DATE...
AND AS I RECALL, SHE IGNORED THEM COM-PLETELY ...!
Can't blame her. Nino wouldn't know any-thing about flower language ...
I chose a really dramatic one... It's stupid to be so nervous...
AH, NINO !!

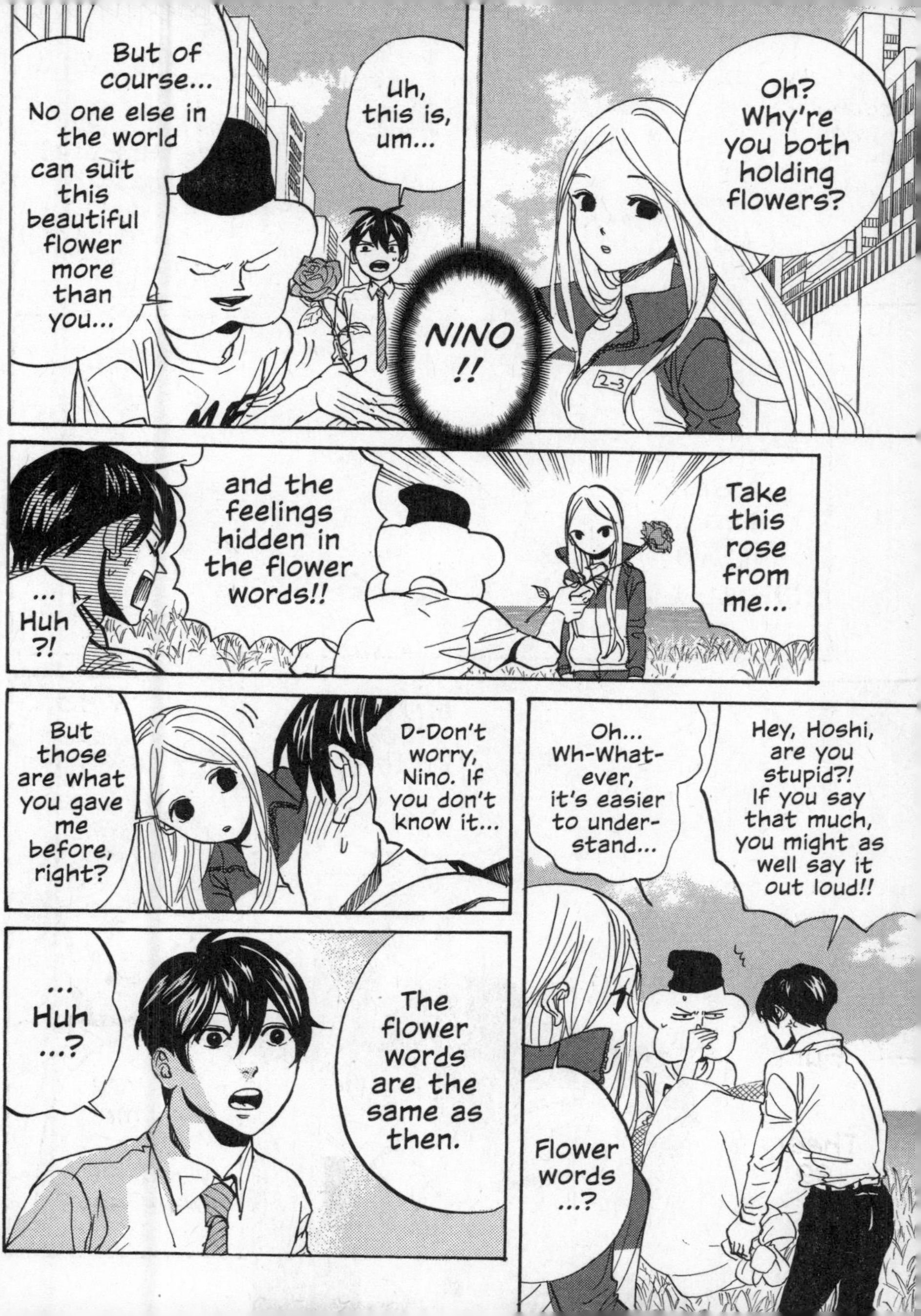
Oh? Why're you both holding flowers?
Uh, this is, um...
But of course... No one else in the world can suit this beautiful flower more than you...
NINO !!
Take this rose from me...
and the feelings hidden in the flower words!!
... Huh ?!
Hey, Hoshi, are you stupid?! If you say that much, you might as well say it out loud!!
Oh... Wh-Whatever, it's easier to understand...
Flower words ...?
D-Don't worry, Nino. If you don't know it...
But those are what you gave me before, right?
The flower words are the same as then.
... Huh ...?

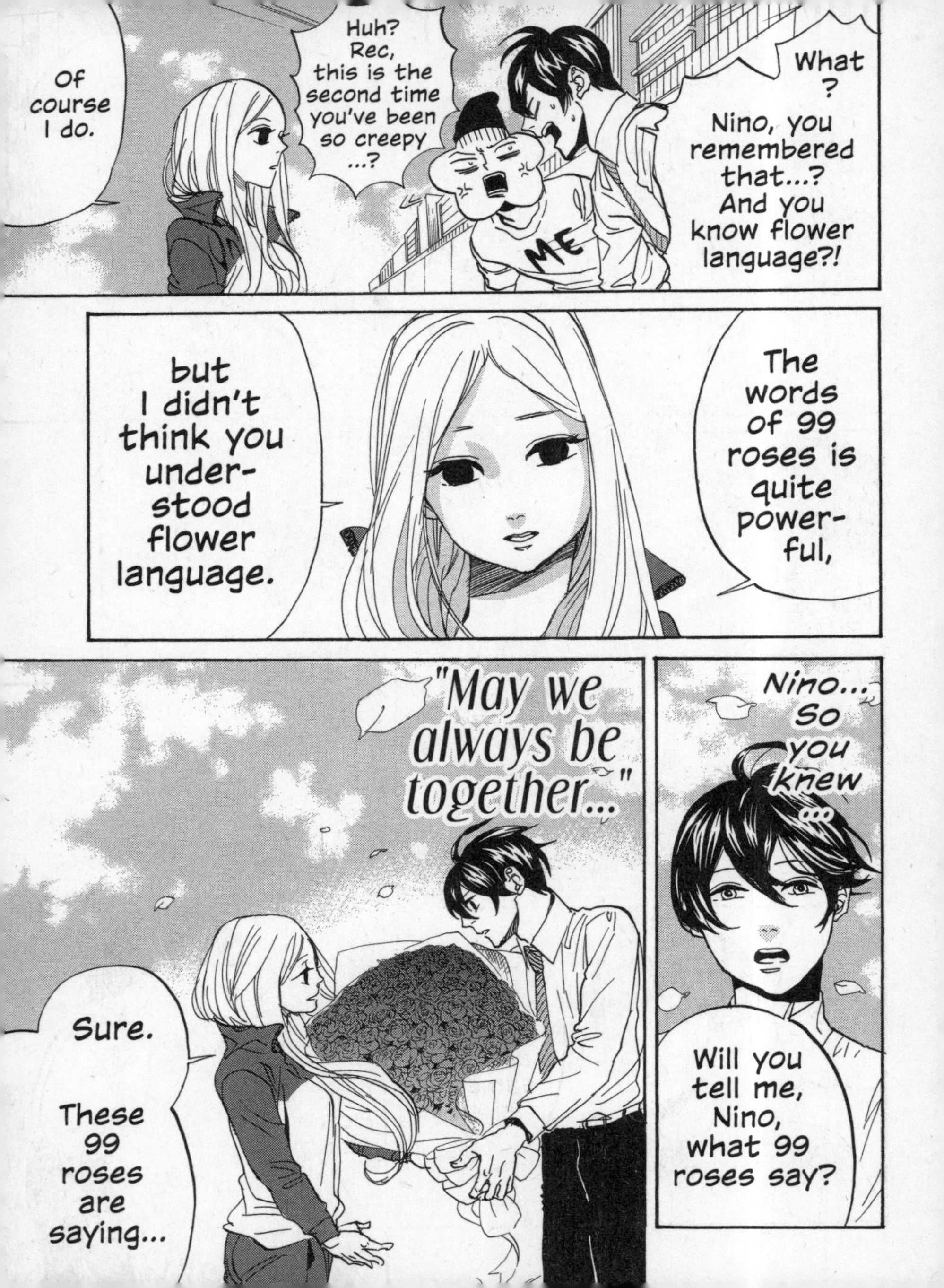
What? Nino, you remembered that...? And you know flower language?!
ME
Huh? Rec, this is the second time you've been so creepy ...?
Of course I do.
The words of 99 roses is quite power-ful,
but I didn't think you under-stood flower language.
Nino... So you knew ...
Will you tell me, Nino, what 99 roses say?
Sure.
These 99 roses are saying...
"May we always be together..."

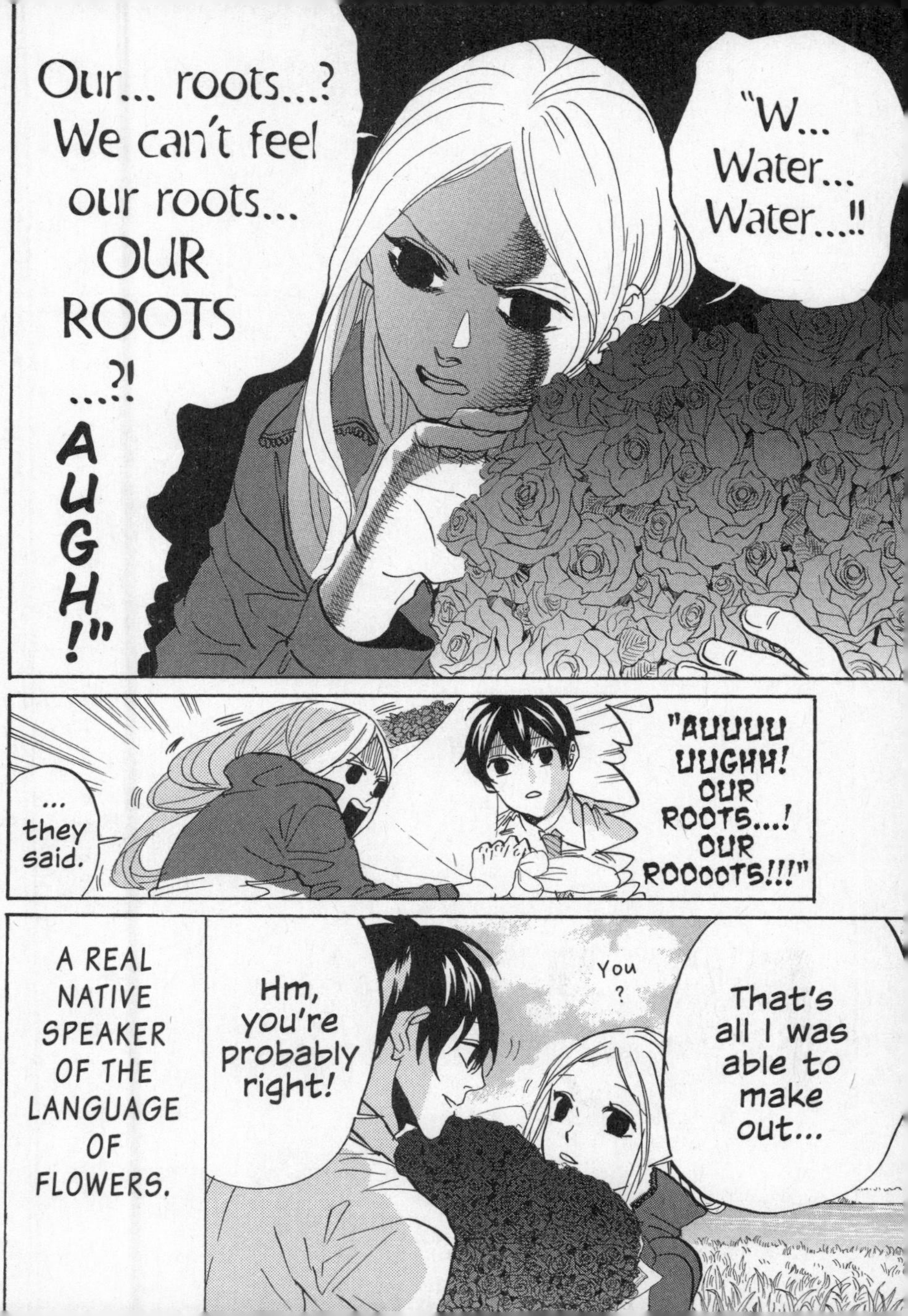
"W... Water... Water...!!
Our... roots...? We can't feel our roots... OUR ROOTS ...?! AUGH!"
"AUUUU UUGHH! OUR ROOTS...! OUR ROOOOTS!!!"
... they said.
That's all I was able to make out...
You ?
Hm, you're probably right!
A REAL NATIVE SPEAKER OF THE LANGUAGE OF FLOWERS.

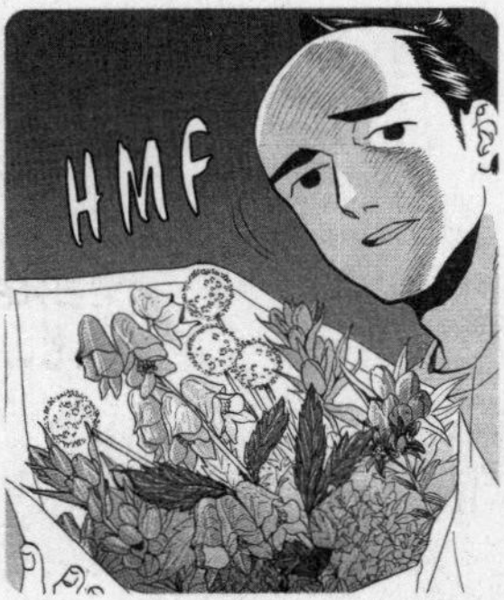
HMF

ARAKAWA
UNDER
THE BRIDGE

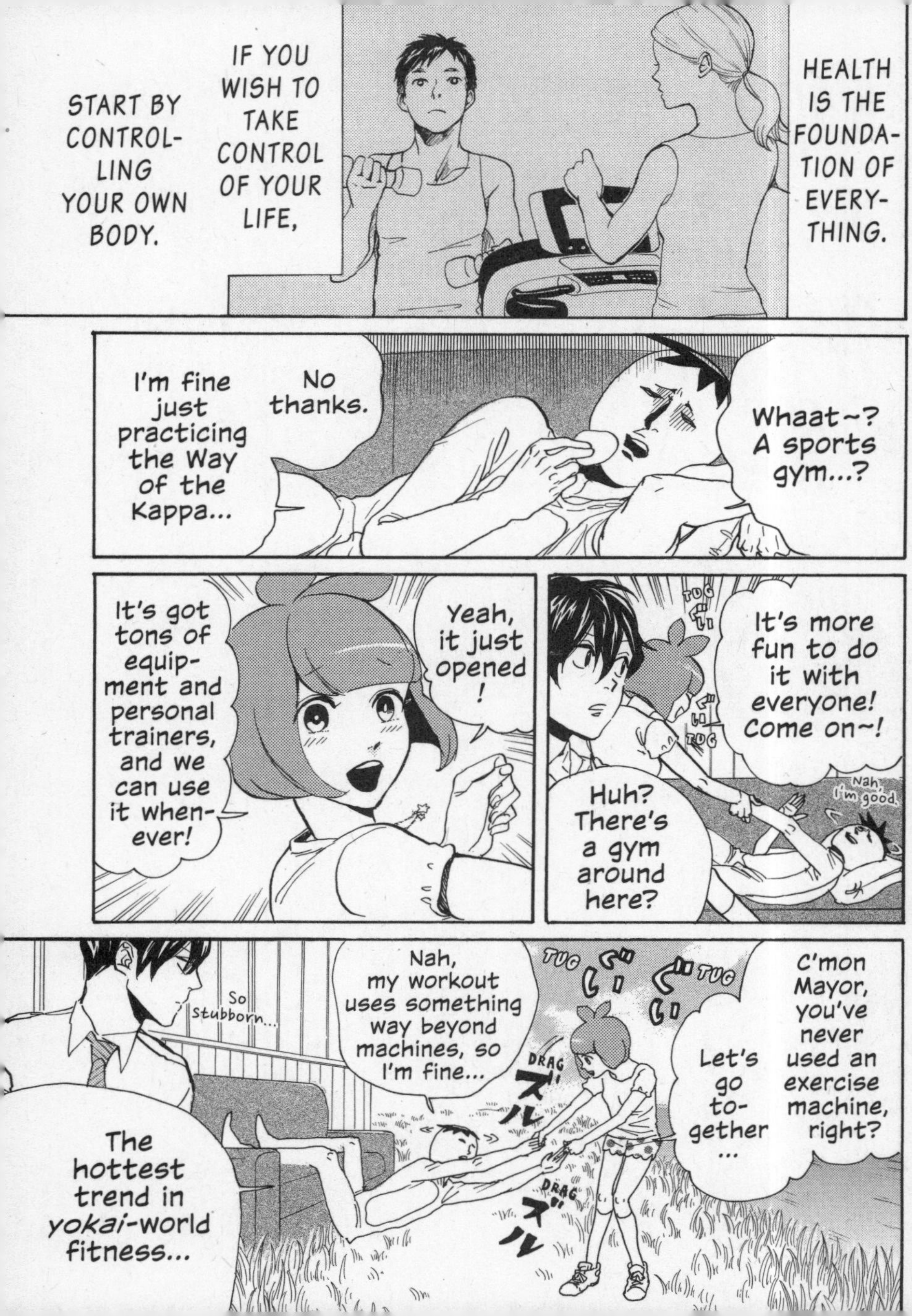
HEALTH IS THE FOUNDATION OF EVERYTHING.
IF YOU WISH TO TAKE CONTROL OF YOUR LIFE,
START BY CONTROLLING YOUR OWN BODY.
Whaat~? A sports gym...?
No thanks.
I'm fine just practicing the Way of the Kappa...
TUG
It's more fun to do it with everyone! Come on~!
TUG
Nah, I'm good.
Huh? There's a gym around here?
Yeah, it just opened!
It's got tons of equipment and personal trainers, and we can use it whenever!
C'mon Mayor, you've never used an exercise machine, right?
Let's go together...
TUG
TUG
Nah, my workout uses something way beyond machines, so I'm fine...
DRAG
DRAG
So stubborn...
The hottest trend in *yokai*-world fitness...

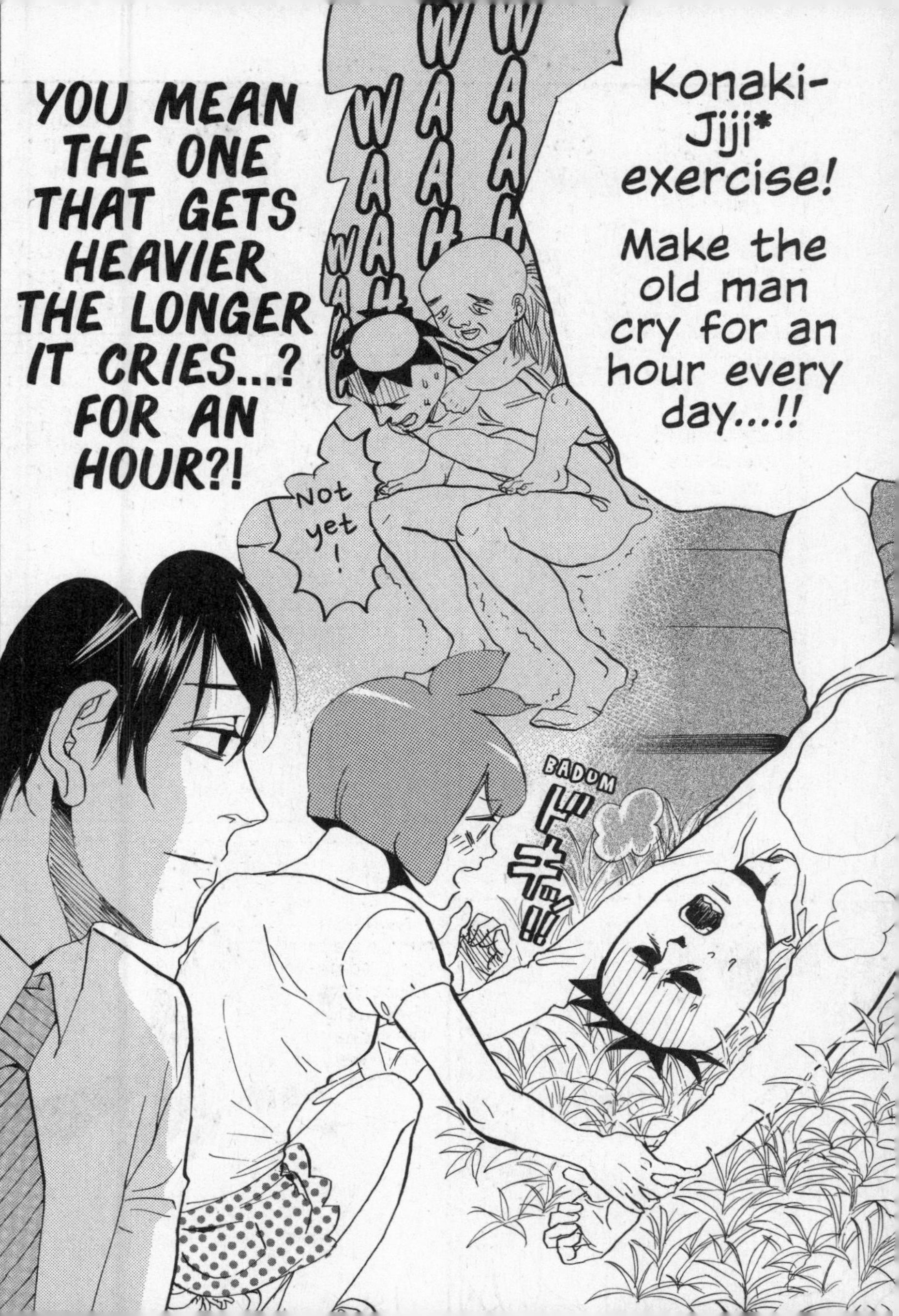
Konaki-Jiji* exercise!
Make the old man cry for an hour every day...!!
WAAAH
WAAAH
WAAAH
YOU MEAN THE ONE THAT GETS HEAVIER THE LONGER IT CRIES...? FOR AN HOUR?!
Not yet!
BADUM

*A ghost in Japanese folklore who looks like a small old man (jiji) that cries like a baby (konaki)

Chapter 367: Tengu Gym

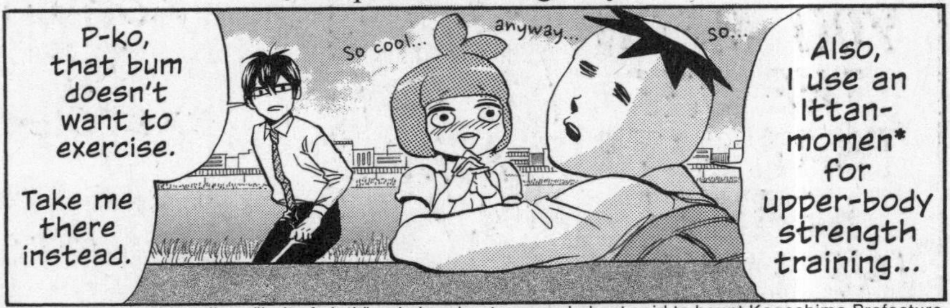

Also, I use an Ittan-momen* for upper-body strength training...
so...
anyway...
So cool...
P-ko, that bum doesn't want to exercise.
Take me there instead.

*Literally, a "bolt of cloth" *yokai*, a sheet-covered ghost said to haunt Kagoshima Prefecture.

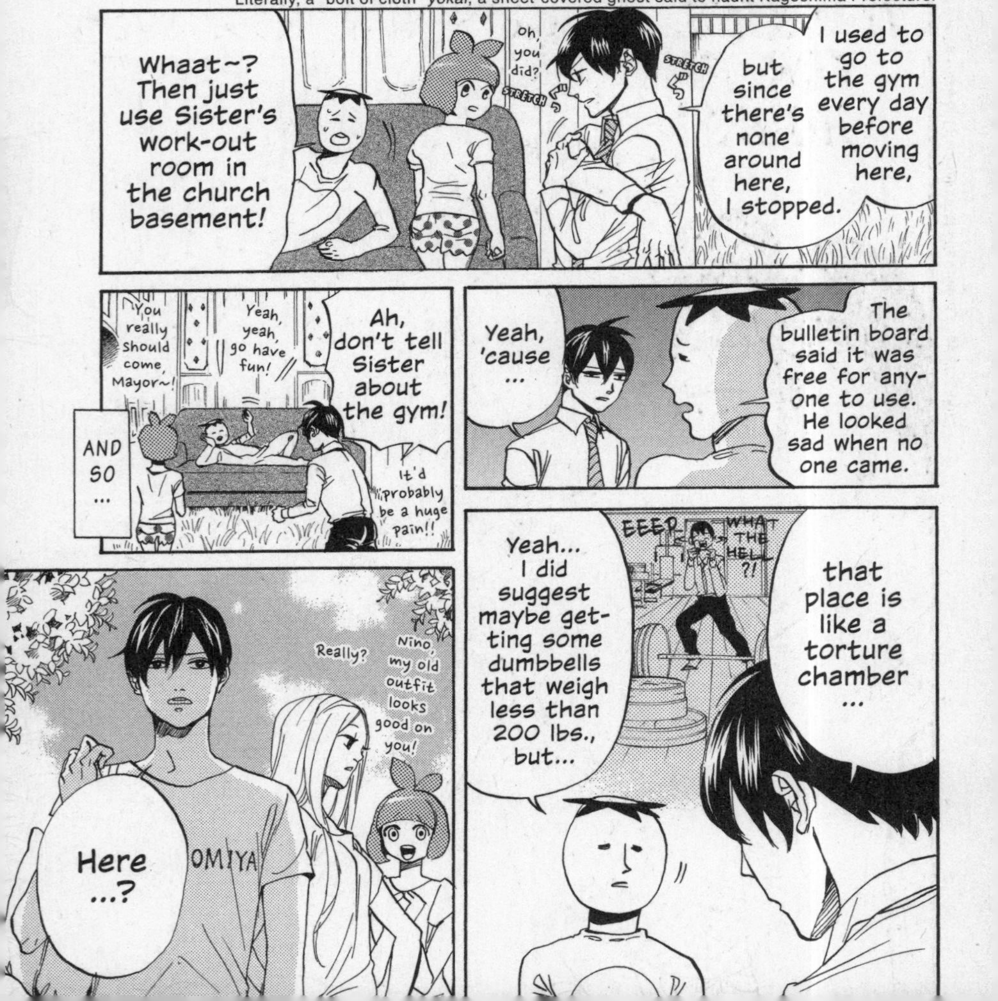

I used to go to the gym every day before moving here,
but since there's none around here, I stopped.
STRETCH
STRETCH
oh, you did?
Whaat~? Then just use Sister's work-out room in the church basement!
The bulletin board said it was free for any-one to use. He looked sad when no one came.
Yeah, 'cause ...
Ah, don't tell Sister about the gym!
Yeah, yeah, go have fun!
You really should come, Mayor~!
It'd probably be a huge pain!!
AND SO ...
that place is like a torture chamber ...
WHAT THE HELL ?!
EEEP
Yeah... I did suggest maybe get-ting some dumbbells that weigh less than 200 lbs., but...
Nino, my old outfit looks good on you!
Really?
OMIYA
Here ...?

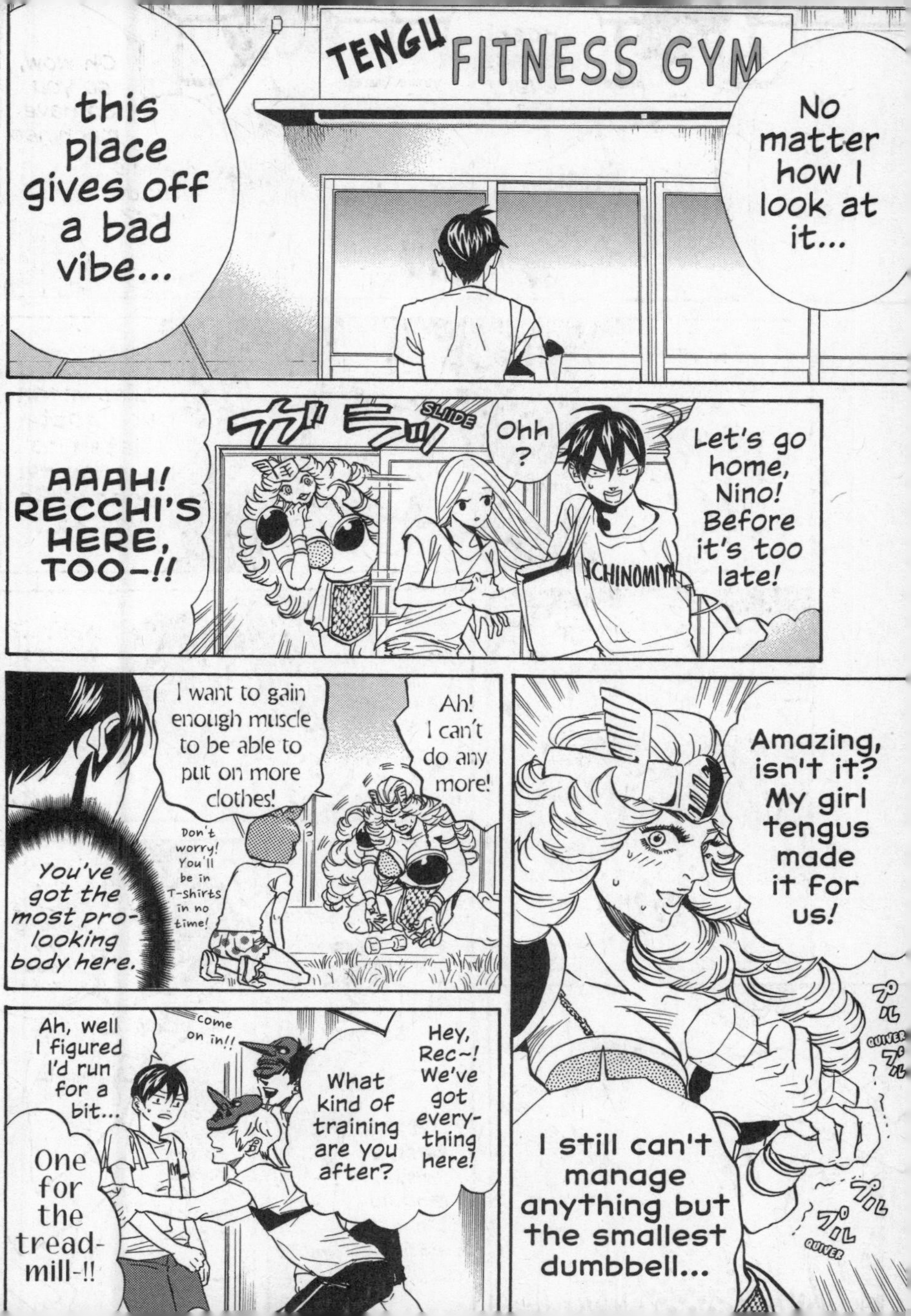
TENGU
FITNESS GYM
No matter how I look at it...
this place gives off a bad vibe...
Let's go home, Nino! Before it's too late!
Ohh ?
SLIDE
ICHINOMIYA
AAAH! RECCHI'S HERE, TOO-!!
Amazing, isn't it? My girl tengus made it for us!
QUIVER
QUIVER
I still can't manage anything but the smallest dumbbell...
Ah! I can't do any more!
I want to gain enough muscle to be able to put on more clothes!
Don't worry! You'll be in T-shirts in no time!
You've got the most pro-looking body here.
Hey, Rec~! We've got everything here!
What kind of training are you after?
come on in!!
Ah, well I figured I'd run for a bit...
One for the tread-mill-!!

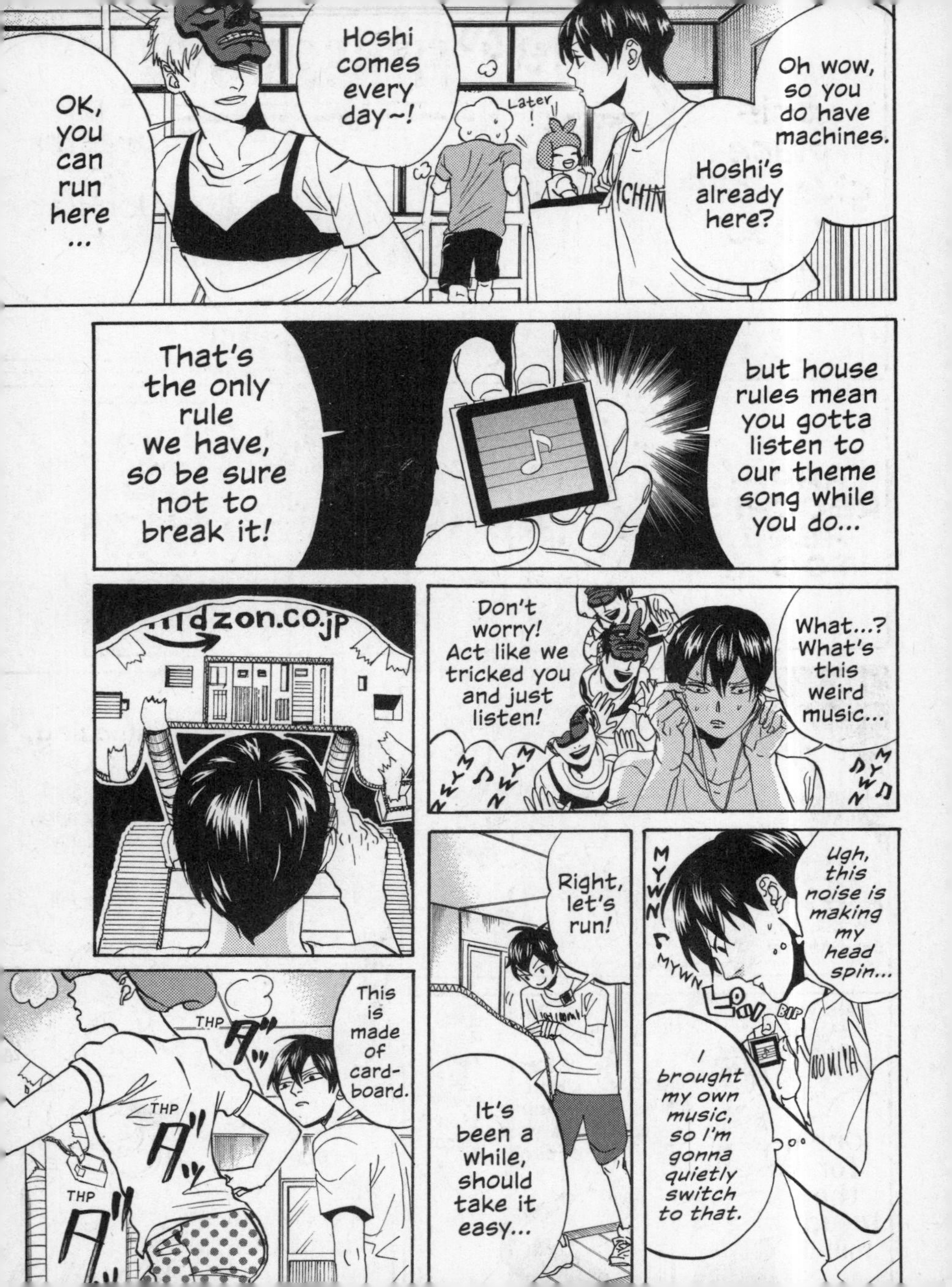
Oh wow, so you do have machines. Hoshi's already here?
Later!
Hoshi comes every day~!
OK, you can run here...
but house rules mean you gotta listen to our theme song while you do...
That's the only rule we have, so be sure not to break it!
What...? What's this weird music...
MYWN
Don't worry! Act like we tricked you and just listen!
MYWN
MYWN
Ugh, this noise is making my head spin...
MYWN
MYWN
BIP
I brought my own music, so I'm gonna quietly switch to that.
Right, let's run!
It's been a while, should take it easy...
This is made of cardboard.
THP
THP
THP

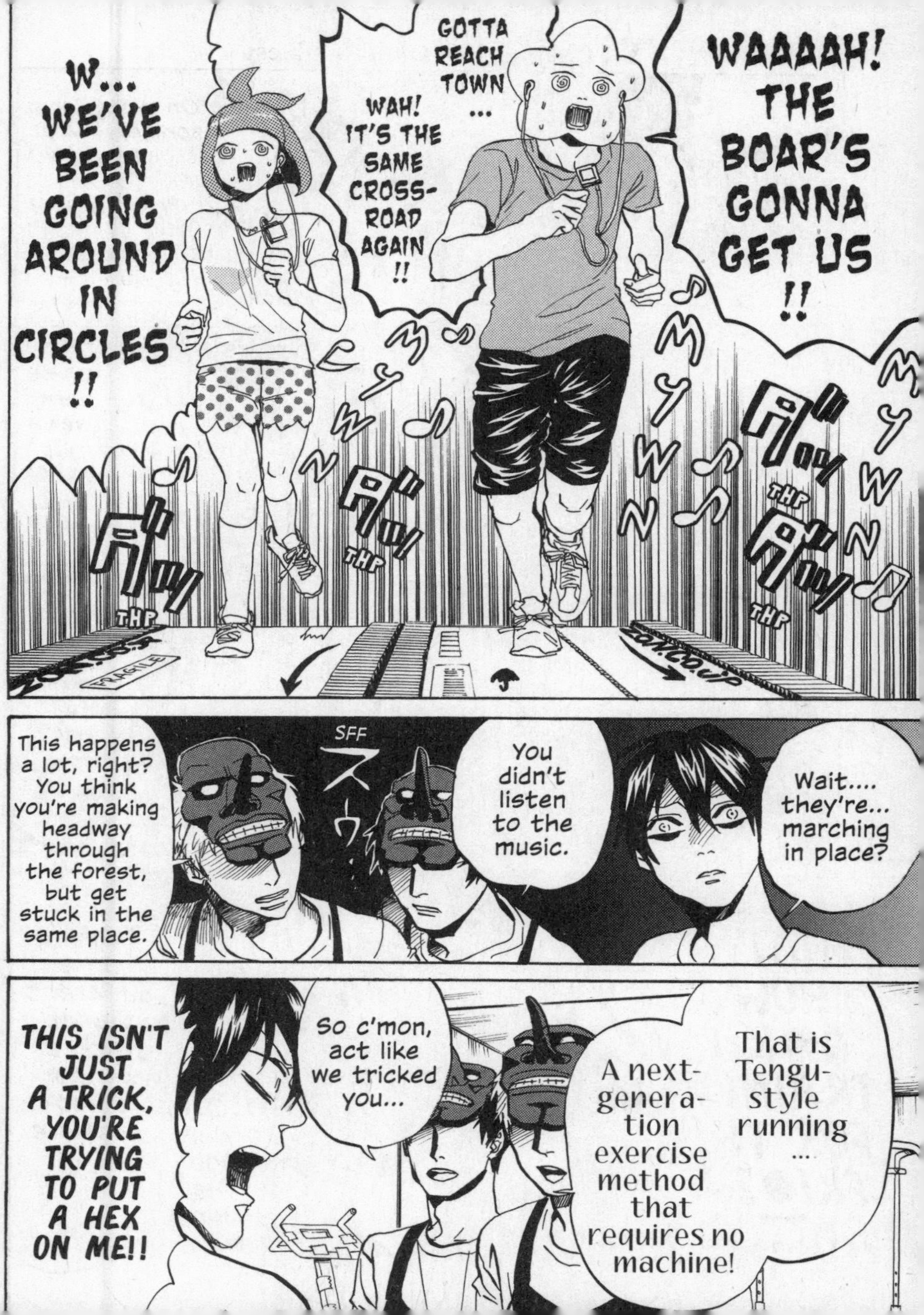
WAAAAH! THE BOAR'S GONNA GET US!!
GOTTA REACH TOWN...
WAH! IT'S THE SAME CROSS-ROAD AGAIN!!
W... WE'VE BEEN GOING AROUND IN CIRCLES!!
THP
THP
THP
THP
FRAGILE
Wait.... they're... marching in place?
You didn't listen to the music.
SFF
This happens a lot, right? You think you're making headway through the forest, but get stuck in the same place.
That is Tengu-style running...
A next-generation exercise method that requires no machine!
So c'mon, act like we tricked you...
THIS ISN'T JUST A TRICK, YOU'RE TRYING TO PUT A HEX ON ME!!

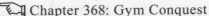

Chapter 368: Gym Conquest

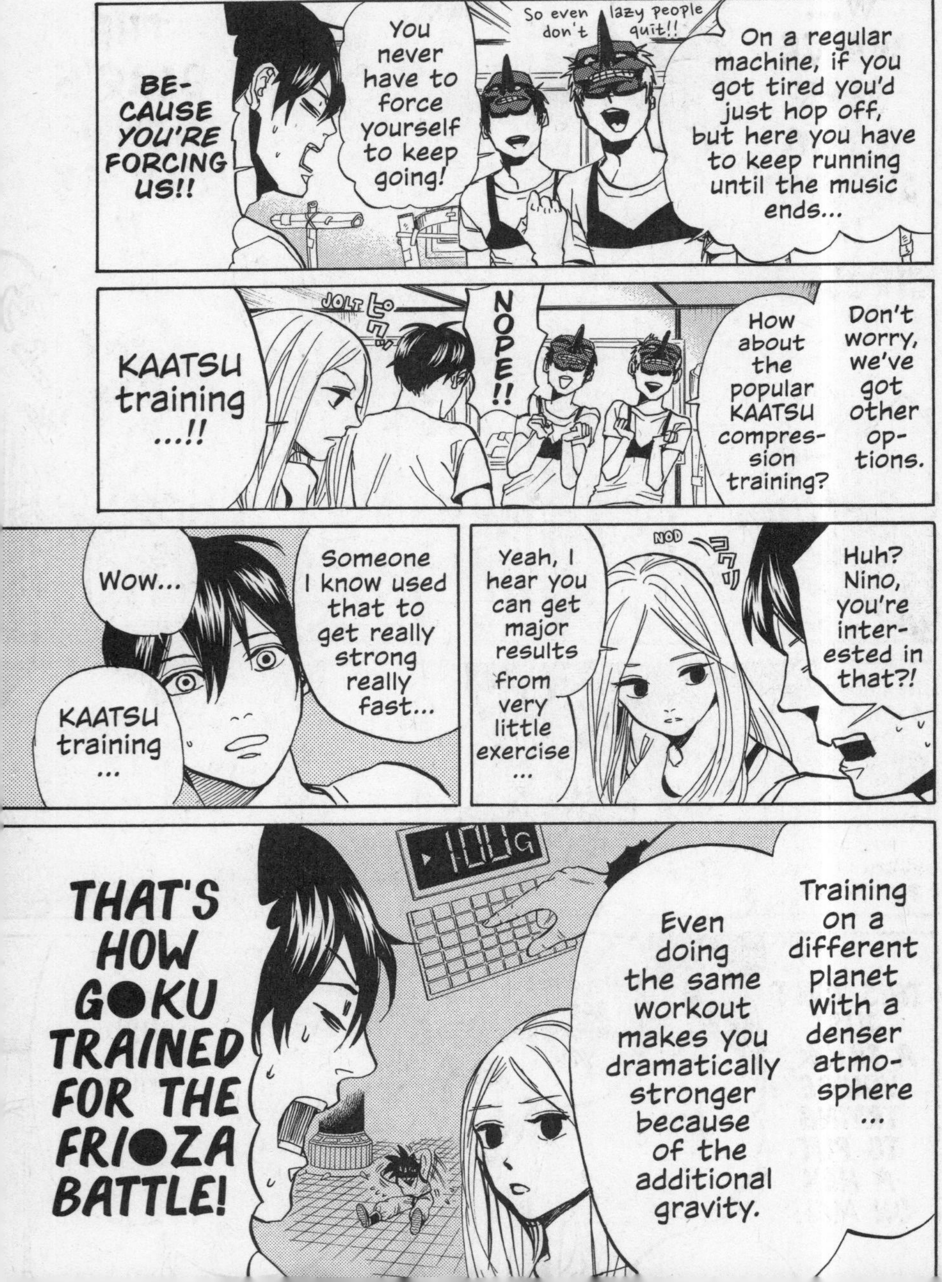

On a regular machine, if you got tired you'd just hop off, but here you have to keep running until the music ends...
So even lazy people don't quit!!
You never have to force yourself to keep going!
BECAUSE YOU'RE FORCING US!!
Don't worry, we've got other options.
How about the popular KAATSU compression training?
NOPE!!
JOLT
KAATSU training...!!
Huh? Nino, you're interested in that?!
NOD
Yeah, I hear you can get major results from very little exercise...
Someone I know used that to get really strong really fast...
Wow...
KAATSU training...
Training on a different planet with a denser atmosphere...
Even doing the same workout makes you dramatically stronger because of the additional gravity.
100G
THAT'S HOW G●KU TRAINED FOR THE FRIOZA BATTLE!

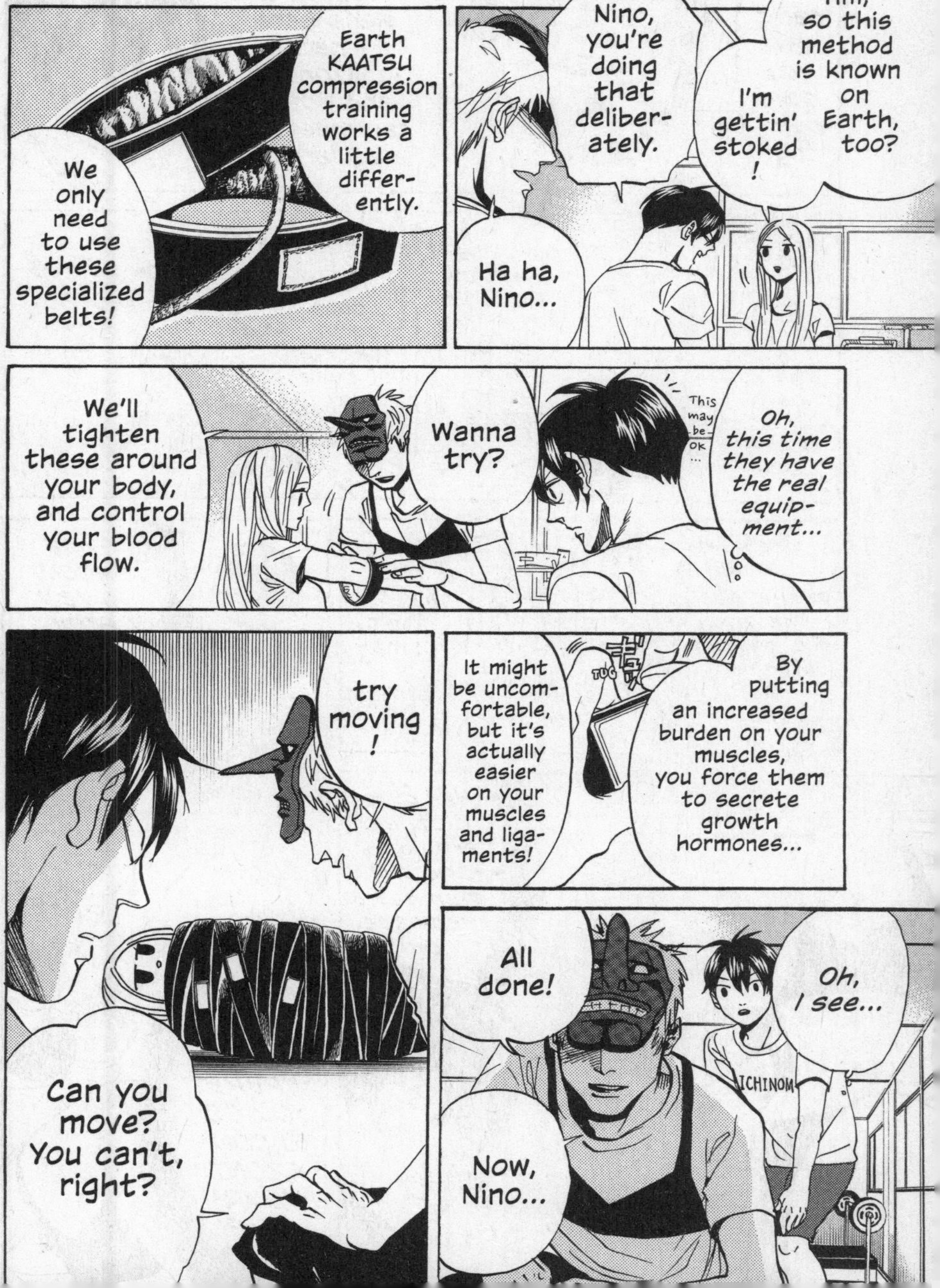
Hm, so this method is known on Earth, too?
I'm gettin' stoked!
Nino, you're doing that deliberately.
Ha ha, Nino...
Earth KAATSU compression training works a little differently.
We only need to use these specialized belts!
Oh, this time they have the real equipment...
This may be OK...
Wanna try?
We'll tighten these around your body, and control your blood flow.
By putting an increased burden on your muscles, you force them to secrete growth hormones...
TUG
It might be uncomfortable, but it's actually easier on your muscles and ligaments!
Oh, I see...
All done!
Now, Nino...
ICHINOM
try moving!
Can you move? You can't, right?

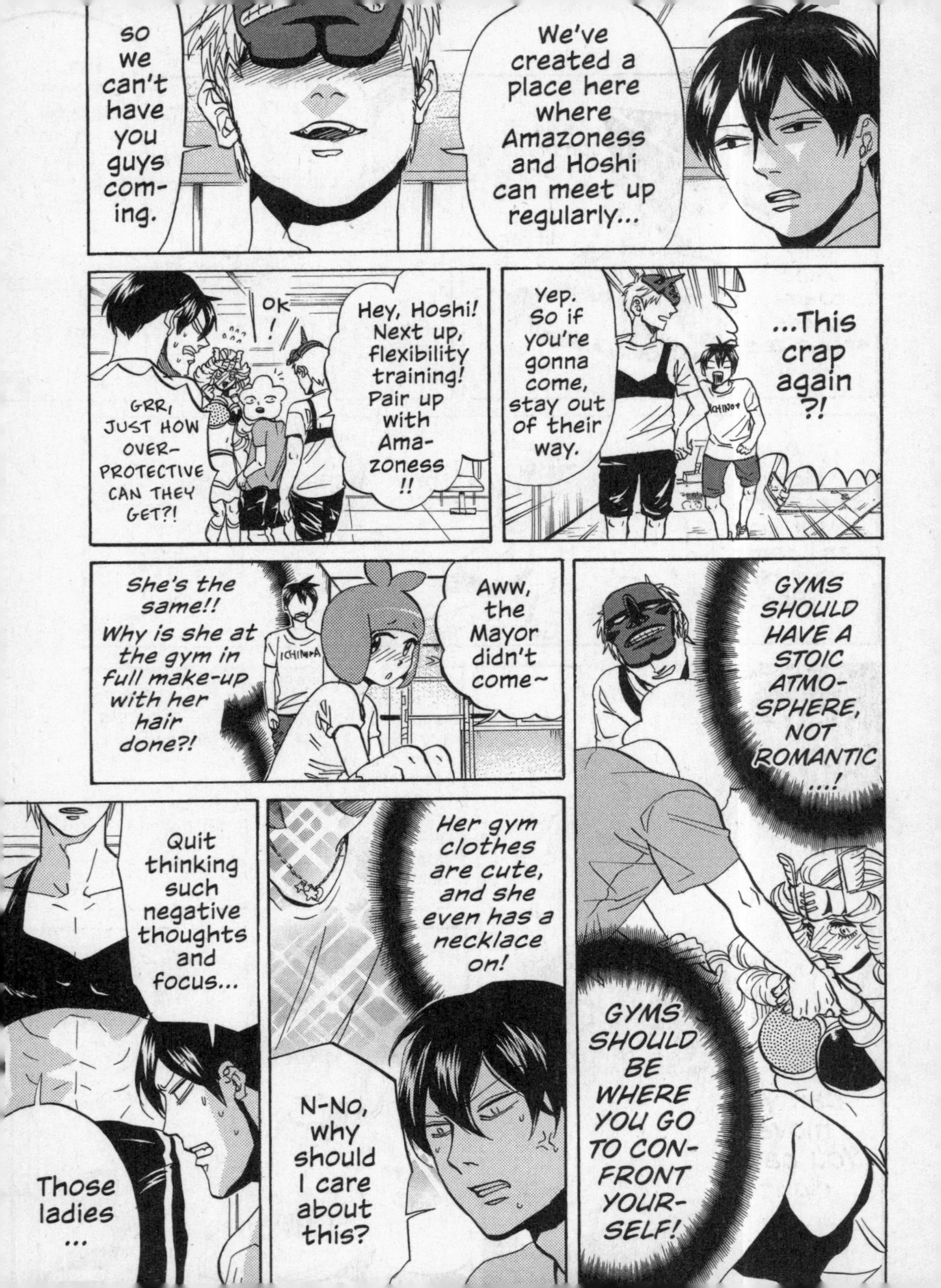
We've created a place here where Amazoness and Hoshi can meet up regularly...
so we can't have you guys com-ing.
...This crap again?!
Yep. So if you're gonna come, stay out of their way.
Hey, Hoshi! Next up, flexibility training! Pair up with Ama-zoness!!
OK!
GRR, JUST HOW OVER-PROTECTIVE CAN THEY GET?!
GYMS SHOULD HAVE A STOIC ATMO-SPHERE, NOT ROMANTIC ...!
GYMS SHOULD BE WHERE YOU GO TO CON-FRONT YOUR-SELF!
Aww, the Mayor didn't come~
She's the same!! Why is she at the gym in full make-up with her hair done?!
Her gym clothes are cute, and she even has a necklace on!
N-No, why should I care about this?
Quit thinking such negative thoughts and focus...
Those ladies ...

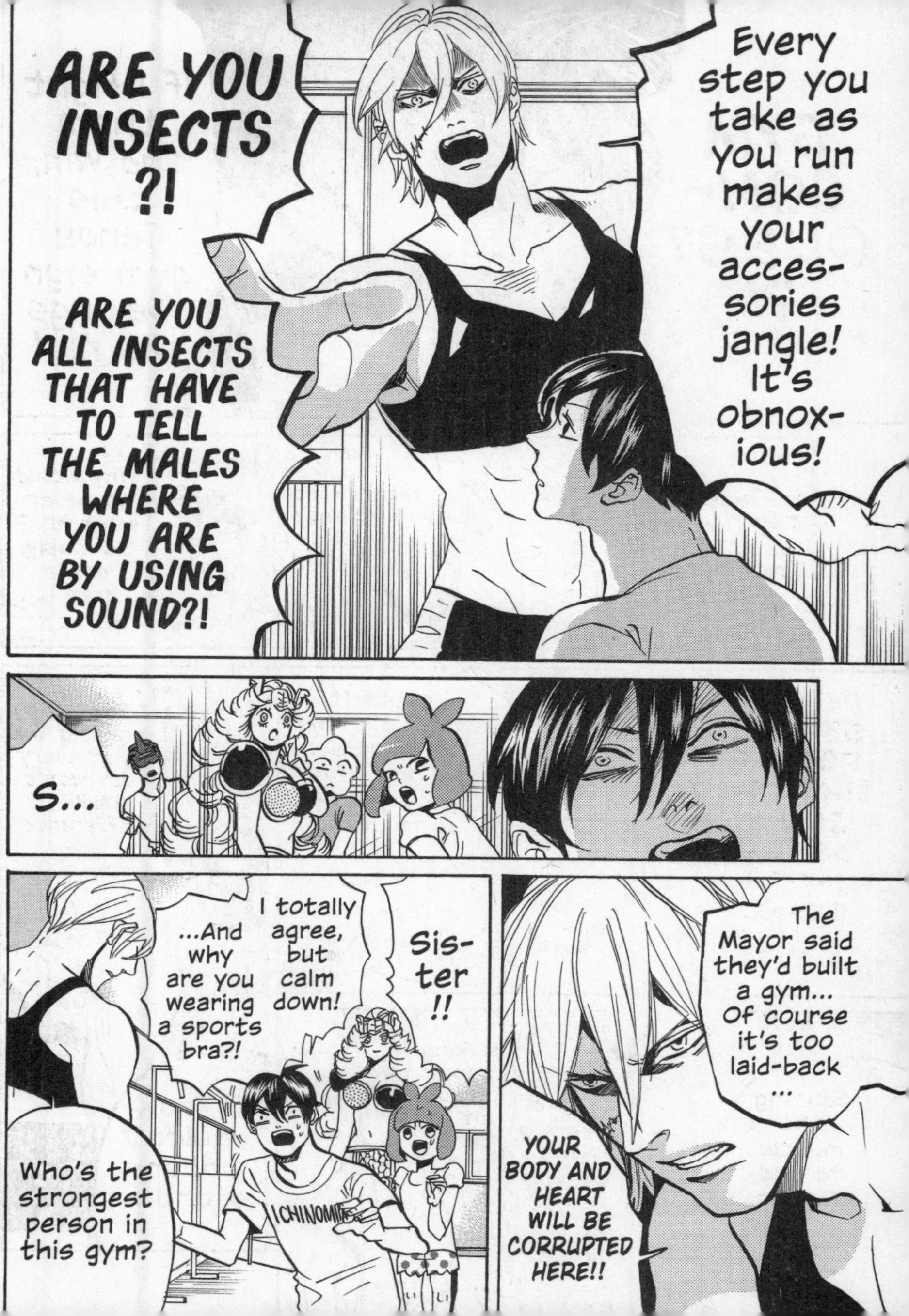
Every step you take as you run makes your accessories jangle! It's obnoxious!
ARE YOU INSECTS?!
ARE YOU ALL INSECTS THAT HAVE TO TELL THE MALES WHERE YOU ARE BY USING SOUND?!
S...
The Mayor said they'd built a gym... Of course it's too laid-back...
YOUR BODY AND HEART WILL BE CORRUPTED HERE!!
Sister!!
I totally agree, but calm down!
...And why are you wearing a sports bra?!
Who's the strongest person in this gym?

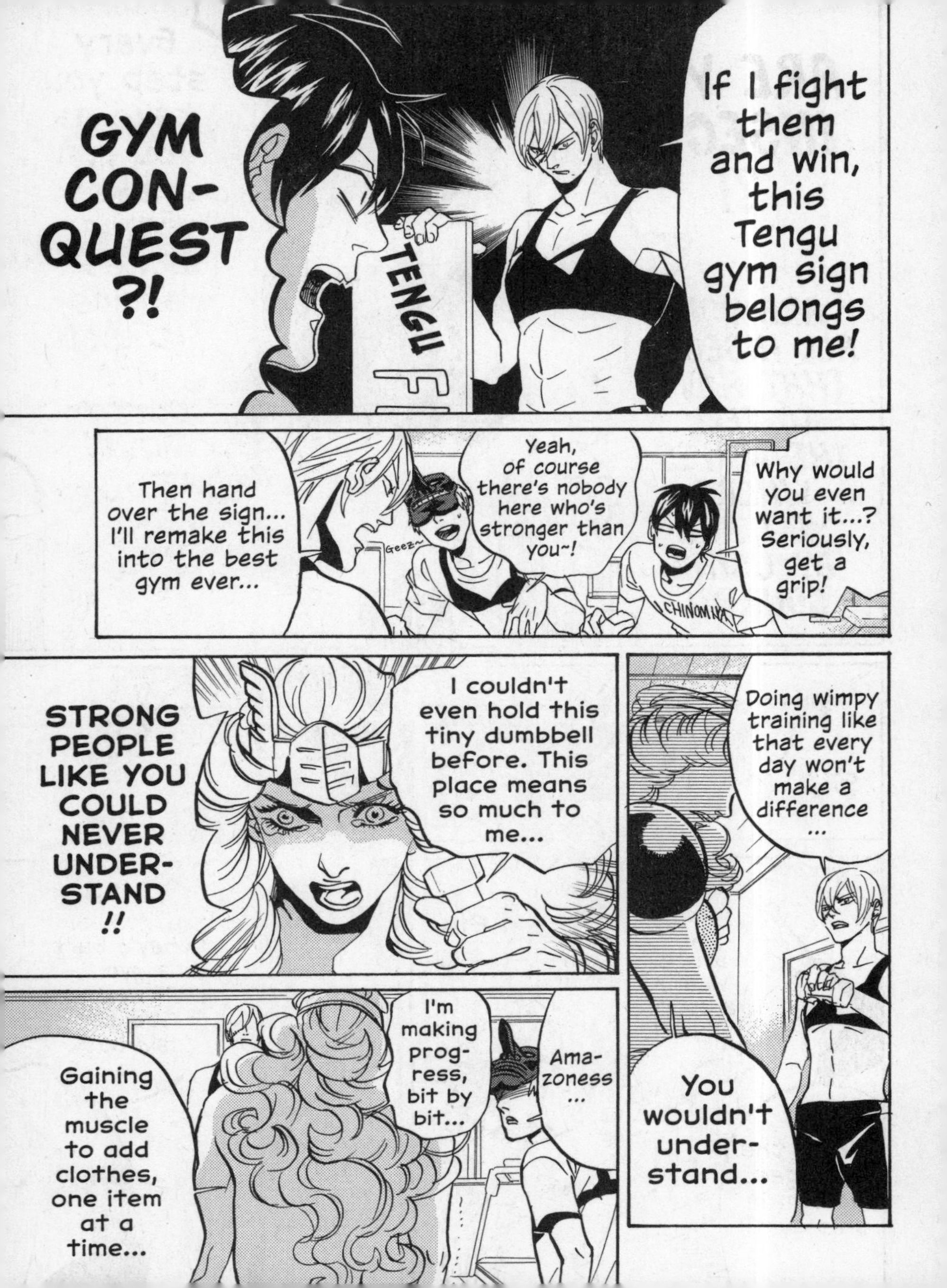
If I fight them and win, this Tengu gym sign belongs to me!
TENGU
GYM CON-QUEST?!
Why would you even want it...? Seriously, get a grip!
CHINOMIYA
Yeah, of course there's nobody here who's stronger than you~!
Geez~
Then hand over the sign... I'll remake this into the best gym ever...
Doing wimpy training like that every day won't make a difference...
You wouldn't under-stand...
I couldn't even hold this tiny dumbbell before. This place means so much to me...
STRONG PEOPLE LIKE YOU COULD NEVER UNDER-STAND!!
Ama-zoness...
I'm making prog-ress, bit by bit...
Gaining the muscle to add clothes, one item at a time...

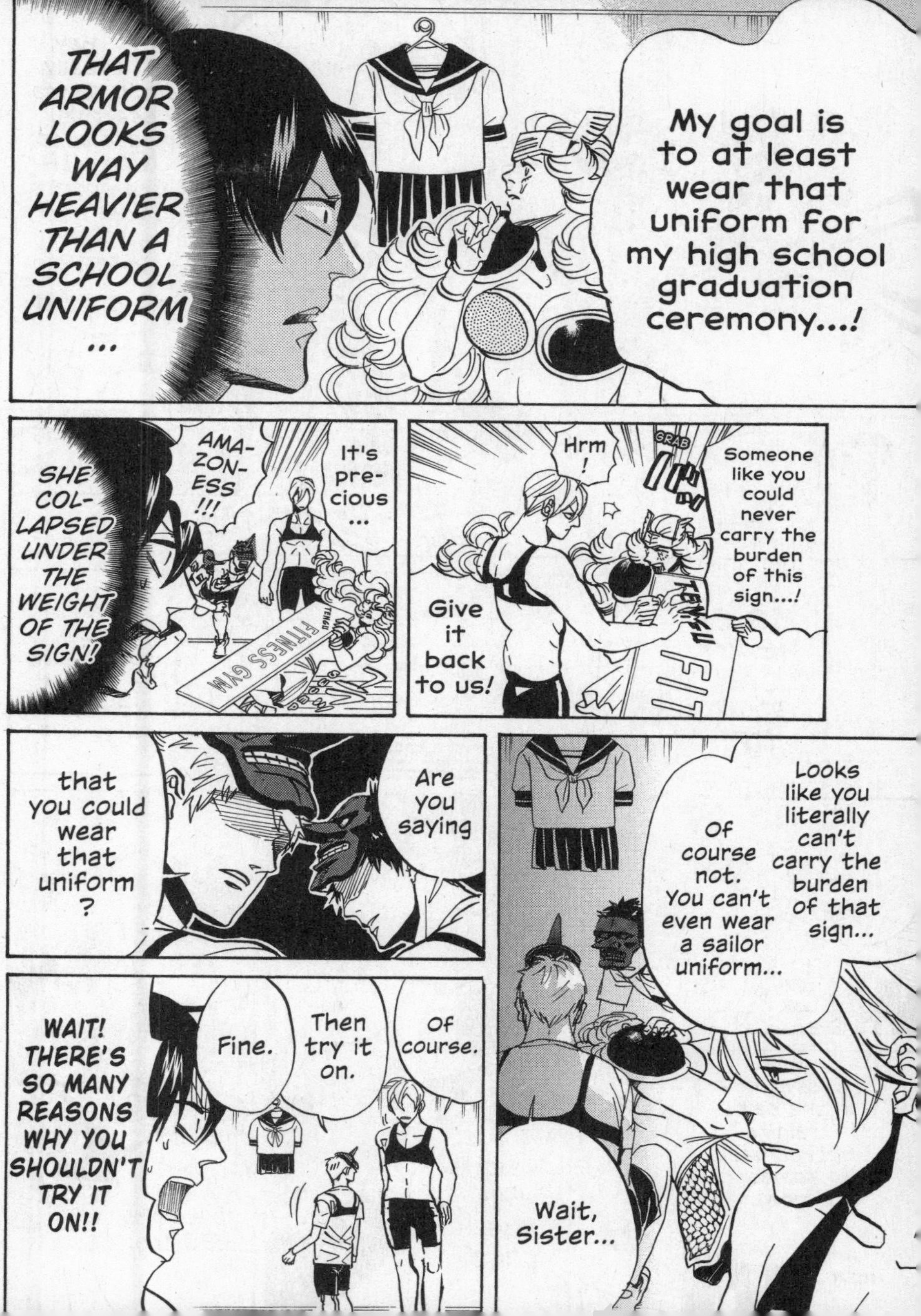
My goal is to at least wear that uniform for my high school graduation ceremony...!
THAT ARMOR LOOKS WAY HEAVIER THAN A SCHOOL UNIFORM...
GRAB
Someone like you could never carry the burden of this sign...!
Hrm!
Give it back to us!
It's precious...
AMAZONESS!!!
SHE COLLAPSED UNDER THE WEIGHT OF THE SIGN!
TENGU
FITNESS GYM
Looks like you literally can't carry the burden of that sign...
Of course not. You can't even wear a sailor uniform...
Wait, Sister...
Are you saying
that you could wear that uniform?
Of course.
Then try it on.
Fine.
WAIT! THERE'S SO MANY REASONS WHY YOU SHOULDN'T TRY IT ON!!

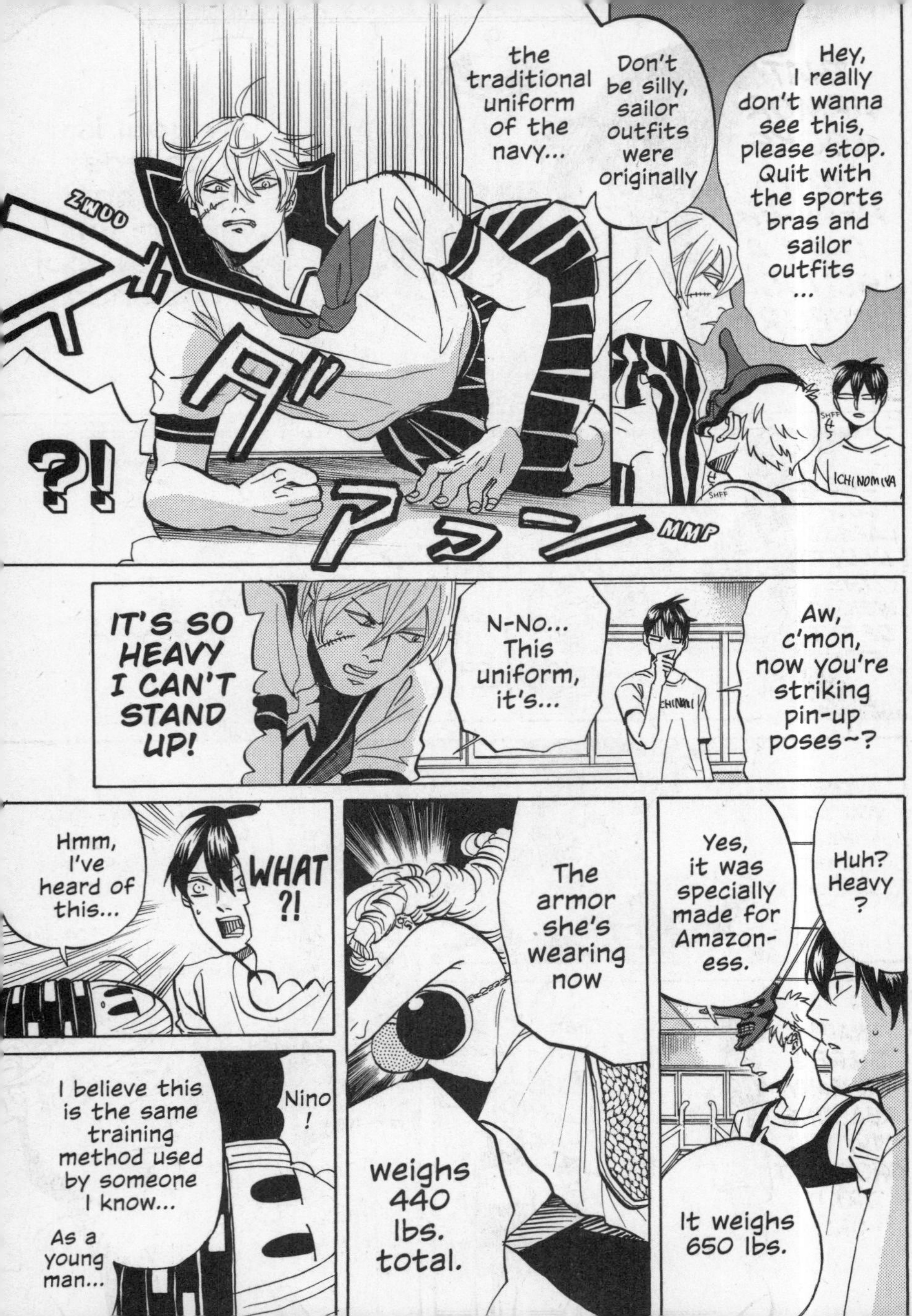

Hey, I really don't wanna see this, please stop. Quit with the sports bras and sailor outfits ...
SHFF
SHFF
ICHINOMIYA
Don't be silly, sailor outfits were originally
the traditional uniform of the navy...
ZWOO
?!
MMP
Aw, c'mon, now you're striking pin-up poses~?
N-No... This uniform, it's...
IT'S SO HEAVY I CAN'T STAND UP!
Huh? Heavy?
Yes, it was specially made for Amazon-ess.
It weighs 650 lbs.
The armor she's wearing now
weighs 440 lbs. total.
WHAT ?!
Hmm, I've heard of this...
Nino!
I believe this is the same training method used by someone I know...
As a young man...

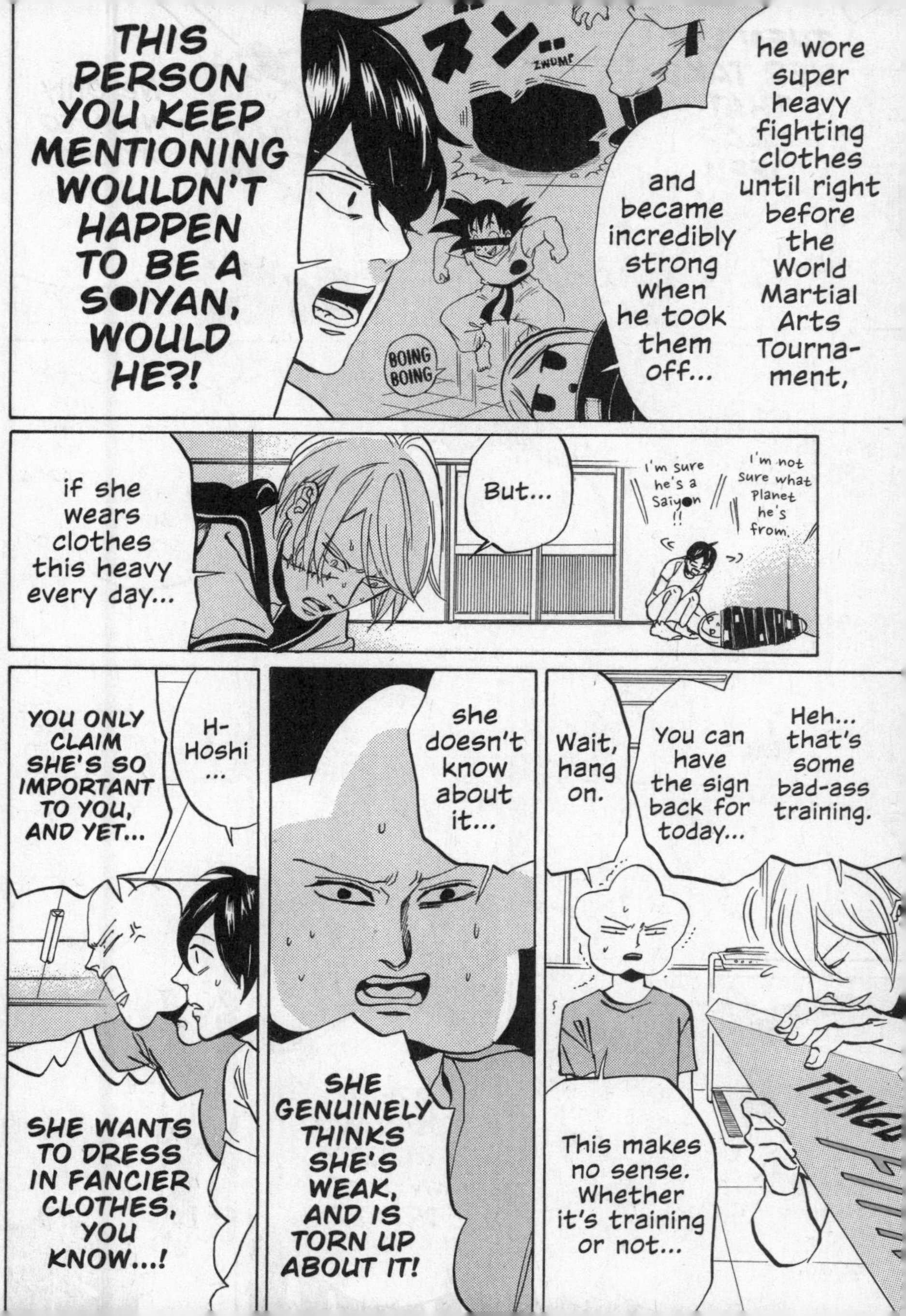

ズン
ZWUMP
he wore super heavy fighting clothes until right before the World Martial Arts Tournament,
and became incredibly strong when he took them off...
BOING BOING
THIS PERSON YOU KEEP MENTIONING WOULDN'T HAPPEN TO BE A S●IYAN, WOULD HE?!
I'm not sure what Planet he's from.
I'm sure he's a Saiy●n !!
But...
if she wears clothes this heavy every day...
Heh... that's some bad-ass training.
You can have the sign back for today...
Wait, hang on.
This makes no sense. Whether it's training or not...
TENGU
she doesn't know about it...
SHE GENUINELY THINKS SHE'S WEAK, AND IS TORN UP ABOUT IT!
H-Hoshi...
YOU ONLY CLAIM SHE'S SO IMPORTANT TO YOU, AND YET...
SHE WANTS TO DRESS IN FANCIER CLOTHES, YOU KNOW...!

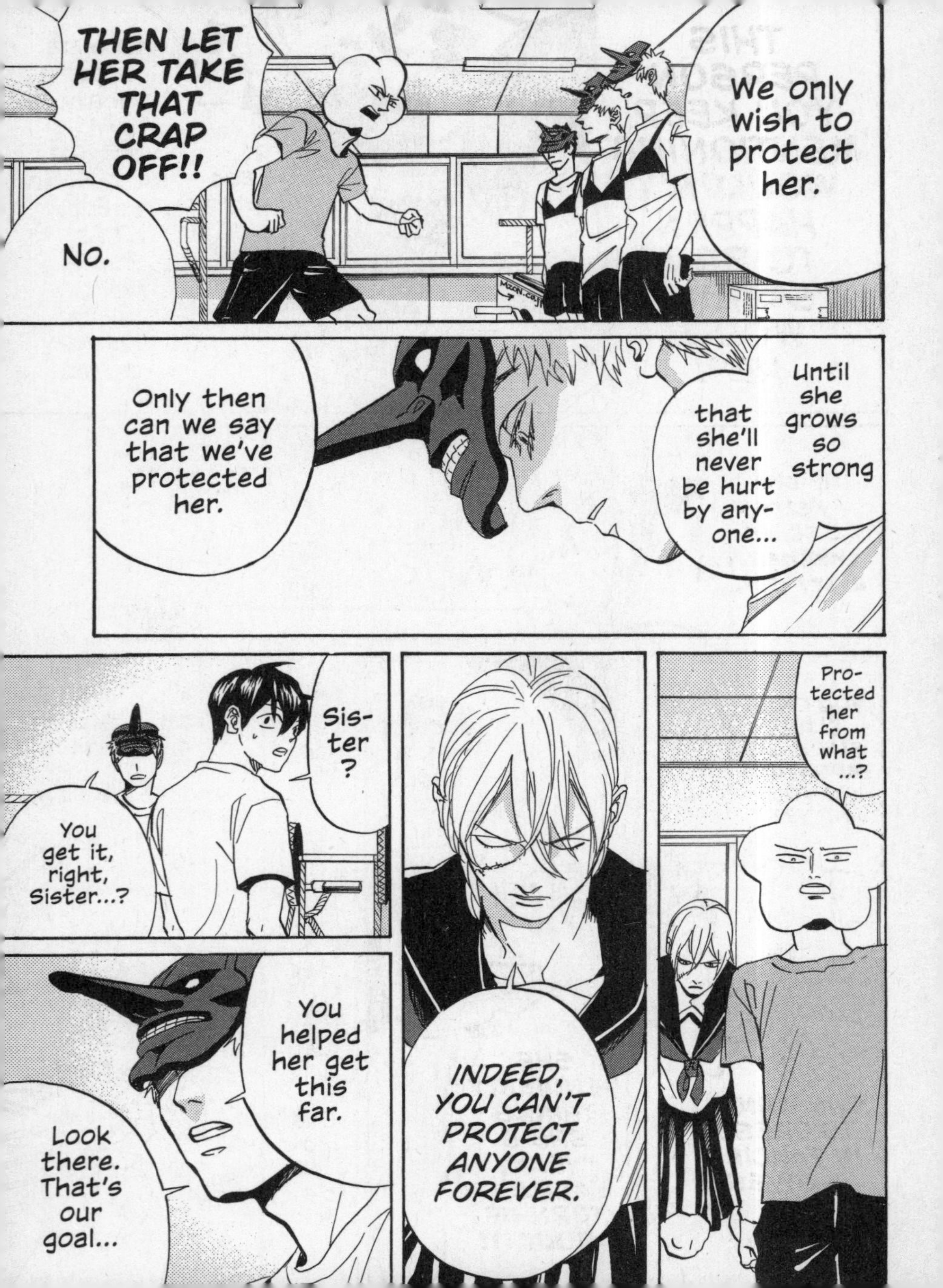
We only wish to protect her.
THEN LET HER TAKE THAT CRAP OFF!!
No.
Until she grows so strong
that she'll never be hurt by any-one...
Only then can we say that we've protected her.
Pro-tected her from what ...?
INDEED, YOU CAN'T PROTECT ANYONE FOREVER.
Sis-ter ?
You get it, right, Sister...?
You helped her get this far.
Look there. That's our goal...

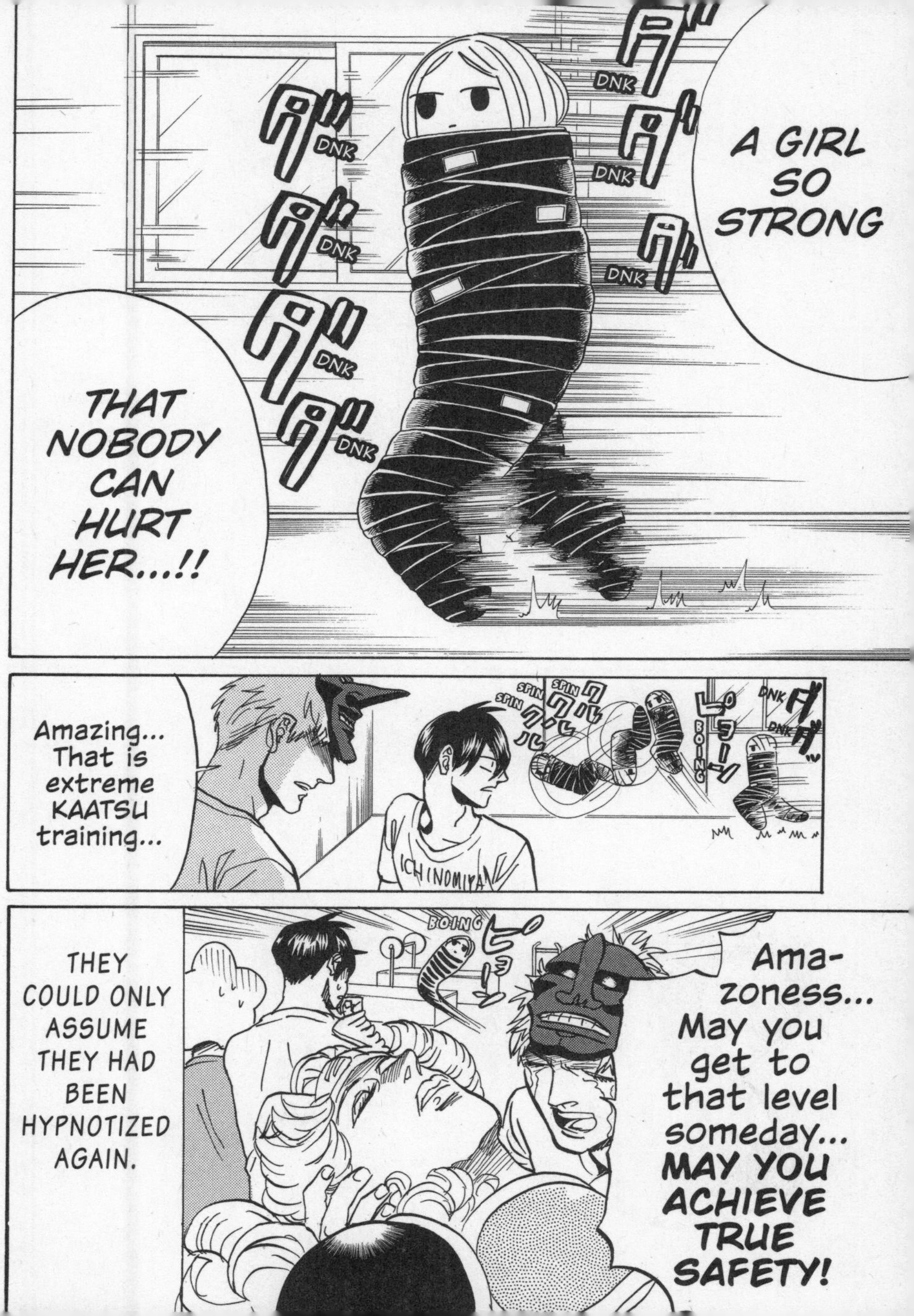
A GIRL SO STRONG
DNK DNK DNK DNK DNK DNK DNK DNK
THAT NOBODY CAN HURT HER...!!
DNK DNK
BOING
SPIN SPIN SPIN
Amazing... That is extreme KAATSU training...
ICHINOMIYA
BOING
Ama-zoness... May you get to that level someday... MAY YOU ACHIEVE TRUE SAFETY!
THEY COULD ONLY ASSUME THEY HAD BEEN HYPNOTIZED AGAIN.

ARAKAWA
UNDER
THE BRIDGE

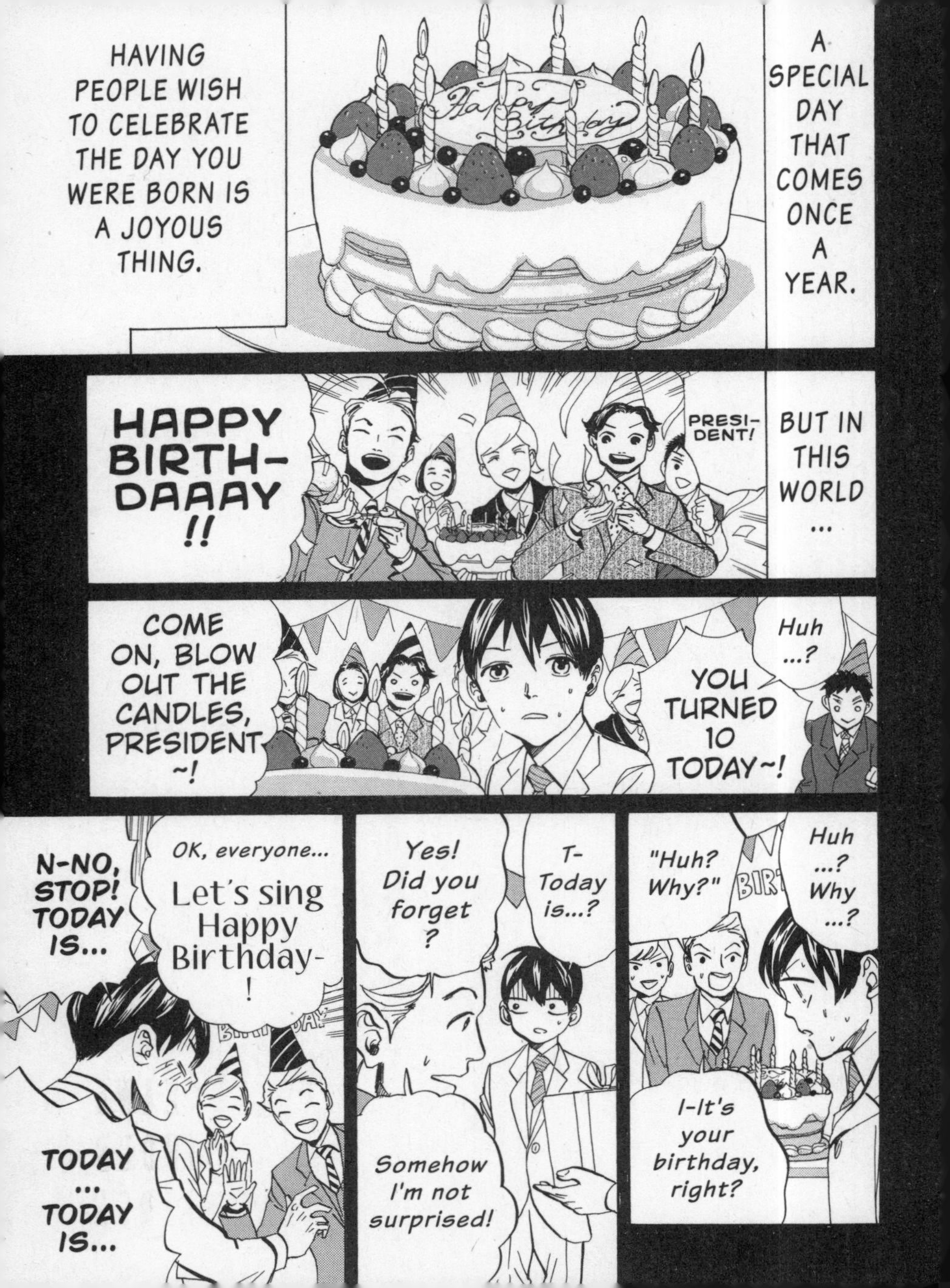
A SPECIAL DAY THAT COMES ONCE A YEAR.
HAVING PEOPLE WISH TO CELEBRATE THE DAY YOU WERE BORN IS A JOYOUS THING.
BUT IN THIS WORLD ...
PRESI-DENT!
HAPPY BIRTH-DAAAY!!
Huh ...?
YOU TURNED 10 TODAY~!
COME ON, BLOW OUT THE CANDLES, PRESIDENT~!
Huh ...? Why ...?
"Huh? Why?"
I-It's your birthday, right?
T-Today is...?
Yes! Did you forget?
Somehow I'm not surprised!
OK, everyone... Let's sing Happy Birthday-!
N-NO, STOP! TODAY IS...
TODAY ... TODAY IS...

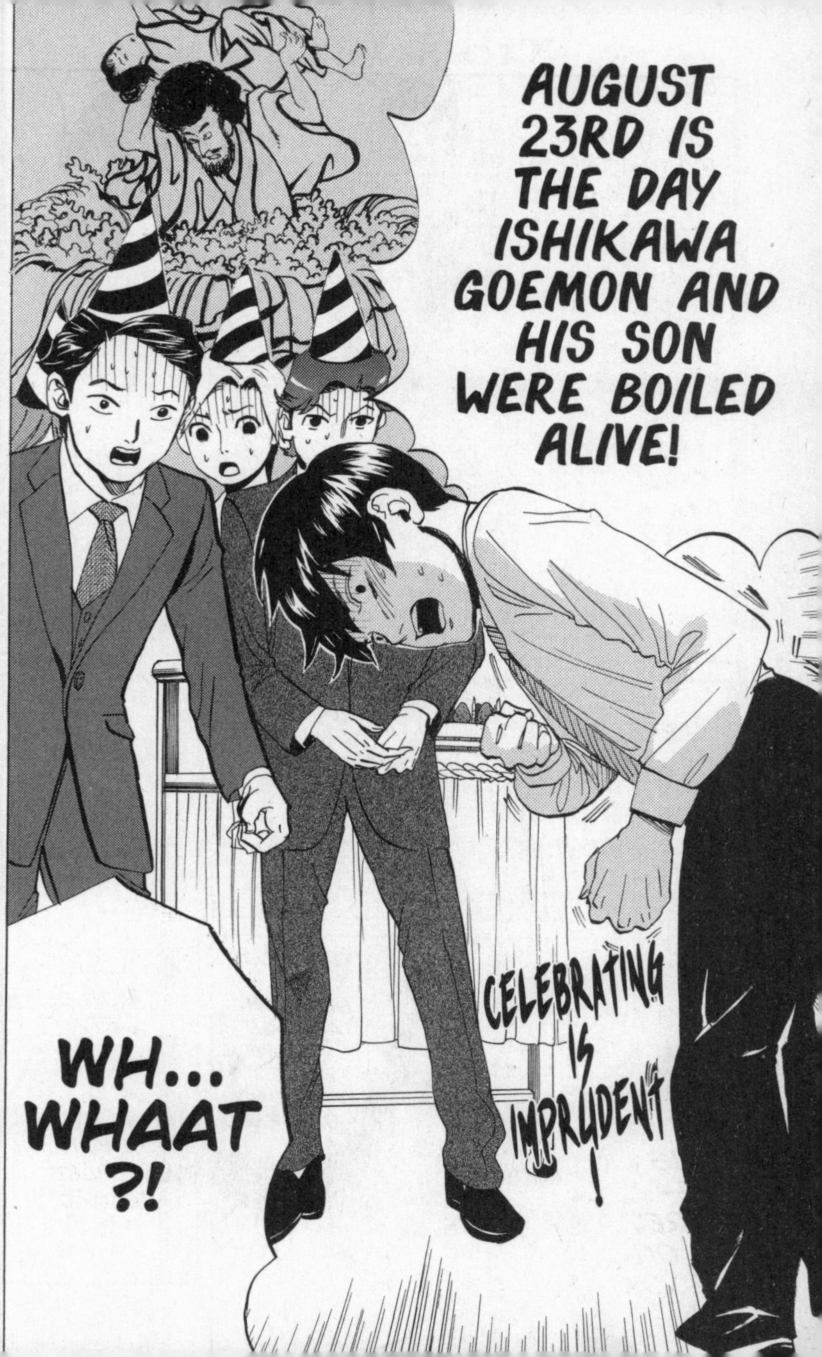
AUGUST 23RD IS THE DAY ISHIKAWA GOEMON AND HIS SON WERE BOILED ALIVE!
CELEBRATING IS IMPRUDENT!
WH... WHAAT?!

THERE ARE PEOPLE WHO CAN'T READILY ACCEPT SUCH GOOD WILL.

*Quasi-legendary figure who was executed for an assassination attempt on Toyotomi Hideyoshi.

Chapter 369: Birthday Party

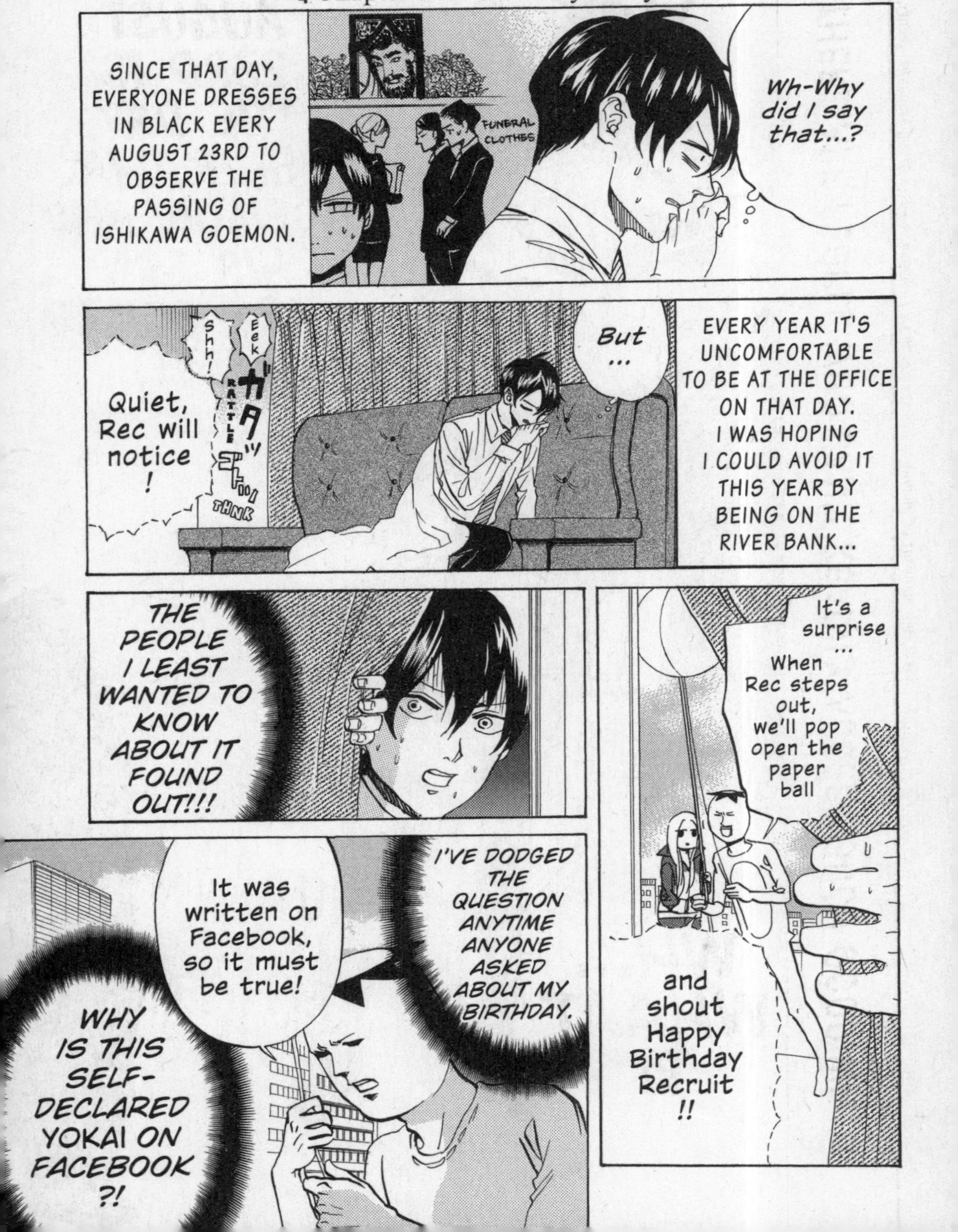

Wh-Why did I say that...?
FUNERAL CLOTHES
SINCE THAT DAY, EVERYONE DRESSES IN BLACK EVERY AUGUST 23RD TO OBSERVE THE PASSING OF ISHIKAWA GOEMON.
EVERY YEAR IT'S UNCOMFORTABLE TO BE AT THE OFFICE ON THAT DAY. I WAS HOPING I COULD AVOID IT THIS YEAR BY BEING ON THE RIVER BANK...
But ...
Eek
Shh!
RATTLE
THNK
Quiet, Rec will notice!
It's a surprise ...
When Rec steps out, we'll pop open the paper ball
and shout Happy Birthday Recruit !!
THE PEOPLE I LEAST WANTED TO KNOW ABOUT IT FOUND OUT!!!
I'VE DODGED THE QUESTION ANYTIME ANYONE ASKED ABOUT MY BIRTHDAY.
It was written on Facebook, so it must be true!
WHY IS THIS SELF-DECLARED YOKAI ON FACEBOOK ?!

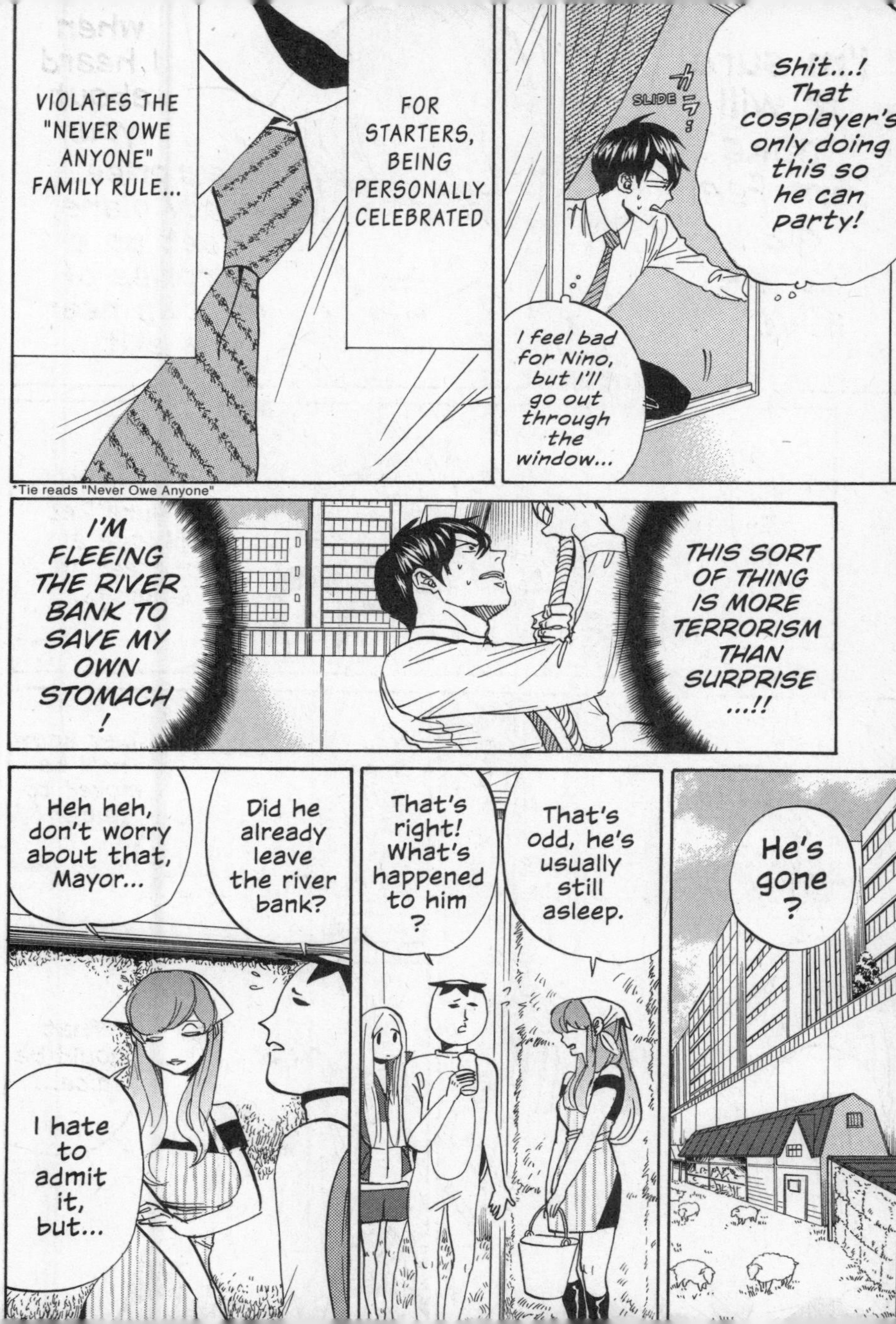
Shit...! That cosplayer's only doing this so he can party!
SLIDE
I feel bad for Nino, but I'll go out through the window...
FOR STARTERS, BEING PERSONALLY CELEBRATED
VIOLATES THE "NEVER OWE ANYONE" FAMILY RULE...
*Tie reads "Never Owe Anyone"
THIS SORT OF THING IS MORE TERRORISM THAN SURPRISE ...!!
I'M FLEEING THE RIVER BANK TO SAVE MY OWN STOMACH !
He's gone ?
That's odd, he's usually still asleep.
That's right! What's happened to him ?
Did he already leave the river bank?
Heh heh, don't worry about that, Mayor...
I hate to admit it, but...

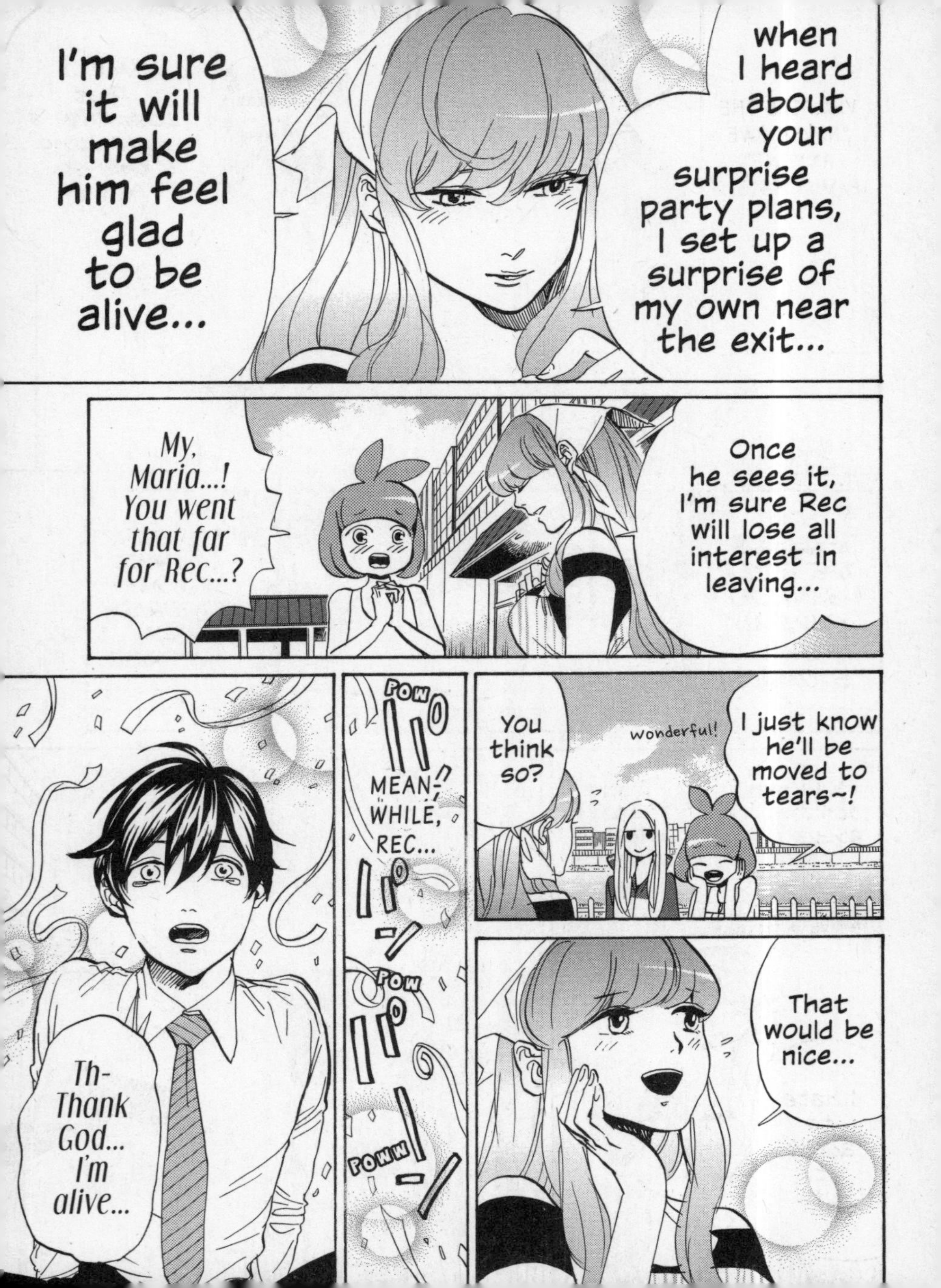
when I heard about your surprise party plans, I set up a surprise of my own near the exit...
I'm sure it will make him feel glad to be alive...
Once he sees it, I'm sure Rec will lose all interest in leaving...
My, Maria...! You went that far for Rec...?
I just know he'll be moved to tears~!
wonderful!
You think so?
That would be nice...
POW
MEAN-WHILE, REC...
POW
POWW
Th- Thank God... I'm alive...

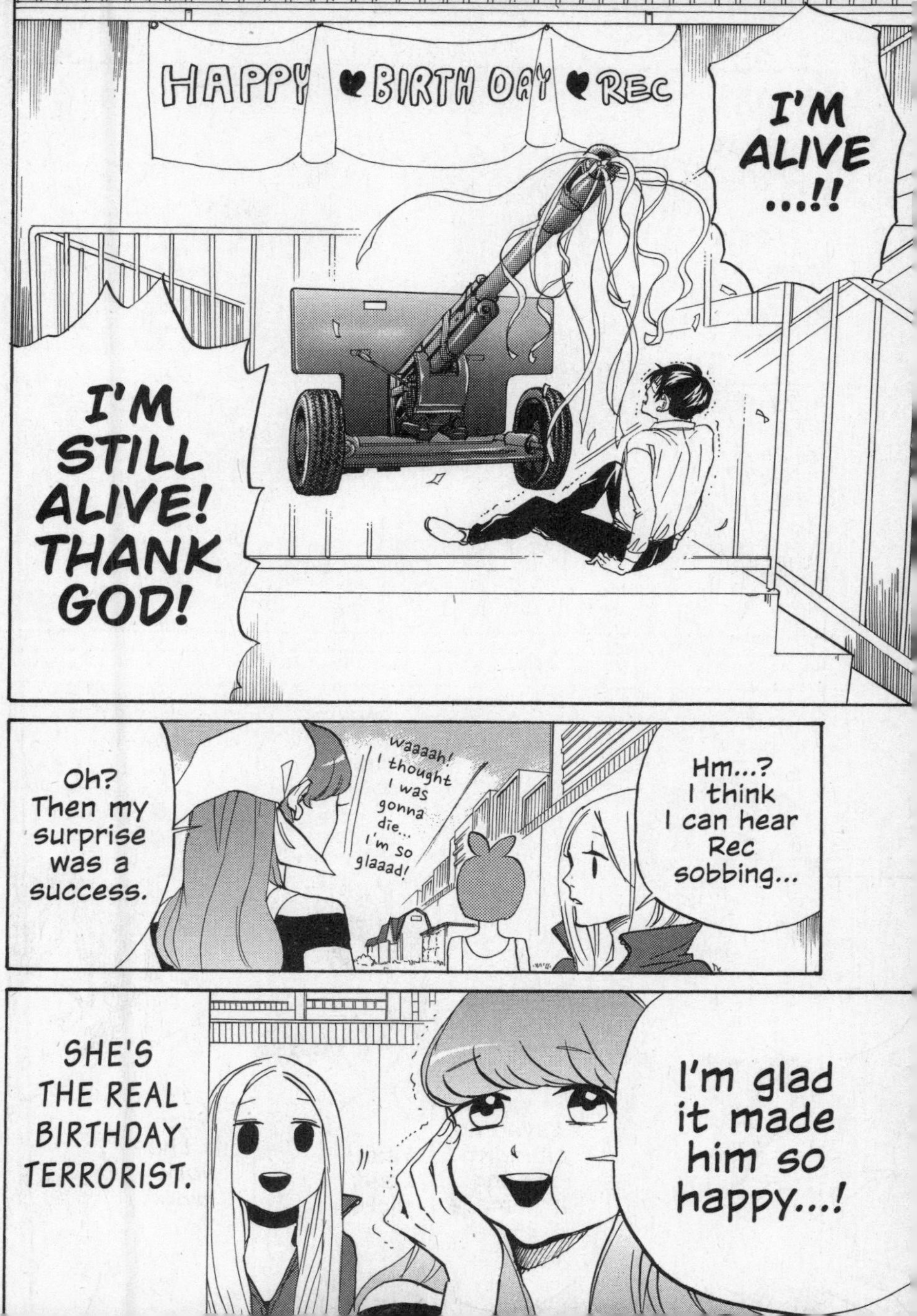
HAPPY ♥ BIRTH DAY ♥ REC
I'M ALIVE ...!!
I'M STILL ALIVE! THANK GOD!
Hm...? I think I can hear Rec sobbing...
Waaaah! I thought I was gonna die... I'm so glaaad!
Oh? Then my surprise was a success.
I'm glad it made him so happy...!
SHE'S THE REAL BIRTHDAY TERRORIST.

Chapter 370: Birthday Present

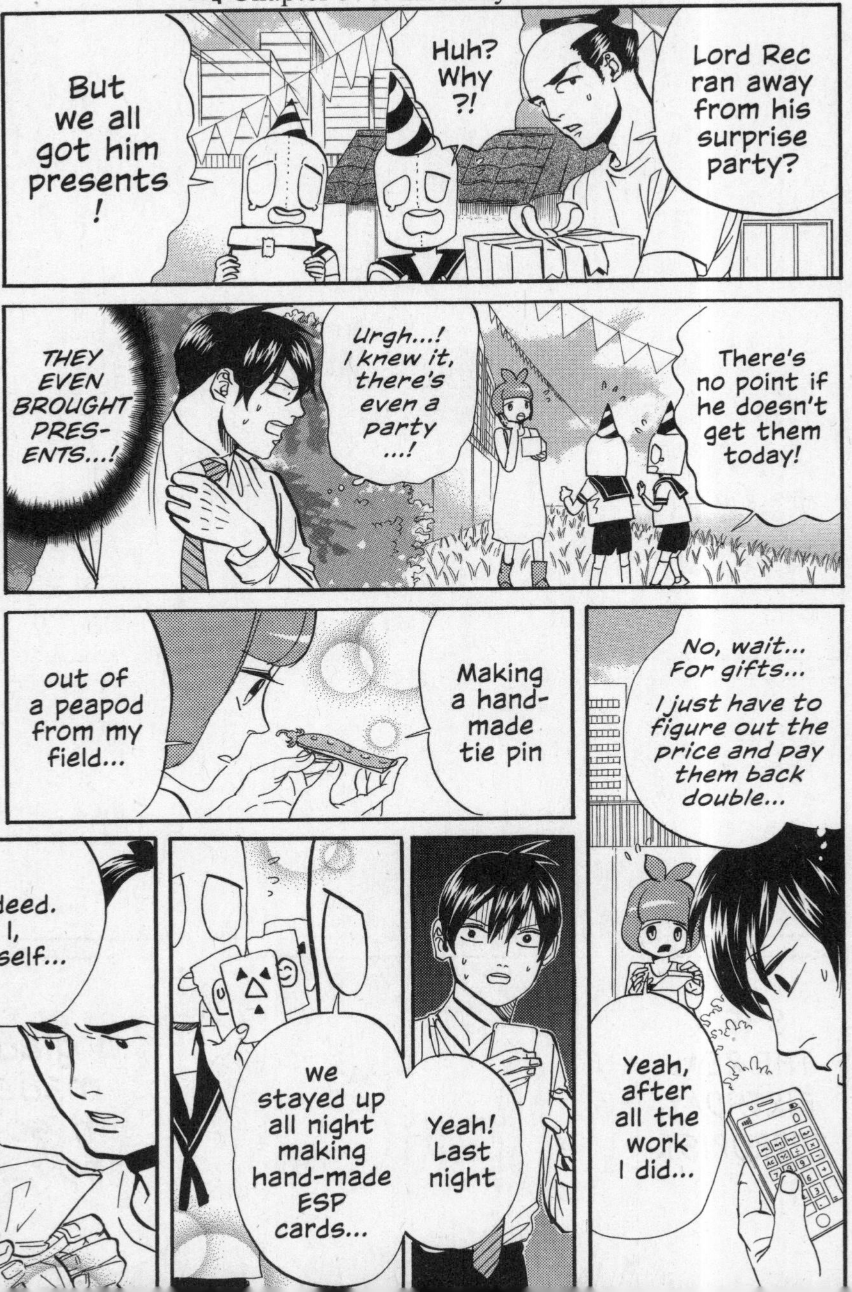

Lord Rec ran away from his surprise party?
Huh? Why?!
But we all got him presents!
There's no point if he doesn't get them today!
Urgh...! I knew it, there's even a party...!
THEY EVEN BROUGHT PRES-ENTS...!
No, wait... For gifts... I just have to figure out the price and pay them back double...
Yeah, after all the work I did...
Making a hand-made tie pin
out of a peapod from my field...
Yeah! Last night
we stayed up all night making hand-made ESP cards...
Indeed. I, myself...

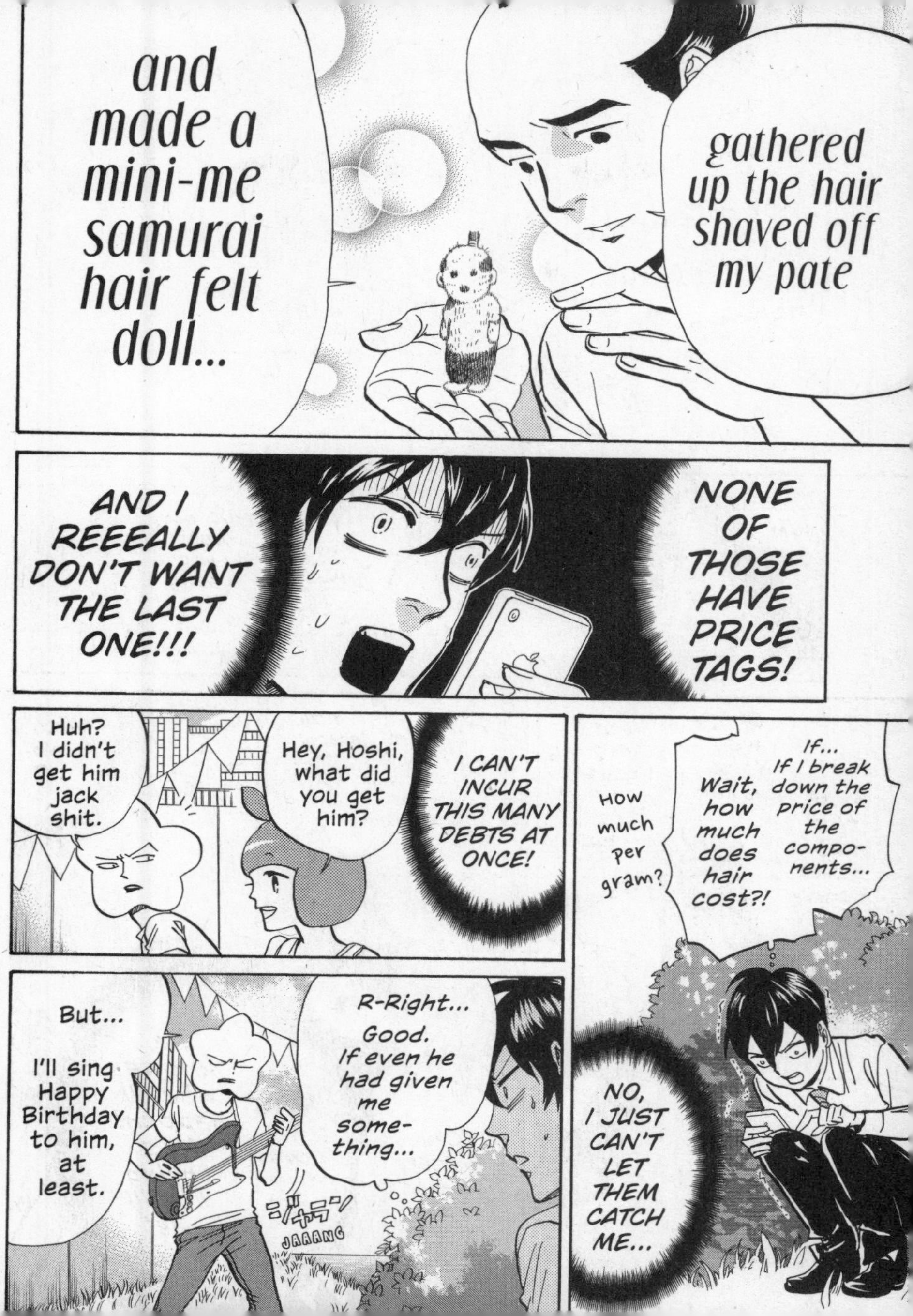
gathered up the hair shaved off my pate
and made a mini-me samurai hair felt doll...
NONE OF THOSE HAVE PRICE TAGS!
AND I REEEALLY DON'T WANT THE LAST ONE!!!
If... If I break down the price of the components...
Wait, how much does hair cost?!
How much per gram?
NO, I JUST CAN'T LET THEM CATCH ME...
I CAN'T INCUR THIS MANY DEBTS AT ONCE!
Hey, Hoshi, what did you get him?
Huh? I didn't get him jack shit.
R-Right... Good. If even he had given me something...
But... I'll sing Happy Birthday to him, at least.
ジャラ〜ン
JAAAANG

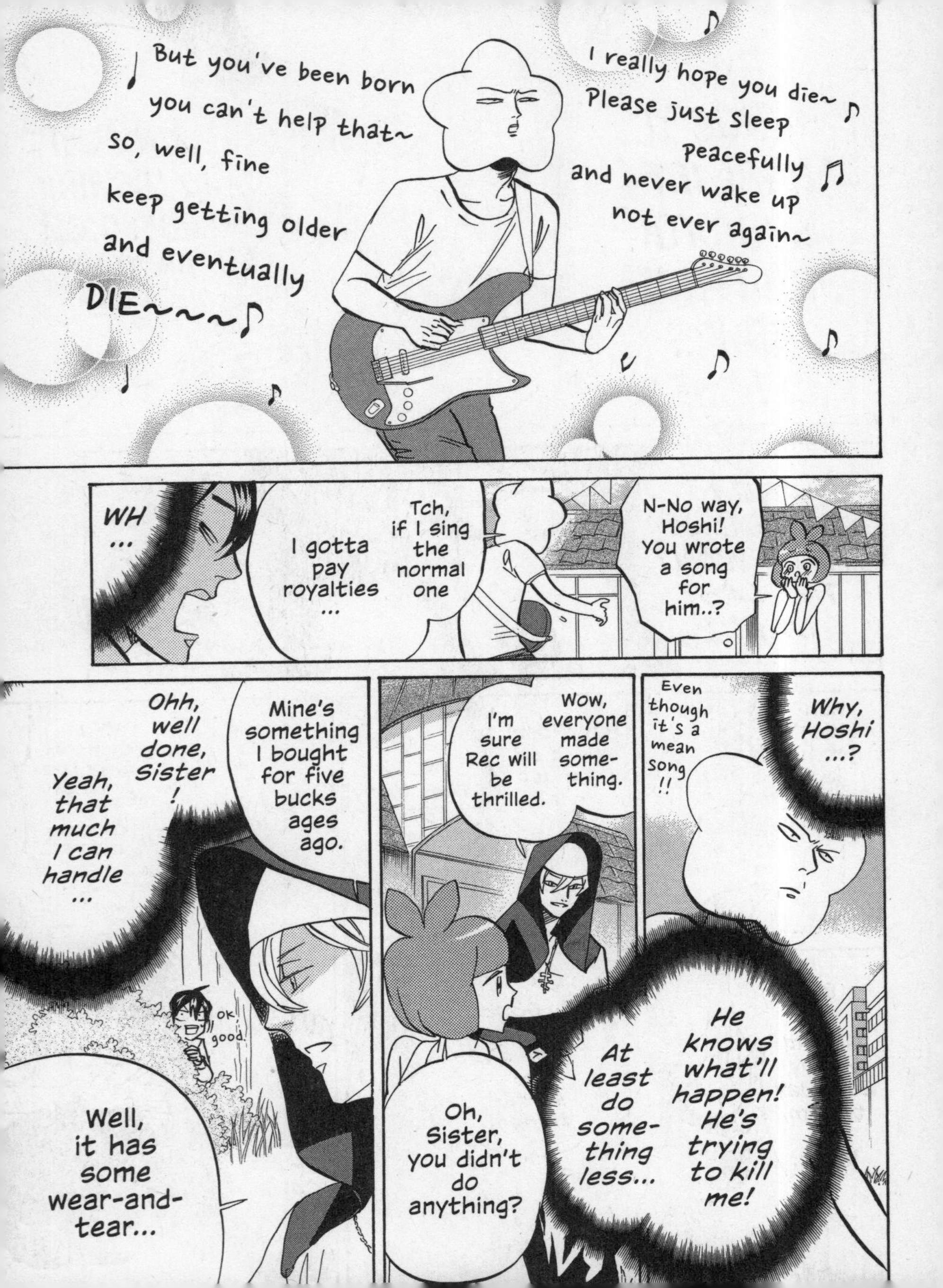
I really hope you die~ Please just sleep peacefully and never wake up not ever again~
But you've been born you can't help that~ so, well, fine keep getting older and eventually DIE~~~
N-No way, Hoshi! You wrote a song for him..?
Tch, if I sing the normal one
I gotta pay royalties ...
WH ...
Why, Hoshi ...?
Even though it's a mean song !!
He knows what'll happen! He's trying to kill me!
Wow, everyone made something.
I'm sure Rec will be thrilled.
Oh, Sister, you didn't do anything?
At least do something less...
Mine's something I bought for five bucks ages ago.
Ohh, well done, Sister!
Yeah, that much I can handle ...
ok, good.
Well, it has some wear-and-tear...

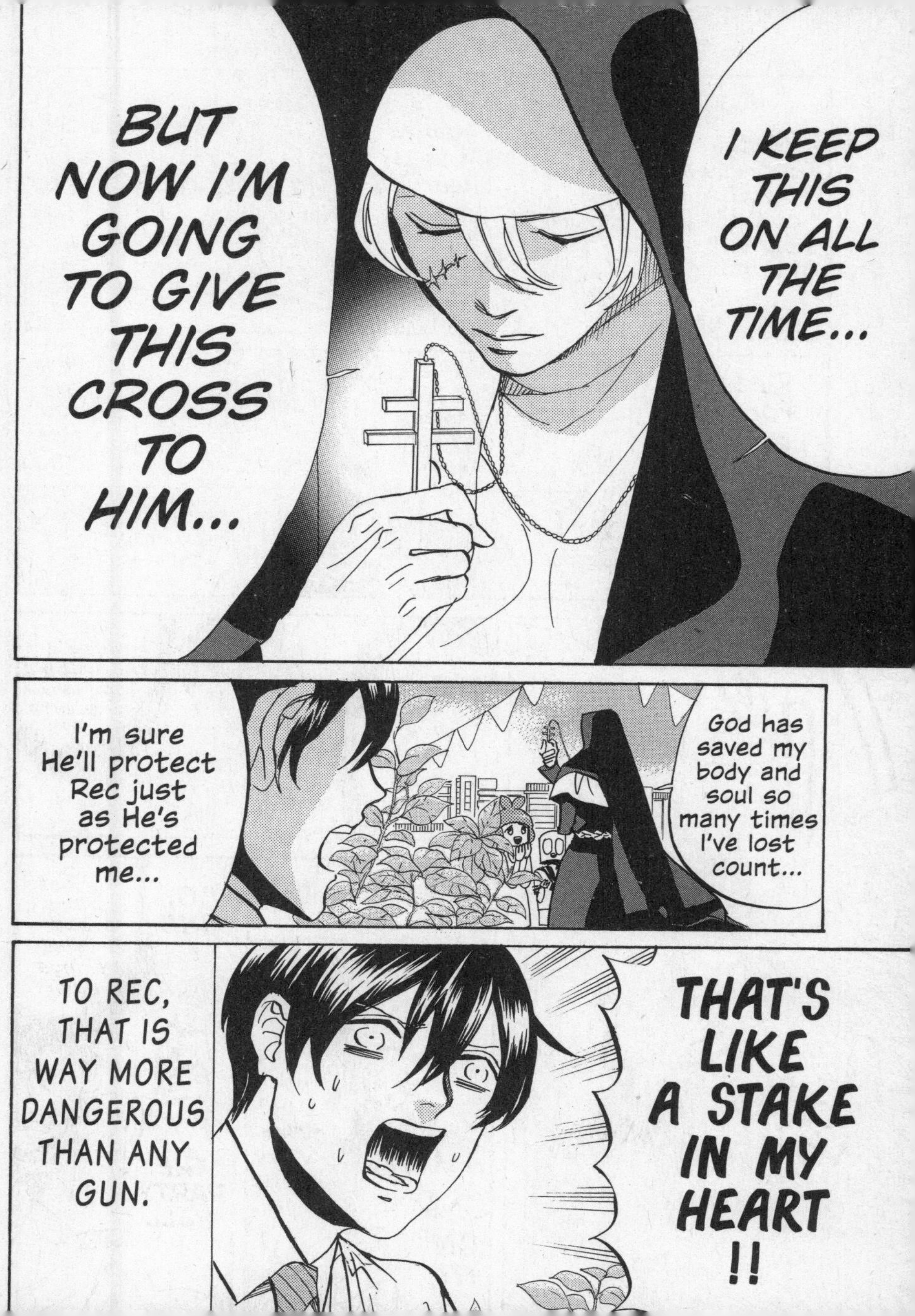
I KEEP THIS ON ALL THE TIME...
BUT NOW I'M GOING TO GIVE THIS CROSS TO HIM...
God has saved my body and soul so many times I've lost count...
I'm sure He'll protect Rec just as He's protected me...
THAT'S LIKE A STAKE IN MY HEART !!
TO REC, THAT IS WAY MORE DANGEROUS THAN ANY GUN.

Chapter 371: Thanks From Everyone

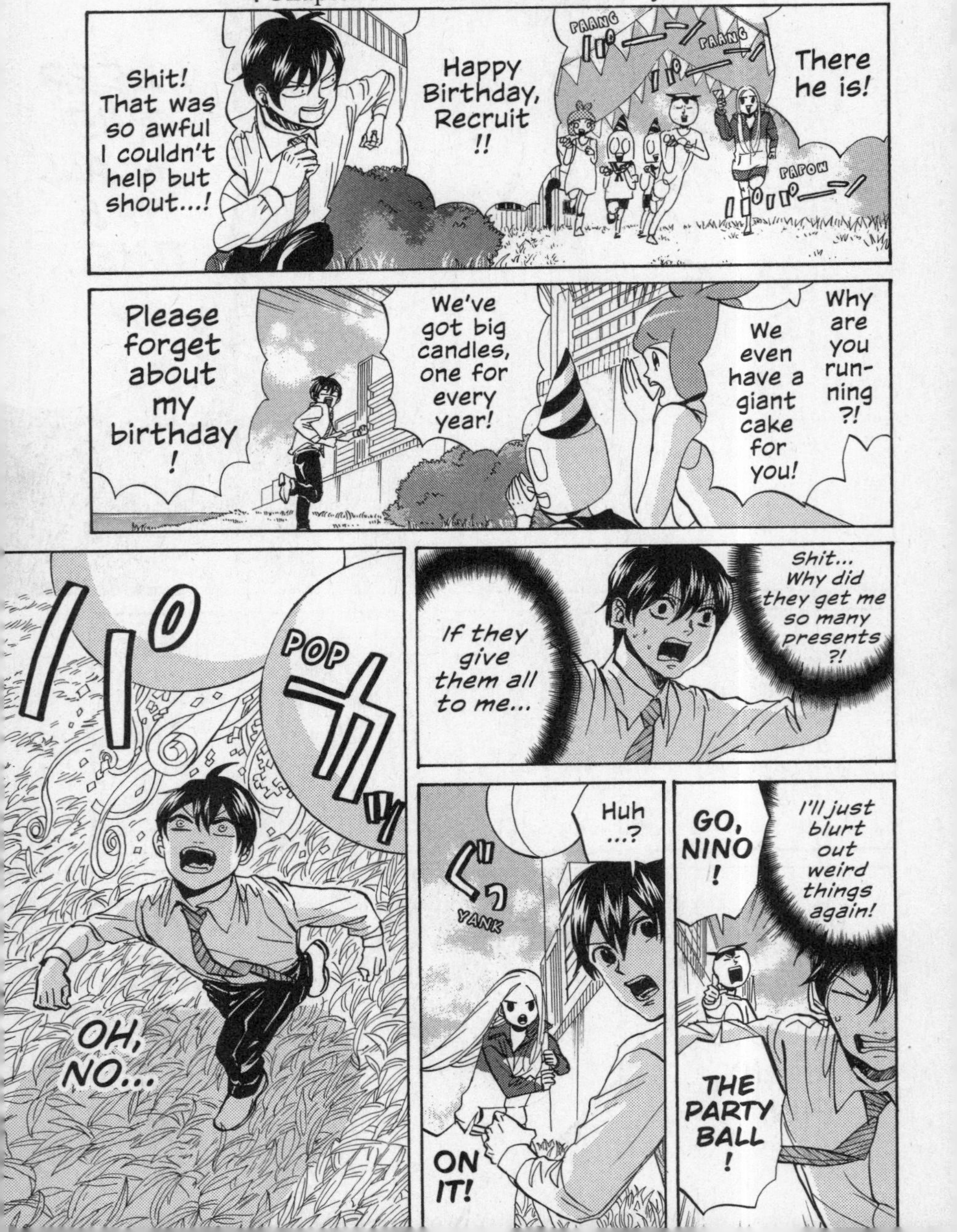
There he is!
PAANG
PAANG
PAPOW
Happy Birthday, Recruit!!
Shit! That was so awful I couldn't help but shout...!
Why are you running?!
We even have a giant cake for you!
We've got big candles, one for every year!
Please forget about my birthday!
Shit... Why did they get me so many presents?!
If they give them all to me...
I'll just blurt out weird things again!
GO, NINO!
THE PARTY BALL!
Huh...?
YANK
ON IT!
POP
OH, NO...

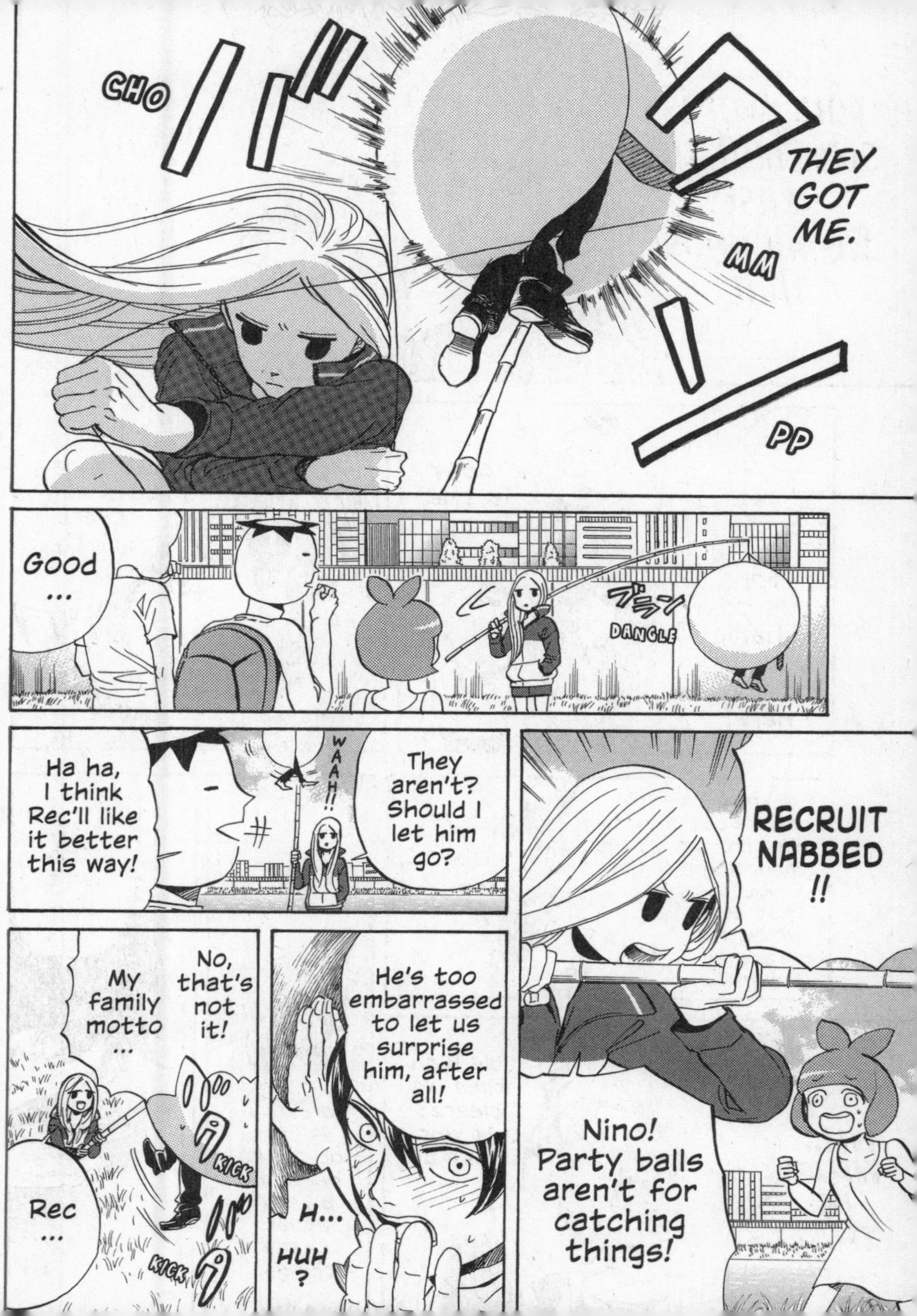
THEY GOT ME.
CHO
MM
PP
Good ...
DANGLE
RECRUIT NABBED !!
Nino! Party balls aren't for catching things!
They aren't? Should I let him go?
WAAH!!
Ha ha, I think Rec'll like it better this way!
He's too embarrassed to let us surprise him, after all!
H...
HUH ?
No, that's not it!
My family motto ...
KICK
KICK
Rec ...

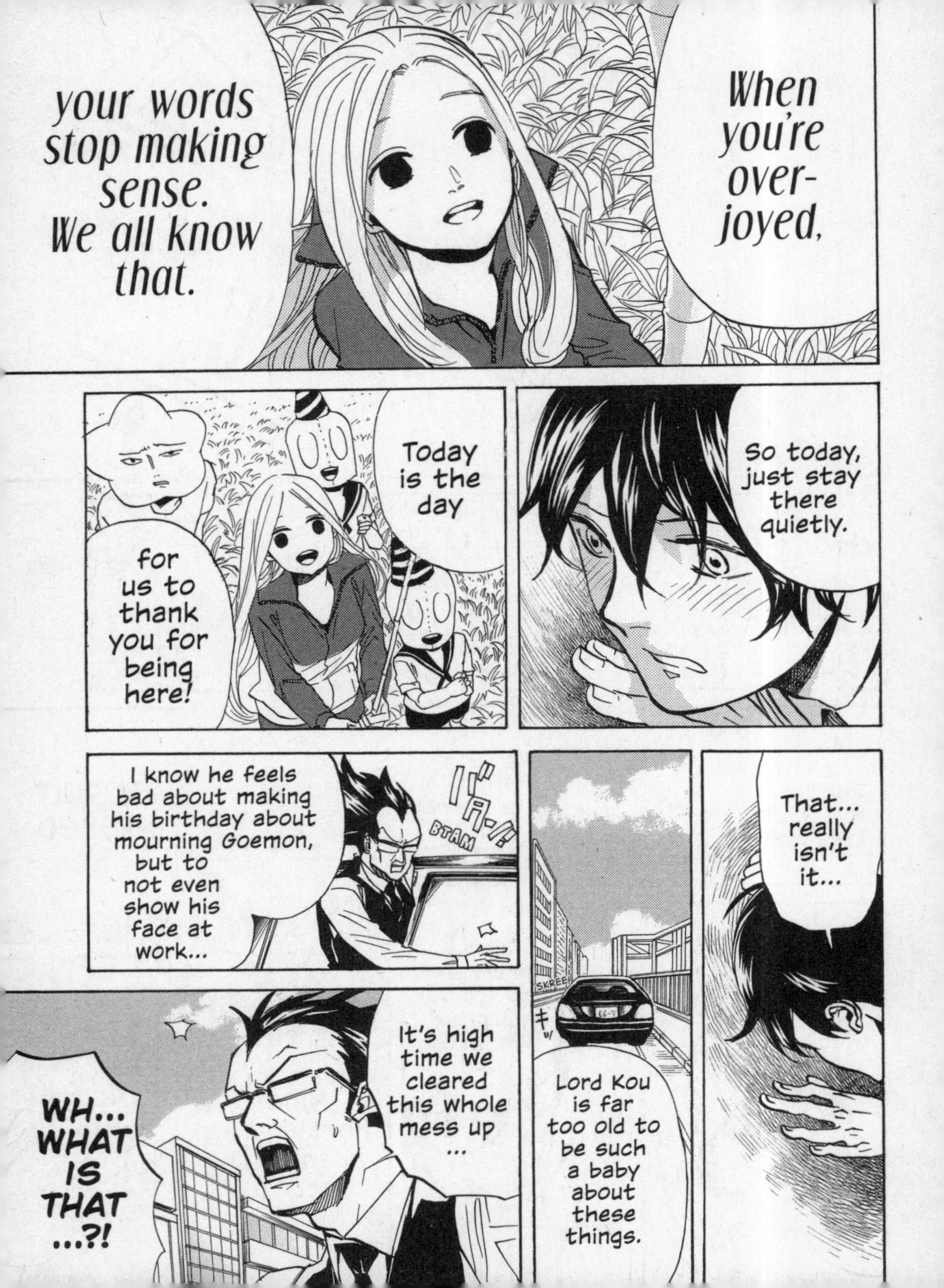
When you're over-joyed,
your words stop making sense. We all know that.
So today, just stay there quietly.
Today is the day
for us to thank you for being here!
That... really isn't it...
SKREE
Lord Kou is far too old to be such a baby about these things.
I know he feels bad about making his birthday about mourning Goemon, but to not even show his face at work...
BTAM
It's high time we cleared this whole mess up ...
WH... WHAT IS THAT ...?!

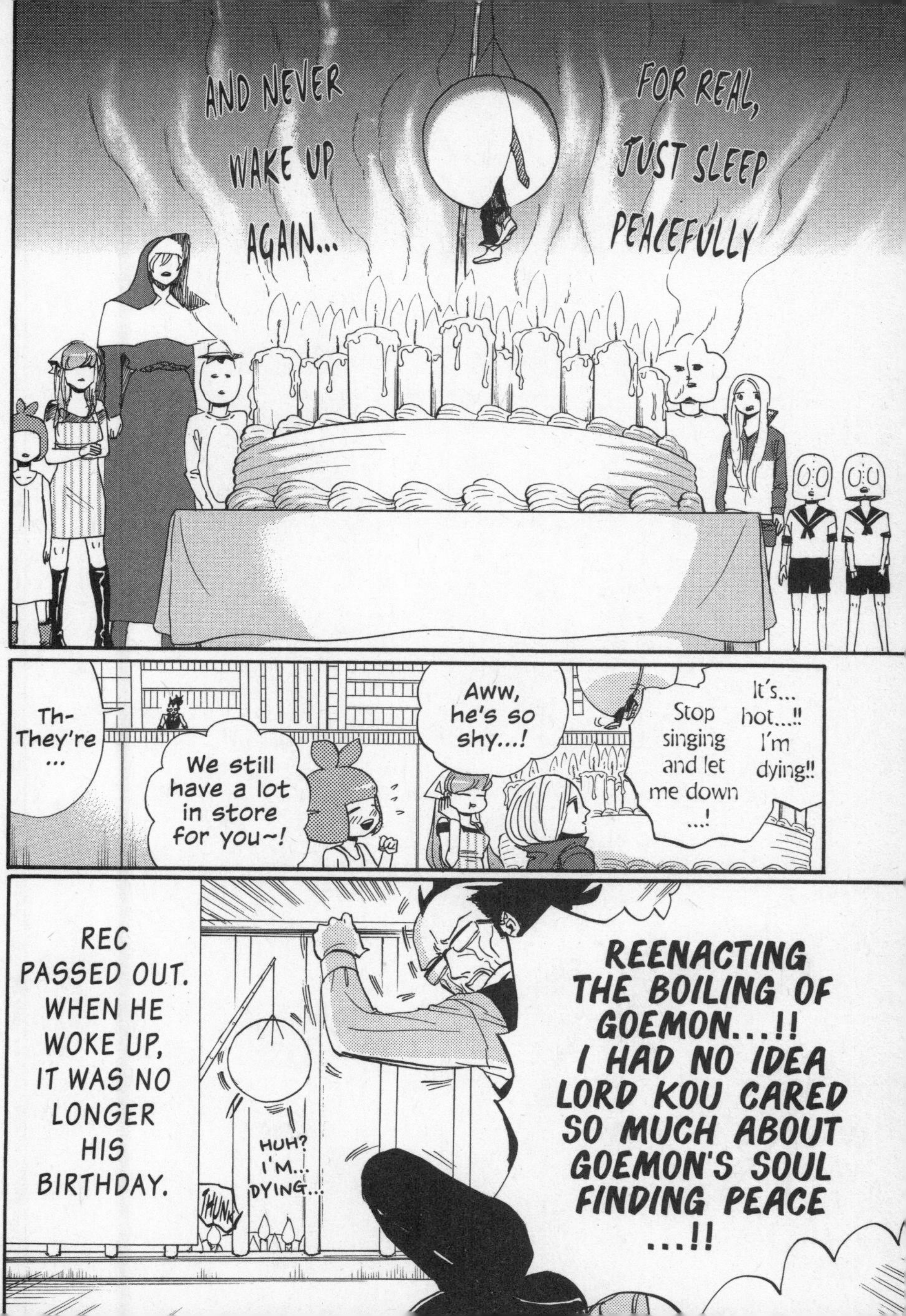
FOR REAL, JUST SLEEP PEACEFULLY
AND NEVER WAKE UP AGAIN...
It's... hot...!! I'm dying!!
Stop singing and let me down ...!
Aww, he's so shy...!
We still have a lot in store for you~!
Th- They're ...
REENACTING THE BOILING OF GOEMON...!! I HAD NO IDEA LORD KOU CARED SO MUCH ABOUT GOEMON'S SOUL FINDING PEACE ...!!
HUH? I'M... DYING...
THUNK
REC PASSED OUT. WHEN HE WOKE UP, IT WAS NO LONGER HIS BIRTHDAY.

ARAKAWA
UNDER
THE BRIDGE

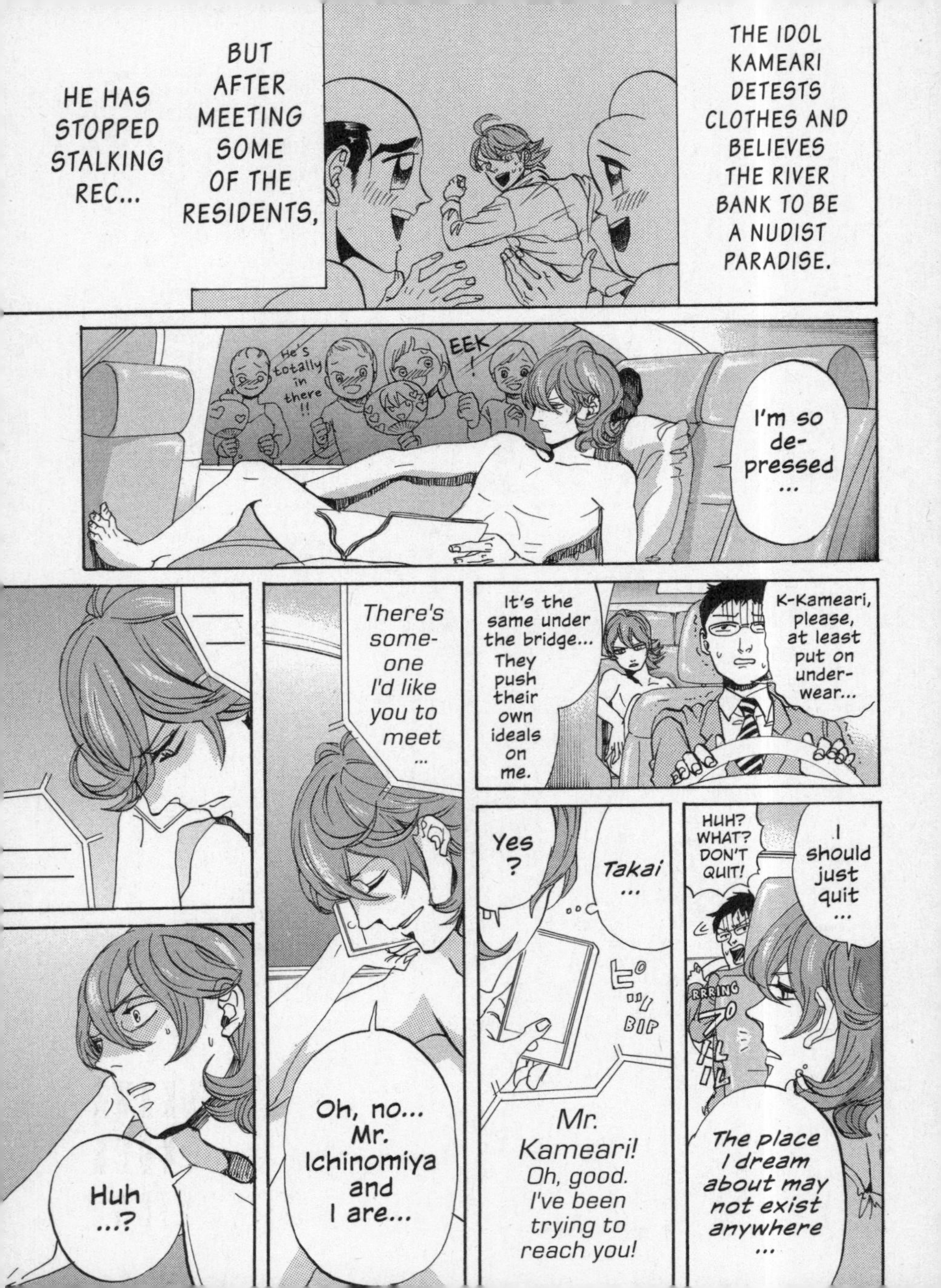
THE IDOL KAMEARI DETESTS CLOTHES AND BELIEVES THE RIVER BANK TO BE A NUDIST PARADISE.
BUT AFTER MEETING SOME OF THE RESIDENTS,
HE HAS STOPPED STALKING REC...
I'm so de-pressed ...
EEK !
He's totally in there !!
K-Kameari, please, at least put on under-wear...
It's the same under the bridge... They push their own ideals on me.
I should just quit ...
HUH? WHAT? DON'T QUIT!
RRRING
The place I dream about may not exist anywhere ...
Takai ...
Yes ?
BIP
Mr. Kameari! Oh, good. I've been trying to reach you!
There's some-one I'd like you to meet ...
Oh, no... Mr. Ichinomiya and I are...
Huh ...?

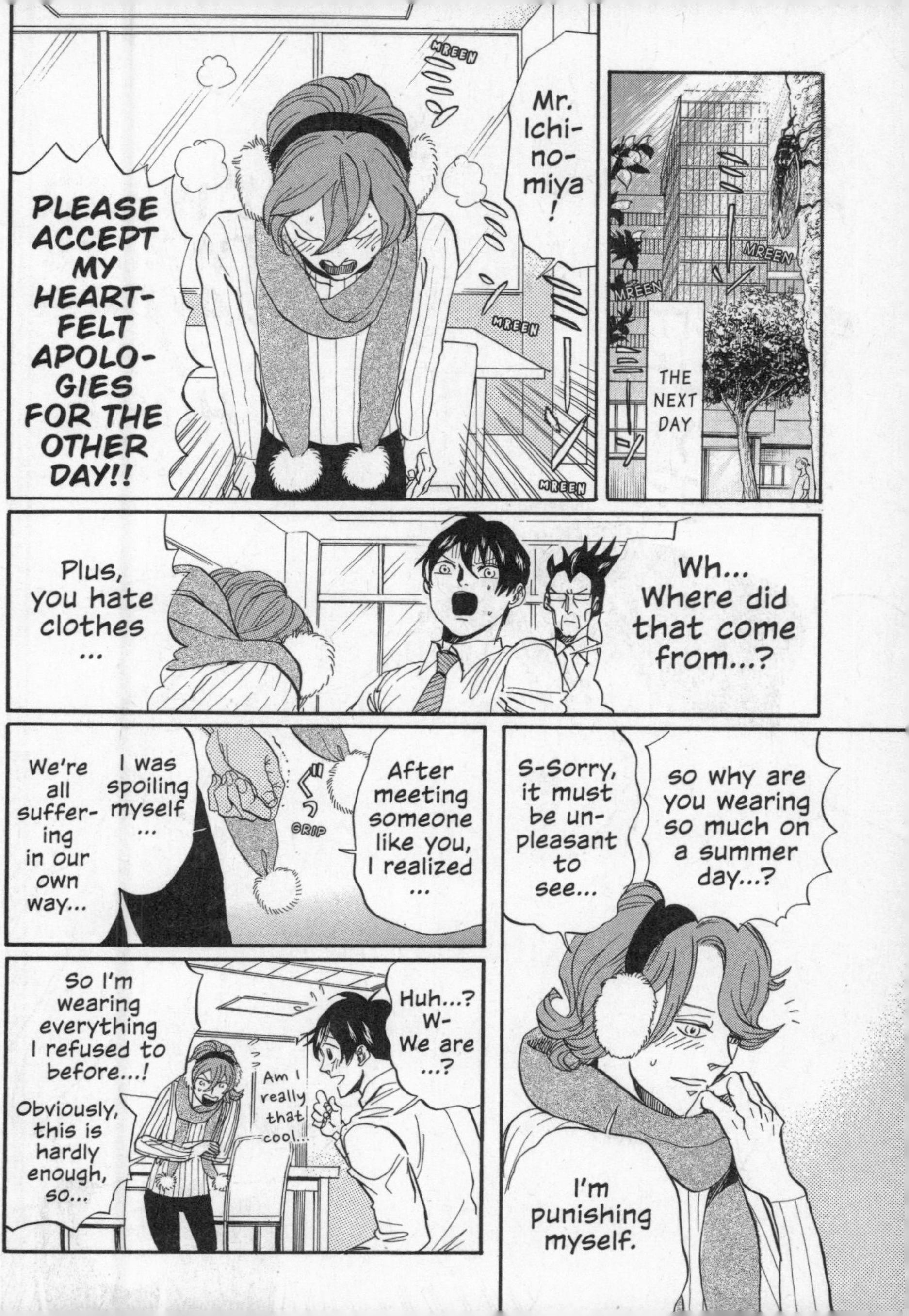

MREEN
MREEN
THE NEXT DAY
MREEN
Mr. Ichi-no-miya!
MREEN
MREEN
PLEASE ACCEPT MY HEART-FELT APOLO-GIES FOR THE OTHER DAY!!
Wh... Where did that come from...?
Plus, you hate clothes...
so why are you wearing so much on a summer day...?
S-Sorry, it must be un-pleasant to see...
I'm punishing myself.
After meeting someone like you, I realized...
GRIP
I was spoiling myself...
We're all suffer-ing in our own way...
Huh...? W- We are...?
So I'm wearing everything I refused to before...!
Am I really that cool...
Obviously, this is hardly enough, so...

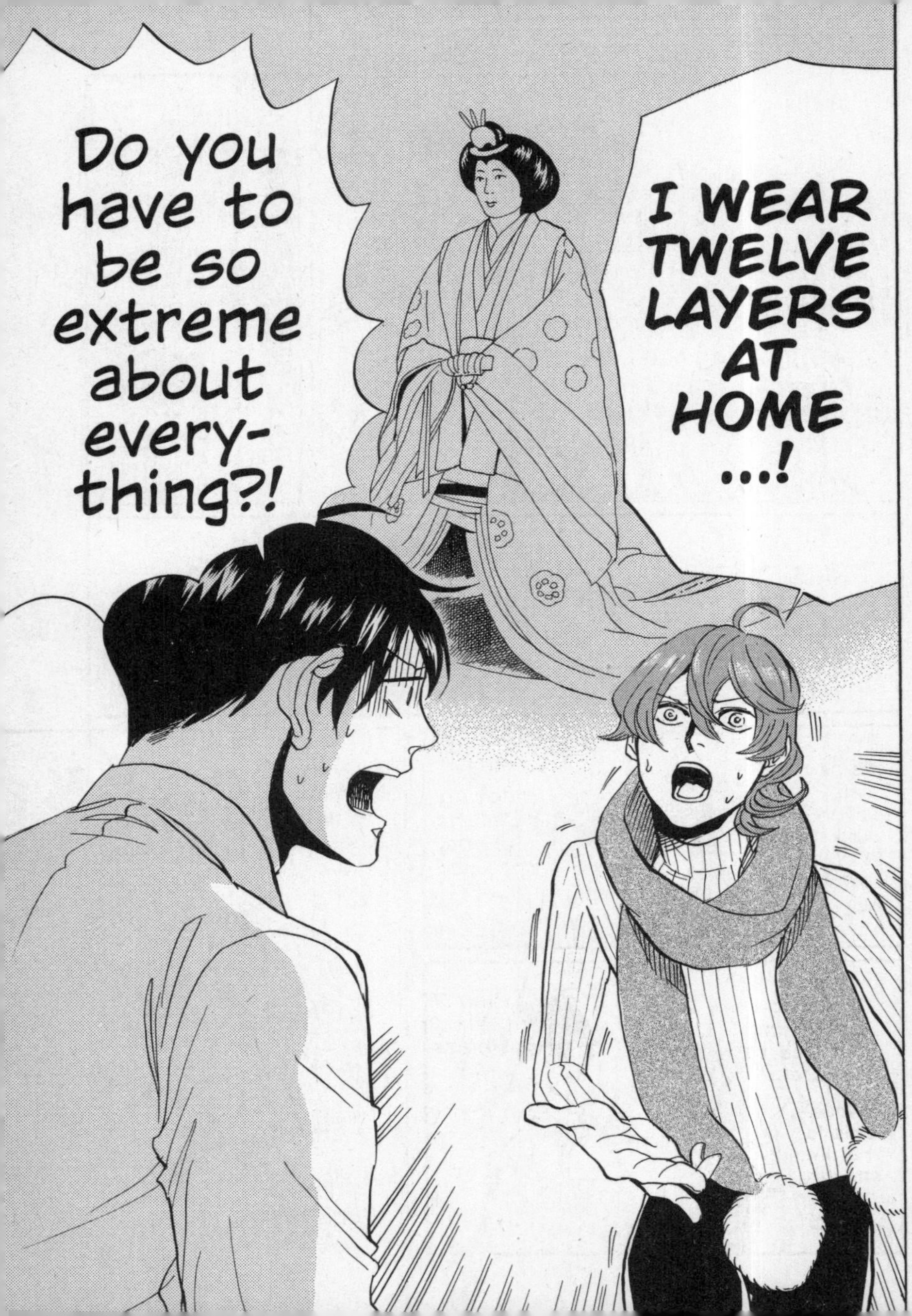
I WEAR TWELVE LAYERS AT HOME ...!
Do you have to be so extreme about every-thing?!

Chapter 372: River Bank Special Concert

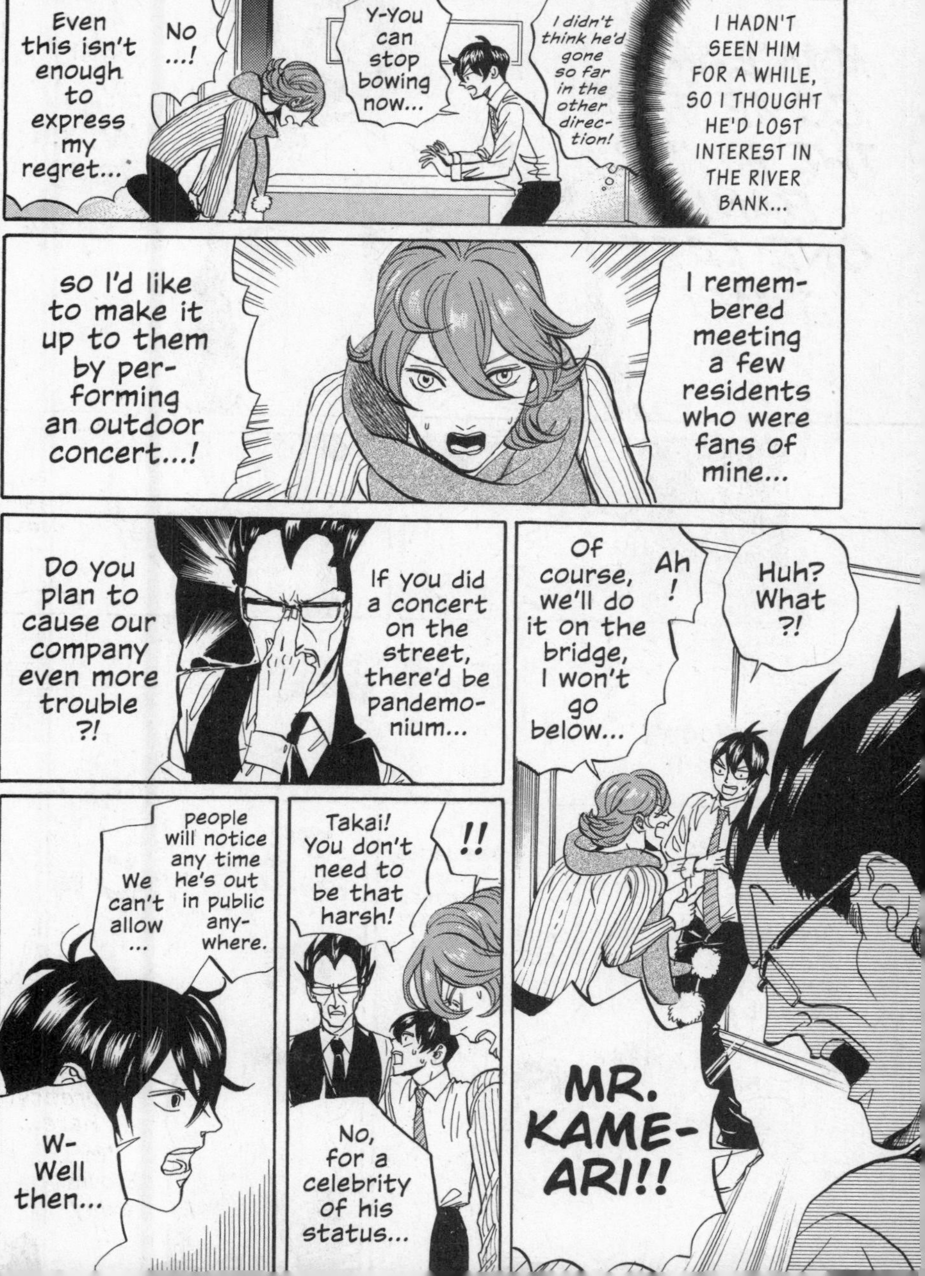
I HADN'T SEEN HIM FOR A WHILE, SO I THOUGHT HE'D LOST INTEREST IN THE RIVER BANK...
I didn't think he'd gone so far in the other direction!
Y-You can stop bowing now...
No ...!
Even this isn't enough to express my regret...
I remembered meeting a few residents who were fans of mine...
so I'd like to make it up to them by performing an outdoor concert...!
Huh? What ?!
Ah !
Of course, we'll do it on the bridge, I won't go below...
MR. KAMEARI!!
If you did a concert on the street, there'd be pandemonium...
Do you plan to cause our company even more trouble ?!
!!
Takai! You don't need to be that harsh!
No, for a celebrity of his status...
people will notice any time he's out in public anywhere.
We can't allow ...
W-Well then...

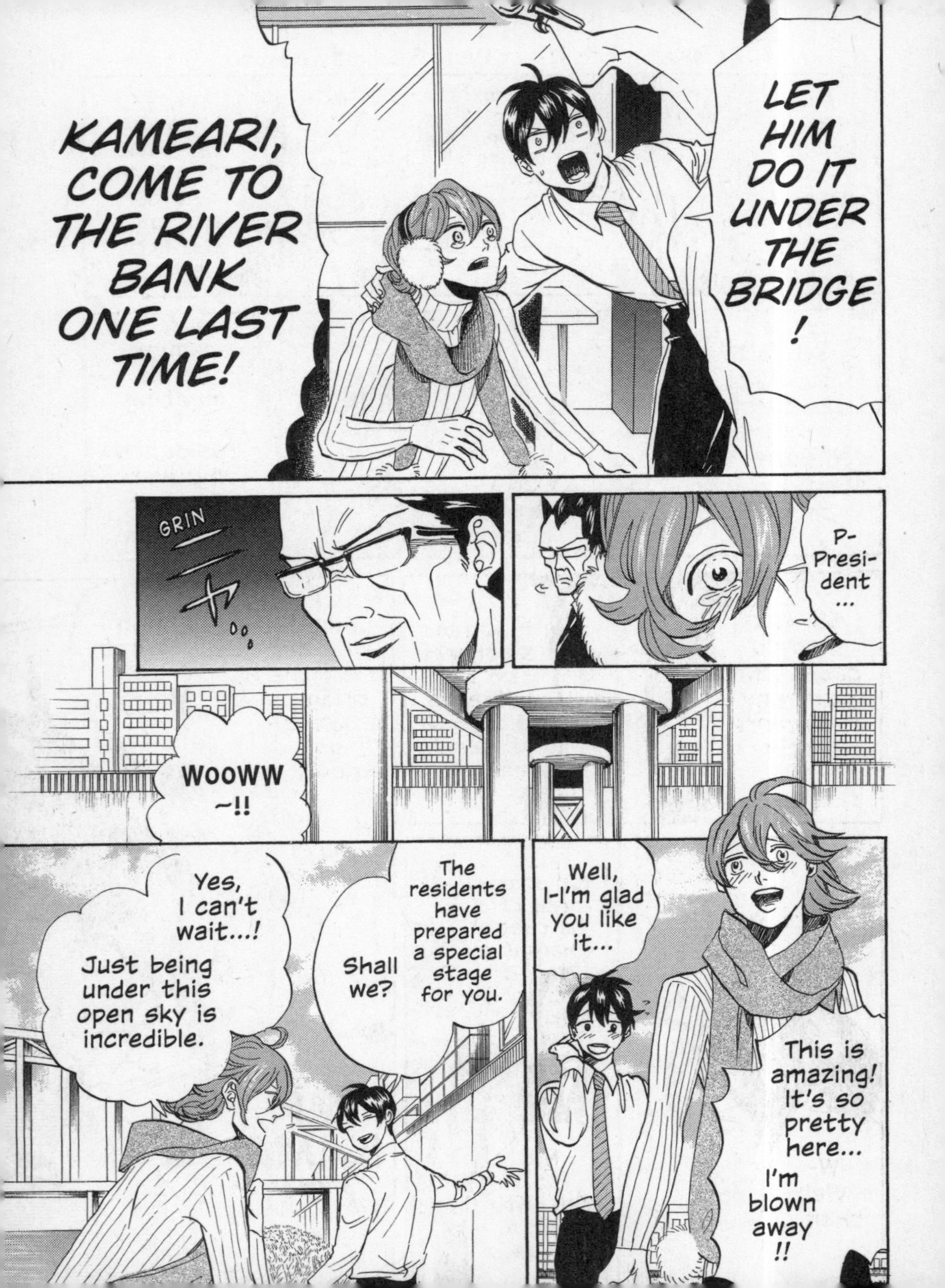
LET HIM DO IT UNDER THE BRIDGE!
KAMEARI, COME TO THE RIVER BANK ONE LAST TIME!
P-President...
GRIN
WOOWW~!!
This is amazing! It's so pretty here...
I'm blown away!!
Well, I-I'm glad you like it...
The residents have prepared a special stage for you.
Shall we?
Yes, I can't wait...!
Just being under this open sky is incredible.

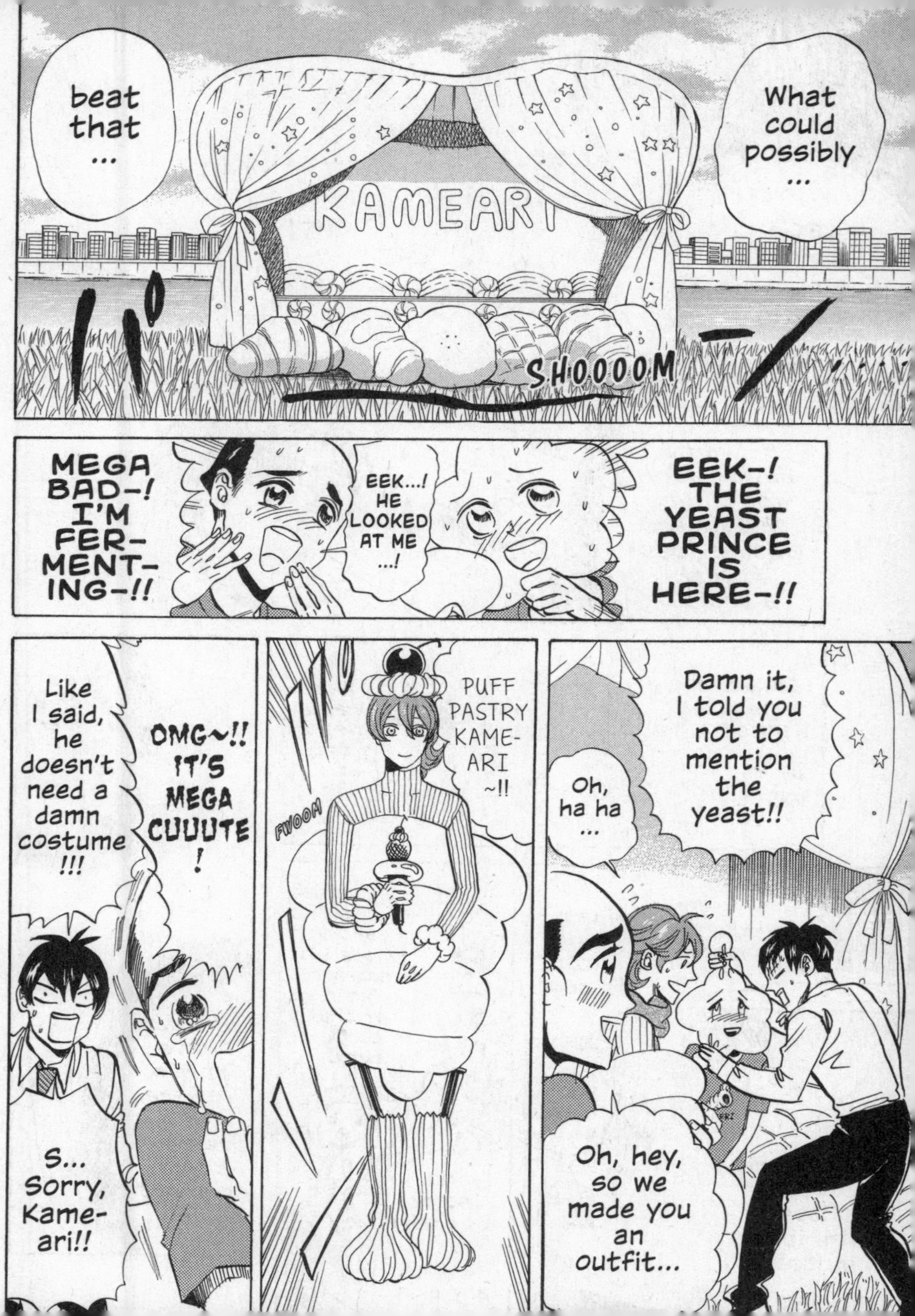
What could possibly ...
beat that ...
KAMEARI
SHOOOOM
EEK-! THE YEAST PRINCE IS HERE-!!
EEK...! HE LOOKED AT ME ...!
MEGA BAD-! I'M FER-MENT-ING-!!
Damn it, I told you not to mention the yeast!!
Oh, ha ha ...
Oh, hey, so we made you an outfit...
PUFF PASTRY KAME-ARI ~!!
FWOOM
OMG~!! IT'S MEGA CUUUTE !
Like I said, he doesn't need a damn costume !!!
S... Sorry, Kame-ari!!

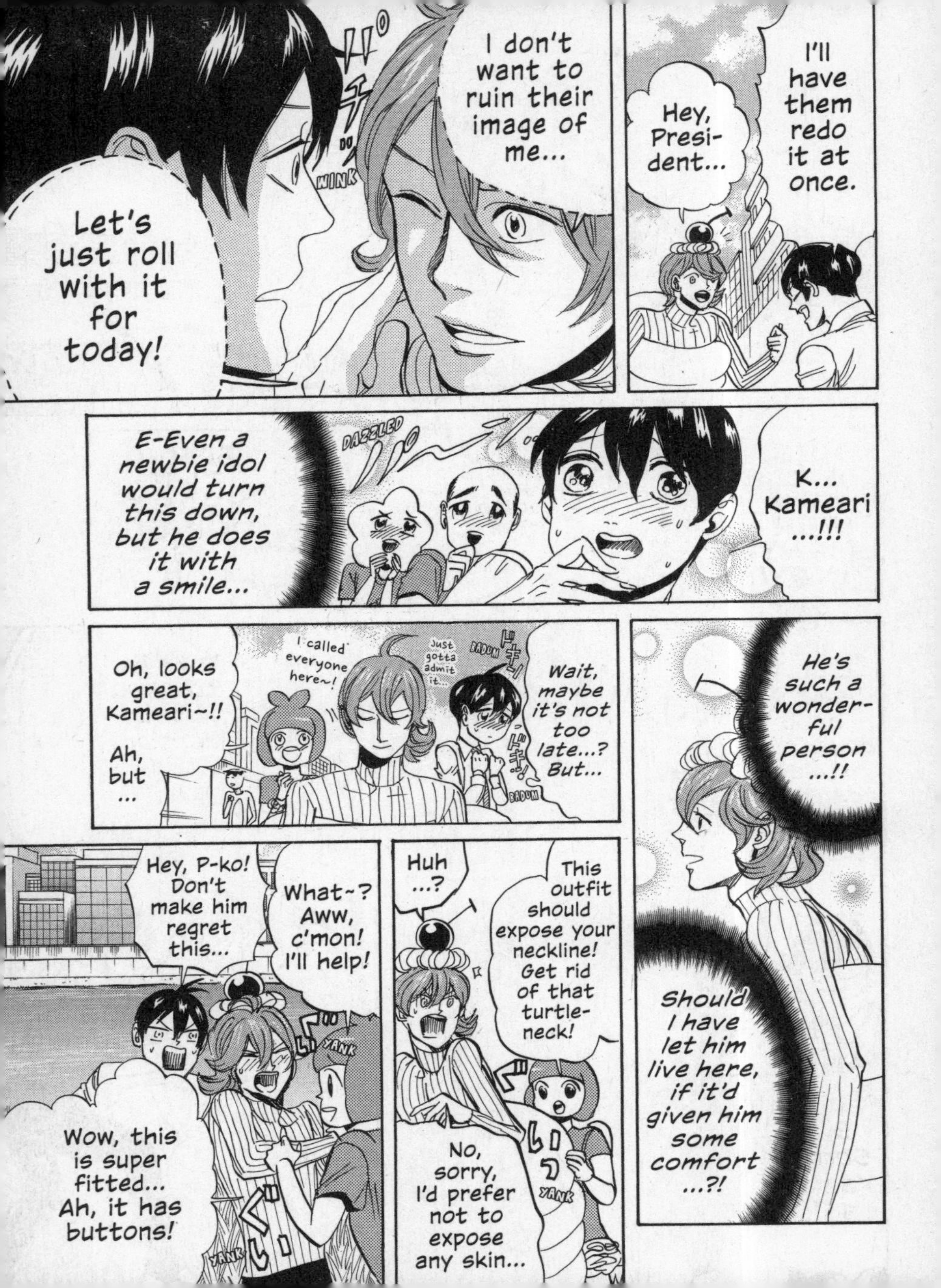
I'll have them redo it at once.
Hey, President...
I don't want to ruin their image of me...
DO
WINK
Let's just roll with it for today!
K... Kameari ...!!!
DAZZLED
E-Even a newbie idol would turn this down, but he does it with a smile...
He's such a wonderful person ...!!
Should I have let him live here, if it'd given him some comfort ...?!
Wait, maybe it's not too late...? But...
BADUM
Just gotta admit it...
BADUM
I called everyone here~!
Oh, looks great, Kameari~!!
Ah, but ...
This outfit should expose your neckline! Get rid of that turtle-neck!
Huh ...?
YANK
No, sorry, I'd prefer not to expose any skin...
What~? Aww, c'mon! I'll help!
Hey, P-ko! Don't make him regret this...
YANK
Wow, this is super fitted... Ah, it has buttons!
YANK

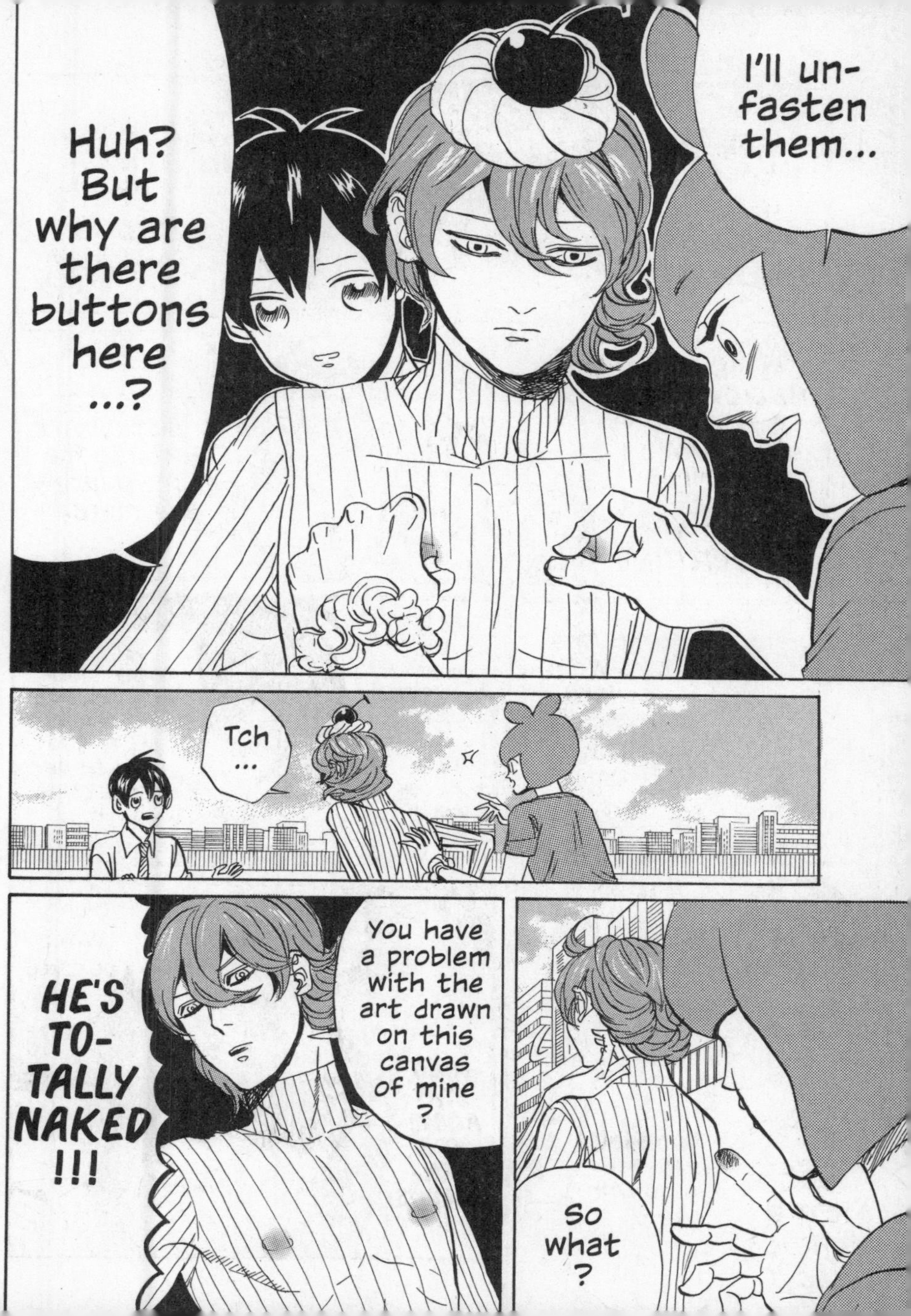
I'll un-fasten them...
Huh? But why are there buttons here ...?
Tch ...
So what?
You have a problem with the art drawn on this canvas of mine?
HE'S TO-TALLY NAKED!!!

☞ Chapter 373: River Bank Democracy

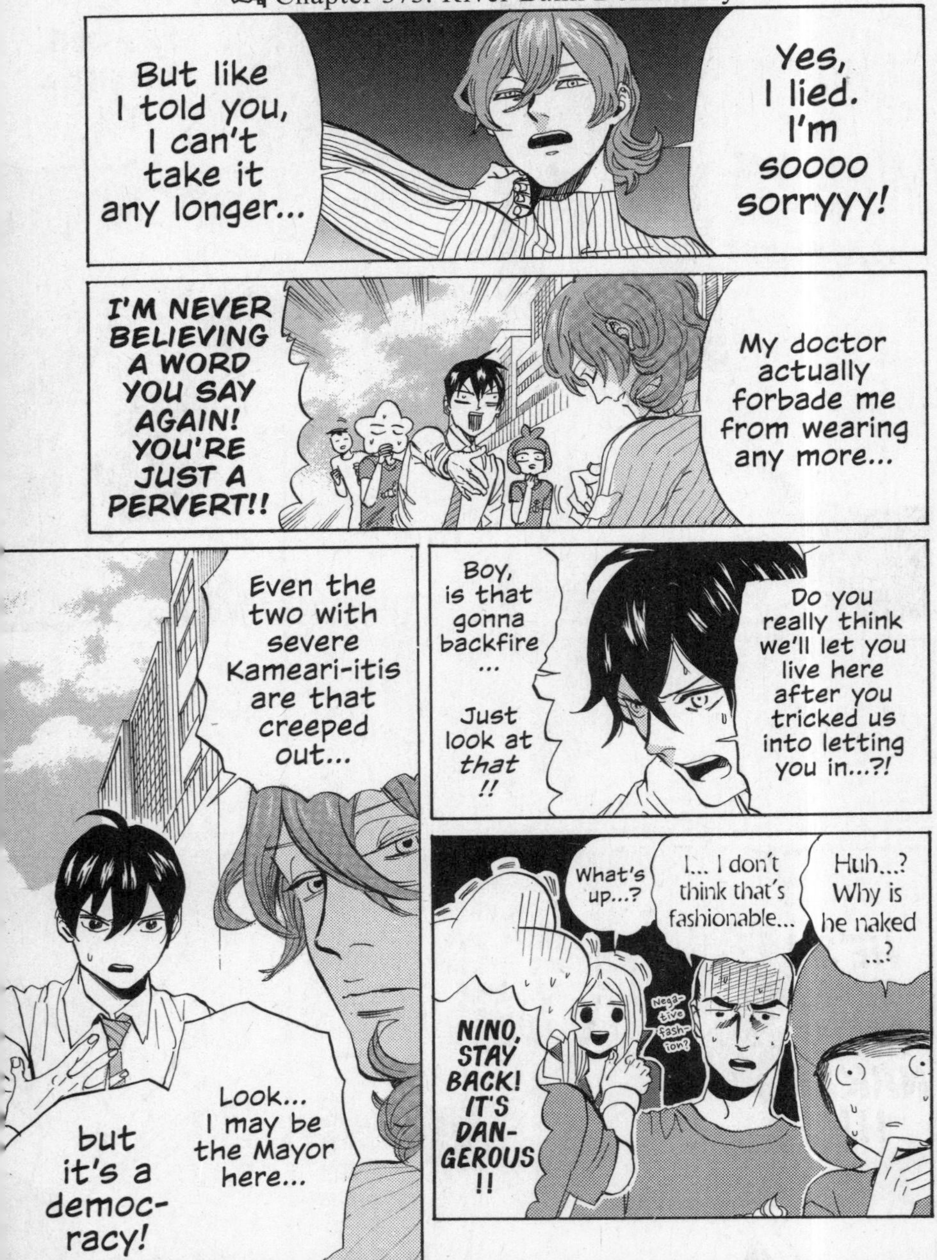
Yes, I lied. I'm soooo sorryyy!
But like I told you, I can't take it any longer...
My doctor actually forbade me from wearing any more...
I'M NEVER BELIEVING A WORD YOU SAY AGAIN! YOU'RE JUST A PERVERT!!
Do you really think we'll let you live here after you tricked us into letting you in...?!
Boy, is that gonna backfire...
Just look at *that*!!
Huh...? Why is he naked...?
I... I don't think that's fashionable...
What's up...?
Nega-tive fash-ion?
NINO, STAY BACK! IT'S DAN-GEROUS!!
Even the two with severe Kameari-itis are that creeped out...
Look... I may be the Mayor here...
but it's a democ-racy!

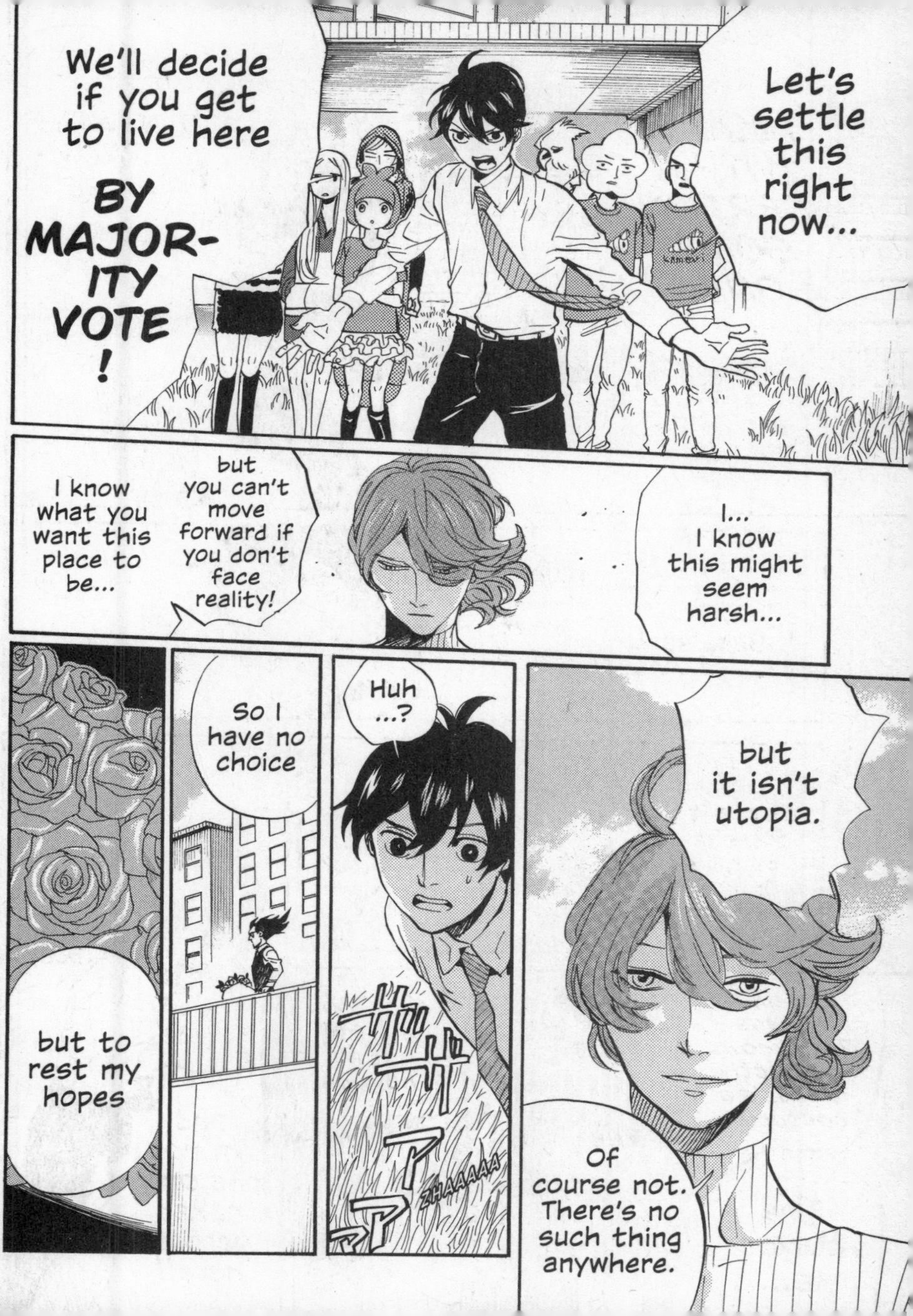
Let's settle this right now...
We'll decide if you get to live here
BY MAJORITY VOTE!
I... I know this might seem harsh...
I know what you want this place to be...
but you can't move forward if you don't face reality!
but it isn't utopia.
Of course not. There's no such thing anywhere.
Huh ...?
ZHAAAAA
So I have no choice
but to rest my hopes

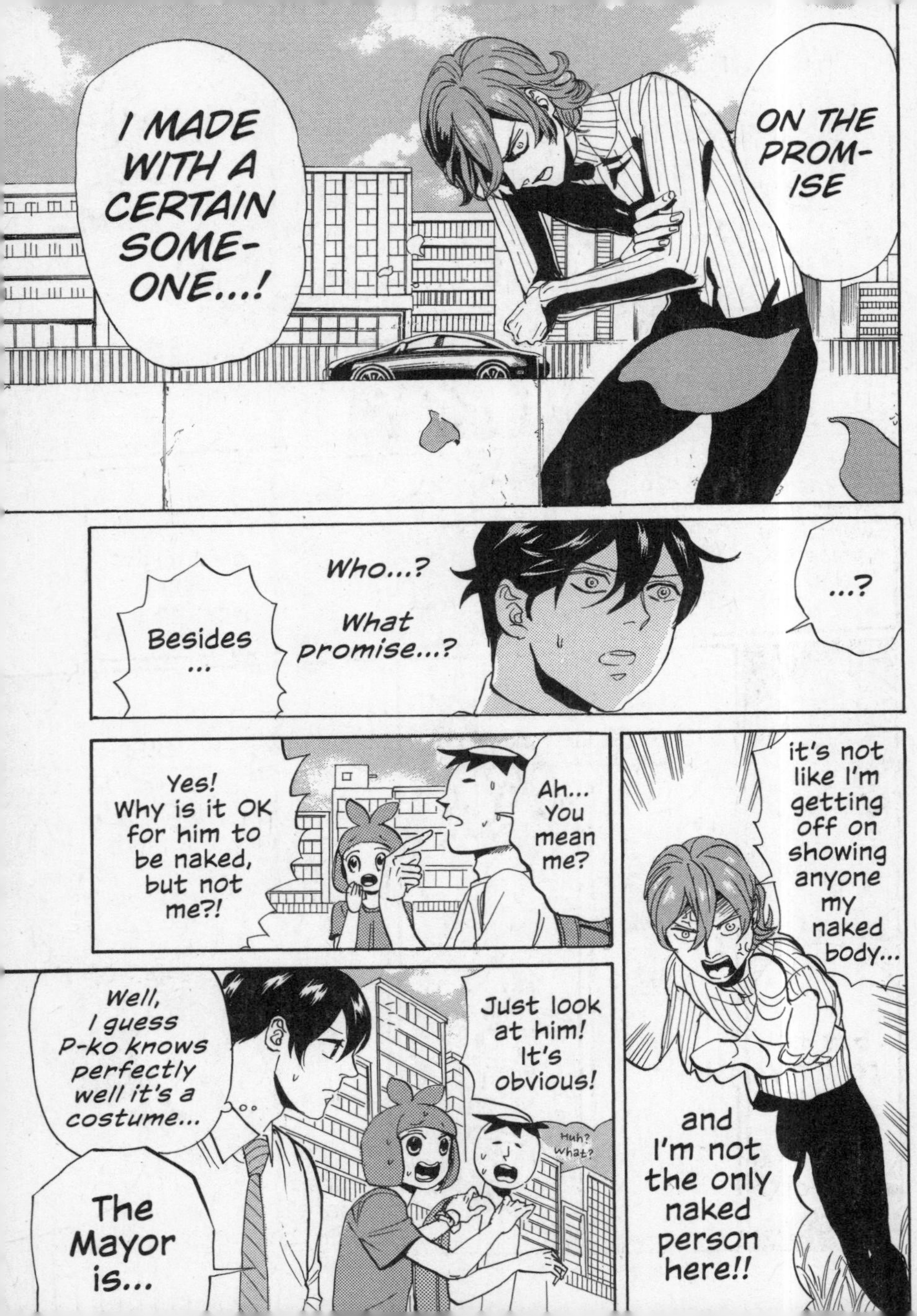

ON THE PROM-ISE
I MADE WITH A CERTAIN SOME-ONE...!
...?
Who...? What promise...?
Besides...
it's not like I'm getting off on showing anyone my naked body...
and I'm not the only naked person here!!
Ah... You mean me?
Yes! Why is it OK for him to be naked, but not me?!
Just look at him! It's obvious!
Huh? What?
Well, I guess P-ko knows perfectly well it's a costume...
The Mayor is...

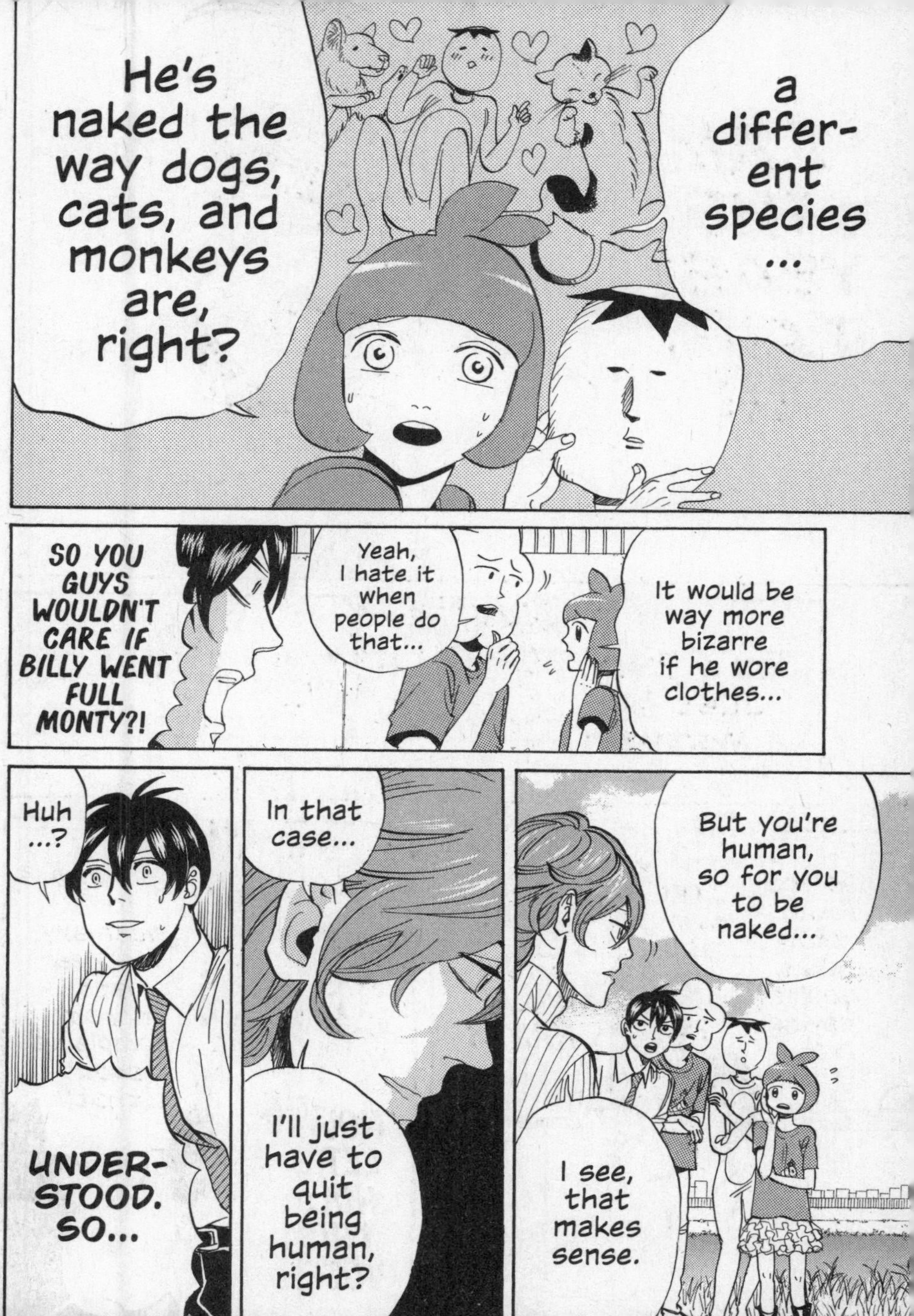
a different-species...
He's naked the way dogs, cats, and monkeys are, right?
It would be way more bizarre if he wore clothes...
Yeah, I hate it when people do that...
SO YOU GUYS WOULDN'T CARE IF BILLY WENT FULL MONTY?!
But you're human, so for you to be naked...
I see, that makes sense.
In that case...
I'll just have to quit being human, right?
Huh ...?
UNDER-STOOD. SO...

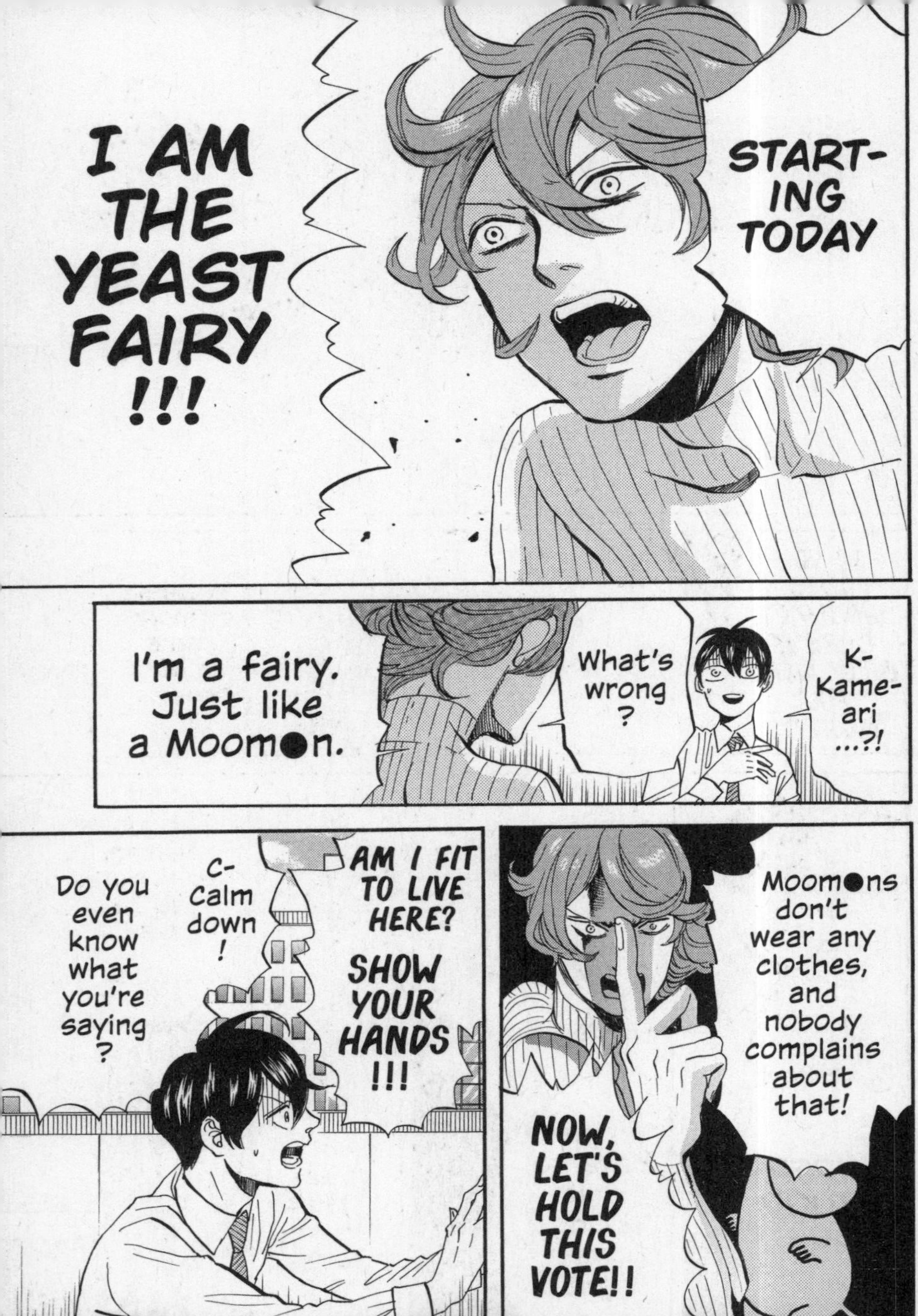
STARTING TODAY
I AM THE YEAST FAIRY!!!
K-Kameari...?!
What's wrong?
I'm a fairy. Just like a Moom●n.
Moom●ns don't wear any clothes, and nobody complains about that!
NOW, LET'S HOLD THIS VOTE!!
AM I FIT TO LIVE HERE?
SHOW YOUR HANDS!!!
C-Calm down!
Do you even know what you're saying?

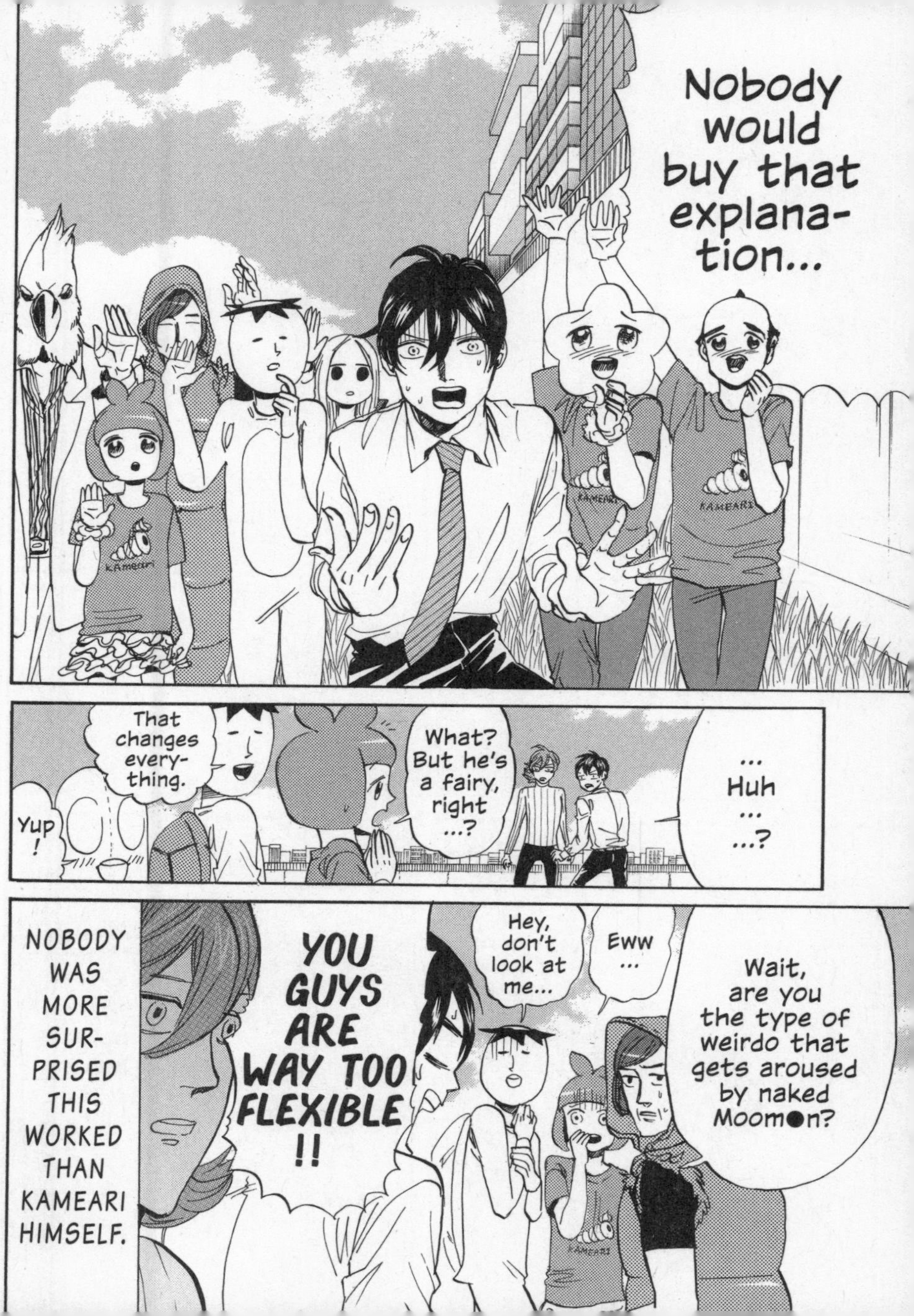
Nobody would buy that explanation...
... Huh ... ...?
What? But he's a fairy, right ...?
That changes everything.
Yup!
Wait, are you the type of weirdo that gets aroused by naked Moom●n?
Eww ...
Hey, don't look at me...
YOU GUYS ARE WAY TOO FLEXIBLE!!
NOBODY WAS MORE SURPRISED THIS WORKED THAN KAMEARI HIMSELF.
KAMEARI

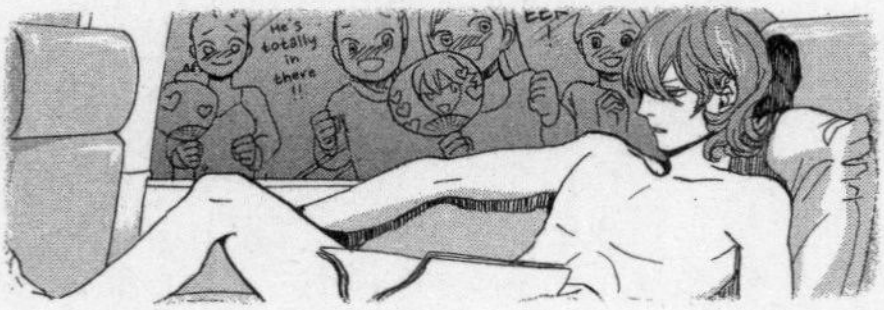
He's totally in there!!

ARAKAWA
UNDER
THE BRIDGE

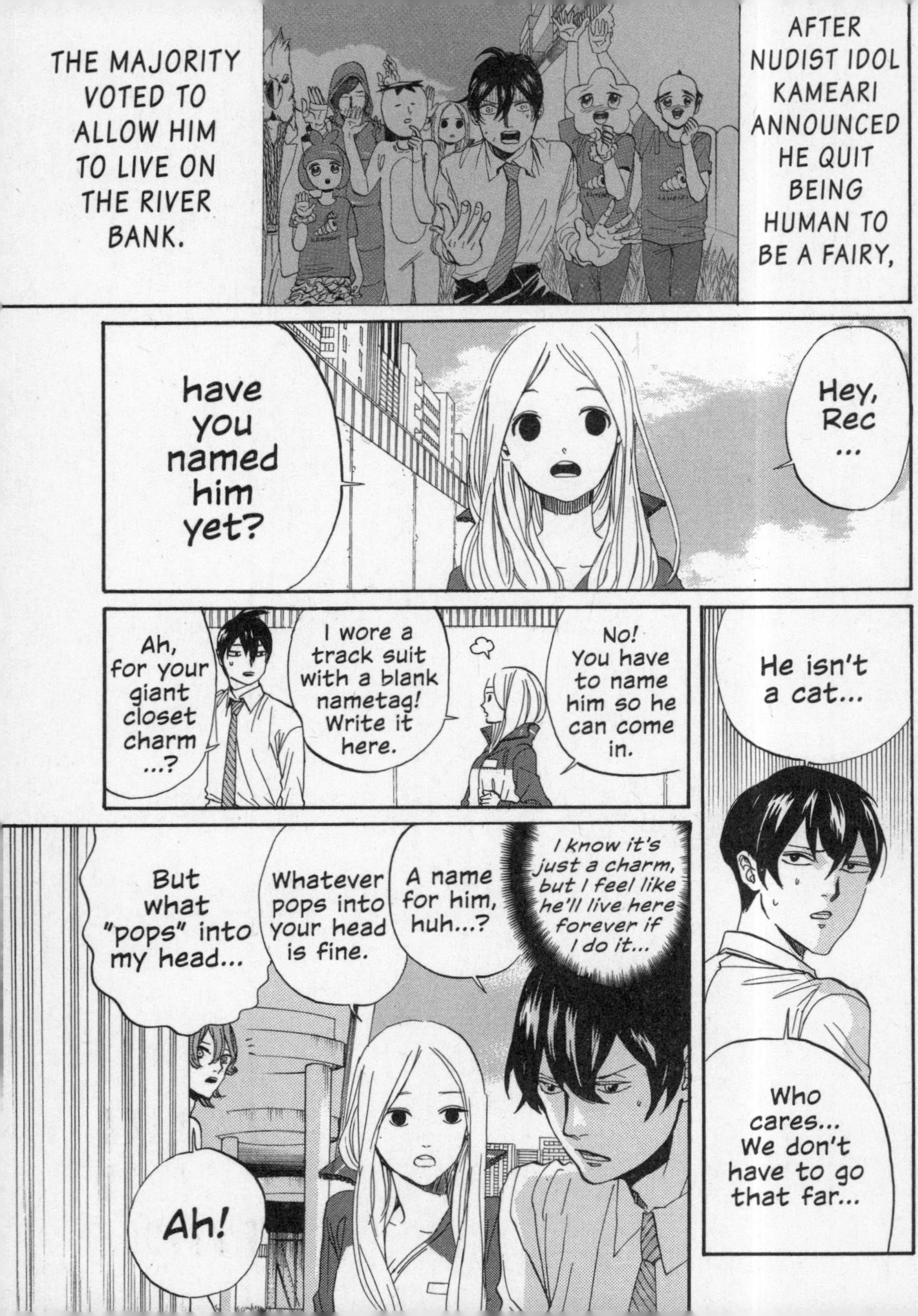
AFTER NUDIST IDOL KAMEARI ANNOUNCED HE QUIT BEING HUMAN TO BE A FAIRY,
THE MAJORITY VOTED TO ALLOW HIM TO LIVE ON THE RIVER BANK.
Hey, Rec...
have you named him yet?
He isn't a cat...
Who cares... We don't have to go that far...
No! You have to name him so he can come in.
I wore a track suit with a blank nametag! Write it here.
Ah, for your giant closet charm...?
I know it's just a charm, but I feel like he'll live here forever if I do it...
A name for him, huh...?
Whatever pops into your head is fine.
But what "pops" into my head...
Ah!

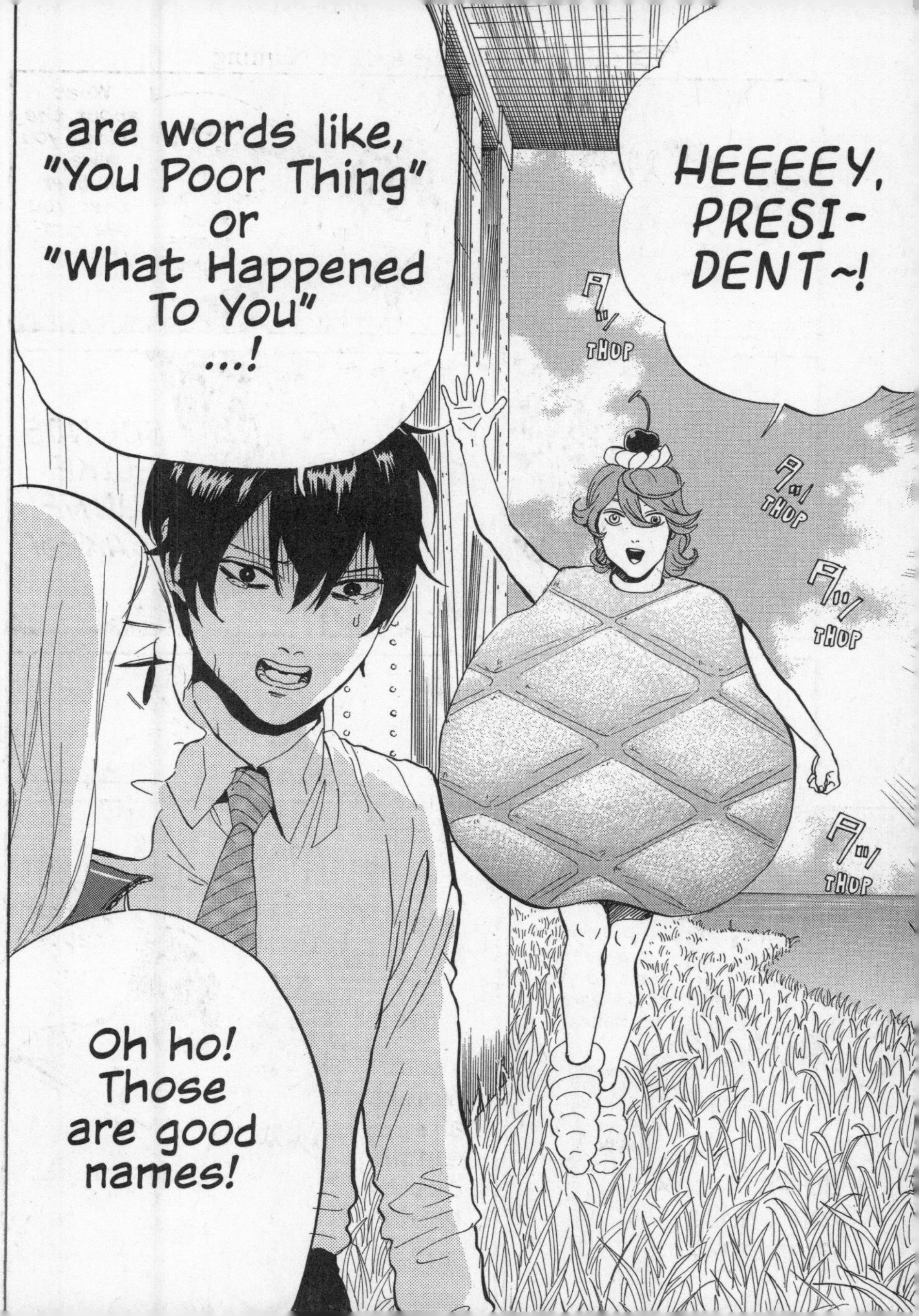
HEEEEY, PRESI- DENT~!
THOP
THOP
THOP
THOP
are words like, "You Poor Thing" or "What Happened To You" ...!
Oh ho! Those are good names!

Chapter 374: The Risk of Naming

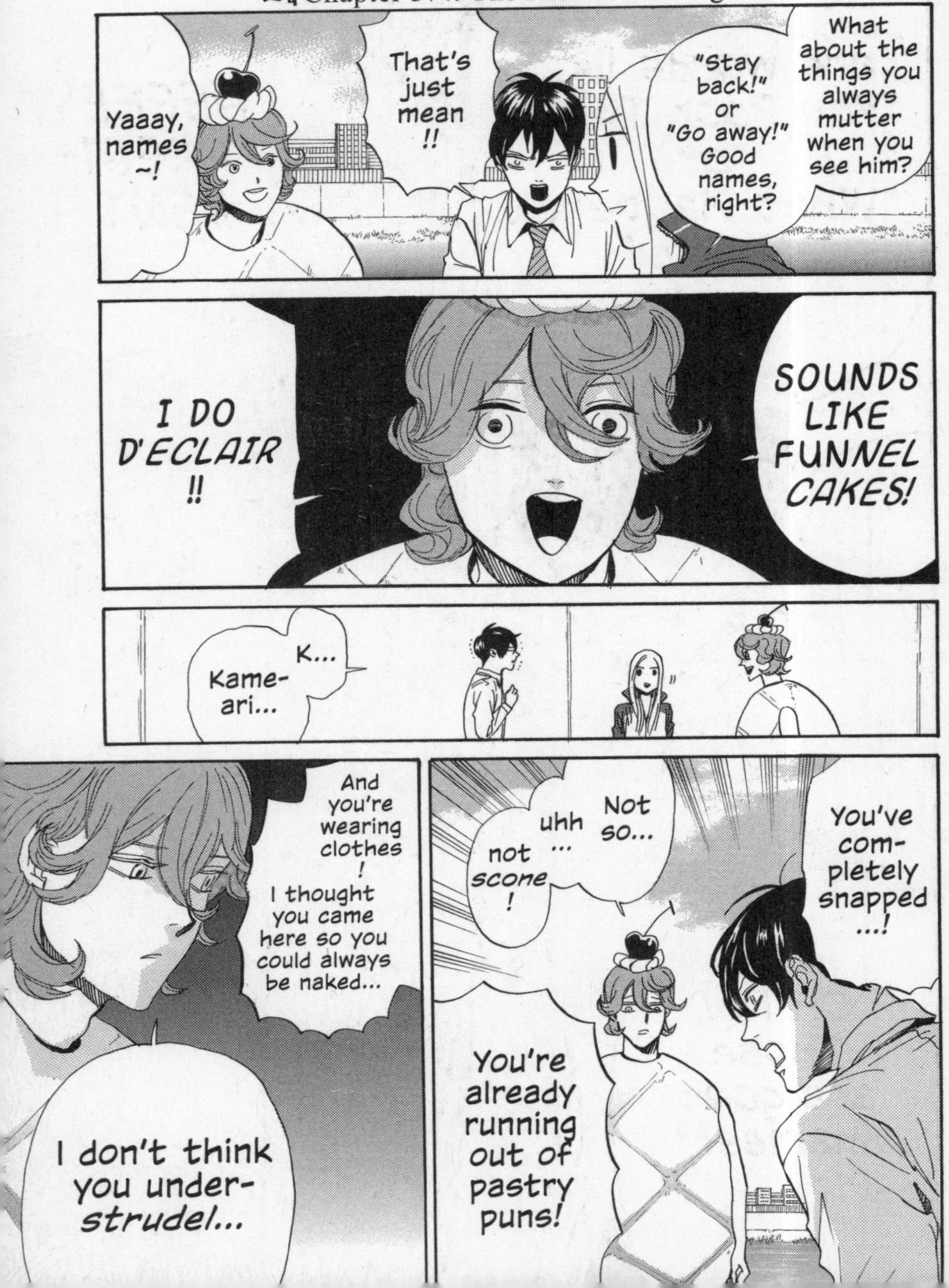
What about the things you always mutter when you see him?
"Stay back!" or "Go away!" Good names, right?
That's just mean!!
Yaaay, names ~!
SOUNDS LIKE FUNNEL CAKES!
I DO D'ECLAIR!!
K... Kame-ari...
You've com-pletely snapped...!
Not so... uhh... not scone!
You're already running out of pastry puns!
And you're wearing clothes! I thought you came here so you could always be naked...
I don't think you under-strudel...

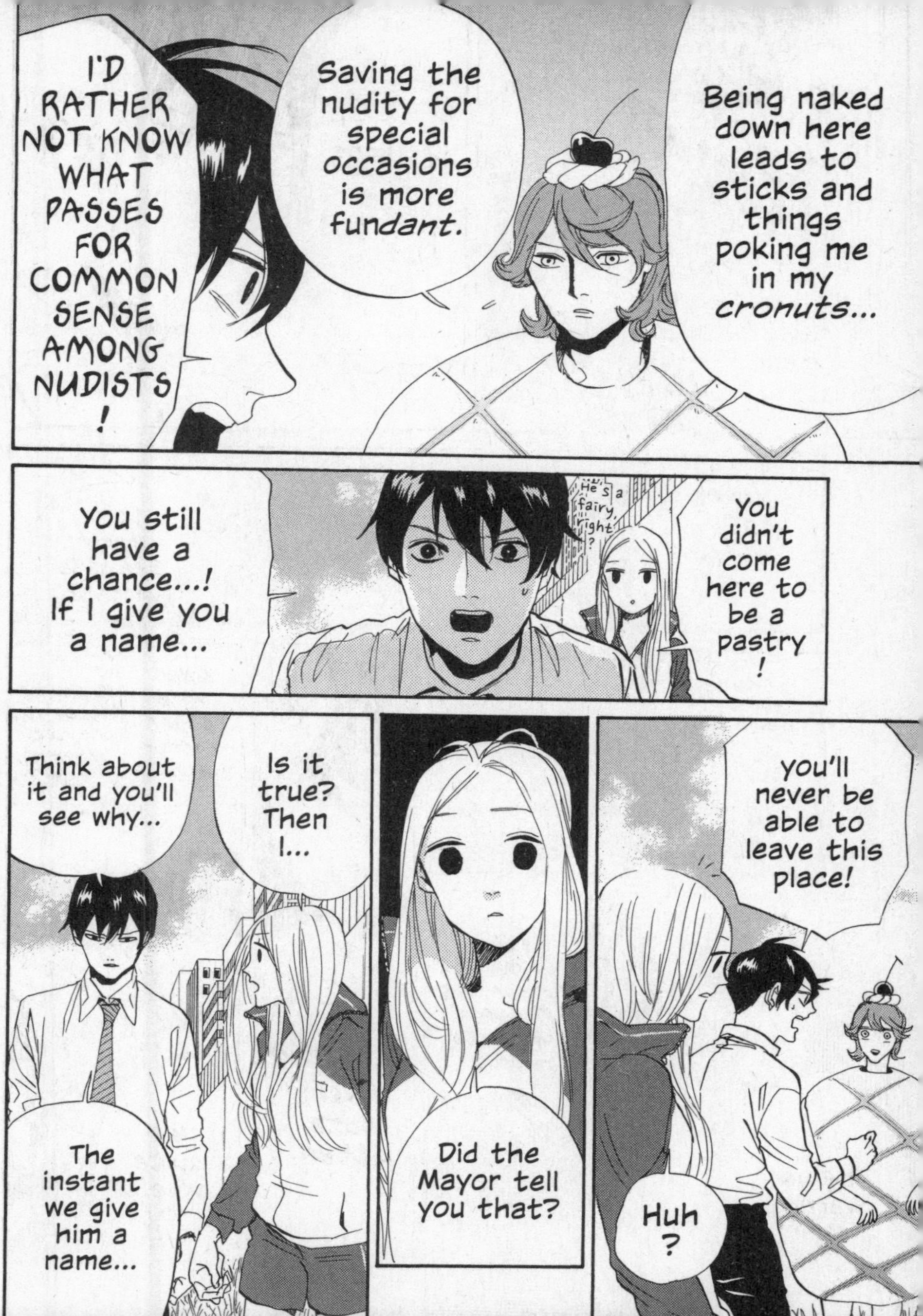
I'D RATHER NOT KNOW WHAT PASSES FOR COMMON SENSE AMONG NUDISTS!
Saving the nudity for special occasions is more *fundant*.
Being naked down here leads to sticks and things poking me in my *cronuts*...
You still have a chance...! If I give you a name...
He's a fairy, right?
You didn't come here to be a pastry!
Think about it and you'll see why...
Is it true? Then I...
The instant we give him a name...
Did the Mayor tell you that?
you'll never be able to leave this place!
Huh?

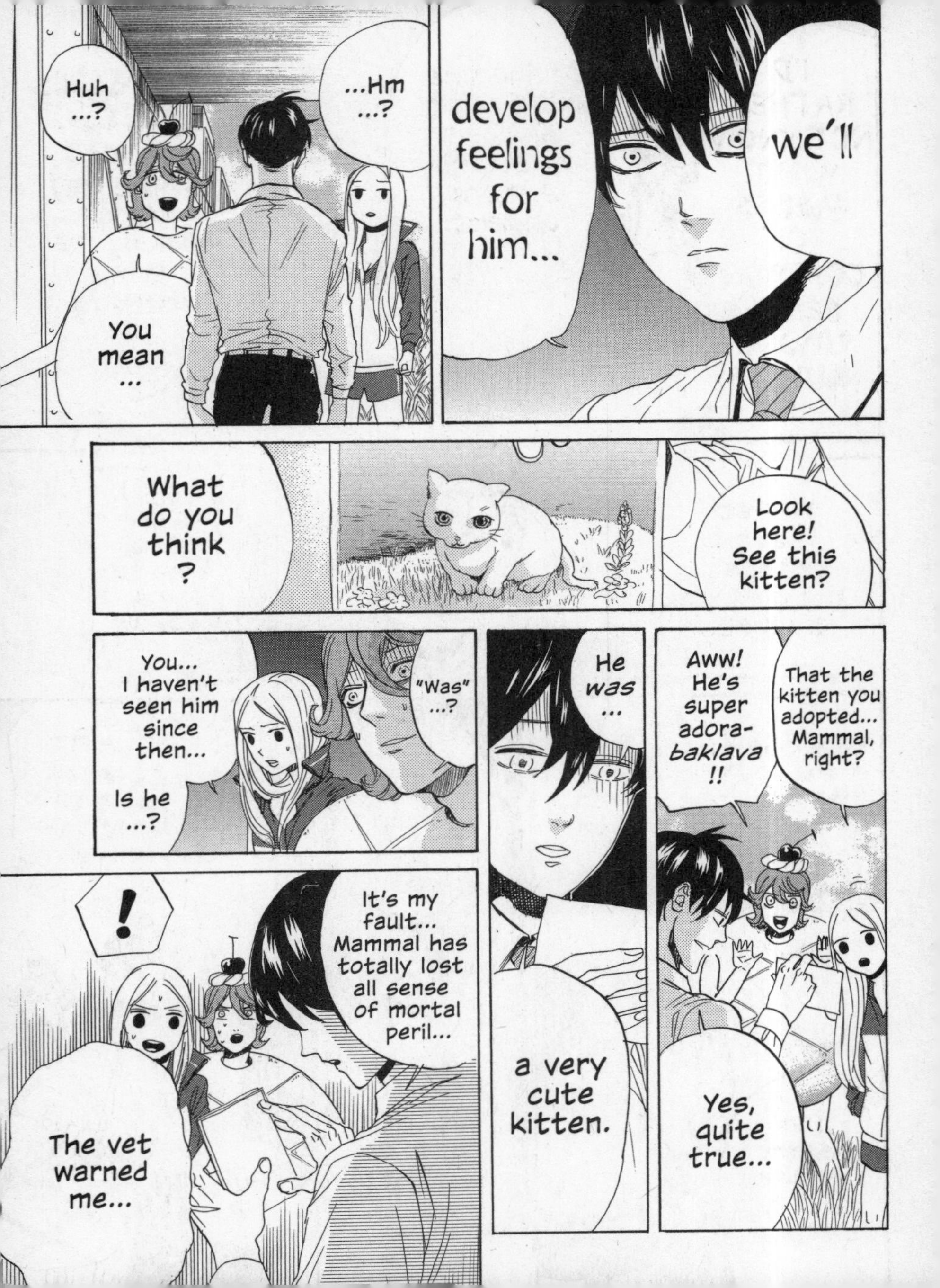
we'll
develop feelings for him...
...Hm ...?
Huh ...?
You mean ...
Look here! See this kitten?
What do you think ?
That the kitten you adopted... Mammal, right?
Aww! He's super adora-baklava !!
Yes, quite true...
He was ...
a very cute kitten.
"Was" ...?
You... I haven't seen him since then...
Is he ...?
It's my fault... Mammal has totally lost all sense of mortal peril...
!
The vet warned me...

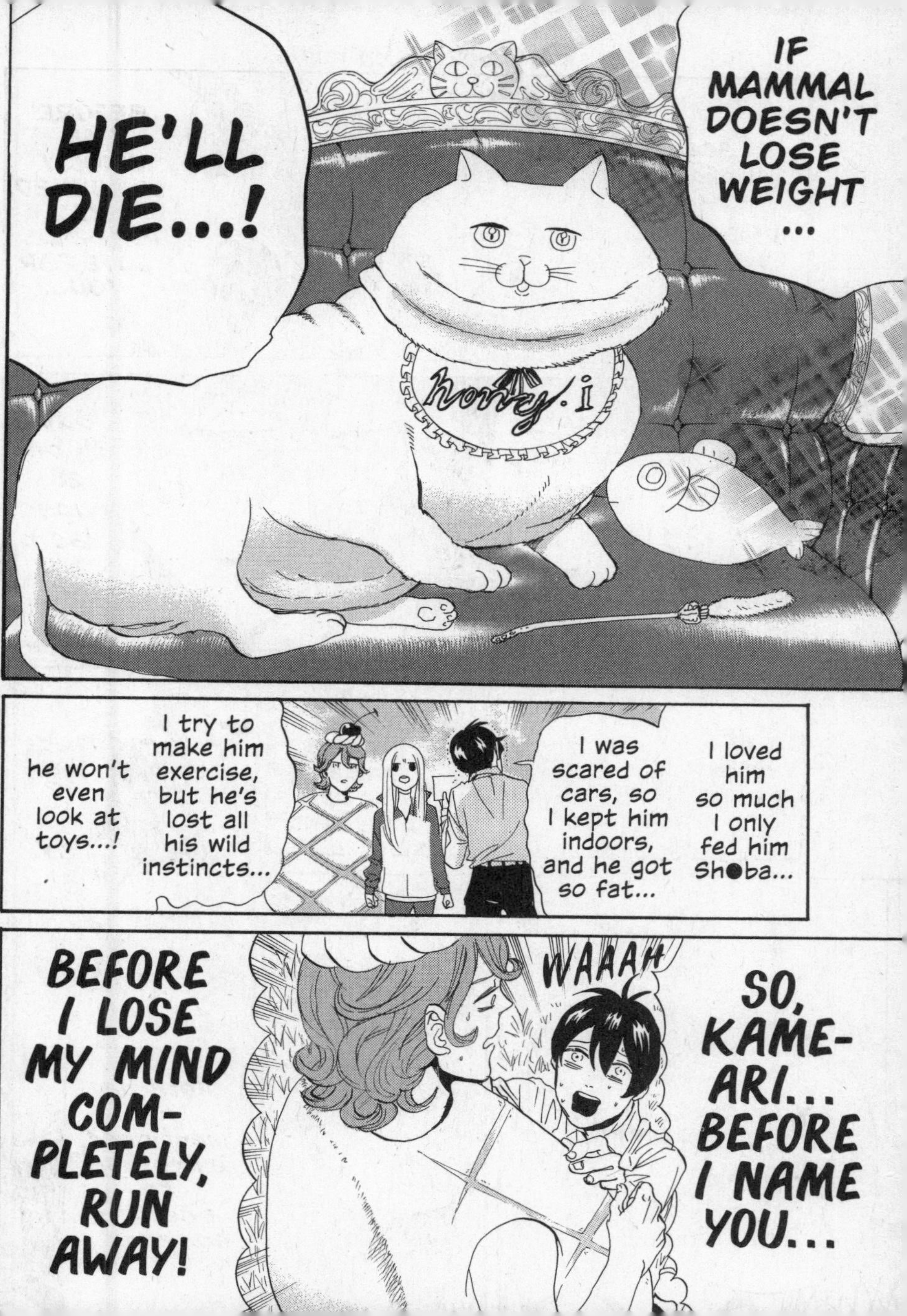
IF MAMMAL DOESN'T LOSE WEIGHT ...
HE'LL DIE...!
I loved him so much I only fed him Sh●ba...
I was scared of cars, so I kept him indoors, and he got so fat...
I try to make him exercise, but he's lost all his wild instincts...
he won't even look at toys...!
SO, KAME-ARI... BEFORE I NAME YOU...
WAAAH
BEFORE I LOSE MY MIND COM-PLETELY, RUN AWAY!

Chapter 375: Ritual

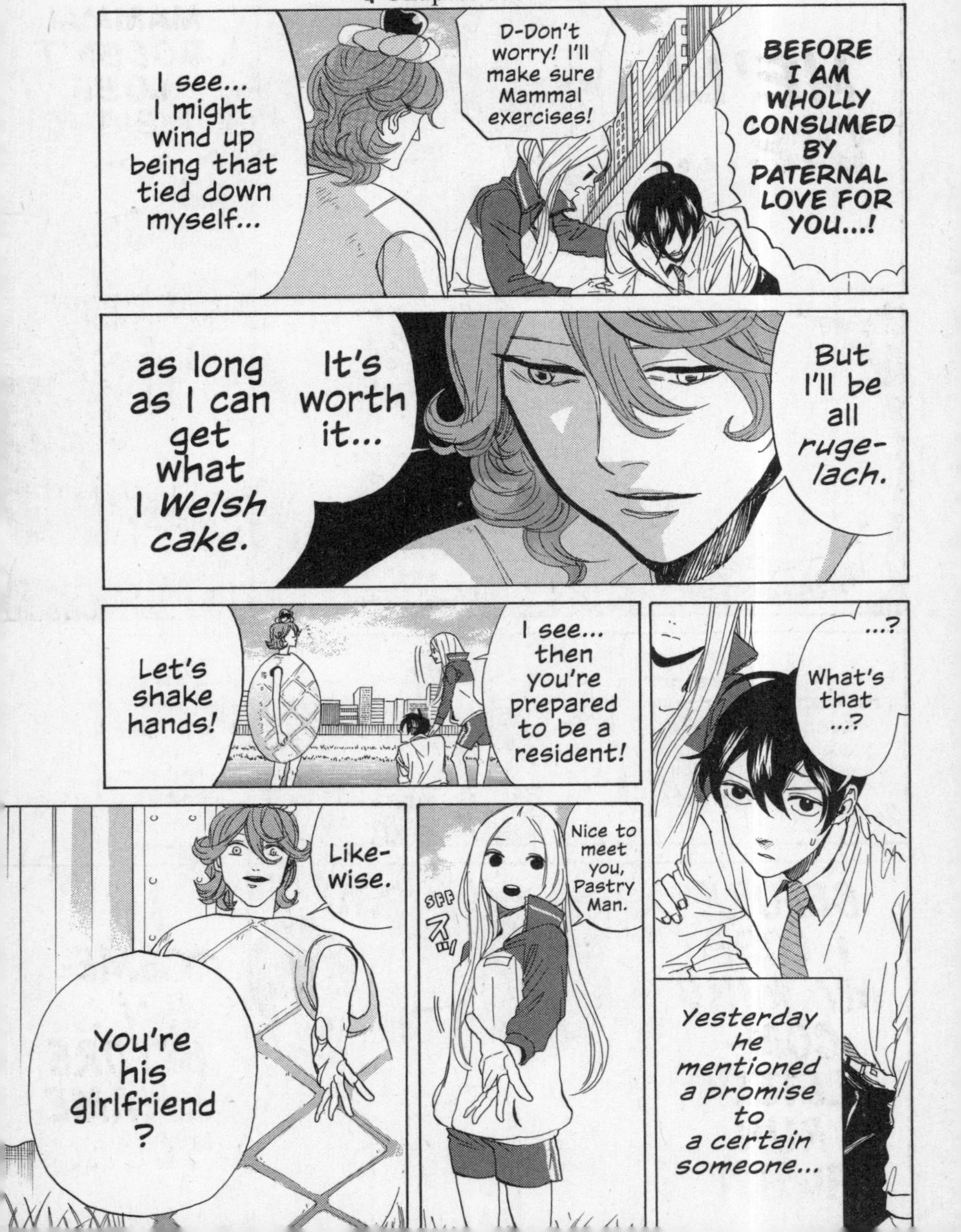
BEFORE I AM WHOLLY CONSUMED BY PATERNAL LOVE FOR YOU...!
D-Don't worry! I'll make sure Mammal exercises!
I see... I might wind up being that tied down myself...
But I'll be all ruge-lach.
It's worth it...
as long as I can get what I *Welsh cake.*
...?
What's that ...?
Yesterday he mentioned a promise to a certain someone...
I see... then you're prepared to be a resident!
Let's shake hands!
Nice to meet you, Pastry Man.
SFF
Like-wise.
You're his girlfriend?

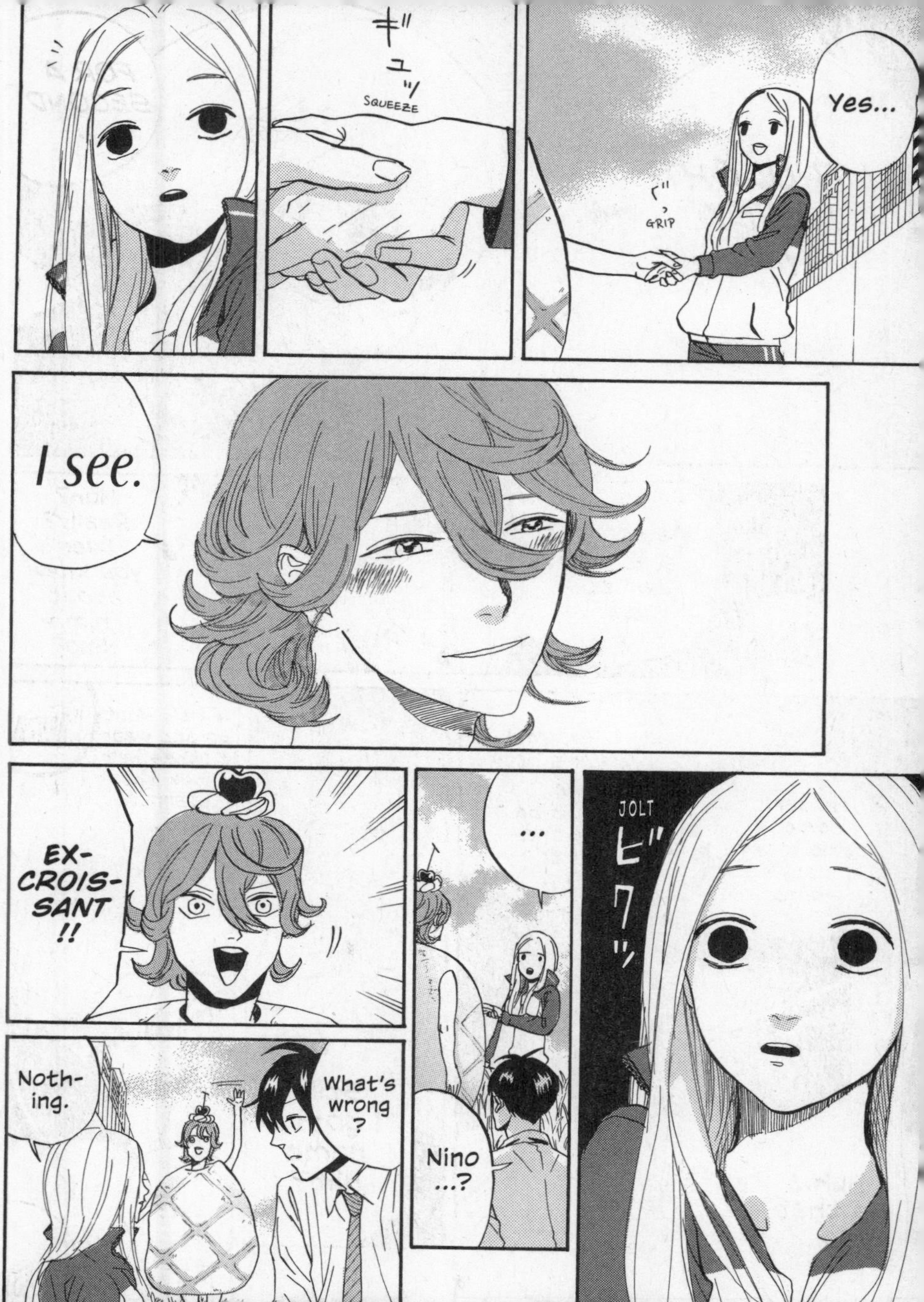

Yes...
ぐっ
GRIP
ギュッ
SQUEEZE
I see.
JOLT
ビクッ
...
Nino ...?
EX-CROISSANT !!
What's wrong ?
Noth-ing.

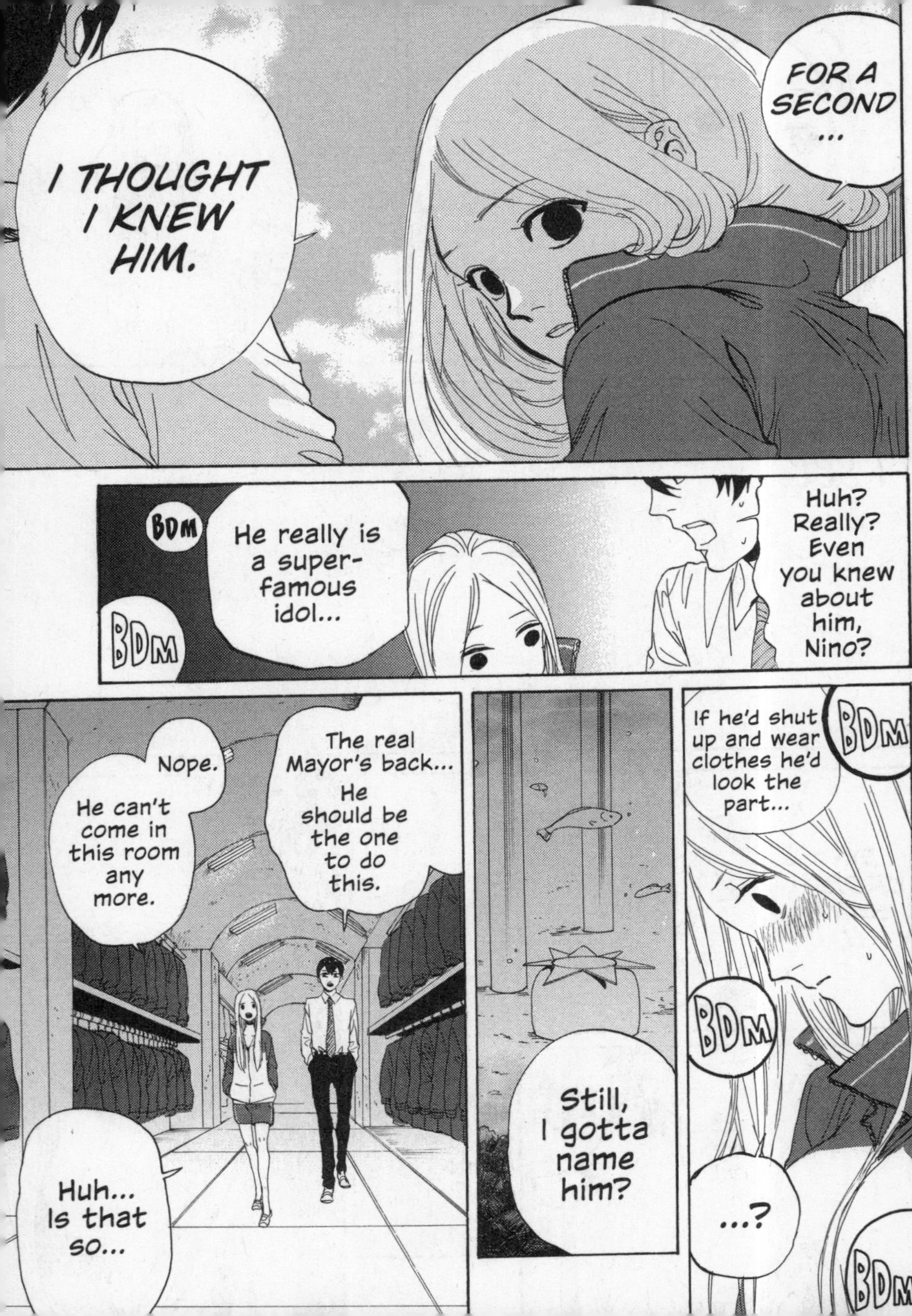
FOR A SECOND ...
I THOUGHT I KNEW HIM.
Huh? Really? Even you knew about him, Nino?
BDM
He really is a super-famous idol...
BDM
BDM
If he'd shut up and wear clothes he'd look the part...
BDM
...?
BDM
Still, I gotta name him?
The real Mayor's back... He should be the one to do this.
Nope. He can't come in this room any more.
Huh... Is that so...

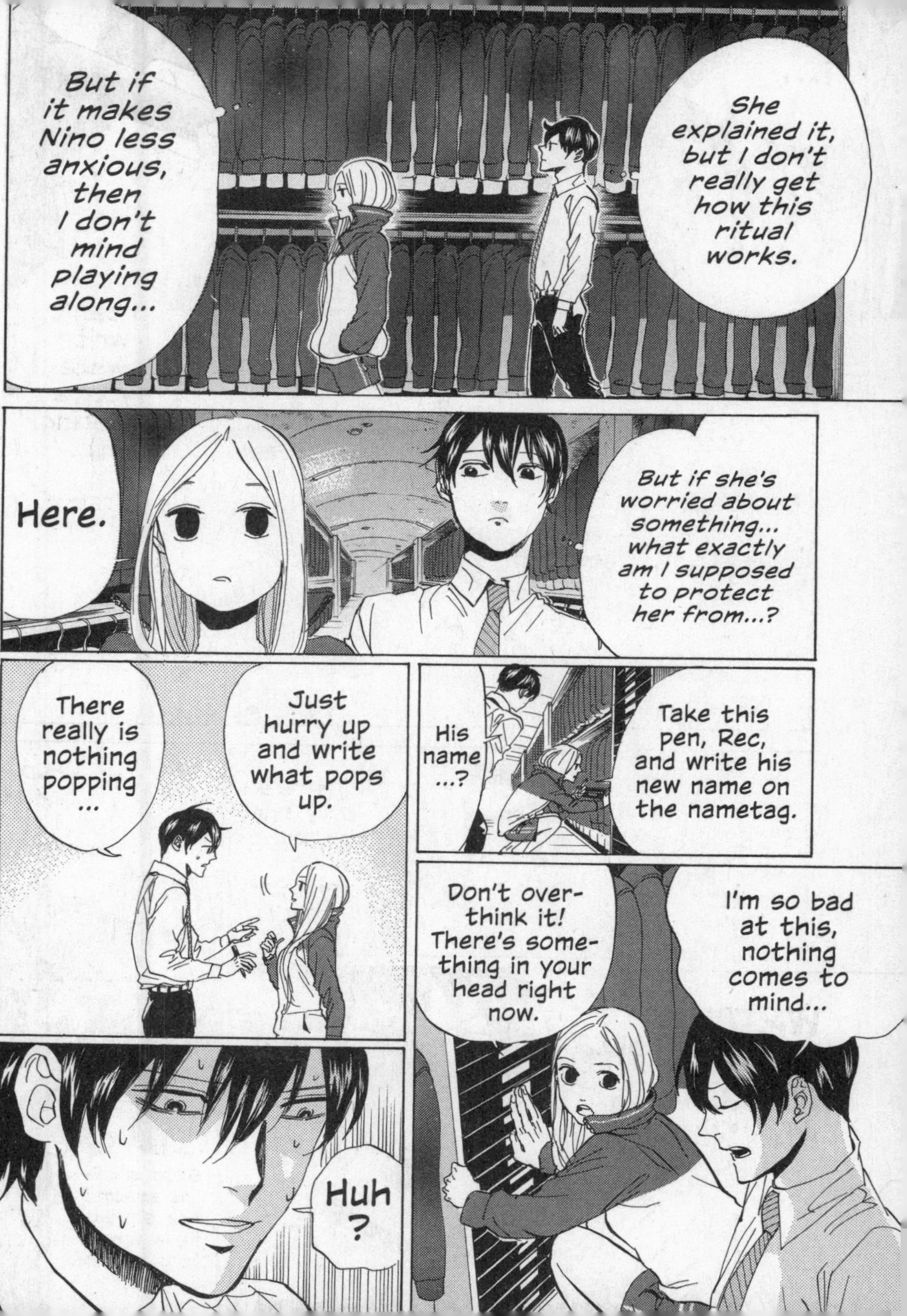
She explained it, but I don't really get how this ritual works.
But if it makes Nino less anxious, then I don't mind playing along...
But if she's worried about something... what exactly am I supposed to protect her from...?
Here.
Take this pen, Rec, and write his new name on the nametag.
His name ...?
I'm so bad at this, nothing comes to mind...
Don't over-think it! There's some-thing in your head right now.
Just hurry up and write what pops up.
There really is nothing popping ...
Huh ?

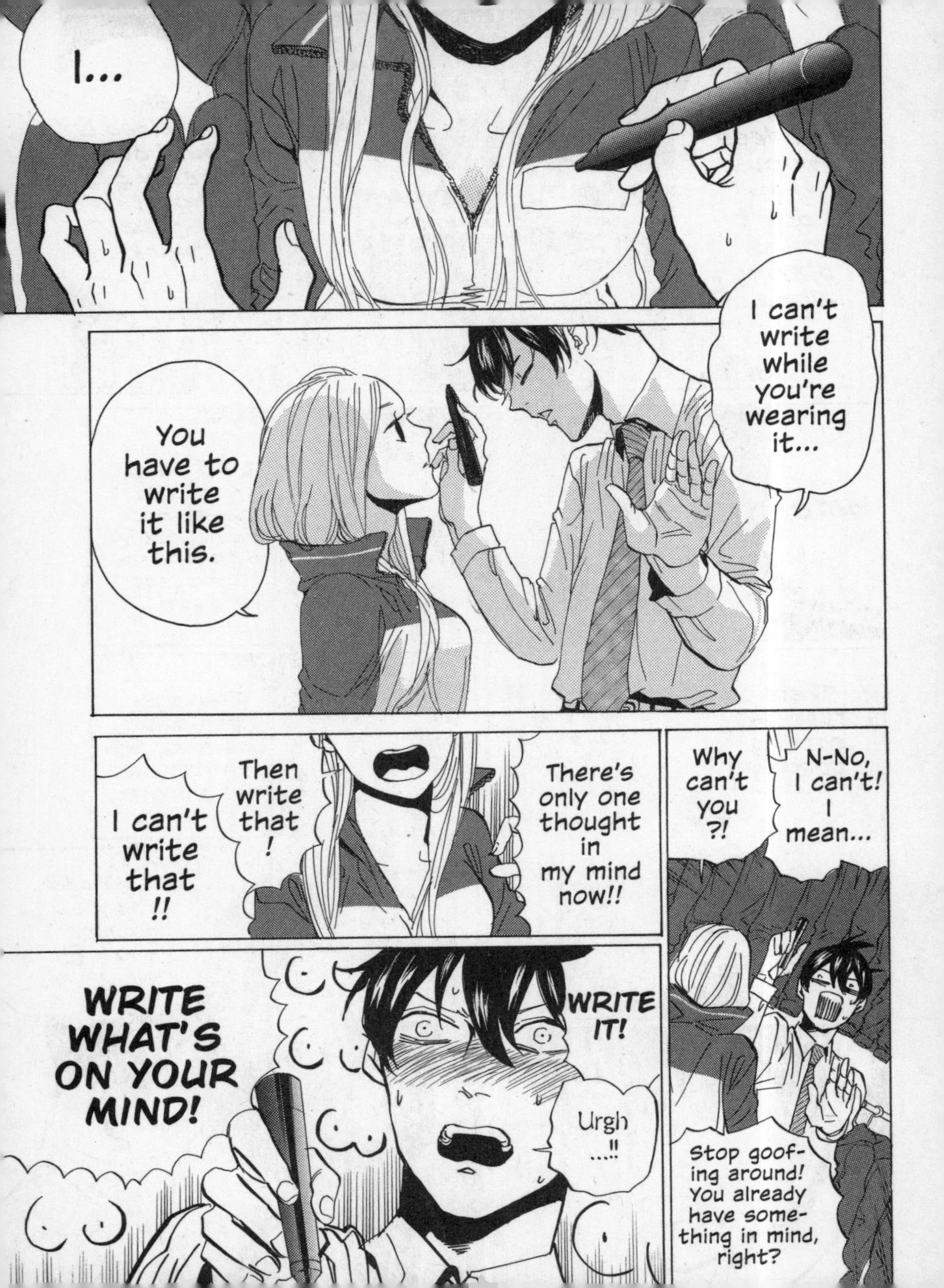

I...
I can't write while you're wearing it...
You have to write it like this.
N-No, I can't! I mean...
Why can't you?!
Stop goofing around! You already have something in mind, right?
There's only one thought in my mind now!!
Then write that!
I can't write that!!
WRITE IT!
WRITE WHAT'S ON YOUR MIND!
Urgh ....!!

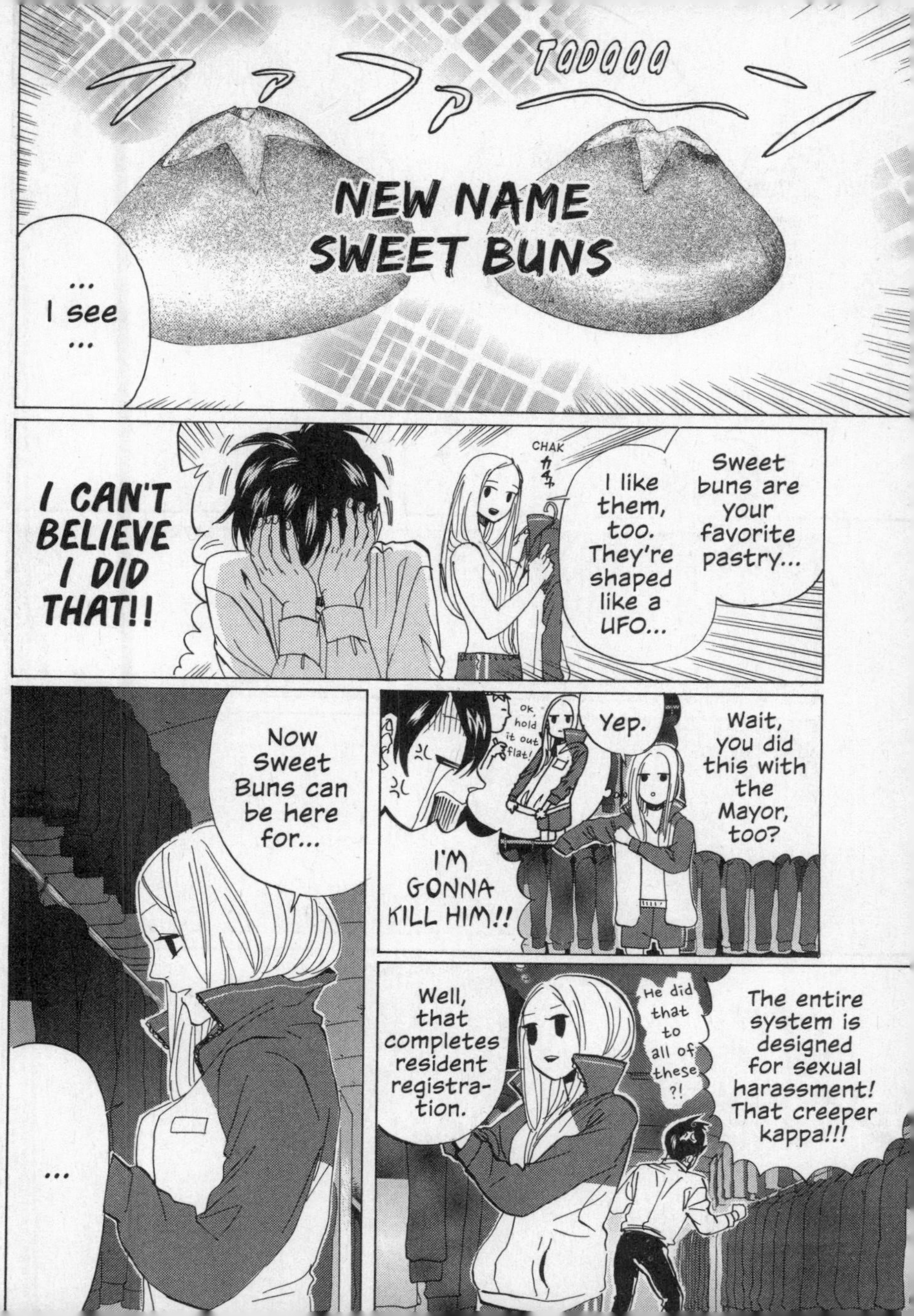
TADAAA
NEW NAME SWEET BUNS
... I see ...
Sweet buns are your favorite pastry...
I like them, too. They're shaped like a UFO...
CHAK
I CAN'T BELIEVE I DID THAT!!
Wait, you did this with the Mayor, too?
Yep.
ok, hold it out flat!
I'M GONNA KILL HIM!!
The entire system is designed for sexual harassment! That creeper kappa!!!
He did that to all of these?!
Well, that completes resident registration.
Now Sweet Buns can be here for...
...

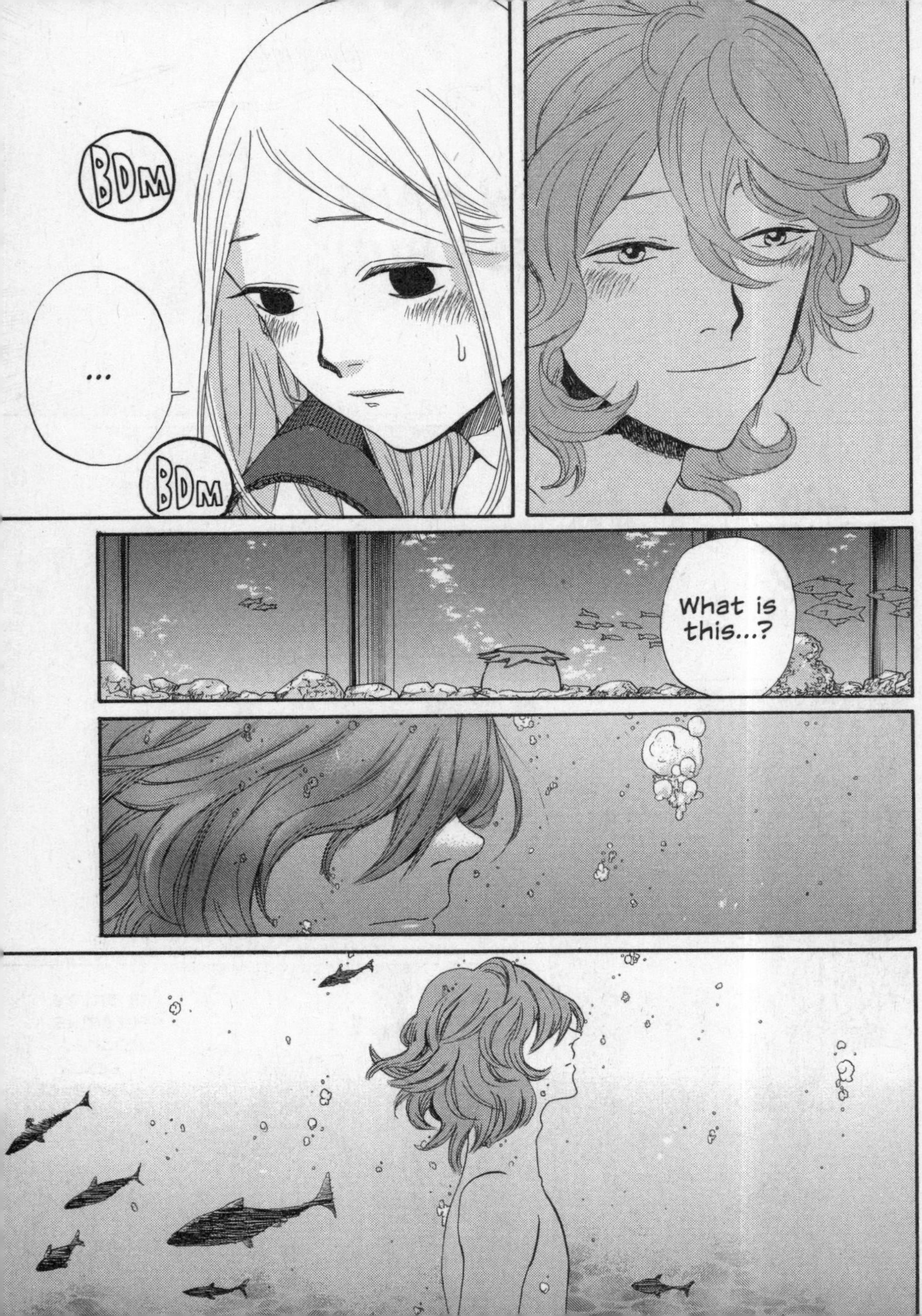
BDm
...
BDm
What is this...?

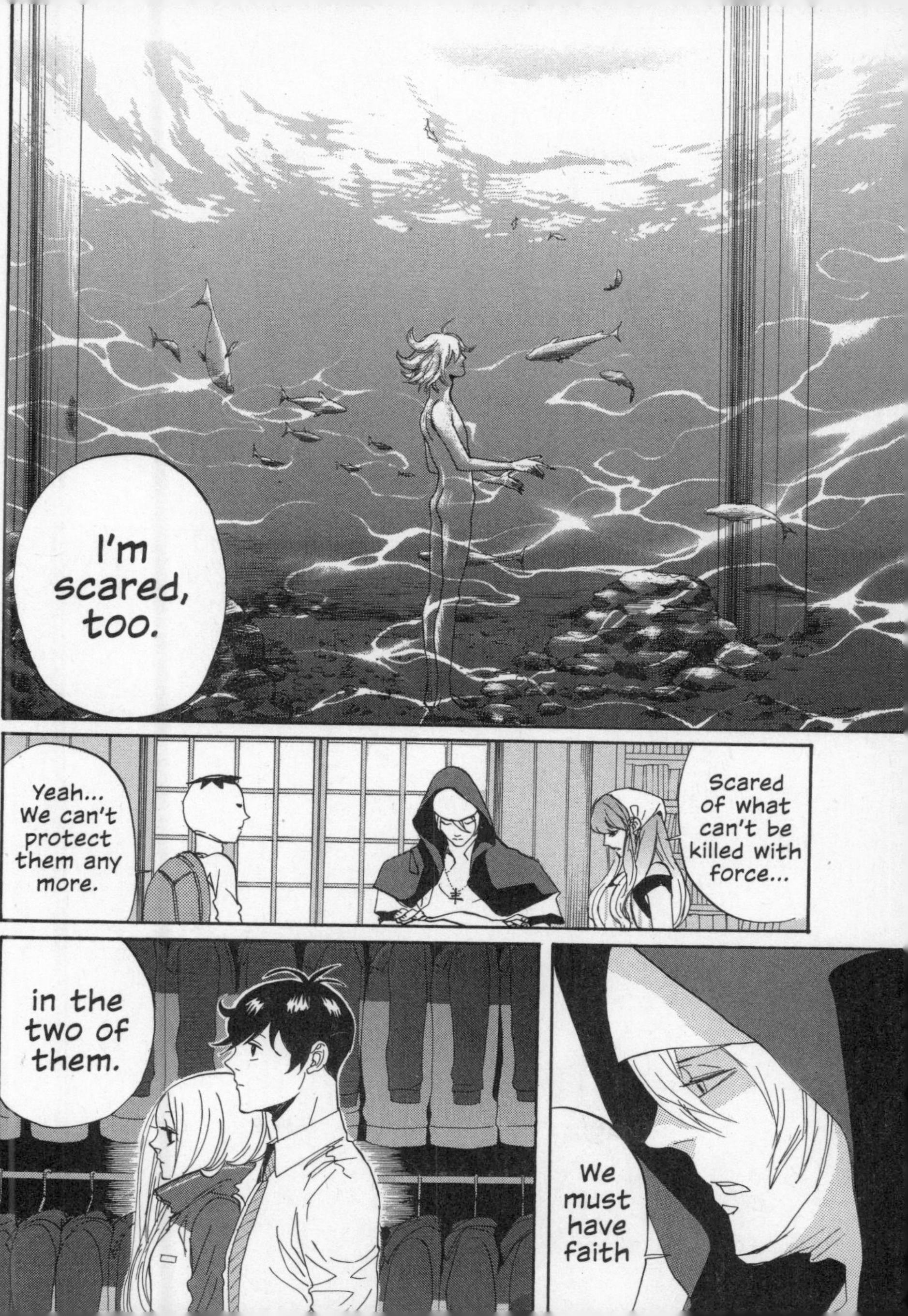
I'm scared, too.
Scared of what can't be killed with force...
Yeah... We can't protect them any more.
We must have faith
in the two of them.

ARAKAWA
UNDER
THE BRIDGE

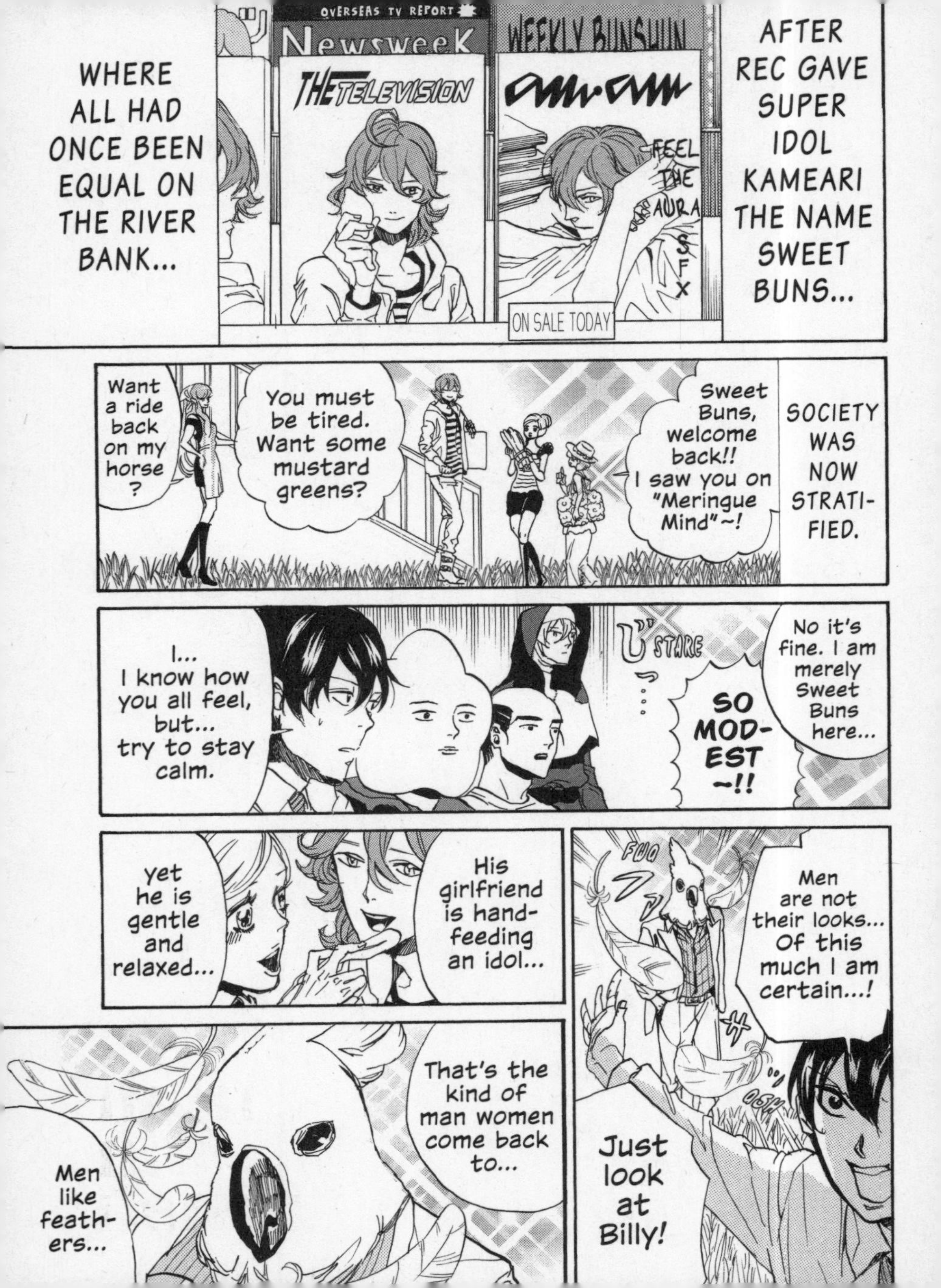
AFTER REC GAVE SUPER IDOL KAMEARI THE NAME SWEET BUNS...
OVERSEAS TV REPORT
Newsweek
THE TELEVISION
WEEKLY BUNSHUN
FEEL THE AURA SFX
ON SALE TODAY
WHERE ALL HAD ONCE BEEN EQUAL ON THE RIVER BANK...
SOCIETY WAS NOW STRATIFIED.
Sweet Buns, welcome back!! I saw you on "Meringue Mind"~!
You must be tired. Want some mustard greens?
Want a ride back on my horse?
No it's fine. I am merely Sweet Buns here...
SO MODEST~!!
STARE
...
I... I know how you all feel, but... try to stay calm.
Men are not their looks... Of this much I am certain...!
Just look at Billy!
His girlfriend is hand-feeding an idol...
yet he is gentle and relaxed...
That's the kind of man women come back to...
Men like feathers...

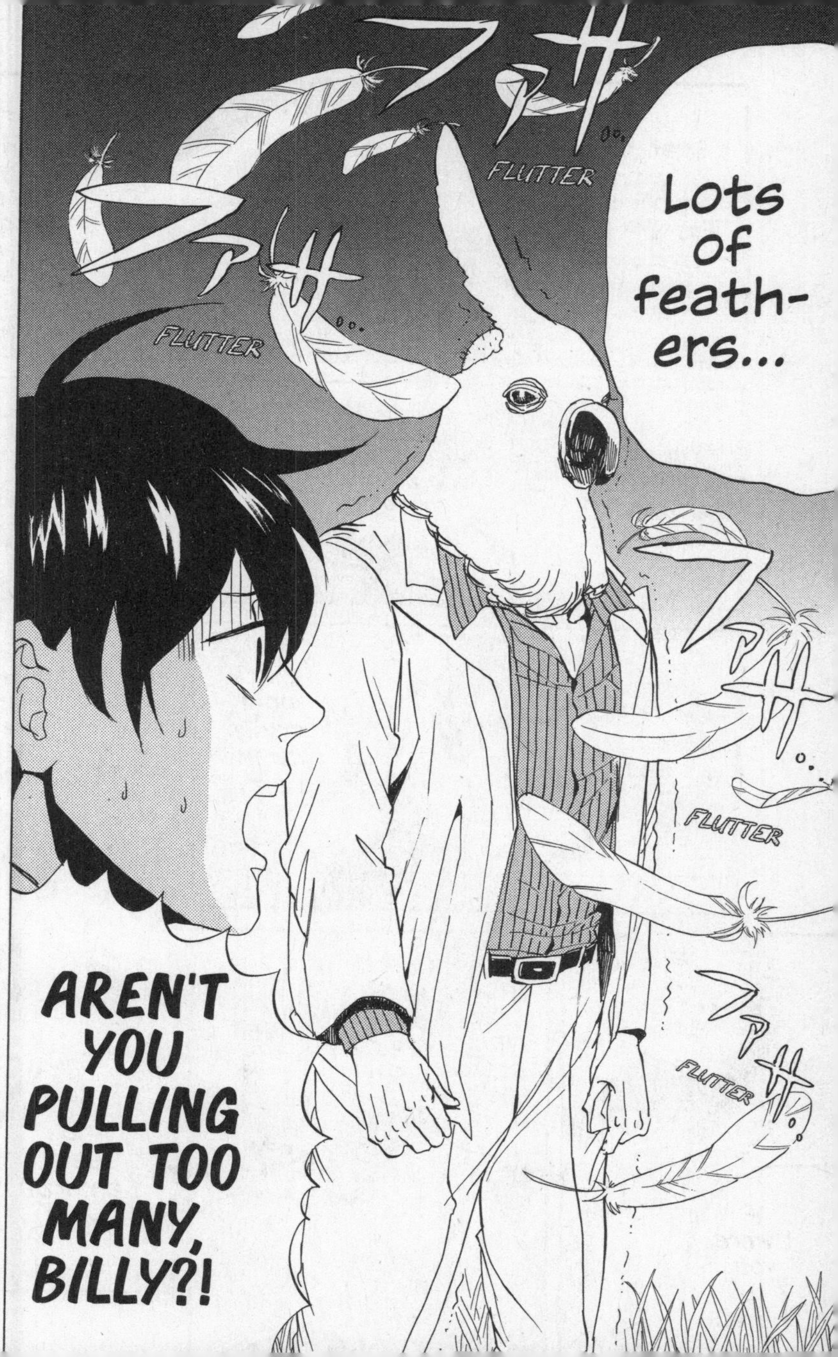

WHITE PARROTS ARE THE ONE BIRD SO DELICATE THEY CAN COMMIT SUICIDE.

Chapter 376: Confidence

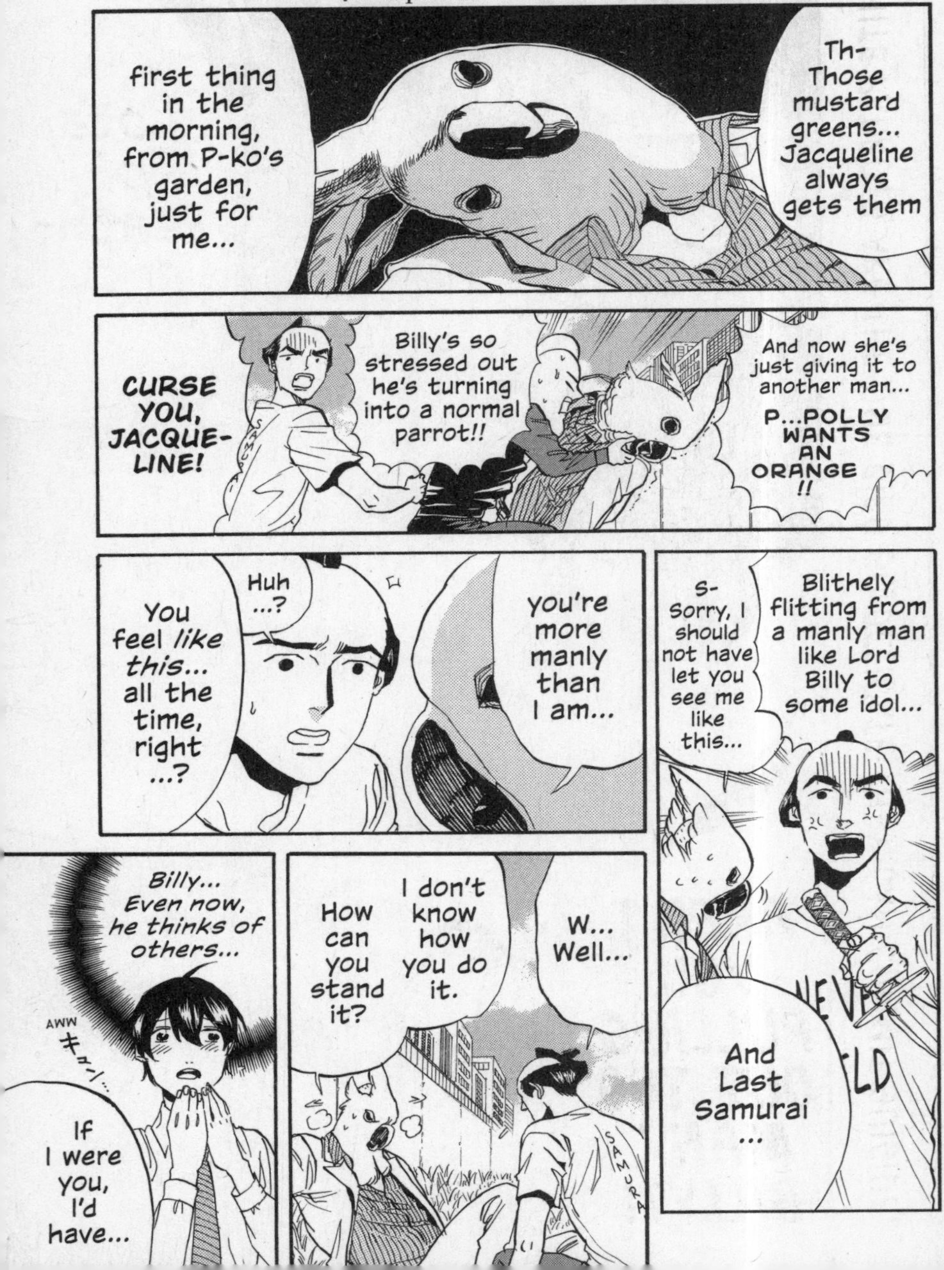
Th- Those mustard greens... Jacqueline always gets them
first thing in the morning, from P-ko's garden, just for me...
And now she's just giving it to another man...
P...POLLY WANTS AN ORANGE !!
Billy's so stressed out he's turning into a normal parrot!!
CURSE YOU, JACQUE-LINE!
Blithely flitting from a manly man like Lord Billy to some idol...
S- Sorry, I should not have let you see me like this...
And Last Samurai ...
you're more manly than I am...
Huh ...?
You feel *like this*... all the time, right ...?
W... Well...
I don't know how you do it.
How can you stand it?
Billy... Even now, he thinks of others...
AWW
キュン...
If I were you, I'd have...

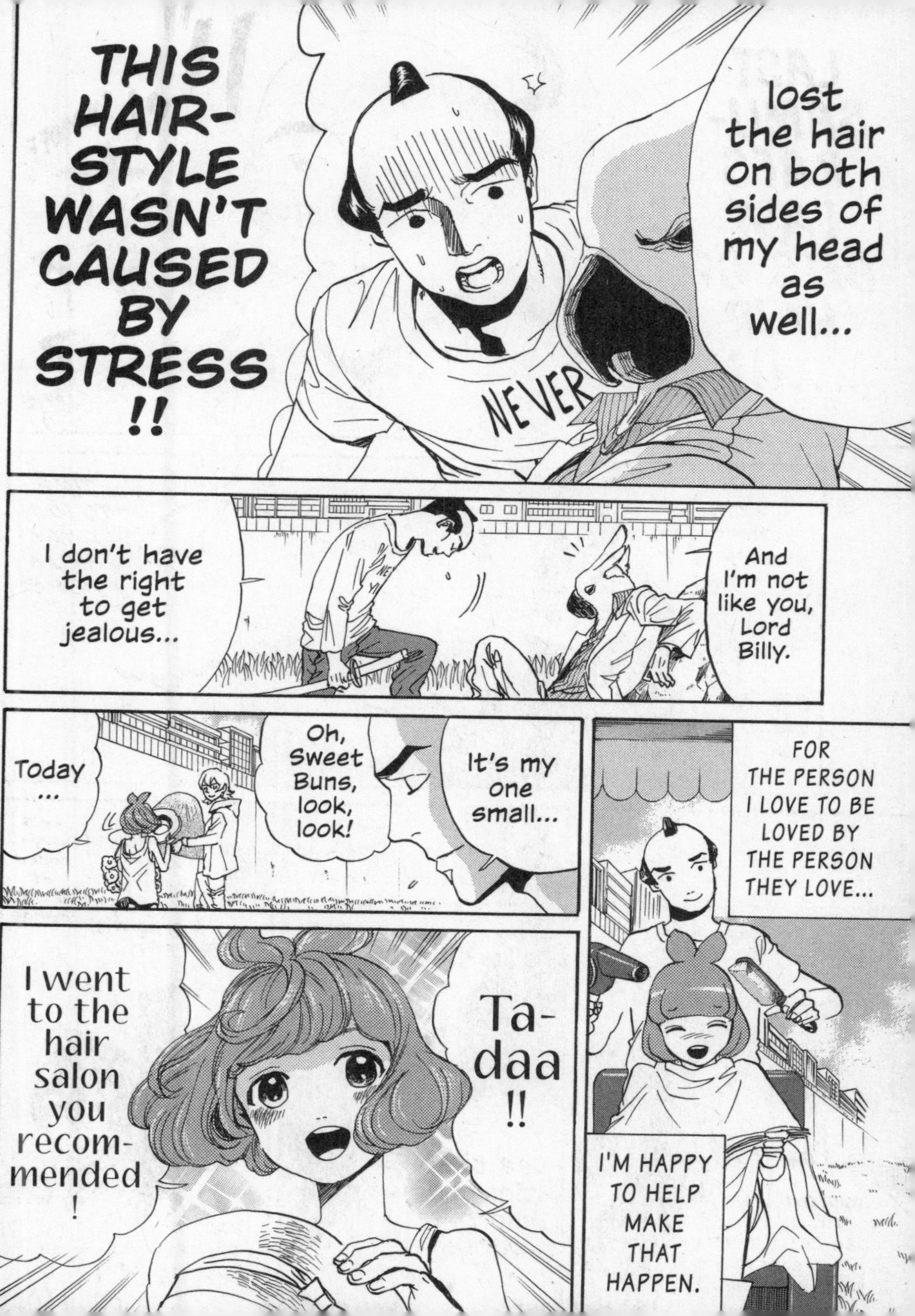
lost the hair on both sides of my head as well...
THIS HAIR-STYLE WASN'T CAUSED BY STRESS!!
NEVER
And I'm not like you, Lord Billy.
I don't have the right to get jealous...
FOR THE PERSON I LOVE TO BE LOVED BY THE PERSON THEY LOVE...
I'M HAPPY TO HELP MAKE THAT HAPPEN.
It's my one small...
Oh, Sweet Buns, look, look!
Today...
Ta-daa!!
I went to the hair salon you recommended!

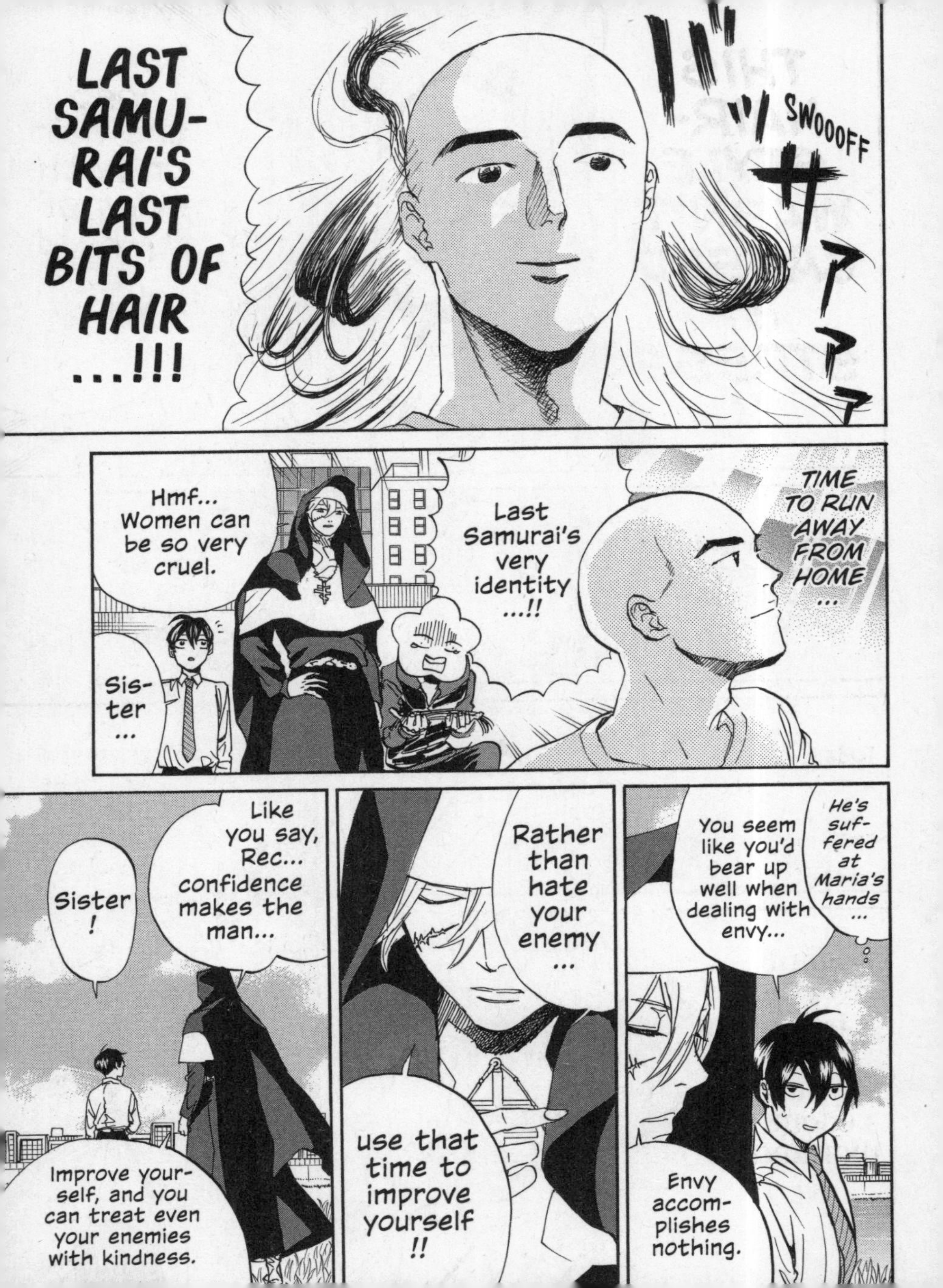
バッサァァァ
SWOOOFF
LAST SAMURAI'S LAST BITS OF HAIR ...!!!
TIME TO RUN AWAY FROM HOME ...
Last Samurai's very identity ...!!
Hmf... Women can be so very cruel.
Sister ...
He's suffered at Maria's hands ...
You seem like you'd bear up well when dealing with envy...
Envy accomplishes nothing.
Rather than hate your enemy ...
use that time to improve yourself !!
Like you say, Rec... confidence makes the man...
Sister !
Improve yourself, and you can treat even your enemies with kindness.

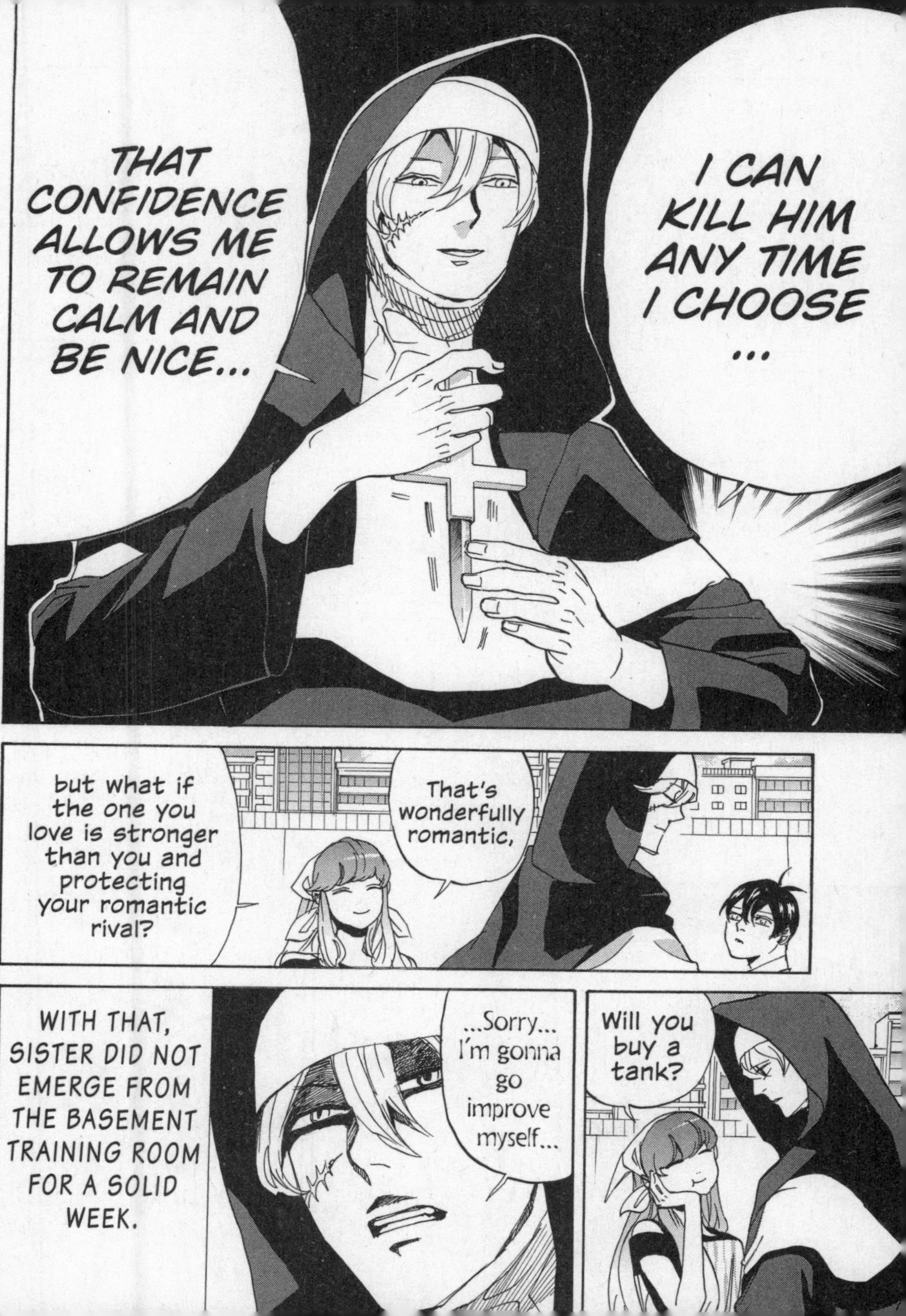
I CAN KILL HIM ANY TIME I CHOOSE ...
THAT CONFIDENCE ALLOWS ME TO REMAIN CALM AND BE NICE...
That's wonderfully romantic,
but what if the one you love is stronger than you and protecting your romantic rival?
Will you buy a tank?
...Sorry... I'm gonna go improve myself...
WITH THAT, SISTER DID NOT EMERGE FROM THE BASEMENT TRAINING ROOM FOR A SOLID WEEK.

Chapter 377: Love in her Eyes

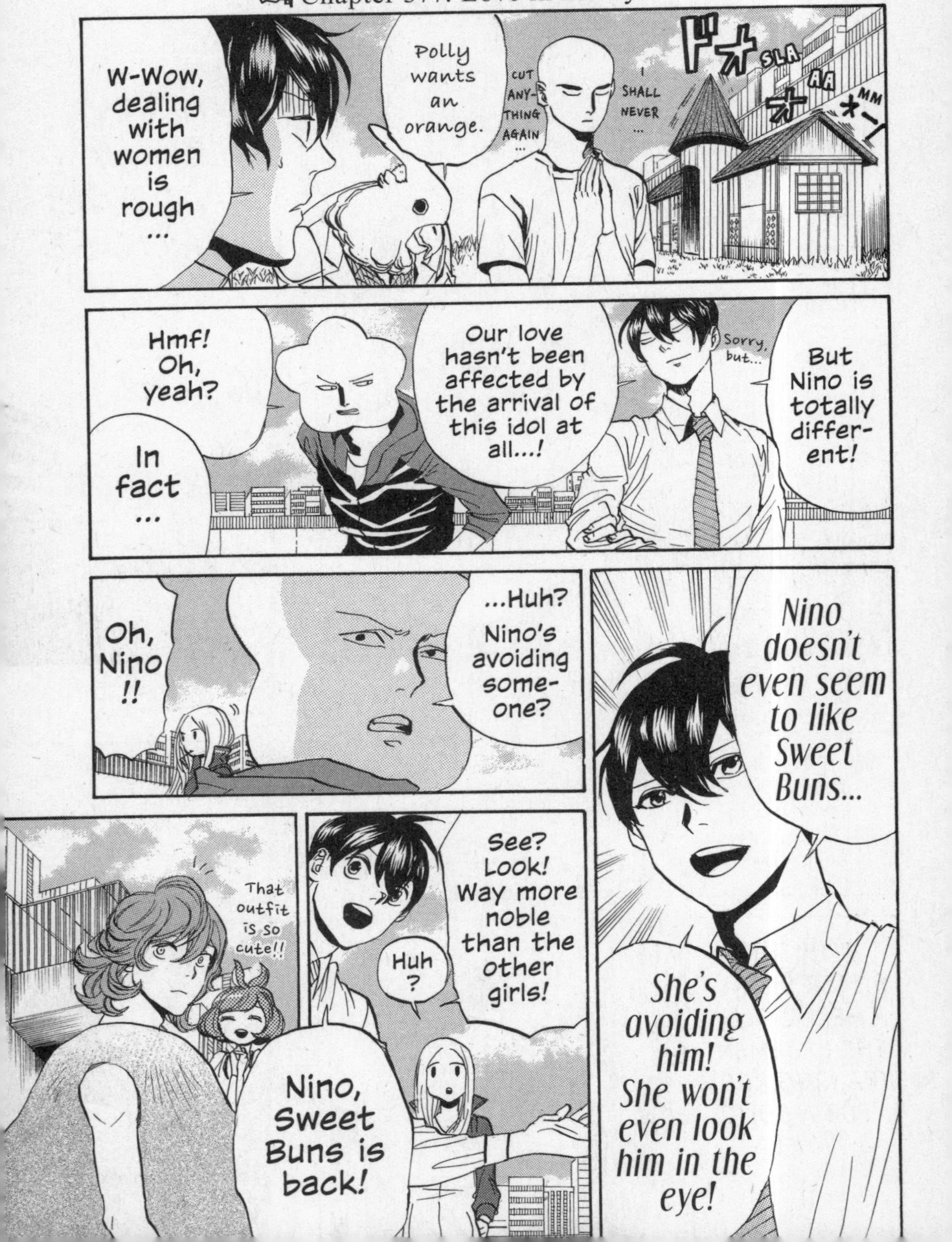

ドオオオー
SLAAAMM
I SHALL NEVER ...
CUT ANYTHING AGAIN ...
Polly wants an orange.
W-Wow, dealing with women is rough ...
Sorry, but...
But Nino is totally different!
Our love hasn't been affected by the arrival of this idol at all...!
Hmf! Oh, yeah?
In fact ...
Nino doesn't even seem to like Sweet Buns...
She's avoiding him! She won't even look him in the eye!
...Huh? Nino's avoiding someone?
Oh, Nino !!
See? Look! Way more noble than the other girls!
Huh ?
Nino, Sweet Buns is back!
That outfit is so cute!!

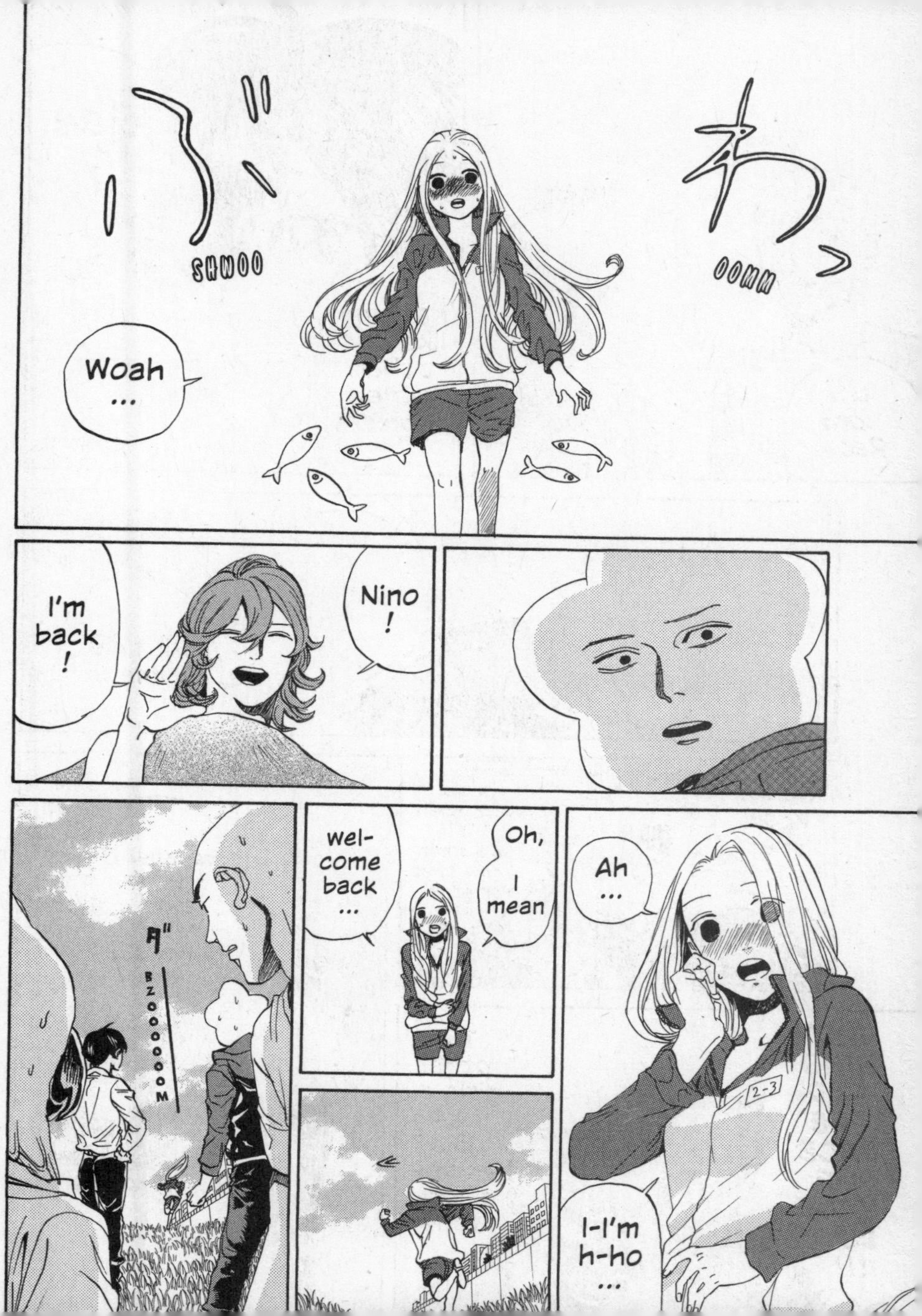
わっ
OOMM
ぶ
SHWOO
Woah ...
Nino!
I'm back!
Ah ...
I-I'm h-ho ...
Oh, I mean
wel-come back ...
ガ
BZOOOOOOOM

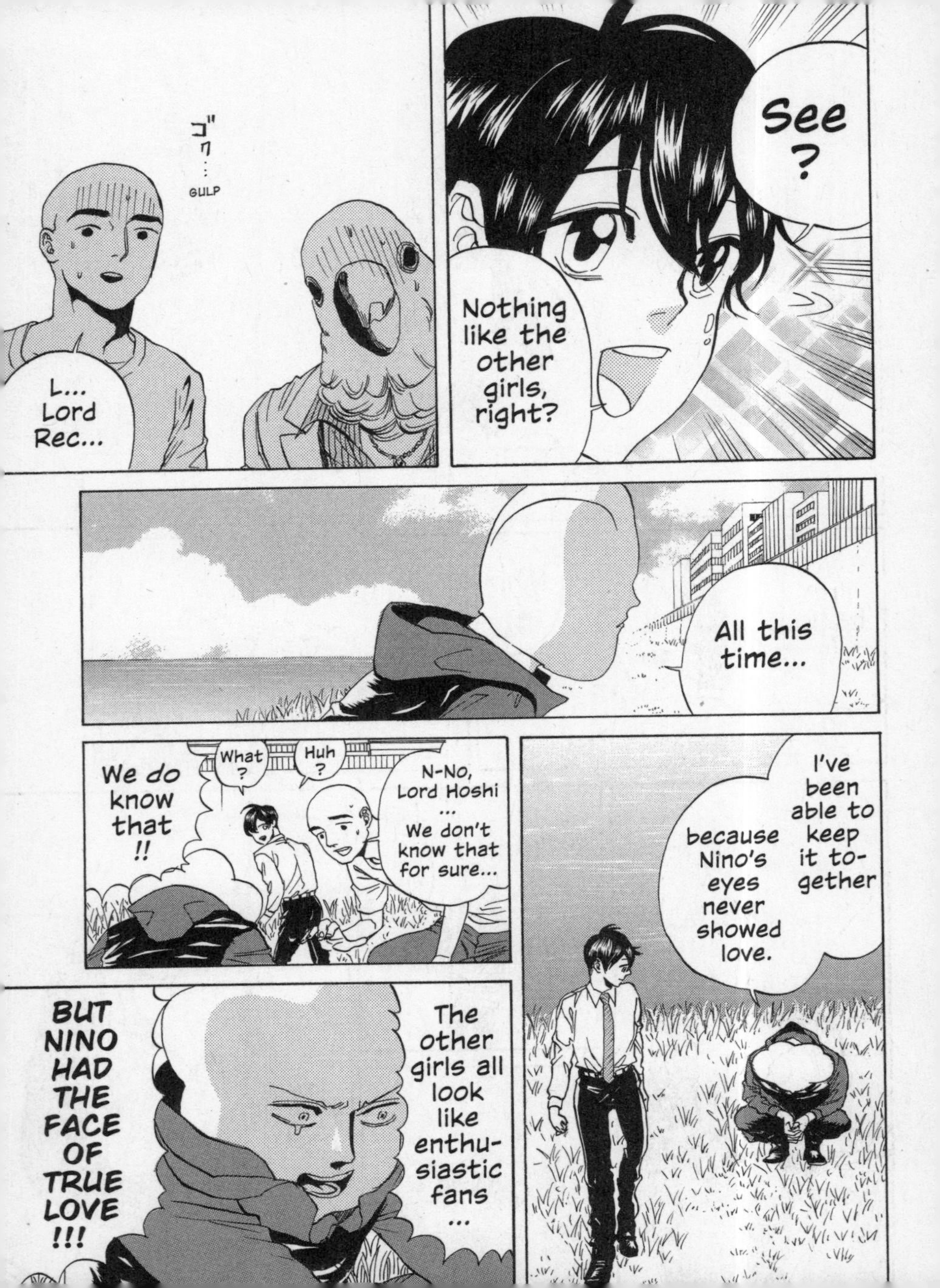
See?
Nothing like the other girls, right?
ゴク…
GULP
L... Lord Rec...
All this time...
I've been able to keep it together
because Nino's eyes never showed love.
N-No, Lord Hoshi ... We don't know that for sure...
Huh?
What?
We do know that!!
The other girls all look like enthusiastic fans ...
BUT NINO HAD THE FACE OF TRUE LOVE!!!

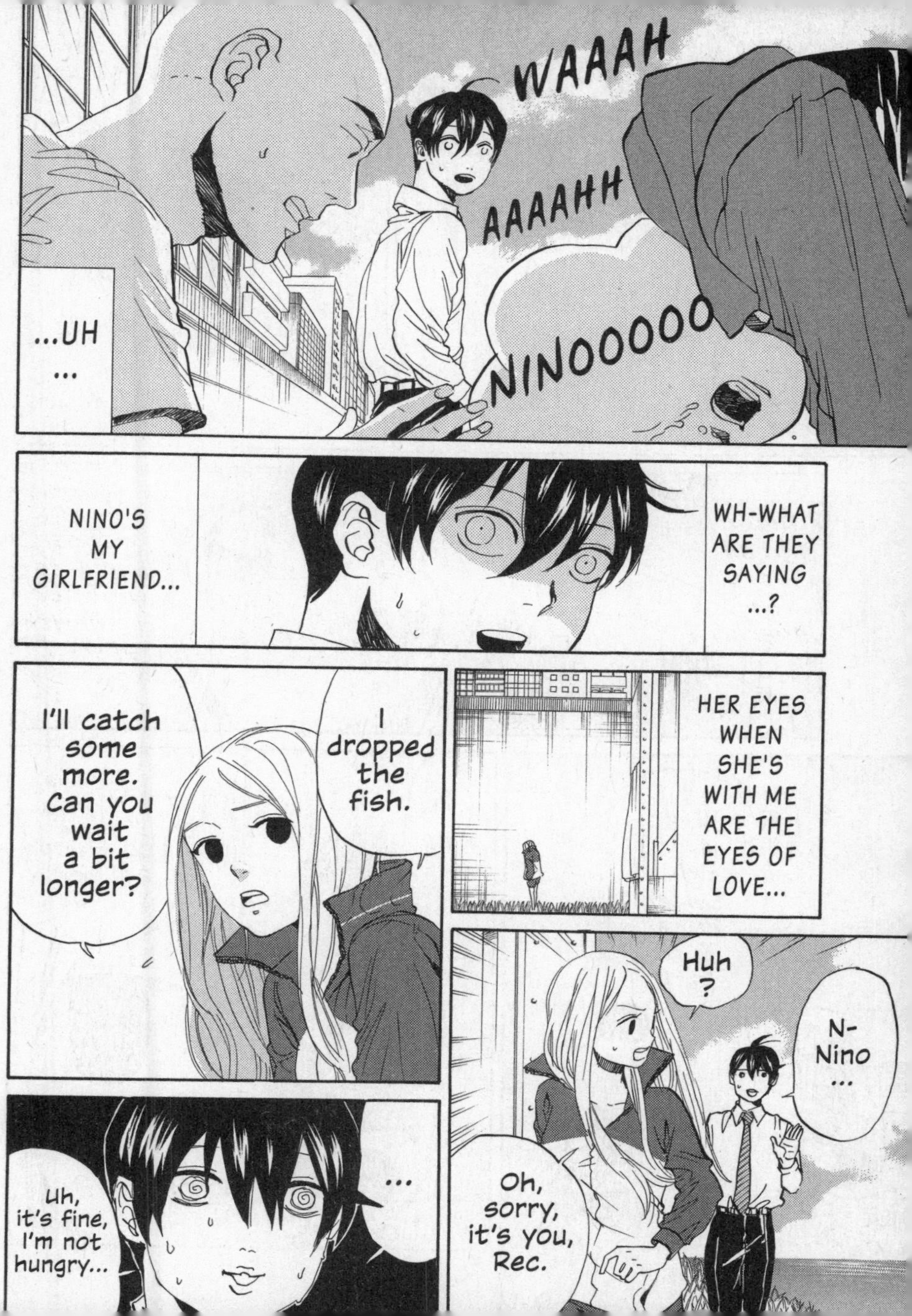

WAAAH
AAAAHH
NINOOOOO
...UH ...
WH-WHAT ARE THEY SAYING ...?
NINO'S MY GIRLFRIEND...
HER EYES WHEN SHE'S WITH ME ARE THE EYES OF LOVE...
Huh?
N-Nino ...
Oh, sorry, it's you, Rec.
I dropped the fish.
I'll catch some more. Can you wait a bit longer?
...
uh, it's fine, I'm not hungry...

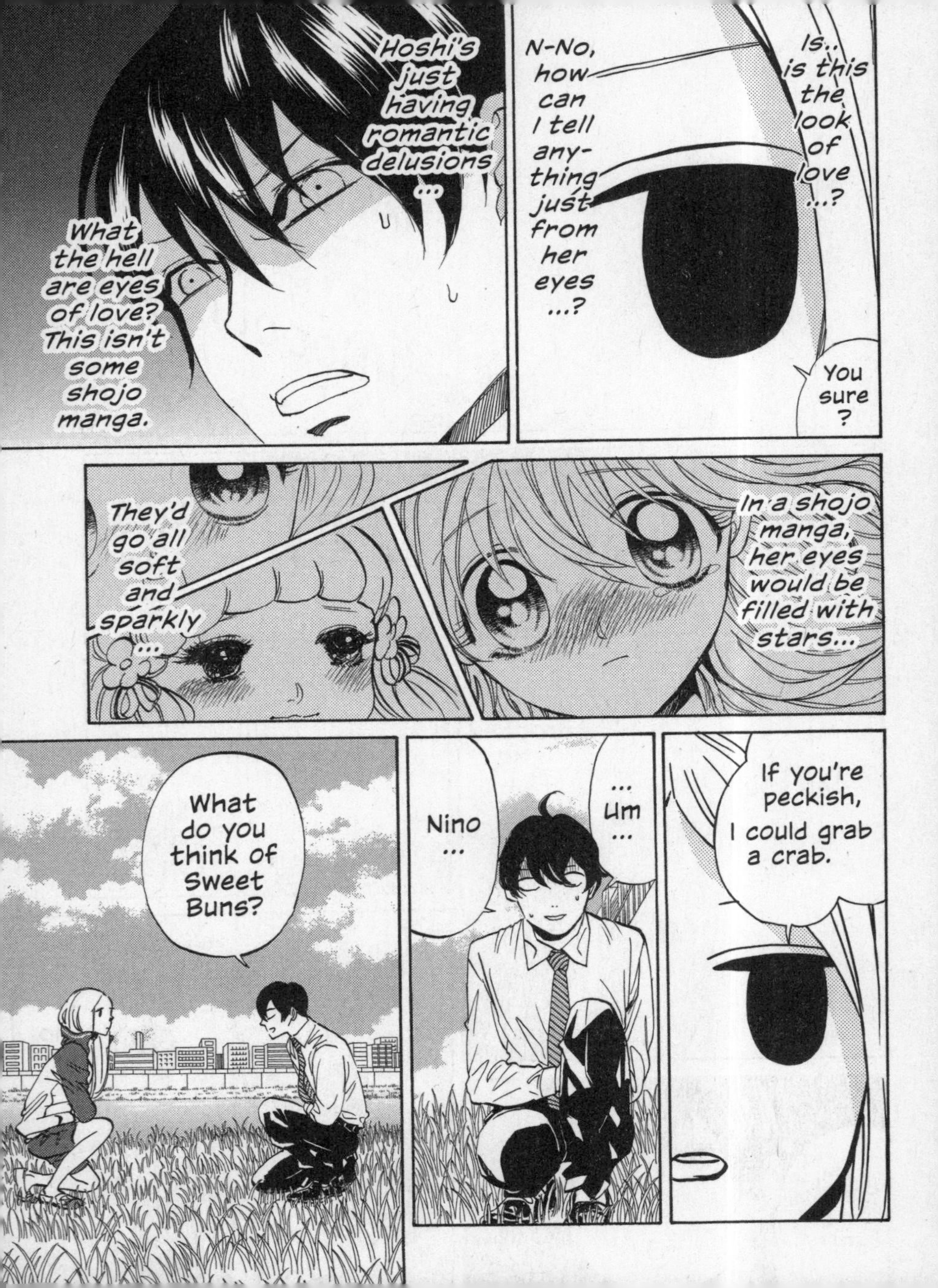

Is.. is this the look of love ...?
N-No, how can I tell any-thing just from her eyes ...?
You sure ?
Hoshi's just having romantic delusions ...
What the hell are eyes of love? This isn't some shojo manga.
In a shojo manga, her eyes would be filled with stars...
They'd go all soft and sparkly ...
If you're peckish, I could grab a crab.
... Um ...
Nino ...
What do you think of Sweet Buns?

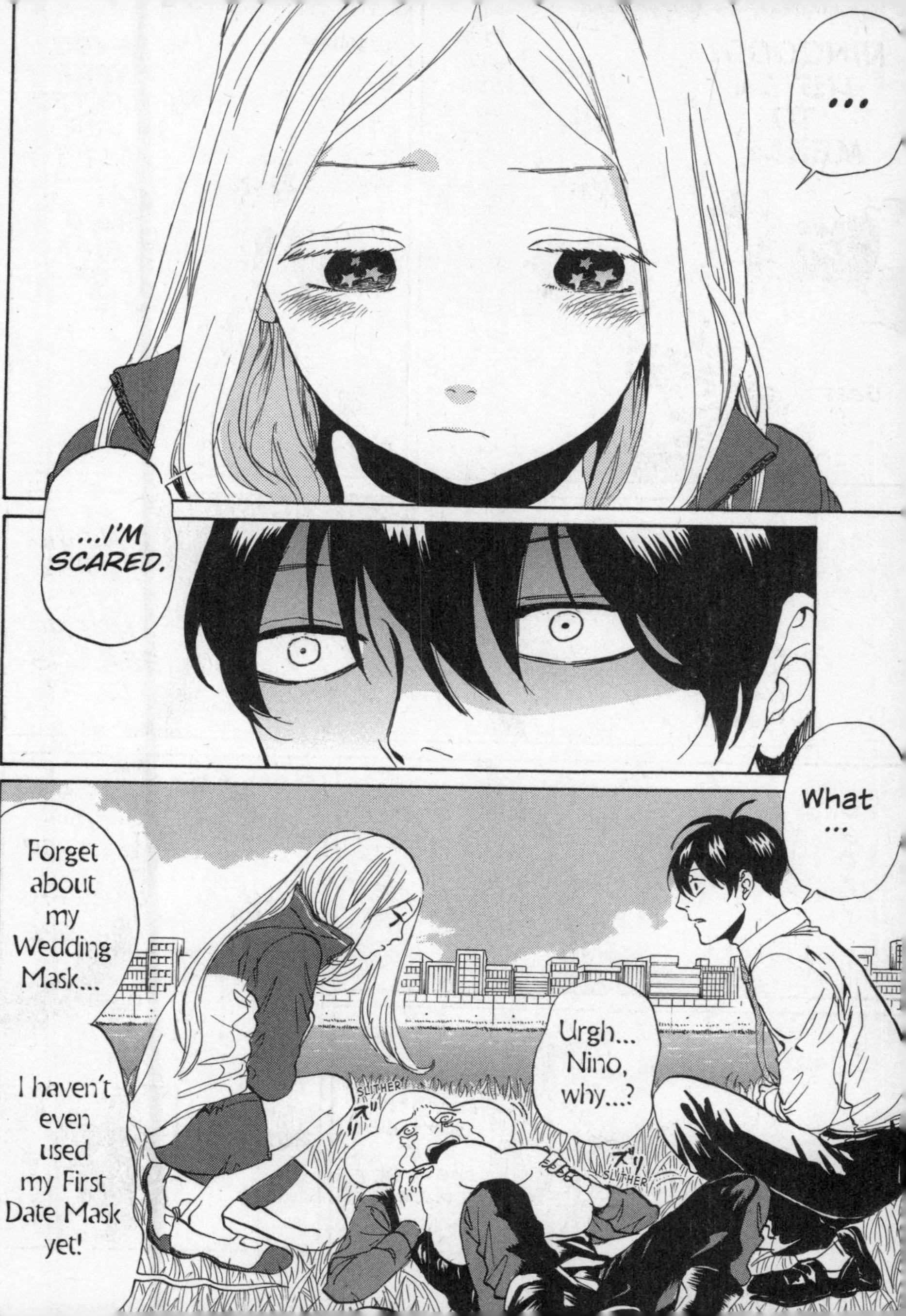
...
...I'M SCARED.
What ...
Urgh... Nino, why...?
SLITHER
SLITHER
Forget about my Wedding Mask...
I haven't even used my First Date Mask yet!

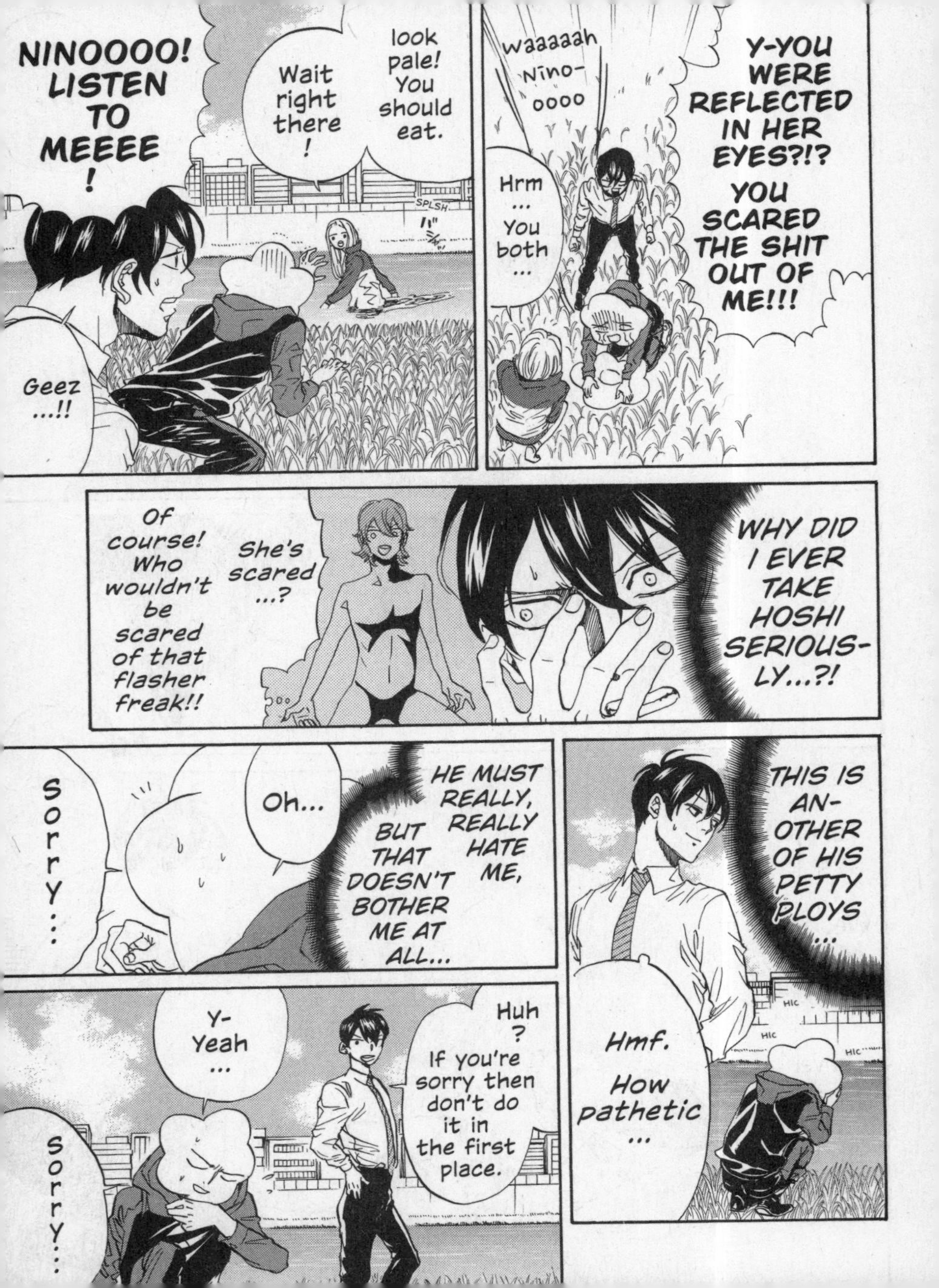

Y-YOU WERE REFLECTED IN HER EYES?!?
YOU SCARED THE SHIT OUT OF ME!!!
Waaaaah Nino-oooo
Hrm... You both...
look pale! You should eat.
Wait right there!
NINOOOO! LISTEN TO MEEEE!
SPLSH
Geez...!!
WHY DID I EVER TAKE HOSHI SERIOUSLY...?!
She's scared...?
Of course! Who wouldn't be scared of that flasher freak!!
THIS IS ANOTHER OF HIS PETTY PLOYS...
HIC
HIC
HIC
Hmf. How pathetic...
HE MUST REALLY, REALLY HATE ME, BUT THAT DOESN'T BOTHER ME AT ALL...
Oh...
Sorry...
Huh? If you're sorry then don't do it in the first place.
Y-Yeah...
Sorry...

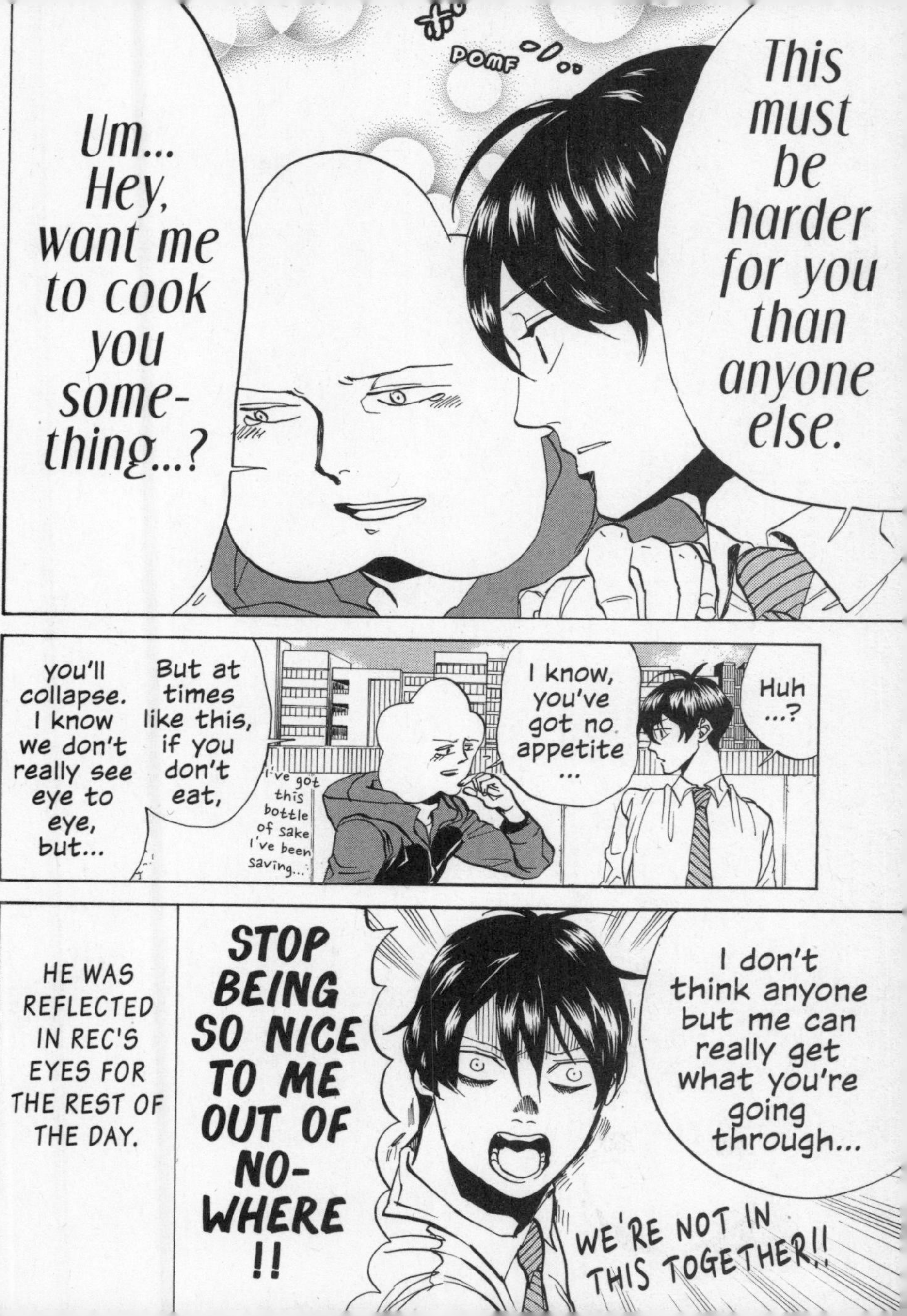
POMF
This must be harder for you than anyone else.
Um... Hey, want me to cook you some-thing...?
Huh ...?
I know, you've got no appetite ...
I've got this bottle of sake I've been saving...
But at times like this, if you don't eat,
you'll collapse. I know we don't really see eye to eye, but...
I don't think anyone but me can really get what you're going through...
WE'RE NOT IN THIS TOGETHER!!
STOP BEING SO NICE TO ME OUT OF NO-WHERE!!
HE WAS REFLECTED IN REC'S EYES FOR THE REST OF THE DAY.

ARAKAWA
UNDER
THE BRIDGE

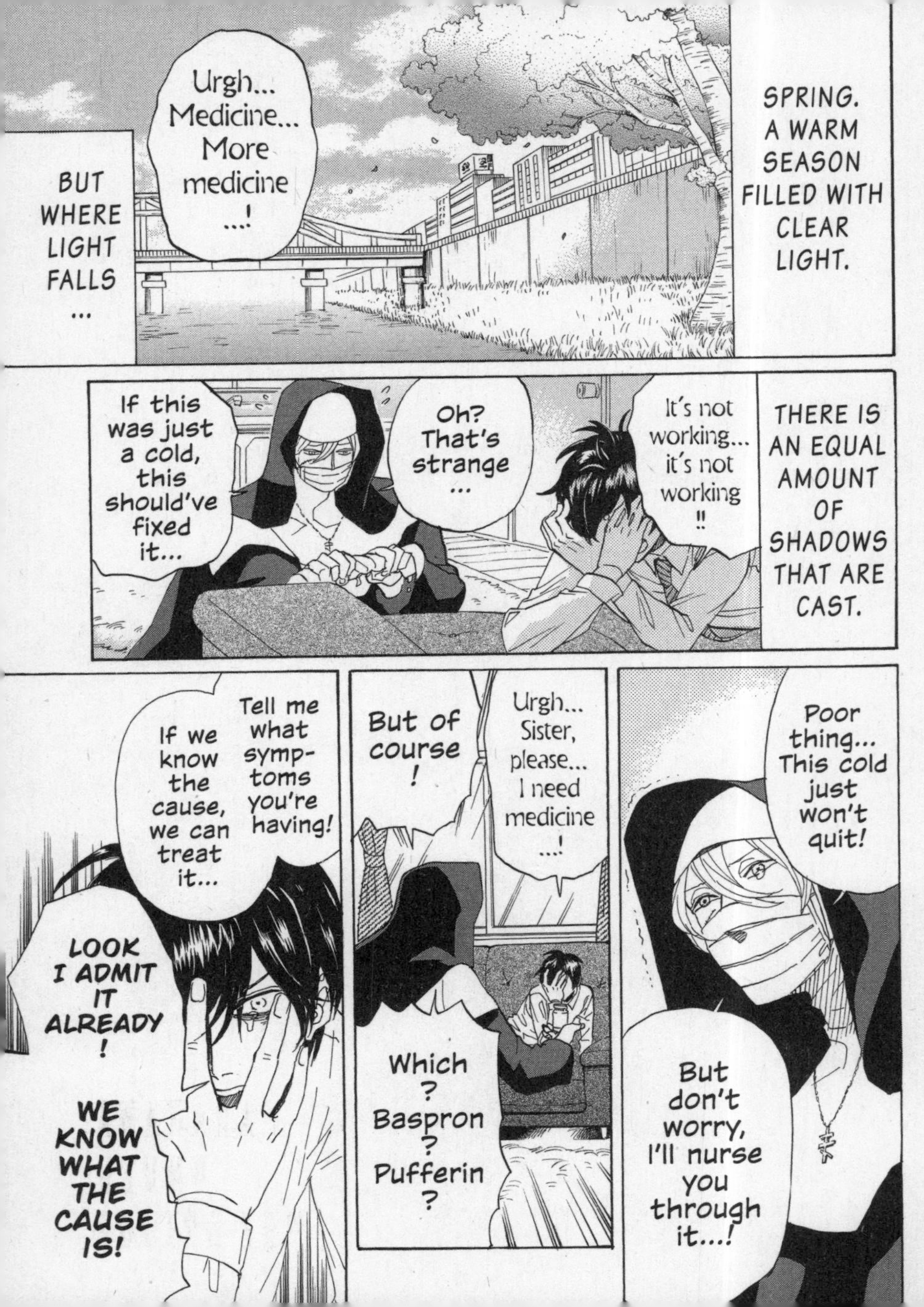
SPRING. A WARM SEASON FILLED WITH CLEAR LIGHT.
Urgh... Medicine... More medicine ...!
BUT WHERE LIGHT FALLS ...
THERE IS AN EQUAL AMOUNT OF SHADOWS THAT ARE CAST.
It's not working... it's not working !!
Oh? That's strange ...
If this was just a cold, this should've fixed it...
Poor thing... This cold just won't quit!
But don't worry, I'll nurse you through it...!
Urgh... Sister, please... I need medicine ...!
But of course !
Which ? Baspron ? Pufferin ?
Tell me what symp-toms you're having!
If we know the cause, we can treat it...
LOOK I ADMIT IT ALREADY !
WE KNOW WHAT THE CAUSE IS!

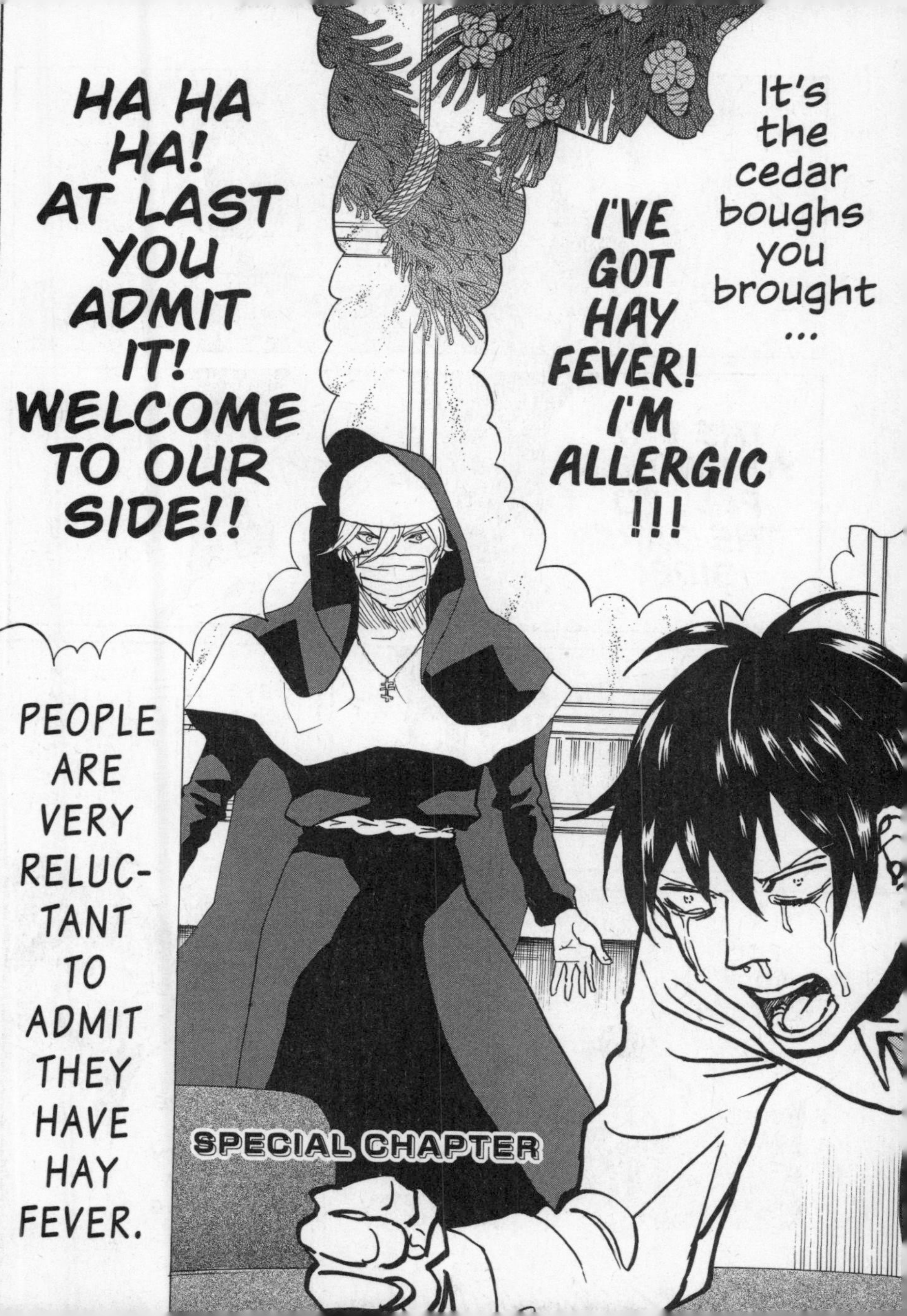
It's the cedar boughs you brought...
I'VE GOT HAY FEVER! I'M ALLERGIC!!!
HA HA HA! AT LAST YOU ADMIT IT! WELCOME TO OUR SIDE!!
PEOPLE ARE VERY RELUCTANT TO ADMIT THEY HAVE HAY FEVER.
SPECIAL CHAPTER

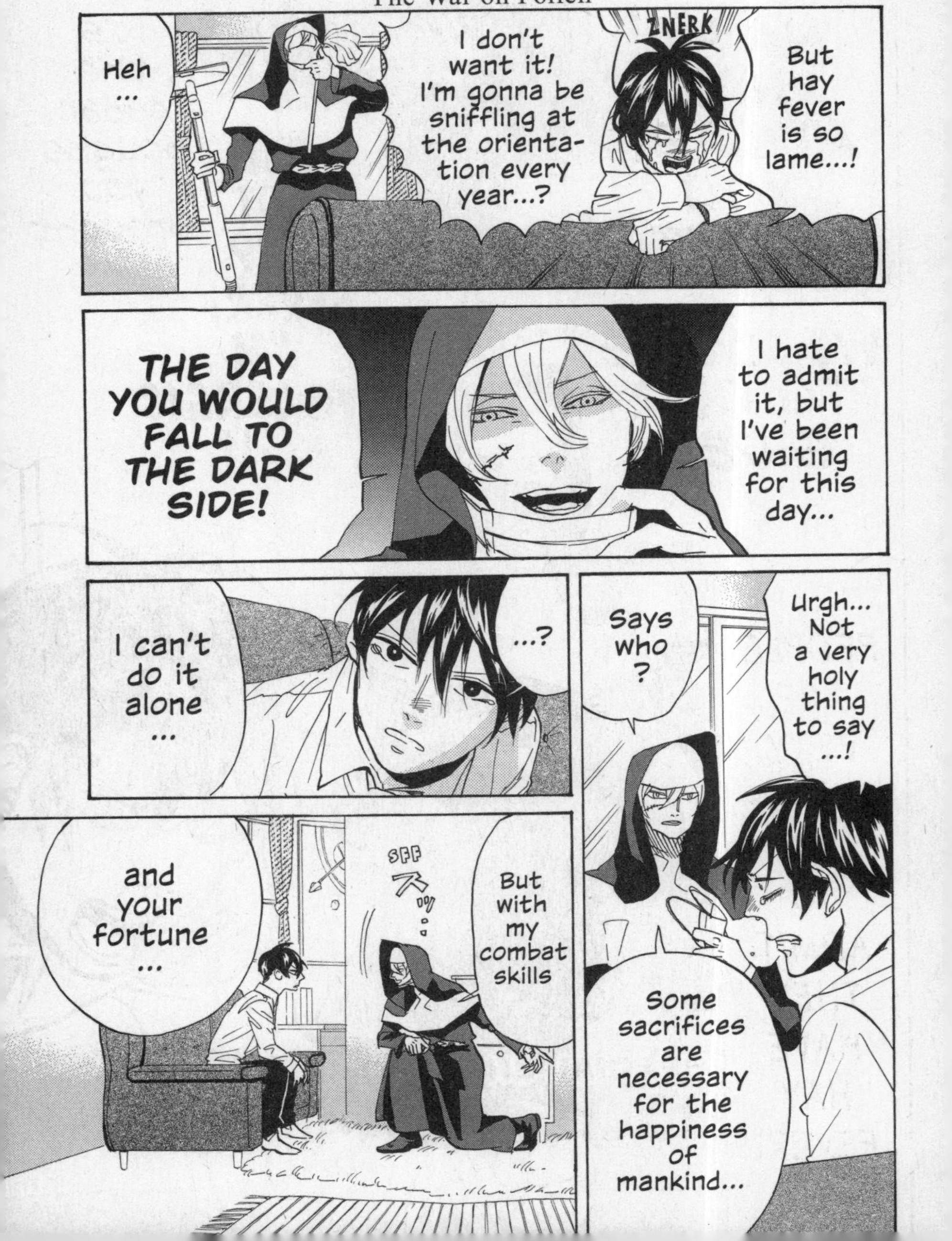
ZNERK
But hay fever is so lame...!
I don't want it! I'm gonna be sniffling at the orienta-tion every year...?
Heh ...
I hate to admit it, but I've been waiting for this day...
THE DAY YOU WOULD FALL TO THE DARK SIDE!
Urgh... Not a very holy thing to say ...!
Says who ?
Some sacrifices are necessary for the happiness of mankind...
...?
I can't do it alone ...
But with my combat skills
SFF
and your fortune ...

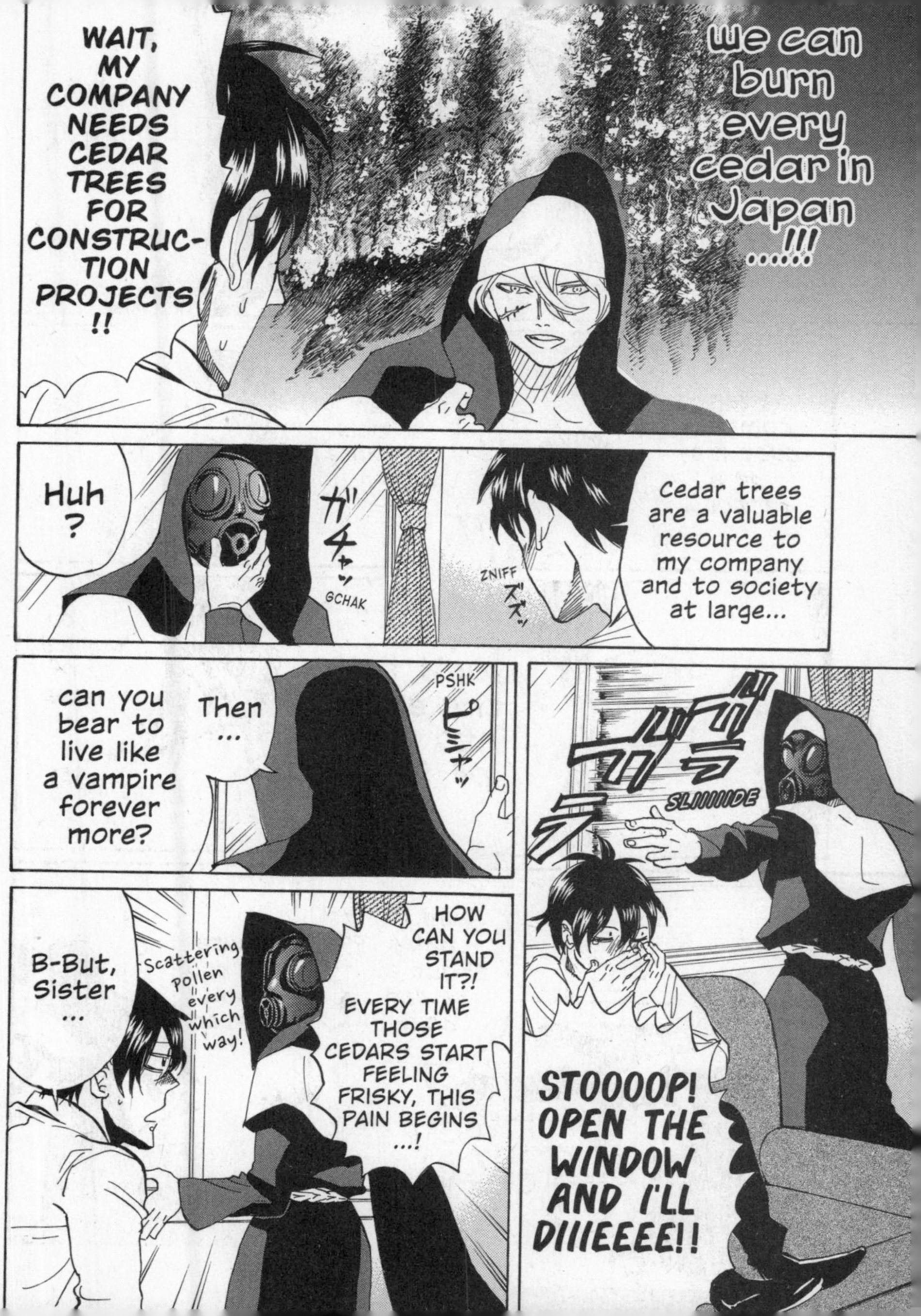
we can burn every cedar in Japan ...!!!
WAIT, MY COMPANY NEEDS CEDAR TREES FOR CONSTRUCTION PROJECTS!!
Cedar trees are a valuable resource to my company and to society at large...
ZNIFF
ズズッ
ガチャッ
GCHAK
Huh?
SLIIIIIDE
PSHK
ピシャッ
Then...
can you bear to live like a vampire forever more?
STOOOOP! OPEN THE WINDOW AND I'LL DIIIEEEE!!
HOW CAN YOU STAND IT?! EVERY TIME THOSE CEDARS START FEELING FRISKY, THIS PAIN BEGINS...!
Scattering Pollen every which way!
B-But, Sister...

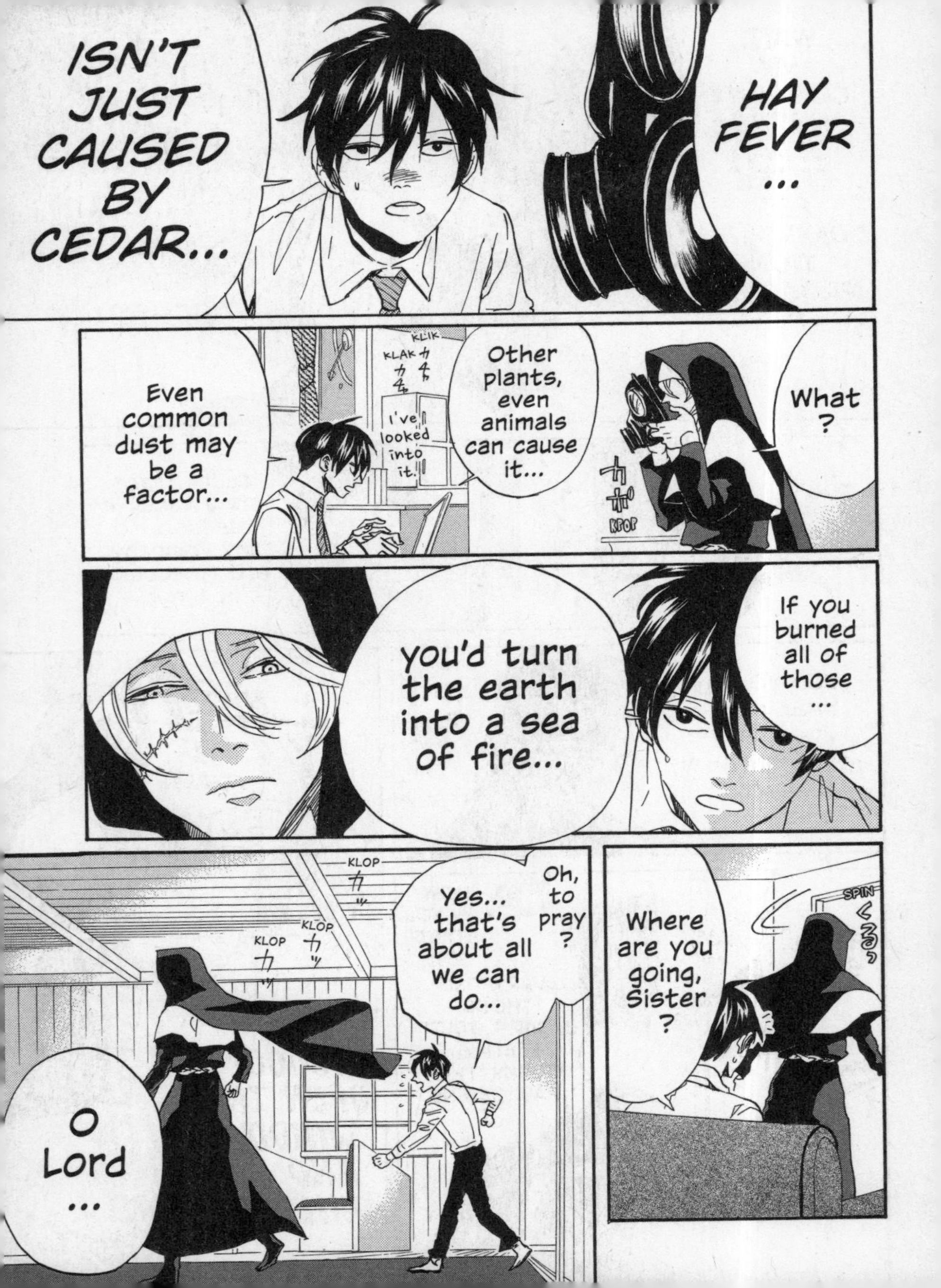
HAY FEVER ...
ISN'T JUST CAUSED BY CEDAR...
What?
KPOP
Other plants, even animals can cause it...
KLIK
KLAK
I've looked into it.
Even common dust may be a factor...
If you burned all of those ...
you'd turn the earth into a sea of fire...
SPIN
Where are you going, Sister?
Oh, to pray?
Yes... that's about all we can do...
KLOP
KLOP
KLOP
O Lord ...

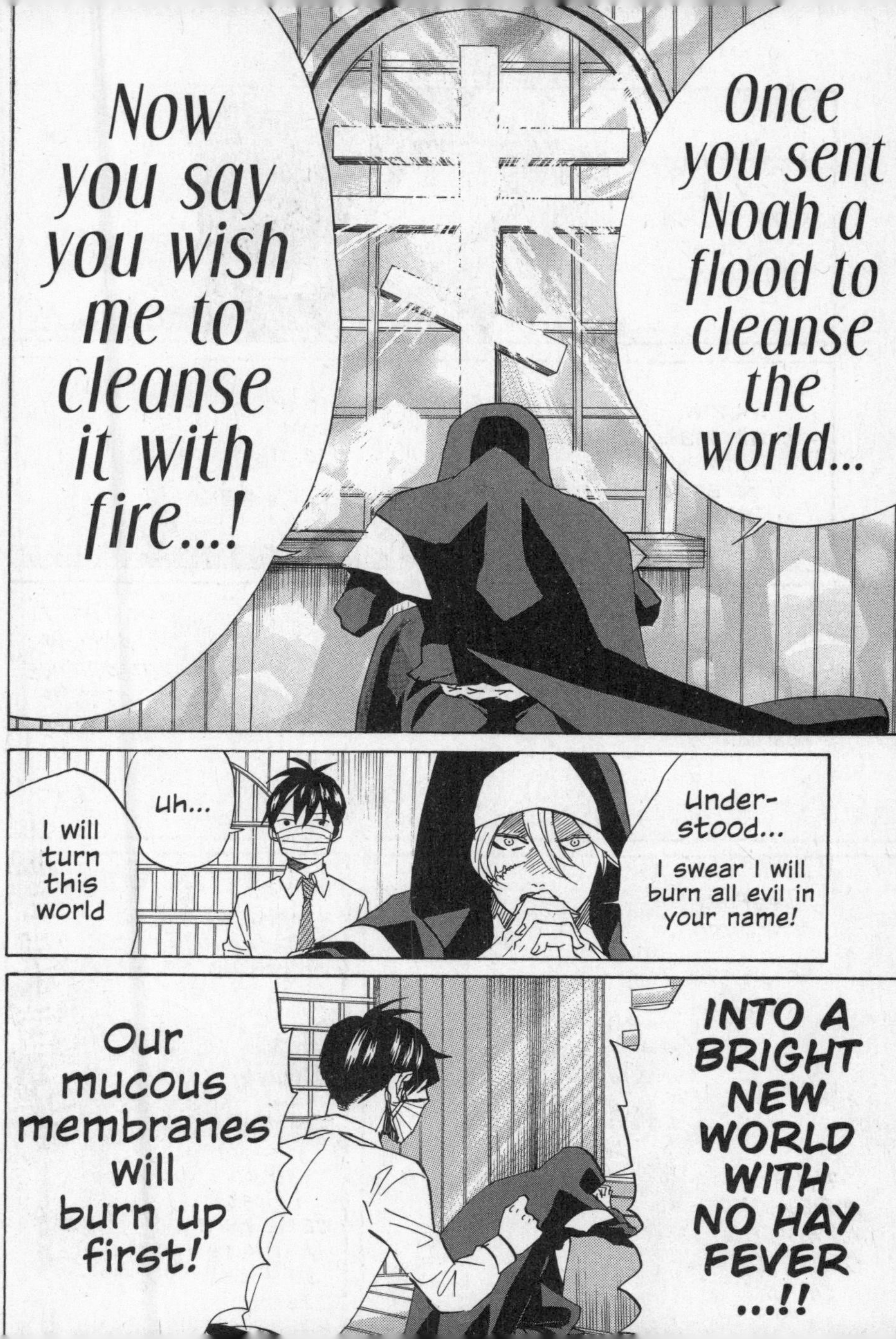
Once you sent Noah a flood to cleanse the world...
Now you say you wish me to cleanse it with fire...!
Under-stood...
I swear I will burn all evil in your name!
Uh...
I will turn this world
INTO A BRIGHT NEW WORLD WITH NO HAY FEVER ...!!
Our mucous membranes will burn up first!

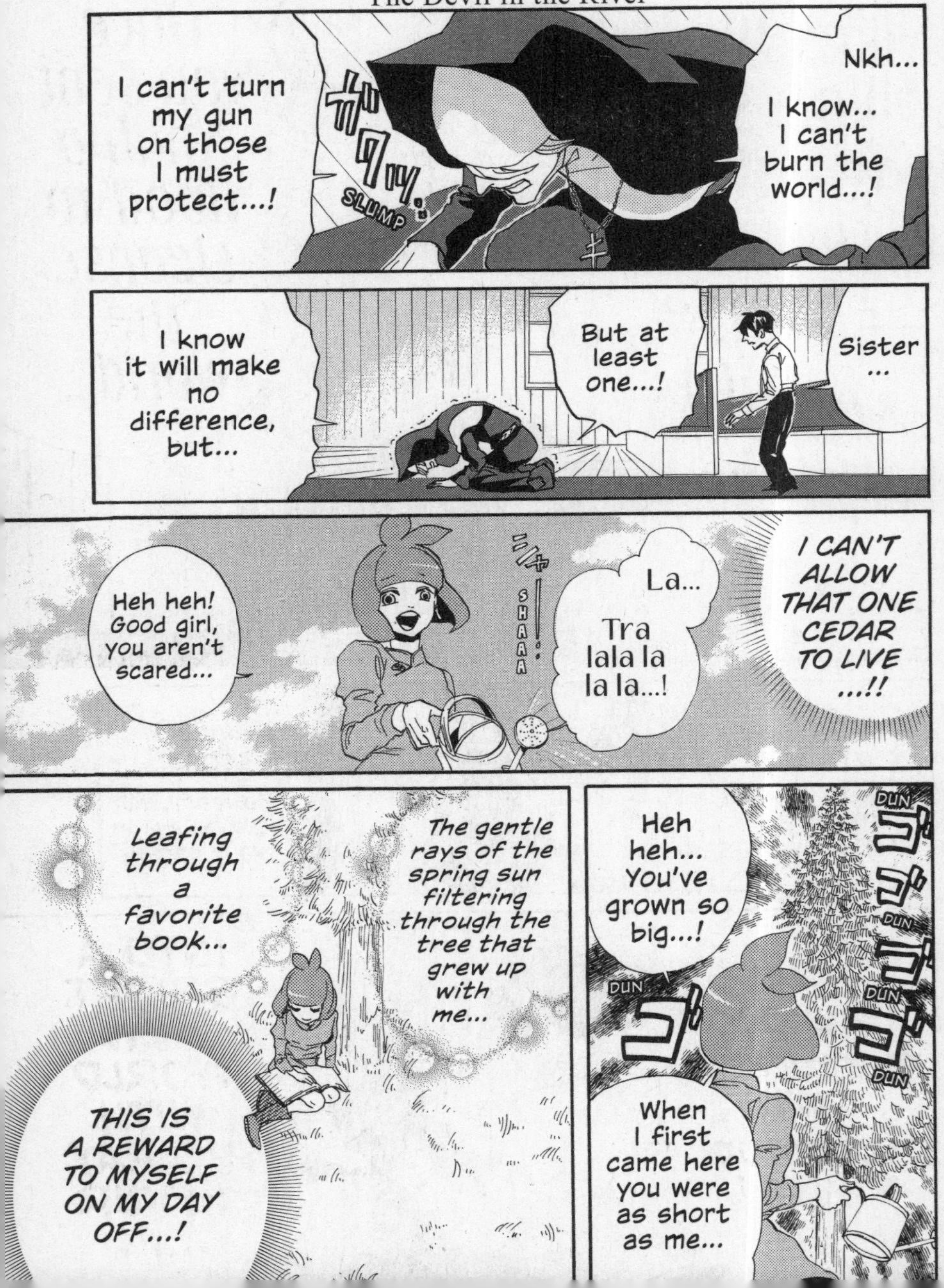
Nkh...
I know... I can't burn the world...!
SLUMP
I can't turn my gun on those I must protect...!
Sister ...
But at least one...!
I know it will make no difference, but...
I CAN'T ALLOW THAT ONE CEDAR TO LIVE ...!!
La...
Tra lala la la la...!
SHAAA
Heh heh! Good girl, you aren't scared...
DUN DUN DUN DUN DUN
Heh heh... You've grown so big...!
When I first came here you were as short as me...
The gentle rays of the spring sun filtering through the tree that grew up with me...
Leafing through a favorite book...
THIS IS A REWARD TO MYSELF ON MY DAY OFF...!

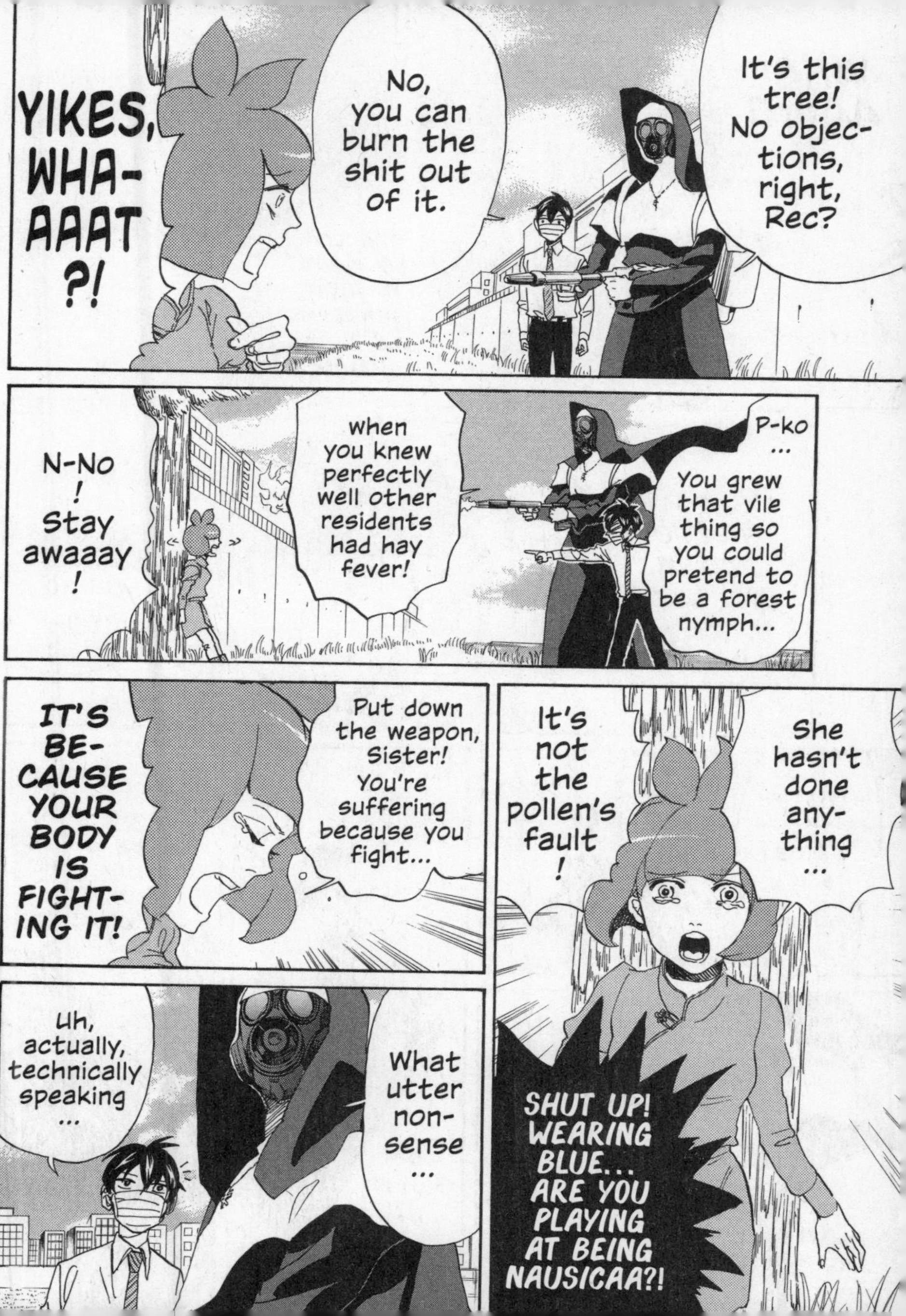
It's this tree! No objections, right, Rec?
No, you can burn the shit out of it.
YIKES, WHAAAAT?!
P-ko... You grew that vile thing so you could pretend to be a forest nymph...
when you knew perfectly well other residents had hay fever!
N-No! Stay awaaay!
She hasn't done anything...
It's not the pollen's fault!
SHUT UP! WEARING BLUE... ARE YOU PLAYING AT BEING NAUSICAA?!
Put down the weapon, Sister! You're suffering because you fight...
IT'S BECAUSE YOUR BODY IS FIGHTING IT!
What utter nonsense...
Uh, actually, technically speaking...

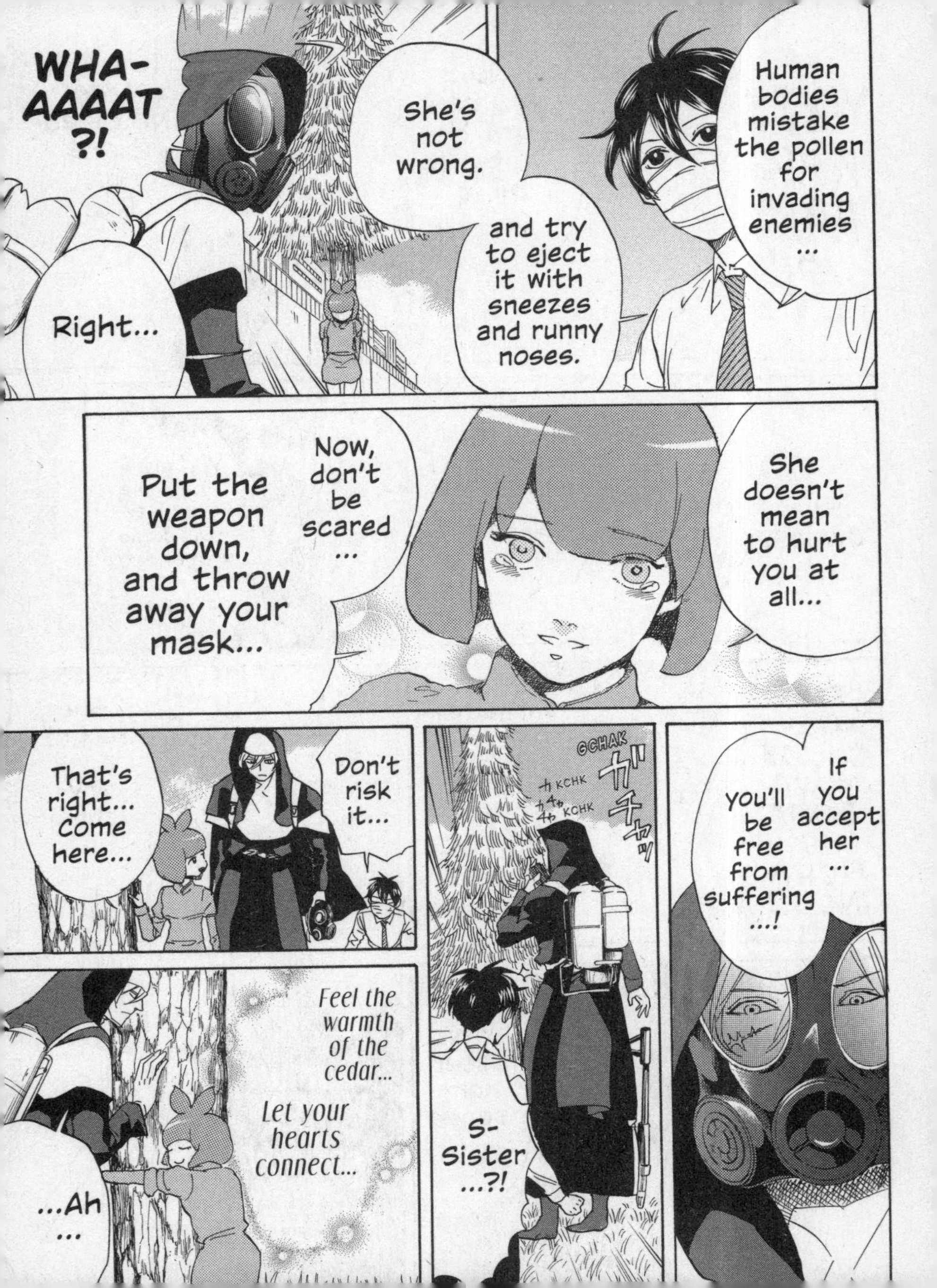
Human bodies mistake the pollen for invading enemies ...
She's not wrong.
and try to eject it with sneezes and runny noses.
WHA-AAAAT ?!
Right...
She doesn't mean to hurt you at all...
Now, don't be scared ...
Put the weapon down, and throw away your mask...
If you accept her ...
You'll be free from suffering ...!
GCHAK
KCHK
KCHK
S-Sister ...?!
Don't risk it...
That's right... Come here...
Feel the warmth of the cedar...
Let your hearts connect...
...Ah ...

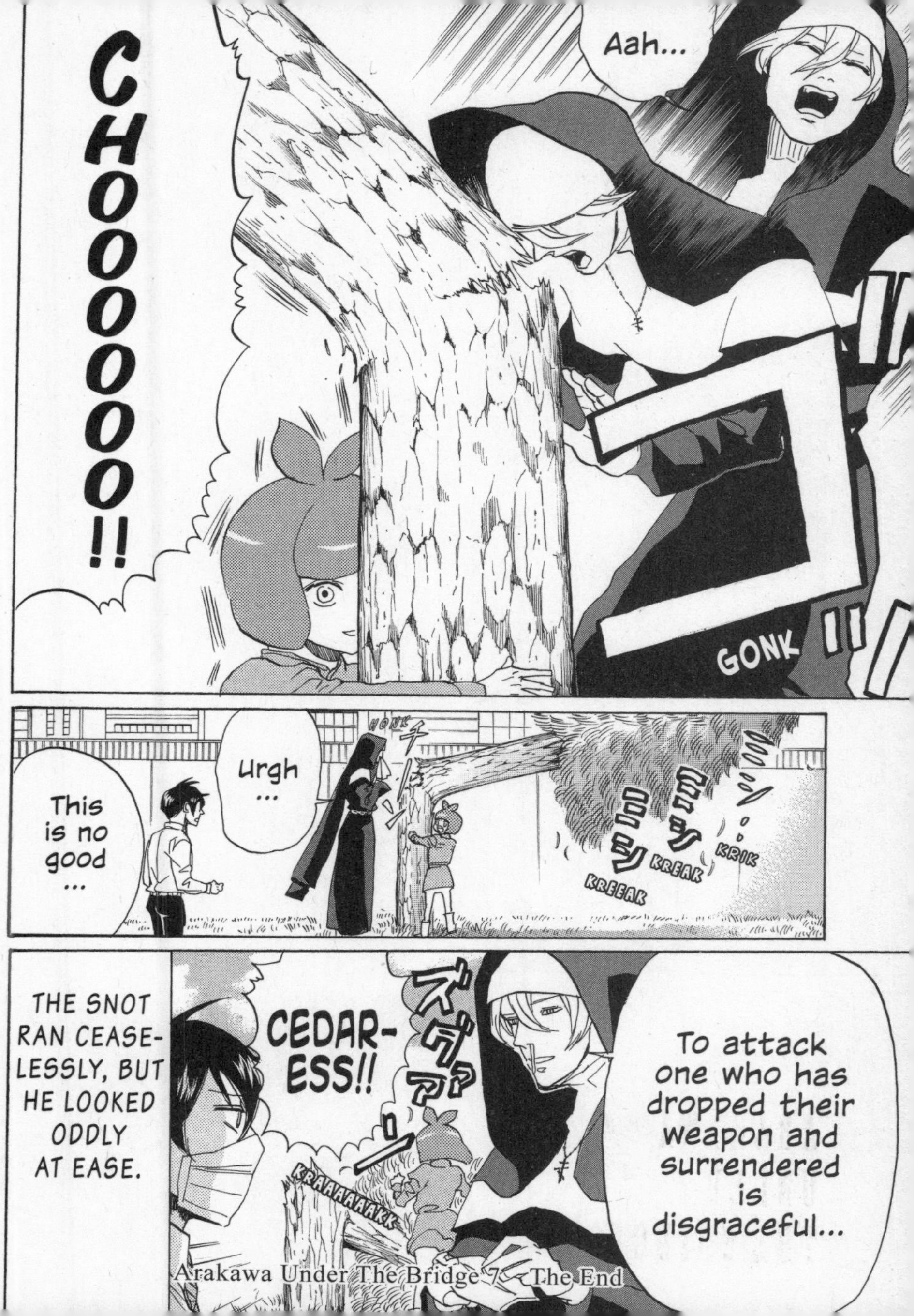
Aah...
GONK
CHOOOOOOO!!
KRIK
KREAK
KREEAK
HONK
Urgh ...
This is no good ...
To attack one who has dropped their weapon and surrendered is disgraceful...
CEDAR-ESS!!
KRAAAAAAAKK
THE SNOT RAN CEASE-LESSLY, BUT HE LOOKED ODDLY AT EASE.
Arakawa Under The Bridge 7 - The End

ARAKAWA
UNDER
THE BRIDGE

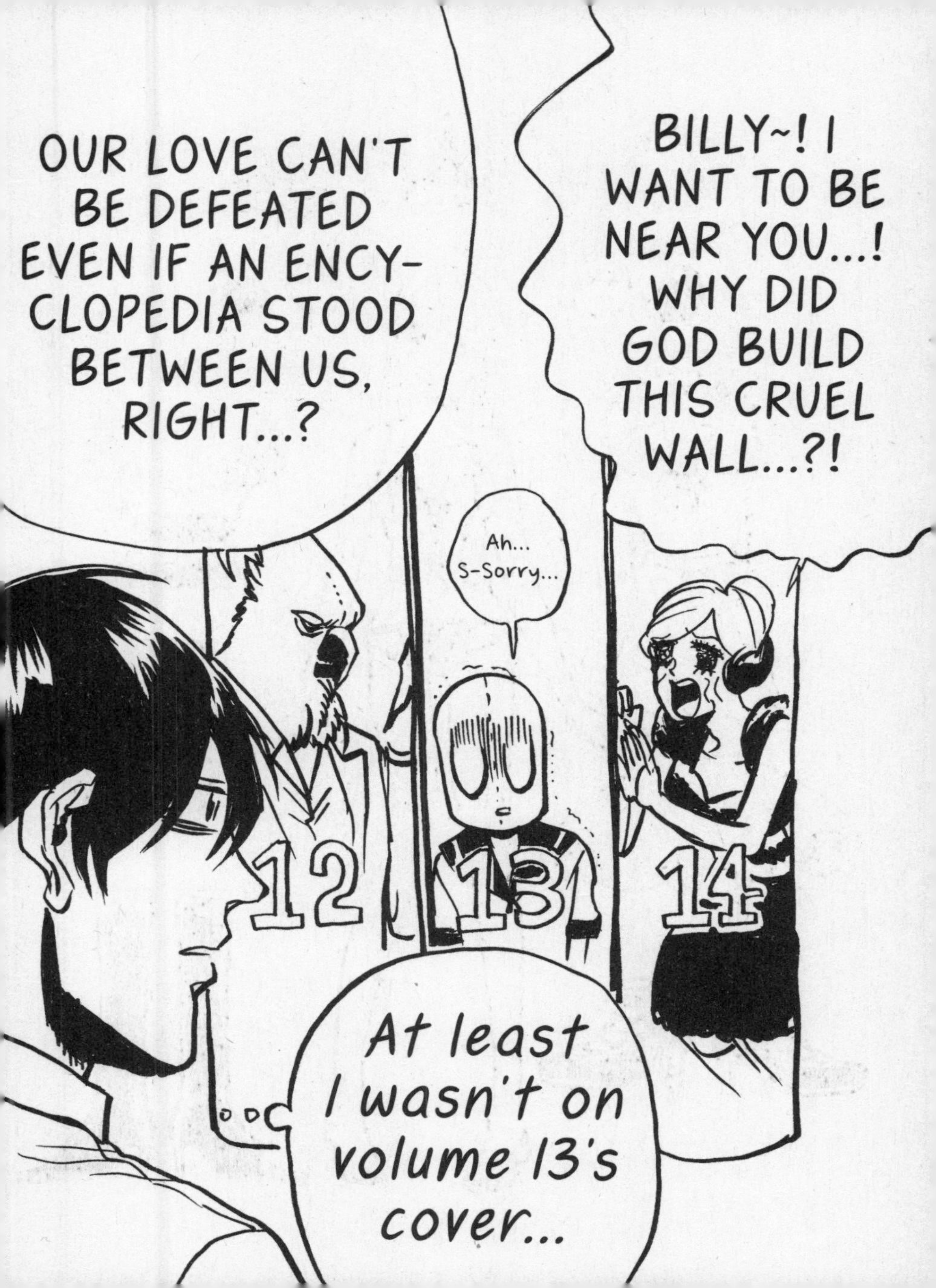
BILLY~! I WANT TO BE NEAR YOU...! WHY DID GOD BUILD THIS CRUEL WALL...?!
OUR LOVE CAN'T BE DEFEATED EVEN IF AN ENCY-CLOPEDIA STOOD BETWEEN US, RIGHT...?
Ah... S-Sorry...
14
13
12
At least I wasn't on volume 13's cover...

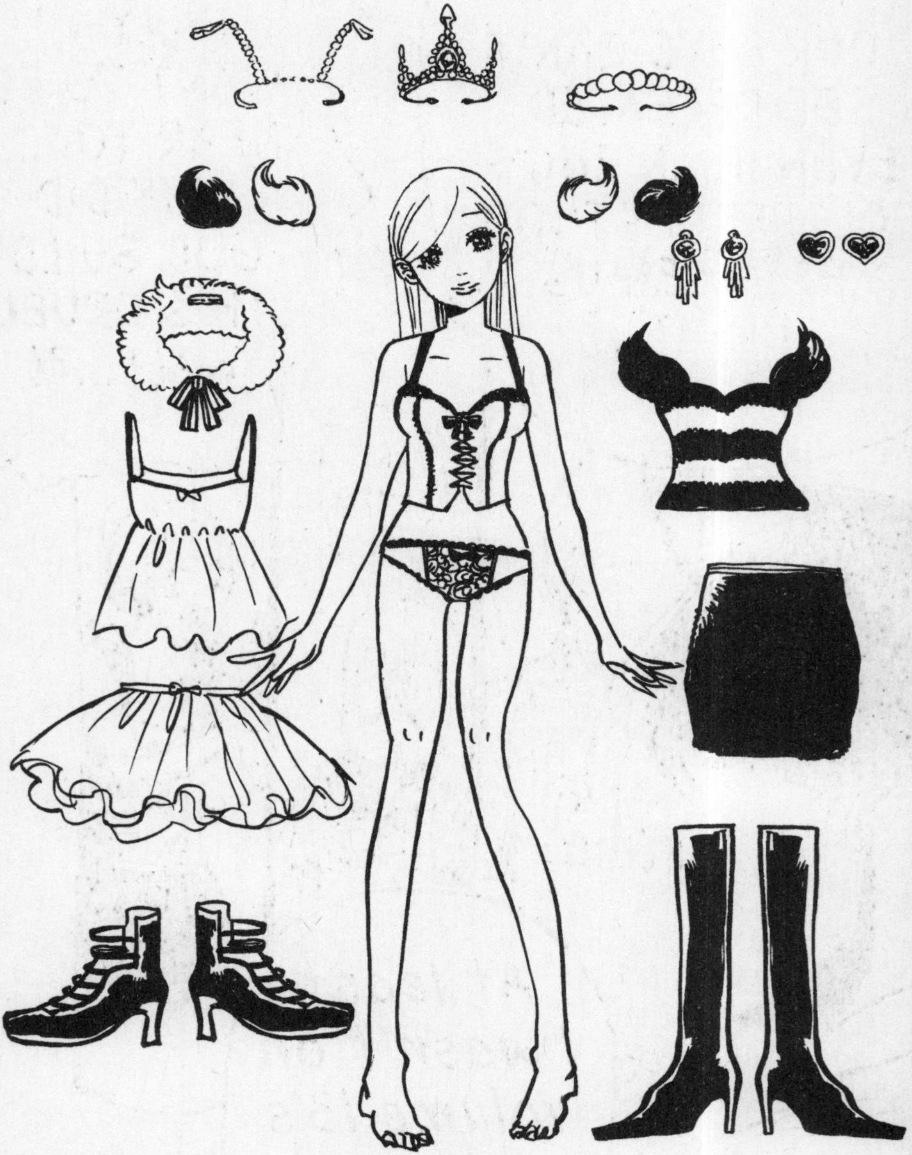

ARAKAWA UNDER THE BRIDGE 7

Hikaru Nakamura

Translation: Andrew Cunningham
Production: Risa Cho
          Tomoe Tsutsumi

Translation provided by Vertical Comics, 2020
Published by Vertical Comics, an imprint of Kodansha USA Publishing, LLC.,
New York

Originally published in Japanese as *Arakawa Andaa Za Burijji 13 & 14*
by SQUARE ENIX Co., Ltd., 2013-2014
Arakawa Andaa Za Burijji first serialized in *Young Gangan*, SQUARE ENIX Co.,
Ltd., 2004-2015

This is a work of fiction.

ISBN: 978-1-947194-46-5

Manufactured in Canada

First Edition

Kodansha USA Publishing, LLC.
451 Park Avenue South
7th Floor
New York, NY 10016
www.vertical-comics.com

Vertical books are distributed through Penguin-Random House Publisher Services.

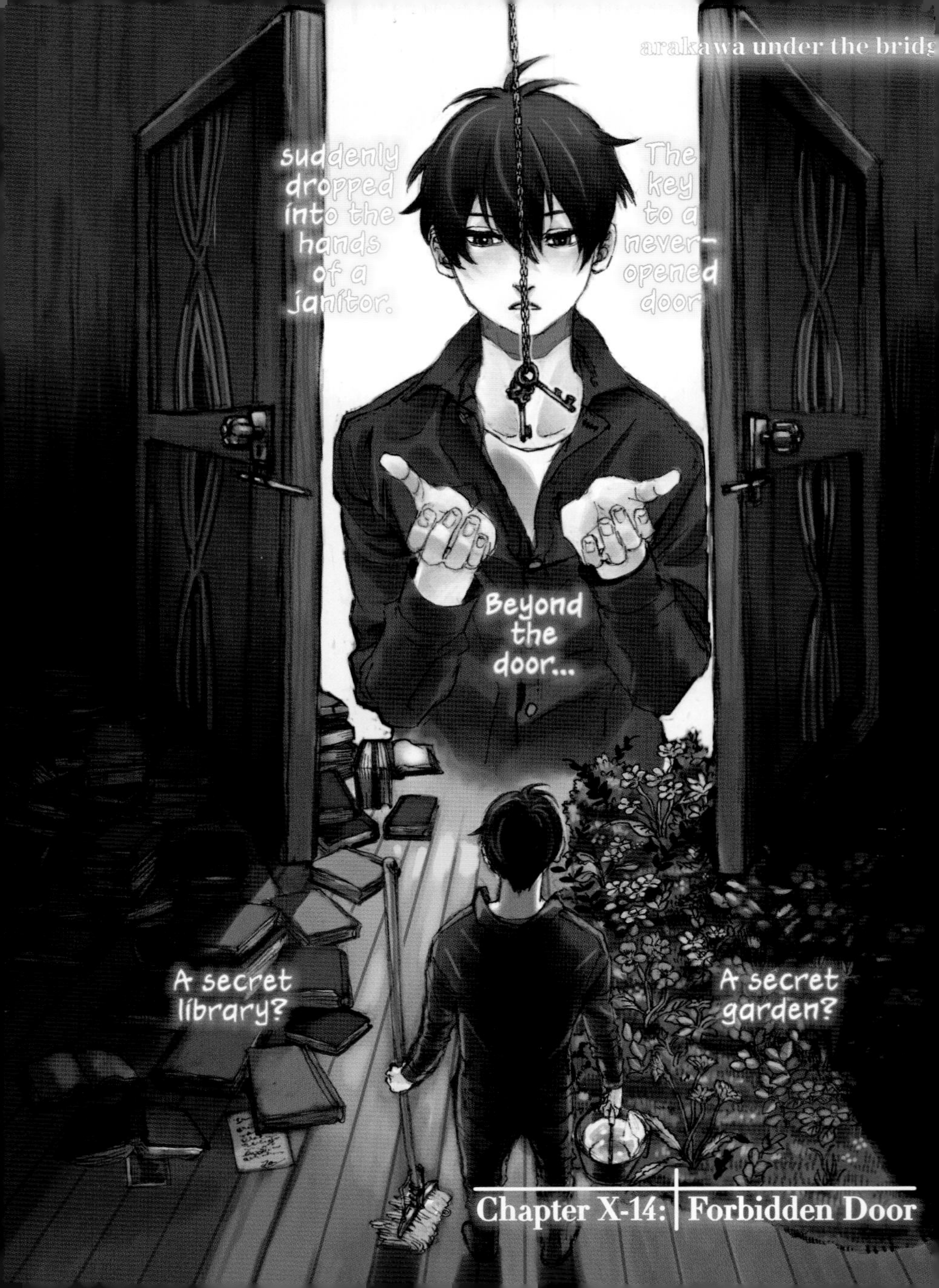
arakawa under the bridg
The key to a never-opened door
suddenly dropped into the hands of a janitor.
Beyond the door...
A secret garden?
A secret library?
Chapter X-14: Forbidden Door

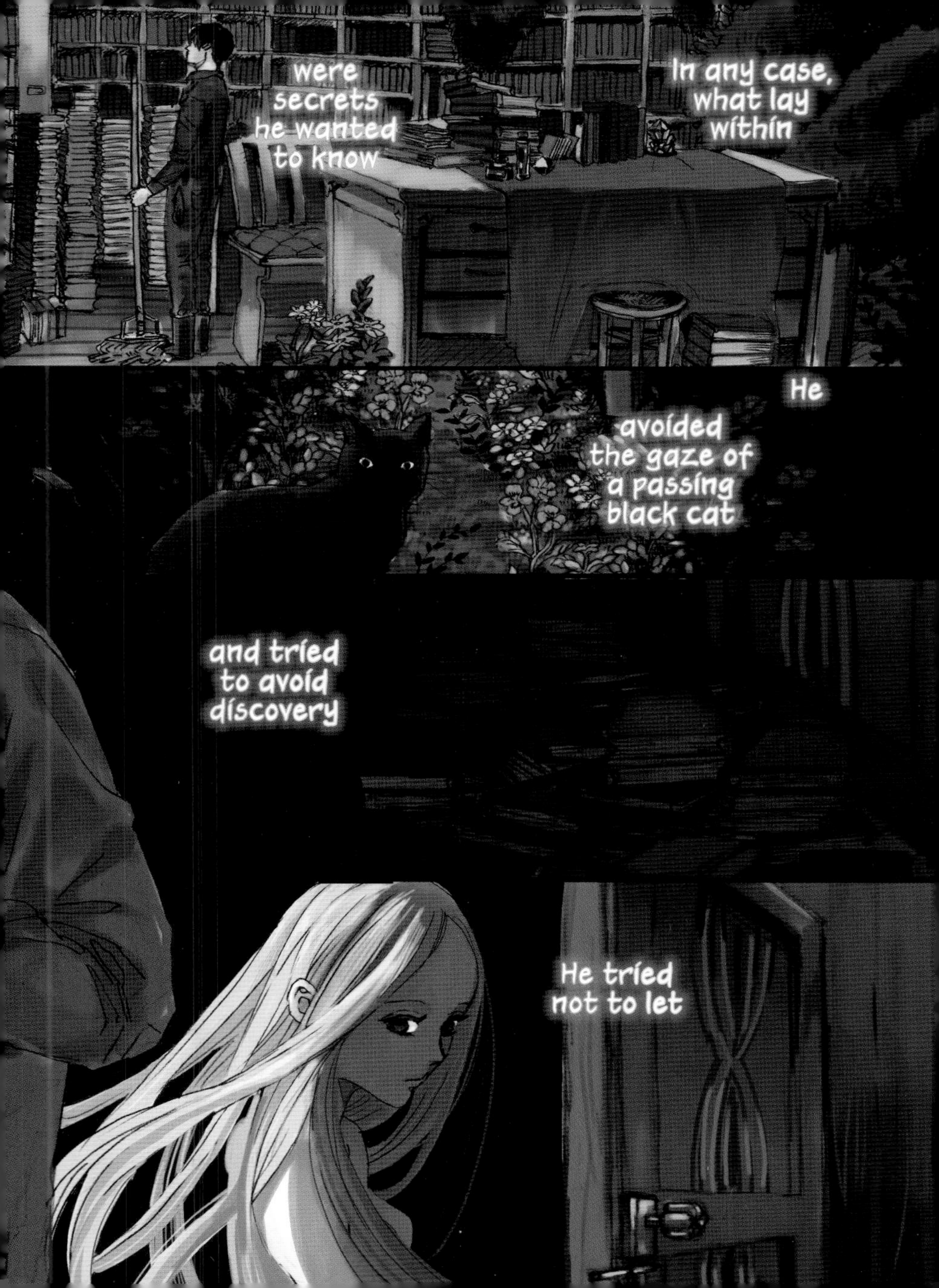
In any case, what lay within
were secrets he wanted to know
He
avoided the gaze of a passing black cat
and tried to avoid discovery
He tried not to let

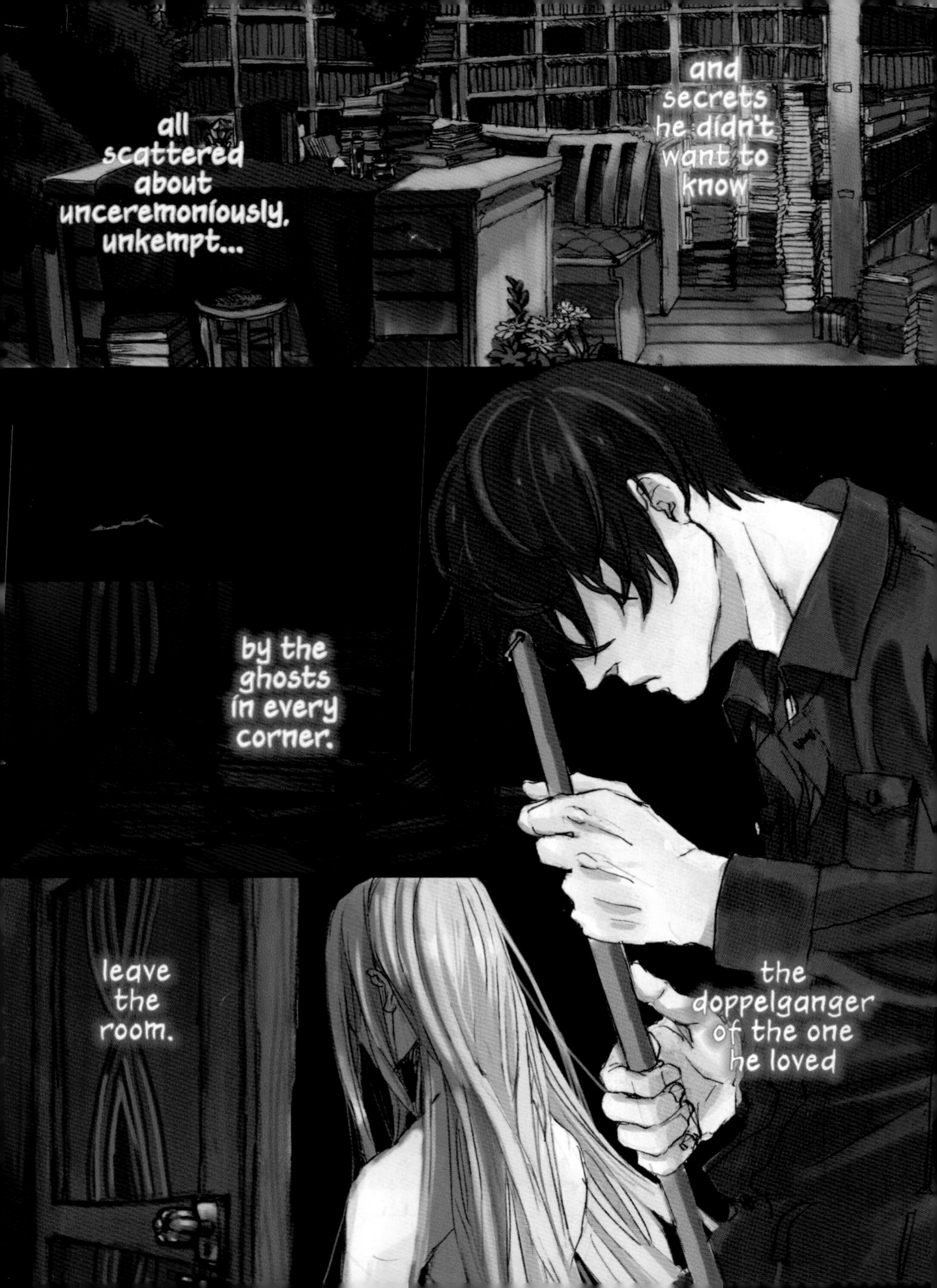

and secrets he didn't want to know
all scattered about unceremoniously, unkempt...
by the ghosts in every corner.
the doppelganger of the one he loved
leave the room.

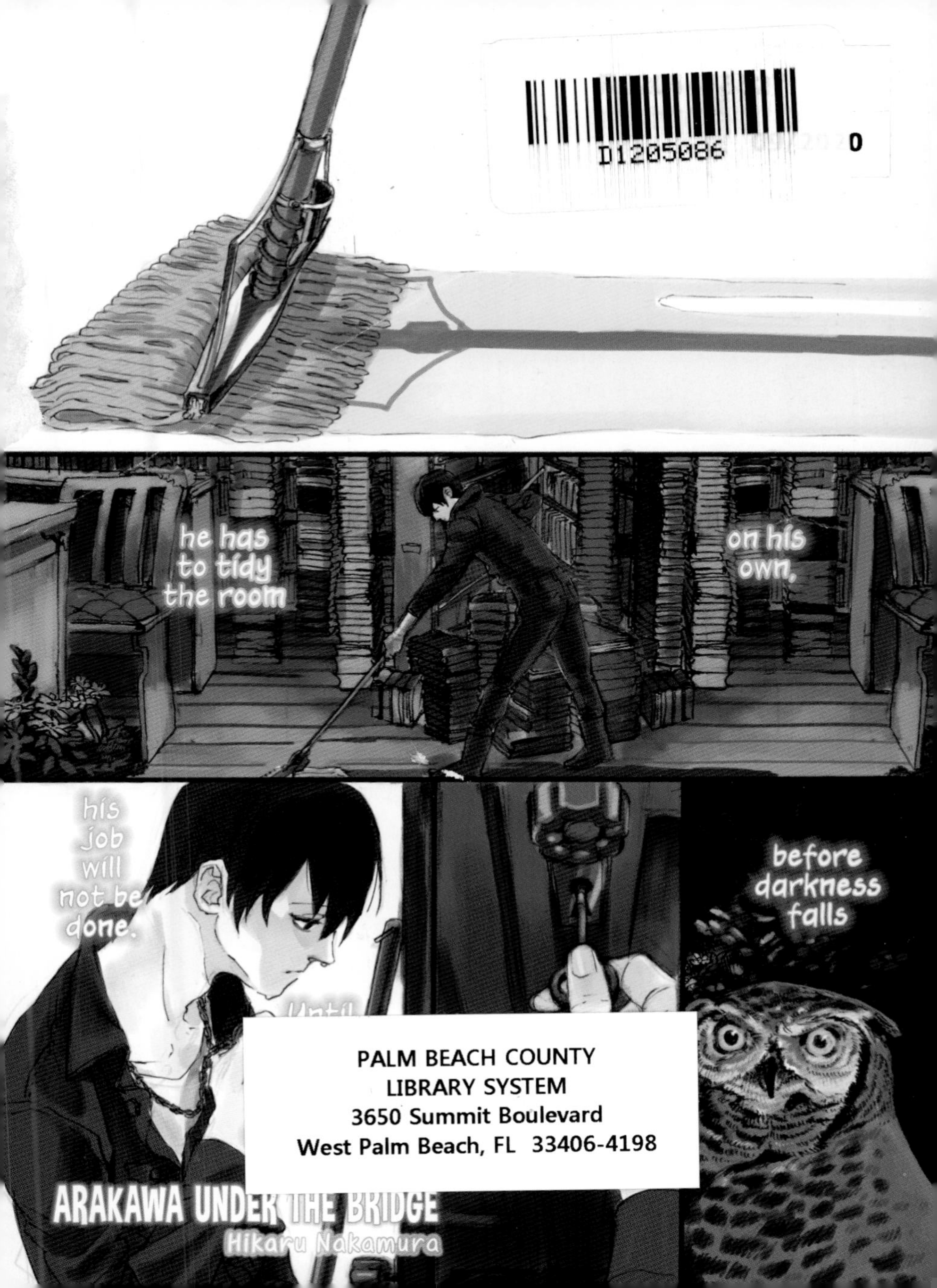
he has to tidy the room
on his own,
before darkness falls
Until
his job will not be done.
ARAKAWA UNDER THE BRIDGE
Hikaru Nakamura